Perspectives on
AMERICAN
RELIGION
and CULTURE

B

Perspectives on
AMERICAN RELIGION *and* CULTURE

Edited by

Peter W. Williams

BLACKWELL
Publishers

2 00,973

P 467

Copyright © Blackwell Publishers 1999; editorial introduction and arrangement copyright © Peter W. Williams 1999

First published 1999

2 4 6 8 10 9 7 5 3 1

Blackwell Publishers Inc.
350 Main Street
Malden, Massachusetts 02148
USA

Blackwell Publishers Ltd
108 Cowley Road
Oxford OX4 1JF
UK

Library of Congress Cataloging-in-Publication Data

Perspectives on American religion and culture / edited by Peter W. Williams.
    p.   cm.
    Includes bibliographical references and index.
    ISBN 1-57718-117-4 (alk. paper). — ISBN 1-57718-118-2 (pbk. : alk. paper)
    1. Religion and culture—United States—History.   I. Williams, Peter W.
    BL65.C8P46   1999
    200'.973—dc21   98-47774
                                               CIP

British Library Cataloguing in Publication Data

A CIP catalogue record for this book is available from the British Library.

Typeset in 10½ on 12pt Sabon by Grahame & Grahame Editorial, Brighton.

Printed in Great Britain by TJ International, Padstow, Cornwall.

This book is printed on acid-free paper.

For John F. Wilson

friend and mentor

Contents

Contributors

Philip L. Barlow is Assistant Professor of Theological Studies at Hanover College in Hanover, Indiana.

Joan L. Bryant is Assistant Professor of African American History at Brandeis University in Waltham, Massachusetts.

Mary Kupiec Cayton is Associate Professor of History and American Studies at Miami University in Oxford, Ohio.

Ava Chamberlain is Assistant Professor of Religion at Wright State University in Dayton, Ohio.

Karla Goldman is Associate Professor of American Jewish History at Hebrew Union College in Cincinnati, Ohio.

R. Marie Griffith is Lecturer in the Department of Religion at Princeton University in Princeton, New Jersey.

Carolyn Haynes is Associate Professor of Interdisciplinary Studies at the Western College Program, Miami University, in Oxford, Ohio.

David L. Holmes is Professor of Religion at the College of William and Mary in Williamsburg, Virginia.

William R. Hutchison is Charles Warren Professor of the History of Religion in America at the Harvard Divinity School in Cambridge, Massachusetts.

Paula M. Kane is the John and Lucine O'Brien Marous Chair of Catholic Studies at the University of Pittsburgh in Pittsburgh, Pennsylvania.

Jeanne Halgren Kilde is Visiting Assistant Professor of Religious Studies at Macalester College in Saint Paul, Minnesota.

Bill J. Leonard is Dean of the Divinity School and Professor of Church History at Wake Forest University in Winston-Salem, North Carolina.

Charles H. Lippy is LeRoy A. Martin Distinguished Professor of Religious Studies at the University of Tennessee in Chattanooga, Tennessee.

Laurie Maffly-Kipp is Associate Professor of Religious Studies and American Studies at the University of North Carolina in Chapel Hill, North Carolina.

Michael D. McNally is Associate Professor of History at Eastern Michigan University in Ypsilanti, Michigan.

Albert G. Miller is Assistant Professor of Religion at Oberlin College in Oberlin, Ohio.

Amanda Porterfield is Professor of Religious Studies at the University of Wyoming in Laramie, Wyoming.

Leonard Norman Primiano is Assistant Professor of Religious Studies at Cabrini College in Radnor, Pennsylvania.

Russell E. Richey is Professor of Church History at Duke University (Graduate Religion Program and Divinity School) in Durham, North Carolina.

Anne C. Rose is Associate Professor of History and Religious Studies at the Pennsylvania State University in University Park, Pennsylvania.

Daniel Sack is Associate Director of the Material History of Religion Project at Columbia Theological Seminary in Decatur, Georgia.

Leigh Eric Schmidt is Associate Professor of Religion at Princeton University in Princeton, New Jersey.

Lawrence W. Snyder, Jr. is Assistant Professor of Religion at Western Kentucky University in Bowling Green, Kentucky.

Stephen J. Stein is Chancellors' Professor of Religious Studies at Indiana University in Bloomington, Indiana.

Mark Valeri is Ernest Trice Thompson Professor of Church History at Union Theological Seminary in Richmond, Virginia.

Mary Jo Weaver is Professor of Religious Studies at Indiana University in Bloomington, Indiana.

Beth Wenger is Assistant Professor of History at the University of Pennsylvania in Philadelphia, Pennsylvania.

Peter W. Williams, editor, is Distinguished Professor of Religion and American Studies at Miami University in Oxford, Ohio.

Introduction

It was not that long ago that one person could aspire to telling, in one volume, the story of the religious experience of the United States. Sydney Ahlstrom, for example, did this masterfully in his *A Religious History of the American People* of 1973, a very large volume that is still extremely useful. Although America's religious landscape has changed significantly in the past quarter century, scholarship on American religion has changed much more dramatically. Not only does our interpretation of the past change as more past accumulates out of the erosion of the present, but new angles of interpretation continue to arise in response to shifts in social and intellectual perspective.

This volume of essays is an attempt to acquaint a variety of readers – university students, academics, and a broader public concerned with religious issues – with the state of the study of America's religious experience today. The authors differ considerably: some are recently minted Ph.Ds, others are in the midst of active careers, and a few have attained senior status. The institutions with which they are associated are scattered across the United States, and range from state universities to seminaries to private colleges to research projects. Their own religious and ethnic backgrounds are similarly varied. Most interesting for our purposes, however, is their range of approaches to the question of how best to study America's religious heritage and contemporary experience.

Before we take a look at the specific topics and approaches they bring to this work, though, it might be useful to address the question of why there has been so much change and variety in the study of American religion in recent years. One source of change lies in the character of the scholars themselves. Prior to World War II, the American academy was dominated by men of Northern European Protestant background, who not too surprisingly were preoccupied with sorting out the roots of their own traditions. Catholic and Jewish scholars, largely employed by institutions of their own traditions, were similarly preoccupied with parochial concerns, some of which would prove seminal in unearthing vital source materials. African Americans and Latinos were extremely scarce in the field until the social upheavals of the 1960s made access to the scholarly community possible to them as well.

Today, scholars from a wide variety of religious and ethnic backgrounds labor together on common terms in universities of various religious origins – Yale, Duke, Notre Dame, Hebrew Union College – and in professional societies – the American Academy of Religion, the American Society of Church History – in which denominational affiliation counts for little. The emergence of a cadre of highly capable historians of Evangelical persuasion in the 1980s also enriched the mixture of backgrounds and motivations at work, and testified to the emergent common understanding of what it meant for the study of religious history to be conducted on a scholarly basis. Religious studies programs in state-supported universities such as those in Chapel Hill, North Carolina, and Bloomington, Indiana, have further demoted the role of religious affiliation in the scholarly process.

This lively and diverse professional community has for the most part come of age in an era of rapidly expanding scholarly activity. Doctoral programs blossomed in the sixties as an expanding university system demanded new talent, and the rapid slowdown of professional opportunities in subsequent decades did little to stanch the flow of aspiring academics into the system. Similarly, colleges and universities that had in the past expected little of their faculty beyond extensive teaching now ratcheted their expectations upwards, so that published research became a necessity for security and advancement even at institutions with previously rather low scholarly profiles. The impact is evident throughout academe, and certainly is apparent in the voluminous book and periodical literature now available on American religious history. During the sixties, a graduate student could master virtually the entire corpus of significant published research in the field. Today, a scholar has to work hard to stay current even in one sub-area of specialization.

Where theological differences separated religious scholars in the past, philosophical and ideological disagreements now shape the way in which American religious history is interpreted. Traditionalist Protestants still sometimes favor a "master narrative," a continuing story with dominant players, conflicts, and progress. Winthrop Hudson's *Religion in America*, originally published in 1965 and now many times revised and expanded in the direction of greater inclusiveness, is perhaps the model of this approach. Ahlstrom's *Religious History*, cited earlier, continued in this tradition, citing Puritanism as the driving force behind American religious, intellectual and cultural development until the election of a Roman Catholic president in 1960 brought an end to the "Great Puritan Epoch." Surveys by Robert Handy, Mark Noll, and others have continued the tradition in emphasizing the development of Protestant thought and institutions as a central motif in American religious life.

A countertrend began to become visible in 1981, with the publication of the first edition of Catherine Albanese's *America: Religion and Religions*. Albanese consciously rejected the centrality of Protestantism as an organizing theme, and instead suggested that America's religious life could be approached as validly through the exploration of any of its constituent religious communities. This new approach began to attract advocates for a variety of reasons: the entry into the academy of a new generation of scholars such as Albanese herself who no longer reflected the northern European Protestant ethos of earlier religious scholars; the emergence into prominence of a variety of religious communities, such as Protestant Evangelicals, Muslims, Hindus, and Latino Catholics; and the impact of Marxist-influenced schools of European scholarship that saw much earlier American historiography as unwarrantedly "privileging" the lives and work of European-descended, politically powerful males as objects of research.

A concomitant trend in religious scholarship was the growing influence of investigative methods that were not primarily influenced by theology and institutional history. The History of Religions school exemplified in the work of the University of Chicago's Mircea Eliade looked less to historical development than to structures of symbolic expression that could be found in religious communities in a wide variety of times and places. An often complementary emphasis derived from the pioneering work of the nineteenth-century French sociologist Émile Durkheim and later by the anthropologists Mary Douglas and Victor Turner, and focused on the correlation of modes of religious expression and activity with changes in underlying social structure. Anthropologist Clifford Geertz emphasized the role of ritual events in providing keys to a broader understanding of the complex interrelationships of a cultural system, a theme taken up by Robert Orsi in his exploration of Italian-American Catholic devotions in his *The Madonna of 115th Street* of 1985.

The recent study of American religion has also incorporated themes developed in American Studies, an interdisciplinary approach to American society and culture. Such themes include an attention to popular culture, in contrast to the thought and work of elites; David Hall made this a major emphasis in his reappraisal of popular elements in colonial New England Puritanism (*Worlds of Wonder, Days of Judgment*, 1989). Of growing interest recently has been material culture studies, as exemplified in Colleen McDannell's *Material Christianity* (1995), in which the author examines the cultural significance of hitherto seemingly trivial phenomena such as parlor Bibles, Catholic shrines, and Mormon underclothing. Regional studies, which have historically focused on the northeastern United States and particularly on New England as a source of religious ideas, more recently have shifted emphasis to the cultural development of such previously neglected areas as the Southwest and its complex Native American and Latino heritage. The closely related area of social history, with its emphasis both on themes of everyday life and on the roles of race, gender, ethnicity, and social class, has also manifested itself in the proliferation of scholarship on women and African Americans in American religious life.

The result of this scholarly explosion has been a "decentering" of the study of American religious life. This is, for example, the conscious objective of Thomas Tweed's 1997 *Retelling U.S. Religious History*, a collection of essays reflecting a wide variety of non-traditional approaches to the subject. Although some scholars argue for such new approaches on ideological grounds, a pluralism in approaches to the study of American religions can be justified purely as a methodological strategy. In any case, the proliferation of scholarly approaches that have blossomed over the past several decades has undoubtedly resulted in the illumination of aspects of America's religious past (and present) that would have been ultimately elusive when viewed through the grids of institutional and theological history. A new synthesis may or may not eventually emerge; in the meantime, however, the student may enjoy the richness of the diversity of intellectual outcomes, always keeping an eye to the themes that may prove central to a new generation's narrative.

The essays that follow were deliberately solicited from a wide range of scholars with an eye to variety both of approach and of subject matter. Some are traditional pieces of historical investigation, probing texts and archives to fill the holes and add nuance to already existing interpretive paradigms. Others move in new directions, either tacitly or overtly exposing the inadequacy of older interpretations. They are grouped into a number of categories that themselves are intended to call attention not so much to overt subject matter – e.g. Catholicism, Judaism, African American religion – but rather to the themes that run across superficially disparate topics. On the other hand, essays from various sections can be regrouped by the reader into different configurations. For example, those by Kane, Primiano, and Weaver can be taken together as an exploration of twentieth-century American Catholic culture from three differing but complementary perspectives. As indicated in the introductory material in several sections, Amanda Porterfield's essay on seminal themes in Puritanism can be used to introduce several lines of historical pursuit. Other themes, such as the transformation of religious communities over time and the interplay between religious movements and their surrounding culture, can be found in many essays. In each case I have tried briefly to provide relevant context, explaining some of the interpretive traditions and issues around each unifying theme, and how each of the included essays relates to that theme. The articles themselves conclude with bibliographical sections which point the way for further exploration in a particular area.

My thanks to Robert Abzug of the University of Texas and Susan Rabinowitz of Blackwells, as well as to the contributors themselves, for making this volume possible.

Peter W. Williams
Miami University, January 1999

Pa

Religious Diversity a

Introduction

Religious and cultural diversity has characterized the people of North America from the very beginnings of the peopling of the hemisphere. Even prior to the arrival of Europeans at the time of Columbus, the North American continent was populated with dozens upon dozens of distinctive Native American groups, each with its own unique culture. Since that time, the territory that eventually became the United States has received immigrants from virtually every part of the globe, each bringing with them their own traditions as well. Although the earliest European settlers were overwhelmingly Protestant, their Protestantisms differed considerably from one another. Catholics, substantially represented among Irish, German, Slav and Italian immigrants during the nineteenth century, manifested great internal ethnic and ideological diversity, as did Jews. By the later twentieth century, immigrants from Asia, Latin America, and the Middle East rounded out the microcosm that the nation in retrospect has always seemed to be in the process of becoming.

This diversity did not take place in an ideological vacuum, however. With the exception of a few unusual souls such as Roger Williams and William Penn, Americans have tended towards ambivalence, if not outright hostility, towards those who differed from them in what they saw to be vital ways – including religion. The hostilities engendered by the Reformation continued to play themselves out on American shores, with religious animus enhanced by ethnic and class antagonisms. The Irish who began to arrive in vast numbers in the wake of the potato famine of the 1840s were not only Roman Catholic in religion, but represented an economic threat to Protestant workers of native birth. Their descendants, who built up a powerful political machine as well as a hierarchical church in Boston, New York, and other major cities, provided further evidence to Protestants that Catholic outsiders were a threat to the principles of the Republic. The "new immigration" that enlarged America's urban population from the 1880s until World War I created further alarm in the minds of nativists, who by the 1920s succeeded in having Congress severely restrict immigration, especially that originating in areas low in Protestant adherence.

Nativism – opposition to and revulsion from the foreign-born – was not the only ideological stance towards newcomers exhibited by "traditional" Americans, however. Henry Ford, for example, staged elaborate pageants at his Detroit factories in which newly Americanized immigrant workers shed the garbs of their native lands and emerged from a "melting pot" dressed as "Americans." The perceived threat to the "American way of life" manifested in the World Wars and the Cold War led to visions of inclusiveness exemplified in World War II combat films. They included an obligatory role call of soldiers or sailors with names like Cohen, Kowalski, and Calabrese as well as Smith and Jones. (African Americans were conspicuously absent, however.) The four chaplains – Catholic, Protestant, and Jewish – later commemorated on a postage stamp who chose to yield their lifevests to sailors on a sinking ship and go down with it dramatized the ways in which a shared patriotism and humanity transcended previously sharply-edged social boundaries. The election of a Roman Catholic president in 1960 further contributed to the erosion of an exclusionary attitude towards religion, as long as practitioners shared a common American set of values and behaviors.

By the 1960s, the success of the civil rights movement had inspired first African Americans and then other marginalized social groups – women, Latinos, Native Americans, homosexuals – to work actively for full social and political empowerment. These "liberation" movements, combined with public disillusionment over both an ill-conceived war in southeast Asia and the dissent it spawned, engendered a significant backlash in the 1970s. This took the form of a resurgence of conservative Republicanism backed by a militant "new religious Right" that attacked difference, not overtly in terms of religion or ethnicity, but rather on moral issues, broadly interpreted. Alliances of conservative Catholics and Jews with previously apolitical Protestant Evangelicals marked an end to some old animosities but introduced new "cultural warfare" as well into the local and national political realm, especially over sexually related issues such as abortion and homosexuality.

Laurie Maffly-Kipp addresses the broad issue of regionalism and more particularly the American West, as the locus for understanding what religious pluralism has meant in the American context. Looking carefully at California in the period following the 1849 Gold Rush, she finds a dynamic interaction among "Anglo" Protestants, Irish Catholics, and Chinese immigrants in which each group has to come to terms with the others as "other." The result was a changing pattern of acceptance and intolerance.

Stephen Stein addresses diversity in American religious life by building on Laurence Moore's earlier demonstration of the significance of outsiders in American religious development. Assuming that religious innovation is a manifestation of cultural health, Stein delineates three areas – social, theological, and ritual – in which new religious movements have provided vital new alternatives to those offered by traditional groups.

William Hutchison deals not only with the particulars of increasing religious complexity, but makes a key distinction between *diversity* – the actual multiplicity of religious communities – and *pluralism* – the cultural attitude that not simply accepts but actually welcomes that diversity. He goes on to reflect on some of the apparent dilemmas that such issues have raised for Americans at the end of the twentieth century.

Charles Lippy focuses on the changing directions of diversity in the decades following World War II, citing population growth, privatization, social and geographical mobility, challenges to authority, and new sources of immigration as key factors. The results have not only been an increase in the variety of religious groups, such as those of Asian origin, but also a new complexity of belief and practice within traditional religious communities.

Chapter 1

Historicizing Religion in the American West

Laurie Maffly-Kipp

When we think about the American West, steepled churches and prayerful priests are probably not the first images to spring to mind. For most Americans, raised on representations of western lands drawn from "spaghetti westerns" and *Bonanza*, religion as a social presence is either absent or at best, serves as a minor and ineffectual player in the early development of western societies. Where lawlessness seems to reign, religion does not command respect. In these renderings, the town preacher or missionary cannot hold a candle to the virile sheriff or itinerant gunslinger, who upholds the values of rugged individualism by dint of physical force.

Reality, of course, cannot measure up to these myths. It is at once more complicated and more elusive, obscured by other impressions. Western regions, we know, have witnessed the flowering of a staggering array of religious groups, from the Mormons to the Branch Davidians. Indeed, the western edge of Euro-American settlement has always provided haven for communitarian religious groups seeking distance from governmental control and oversight. Thus, although religion does not have a strong public voice in our stories of the American West, the western edge of settlement has always served as a refuge for a wide variety of religious beliefs and practices; it has been a veritable seedbed for religious ferment. People moved to the region not simply to escape traditional authority, but to embrace other kinds of controls and powers. And so we are left with a conundrum: how could there be so many religious people if religion as a social force is such a minor character in western communities?

One answer is that historians of the American West simply have not found a compelling and dramatic way to recount an intricate and multifaceted story. We have no simple concept or narrative "errand" that captures the essence of this wilderness, in the way that historian Perry Miller immortalized the establishment of Puritan New England as an ideologically driven mission (although later scholars have questioned the simplicity of his account as well); no one heroic religious tradition fighting back the chaotic underbrush of a remote and isolated continent to establish a sense of moral order. If Puritan clergy served as the moral equivalent of the western sheriff, fending off heterodoxy and lawlessness, there is little apparent need for religious authority in the individualistic West, and less need to tell the stories of those religious "outsiders." Yet how, then, to explain the pull of western religious life?

Looking at the history of western settlement in a single location may help explain the apparent discrepancy between the vibrant and various spiritual lives of westerners and the lack of a "public" religious voice in western communities. There have been many errands to the wilderness of the American West. Variety, to be sure, has always been the overriding characteristic of the frontier experience; the notion of the frontier itself indicates a situation of cultural contact, a region of exchange, negotiation, and conflict. If we begin an analysis of religion in the West, then, by looking at religious exchange and contact instead of emphasizing the imposition of moral authority (be it by the minister or the sheriff), what might we see?

While we cannot tackle the entire trans-Mississippi West at once, one series of events from California in the late nineteenth century suggests ways of characterizing the unfolding of religion in western communities as they were first populated and settled by large numbers of people. Colonization occurred at different times in different areas of the American West, and gave birth to a variety of types of frontiers, but the features that marked nearly every area of settlement were cultural variety and transiency. Nowhere was this more true than in the first years of California settlement beginning in the mid-nineteenth century. Immigration began in earnest in 1848 with the rush for gold, but continued throughout the next several decades as people descended on the Pacific Coast from around the globe.

Along with their pickaxes and pans, they brought with them all manner of religious beliefs and behaviors. Roman Catholics from Spain had settled in the area for over a century, but their numbers were soon eclipsed by thousands of Irish, Mexican, Peruvian, and Chilean Catholics. Chinese migrants who practiced a mix of folk religions, Buddhism, and Taoism also came to California. The many Europeans and Euro-Americans moving into the region included Protestants from many different denominations as well as Catholics and Mormons. By all accounts, there were also many settlers whose religious practices defied classification, including, according to one Methodist minister, "jugglers, astrologers, conjurers, magicians, fortune-tellers, necromancers, wizards, witches, 'mediums,' " and "familiar spirits under any cognomen whatsoever." All of these new arrivals encountered a visible but receding American Indian population with its own distinct religious practices.

In much of the literature published in the early decades of this settlement, we see the attempt to come to terms with religious variety and cultural mobility, and the desire to find a way to conceptualize it. In 1877 Otis Gibson, a Methodist minister who had come to California to evangelize newly arrived Chinese migrants, published *The Chinese in America*. It might more appropriately have been titled *The Chinese in Northern California*, given that all of the examples upon which Gibson drew were collected from his experiences in that western region. Writing in the midst of a highly volatile anti-Chinese campaign, one that culminated in 1882 with the suspension of immigration rights for Chinese laborers, Gibson endeavored to give a "fair and impartial presentation" of the customs, habits, and character of the Chinese, even as he desired to show that they were a people in need of the "blessings" of Christian civilization.

Many scholars have discussed the ethnic and racial dimensions of the anti-Chinese movement in California. Generally, they have interpreted the religious rhetoric of the movement, as well as the participation of Protestant ministers and Catholic priests on opposing sides, as merely a function of economic battles. Labor competition is surely an important part of the story. But we must also take seriously the religious commitments and concerns voiced by participants. Gibson's book, perhaps the most widely circulated study of religious variety in California during this period, tells the story of the anti-Chinese movement, and reveals many of the dilemmas and ambivalences of religious practitioners in this highly diverse and mobile society. In an important sense, *The Chinese in America* serves as a prism through which the light of California's religious diversity was refracted.

Born in Moira, New York, Gibson had come to California by way of a decade-long Methodist missionary tour in Foochow, China. There he had founded a school for boys. When his wife became ill he requested a domestic post, and was sent to head the Methodist mission in California in 1868, where he remained until his death in 1889 (Seager 1959: 54). Like many evangelical Protestant missionaries in western towns, Gibson predicted great things for California, and was especially inspired by its proximity to a Pacific world. So convinced was he of the superiority of a Protestant belief system that he simply assumed Chinese arrivals would want to adopt its values.

With the opening of China (and later Japan) to economic trade and migration in the 1850s and 1860s, the presence of the Chinese on the Pacific Coast had increased dramatically. As was true of other California immigrants, it was not yet a population looking for permanent settlement. Fleeing poverty and unrest in the Pearl River Delta region of Kwangtung province, and seeking a livelihood to support their families back home, male Chinese workers indentured themselves to agents in Hong Kong, who then sent them in companies to South or North America, Australia, Africa, New Zealand, and Southeast Asia. Of the 30,000 or more Chinese who had migrated to California by 1860, most became miners. Later, with the advent of railroad construction, many Chinese laborers moved with the work force to towns along the railroad lines, but the vast majority remained in California, which they dubbed the "Golden Mountain" (Fields 1981: 73–5).

Missionaries like Gibson took it as their task to convert these Chinese arrivals to Christianity. They saw in the East Asian migration a confirmation that God was to bring about a new, purified Protestant civilization on the Pacific, one marked by its racial and ethnic diversity but united in a trans-cultural commitment to Christian values. California could thereby be a staging area for later missions abroad: first, migrants would be converted to Christ, then they would return to their countries of origin and spread the Gospel all around the world. "The Pacific Coast is the theological equator," boasted one minister, pointing to the fact that all cultures and belief systems were meeting in California (Thomson 1867: 61).

Protestant leaders were far from united about the providential nature of the Asian migration, however. While a vocal group supported the rights of the Chinese to immigrate to the United States, others sounded alarm bells. American historians have examined at length the tendency to characterize the western frontier as "virgin land," as space untainted by civilization or previous history. Some clergy did likewise, painting the immigration of non-Protestants as the corruption of innocence and purity, virtues that could only be preserved if ministers could ably "defend the honor" of the region. Chinese temples of worship on Christian soil were a particularly startling symbol of spiritual perversion. Other Protestant leaders used the metaphor of plague to describe the Chinese presence, as when the Reverend J. C. Holbrook observed that "the inhabitants of China . . . are pouring in upon this State, not by hundreds, merely, but by *thousands upon thousands*. . . . There is a prospect that they will overrun the State like the pests of Egypt" (*Home Missionary*, August 1859).

The realities of religious diversity and the face-to-face encounter with people of non-Christian beliefs confounded even the Chinese supporters. Gibson's study reveals as much. His description of Chinese religious practices and beliefs was on the whole sympathetic, and meant to convince a skeptical Protestant public about the importance of his evangelical labors. On the one hand, Gibson "domesticated" the Chinese by imbuing them with values familiar to Protestant readers: he pointed out that they came from a country with a government that is "Abrahamic or Patriarchal in theory" (Gibson 1978: 24). Despite poor living conditions, the Chinese were "clean and tidy" people, and thrifty with their money. They work hard, he added, and are "patient and constant" in their labors. "They are like us," Gibson seemed to be telling his readers. And with Christianity, presumably, they would become even more like Euro-Americans. Missionaries, in other words, favored *cultural* diversity as along as migrants remained "well-behaved" and practiced a religion that the clergy recognized as suitably Protestant. As the editor of the Methodist *California Christian Advocate* put it, "So long as they are industrious and quiet, we do hope the great American principle – equality before the law – will be held inviolate" (*Advocate*, June 10, 1852).

But Gibson's portrayal also made Chinese practices seem exotic, in a mix of impressions that was alternately voyeuristic and repelled. He was particularly disgusted that one of the first Protestant churches in San Francisco had been converted into a "temple for heathenism," and he characterized Chinese worship as "grotesque." But the novel sights, sounds, and smells of temple rituals and Chinese theater also held their share of fascination; Gibson openly marveled at the mysterious "joss houses" with their "goddesses and attendant divinities, and tablets and inscriptions, and incense sticks and incense urns and elaborate carvings in the most grotesque of designs" (1978: 72–3). His book described at length Chinese barbershops, theaters, temples, restaurants, and gaming houses. Other missionaries, too, penned articles for local papers that explicated in exquisite detail the sights, sounds, and smells of Chinese practices. The fact that worshippers visited the dimly-lit shrines and temples at all hours, bringing with them offerings of food, piqued the interest of a people accustomed to the recognizable patterns of weekly worship in well-lit edifices. The line between curiosity and participation, moreover, frequently blurred. By the 1870s some Euro-Americans had become involved in traditional practices such as celebrating the Chinese New Year: they exchanged gifts with local Asian merchants, joined parades, and shot off firecrackers in celebration (Takaki 1989: 120).

Even for those most devoted to spreading a Protestant faith, then, the encounter with religious diversity was met initially with a mix of reactions: fear, fascination, repulsion, and even grudging respect. The Chinese also greeted the religious milieu with a variety of responses. Most newcomers were peasants or laborers, for whom the migration reflected a family decision and months of careful preparations. But their lives were not entirely their own: the credit-ticket system provided them passage and work upon arrival, but it structured their social and religious lives in California in ways unseen by most Euro-American observers. Kinship associations and district companies (based on places of origin in China) provided mutual aid, fellowship, and space for worship. Some company buildings even set aside a special room for the worship of spirits of deceased members (Tsai 1986: 48–9).

While a significant minority did convert to Christianity through the agency of the Protestant missions, and some even became preachers in their own right, the vast majority found their religious lives severely disrupted by migration. Popular Chinese religious practices represented a highly syncretized blend of ancestor worship, animism, Taoism, Buddhism, and Confucianism. Their gods were transportable, inasmuch as worship took place in autonomous shrines without need of supervision by resident priests or connection to a religious hierarchy. But the lack of a close-knit family and clan structure in California made it hard to fulfill religious obligations, many of which were dependent on domestic rituals conducted by women within the home. Migration also severed the close connection between religious practice and the lived environment, since Chinese custom dictated that burials and offerings to ancestors be located in auspicious sites close to family dwellings. As Gibson noted, Chinese religious practices flourished in California, but the transiency of the migrant population made it difficult to establish an organized religious life with a public voice.

Yet if Gibson saw difficulties in converting non-Christians to a Protestant faith, if mobility and religious heterogeneity created a problem for his evangelization of the Chinese, his study reveals that he encountered even more difficulty with Euro-American settlers in the state. Along with other ministers, Gibson lamented the failure of morals of former churchgoers who, upon arrival in California, seemed to let their Christian principles fall by the wayside. "How our civilization must shine in the eyes of those poor underground Chinamen!" Gibson remarked sarcastically. He countered criticisms of Chinese houses of prostitution by pointing to the "Christian saloons" and gaming houses that abounded in San Francisco. Society was so unsettled, he noted, and the possibility of fortune so seductive, that it kept people "in a restless, feverish state of mind" (Gibson 1978: 94, 160).

What Gibson could not see was that Euro-American religious systems were just as disrupted by western transplantation as were those of the Chinese. Many ordinary Euro-American settlers did, however, maintain an intense religiosity, praying and writing home to family members about their deepest spiritual hopes and fears. But the circumstances of their lives and the relatively small number of churches and ministers made regular attendance at worship, as well as other public expressions of religious adherence, difficult to accomplish. Like the Chinese during the early decades of settlement, many Euro-Americans in California lived lives in a state of anticipation and displacement, awaiting a time when they would be reunited with their "real" homes and families, and when religion could once again become a matter of routine (Maffly-Kipp 1994, ch. 5). As a result of this initial transiency, the number of church members in California, as well as that in other western states, would never match that of the eastern United States. Well into the twentieth century, the American West would remain the least "churched" region of the country.

Yet just as a prism disperses a beam of light, revealing the component colors within it, so Gibson's study exposed other fears. Despite the moral threat of "heathen" Chinese and lapsed Protestants, the imminent hazard expressed in nearly every chapter of Gibson's work is the danger posed by local Roman Catholics. While other migrants presented a challenge to missionary success, the growing Catholic presence in California – particularly the Irish Catholic community – seemed a still greater peril to many Protestants. Gibson took advantage of every opportunity in his work to criticize "papists." He blamed much of the anti-Chinese sentiment in California on the Irish, a people whose habits he depicted as every bit as unsavory as those of Asian migrants. In countering criticisms of the Chinese presence, he turned each one back upon the Catholics: Chinese workers, for example, may not have been as physically robust as the Irish, but they were more reliable and less taken to drinking (a common Protestant stereotype of Catholics). When describing gangs, hoodlums, or other undesirables, he endowed them with Irish brogues, and commented pointedly on the high number of Irish populating the local prison.

Gibson was certainly correct that many Irish Catholic workers, fearful for their jobs, joined in the anti-Chinese movement, a political force that gained momentum through the 1870s. And his fears unquestionably reflected a Protestant sense that the organizing powers of the church hierarchy would afford Catholics a public voice that Protestants, because of their relative disorganization and diffusion into rival denominations, could not match. Like other migrants, many Catholic settlers discovered on the west coast a place to achieve the kind of economic and social status unavailable to them elsewhere. As historian James Walsh (1980) has shown, most Irish immigrants came not from Europe but from other states in the union. They tended to be older, on average, than members of other migrant groups, and they brought their families with them. In cities such as San Francisco they found a level social playing field, with no entrenched elite that could confer an inferior status upon them as new arrivals, and thus they quickly moved into positions of wealth and political authority in the young state.

Religiously, given their family-based movement, they were also more equipped than their Protestant or Chinese counterparts to replicate and bolster the organizational structures of religious life. The Spanish had introduced Catholicism to California several centuries earlier through its mission system, by which the Spanish government organized local native populations throughout the region into productive labor forces. But with the return of California to Mexican control in the 1820s the mission system had fallen into disrepair, and Catholic priests retained merely a nominal presence among the small and highly dispersed local populations of "Californios." Only after the scramble for gold began in 1848, and the Irish immigrants started pressing for schools and priests to minister to their needs, did the Church once again send labor and financial support to the region. From the first days of Irish settlement local Roman Catholics secured a public presence that rivaled Protestant attempts at establishment. In short order they built a religious infrastructure of schools and parishes to minister to the needs of the growing Catholic population.

Despite their opposition to Chinese immigration, however, and Gibson's comments notwithstanding, Catholic leaders did appreciate and even champion cultural diversity in California. They simply conceived of variety in ways that differed dramatically from the trans-cultural Protestant paradise envisioned by Gibson and his colleagues. Recipients themselves of considerable religious persecution in eastern states, the Irish valued California precisely for its public toleration. The editor of the San Francisco *Irish News* boasted that "San Francisco is a cosmopolitan city." He attributed that generous spirit to the heterogeneity of the region: "It is difficult for a clergyman of any denomination to make an oration for an hour or two without spicing it pretty freely with his own peculiar orthodoxy . . . which may be distasteful to many of his hearers" (Burchell 1979: 179). Nonetheless, he noted that such candor was tolerated and even encouraged.

Yet for many Catholics, generosity ceased when they felt that their access to jobs was threatened by the arrival of cheaper Chinese labor. Seeing this as an economic issue, most did not make the conceptual connection between anti-Chinese sentiment and the religious toleration they enjoyed. They instead saw themselves as the religious victims of Protestant passion, as they had been in the East; this identification may well have made it impossible for them see themselves as persecutors. On the contrary, most Irish felt that it was Protestant missionaries who were violating the spirit of toleration through their public condemnations of the Catholic Church.

It might be said that Protestants, Chinese, and Irish Catholics, viewing the same phenomenon of religious and cultural diversity, all had different opinions about the appropriate form that such pluralism should take. Based on their own past experiences of the public role of religion and the present exigencies of their migrant communities, these differences became increasingly apparent as the anti-Chinese movement gained momentum. For Protestants, ethnic variety in the form of cultural practice was acceptable, and was even a positive sign of spiritual progress, as long as migrants upheld traditional evangelical beliefs. Thus Otis

Gibson took exception to criticisms of the Chinese custom of wearing their hair in "cues": true religion, he observed, required a change of heart rather than a change of hairstyle. Catholic practice, however, inasmuch as it seemed to threaten the Protestant sense of social order, could not be tolerated. The Chinese, for their part, differed amongst themselves about how best to live in a heterogeneous community. Some felt that conversion to Christianity served as an important signal of assimilation, while many others preferred to live alongside Catholics and Protestants in their own cultural enclaves. For them, pluralism would allow for a continuation of traditional and highly diffuse practices in a new setting, an approach to diversity symbolized best by the appropriation of Protestant churches for Chinese worship. For Catholics, California presented a new opportunity to establish a strong religious and political voice without persecution, a possibility denied them in the eastern United States. They did not read into their own battles over labor a religiously-based intolerance of the Chinese; instead, they saw themselves as the victims of exclusionary policies promulgated by narrow-minded Protestants.

The political battle over the "Chinese problem" was shot through with religious import, exposing fundamentally conflicting versions of pluralism and the place of religion in public life. When violence erupted, it took highly symbolic forms. In the summer of 1869, vandals burned to the ground the Methodist Church in San Jose, California, which housed a Sunday School for Chinese immigrants. Less than a decade later, in 1876, Otis Gibson was hanged in effigy and symbolically burned at the stake by protesters, including some prominent state politicians. That same year the Presbyterian pastor William Brier was accosted by a lawyer for the prosecution after testifying before the Congressional Joint Commission of Investigation of Chinese Immigration. Numerous Chinese Protestant teachers were attacked and harassed by Euro-Americans, and "joss houses" (temples) in San Francisco's Chinatown burned. And the persecution of Chinese began to take on a ritualized quality of its own: groups of men would line up at the San Francisco docks to await the arrival of incoming boats from East Asia, and would stone and jeer at Chinese newcomers (Markus 1979: 61).

But it is important to note that Chinese laborers and Protestant missionaries were not the only victims of religious hatred. Gibson, after all, launched multiple attacks against the Catholics in the course of his own work. In 1873, during a public rebuttal of the Jesuit Father John Bouchard's criticisms of both the Chinese and Protestant missionaries, Gibson declared that the *real* war should be waged not against the Chinese, but against the "class of foreigner" that was trying to undermine the basic freedoms of American life. He accused Catholics of wanting jobs so that they could place their money right into the coffers of the church, in order to "aid in building up the traditional institutions of Popery in our midst" (Gibson 1978 [1877], p. 253). All parties seemed to see religious bigotry and hatred in the actions of their opponents, fashioning themselves as the "true" pluralists.

Protestant missionaries, lacking the support of their own congregants, ultimately renounced their struggle to define pluralism in terms that would include the Chinese community (albeit a Christianized one). Tired of the incessant conflict and frustrated over the failure to convert more Chinese to the Protestant faith, evangelical missionaries like Otis Gibson eventually changed their public stance. Shortly after the publication of his book, the San Francisco Chinese Methodist mission was attacked by a mob, and his ministerial colleagues one by one fell silent or renounced their former views about the importance of work among the Chinese. In 1881, Gibson stunned his clerical colleagues by supporting immigration restrictions on East Asians, and by asserting that Asian settlers should be compelled to cut their cues and adopt foreign dress. Branded by Catholics and many other Protestants as hopelessly old-fashioned and out of step with "enlightened" views on religious diversity, missionaries abandoned their own dreams of a pan-Pacific Protestant society. The conceptual tide that they could not stem soon assumed the force of law: owing in large measure to the escalating social violence in California, in 1882 the United States severely restricted the immigration of Chinese.

This early battle over cultural diversity ended in what one scholar has referred to as a "cosmopolitanism of stalemate," a tacit agreement on the part of Protestants and Catholics, both of whom wanted to make some claim to public authority in this newly emerging society, to sacrifice one kind of diversity for another. The Chinese, the group perhaps least able to stake a claim to social status in California, lost all rights to expression in exchange for a "progressive" model of toleration that stopped abruptly at the edge of the Pacific, excluding entirely the beleaguered Chinese community. Ironically, Californians in the ensuing decades would continue to celebrate the triumph of an unusual degree of religious clemency, turning an ugly battle into a badge of virtue. As the Catholic priest Hugh Quigley remarked about the state, "People here, even in religion, have come to the conclusion to 'live and let live,' and their common sense teaches them that to attack your neighbour's religion or his character is a pitiable way to defend your own" (Burchell 1979; 6). Matters spiritual increasingly came to be seen as an affair of individual conscience, in an agreement that was celebrated by Catholics, Protestants, and Jews alike. But it was generosity with a cost.

Exploring the multiple dimensions of stories like this one reveals a tangled skein of religious errands that met on the shores of the Pacific. As was true in many other societies on the western frontier in the early years of settlement, religious pluralism was less of a preconceived, static condition and more of a political construct that had to be negotiated and contested. Forged in an atmosphere of "intimate contact and appalled rejection," as the theorist Christopher Herbert has put it (1991: 171), missionaries and other migrants forged a new definition of diversity. While many other skirmishes occurred on the road to religious toleration in California, the anti-Chinese movement reflected a turning point in the campaign. Repudiating the model of an established church or even a *de facto* religious authority, Protestants and Catholics suspended long-standing feuds and joined forces to expel what they saw as an even greater threat to a Christian social order. Their *détente* came at the expense of Asian migrants.

Analysis of this particular moment of western history also suggests that the singular blend of individual, sometimes highly idiosyncratic, piety and public toleration that has distinguished religion in the American West is an amalgam forged through conflict, opposition, and negotiation. Westerners have fought over religious differences, but they have also exchanged and recombined religious practices in unique ways. Repression and violence have been wedded to cultural improvisation and creativity. The relative lack of an authoritative religious voice has enabled subjugation as well as inventiveness.

Some of what Gibson, for example, interpreted as the failure of lay Protestant morals, may also have represented the emergence of new religious impulses. Physical movement itself raised the possibility of new admixtures. In a series of articles published in the *California Christian Advocate* in the 1850s, a lay traveler coming to California recounted his sojourn in Rio de Janeiro, where he became fascinated by local Catholic practices. In a transformative moment, upon entering a small chapel, he was awed by a statue of the virgin on the altar, "a beautiful brilliant upon her breast dazzled the eye with its brightness." "For hours I wandered from room to room," he continued, "leaving with regret at a late hour." In reflecting on his adventures, the traveler admitted that there was much about Catholicism he disliked; still, he acknowledged, "I doubt not but through God's grace their religion will be found to have a saving power in it" (*Advocate*, September 16 and 22, 1852). Religious identity, here as well as elsewhere, was forged and recreated through opposition and contact.

The settlement of California marked the first time that Euro-Americans encountered large numbers of Asians on their own soil, and for this reason, the story of the development of religious pluralism on the Pacific Coast is distinctive. But in other respects, lending this historical perspective to our impressions of religion in the American West propels us eastward once again, where we may now choose to ask different questions of traditional accounts. Perry Miller ended his famous essay "Errand into the wilderness" with a notably romantic line about the Puritan experience in the New World. Describing the failure of the English Reformation to confirm the Puritans' understanding of the world, Miller remarks that the migrants were thereafter forced to search within themselves to make meaning out of a new land: "Having failed to rivet the eyes of the world upon their city on the hill, they were left alone with America" (Miller 1998: 41).

Despite the intrigue evoked by this image of a collective lone gunslinger on the continent, we would do well to pay more attention to the other settlers in town. New England was home to other inhabitants, and it is certainly true that they had their own errands that bear recounting. But even more fundamentally, the heterogeneity of the western frontier may also indicate that religious meaning never has been made in cultural isolation or within a communal self. It has been made in specific places and times, in conjunction with those religious "others" whose beliefs and practices Americans have confronted. If pluralism has always been a feature of the American religious landscape, then we are in essence products of negotiations, disagreements over, and exchanges between, meanings and social values.

BIBLIOGRAPHY

Barth, Gunther (1964) *Bitter Strength: A History of the Chinese in the United States, 1850–1870*, Cambridge, Mass.: Harvard University Press.

Burchell, Robert A. (1979) *The San Francisco Irish, 1848–1880*, Manchester: Manchester University Press.

Chan, Sucheng (1986) *This Bittersweet Soil: The Chinese in California Agriculture, 1860–1910*, Berkeley, Calif.: University of California Press.

Fields, Rick (1981) *How the Swans Came to the Lake: A Narrative History of Buddhism in America*, Boulder, Col.: Shambhala Publications.

Gibson, Otis (1978) *The Chinese in America*, New York: Arno Press first published Cincinannti, 1877.

Herbert, Christopher (1991) *Culture and Anomie: Ethnographic Imagination in the Nineteenth Century*, Chicago: University of Chicago Press.

Maffly-Kipp, Laurie F. (1994) *Religion and Society in Frontier California*, New Haven, Conn.: Yale University Press.

Markus, Andrew (1979) *Fear and Hatred: Purifying Australia and California, 1850–1901*, Sydney: Hale & Iremonger.

Miller, Perry (1998) "Errand into the wilderness," in Jon Butler and Harry S. Stout (eds) *Religion in American History: A Reader*, New York: Oxford University Press, pp. 27–41.

Minke, Pauline (1974) *Chinese in the Mother Lode 1850–1870*, San Francisco: R & E Research Associates.

Seager, Robert II (1959) "Some denominational reactions to Chinese immigration to California, 1856–1892," *Pacific Historical Review* 38, pp. 49–66.

Takaki, Ronald (1989) *Strangers from a Different Shore: A History of Asian Americans*, Boston, Mass.: Little, Brown & Co.

Thomson, Bishop E. (1867) Minutes of the California Annual Conference, Methodist Episcopal Church, vol. 1 (1855–72).

Tsai, Shih-Shan Henry (1986) *The Chinese Experience in America*, Bloomington, Ind.: Indiana University Press.

Walsh, James P. (1980) *America and Ireland, 1776–1976: The American Identity and the Irish Connection*, ed. David Noel Doyle and Owen Dudley Edwards, Westport, Conn.: Greenwood Press.

Woo, Wesley (1984) "Protestant work among the Chinese in the San Francisco Bay area, 1850–1920," Ph.D. dissertation, Graduate Theological Union.

Chapter 2

Religious Innovation at the Edges

Stephen J. Stein

In a brilliant and provocative book published in 1986, R. Laurence Moore examined the phenomenon of "religious outsiderhood" in America and concluded that "outsiderhood is a characteristic way of inventing one's Americanness" (p. xi). Moore's volume challenged a number of prevailing assumptions about writing the religious history of the United States, including the notion that the religious culture of a few principal Protestant denominations is what is significant in the story. Called by many the "mainline," these select Protestant churches became the measure of what was natural, appropriate, and acceptable religion. Religious groups not part of this narrow band of denominations were by implication "outsiders" and, accordingly, less legitimate and certainly less American. By the time that Moore finished his volume, he had exposed the arrogance of those who blindly subscribed to this myopic historiography and thereby enriched our understanding of the role that outsider religious groups have played in America.

Using a broad, dynamic definition of outsiderhood, Moore demonstrated that Catholics, Jews, Mormons, fundamentalists, blacks, and a host of smaller sectarian communities have at one time or another, and in one place or another, occupied the position of outsiders. Yet these groups, he argued, more than the declared mainstream communities, energized the American religious scene. Therefore any effort to understand America's religious history that ignores outsiders does so at considerable peril.

Moore's study, it might be argued, marked a turning point in the historiography of American religious history. While not alone in his critique of the field, he was more direct than most in his challenge to the dominant assumptions informing a great deal of the work being done on America's religions. Furthermore, and importantly, Moore was not making his case in order to plead for special consideration of one or another denomination. He came to his task with no narrow theological or denominational agenda. His take on outsiderhood was broad, neutral, and "ecumenical," if we may use this last term in a very different way than it functioned in his critique of the hegemonic Protestant historiography. Moore's work has contributed to the creation of an increasingly favorable climate for research on religious outsider groups in America, especially research carried out by scholars who are not members of those traditions. The last two decades of the twentieth century, in fact, have witnessed an explosion of such publications.

Simultaneously, a widespread search has been under way for new explanatory models and alternative narratives for America's religious history. As a result, numerous proposals are now being offered. One collection of such efforts is the volume entitled *Retelling U.S. Religious History*, edited by Thomas A. Tweed (1997). In his introduction Tweed describes the debate that pits those who favor "comprehensive narratives of American religion" (even if they focus "disproportionately on male, northeastern, Anglo-Saxon, mainline Protestants") against those who desire totally "new stories" because the latter believe that the old narratives obscure and distort (p. 3). Fortunately, these are not the only options available to historians.

To his credit, Tweed acknowledges the challenge facing everyone who tries to embrace the full spectrum of religious peoples in America. Unfortunately many, if not most, of the proposed "new narratives" lack comprehensiveness, and therefore they too obscure and distort, falling into the very trap their authors wish to avoid. The new narratives often fracture the story of America's religious history into small pieces by their focus on special interests. For instance, the corrective to a narrative biased in favor of males is hardly a story focused exclusively on females. The remedy for an account that focuses only on Protestants is not a narrative that excludes Protestants. Similarly, the problem of ignoring religious outsiders in the story of America's religions is not solved by writing about such outsiders in isolation from religious insiders. Inclusion and integration are the proper goals for writers of American religious history.

This essay about religious innovation is premised on the principle that it is impossible to understand outsiders without a clear appreciation for the ways they dissented consciously from the mainstream. Any effort to tell the story of religious people at the edges must deal with both the margins and the mainstream, for tension and dissent are at the heart of the outsider experience. In what follows, I explore this inclusive approach to outsiderhood by examining select examples of beliefs, practices, and rituals in religious communities at the edges.

One religious community's orthodoxy is often another religious community's heresy. Theological innovation, frequently a primary reason for a group's separate existence, is a defining characteristic of many religious outsiders. What makes such theological innovation possible? Groups at the edges frequently derive distinctive theological ideas or beliefs from visions, revelations, and intuitions received by their founder or charismatic leader. In that process formal doctrinal assertions are usually secondary to the primary religious experiences. Sometimes written versions of both the primary experiences and the secondary accounts take on the status of sacred texts. Numerous examples of such scriptural writings exist among outsider groups in America.

The most prominent new "bible" in the United States is the *Book of Mormon*, which, according to the Latter-day Saints, is the product of a divinely-guided translation process carried out by Joseph Smith (1805–44) in the closing years of the 1820s. Mormons describe this third "testament" as Smith's "translation" of tablets providentially preserved from ancient times. The published volume tells a story of pre-Columbian inhabitants in the Americas. Non-Mormon critics, by contrast, characterize the *Book of Mormon* as a fictive reflection of widespread religious concerns in nineteenth-century America. Both perspectives underscore the critical role this scripture played in the initial definition of the LDS church and its continuing importance as a distinctive marker, setting Mormons apart from other Christians who also accord the scriptural principle primacy in their religious life.

Even more significant for theological innovation in the early Mormon community were revelations received by Joseph Smith, some of which were published in 1833 as the *Book of Commandments*, and then later as *Doctrine and Covenants*. Specific revelations address a variety of theological concerns and demonstrate how Smith's religious experiences gave rise to doctrines peculiar to Mormonism. For example, Section 131 in *Doctrine and Covenants*, dated May 16–17, 1843, contains the following declaration: "There is no such thing as immaterial matter. All spirit is matter, but it is more fine or pure, and can only be discerned by purer eyes." This metaphysical observation had direct implications for Smith's ideas concerning the nature of God.

In April of the same year, Smith had recorded an unusual view of the godhead. On the basis of a revelation, he stated that God the Father "has a body of flesh and bones as tangible as man's," as does God the Son (Section 130). In the same revelation he was also told that the third member of the Trinity, the Holy Ghost, does not have "a body of flesh and bones, but is a personage of Spirit," thus facilitating the indwelling within individuals. These assertions corresponded with Smith's account of his First Vision in 1820 when two "personages," the Father and the Son, appeared to him and instructed him regarding the unsatisfactory character of the established denominations. Even though his celebrated First Vision did not figure publicly in the history of Mormonism until years later, its sharp critique of the existing churches operated as a formative negative principle in the earliest years of the infant movement.

Sections 130 and 131 together give voice to a very unconventional view of God. For Smith, God was a material being, similar to humans. Even the Holy Ghost, or Holy Spirit, was spirit in name only, for spirit is but a "more fine or pure" form of matter. Smith's view cut deeply against the grain of traditional Christian beliefs that declared God's nature to be wholly Other and comprised of spirit. It is the traditional doctrine of God's nature as spirit that makes the idea of the Incarnation of Christ such a dramatic act of love and condescension for many Christians. In Mormon theology the concept of Incarnation fades in significance because God's nature is already "flesh and bones." When measured against prevailing Western Christian traditions, Mormon orthodoxy was heresy of the first order.

This notion of the materiality of all existence, including God, became foundational for Mormonism. On it Smith built a soteriology that begins with preexistent souls literally fathered by God, combines them with mortal bodies that undergo a period of probation on earth, and ultimately bestows their due reward in the heavenly spheres. The sense of possibility open to humans is explicit in the Mormon assertion: "As man is, God once was; as God is, man may be." The concept of "eternal progression" allows humans to rise to spiritual heights so that they too may become gods, thus further blurring the line between the Creator and the creature. In sum, Latter-day Saint theology is filled with beliefs radically different from the Christian traditions that preceded Mormonism. It was, in part, that radical difference that made Mormonism distinctive and appealing to those who accepted it, most of whom came out of the "orthodox" religious traditions in both the United States and western Europe.

The Church of Christ (Scientist), another significant outsider religious group in the United States, also holds dissenting beliefs about God, human existence, and salvation. This community arose during the last quarter of the nineteenth century, some fifty or so years after the beginnings of Mormonism. Mary Baker Eddy (1821–1910) was the shaping force behind Christian Science, but the process leading to her innovative theological notions differed markedly from that in Mormonism. In Eddy's case, study and reflection, writing and rewriting, marked the development of doctrine. Her ideas emerged from the crucible of her own experience. Years of physical and psychological suffering gave her cause to consider carefully both the religious and the medical orthodoxies of her day, and she rejected them. After experimenting with the variety of available spiritual and healing options, she turned to the study of the Bible and, in particular, to the accounts of Jesus' miracles.

Christian Scientists speak of Eddy's "Great Discovery" in 1866 following a serious accident as her moment of insight, a discovery that reoriented her understanding of reality. Critics of Eddy suggest that her relationship with Phineas Parkhurst Quimby, a mental healer in Portland, Maine, was the critical factor in her changing views. Regardless of the origin of her ideas, Eddy came to regard the notion that humans are material organisms as the fundamental error. Rather, as she later stated, "Man is not matter; he is not made up of brain, blood, bones, and other material elements. . . . Man is idea, the image, of Love; he is not physique" (*Science and Health*, p. 475). Even more, she wrote, "Man is God's image and likeness . . . (*Miscellaneous Writings, 1883–1896*, p. 183, quoted in Gottschalk 1973: 61). Therefore all that can be affirmed concerning the goodness of God is true also of humans.

Eddy's view of God and of humans rested on her metaphysical affirmation concerning the unreality of matter. "Mortal mind" produces a misleading "error" that blinds individuals to the truth that they are in the image of God, or Divine Mind, and therefore equally perfect, spiritual, and eternal. The task confronting humans is to recognize the fallacy of materiality and to "demonstrate" their true spiritual nature. When truth is discovered and illusion is revealed as false, then sin, sickness, and death vanish. Divine Science dispels error and leads to understanding, which is salvation.

Through her many publications, but most of all in the textbook she authored, *Science and Health with Key to the Scriptures*, which has become scripture for Christian Scientists, Eddy created a distinctive Christian Science vocabulary. She redefined many conventional religious terms, constructing her own theological lexicon. For her "science" was not empirical experimentation, but spiritual demonstration of perfection. For her the Trinity was not Father, Son, and Holy Spirit, but rather Life, Truth, and Love – synonyms for God, or three essential qualities of the infinite. For Eddy God was not only Father, possessing masculine qualities, but also Mother, possessing feminine characteristics, as is evident especially in the love of God.

Christian Science established itself in the closing decades of the nineteenth century as a radical alternative to both mainstream religion and to conventional medicine. At a moment in the United States when material success seemed all-important, when the new sciences of biology, geology, sociology, and psychology were capturing the public imagination, when allopathic medicine was consolidating its cultural position, and when the so-called mainline Protestant churches still exercised a kind of religious hegemony, at precisely that moment Eddy appeared on the scene, challenging a variety of the fundamental premises of the day. Christian Science beliefs made sense to Americans in the decades surrounding the turn of the twentieth century, in part, because they were directly in tension with widespread views found throughout society at the time but not universally accepted. This sense of an alternative was central to the theological appeal of Christian Science.

One religious community's virtues are often another religious community's vices. Social innovation, a second defining feature of religious outsiderhood in America, is frequently another reason for the separate existence of groups. What makes such social innovation possible? Unique or dissenting social practices sometimes derive directly from visions, revelations, or intuitions received by the founder or leader, but just as often the justification or rationalization for dissenting behavior follows rather than precedes its institutionalization. In America a variety of factors has contributed to social experimentation by religious outsiders, including the existence of seemingly endless open space on the geographical margins of society, the abundance of natural resources throughout the continent, and the constitutional guarantee of the free exercise of religion. Among outsider groups few social practices have been more innovative and controversial than those involving alternative patterns of family life, including dissenting views on marriage, sexuality, and gender.

The Shakers, formally known as the United Society of Believers in Christ's Second Appearing, were one outsider religious group that developed very unconventional social practices. Some of their most unusual activities were not established by their founder, but rather evolved in the community with the passage of time. The American founder of the Shakers was Ann Lee (ca. 1736–84), an unlettered English charismatic figure who emigrated to America in 1774, led by visions and because of the opposition to her small following in England. Lee's unsuccessful marriage and her misfortunes in childbirth deeply influenced her. Her public proclamation challenged hearers to strive for purity and the higher life by putting aside carnal concerns. Yet during Lee's lifetime most of her followers continued to live in conventional family units. After Lee's death, however, her successors gathered the Believers into communities formed on the principles of mandatory celibacy, physical separation of the sexes, and spiritual families replacing biological units. Elders and eldresses assumed parental roles; husbands and wives who converted to Shakerism became as brothers and sisters; children were raised by designated caretakers in common circumstances; and the whole community came to view itself as an extended family whose heavenly parents included Jesus and Ann Lee. Sexual relations were identified with the original sin of Adam and Eve; renunciation of sexual relations (what Believers called "bearing the cross") became the greatest challenge of the Shaker lifestyle.

Community structures mirrored the social realities implied by the collective commitment to celibacy. Rules and regulations codified in the "Millennial Laws," first written down in 1821, governed all aspects of life. Physical separation of the sexes was accomplished by constructing living quarters that had separate entrances and staircases. Social intercourse between men and women was carefully supervised by the leadership. Uniform clothing and communal property eliminated marks of distinction among the members. A strong sense of gender equality accompanied these social practices, derived in part from the fact that the founder was a woman and by subsequent commitments made by later Shakers. The Believers, for example, interpreted the creation story in Genesis as affirming the dual nature of all creation patterned after the duality of God. That judgment reinforced the high estimation for the place of women in the society; men and women both exercised leadership and authority within the community.

The social arrangements among the Shakers contrasted sharply with prevailing mores in American society during the nineteenth century, a time when families were large, the appropriateness of sexual relations rarely questioned, patriarchy dominant, and women subordinate. Again the alternative character of Shakerism attracted many to the movement.

Another group of religious outsiders whose views on marriage, family, and gender issues were in fundamental tension with the dominant social patterns in the larger society was the twentieth-century community known officially as the Peace Mission Movement; it was comprised of the followers of Father Divine. Divine, born George Baker (1879–1965), was an African-American laborer who was part of the mass migration of blacks from the South. He emerged on the public scene as an itinerant minister known at one point as the Messenger, appearing first in the Baltimore area, then throughout the South, and later in New York City. Another name change, to Reverend Major Jealous Divine, and another relocation, this time to Sayville, Long Island, set the stage in the years after 1919 for the emergence of Baker as Father Divine and his wife Peninniah as Mother Divine. From these less-than-promising circumstances over a period of several years he built a unique religious community.

It is difficult to overstate Father Divine's role in the life of this outsider group. He presided over all its activities. He provided for the physical and emotional needs of those attracted to him and his teachings. The movement expanded from serving free meals to those who were hungry and assisting others seeking employment, to a full communal organization with residential sites located in major urban centers across the country. There members lived together and gave their time and possessions to Father Divine. Early in this evolution of the community, conflict developed between Divine and Sayville authorities. Arrest and conviction for maintaining a public nuisance, followed by the sudden death of the trial judge and the overturning of the conviction, catapulted Divine into the public eye. He capitalized on the publicity and moved forward, building his distinctive community during a period of American history when economic circumstances were inflicting severe hardship on many of the blacks who had migrated to northern urban centers.

The social program of the Peace Mission Movement rested on Divine's expanding claims that increasingly included declarations of divinity. The name change from "Reverend" to "Father" signaled the public emergence of his persona as a savior figure. His message was one of liberation and redemption for those who believed in him. But it also included a series of demands: he called for African Americans, who formed the bulk of his followers, to reject the negative features of the social environment in which they found themselves, namely, the poverty and oppression of their segregated world.

The Peace Mission Movement was fundamentally countercultural. Father Divine proclaimed that there was no color line in the new family over which he and Mother Divine presided as spiritual parents. All who became part of the community were God's children regardless of skin color. In fact, within Divine's kingdom the use of the words "black," "white," or "Negro" as racial markers was strictly prohibited. Significantly, with the passage of time, whites as well as African Americans joined the movement. Divine welcomed into his community all who needed food and lodging; he provided those necessities free of charge to those unable to pay. In turn, he asked of them commitment, affection, and dedication. On this basis a strong economic communal organization arose which provided for the needs of its members. The community's resources came from the contributions, both money and labor, of Divine's followers, as well as from enterprises that Divine established, including restaurants, hotels, garages, and other independent businesses.

The Peace Mission Movement also restructured social relations among its members. In this community sexual relations were forbidden. Traditional marriages were condemned; Father Divine demanded that his followers be celibate. When married couples came into the movement, they separated and became as brothers and sisters – which was also the common form of address among all members. The only exception to this prohibition of marriage was the union of Father and Mother Divine, but even in that case it appears that sexual relations were not part of their marriage. In the Peace Mission Movement, gender was another boundary marker setting members off from the larger society. Divine minimized distinctions between men and women; he often spoke of himself in feminine terms. Women who joined this community received a measure of respect not commonly accorded them in the larger society, especially in the case of African-American women who often worked in menial service jobs.

The Peace Mission Movement constituted an alternative world to that existing in the larger society. Father Divine constructed this new world from a variety of different sources, including New Thought ideology. From the latter he appropriated the notion of the creative power of the mind and the attendant prospects for health, prosperity, and power. New Thought affirmed the significance of an indwelling presence within individuals. For Divine and his followers this positive outlook helped to overcome their negative circumstances. He structured life within the Peace Mission Movement on this outlook. For example, there was no official place in this world for sickness or disease. In the words of Divine, "I have limitless blessings to bestow upon mankind, spiritual, mental, material and social. All that is necessary is the understanding of the spirit of the consciousness of the presence of God. I have healing for you all. It is not necessary to contact me personally" (Weisbrot 1984: 50). There were no doctors or prescriptions, nor any need of the same, once members fully realized God's presence in their midst. The ultimate measure of this alternative outlook was denial of the reality of death. The Peace Mission Movement took no public recognition of deaths, made no provision for mourning, held no funerals – until the death of Father Divine himself. After his death an elaborate ritual meal was celebrated at which it was affirmed that because Divine was God, he was now present spiritually, rather than physically.

Father Divine was buried at his Woodmont estate in a Philadelphia suburb. Mother Divine, the second Mother Divine – a former secretary, Sweet Angel, whom Father Divine married after the death of Peninniah – stepped into the position of sole leader of the movement at a time when it had shrunk to a mere shadow of its former size. By the 1960s the Peace Mission Movement no longer presented an attractive alternative for most Americans, black or white.

One religious community's rites are often another religious community's wrongs. Ritual innovation, a third defining feature of religious outsiders in America, is another reason for creating separate communities. What makes such innovation of a ritual kind possible? Distinctive rites frequently embody the formative theological ideas of religious outsiders or reflect their unconventional social practices. Sometimes such ritual expressions are the product of the experiences and ideas of the founders, but in many situations religious ceremonies evolve with the passage of time, arising perhaps from the life experiences of community members. Rituals are powerful forces in the construction and confirmation of the collective identity of religious outsiders.

The Quakers, formally the Religious Society of Friends, provide one striking example of the power of the ritual setting. The Friends, one of America's oldest and most significant outsider communities, originated from the religious experiences of their English founder George Fox (1624–91). Fox, a religious rebel who abandoned the conventions of English church life in pursuit of spiritual enlightenment, came to the conviction that truth is accessible to each individual by means of God's inner voice, or the Inner Light of Christ. When he began proclaiming his ideas in public, he encountered violent opposition and imprisonment. Undeterred by persecution, he attracted followers of equal moral earnestness and devotion. His travels on behalf of the Quaker cause – a name associated with the young movement because of ecstatic trembling that occurred during their meetings – included a trip to the English colonies in America in

1671–3. William Penn, the proprietor of the Pennsylvania colony founded in 1681, was a member of the Society of Friends. His "Holy Experiment" reflected Quaker principles and beckoned as a haven for Friends.

The Quaker principle of the Inner Light led directly to worship patterns strikingly different from those in other churches at that time. Quaker meetings were held in plain meetinghouses that bore little resemblance to the Roman Catholic cathedrals of medieval Europe or even the Protestant church buildings of the Reformation era. They contained neither an altar for celebration of the Eucharist nor a pulpit for proclamation of the Gospel. When Friends gathered for worship, they waited silently for a leading from God. No fixed or formal sequence of activities occurred on each occasion. The Quakers rejected a set liturgy, chanting or hymns, sacraments, and sermons. No priest or minister presided because all men and *women* alike might testify in the meeting as they were given inner guidance. Even children might become the voice of God to the assembly.

This informal participatory ritual was driven by a deep antagonism toward the more conventional worship practices of the day. Fox and his followers heaped scorn and ridicule on the "steeplehouses" (church buildings) of other Christian communities, calling them "idolatrous temples" made with hands. Friends were themselves to be living temples dedicated to the service of God. Sacraments and other traditional rituals were rejected as unnecessary physical manifestations of inner realities. Fixed theological formulas or creeds stifled the power of the Christ Within. Prepared sermons were the opposite of the impulses of God given to individuals. Priests and ministers were denounced as hirelings. Quaker rituals – even though Friends would not have used that language to describe their worship practices – were defined by their diametrical opposition to the worship conventions of the day.

Other aspects of Quaker behavior also reflected the Friends' views on proper worship. The act of testifying or witnessing to the Truth – the essence of worship – was not confined to the meetinghouse. Friends were to embody the principle of truth in their daily activities. The plain style of speech and dress was one such testimony. Addressing all people alike was one manifestation of the principle of spiritual equality. Quakers refused to take oaths, for they found such swearing by God's name offensive and unnecessary because they were always to speak the truth. Likewise, social rituals that reflected distinctions among people were rejected, such as removing the hat in the presence of someone of higher rank or social status. Since even slaves possessed the Inner Light, opposition to slaveholding became a matter of debate among Quakers long before it was a general issue of concern in American society. Fox's movement embodied a radical critique of authority and hierarchy. Decisions in the meeting were made by consensus rather than by clergy or bishops.

With the passage of time the Quakers fell under the influence of other Christian traditions, especially evangelicalism. During the nineteenth century the Quaker movement in America divided on several religious issues, including the role of the Bible in the Christian life, the legitimacy of a paid clergy, and the nature of worship in the meeting. Nevertheless, all Friends maintained a commitment to the power of Christ Within in worship, even though not all maintained primitive meetings.

Another family of religious outsiders noted for innovation of a ritual kind is the cluster of Pentecostal churches that has developed during the twentieth century. Pentecostals share with the Quakers a negative critique of the worship practices in established mainline churches. Both groups rejected formal, structured, and liturgical patterns of worship in favor of free spiritual expression. Nevertheless, they carried their innovation in opposite directions. Quakers "waited" on the Inner Voice; Pentecostals actively sought out the Spirit's presence.

The theological principle at the heart of Pentecostal worship – the presence of the Holy Spirit in the life of the Christian – has unified the family of diverse denominations identified with American Pentecostalism. From its earliest manifestations in the ministry of Charles Parham (1873–1929) in Topeka, Kansas, and his subsequent itinerancy throughout the mid-section of the United States, as well as in the Azusa Street revival of 1906–9 in Los Angeles under the charismatic leadership of William Seymour (1870–1922), until the present day when celebrity-like televangelists command huge media audiences, the Pentecostal movement has affirmed that a second intense spiritual experience must follow conversion, namely, the baptism of the Spirit. The latter is commonly evidenced by the "gift" of speaking in tongues, or glossolalia. Tongue-speaking, according to Pentecostals, is one of the gifts of the Spirit enumerated and described in the New Testament. The twentieth century has given rise to a host of distinct Pentecostal denominations in America. Many of these organizations are very small; several are very large, including, for example, the Assemblies of God and the Church of God in Christ. A number of theological differences distinguish the groups from one another, yet all accept this cardinal principle.

In the earliest decades of the twentieth century, Pentecostals gave free reign to the gifts of the Spirit in their worship. They rejected everything that might be seen as inhibiting of the Spirit's operation and turned instead to the primitive church in the New Testament as their model. Observers often described their worship gatherings as filled with a cacophony of sounds and confusing ecstatic behavior. Preaching, testifying, witnessing, prophesying, praying, singing, healing – all of these activities came under the influence of the Holy Spirit. Men, women, and children might be the chosen instruments. Ministers did not attempt to control the flow of the services which often went on for long periods of time. The physical setting mattered little to Pentecostals. Often storefronts or other locations not distinctly set aside for religious purposes served as "churches." In these locations Pentecostal worship was spontaneous, participatory, and improvisational.

The passage of time has witnessed some accommodation to more conventional worship patterns, but Pentecostal ritual still remains the province of the Spirit. Powerful charismatic figures, both men and women, preside in these situations, but they are unable to restrict the movements of the Spirit. Music has emerged as a central element of Pentecostal worship, often involving instruments not commonly found in other churches. Healing, too, has become a common feature in the ritual context, whether carried out by prayer alone or by miracle-working through the laying on of hands. Scores of Pentecostal leaders – for example, Aimee Semple McPherson, William Branham, Oral Roberts, Jimmy Swaggert – have achieved prominence as successful healers.

The diversity within the Pentecostal family sometimes is evident in controversies regarding worship practices. For a very few within the movement, the scriptural principle associated with Mark 16:8 allows the handling of poisonous snakes or the drinking of dangerous liquids as a sign of true belief. These unusual practices, which have received more attention from the media than they deserve, most Pentecostals roundly condemn. In general, the passage of time has seen a movement toward moderation and the mainstreaming of Pentecostal rituals, thus reducing somewhat the degree of distinction from other denominations.

This exploration of innovation among select groups confirms the insight that "contests" between insiders and outsiders gave shape and form, content and substance, to the religious beliefs, practices, and rituals of outsiders. Mormon beliefs arose in a context of competing religious claims and aroused immense hostility. The theological affirmations of Christian Science evoked vigorous opposition and scorn from its early opponents. The social practices institutionalized by the Shakers in the nineteenth century offended many Americans and produced repeated outbursts of violence against the Believers. The communal practices of the Peace Mission Movement were denounced by critics who charged Father Divine with manipulating gullible followers. Quaker worship was dismissed as "enthusiasm" by the clergy of the other Christian denominations. Pentecostals were ridiculed as "Holy Rollers" because of the centrality of ecstatic experiences within their services.

Yet this opposition did not destroy these outsider groups. Instead, it often had the effect of publicizing and solidifying the movements. Leaders and members alike turned the conflict to advantage, for it provided an occasion to feature the serious religious alternatives these outsiders groups represented – whether in the area of beliefs, practices, or rituals. These "contests" also became the occasion for outsiders to sharpen the sense of being "other" – different from the insiders. The sense of embodying an alternative way of being religious has been and remains a critical component of religious outsiderhood. In a world that identifies with product diversification, religious diversification has become an equally attractive American option. Outsider religions provide new options in the spiritual marketplace of America.

The growth of new religions is rarely a parthenogenetic process. On the contrary, the creativity and invention manifested among such groups commonly arises in a context of contact with other religions and results from the appropriation, adaptation, or rejection of religious elements from those communities. Religious groups at the edges define themselves in relationship to others, not in isolation from them.

Some special ironies attach to the situation of religious outsiders in American culture. In our society generally, we laud and applaud risk-takers, pioneers, those at the cutting edge, those who set the pace. Our historical narratives, for example, romanticize the pioneers who left the settled communities and broke new trails in the wilderness. Scientists who discover medical breakthroughs we hail as miracle-workers in lab coats and reward with Nobel Prizes. Astronauts willing to travel in outer space we celebrate as folk heroes. But the same attitude does not operate in the area of religion, where caution seems the order of the day. Tradition is preferred over innovation, orthodoxy over heresy, the conventional over the radical, the predictable over the spontaneous. In a word, religious insiders still enjoy greater public favor even though, in the history of religions in America, the innovative edge clearly goes to religious outsiders.

BIBLIOGRAPHY

Anderson, Robert Mapes (1979) *Vision of the Disinherited: The Making of American Pentecostalism*, New York: Oxford University Press.

Arrington, Leonard J. and Bitton, Davis (1979) *The Mormon Experience: A History of the Latter-day Saints*, New York: Alfred A. Knopf.

Bednarowski, Mary Farrell (1989) *New Religions and the Theological Imagination in America*, Bloomington, Ind.: Indiana University Press.

Brewer, Priscilla J. (1986) *Shaker Communities, Shaker Lives*, Hanover, NH: University of New England Press.

Conkin, Paul K. (1997) *American Originals: Homemade Varieties of Christianity*, Chapel Hill, NC: University of North Carolina Press.

Gottschalk, Stephen (1973) *The Emergence of Christian Science in American Religious Life*, Berkeley, Calif.: University of California Press.

Hamm, Thomas D. (1988) *The Transformation of American Quakerism: Orthodox Friends, 1800–1907*, Bloomington, Ind.: Indiana University Press.

Harrell, David Edwin, Jr. (1975) *All Things Are Possible: The Healing and Charismatic Revivals in Modern America*, Bloomington, Ind.: Indiana University Press.

Melton, J. Gordon (1986) *The Encyclopedia of American Religions*, 4th edn, Detroit, Mich.: Gale Research.

Miller, Timothy (ed.) (1995) *America's Alternative Religions*, Albany, NY: State University of New York Press.

Moore, R. Laurence (1986) *Religious Outsiders and the Making of Americans*, New York: Oxford University Press.

Peel, Robert (1987) *Spiritual Healing in a Scientific Age*, San Francisco: Harper & Row.

Shipps, Jan (1985) *Mormonism: The Story of a New Religious Tradition*, Urbana, Ill.: University of Illinois Press.

Stein, Stephen J. (1992) *The Shaker Experience in America: A History of the United Society of Believers*, New Haven, Conn.: Yale University Press.

Tweed, Thomas A. (ed.) (1997) *Retelling U.S. Religious History*, Berkeley, Calif.: University of California Press.

Watts, Jill (1992) *God, Harlem U.S.A.: The Father Divine Story*, Berkeley, Calif.: University of California Press.

Weisbrot, Robert (1984) *Father Divine: The Utopian Evangelist of the Depression Era who became an American Legend*, Boston, Mass.: Beacon Press.

Chapter 3

Diversity and the Pluralist Ideal

William R. Hutchison

Introduction: A Pluralism "Struggling to be Born"

Hector St John de Crèvecoeur, the immigrant "American farmer" who published admiring reflections on the American society of the 1780s, expressed special wonderment about religious conditions. He was intrigued, above all, by two characteristics for which, today. we would use the words "diversity" and "pluralism." ("Pluralism," a modern term for a very old ideal, in this context means the celebration or at least genuine acceptance of diversity.) Crèvecoeur marveled at the very existence, within one country or colony, of widely differing forms of Christianity; but he was also greatly impressed by the degree to which these differences seemed to be accepted, or even taken for granted.

Asking his mostly-European readers to accompany him, in their minds, down what he portrayed as a typical country road, the genial author pointed first to the prosperous farm of "a Catholic, who prays to God as he has been taught, and believes in transubstantiation." This hard worker and good family man was entirely accepted. "His belief, his prayers offend nobody."

According to Crèvecoeur, the same was true of every householder on the road: the "good honest plodding Lutheran," the fiery "seceder" with his well painted house, the "Low Dutchman" who adhered to a rigid Calvinism but seemed more preoccupied with his "waggon and fat horses." Everyone tolerated and respected everyone else. "Persecution, religious pride," and other inanities that "the world commonly calls religion" had been left in Europe. If these colonists "are peaceable subjects, and are industrious, what is it to their neighbors how and in what manner they think fit to address their prayers to the Supreme Being?"

Although this depiction appeared in an extraordinary piece of literature, it was otherwise far from unusual. Throughout the nineteenth century especially, the idea that religious diversity and religious pluralism were practically the same thing – that in America the second followed the first inevitably if not immediately – was reiterated endlessly in print, in song and in the visual arts. In their Thanksgiving and patriotic hymns Americans sang about a pluralist ideal that had beckoned "our exiled fathers" to the North American continent and then had been realized gloriously as they beat "a thoroughfare for freedom . . . across the wilderness." In popular paintings like Edward Hicks's *Peaceable Kingdom*, cultures as distinct from each other as those of Native Americans and European Americans were depicted as dwelling together like the lion and lamb of biblical prophecy.

However implausible – given the sporadic persecutions and the persisting exclusions or aggressions in American culture and religion – such dreams of concord remained vivid well into the twentieth century. By the latter decades of that century, however, historians and others were treating them as largely erroneous. The idea that diversities had normally been accorded a pluralistic response was, they argued, not so much a dream as a delusion, and a serious one. Sydney Ahlstrom of Yale University, in a magisterial history of American religion published in 1972, went so far as to assert that religious pluralism, although it might be emerging in the post-1960 era, had been, at most, "struggling to be born" up to that time.

Long-dead historians and religionists doubtless stirred in their graves as this heresy was committed to print; and live politicians, had they been reading tomes like Ahlstrom's, might have proposed punitive legislation. As it was, scarcely anyone noticed. A great American certitude, it seemed, had become uncertain.

Why such a reversal? The explanation, I think, is that the pluralist ideal had become steadily more encompassing and more demanding. Ideas about what it means to accept or honor diversity had changed substantially since Crèvecoeur's time, and even since the early twentieth century. The result was that, seen in relation to definitions of pluralism that were taking hold by mid-century, the record so proudly hailed under earlier definitions had come to seem problematic.

Until at least the latter part of the nineteenth century, the society's honoring of diversity had meant little more than the absence or overcoming of religious persecution. Stated affirmatively, it had meant legal toleration or, more broadly, tolerance. And by such standards the American record, while more mixed than the popular mythology imagined, was the best, or certainly among the best, that could be found either in Western or in non-western societies. So long as toleration was the criterion, one *could* claim that lion and lamb had lain down together in the expanses of America.

Gradually, however, the requirements – what it took, so to speak, to be accounted a pluralist – had become more rigorous. Broadly speaking, this had happened in two stages. "Tolerated" religious and cultural groups (for example, Catholics, Jews, African Americans, and women) had pressed first for what might best be called "inclusion," and then, by the mid twentieth century, for something more than inclusion. By the time when Ahlstrom issued his judgment, pluralism had come to mean not just toleration, or tolerance, or even inclusion; it had come to mean equal participation. By then, a card-carrying pluralist was someone for whom it was not enough to say that everyone should, so to speak, be allowed to attend the meeting and join the discussion. Pluralism had come to mean an equal, or at least a proportional, right to set the meeting's agenda.

Given this latest understanding of what it means to accept and celebrate diversity, the American record seemed in need of careful reassessment – in need of a reality check. In the balance of this essay I shall try to sketch the newer conceptions of the American religious past that have emerged from that kind of reappraisal.

The Great Diversification

Despite a tendency to think of the demographic changes of the late nineteenth and late twentieth centuries as the most dramatic in American history, those that occurred soon after the founding of the Republic were just as rapid and far more traumatic. In religious terms: a country whose European population in 1800 had been almost entirely Protestant Christian became, within a very few decades, something closer to the 60 percent Protestant society of modern times.

Much of the "trauma" is attributable to the fact that the changes, whatever their exact magnitude, burst upon a society that for two centuries had been strikingly homogeneous. Not only had the European component in colonial society been more than 95 percent Protestant in background; the toweringly dominant Protestants had been less diverse than popular and scholarly depictions have led us to suppose. At least 90 percent of the European population had come out of the Calvinist rather than the Lutheran side of the Protestant Reformation; and 85 percent were *English speaking* Calvinist Protestants. The contributions of colonial "outsiders" – non-Christans, sectarian groups, dissenters of all kinds – far outran their numerical strength, but that strength was indeed very limited. Jews in 1780 could claim only five of the 2700 religious congregations in the colonies; and that miniscule number was more typical, among "outsider" groups, than the 300 congregations of the Quakers or the thirty-one churches of the Moravians. A fundamentally like-minded, like-speaking colonial population had spent two centuries constructing a culture to its own specifications.

Against this background, the era that followed stands out, first of all, as one of unusually rapid growth. While the Indian and African populations declined between 1800 and 1860 – the first numerically, the second proportionally – the European component increased by a factor of nearly six. The 3 million immigrants who arrived in just one ten year period (mid-1840s to mid-1850s), and who added themselves to a population of only 20 million, represented by far the largest proportional increase experienced in any period of American history.

But these were not simply new people; to an unprecedented degree they were "different" people. Although Englishmen and Scots continued to immigrate in large numbers, a huge portion of the immigrants, and of those added by territorial expansion, seemed, to older-stock Americans, nearly as exotic as Russian Jews would appear to Americans in the 1890s.

With respect to religious change: it was a matter of some significance that the "Lutheran" component in American Protestantism grew from 50,000 to 250,000, and that Jewish numbers grew at the same rate as the general population. But the most striking and portentous statistics by far were those that showed a Roman Catholic increase that was roughly eight times faster than overall population growth. In view especially of deepseated anti-Catholic feelings that in some respects were more bitter than those that targeted Jews or Muslims, one can indeed argue that the "shock to the system" administered in this era was and remains unparalleled in the American experience.

"Just Behave Yourself":
Conditions of Acceptance in Early American Society

How well did Americans, in response to this process of radical diversification, meet the promises of toleration and tolerance enshrined in their founding documents and loudly trumpeted in their nationalistic rhetoric? Faced with the evidences of extreme anti-Catholic and anti-immigrant feeling and activity, the historian is tempted to answer simply, and flippantly, "Not very well." Like most societies faced with similarly rapid social change, nineteenth-century Americans greeted newcomers more often with resistance and apprehensiveness than with cordial acceptance.

Yet the picture is a mixed one. Concessions to dissent and outsidership were sufficient to enhance the American reputation and self-image regarding religious toleration. In a longer view, moreover, even the narrow and otherwise minimal pluralistic advances of this era provided models for later, wider application.

Most such advances occurred within the cultural mainstream, that is, within long-established groups of West European and Protestant background. Among the ethnically privileged, dissent and innovation not only were broadly protected in a formal sense; they were accorded a degree of popular acceptance and, in some cases, respect that was quite unusual, and therefore justly celebrated, in and beyond the western world.

Even within the mainstream, however, there were limits: limits measured less by doctrinal dissent, disruptive as that could be, than by divergence from behavioral norms. Pew-holders and preachers in mainstream churches were less likely to be contemptuous of theological liberals or radicals than they were of frontier revivalists. The latter, though generally more orthodox in doctrine than liberals, were accused of employing methods that induced harmful or even licentious behavior. And among the utopian or otherwise radical communities of the time, the ones that experienced actual persecution were those like the polygamous Mormons, or the "free-loving" Oneidans of upstate New York, who were seen as engaging in outrageous personal and group practices.

Behavior as a criterion for acceptance stands out most plainly in these differential responses to dissenters who resembled the American majority in ethnic origins and class distribution. But it was also an important, sometimes decisive, litmus test in relation to those perceived as ethnically different and in other respects "not our sort of people."

Here one's attention is drawn to the especially virulent and widespread unwillingness to extend tolerance to Roman Catholics. Nativism, the organized opposition to new-stock immigrants and most especially to Catholic immigration, spawned a political party in the 1840s and 1850s. It also gave rise to occasional violence, including the notorious burning of a nunnery in Charlestown, Massachusetts, in 1834. More generally, however, it was a matter of anti-Catholic and anti-immigrant organizations, of social exclusion, of pressure against establishment of Catholic schools, and above all, of anti-Catholic propaganda that was frequently vicious.

In that propaganda, one does find an obsession with behavior, most especially sexual behavior. The allegations concerning Catholic clergy and the members of Catholic orders were even more severe and sinister than the charges against Mormons or Oneidans, and were less grounded in any sort of evidence. *The Awful Disclosures of Maria Monk* (1836), supposedly penned by an escapee from a Montreal nunnery, was only the most widely circulated item in an entire genre of subliterature that purported to show priests, monks, and nuns in general debauch and in very specific sexual transgressions.

Those seen as behaving themselves, on the other hand, could hold strongly dissenting beliefs, such as those of nineteenth-century Quakers or Unitarians, with little fear of derision and almost no danger of persecution. Even serious misbehavers (Catholics, Mormons) and those with inconvenient habits (such as those of Jews and Adventists who celebrated the Sabbath on the wrong day) tended to gain acceptance insofar as they could see fit to alter their practices. Crèvecoeur's observation – So long as someone is a good sturdy farmer and a family man, who cares what he believes, or whether he believes anything at all? – seemed to be validated, fifty and sixty years later, on the larger stage of the early American republic.

If you were some kind of national hero, that helped too. A number of military and political figures, from Thomas Paine and Ethan Allen in the Revolutionary period to "Colonel Bob" Ingersoll after the Civil War, found it entirely possible to be outspoken detractors of the faith supposedly held dear by the vast majority of their countrymen. To be sure, they were denounced and caricatured; little children were warned against the wickedness that allegedly had destroyed "Mad Tom" Paine and others of his ilk. Their schoolbooks also, however, printed the elegant Romney portrait of Paine in sections on the Revolution, along with pictures of the heroic Allen with sword or musket in hand.

In sum, if you were a cultural insider, you could be about as different as you wished in actual religious views. If you were an outsider, acceptance depended to a large extent upon your willingness to become assimilated, especially in matters of religious and general behavior.

The pluralist ideal, therefore, had both failed and succeeded during the early decades of the Republic. Even toleration – first-stage pluralism – had been withheld in the cases of Mormons, Catholics, non Europeans, and some religious radicals. But with a right of dissent clearly embodied in the founding documents of the nation and most of its states, and with dissent itself selectively encouraged, commitments had been created that could not be expunged or entirely ignored.

Marching to Zion: The "Protestant Establishment" as a Unitive Force

With respect to the church–state separation that was foundational for pluralist advances, a funny thing happened on the way to the twentieth century. The Americans, who were famous, and notably self-congratulatory, for having over-thrown establishments or left them behind, managed to develop an impressive functional equivalent for an Established Church. Americans, as the future Cardinal Newman wrote in the 1830s, liked to think their religious life was not, "like ours, enslaved to the civil power"; yet their churches were beholden to public opinion, which in a democracy is "the civil power in another shape." And a British Congregationalist delegation reported that while the United States had no law for the regulation of the Sabbath, "public sentiment secures its sanctifi-cation better with them than with us." Such observations were standard.

If the American form of religious establishment lacked the focus and concrete-ness of, say, an Anglican Church, neither was it something as elusive as "public sentiment." It was a highly structured affair. On the institutional side, it involved the more powerful denominations, especially those of the Baptists, Con-gregationalists, Episcopalians, Methodists, and Presbyterians; it expressed itself in a multitude of voluntary associations devoted to missions, peace, temperance, and other kinds of moral and social reform. Terms like "establishment" also denoted cultural, literary, educational, and journalistic entities that were Prot-estant in leadership and outlook; and a personal network of Protestant elites that extended across the churches, dominated most of the nation's political life, and managed virtually all of the "secular" institutions and social movements in American society.

But observers at the time, and historians later, were not mistaken in placing an emphasis on public opinion – or, more broadly, on a Protestant ethos – that pervaded establishment structures and, through them, made itself felt throughout the society. As Catherine Albanese puts it with reference to this era, "Prot-estantism meant acknowledged ways of thinking and acting supported by most institutions in the society." It was a "majority tradition [that] acted in subtle and not so subtle ways to wear away the sharp edges of separateness" (1992: 398).

Among those ways of thinking and acting, four that were intricately inter-woven seem especially important: individualism, moralism, activism, and millennial optimism. The first, in its religious formulation, referred funda-mentally to the responsibility of the individual to work out his or her own salvation. The second, moralism, entailed the saved person's responsibility to save others and by extension implied society's obligation to persuade, aid, and sometimes coerce its members toward redemptive moral choices.

Activism, the tendency to define religion more as action than as contemplation or as either doctrinal or liturgical regularity, was an especially visible and ubiq-uitous trait – so much so that, in both Protestant and Catholic Europe, "activism" and "Americanism" tended by the twentieth century to become synonymous terms. And finally, American forms of millennial optimism, a more-than-ordinary faith that the coming of God's kingdom on Earth is inevitable and imminent, made themselves felt around the world as the American churches assumed the leading role in foreign missions.

Throughout American history, but especially during the later years of the nineteenth century, some sought to make this virtual establishment into the genuine article. Usually this meant, above all, a determination to write allegiance to Jesus Christ into the United States Constitution; the "Christian Amendment" movement of the 1870s gained respectful, if ultimately unfavorable, attention in such forums as the Senate Judiciary Committee.

By and large, however, hegemonic Protestantism flexed its muscles, and avoided thoroughgoing adjustments to diversity, through subtler (and usually less conscious) processes than either nativist assaults or Christian amendments. The Protestant establishment offered leadership, provided a frame for societal and moral unity, and proclaimed an important version of the American promise (one that already rang hollow in the ears of some inhabitants) that outsiders possessed of diligence and adaptability could become insiders.

This establishment also exercised its own capacities for adaptation, with results that cut both ways in their relations to the pluralist ideal. The changes associated with terms such as Progressive Orthodoxy, New Theology, Modernism, and Social Gospel represented gains, certainly in the proverbial "long run," for religious and cultural pluralism. Theological liberalism, in the course of its relentless campaign against doctrinal, credal, and other formalisms, managed to blur the boundaries separating religions as well as those that divided the religious from the secular. The Protestant social gospel (which was closely entwined with liberalism even though many liberals ignored it) supported pluralist advances by placing a powerful new emphasis on Christianity as a matter of ethics, thereby opening the way to increased collaboration with Catholics, Jews, and other non-Christians. In addition, the social gospelers – even though later generations would fault them for insufficient concern about racial issues – forged linkages with African Americans as well as with ministers and laypeople in white "ethnic" communities.

Yet liberal and social gospel adjustments also strengthened and helped perpetuate the Protestant establishment. The social gospel, for example, although it may not have represented a majority in the Protestant churches, did get written into the official programs of most of them, as well as into the foundng documents of their federative organizations. It was, moreover, closely associated with a Progressive Movement that, for several decades after Theodore Roosevelt's ascension to the Presidency in 1901, played a leading role in "mainstream" politics and culture.

"Inclusion": Melting Pots and Trojan Horses

Although the Protestant establishment was thus a powerful, persisting, and massively institutionalized embodiment of the unitive impulse, the countervailing pluralist ideal remained alive and healthy throughout that establishment's finest hour: the late nineteenth and early twentieth centuries.

The process of ethnic and religious diversification continued, during these years, in highly visible and much publicized ways. Between 1850 and 1920 the Roman Catholic presence in the United States expanded at nearly three times the rate of overall population growth. Jews, although as late as 1920 constituting only 3 percent of the population, increased their numbers spectacularly (from 50,000 to more than 3 million) over the same period. As in the past, moreover, the newcomers were "different" as well as numerous. Like incoming Irish Catholics or German Jews a half-century earlier, the Catholic and Jewish immigrants of this later period differed from their predecessors culturally and religiously. Unlike those predecessors, in the Jewish instance at least, they also differed in class standing from those already in America. As all this was happening, anti-foreign reactions continued and in fact became nastier and more virulent, the anti-immigrant brigades having acquired weapons of biological racism that earlier had been utilized principally against African Americans. Pluralist alternatives, however, also managed to keep pace with the changes, and in some respects did more than keep pace. Spurred by the continuing diversification and provoked by the various forms of negative response to it, pluralists found themselves nudged beyond mere toleration into relatively new stances best characterized by terms like "inclusion." This was evident in three distinct, though also overlapping, arenas: within Protestantism, and in the larger fields of American and world religious relationships.

Within American Protestantism, newly explicit pleas for "inclusion" were evident in repeated demands by women and African Americans, and by others arguing on their behalf, for individual and collective recognition. The talented Methodist leader Anna Howard Shaw was both an advocate and an exemplar in the cause of women's ordination. Highly organized and effective women's mission organizations fought for full inclusion in their various male-dominated denominations.

Spokespersons such as Elizabeth Cady Stanton, W. E. B. DuBois, and the black educator Theophilus Steward went farther, calling not merely for recognition of the traditionally shunned within the structures of American Protestantism, but also for the "inclusion" of sharply divergent attitudes toward the Bible (Stanton), toward the social mission of the Church (DuBois), and toward the millennial meaning and future of America (Steward).

Such forms of advocacy, together with what many could see as a simple logic calling for the inclusion of major constituencies in the councils of the Protestant establishment, produced substantial, if still limited, gains for intra-Protestant pluralism. For example, although precious few women gained ordination in this era, their missionary and other organizations were gradually incorporated into denominational structures. And the new Federal Council of Churches (1908) included black denominations whose participation had scarcely been considered, let alone effected, in the case of the Evangelical Alliance, the FCC's nineteenth-century predecessor.

On the broader stage of American religion, increased inclusiveness was signaled in the early years of the century when non-Protestant leaders such as James Cardinal Gibbons achieved something like parity with their Protestant

counterparts as influential figures in American society. In 1917–18, the participation of Catholics and Jews in a major war effort was not only more visible and
acknowledged than in past instances; in very practical and statistical terms it was
more of a reality. Catholics and Jews together constituted roughly a third of the
total force of wartime chaplains. Equally unprecedented was the high degree of
interreligious collaboration among such wartime agencies as the National
Catholic War Council, the (Protestant) Wartime Commission of the Churches,
the Jewish Welfare Board, and an impressive number of non-denominational or
secular agencies in which Protestants and non-Protestants served together.

Here it is useful to glance ahead, beyond the 1870–1920 period. Taking
the wartime interfaith manifestations as a starting point, one can follow a
well-marked trail of advances for both tolerance and inclusion: from the
Protestant-sponsored Goodwill Movement of the 1920s, through the founding
in the interwar period of such institutions as the National Council of Christians
and Jews, into another wartime and postwar period in which terms like "Judeo-
Christian tradition" and "Triple Melting Pot" came into vogue as signifiers for
the inclusiveness that Americans aspired to and, by and large, believed they had
achieved. In the Second World War, even more than in the first, the need for solidarity against "the common enemy" was a powerful motive and talking point.
"Godless Fascism" (later rechristened as "Godless Communism") did as much
as homegrown pressures could do to advance triple-melting-pot inclusiveness –
and did it far more rapidly.

"Inclusion" was also, around the turn of the century, an increasingly important
component in a panoply of changing attitudes toward world religions. The most
concentrated, and also most celebrated, illustrations of this came in connection
with the "World's Parliament of Religions" that was one feature of the
Columbian Exposition at Chicago in the summer of 1893. Nearly forty of
the Parliament's 216 principal participants were Jewish, Orthodox, or Roman
Catholic; and this in itself bespoke the new inclusiveness. That eight other world
religions, from Buddhism through Zoroastrianism, were also represented prominently and in significant numbers (a total of twenty-eight featured speakers) was,
for that time, a truly spectacular happening.

From the point of view of any pluralist or proto-pluralist ideal, the foregoing
instances represent the good news of that ideal's hard-won triumphs. The not-
so-good news, especially from a later and therefore privileged vantage point, is
that substantial segments of American and world religion – indigenous American
Indian or African religions, for example – were not certified as candidates for
inclusion.

Equally problematic, in that same perspective, was the fact that the model for
inclusion was thoroughly assimilative. Even for the newly included, acceptance
and recognition came on someone else's terms; and those terms for the most part
involved subordination, or the sacrifice of individual and group identity, or very
often both. Women's organizations and black denominations were not so much
incorporated in the dominant structures of American Protestantism as swallowed
up by them or subordinated within them. And the celebrated "melting pot," in
its religious as in its general functioning, was really what social critics were calling

it by the middle years of the century: a "transmuting pot." As the sociologist Will Herberg put it in the 1950s, newcomers had quite regularly been "transformed and assimilated to an idealized 'Anglo-Saxon' model."

Similarly, the World's Parliament of Religions, despite the unprecedented cordiality of its outreach to the so-called "great religions," was directed for the most part by Protestant Christians who believed "the world's" exposure to the West, whatever other good things it might do, would speed that world's conversion to Christianity. The Parliament, typically for this inclusionist era, presented itself as an Olympics to which nearly everyone was invited, but in which Protestant Americans quite definitely expected to win the gold medals.

For these and other reasons, the "melting pot" model for inclusiveness – which can be seen as operative in all these various contexts – was to become an obvious and easy target for criticism. This was not just because the "melting" process had, in practice, lacked the kind of mutuality the metaphor implied. It was also because so many Americans came to believe that a formula constantly touted as respectful of diversity was not that at all; at most, it valued the kind of diversity that one views, so to speak, in a rear view mirror. *E pluribus unum,* in religious as in other applications, expressed gratification not that "we are many" but that "we were many."

What seems equally obvious, however, is the importance, indeed the indispensability, of this inclusionist stage in the developing story of a religious pluralism "struggling to be born." The inclusionist formulation, wherever translated into reality, brought with it unintended consequences. As Catholics, Jews, and even African Americans achieved varying degrees of inclusion in American society, the ground was being prepared for benefits not written into the inclusionist contract. The newly included did have voices, and in a good many cases (a Stanton, a Steward) these were voices that spoke of a different Christianity or a different America. And a few voices, such as that of the Swami Vivekananda at the Chicago meetings, made the case for new orderings of the world's religions and cultures.

The developing structures of interchurch and interfaith relations could be, and were, still dominated by white mainline Protestantism. Vehicles of inclusivist modernity like the Chicago Fair and its Parliament of Religions could be, and were, decorated all over with the trappings of an insistence on American, western, and Christian supremacy. Yet many of these engines of a carefully limited inclusivity proved to be Trojan horses wheeled into the very center of the American and western establishments.

Who Writes the Agenda? Pluralism as "Participation"

"Don't change your name!"

The stand-up comedian Shelly Berman, in the 1950s, recalled this as his immigrant father's parting shot after the father had conferred a most reluctant blessing on young Shelly's plans for an acting career. The phrase could be inscribed over the gateway into the America of the later twentieth century.

If it were, however, one would need to understand this admonition's broader and more fundamental meanings. It reflected the relatively new sense that Bermans and Epsteins, as well as Müllers and Svensons, might no longer need to Anglo-Saxonize their names; and it heralded a time, just ahead, when women might make a somewhat similar choice – might "keep their names." But it also, rightly understood, represented encouragement for African Americans or Native Americans who might wish to make precisely the opposite choice as part of an effort to repossess some parts of a world they had lost. The broader assurance embedded in a punch line like Berman's was, "You can change your name or not, become thoroughly assimilated or not. The idea is that it's your decision."

From that point – the point at which rights to the retention of individual and group identity are allowed in the same measure to Jews or Slavs or Africans as to white Anglo Saxons – it was only a short distance to a demand for an equal, or at least a proportional, responsibility for setting the society's agenda. It was only a short way, in other words, to the kind of "pluralism" Ahlstrom and others had in mind when they wrote of promises not kept and of destinies not made manifest.

These broader messages – "it's your decision," "it's okay to be different" – were also conveyed in some parts of Will Herberg's observations, in his *Protestant-Catholic-Jew* (1955), concerning a "triple melting pot." What that new metaphor meant, among other things, was that it had become okay to return to the religious portions of one's ethnic heritage. There were now three ways to be an American instead of just one.

But formulations like this also evoked an almost immediate, troubled, response: "*Only* three ways to be an American?" Before the ink was dry on the pages of Herberg's book, African Americans and others were posing such questions with some vehemence.

As the pleas concerning individual and group identity widened, they also achieved a new depth and intensity in the thought of many activists, and of intellectuals like the writer James Baldwin. Baldwin asserted that he had been unable to become a writer at all, let alone a successful one, until he found a way to shake off the identity imposed upon him by others. As he told Studs Terkel in a 1961 interview:

> I really began to go a little out of my mind because I obviously wasn't white . . . but I didn't quite know anymore what being black meant. I couldn't accept anymore what I'd been told; all you're ever told in this country about being black is that it's a terrible, terrible thing to be. Now, in order to survive this you have to really dig down into yourself and recreate yourself according to no image which yet exists in America . . . You have to decide who you are, and force the world to deal with *you* – not with its idea of you.

A stage that had been set by such appeals and by the activism of the civil rights and Black Power movements was broadened further after the liberalization of immigration laws in 1965. In religious terms, the renewed welcome to immigrants meant that the numbers of Hindus and Buddhists rose, in the quarter-century after 1965, from a few thousand of each to a half million of each. By the 1990s there were far more Hindus than Quakers, many times more Buddhists than Unitarians. As for Islam: although good estimates were especially difficult to achieve, it seemed clear that if one counted both immigrant and African American Muslims, the Islamic component in American religion had become comparable in size to the Jewish, and that Muslims were more numerous than Presbyterians or Episcopalians.

Responses to this latest stage of diversification ran the familiar gamut from enthusiastic welcome, through grudging acceptance, to anguished resistance and beyond; but the negative responses were more complex than in the past. This was not so much because the newcomers seemed more exotic than their predecessors (as newcomers always had), and not just because the pluralist ideal was groping its way beyond mere inclusion. What especially complicated the adverse or cautionary responses of the 1960s and after was the recognition that, as a former divinity school Dean put it, "in ever larger areas of our country, the Protestant – indeed the Christian – franchise has expired" (Keck 1993: 74). Perhaps, as my own historical treatment would suggest, the "real" decline of Protestantism had occurred in the first half of the nineteenth century; but if so, coming to terms with such a wrenching reality was the more difficult for having been so long delayed. Protestant America had been in denial for a very long time. Working its way out of denial was not a simple or tranquil process.

In any case, the several forms of resistance to the new pluralism displayed elements of bewilderment, nostalgia, and resentment that had been less prominent in earlier stagings of the adjustment to diversity. Yet this is not to say that uneasiness about pluralism was simply reflexive, or sheerly negative and adversarial. It was indeed more complex than that. Along with genuine, and of course long-standing, commitments to the truth claims of Christianity or Judaism, reservations about pluralism reiterated the venerable and very respectable insistence on a society's imperative need for unity. Many religionists, but also many "secular" observers of American religion and society, looked askance at the new and fuller pluralism because of real anxiety about what they saw as serious threats to a social and moral cohesion already imperiled, if not destroyed, by other elements of modernity. Doubts about pluralism, and about what came to be called "multiculturalism," at their best embodied genuine uncertainty – ambivalence might be an apter term – about the possibility of maintaining any kind of moral consensus in a society that, it was thought, was about to divide itself into "identity groups" each of which would then insist upon its own agenda and its own vision for America.

Evangelicals, who by this time could claim something like majority status within Protestantism, were especially prominent among those who voiced these measured reservations concerning pluralism. Many evangelicals, with some support from within "liberal Protestantism," argued that America had been founded, whether officially or otherwise, as a Protestant Christian country; and that, however cordially one might welcome those who had arrived since about 1820, Protestant Christianity must still somehow provide the kind of cement that holds a society together.

On the far right flank of this new evangelicalism were people and organizations that omitted the "somehow." The smaller but far more publicized "Christian right" stood ready, like its nativist forbears, to write Jesus Christ into the United States Constitution and to deal with diversity by subordinating "outsiders" or, in the case of pesky unwanted immigrants, sending them back where they came from.

Typical of such extreme restatements of the unitive ideal was the outburst of one Robert Hoy at a meeting, in December 1997, of President Clinton's Advisory Council on Race. Mr Hoy grabbed the microphone to complain that "there's no one up there [in Washington] that's talking about the white people. We don't want to be a minority *in our own country*." (The emphasis is added, but quite possibly was in the spoken statement.) During a further shouting match after Mr Hoy had been ousted from the meeting, he defended his intervention by warning that whites were in danger of losing "our homeland."

Whether or not Hoy also felt that Christian Americans were losing "their" homeland to Buddhists and Muslims is not recorded, but clearly that sort of fear was in the minds, and frequently in the utterances, of the extreme right – non-religious as well as religious.

Whose America? Options at the Close of the Century

What are the options, as the twentieth century ends, for an American religious polity substantially torn – though not at all for the first time – between plural-istic and unitive responses to diversity? They would seem to be, at one extreme, acceptance of pluralism itself as the sole common value for the society at large; and at the other, a return to the kind of unitive ideal that, even in expanded form, would repristinate and enforce the common values of an older "Protestant America." But most commentators on such matters appear to agree with the view of Nathan Glazer, one of the sociological critics of the newer pluralism, that pluralism as *the* central principle would ensure divisiveness, while the other extreme – a return to Protestant or triple-melting-pot America – is not really an option.

What then? What is to be thought and done? Some occupants of the same moderate center that Glazer represents want "to have it both ways," and con-sider it both necessary and possible to achieve such a feat. The society and its religions, they believe, can embrace pluralism as a primary value and still take seriously the importance of societal unity and the need for moral cohesion. Such a formula, they argue, will be no more but also no less realizable than other reso-lutions (governmental, for example) that produce working relations between competing principles of freedom and order.

But can any set of believers, culturally dominant or not, accept formulas that appear to take their own truth claims as less than absolute? For many people who have pondered these matters carefully and sympathetically, the answer has to be No. They are sure that the newer pluralism will lead only to a lowest-common-denominator religion, an utter evacuation and flattening out of belief.

To others, however, it is not obvious that pluralism, even in its most "modern" forms, disallows or discourages firm convictions. In fact, some of them argue, it means just the opposite: although pluralism mandates respect for the firmly held beliefs of others, it also demands that this sort of respect be reciprocated. Pluralism enables the Christian or other believer to say, "You need not, in this society, surrender your deepest convictions; nor shall I surrender mine."

However one comes down on that very fundamental issue, it can scarcely be said that the "new" pluralism is a wild or untraditional formulation. It is as venerable as the insistence of Christianity and other faiths that "only God is God," and that religions, as well as the cultures and kingdoms of this world, are therefore penultimate.

BIBLIOGRAPHY

Ahlstrom, Sydney E. (1972) *A Religious History of the American People*, New Haven, Conn.: Yale University Press.

Albanese, Catherine L. (1992) *America: Religions and Religion*, 2nd edn, Belmont, Calif.: Wadsworth.

Baldwin, James (1961) *Nobody Knows My Name: More Notes of a Native Son*, New York: Dial.

Billington, Ray Allen (1938) *The Protestant Crusade, 1800–1860*, New York: Macmillan (early nineteenth-century nativism).

de Crèvecoeur, Hector St John (1782) *Letters from an American Farmer*, London.

DuBois, W. E. B. (1911) "Jesus Christ in Georgia," *The Crisis* 2 (June).

Glazer, Nathan (1997) *We are all Multiculturalists Now*, Cambridge, Mass.: Harvard University Press.

Herberg, Will (1955) *Protestant-Catholic-Jew: An Essay in American Religious Sociology*, New York: Doubleday.

Higham, John (1955) *Strangers in the Land: Patterns of American Nativism, 1860–1925*, New Brunswick, NJ: Rutgers University Press.

Hill, Patricia (1984) *The World their Household: The American Woman's Foreign Mission Movement and Cultural Transformation, 1870–1920*, Ann Arbor, Mich.: University of Michigan Press.

Hutchison, William R. (ed.) (1989) *Between the Times: The Travail of the Protestant Establishment in America, 1900–1960*, Cambridge: Cambridge University Press.

Keck, Leander E. (1993) *The Church Confident*, Nashville, Tenn.: Abingdon Press.

Moore, R. Laurence (1982) *Religious Outsiders and the Making of Americans*, New York: Oxford University Press.

Seager, Richard H. (1995) *The World's Parliament of Religions: The East/West Encounter, Chicago, 1893*, Bloomington, Ind.: Indiana University Press.

Showalter, Nathan D. (1998) *The End of a Crusade: The Student Volunteer Movement for Foreign Missions and the Great War*, Lanham, Md.: Scarecrow.

Stanton, Elizabeth Cady (1895–8) *The Woman's Bible*, New York.

Steward, Theophilus G. (1888) *The End of the World; or, Clearing the Way for the Fullness of the Gentiles*, Philadelphia, Pa.

Chapter 4

Pluralism and American Religious Life in the Later Twentieth Century

Charles H. Lippy

Pluralism and diversity initially described American religion because of the sheer number of Christian groups cropping up among Europeans in the English colonies that became the United States. That multiplicity of religious groups fed into the image of the United States as a nation founded on the principle of religious freedom; since so many diverse religious communities flourished, religious liberty must have been a given. That perspective, however, distorts the historical record, for it overlooks the hostility between religious communions that once prevailed and the struggle of groups such as the Quakers to gain acceptance.

Accidents of circumstance contributed more to the traditional understanding of religious pluralism, for when the colonies were settled, most Europeans believed that religious uniformity was necessary for political stability. In North America, patterns of settlement, and the need to have a critical mass of colonists, undermined and eventually destroyed that assumption. The Puritan commonwealths in New England, for example, had theological roots in the Reformed tradition and an ecclesiastical style emphasizing congregational autonomy. But they were exceedingly reluctant to let those who thought differently settle among them, lest their own truth be contaminated. Some who differed simply moved to nearby places where Europeans had not settled. Perhaps the most well-known example was the seeker Roger Williams, who in exile from Massachusetts Bay established his own colonial enterprise in Rhode Island where greater religious liberty prevailed. Southern colonies were at first inclined toward the Church of England, the parent of Episcopalianism, though in the Carolinas, for example, the need to attract a sufficient number of European settlers to make the colonial effort successful, required broader toleration. Consequently, Charleston, South Carolina, became home to one of the earliest Jewish communities in the colonies. African immigrants, most brought as slaves, fused native tribal expression with the Christianity they were presented, particularly after the Great Awakening in the eighteenth century, to give pluralism another dimension.

A prominent English Catholic family hoping to create in Maryland a haven for their co-religionists also found that if only Catholics settled there, the colony would not survive economically. Quaker William Penn used his colonial enterprise as an experiment, welcoming virtually any religious community so long as peace prevailed. That openness meant that by the end of the colonial period, Pennsylvania, not Maryland, would boast the largest Catholic population in the colonies. In the eighteenth century when Scots-Irish immigrants came in large numbers, they planted their more Presbyterian ways wherever they settled. New York furthered the pattern of colonial diversity in part because it was first controlled by the Dutch, who brought another brand of the Reformed heritage with them.

In sum, the vast amount of land apparently open to European conquest gave people the space to plant settlements where their own religious views would prevail, and the need in the early colonial days to ensure that there were enough settlers to guarantee success meant welcoming persons of diverse religious backgrounds, albeit sometimes reluctantly. In many colonies, tax monies were used in some way to provide support for religion, but when the US Constitution was drafted in 1787, the prevailing pluralism made it impossible to identify one religion or even one form of Christianity as the official religion of the new nation. The "separation of church and state" later generations would find in the First Amendment to the Constitution nurtured an atmosphere where pluralism continued to flourish. As the denomination became the accepted form of religious institution and the number of denominations multiplied, pluralism usually came to denote the vast number of Christian groups that each found a niche in American religious life.

Other forms of pluralism are also part of the historical picture. As immigration continued, new religious expressions emerged. In the nineteenth century, numerous utopian communities, millennialist groups, and Christian sectarian experiments added to the primary, Protestant-based pluralism. American Catholicism, although struggling to be one church, experienced a different sort of pluralism, one that revolved around ethnicity. Irish Americans dominated the Catholic hierarchy, but Irish Catholics had a flavor to their religious life uniquely their own, as did German Catholics, Italian Catholics, Czech Catholics, and every other ethnic community. Among some American Protestants, ethnic diversity led to multiple denominations that shared a common history, but maintained some distinctions based on use of a European language in worship. American Lutherans provide a convenient example. Until well into the twentieth century, the large number of Lutheran denominations reflected the ethnic origins of each group; there was, for example, a denomination that was Swedish American and another that was Finnish American. Jewish immigrants, while more diverse ethnically by the end of the nineteenth century, brought a pluralism to their religious heritage that loosely resembled that of the Protestant denominations, although internally the major distinctions among Orthodox, Conservative, and Reform Judaism had to do with personal adherence to the traditions of Torah.

Until the mid-twentieth century, then, religious pluralism in the United States usually referred to the large number of different religious groups that had found a home in the nation. Most often, it highlighted the variety of Protestant denominations that, when their numbers were combined, dominated public religious life. But pluralism also echoed the range of ethnic communities that nurtured the myth of the "melting pot" in American life. Sometimes it reflected diverse attitudes of adherents towards their own tradition. In every case, the presumably neutral stance of the government towards religion and the fact that no single group constituted a majority religion or denomination helped sustain pluralism. In the latter half of the twentieth century, however, pluralism has taken many new faces. It now signals that all the major religious traditions of the world have faith communities functioning in the United States. As well, contemporary pluralism encompasses the diversity in approaches to worship and to personal spirituality, not just denominations or groups. What has given pluralism so many new faces?

In the half century since World War II, at least five interrelated factors have worked together to unveil many new faces of American religious pluralism. The first is the significant population growth in the first two decades or so after the war that gave the nation the "baby boom" generation. Boomers, as those before them, tended to withdraw from active involvement in organized religion in late adolescence and young adulthood, but then demonstrated a rebirth of interest in the religious and spiritual when reaching middle age and raising a family. What marked this generation as different, however, was the ways in which they returned to religion. Thousands spurned the religious communities of their childhoods and turned in new directions; thousands jettisoned traditional religious institutions altogether, looking for a personal spiritual path that endowed life with meaning and purpose.

Intertwined with this shift is the increasing privatization of vital religiosity in the later twentieth century. Sociologists have long claimed that one feature of highly complex societies (which emerge because of urbanization and industrialization like that which changed the character of American life between 1870 and 1920) is just such privatization. In daily life, individuals are involved with an increasing number of social institutions and agencies, relate to more and more persons with whom they have at best secondary relationships, and receive signals about values and meaning from a host of sources. In the last category, the monumental changes in communications media in the twentieth century are especially significant. Radio, television, and then various means of electronic communication have brought the world into the private home. Individuals are free to pick and choose what they see and hear and where they seek out meaning, without having to be part of a social institution such as a religious congregation. Consequently, people create intensely personal (and hence private) belief and value systems, their own religious worlds to which they turn for direction in life. That individualism represents yet other face of pluralism.

The end of World War II also launched a time of significant economic growth that, while neither continuous nor uniform in its impact, created unprecedented educational and vocational opportunities for millions. That combined with the reintegrating of former military personnel into the civilian labor force to spur greater mobility in every sense of that word. Americans moved to new geographic locations in ever greater numbers to take advantage of educational or employment opportunities. Religious institutions that counted on a parish or community of nearby residents as their membership base often saw their neighborhoods vanish or the composition of the population rather shift, so that they lost their natural constituency. More striking, when people moved to new locations they did not take denominational loyalty with them. Denominational switching became normative, not exceptional. Marriage across denominational lines and across boundaries of religious traditions increased, often nudging families of "mixed marriages" into new religious communities or none at all. Into that gap stepped many new options, adding to the faces of American religious pluralism.

In the midst of these shifting currents in American common life came fresh challenges to established authority. In the 1960s three movements were prominent: the civil rights movement, the women's movement, and the anti-war movement that protested American military engagement in Vietnam and Southeast Asia. The challenge of the civil rights movement to governmental authority that supported racism and discrimination easily transformed itself into a challenge toward all established authority, including such religious authorities as creed, church, and clergy. The same holds for the women's movement and the anti-war movement. As traditional religious authority came under scrutiny, once-secure religious institutions saw their foundations shattered; their rebuilding added fresh dimensions to American religious pluralism.

Finally, the half-century after World War II brought significant changes in the sources of immigrants entering the US. The roots lie with returning World War II military personnel, since thousands of those who served in the Pacific brought home spouses who were Asian. Military engagement in Vietnam also introduced millions of Americans to Asian cultures, and subsequent business connections cemented ties across that one-time cultural divide. By the last decade of the twentieth century, immigrants from the Middle East, Asia, and Latin America vastly outnumbered those coming from Europe and Africa, the two major sources of immigrants in past centuries. The new immigrants, like those of previous generations, brought their own religions and religious styles with them, but here there was difference. In earlier generations the religion of most of the immigrants was some variation of Protestantism, some ethnic variety of Catholicism, or some brand of Eastern Orthodox Christianity or Judaism; now immigrants were Hindu, Buddhist, Muslim, or from other traditions that formerly had been a very minor part of American life. Pluralism was taking on yet another layer of meaning.

What specific forms did this new pluralism take? Two movements in the 1960s and 1970s, one concrete and one more amorphous, illuminate some of the new faces pluralism took in the second half of the twentieth century. The more amorphous is the resurgence of Evangelicalism in American Protestantism that was so pronounced as to lead *Newsweek* magazine to dub 1976 the "year of the evangelical." The more concrete is the Second Vatican Council, a gathering of Roman Catholic clerical leaders from around the globe called by Pope John XXIII. It held several extended sessions in Rome from 1962 through 1965 to update Roman Catholic practice and open new vistas for the Roman Christian tradition.

Evangelicalism in American Protestantism had been a sleeping giant for half a century before its power became evident. Analysts and religious leaders alike dismissed evangelicalism and its religious cousin, fundamentalism, after the Scopes trial of the 1920s and the failure then of fundamentalists to gain control of the bureaucracies of some long-established denominations. But evangelicals, still regarding an inner experience of conversion as basic to the religious life, had built numerous networks, from publishing houses to Bible colleges, institutes, and colleges, that had reinforced the plausibility of the evangelical style and the integrity of maintaining an evangelical identity.

By the 1970s, two factors converged to bring evangelicalism to center stage. One was the increasing popularity of evangelists who mastered the medium of television. Although financial and personal scandal would partially, although only temporarily, undermine the vitality of the genre of evangelistic religious television (televangelism), by the 1970s personalities such as Pat Robertson, Jim and Tammy Faye Bakker, Oral Roberts, Jimmy Swaggart, and the more main-line Robert Schuller claimed the support of millions through their television and related religious empires. Readily drawing on an evangelical, often Pentecostal vocabulary, televangelists helped popularize the idea of being "born again" and of regarding a vital, personal relationship with God through Jesus Christ almost as a panacea for personal and social problems. Televangelism also buttressed the increasing privatization of vital religiosity, for individuals watched the television preachers in the privacy of their own homes, frequently supplementing what they received from the religious groups with which they remained affiliated with beliefs taken over from the televangelists, to create personal religious worldviews.

The other factor that gave evangelicalism a boost came from the political sector. In the 1976 presidential campaign, Democratic candidate Jimmy Carter unabashedly spoke of being born again and of the importance of religious faith in shaping his values and political views. Having someone of that stature proclaim an evangelical identity gave the movement plausibility. Evangelicals also edged into the political arena through groups such as the Moral Majority (founded by independent fundamentalist Baptist preacher, and television personality Jerry Falwell) and the Christian Coalition (started by televangelist Pat Robertson and guided for several years by Ralph Reed). These groups brought a kind of pluralism to evangelicalism itself. Historically evangelicals shied away from political activity because they saw society as an arena fraught with evil. Traditionally evangelicals insisted that the only way society could be transformed was through the conversion of the individuals who made up society. Groups like Moral Majority, Christian Voice, Roundtable, and Christian Coalition took a different approach, by vigorously lobbying in support of legislation that reflected their understanding of moral values and working for candidates for public office whose views mirrored their own. Not all evangelicals were comfortable with this approach; the differences internal to evangelicals when it came to politics gave a pluralistic cast even to evangelical public life.

The evangelical resurgence brought new dimensions to American religious pluralism in other ways. Evangelicalism ignored denominational boundaries.

Evangelicals appeared in all of the long-established denominations as well as in those groups, usually smaller, historically aligned with evangelicalism or fundamentalism. Observers recognized that evangelicals had more in common with each other, regardless of denominational affiliation, than with non-evangelicals within their own denomination. Consequently, the evangelical renaissance contributed to the gradual demise of the denomination as the basic organizational unit of Protestantism. Evangelicalism also enriched pluralism through its emphasis on feeling. Since the eighteenth century Enlightenment, rationalism and an appreciation of scientific method thought had gained great currency in American intellectual life. Theologians had expended tremendous energy recasting doctrine in rationalistic terms. The evangelical renaissance, while not casting reason aside, gave fresh credibility to feeling, to inner experience, to a personal apprehension of the Divine not subject to verification by the canons of reason.

The more concrete phenomenon of the Second Vatican Council gave pluralism new meaning within Roman Catholic circles. Vatican II was the first general council of the Roman communion in nearly a century. When Vatican I met in 1870, the church was poised very differently. Church leaders then were concerned more about the erosion of the papacy's political influence in Italian affairs; in most matters of belief and practice, the church continued to endorse formulations that in many cases dated back to the sixteenth century. In the 1960s, the concern was to formulate statements of belief and practice in the language of the twentieth century, not the sixteenth, and to probe ways the message and mission of a global religion could be relevant to contemporary local needs and issues. The council called for greater lay participation in setting local programs, use of the vernacular in celebration of the mass, and other reforms that would give Roman Catholicism a distinctly modern cast. Some believed that the council opened doors for more radical change from the church's past. Soon there were calls to ordain women to the priesthood, rethink the church's ban on artificial means of contraception and abortion, abandon insistence on a celibate priesthood, and allow more vocal participation of church leaders in the political life of the nation.

The result was the emergence of a new pluralism internal to the Catholic church, much of which directly or indirectly had to do with authority. Some lamented the loss of all that was familiar because of changes from Vatican II; they longed to return to or at least continue traditional ways. Others believed that the changes approved by the council had not gone far enough, although some wished to accept church authority on matters of doctrine while giving considerable latitude to individuals when it came to views on social issues. Many of this group bemoaned Pope Paul VI's reaffirmation of church teaching banning contraception, and his and Pope John Paul II's insistence on a celibate male priesthood. Pope John Paul II also forbade priests to hold public office, while encouraging them and other church leaders to become politically active in support of policies that mirrored church teaching. Yet another face of pluralism internal to Catholicism came with the millions of American Catholics who continued to identify themselves as Catholic, but who ignored church teaching on matters such as contraception and abortion. The Roman Catholic church might be one church, but Catholics had many faces and sometimes held contradictory beliefs.

Vatican II had repercussions well beyond Roman Catholicism in the area of liturgical reform and renewal. In the Catholic tradition, that meant not only using the vernacular as the language of worship, but having the priest celebrate the mass facing the congregation and laity reading Scripture and assisting in the distribution of the communion elements. In the third of a century since Vatican II, other changes have come to Catholic worship, enriching the pluralism that prevails. One is the result of increasing Hispanic influence as the growing numbers of Mexican, Cuban, and other Latin American Catholics make their presence felt in American Catholic life. The Hispanic influence brought a new ethnic pluralism to Catholicism, a new indigenous heritage to incorporate into worship. A host of "folk" masses and masses with rock music accompaniment have shattered forever the image of Catholic worship as somber and foreboding. A few congregations still offer the Latin mass from time to time. In a church where uniformity once prevailed with the Latin mass as its centerpiece, there is now variety and diversity. Pluralism has come to Catholic worship life.

The liturgical renewal prompted by Vatican II also led many Protestants to rethink approaches to worship. Many of the denominations in the "free church" tradition, where fixed liturgy was scorned, slowly made greater use of liturgical form and experimented with worship styles. Through the National Council of Churches, many Protestant denominations developed a common lectionary or cycle of Scripture readings for use in worship. Whereas a half century ago there would have been obvious differences between Episcopal worship and Methodist worship, for example, in many communities greater sensitivity to liturgy and the use of the common lectionary has muted them. The lessening of differences has furthered the erosion of denominational loyalty. If there is nothing distinctive about the worship life of a particular denomination, then denominational switching is less problematic.

Considerable pluralism remains among Protestants when it comes to worship. The birth of the megachurch, symbolized in Willow Creek Community Church in South Barrington, Illinois, inaugurated approaches to worship clustered under the rubric of "contemporary Christian worship." Willow Creek pioneered the "seeker service" that replaced traditional worship. With its the casual atmosphere and minimal use of overt Christian symbols and content, the seeker service was developed as a result of market research. Surveys conducted within what once would have been called Willow Creek's "parish" revealed that many of the baby boomer generation were alienated from traditional churches because of their formality and perceived sterility. Yet they were seeking some spiritual nurture that resonated with the highly complex lives they led. Another influence shaping this new worship form was television; many televangelists adapted the variety show format for their programs, relying on its fast pace and upbeat mood to sustain viewers' attention. In contemporary Christian worship, electronic sound systems replaced organs, words of praise choruses flashed on screens became new versions of the hymnal, talks on dealing with "real life" problems like courtship and marriage or job-related stress superseded sermons on sin and salvation, auditoriums with theater seats became the new pews filled by women and men in jeans or shorts rather than their "Sunday best." Worship had become pluralistic in new ways.

To casual observers, contemporary Christian worship seems interchangeable with another mode that became increasingly vital within both Protestant and Catholic circles in the second half of the twentieth century. In the 1960s a burst of fresh interest in charismatic gifts, the several spiritual phenomena outlined in the New Testament but usually identified with glossolalia or speaking in tongues, moved Pentecostal worship styles from a handful of small denominations and independent churches into the Christian mainstream. Hands raised signifying submission to the Almighty became as familiar a sight as heads bowed in prayer. If speaking in tongues still remained extraordinary, the expectation of direct manifestation of the power of the Holy Spirit did not. Historians linked neo-Pentecostal charismatic worship to patterns associated with early nineteenth-century frontier camp meetings and African-American churches, for exuberant enthusiasm filled them all. But whereas camp meeting worship became more subdued as the city swallowed the frontier, and African-American worship some-what more muted as people moved up the socio-economic ladder, Pentecostal Christians, Protestant and Catholic alike, believed that the dimension they added to pluralism in American worship would endure till the end of time. Even among the congregations that retained or revived traditional forms, contemporary Christian worship and neo-Pentecostal styles had an impact. Attire appropriate for worship became more casual. In many churches, recorded music sup-plemented traditional organ and choir. Preaching resounded with popular psychology as much as it proclaimed the Word. By the end of the twentieth century, Christian worship in America evinced a pluralism unmatched in earlier generations.

Out of this pluralistic worship ethos came a new genre of religious music, often called contemporary Christian music. Like the format of much worship, it clearly received as much of its impetus from the secular culture as from traditional re-ligious sources. Instrumentation, rhythmic patterns, and presentation mirrored secular musical forms from classical "rock and roll" to "heavy metal." Some radio stations devoted the bulk of their programming to contemporary Christian music; casual listeners were hard put to distinguish between their offerings and those proffered by stations playing "Top Forty" secular hits. Singer and composer Amy Grant became one of the first "cross-over" artists because her lyrics and style appealed to both religious and secular audiences. Grant had re-ligious albums that topped best-selling charts when, in recognition of her broad audience, she began to write songs about secular love. Although this affirmation of her own of cross-over appeal chagrined some religious critics, it illustrates the collapsing of boundaries between the sacred and the secular in the pluralistic culture of the late twentieth century.

If some Protestant worship expressions echoed the affective exuberance once characteristic of African-American churches, African-American religious life itself manifested other nuances of the multifaceted pluralism of the age. Kindled by the civil rights movement of the fifties and sixties was a quest to explore and reaffirm dimensions of African life and culture. Black thinkers such as James Cone offered a distinctive theology based not just on traditional Christian thought, but on African spirituality and the unique history of African Americans, a people for whom slavery shaped a collective identity. More to the point was the emergence of a distinctive holiday, Kwanzaa, grounded in African celebrations of the harvest of the first crops. The festival, part of African-American culture since 1966, roughly coincides with Christmas. Kwanzaa thus illustrates yet another face of pluralism, the eclectic fusion of religious features of African tribal life, Christian expression, and the distinctive African-American experience.

The pluralism that came to American Judaism in the later twentieth century was of yet another sort. The massive wave of immigration that endowed American Catholicism with rich ethnic diversity also brought dramatic growth to American Judaism. Until the later decades of the nineteenth century, the bulk of the small American Jewish population had Germanic origins. They were quick to imbibe the heady wine of Enlightenment rationalism and to take advantage of the lack of legal constraints on Jewish identity afforded by the First Amendment. Like many of their German counterparts, they began to rethink what it meant to be a Jew in the modern world. Much traditional belief and practice, such as adhering to the dietary codes of the Hebrew Bible, seemed to set Jews apart, rather than facilitate participation in the larger culture. Those eager to fit in were often willing to jettison such practices. The result was Reform Judaism. Immigrants of the later nineteenth and early twentieth centuries, overwhelmingly of central, southern, and eastern European stock, provided other models for how to be Jewish and American. Those insisting on strict adherence to tradition became known as Orthodox Jews. Between Orthodox and Reform stood Conservative Judaism. Conservative Jews (unlike Reform but in tandem with Orthodox) might adhere strictly to dietary regulations in their own homes, but elsewhere (like Reform but unlike Orthodox) would eat food prepared in non-kosher kitchens; Conservative Jews might still refuse to eat food that was taboo, though few Reform Jews would. Because these three communities looked like denominations, they gave one kind of pluralistic cast to American Judaism. But beneath them lurked an ethnic diversity that still generally reflected country or region of ancestral origin in Europe.

The new pluralism that came to American Judaism in the later twentieth century gave a different nuance to ethnicity. Ties to lands of ancestral heritage naturally dwindled as succeeding generations, born in the US, assimilated into American culture, defined themselves as Americans, and married outside any Jewish community with great frequency. Some believed interfaith marriage the primary force transforming the understanding of ethnicity. In interfaith households, adherence to distinctive Jewish practice was often minimal; developing a Jewish religious identity became a challenge for those born into such families. Since the primary locus of Jewish practice remains the home, not the synagogue, the same forces pushing privatization in other religious communities worked especially effectively in American Judaism. Without a ghetto culture to buttress religious practice even within the home, it was easy to let strict practice lapse. Scholars have written of "secular Jews," an oxymoron if Judaism denotes only a religious heritage. Yet increasing numbers of Jews looked at Judaism as an ethnic heritage, not a religion. Hence ethnicity no longer referred only to place of ancestral origin, but also to the cultural sensibilities shaped by a religious tradition, which endure independently of religious practice. Conservative, Reform, and Orthodox communities continue to dominate organized American Judaism, but a new pluralism differentiates between those Jews who practice Judaism as a religion and those who do not.

The new faces of pluralism come into sharpest relief in looking at the impact of changing patterns of immigration on American religious life in the last half of the twentieth century. Statistics indicate that total immigration from Asia in the 1980s was five times what it was in the 1960s. For India, the increase was tenfold. More than one-quarter of all Asians who immigrated to the United States after 1820 came in the 1980s. Not all are from the Far East. Between 1980 and 1990, for example, the number of people living in the US who were born in Iran grew by two-thirds. Overall numbers may yet be modest, compared with the much larger immigration that brought such rich ethnic diversity to American Catholicism and Judaism between 1880 and the outbreak of World War I. But the effect of this recent immigration is equally as profound.

Like earlier immigrants, those coming from Asia brought religion with them. The difference was that the faiths transplanted to American soil from Asia bear little relation to those in the Jewish or Christian traditions, unlike those of an earlier day. Offshoots of many of these traditions – sects of Buddhism, Chinese religions, Hinduism, Sikhism, Islam – existed in the US earlier; some religious institutions identified with those traditions emerged after the World's Parliament of Religions in Chicago in 1893. But with the exception of a very small number of Chinese and Japanese immigrants who settled mostly in the western US and several thousand who married US military personnel stationed in Asia during World War II, the Korean War, and the conflict in Vietnam, most of those attracted to the various Asian religions were not of Asian stock. Part of what piqued the curiosity of the American public when groups such as the International Society for Krishna Consciousness (Hare Krishna) became commonplace in the 1960s was the way they drew on native-born Americans to swell their ranks. Another dimension of the new pluralism centers on the awareness that now, in contrast, practitioners of these Asian faiths are Asian Americans or Asians by birth, not converts from some other faith.

The more visible presence of Asian religious traditions has added to the pluralism of American worship life in ways other than those already discussed. Hindu immigrants became as inveterate temple builders in the United States as in India, providing followers with sacred space where the aroma of incense mingled with the sounds of Sanskrit chant, as priests petitioned the gods and blessed the faithful. The steady growth of Islam in the United States brought a demand for mosques where the devout could gather on Fridays for prayer and instruction in the ways of Allah revealed in the Qur'an and Muslim law. Theoretically any building can function as a mosque, but in most American cities with populations over 50,000, by the 1990s single-purpose structures served as mosques, where Muslim men prayed and studied. Less prominent, but nevertheless firmly planted on American soil in the later twentieth century were temples or centers for Buddhist worship and meditation. At the close of the twentieth century, pluralism denotes the multiplicity of world religions at home in the US as well.

Expressions of personal spirituality have also taken many new forms in the later twentieth century. Among American Protestants in the early part of the century, disciplines like prayer, Bible study, and meditative reflection shaped personal spirituality. Denominations and ecumenical agencies prepared materials, such as the popular devotional guides *Our Daily Bread* and the *Upper Room*, for personal use. Much Roman Catholic spirituality also focused on exercises with a long history: saying the Rosary, doing Novenas, fasting or at least abstaining from meat on particular holy days, joining in festivals honoring patron saints, perhaps taking an occasional pilgrimage. Traditional disciplines stretching back centuries, such as daily rituals of prayer, molded Jewish personal spirituality for the devout.

Here, too, the baby boomer generation left its mark, for as the boomers moved into adulthood, the traditional disciplines informing personal spirituality were frequently jettisoned. For some, an eclectic spirituality became primary. Ongoing interest in Eastern meditation disciplines meant that scores of persons combined yoga with Bible reading, for example. Others drew on so-called New Age techniques, but often blended them with a variety of other spiritual exercises to fashion an idiosyncratic personal religiosity. When sociologist Robert Bellah and his associates examined religious commitment in the 1980s, they reported one subject, a woman named Sheila, who identified her personal religion as "Sheilaism," exemplifying individualistic spirituality in the extreme.

In the wake of the feminist movement, many women began to seek spiritual wholeness through rituals and forms unique to women's experience, many with a lineage stretching back to pre-Christian goddess and fertility religion. In cities and forest glens across the nation, circles of women celebrated the goddess and covens performed the ancient rituals of wicca. Writers such as Starhawk and Z. Budapest prepared guidebooks to assist women in executing rituals grounded in female life experience. Even within the churches, growing concern for use of gender-inclusive language revealed feminist influence. Catholic and Protestant theologians alike offered interpretations of the role of the Virgin Mary, the mother of Jesus, for speaking to women's concerns and for informing Christian spirituality more generally. Protestant women from many denominations gathered at Reimagining Conferences in the 1990s which, although controversial because of the presumed challenges they represented to male-controlled denominational leadership and traditional ways of thinking, attempted to find in the biblical heritage the feminine face of God.

Some critics naively lumped the concern for female spirituality with the debates over sexuality that pervaded American religion and American society in the closing decades of the twentieth century. Only a very small minority of those seeking spiritual wholeness through pursuit of the goddess were lesbians, but feminists were perhaps more inclined than the population as a whole to regard lesbian sexual orientation as an authentic identity for some women. Gay men, bisexuals, and transgendered persons also began to seek spiritual nurture more openly and directly, rejecting the assertions of most religious institutions that same gender sexual activity was aberrant and sinful. Another aspect of the pluralism pervading late-twentieth-century American religious life revolved around the many groups existing within the older denominations that cultivated the religious life of the various homosexual communities, such as Dignity among Roman Catholics, Affirmation among United Methodists, and Integrity among Episcopalians. Some Protestant congregations welcoming homosexuals into their religious life formed networks through such organizations as the Presbyterians' More Light congregations or the Open and Affirming con-gregations of Unitarian Universalists. One new denomination, the Universal Fellowship of Metropolitan Community Churches, was founded in the late 1960s primarily to minister to the spiritual needs of gay men, lesbians, bisexuals, and transgendered persons.

By the 1990s, concerns for male spirituality distinct from issues of sexual orien-tation were becoming more evident. Since the 1950s there had been small prayer groups for men that frequently crossed denominational lines and often included Catholic as well as Protestant members. Some of the earliest drew from the neo-Pentecostal and charismatic renewal efforts. The Full Gospel Business Men's Fellowship International is one example; more moderately evangelical in style was the Christian Business Men's Committee and its local affiliates. The rethinking of gender roles in the larger culture stimulated efforts to provide fresh expressions of a distinctly male spirituality. In the 1990s, the Promise Keepers movement, founded by former University of Colorado football coach Bill McCartney, emerged as the most prominent. Dedicated to bridging racial and denominational lines, Promise Keepers packed thousands of men into football stadiums and other sports arenas at mass rallies. As with other groups, local affili-ates emerged, sometimes identified with particular Protestant congregations, but sometimes crossing faith lines.

Larger churches, including the megachurches that boasted 10,000 or more members, responded to this thirst for personal spirituality by organizing small groups. Sociologist Robert Wuthnow highlighted the prominence of small groups, which often use methods first developed by Alcoholics Anonymous, in giving persons both a firm sense of identity and spiritual strength. Few religious communities failed to develop some sort of small group, cell group, support group, or recovery group program to respond to the spiritual yearnings of the age. Many of the megachurches eschewed affiliation with an established denomi-nation, thereby contributing to the erosion of the denomination as the primary institutional expression of religion in the US. For the millions drawn to the small groups, loyalty is often to the small group itself, not to the church that sponsors it, whether denominationally-affiliated or not. The profusion of small groups signalled yet another face of late-twentieth-century religious pluralism in the US.

The Europeans who first settled what became the United States never en-visioned a nation where diversity would characterize religious life. Those who sought freedom for themselves were rarely tolerant of alternative perspectives. Yet by the time the American nation achieved its independence, a certain style of pluralism already prevailed in the religious sphere, albeit one that generally signaled the variety of Protestant denominations that were all flourishing. Over the years pluralism has remained constant, but moved in many new directions. In the last half of the twentieth century, pluralism revealed so many new faces that both the public and private character of religion looked different than they had when the century began.

BIBLIOGRAPHY

Bellah, Robert, Masden, Richard, Sullivan, William M., Swidler, Ann, and Tipton, Steven M. (1985) *Habits of the Heart: Individualism and Commitment in American Life*, New York: Harper & Row.

Fulop, Timothy, and Raboteau, Albert G. (eds) (1997) *African American Religion: Interpretive Essays in History and Culture*, New York and London: Routledge.

Hoge, Dean R., Johnson, Benton, and Luidens, Donald A. (1993) *Vanishing Boundaries: The Religion of Mainline Protestant Baby Boomers*, Louisville, Ky.: Westminster/John Knox.

Neusner, Jacob (ed.) (1994) *World Religions in America: An Introduction*, Louisville, Ky.: Westminster/John Knox.

Roof, Wade Clark (1993) *A Generation of Seekers: The Spiritual Journeys of the Baby Boom Generation*, San Francisco: HarperSanFrancisco.

Roof, Wade Clark and McKinney, William (1987) *American Mainline Religion: Its Changing Shape and Future*, New Brunswick, NJ: Rutgers University Press.

Webber, Robert E. (1996) *Blended Worship: Achieving Substance and Relevance in Worship*, Peabody, Mass.: Hendrickson; first published as *The Worship Phenomenon*.

Wuthnow, Robert (1988) *The Restructuring of American Religion: Society and Faith Since World War II*, Princeton, NJ: Princeton University Press.

—— (1993) *Christianity in the Twenty-First Century: Reflections on the Challenges Ahead*, New York: Oxford University Press.

—— (ed.) (1994) *"I Came Away Stronger": How Small Groups are Shaping American Religion*, Grand Rapids, Mich.: Eerdmans.

Part II

Religious Roots of American Culture

Introduction

One persistent and fertile source of controversy in the study of American religion has to do with the long-term effects of early religious cultures on the subsequent development of religion and, more broadly, the dominant culture of the United States. The German sociologist Max Weber argued long ago in his *The Protestant Ethic and the Spirit of Capitalism* (1904) that there was a direct if somewhat ironic relationship between the emergence of Protestant Christianity during the Reformation era and the subsequent dominance of capitalism as the economic system of the West. Sydney Alhstrom's *A Religious History of the American People* (1972) made a related argument that Anglo-American Puritanism, a variety of Calvinism, had a similarly long-reaching impact on the shaping of American life in its instilling of a mindset about the relationships between the individual, the divine, and the social that long outlasted its institutional existence, and only recently came into serious eclipse.

Some scholars have stressed novelty and diversity as dominant themes in American religious life; however, a case can still be made that the persistence of certain themes unfolded in the earliest Euro-American religious cultures must also be taken into account in understanding the complicated role that religion has played in the development of a distinctively American culture, however complex that culture may now in fact be. In the broadest terms, "continuity and change" can be posited as a methodology for looking at any kind of history: in almost any enduring society, some things endure while others change. Perhaps a dialectical model is the most useful here: while Puritanism, for example, has over the decades continued to exert a shaping force on the American experience, it has only been able to do so while forces of change have steadily eroded its original character and context. These agents of change include democracy and a market economy. Ironically, argue some, the roots of these forces may lie implicit in the tensions within colonial Puritanism itself.

The New England Puritans were also a self-definedly elitist society, a characteristic generally frowned upon by recent generations of interpreters. Where 1950s scholars may well have found the prominence of intellectuals in such a society attractive, their successors have often chosen to stress the currents of popular belief and practice that existed in tension with the elite "party line," and in which the elite themselves may have participated to some degree. Similarly, the planter elite that dominated the life of the established Anglican churches of Virginia during much of the colonial period do not inspire affection among many of our contemporaries (except, perhaps, their multitudinous descendants), and latter-day "elite" denominations – Episcopalians and Presbyterians – continue to bemoan their fall from influence in a society in which newly empowered conservative religious groups seem to exert a conspicuous and, for some, an alarming influence. Nevertheless, the number of Episcopalians in Congress continues to outnumber by far that of Pentecostals – although, in the late 1990s, virtually all of the leadership positions in both Executive and Legislative branches of the Federal government are held by Southern Baptists.

Finally, both New England Puritans and Virginia Anglicans enjoyed the status of *established* churches – that is, they were exclusively recognized and supported by their colonial governments, while competing religious groups were at best tolerated and sometimes, as in the case of Quakers who made periodic incursions into the Bay Colony, actually executed. The First Amendment to the Constitution definitively ended such establishments of religion, and all of the states had adopted similar provisions within a half-century. However, the normative character of Christianity has never disappeared from our discourse and remains problematic in today's society, as evidenced in continuing attempts to amend the Constitution to authorize prayer in public schools.

The persistence of the influence of the colonial religious elites into modern time through change and storm is addressed by several contributors. In each case, however, the irony that colonial historian Perry Miller saw as so central in Puritanism's metamorphoses ultimately prevails: things rarely turn out in the long run the way early religious leaders foresaw.

David Holmes discusses the Anglican establishment of colonial Virginia, outlining its distinctive practices of worship and polity; relating these to the class structure with which that church was intimately associated; and reflecting on the long-term consequences of that establishment status for their longer-term fortunes in American society after they had become known as Episcopalians.

Amanda Porterfield begins with the case of Anne Hutchinson, who was banished by the leadership of the Puritan Massachusetts Bay Colony for heresy when she maintained that she and her followers were directly inspired by the Holy Spirit. Porterfield argues that both Hutchinson, who stood for the immediacy of religious experience, and her opponents, such as the colony's governor John Winthrop, who stood for religion as a support for the social order, were both ultimately victorious in shaping American religion in such surprisingly disparate venues as late-twentieth century Buddhism and Roman Catholicism.

Mark Valeri takes on the venerable Weber thesis, arguing that American Puritans ultimately did contribute to the economic and ideological triumph of capitalism in America, but only after many decades and considerable intellectual adjustment. Ultimately, argues Valeri, latter-day American Calvinist divines such as John Witherspoon endorsed free market economics only after they had abandoned traditional social ethics in favor of the new universalism embodied in Enlightenment thought.

Chapter 5

The Anglican Tradition in Colonial Virginia

David L. Holmes

"An establishment in a healthy condition," Richard Hofstadter writes of established churches,

> is intimately linked, as was the Church of England, at home, to the power of the state. Its ranks supply a parallel hierarchy of authority, which both supports and is supported by the secular power. . . . It commands the ready and willing allegiance of the majority of the population, for whom it is the inherited, the normal church; the agencies of education, charity, and welfare are in its hands; its local churches stand at the center of community life, and in the rhythms of daily existence it supplies the beat and tolls the bells. It is the core of the whole national system of values, spiritual, intellectual, and political, and it provides them with their distinctive texture.[1]

Hofstadter's statement applies not only to the Church of England but also to the Church of England in the colony of Virginia. It is important for readers to understand some truths about this religious establishment that formed Virginia.

First, the Virginia establishment was Anglican: the faith of the Church of England. Nonconformists (or Protestants who declined to conform to the Church of England) were tolerated from the late seventeenth century on, but were subject to restrictions; Roman Catholics and Jews lacked religious rights. Although a few Roman Catholics not only lived in Virginia across the Potomac from Maryland but also served in the General Assembly, they did so only because the Anglican establishment looked the other way.

Second, the Anglicanism of Virginia was of the Protestant variety. In various places and at various times in church history, certain Anglican churches have stood very close in outlook and practice to Roman Catholicism or to Eastern Orthodoxy. In the 1990s, visitors at an Episcopal service experience worship that is similar to the worship of Lutheranism or Roman Catholicism. The product of influences ranging from apostolic to medieval to Reformation Christianity, emphasizing the authority of Scripture as primary but leaving a place for tradition and reason, the Anglican tradition is like the color purple: having both red and blue qualities, but being a third color. Blending Catholic and Protestant influences, it can emphasize one part of its tradition over another.

But in the eighteenth century, Anglicanism existed in a Protestant mold. For the three hundredth anniversary of the College of William and Mary in 1993, a group of church historians reproduced an eighteenth-century Anglican Sunday service in the College's chapel in the Sir Christopher Wren Building. William and Mary was the Anglican college of Virginia and of the South. Those who participated in the service gained a new insight into colonial American Anglicanism. The service turned out to be an extremely biblical, word-centered service. It included few sacred gestures, little pomp, little concern with ecclesiastical millinery, and little sense of the priestliness that has sometimes characterized Anglicanism.

Rather, the colonial Anglican service was suffused with a concern for the read, preached, and sung Word. Invitations, exhortations, readings, creeds, psalms, prayers, sermon, and final prayers and blessing: that was what the service consisted of. And so the second truth is that the worship experienced by colonial Virginians who attended their established church was closer to the worship of the New England Puritans than it was to the worship of the Lutherans or Roman Catholics of colonial America.

A third truth is that the Anglicanism of Virginia was formal, worldly, aristocratic, decorous, and dependent upon literacy. As a direct result, the established church of Virginia gained little more than the superficial loyalty of Virginia's common people. Thus when religious freedom came to Virginia in the 1780s, the common people left the newly-independent Episcopal Church of Virginia just as soon as they could.

All Christian denominations seem to have characteristics that appeal to some people and at the same time are drawbacks for others. What might be some typical examples? For the Quakers, the aspect that was both a strength and a liability seems to be silent worship. For the Baptists, it seems to be the authority of Scripture. For Roman Catholicism, it has surely been papal authority. For Eastern Orthodoxy, it has probably been the rootage in the councils and practices of antiquity.

What about Anglicanism? For Anglicanism the central characteristic that has been at the same time both an asset and a millstone seems to have been formality, decorum, and an appeal to the upper strata of society. In century after century, Anglican worship and piety has appealed to three kinds of people above all: to the literate and educated, to the wealthy and professional, and to the aesthetically sensitive. (In both England and colonial Virginia, the Church of England also appealed to the patriotic instincts of the citizens. Although that appeal persists to some extent in England in the 1990s, the Revolutionary War eradicated it in Virginia.)

No one can dispute that a built-in attraction to the educated, cultured, and economically comfortable members of society gives a church power and influence in society. But at the same time, such a church will at best fail to attract, and at worst repel, the majority of any population.

And that is precisely what has happened in the last two hundred years in the United States to the Church of England. Renamed "the [Protestant] Episcopal Church" in the 1780s (for the name of "England" was no longer in good standing among Americans), it contained within its membership eleven presidents of the United States. The number rises to twelve if Thomas Jefferson: a Deist who was not only raised in the established church of Virginia but also attended Episcopal services regularly, is counted.

Almost one-half of the chief justices of the US Supreme Court and one-third of its justices have been Episcopalians. Episcopalians have been represented disproportionately in the U.S Senate, in the US House of Representatives, and in the presidencies and on the boards of Fortune 500 companies. Until well after World War II, Episcopalians dominated the officer class of the American armed forces. The Gulf War of 1991, for example, was essentially planned by Episcopalians; President George Bush, Secretary of State James Baker, Secretary of Defense Richard Cheney, and Chairman of the Joint Chiefs of Staff General Colin Powell were all communicants of the church.

But the newest information shows that the Episcopal Church – the church that was established as the Church of England during the colonial period in Virginia, North Carolina, South Carolina, Georgia, Maryland, and lower New York – now ranks in size somewhere between twelfth and fourteenth among American denominations. Thus in the 1990s this former established church has become very much of a minority faith in America, though it retains strength among the professional, educated, and wealthy classes. Any one who seeks to understand the history of the Church of England in Virginia should keep this strength and weakness of the Anglican tradition very much in mind.

Anglicanism was the established faith of colonial Virginia. That it was the official state church meant that throughout the colonial period, the General Assembly of Virginia legislated for Anglicanism, supported it through taxation, and protected it against competition.

In one way, it is good to have state churches, for they solve a number of ethical and financial problems. State churches were, in fact, the model in Christianity from the fourth century until well after the Reformation. Some still exist in Europe.

But the interesting fact is that established Christian churches do not seem to do well over a long period of time. In the 1990s it is difficult, in fact, to think of a single country where an established church exhibits a healthy church life. In every country where Christianity has become the established faith, except perhaps Poland, the Christian salt in time seems to have lost its savor. And many historians would say that Poland became an exception because its Roman Catholic faith became identified with the patriotic defense against the efforts of Eastern Orthodox Russians, Protestant Prussians, and Marxist atheists to convert the nation. In any event, colonial Virginia was no exception to the general rule that established churches ultimately do not flourish.

From 1607 on, the established church grew: first at Jamestown, and then in ever-widening settlements along Virginia's rivers. Whenever settlers moved too far from existing courthouses and parishes, the Assembly simply established new counties and new parishes.

What was a *parish*? A parish was simply a geographical district, perhaps 150 square miles in size. Thomas Jefferson's county, Albemarle, contained two parishes, and that was the normal pattern. Sometimes, however, a parish would be coterminous with a county, or it would stretch across parts of two counties.

Each parish would contain anywhere from two to four churches, and occasionally more. Near its center the parish would have a *glebe*: a church farm of two hundred or more acres. The priest or minister of the parish, called the *rector*, would live on this glebe in the manner of the plantation gentry. If he had an assistant, that priest would carry the title of *curate* or *vicar* and live elsewhere in the parish. Usually the rector would have slaves to work his glebe farm; its income, like his income from wedding fees, was considered part of his *perquisites*. In addition, since Virginia had no public schools, many rectors also operated academies on their glebes.

Riding out from his glebe, the rector would rotate his services among the churches in his parish. When the rector was not scheduled to be at a church, a layreader called the *clerk* (spelled "clerk," but pronounced "clark") would read the prescribed service from the Book of Common Prayer. The official service book of Anglicanism, the Book of Common Prayer, contains the forms for daily and Sunday worship and for such rites as baptism, matrimony, and burial of the dead.

The ideal of the Virginia parish system was to have a church not more than about six miles – easy riding distance, and manageable walking distance – from every home. Certain unwritten rules guided the location of these churches. *Vestries* (about whom more later) located churches adjacent to centers of population or of population growth; adjacent to navigable rivers or to main roads; near crossroads when they were available; and on land that had a potable water supply (for people and horses required water). The journals that have survived from colonial Virginia – such as that of Philip Vickers Fithian, a Presbyterian graduate of the College of New Jersey who came to Lancaster County, Virginia, just before the Revolution to tutor the family of Robert Carter – reveal colonial Virginians going to church on Sunday by horse, by boat, or by walking.

Today most of the colonial churches of Virginia have disappeared. But visitors to the state can still view the remnants of the colonial parish system aong the banks of the great Tidewater rivers. The James, the York, the Potomac, and above all the Rappahannock rivers still display either Episcopal churches dating from the colonial period or historical signs marking where colonial churches once stood.

As the population of colonial Virginia increased and spread, the number of parishes grew. By 1784, the year that the Revolution officially ended and that the Church of England was officially *disestablished* (or dispossessed of state support) in Virginia, the state had 107 parishes stretching as far as Kentucky (which consisted of one parish served by one rector).

As the parishes of the established church of Virginia multiplied, so did the

number and size of the churches in them. By the eighteenth century, Virginia was
dotted with substantial churches of frame, brick, or stone built on the English
pattern. The seventeenth-century churches were gothic in style, but most of the
churches built during the colonial period were Georgian. And "Georgian" meant
what a visitor sees upon arrival in Colonial Williamsburg: it means symmetry,
and clear glass, and Flemish bond brickwork, and beaded wood siding, and orna-
mental entries. Some of these colonial Anglican churches bore unintentionally
humorous names. The colonial records of Virginia display such names as
Pohick Church, Beaver Dam Church, Difficult Church, Cattail Church, Turkey
Run Church, Rattlesnake Church, and even Cheesecake Church – the latter a
corruption of an Indian name.

This growth of parishes in the colonial Church of Virginia led to the vestry
system. What was a *vestry*? In the seventeenth century the General Assembly of
Virginia created groups of men – always men, always white men, usually wealthy
white men, and often twelve in number – called "gentlemen vestries" to run the
individual parishes. The powers of these vestries were immense. They levied
the taxes that paid for the churches, clergy, and welfare system of the parish; they
administered the welfare system; they watched over morality; and they hired and
fired the clergy.

How were these vestries selected? Initially they were appointed or elected. But
early in their history, colonial Virginia's vestries became closed, self-sustaining
corporations. When one of the vestrymen died or resigned, the others simply
elected his replacement.

And so in parish after parish throughout colonial Virginia, there came to be
family seats on the vestry – seats reserved for the Carters, or for the Tayloes, or
for the Randolphs, or for the Byrds, or for the Lees, or for the Talliaferros, seats
passed on from oldest son to oldest son, or, when no male issue existed, to
sons-in-law or to cousins. Thus from the 1660s through to the end of the
Revolutionary War, family after family in Virginia controlled one-twelfth of
the power in their parish.

The effect of this vestry system on Virginia for almost two hundred years after
the Revolution cannot be exaggerated. During the colonial period, the economically leading families controlled both the religious and the political establishment.
After the Revolution, they continued to control the politics of the state, except
during the brief period of Reconstruction following the Civil War. Throughout
Tidewater and Piedmont Virgina, there were old families with power; there were
inherited seats on the parish vestry; and it was very difficult for others to change
the grooves.

For much of the twentieth century, for example, politics in Virginia was
controlled by what Virginians called the "Byrd Organization." The candidates
backed by Harry Byrd, Sr. or Jr. (both of whom served as US Senators from
Virginia, the latter resigning to allow his son to continue in his place) were generally not only nominated but also elected to political office. To historians it was
unsurprising that the Byrds were not only Episcopalian but also descendants of
an influential colonial family.

The vestry system – run by what one might call "the old courthouse vestry crowd" – held great advantages. It put the leading landowners on the side of the church, which is usually very helpful to a church body. In addition, it caused economically comfortable Christians to receive hands-on experience of human need and suffering, which has not always been the case in history. By law the General Assembly made illegitimate children, Downs-syndrome children, widows, orphans, elderly, and handicapped the responsibility of the vestries in every parish. By law the two leading figures on the vestries – called the *church-wardens* – had to get involved with such cases. And so they received an introduction to reality and to suffering.

Yet if the vestry system had certain clear advantages, it also carried with it at least four overriding disadvantages that in time undermined the established church of Virginia. First, it identified Anglicanism with the policy of taxation without representation. This association of the established church with England assisted its collapse during and after the Revolution, even though the majority of its clergy and the overwhelming majority of its laity were patriots. This fact needs to be emphasized: Virginia Anglicans, clergy and laity alike, supported the American side during the Revolution. Thus the subsequent collapse of Anglicanism in Virginia had nothing to do with political Toryism.

A second disadvantage of the vestry system was that parish morality suffered. The vestries tended to hire clergy (generally graduates of Oxford, Cambridge, William and Mary, or one of the Scottish universities) only on renewable one-year contracts. Whether married with families or single, few of the clergy were therefore free from concerns about their economic and job security. Under such circumstances, only a few John the Baptists in the colonial ministry dared to speak out against cockfighting and carousing and gambling when their leading parishioners were themselves doing these things.

As a result, Virginians who wished for a sterner biblical morality, and who wanted the Church of Jesus Christ to distinguish itself from the worldly society around it, looked for another interpretation of Christianity. When the Presbyterians, Baptists, and Methodists – all of whom then enforced a stern ethical discipline on their members – entered the state, they had a built-in appeal.

A third liability of the vestry system was that it left the Anglicans of Virginia (called "Episcopalians" after the Revolution) without the knowledge of how to support a church voluntarily once their church lost its state props. As far as scholars can tell, collections – in the form of a special offering for the poor – were taken in the Anglican churches of colonial Virginia only once a year. Other than that, a vestry would simply send an annual bill, enforceable by the sheriff, for a resident's share of parish expenses.

Thus from the 1780s on, when Anglicanism was disestablished and its support by taxation ended, the remaining Episcopalians of Virginia encountered great difficulty in keeping their churches and clergy solvent. An analogy is what would happen to the roads or courthouses of the United States today if government did not require citizens to pay for them by levied taxes. A fair guess is that some or many would decay or crumble.

And precisely that happened to most of Virginia's colonial Anglican churches after the Revolution. The yeoman and less propertied classes went off to the evangelical denominations or to the Enlightenment-centered religion of reason called Deism. Many of the wives of the gentry tried to stay with the Episcopal Church. But the backbone of the parishes since the seventeenth century, the male planter class, became so influenced by Deism that they saw no real need for the church to continue. And so in parish after parish in Virginia, from the 1780s on, the Episcopal Church died out.

Finally, the fourth disadvantage of the vestry system was perhaps its most harmful. Above all, the vestry system made the Anglican Church conspicuously the church of the aristocracy. The vestries ran the parishes subject only to the laws passed by the General Assembly. The General Assembly was composed of the same people who served on the vestries. Consequently the more than 90 percent of colonial Virginians who were not gentry had virtually no say in the affairs of their own established church.

Thus in the years just before the Revolution, when the Baptists and Presbyterians and Methodists began to appear in Virginia in increasing numbers, their appeal was clearly immense. These evangelical denominations allowed the common people to play a role. The Baptists and Methodists (who in that period emphasized the converted heart over the schooled head) even allowed uneducated men to enter their ministry. Why, then, especially now that the colonies were separate from England, should a Virginian continue to belong to the former Church of England?

Nevertheless, twentieth-century readers should not be too hard on the Anglicanism of colonial Virginia. Until relatively recent years, precisely this kind of established church was common in Europe. To play a role in church life in Europe, common people had to join such movements as the Mennonites, Brethren, or Baptists, if the law permitted them to. From Spain to Sweden, established churches throughout Europe were run not only *by* but also in many ways *for* the political establishment. Thus the state church system of colonial Virginia has to be seen against the backdrop of all the state churches of its time. And in the comparison, it may not come off badly at all.

It would be hard to exaggerate the role the establishment and class played in the problems of Anglicanism in Virginia. When historians rotate the established church under the prism of class structure, they have to be struck by the extent to which the element of *class* influenced even the established church's worship and architecture.

What do scholars know about the worship and architecture of colonial Virginia Anglicanism? In warm weather the Anglican churches of Virginia held their services at 11 a.m.; in cold weather, they were delayed until 12 noon. These times were chosen out of consideration for farm chores, for travel time, and for warmth. They were, in fact, the same times that generally obtained at churches in rural Europe.

Colonial Virginians tended to arrive at church early, for Sunday services provided a chance for isolated people to socialize. The picture one gets of an Anglican service in colonial Virginia is that of liveried servants taking care of carriages and horses, of well-dressed people standing in the churchyard chatting, of men discussing politics or horses, of sedate worship. Returning to his native

New Jersey for a visit and attending his home Presbyterian church, Fithian is struck by the difference between worship there and in Virginia. "How unlike Virginia," he writes:

> No rings of Beaux chatting before and after Sermon on Gallantry; no assembling in crowds after Service to dine and bargain; no cool, spiritless harangue from the Pulpit; Minister and people here seem in some small measure to reverence the Day, while in Virginia they neither do the one or the other.[2]

A middle-colonies version of Puritan, Fithian arrives in Virginia curious about its established Anglican church. From his ascetic Calvinist fellows at Princeton, he has heard many stories about it, virtually all of which have equated Virginia with Las Vegas. Given not only the contemporary Presbyterian commitment to spiritual discipline but also their opposition to worldly amusements, he would have heard even more critical comments about Roman Catholicism in Europe. After arriving in Virginia, the new tutor initially attends Anglican churches almost every Sunday.   But by the mid-point of his stay, he begins to read Calvinist theology in his room on Sunday rather than ride to Anglican services. Why? The reason seems to have much to do with that Anglican strength-cum-liability of class, formality, and especially worldliness. The combination seems to have repelled Fithian; for him Christianity was a serious, even grim, religion.

What else did the typical Anglican churchyard in Virginia contain besides chatting beaux? Churchyards seem to have have had some or all of the following: springs, for water; mounting blocks, for riders; benches, for sitting; a sundial, for time; a graveyard, for burials (usually of the lesser parishioners, the leading ones preferring burial in the family graveyard on their estate); a churchyard wall (generally for protection of the graves from animals); and a vestry house (for meetings of the vestry). Generally only one church in a parish – the church viewed as the principal church – would have such a house.

As for the church buildings, the canon law of the Church of England (which applied to all Anglican colonies) required them to be *oriented* – that is, the table-altars were set at the east, or orient, end. Thus when visitors enter such colonial Episcopal churches as Bruton Parish Church in Colonial Williamsburg or Christ Church in Alexandria today, they face east. This practice of orientation has nothing to do with facing Jerusalem. Rather, it goes back beyond Christianity to the pagan worship of the rising sun and was something the Church of England inherited from Roman Catholicism.

Ironically, in Virginia from about 1670 on, the orientation of the Middle Ages ran into the word-centered churches introduced to Anglicanism by Christopher Wren (1632–1723). Wren's designs for churches influenced all of Anglicanism. He believed in what he called auditory churches – that is, churches where everyone could not only hear the readings, sermons, and prayers but also see the parson who read or preached them. The churches Wren designed were word-centered, light-filled, unmysterious churches, like St Paul's Cathedral in London. They replaced the dark and mysterious Gothic churches that Anglicanism had in-herited from the medieval period – churches in which, in Wren's experience, worshipers often could neither hear nor see, and hence tended in such cases to be spectators, rather than participants in worship.

In the colonial period Anglican services did not revolve around the table-altar, as they do today. Only on the relatively few Sundays a year on which a rector administered the Holy Communion would he perform any part of the service from the table-altar. On all other Sundays, the rector (or clerk, in his absence) would lead the entire service from the high pulpit.

Where would that pulpit be located? The answer is that in an auditory church, it would usually be located roughly equidistant from all points. Hence it would normally be placed at the mid-point of the north wall. That is where it originally was located at Bruton Parish Church, and that is where it still is located in such restored Virginia churches as St. Peter's Church, New Kent County. Alternatively, if the church were shaped like a cross – if it were, that is, a *cruciform* church – the pulpit would be located at one of the points where the transepts intersected the main church. That is where the pulpit is located in Christ Church, Lancaster County, one of the few colonial churches in Virginia to have escaped change since its construction. It is also where the pulpit came to be located at Bruton Parish Church.

As for the pews in these churches, class considerations influenced the seating. Today many churches cannot persuade worshipers to sit in the front pews, but in the colonial period the rule was: the closer a pew to the table-altar or pulpit, the higher the rank; the further away, the lower the rank. In the very back of the churches, the poor sat on plain benches.

The pews were box pews with high sides for protection against the cold. Since they had seats on three sides, worshipers could shift in different directions. But if the pews were crowded, the parson would have to read the service and to preach while facing the backs of a certain number of his congregation. Engravings by William Hogarth depicting worship in English churches of the time show exactly that situation.

What posture would Virginia's Anglican worshipers use to pray in these pews? Here the evidence is confusing. Letters, diaries, or church records exist that seem to suggest parishioners in Virginia kneeling and looking straight ahead. Other sources clearly describe worshipers kneeling but turning around to support their arms on the seats of the box pews during prayers. Still others mention some worshipers not kneeling but rather sitting with bowed head – and certainly that has always been the case with many of the elderly in congregations. Finally, Eleanor Parke Custis, the ward of George Washington, insisted that Washington always stood in church for prayers. Thus the recurrent image a researcher gets of a Virginia congregation at prayer is that of the first families of of Virginia all facing in different directions, and sometimes nose to nose, with Washington and his aides resolutely standing.

What about African Americans? The Society for the Propagation of the Gospel (SPG) – the overseas missionary society of the Church of England, founded in 1701 – required its missionaries to work with slaves. But SPG missionaries went only to colonies where the Anglican churches were struggling, and Virginia's established, state-supported parishes needed no such assistance. The Virginia

Anglican clergy who did attempt to evangelize the colony's slaves (Morgan Godwyn is the most noteable example) frequently ran into indifference or outright opposition on the part of the slave owners.

Relatively few African Americans therefore attended Anglican services. The few who did sat or stood in the back or outside the windows. Some may also have sat in galleries, though that tradition is currently undergoing re-examination. Visitors to colonial churches should not assume that a gallery was a *slave gallery*. In reality, seating in galleries in the Anglican churches of colonial Virginia could cover the entire social spectrum. A Virginia church might have a gallery reserved for students from the parson's academy, several galleries erected by families for their exclusive use (much like boxes at the opera), and perhaps a gallery reserved for slaves. Seating in boxes and galleries was once common practice in Europe. One seventeenth-century Lutheran church in Dresden, Germany, for example, had several tiers of galleries.

In the established church of colonial Virginia, no procession began the services each Sunday. The rector and the clerk, both wearing wigs, gowns, and neckbands (all of which identified them with the gentry and the educated class), simply arrived and took their places in the pulpit. This pulpit had several levels, or decks. From the bottom deck, the clerk led the singing and responses. From the middle deck, the rector read the service. From the top deck, he preached the sermon. If the church had a two-decker rather than a three-decker pulpit, the rector read the Prayer Book service as well as preached from the second deck.

The service came from the Book of Common Prayer of the Church of England, a book that replaces the drama and gestures of medieval Roman Catholicism with something that is very Protestant: *words*. The Book of Common Prayer is a monument of English prose, but a monument that is predicated upon literacy. Hence in colonial Virginia, where not only one quarter of the white population but also most of the black population were illiterate, Anglican worship inevitably had limited appeal.

What form of worship might have appealed to more of the population? The mystery and ritual of Tridentine Roman Catholicism – the medieval form of Christian worship, codified by the sixteenth-century Council of Trent, with much of the mass in Latin – was not present in colonial Virginia. But as the eighteenth century went on, evangelical "hot-Gospel" Protestant denominations came into the colony. Their emotional services appealed to the less literate classes of Virginia, though they repelled most of the gentry.

As for the sermons preached from these Anglican pulpits, the primary sources describe them not only as lasting fifteen to twenty minutes but also as being dry in content and read from a manuscript. To colonial Presbyterians, Baptists, and Methodists, fifteen or twenty minutes was simply too short a time for a proper sermon, for then – as today – evangelicals viewed the sermon as a teaching and converting mechanism. That the colonial Virginia rectors tended to embroider and to enlarge when they published their sermons has misled some writers into thinking that Anglican sermons were lengthy. The diarists and letter writers of colonial Virginia clearly indicate that few Anglican sermons lasted as long as the sermons in other Protestant denominations of the time.

Writers sometimes overlook that Anglican sermons almost had to be relatively brief, precisely because the services from the Book of Common Prayer were long. John Wesley's journal indicates that his typical Sunday service as an Anglican priest in Savannah lasted ninety minutes. When on four or more Sundays a year, the holy communion service was added to it, the Anglican service stretched to two hours. To be sure, the worshipers of colonial America had more patience for lengthy services than twentieth-century worshipers have. But keeping the sermons relatively brief represented one way for the Anglican clergy to shorten worship. Evangelical denominations did not worship out of a printed mass or common prayer book and therefore had more liberty in adjusting the length of their services to compensate for a long sermon.

As for music, a small number of Virginia's Anglican churches had organs, but the vast majority did not. Like the Puritans, the congregations sang only Psalms, for Psalms were taken from the Bible and hence viewed as divinely inspired (unlike hymns, which were written by humans). In some few parishes, the sources indicate that a choir sat by the organ in the west gallery. Fithian and others mention that only the clerk and a few members of a typical congregation sang the Psalms.

So much for the history and life of Virginia's colonial church. It was a genteel church; even in the back pews, appearance, clothes, manners, and decorum were important. Formality, decorum, and literacy characterized its worship. When holy communion was celebrated, congregations generally received it roughly in order of class rank. Again, it should be noted that the same practice of receiving the bread and the wine according to rank seems to have gone on in many of the class-centered churches of Europe during the same centuries. Nowhere did a peasant blunder up to the altar ahead of the baron and the baroness. Whatever Jesus of Nazareth may have thought of class structure, most of Christendom came not only to affirm it but also to embrace a hierarchy of such titles as "Reverend," "Very Reverend," "Rt. Reverend," and "Most Reverend" for the clergy.

Nevertheless, the real question for colonial Virginia religion may be: what did ordinary, lower-class, black or white Virginians *feel* when they attended Anglican worship, as by law they had to do at least periodically? Could they escape their subordinate status even then? And if they could not, did their sense of subordination interfere with their worship? Did it, that is to say, *trouble* them?

Because if readers remove the colonial gentry and place the Virginia poor on center stage, they may begin to understand why the common people of Virginia left the Anglican tradition and on the whole never returned again. They may begin to understand, too, why in the centuries since the Revolution the Episcopal Church has never quite been able to attract the lower middle and lower economic and social classes in the United States.

As this chapter said at its start, Anglicanism tends to appeal to the economically comfortable, to the cultured, to the aesthetic, to the professional, and to the intellectual – and that's a clear *strength*. As the saying goes, it's hard work, but somebody has to do it. And in the minds of many observers, the Anglican tradition has done it well since the colonial period, inspiring and nurturing millions of Americans. "Something deep in me responds to the sweet and tempered ways of the Episcopal Church," a convert from another denomination once wrote:

> Its atmosphere of reverence, its ordered and stately worship, its tradition of historic continuity, linking today with ages agone; its symbols which enshrine the faith of the past and the hope of the future; its wise and wide tolerance; its old and lovely liturgy . . . the organized mysticism of its sacraments – all these things of beauty and grace move me profoundly.[3]

Yet to read these words is to come face to face with the problem, for their author was a highly educated, cultured, urbane, upper-middle-class man who moved in the world of civic affairs, museums, and libraries and who was viewed as an intellectual in his former denomination. The words are not those of an assembly-line worker, a small farmer, a clerk in a convenience store, or a typical fan at a professional football game. A church that offers "ordered and stately worship . . . tradition . . . historic continuity . . .symbols . . .wise and wide tolerance . . . old and lovely liturgy . . . organized mysticism . . . [and] things of beauty and grace" will inevitably appeal only to a minority in American society. Religious people of other sensibilities and circumstances, those who were once called "common folk," will tend to abstain from such a church if they have that option.

And a mass departure from the church of their ancestors is precisely what did occur among Virginians in the 1770s and 1780s. Again, the exodus had no relationship to the established church's record in the Revolutionary War. A solid majority of Anglican clergy and the overwhelming majority of Anglican laypeople in Virginia were patriots; Anglicans from Virginia took leading roles in the affairs of the new republic.

Rather, the departure occurred because the hold of the established church on the affections of the populace had become increasingly feeble as the colonial period progressed. The established church had done its best to give Virginians spiritual guidance and reassurance in an uncertain world, but it was not quite the interpretation of Christianity the majority of Virginians desired. At the start of the Revolutionary War, the General Assembly ended the tax support of the church. At the end of the Revolution, it fully disestablished the church and required it to compete with other denominations on an equal basis. Before, during, and after the war, the majority of Virginians left the former established church for other interpretations of Christianity. Or they left it for no church, since the Enlightenment faith of Deism gained many adherents in Virginia.

Two denominational offspring of the Great Awakening, the Baptists and the Methodists, became the popular churches in the Commonwealth of Virginia. In church statistics drawn up in the 1990s the various Baptist groups have more than thirteen times as many adherents in Virginia as the Episcopal Church, and the various Methodist churches have four times as many.

As the twentieth century ends, Virginia has no more than several hundred thousand Episcopalians in a population of six and a half million. Once the church of the vast majority of Virginians, the Episcopal Church ranks fifth among the families of churches in the 1990s, after the Baptists, Methodists, Roman Catholics, and Presbyterians. Nevertheless, it has continued to be a respected, influential denomination in its former stronghold. But its strength – the strength that is simultaneously its abiding handicap in terms of growth – is that it is composed largely of the economically comfortable and the professional, gentry, merchant, and educated classes.

If the readers of this chapter had lived in Virginia in 1750, the odds are overwhelming that they would have been Anglicans. The odds are also high that they would have had a religious affiliation other than Episcopalian if they had lived in Virginia in 1850. To be sure, the former state church of Virginia survived. After 1811 it even adopted the evangelical methods of the first and second Great Awakenings in an effort to bring back Virginians to the church of their ancestors. But the former established church, which for almost two centuries, in Hofstadter's memorable words, had been "the inherited, the normal church [which had stood] at the center of community life . . . and supplied the beat and tolled the bells of daily existence" was never able to regain its former hold on the populace of Virginia.

What is often overlooked is that it probably never had a substantial hold to begin with.

NOTES

1 Richard Hofstadter, *America at 1750* (New York: Knopf, 1971), pp. 204–5.
2 Philip Vickers Fithian, *Journal and Letters of Philip Vickers Fithian: A Plantation Tutor of the Old Dominion, 1773–1774*, edited by Hunter D. Farish (Williamsburg, Va.: Colonial Williamsburg Inc., 1965), p. 100.
3 Joseph Fort Newton, *River of Years: An Autobiography* (Philadelphia, Pa.: J. B. Lippincott Company, 1946), pp. 234–5.

BIBLIOGRAPHY

Billings, Warren M., Selby, John E., and Tate, Thad W. (1986) *Colonial Virginia: A History*, White Plains, NY: KTO Press.
Bond, Edward L. (1995) "Religion in seventeenth-century Virginia: myth, persuasion, and the creation of an American identity," Ph.D. dissertation, Louisiana State University.
Brydon, George MacLaren (1947–52) *Virginia's Mother Church*, (2 vols), Richmond, Va.: Virginia Historical Society.
Fithian, Philip Vickers (1965) *Journal and Letters*, ed. Hunter D. Farish, Williamsburg, Va.: Colonial Williamsburg Foundation.
Gaustad, Edwin S. (1994) *Revival, Revolution, and Religion in Early Virginia*, Williamsburg, Va.: Colonial Williamsburg Foundation.
Holmes, David L. (1993) *A Brief History of the Episcopal Church*, Valley Forge, Pa.: Trinity Press International.
Isaac, Rhys (1982) *The Transformation of Virginia, 1740–1790*, Chapel Hill, NC: Institute of Early American History and Culture.
Jefferson, Thomas (1954) *Notes on the State of Virginia*, ed. William Peden, Chapel Hill,

NC: Institute of Early American History and Culture.

Rose, Robert (1977) *The Diary of Robert Rose: A View of Virginia by a Scottish Colonial Parson, 1746–1751*, ed. Ralph E. Fall, Verona,Va.: McClure Press.

Upton, Dell (1997) *Holy Things and Profane: Anglican Parish Churches in Colonial Virginia*, New Haven, Conn.: Yale University Press.

Chapter 6

The Puritan Legacy in American Religion and Culture

Amanda Porterfield

When Anne Hutchinson faced John Winthrop, the Governor of the Massachusetts Bay Colony, in the Newtown court near Boston in November 1637, he accused her of having "troubled the peace of the commonwealth and the churches here." He explained that the court had summoned her, "to understand how things are, that if you be in an erroneous way we may reduce you . . . so you may become a profitable member here among us." Or "if you be obstinate in your course," he went on, clarifying her alternatives, "then the court may take such course that you may trouble us no further."

Hutchinson proved to be obstinate in the eyes of the court. Banished from Massachusetts, she sought refuge in Rhode Island and then in New York, where she was killed in an Indian attack in 1643 during the Dutch–Indian War. The reason given for her banishment was clearly stated. In questioning the authority of ministers supposed to be her teachers, she had threatened the social order. And this social order was not as firmly established as the governor and magistrates would have liked it to be. Elections were tumultuous, merchants chafed against restrictions on their businesses, laws were sometimes ignored, confusion existed about who could vote, and the governor was not always treated with respect. Then there were primitive living conditions to contend with, along with isolation from England, which stirred loneliness and made it difficult to keep abreast of politics. In addition to the ever-present danger of Indian attack, all of these things contributed to an underlying anxiety about whether or not coming to the New World had been a good idea after all. In condemning Hutchinson for acting "more like a husband than a wife" and for speaking up in a way "not fitting for your sex," the Puritan leadership was trying to affirm the fundamentals of Puritan culture and stem the tide of disorder and confusion. In this effort they quashed women's right to religious speech and sent a clear message about the importance of patriarchal religious authority as a mainstay of social order.

In addition to its impact in clarifying official Puritan norms for gender roles, the trial represents an important set of American ideas about the relationship between religion and civil society. On the one hand, the verdict sent a clear message that individual religious expression should not be allowed to undermine social order. On the other, the distinction implicit in Hutchinson's trial between antisocial and prosocial forms of individual religious experience was part of a larger process of establishing individual religious experience as part of the groundwork of social order. Thus Hutchinson rose to influence in Massachusetts because her ideas grew out of the very commitment to the individual as recipient of grace and exponent of faith upon which the whole enterprise of Puritan religious thought was predicated.

To an important extent then, Hutchinson's ideas corresponded with those of the Puritan elite. They all understood grace to be a powerful process that transformed individuals into faithful Christians and enabled them to covenant together to establish virtuous families, churches, and communities. As a result of this understanding of how grace worked through individuals to create good societies, they believed that government should flow out from the consciences of Christian individuals and not be imposed on them by hostile authorities. Thus government should be moral and just – and should not hamper the expression of religious truth. Put more specifically, the government of Massachusetts Bay should contribute to the development of the religious principles that Puritans in England had not been free to fully express or implement in England. Thus religious freedom was an important principle for the Puritan leadership in Massachusetts, even though it was defined in terms of freedom to express what the leadership deemed to be religious truth.

The governors and magistrates of Massachusetts Bay defended their moral judgment in banishing Hutchinson by asserting that they had simply acted the part of a wise physician who cuts off a gangrenous limb to save the rest of the body from infection. But questions about their judgment have dominated interpretations of the trial at least since the early nineteenth century, as have questions about their hypocrisy in persecuting members of their own society for religious beliefs deemed hostile to the state, as they themselves had sometimes been persecuted in England. The notoriety of the trial in American literature and historiography only underscores its importance as a landmark in discussions about the relationship between religion and civil society.

The issues raised in the Hutchinson trial have continued to be raised in American religious history. Moreover, the temporary resolution of these issues in the verdict against Hutchinson helped determine the place that New England Puritanism would occupy in American history. The verdict against Hutchinson has contributed significantly to the tendency to stigmatize the Puritans as hypocritical bullies, a tendency which in turn has contributed to that persistent struggle for freedom from external authority so characteristic of American culture. Denouncements of the complacency engendered by adherence to established authority erupted in the dramatic expressions of religious concern that characterized the revivals of first and second Great Awakenings in the eighteenth and nineteenth centuries. In a related vein, resistance to accepting truth secondhand figured prominently in the growth of American Transcendentalism and its influence on American culture. As the Transcendentalist leader Ralph Waldo Emerson said to prospective ministers in his controversial "Divinity School Address" of 1838, "Truly speaking, it is not instruction, but provocation, that I can receive from another soul. What he announces, I must find true in me, or wholly reject; and on his word, or as his second, be he who he may, I can accept nothing" (1983: 79).

This emphasis on the primacy of personal experience and readiness to resist convention has come to the fore in numerous times and places, including in the enthusiasm for intellectual freedom among writers and social activists of the early twentieth century, who produced diatribes against Puritans as authoritarian, sexually repressive, and constantly on the lookout for anyone who might be having fun. It has also nurtured the penchant for religious experimentation expressed in William James's *Varieties of Religious Experience*, Jack Kerouac's *Dharma Bums*, and Annie Dillard's *Pilgrim at Tinker Creek*, to name but three of many titles that might be cited. In the 1960s, emphasis on the authority of the individual to resist the status quo surfaced in protest marches against the military-industrial complex and its war in Vietnam, in which Lyndon Johnson played the morally bankrupt defender of social order to millions of rebellious and religiously inspired college students.

The Hutchinson trial helped to shape this cultural mentality of fierce individualism. During the trial, asked why she had befriended John Wheelright, a minster officially censored for criticizing other ministers in New England, and why she continued to support him, Hutchinson famously replied, "That's matter of conscience, Sir." In defense of her reliance on conscience, she invoked her experience of the Holy Spirit, claiming that she experienced the Spirit's "immediate revelation" and that she believed it had as much authority as the revelations described in Scripture.

But while the claim about the Holy Spirit speaking directly to her soul marginalized her in the eyes of the governor and magistrates of Massachusetts Bay, in much of what she said, she agreed with the teachings of her own minister, John Cotton, whom she and her husband had followed to America from Lincolnshire, England. Cotton was held in the highest respect by Puritans in both England and America and his perspective on the Holy Spirit and its validation of personal religious experience was quite similar to Hutchinson's. He stressed the difference between the vital experience of grace and the mere hope of grace, which typically entailed conformity to the outward demeanor and behavior conventionally associated with grace. In his focus on the need for experiential assurance of grace, he stressed the importance of having a "Seal of the Spirit," an event beyond conversion that gave the soul indissoluble union with God and everlasting life.

Both in the radical way that Hutchinson and Cotton expounded it and in somewhat more conservative forms expounded by other Puritans, the emphasis on personal religious experience was a distinguishing aspect of Puritan thought. Thus Puritans differed from many other Christians of their time in their intense interest in the Holy Spirit, its transformative power in the lives of individuals, and in the authority it imputed to subjective experience. As the British historian Geoffrey Nuttall demonstrated, the spectrum of Puritan thought, ranging from radical to moderate to conservative, was defined by the degree of emphasis on the authority of subjective experience of the Holy Spirit. In other words, all Puritans agreed on the primacy of individual experience, although they disagreed with each other on questions about how spontaneous it could be, and how independent of scriptural authority it could be, and still be authentic. But as a cultural group, it is the Puritans who introduced belief in the primacy of internal experience into American religious life.

Somewhat ironically, along the radical end of the Puritan spectrum, this emphasis on personal religious experience involved the idea that important aspects of this experience were *impersonal*. Thus Hutchinson believed that she had been "sealed with the Spirit," meaning that any sense of a distinct spiritual identity of her own had been obliterated and that God spoke directly to and through her. Because she believed that the personal identity of the true Christian became swallowed up in the Spirit, she rejected the belief in personal immortality and bodily resurrection to which more conservative Puritans adhered.

Two hundred years later, Emerson and his fellow Transcendentalists contributed to the popularity of this kind of religious radicalism and developed it in a much more thoroughgoing way. Inspired by Romantic writers, especially Samuel Taylor Coleridge and Thomas Carlyle, and by the first English translations of Hindu and Buddhist scriptures, the American Transcendentalists came to define God as the flow of consciousness underlying all reality and to celebrate the religious genius of writers, artists, and philosophers who summoned their attention to this all-pervading but finally impersonal divine. In the Transcendentalist schema, this self-reliance was not narcissistic or antisocial. Rather, attunement to oneself and confidence in the authority of one's feelings and intuitions ushered one into a deep kinship with others associated with respect for the underlying spiritual intelligence coursing through one and all.

In recent years, this concern to intuit the underlying flow of spiritual intelligence or energy has become commonplace and even conventional. Partly as a result of this cultural triumph of Transcendental spirituality in our own day, openness to religious experience has advanced in unprecedented ways, melting boundaries between denominations and enabling individuals to incorporate various aspects of different faith traditions into their own personal spirituality. Conceptions of divine reality as an impersonal flow of spiritual energy work to equalize all religious traditions as well as to validate internal experience as the apotheosis of religious authority.

Two recent examples begin to illustrate the pervasiveness of this distinctive American phenomenon. In both cases, the vigorous development of what we might call post-Protestant individualism has coincided with a dramatic increase in religious pluralism in the United States and with an equally dramatic decline in control over American culture by what we used to call mainstream Protestant churches. As Protestant institutions have lost their hold over American culture, it has become easier for members of other religious traditions to embrace the emphasis on internal experience that has seeped into American culture from Protestantism.

To take one example, some of the current trends in Roman Catholicism in the

United States exemplify this characteristically American emphasis on internal authority. As many observers have noted, American Catholics are more willing than Catholics in other parts of the world to make personal decisions about which official teachings of the Church to embrace and which to overlook. Thus many American Catholics reject the idea that to be good Christians they must obey the Church's official ban on birth control. The relatively strong support for women's ordination among American Catholics, despite the Pope's insistence that the subject cannot even be discussed, is another example of the reliance on personal experience and judgment in religious matters. The same individualistic tendency is evident in the growing trend among American Catholics to choose a church on the basis of how it fits one's own personal outlook rather than to attend the church to which one is assigned as a result of residence in a particular parish neighborhood. This penchant for personal choice on religious issues is a matter of great concern to the papal hierarchy of the church as well as to a vocal minority of conservative American Catholics who oppose this Americanization process and wish to draw their co-religionists into more complete acceptance of the magisterium of the church.

In considering these developments, it is important to recognize that Catholicism carries its own strong emphasis on conscience and personal religious experience and that these elements have not been created by exposure to American culture but only reinforced and brought to expression in interesting new ways. In this regard, one might point to the flourishing of Catholic feminist theology in the United States today as an example of how the American emphasis on the authority of personal experience has combined powerfully (some would say explosively) with old ideas about womanhood and sacramentality and with newer ideas about justice and liberation also at work in Catholic theology. One might also point to the revitalization of Catholic spirituality among young people both in the United States today and in other parts of the world where the "youth culture" shaped by American media is strong. This revitalization movement is rooted in forms of Christian spirituality that predate the existence of American culture. But the catalyst that helps to make these forms of Christian life so attractive today is the current widespread interest in spirituality in American culture, and the distinct preference for spirituality over religion, which is rooted in the deep-seated American tendency to elevate the authority of personal religious experience and to expect established religious authority to nurture and protect that experience.

Elements of the same individualizing process can be found in Buddhist communities in the US. This is a particularly interesting example because, for more than a century, American interpretations of Buddhism have contributed to the liberalization of American ideas about divine reality, which now, today, are contributing to the liberalization of Buddhism. Thus Americans committed to the authority of internal experience invoke Buddhist ideas about internal experience to democratize Buddhist traditions. This democratization process is manifest in women's efforts to achieve parity as students and teachers in Buddhist communities and in their criticism of male-dominated religious authority. While women have participated actively in Buddhism since its founding in India in the fifth century before the Common Era, they have often been presumed to be born to a lower state than men and any wisdom they may have offered has often been presumed to be limited to women's issues. In the western world today, and especially in the United States, many Buddhists have challenged these traditional assumptions and linked their overturning to the progressive evolution of worldwide consciousness. As one American woman, Karma Lekshe Tsomo, expressed the point, "The Buddha's words were meant to be tested and verified through one's own practice experience." Invoking Buddhist ideas to challenge Buddhist traditions, Tsomo argues, "We are not being asked to believe anything or accept anything (particularly not to buy something simply because a man said it, however enlightened he may have been)." Relying on their own practice experience, "American women, having broken with a patriarchal path, are creating their direction, incorporating wisdom wherever they may find it." If the words of these women "lack some of the weight and depth of tradition," the role of these women in Buddhism's development is crucial, Tsomo argues, because "their viewpoint may be fresher, more personal, more dynamic" (1995: 157–8).

The democratizing tendency has been especially dramatic in Zen, which has been part of American culture since the late nineteenth century and is probably the form of Buddhism most firmly ensconsed in the United States. The democratizing of Zen is manifest not only in the emergence of female roshis (or teachers) but also in the concept of "everyday Zen," which loosens religious practice and the experience of enlightenment from the formalized structures of monkhood and monastic life associated with Japanese culture. Everyday Zen is the discovery of religious practice and experiences of enlightenment in the ordinary American work of keeping a home, raising children, and holding down a job. Of course Buddhism has always concerned itself with the meaningfulness of ordinary life and with the "middle way" between denying the needs and pleasures of life and overindulging them. Famous pictures of the Sixth Ch'an Patriarch, Hui Neng, chopping bamboo at the moment of enlightenment provide just one example of this respect for mundane tasks. But while this respect for the mundane was studiously cultivated by monks whose lives were quite different from those of other people, in the American context, Zen has become an aid to ordinary life. Thus in America, the long-standing Buddhist respect for ordinary tasks has developed into a more democratic respect for ordinary people. The social and religious distance between monks and laity has shrunk. Some of the strict, authoritarian, male-oriented and male-dominant structures of Japanese Zen have weakened in the United States, and both the teaching and the practice of Buddhism have become more open and egalitarian.

In considering the development of Buddhism in America, it is important to recognize that Buddhism carries its own focus on the primacy of inner experience and that this focus has not been created as a result of Buddhism's exposure to American culture but only brought to new forms of expression. Buddhist and American ideas about the authority of inner experience have combined to create more egalitarian approaches to Buddhist practice, which incorporate respect for women as teachers and for the spiritual value of everyday tasks that women ordinarily perform. Along with this democratizing process, the fundamental Buddhist commitment to the authority of inner experience has flourished in the context of a wide ranging and widespread interest in spirituality in the United States today, which has emerged out of a long-standing interest in the primacy of personal religious experience rooted in Puritan ideas about the Holy Spirit and the transformative power of grace.

As these two examples illustrate, the American commitment to the primacy of personal experience has taken on a life of its own quite independent of validation by any Protestant institution, as a consequence of being appropriated, owned, and elaborated upon by different religious groups. These examples also suggest how a deeply related commitment to the connection between religion and civil society has also been appropriated, owned, and elaborated upon by different religious groups as they have developed in the context of American culture. To better appreciate the nature of this connection between the American commitments to the primacy of religious experience and to religion's importance in building and maintaining civil society, it is useful to return to the trial of 1637.

The principal objection raised against Anne Hutchinson in that trial was that her religious activity and religious speech threatened the social order. But this objection was not simply a religious defense of an authoritarian political system and social order, although it has often been interpreted that way. The theology at work in the verdict against Hutchinson also involved commitment to the idea that grace enabled individuals to lead lives that were morally upright but also beneficial to the well-being of others and to society as a whole. In contrast to Luther's idea that God's law was impossible for anyone to fulfill, Puritan theology made religion an enabler of social virtue. Puritans understood the covenant of grace to be an agreement between God and each saint that enabled each saint to fulfill God's law. This concept of religion as an enabler of social virtue led Puritans to believe that if a society of saints could be created in New England, then the government of this society could concern itself not with defining religion but with pulling out any weeds that threatened to overrun religion or hamper its propagation in the larger world.

Hutchinson and her teacher John Cotton shared this vision of Christian society with other New England Puritans. In fact, their commitment to the sealing of the Spirit developed out of their belief that the great majority of emigrés to New England were already converted and that the community as a whole was ready to take the next step forward in religious growth and power. More moderate Puritans like John Winthrop were not so sure. They were more hesitant to affirm the sanctity of their own souls and those of their neighbors. They were especially dubious about the sanctity of Anne Hutchinson. She seemed to them to be arrogant. As well as being irritating, that perceived arrogance undermined her implicit claim to be a saint.

From the judges' perspective, the difficulty with Hutchinson was that her claim to religious truth appeared to be bogus. They believed it was bogus because it was harmful, unprofitable, and irritating. She was censured not only because she claimed to have experiences of immediate revelation from the Holy Spirit that the judges believed to be delusional, but also because her criticism of New England's religious teachers was judged to be harmful to religious life in New England and to the social order designed to support and express it.

Implicit in the judgment against Hutchinson was the belief that a relationship existed between the transformative power of personal religious experience and the construction of civil society. In the civil society the Puritans hoped to build, personal religious experience was the ultimate source of all virtue. The institutions of society, like churches and civil government, had mediating functions: they involved social covenants that protected, supported, and developed the implications of the covenants of grace that existed, and would exist in the future between God and his saints. But within this understanding of the relationship between authoritative personal experience and civil society, there was also tension and at least potential conflict as well. While civil society grew out of individual virtue and government was supposed to play a protective and supportive role in that process, individual expression on religious subjects was not always virtuous or beneficial to society and government reserved the right to prohibit and punish attacks on life, safety, and civil order, even if those attacks claimed to be religiously motivated.

In the verdict against Hutchinson, the government drew a hard line against religious dissent and strenuously insisted on its danger to social order. This hard line obscures the important point of similarity that exists between the ideas at work in the verdict against Hutchinson and later conceptions of religion's role in civil society that have become institutionalized in the United States. For example, the difference between the Puritans' intolerance of religious dissent and the Constitution's guarantee of religious freedom cannot be denied. But this difference can obscure the important similarity between the Puritans' belief in the role of personal religious experience in the construction of civil society and the belief advanced by James Madison and other founders of the United States government that freedom of religion was the most basic of all freedoms essential to civil society, that moral virtue and social commitment often grow out of personal religious commitments, and that one of government's most basic functions was to guarantee each individual's right to the expression of religious beliefs. Without minimizing the difference between Winthrop's intolerance of religious dissent and Madison's commitment to religious freedom, we can see how Madison's emphasis on the necessity of religious freedom for a healthy society grew out of the English Protestant idea that grace enables individuals to fulfill God's law and to covenant together in associations that construct civil order.

Embedded in the Constitution and still at work in American culture is the expectation that religious life, whatever particular beliefs and rituals it involves, should be beneficial. This expectation of religion's beneficence helps to explain the extraordinarily high degree of tolerance for religious diversity that exists in the United States. To a remarkable extent, it doesn't really matter *what* you believe. But the nonjudgmentalness of your neighbors and fellow-citizens in this regard should not be mistaken as an expression of their indifference to religion or lack of appreciation for its possible importance in your life. It is rather an expression of the pragmatic orientation to religion that pervades American culture. Most Americans expect religion to be a positive influence in society, at least by helping the believer live a better life. Their tolerance disappears when religion appears to be harmful, as it did when David Koresh led the Branch Davidians in seemingly dangerous and unwholesome directions, or when Jehovah's Witness parents refuse to allow doctors to give their child a blood transfusion, or when Somalian immigrants perform ritual clitorectomies on girls in their community, or when Hari Krishna chanters impede business travel in airports. Ours is not a culture where religious asceticism, flagellation, immolation, mutilation, or intrusion in other people's lives are exalted or admired as they have been in other times and places.

Expecting religion to be prosocial and personally beneficial is an outgrowth of the pragmatism of American culture, which has roots in the Anglo-Protestant concept of grace as an enabler of moral virtue. As Max Weber discerned a hundred years ago, there is a real compatibility between Reformed Protestant theology and the for-profit mentality of investment capitalism. The Reformed Protestant expectation that religion be personally and socially beneficial was at work in the trial of Anne Hutchinson and in the argument against her, which focused on the dangerousness of the errors she promulgated for others in the commonwealth and on her failure to "become a profitable member here among us."

As in the case of the commitment to the primacy of spiritual experience, the closely-linked commitment to religion's social and personal profitability is a feature of American culture that has come to be appropriated by members of many different religious traditions. And this appropriation process has accelerated in the late twentieth century as a result of the increasing diversity of American religious communities and the decline of Protestant church control over the larger culture. A brief revisiting of the two non-Protestant traditions previously discussed will begin to illustrate how the pragmatic approach to religion associated with Puritanism has now come to expression in other traditions.

In the current renewal of Catholic spirituality, interesting discussions have developed about the transformative effects of that spirituality in the lives of individuals and in the larger society they inhabit. This effort to identify the social and personal benefits of Catholic spirituality stands in some contrast to earlier emphases on the inherent beauty of Catholic spirituality and on the role of devotional piety in increasing one's union with God in the midst of earthly deprivation and suffering. Of course prayers to saints were often appeals for blessings in this life, but the main thrust of many forms of Catholic spirituality was often contemplation of the divine, regardless of practical benefit.

At numerous Catholic colleges and universities in the United States, interpretation of the meaning of Catholic spirituality has become less otherworldly and more pragmatic since the 1960s. For example, at one Catholic university in the late 1950s, several student groups existed for the purpose of developing Catholic spirituality. One of these groups focused primarily on pious devotions to the Virgin Mary and two others concerned themselves with assisting at masses and helping to maintain numerous chapels on campus. In the late 1960s, some of the members of the sodality devoted to Mary were pacifists opposed to the war in Vietnam. In addition to speaking out on campus against the war, they became committed to the concept of social reform and instituted a variety of community action programs in conjunction with classroom seminars on social policy and Christian thought, which came to be taught by professors for academic credit. But the program ran into difficulty when it became clear that the voluntary service the students were performing in the community did little to bring about the social transformation recommended in seminar readings. After considerable discussion, it was agreed that the program's real impact was not on the community immediately off-campus but on the lives of the students taking the course. Upon this discovery, the focus of the seminars changed to emphasize the personal and social responsibilities of each student and the relationship between these responsibilities and each student's own development in Christian spirituality. With the help of new seminar readings, students are now encouraged to see the poor they encounter in their volunteer work as brothers and sisters in God and to commit themselves to lives that reflect this sense of human community. The program generates experiences of personal transformation in many students each year and the university relies on the program as a means of recruitment and retention.

Many apsects of Catholic theology have contributed to the development of this program. Among the most important of these, a commitment to exercise "a preferential option for the poor" has become especially important. At the same time, the relatively recent effort to concentrate on the social and psychological benefits of Catholic spirituality and to define spirituality, at least to some extent, in those terms, reflects Catholic appropriation of the pragmatic expectations for religion that pervade American culture. Not by coincidence, these expectations have reshaped the meaning of Catholic spirituality at a time when Protestant control over American culture has declined, as Catholicism has moved from the margins into the mainstreams of American culture, and as the wealth and professional status of American Catholics has increased dramatically.

A similar attentiveness to the pragmatic benefits of spirituality characterizes the development of Buddhism in the United States. As observers have noted, Americans interested in Buddhism often interpret it as a way of learning how to savor, treasure, and make the most of life. And people who first encounter Buddhism in the United States often focus on its practical benefits and either celebrate or question its usefulness. For example, Sylvia Bornstein's book, *It's Easier Than You Think: The Buddhist Way to Happiness*, shows how Buddhist teachings can help relieve stress and cultivate the goodness of life. As Rick Fields observed in a comparison between American and Burmese practitioners, "the Burmese had more faith in the practice to begin with and so didn't worry so much about whether what they were doing would be effective." Among other things, this meant that "the Burmese were able to develop concentration in the initial stages much more quickly." In contrast, many Americans do not progress "very far beyond the hurting knee state" (1992: 322).

This interest in the effects of Buddhist practice can involve an impatience that limits religious experience. But it can also extend that practice in interesting new ways. For example, in *Instructions to the Cook: A Zen Master's Lessons in Living a Life That Matters*, Bernard Glassman shows how the Buddhist metaphor of life as a meal yields helpful recipes for good business management. Glassman is a Zen roshi, baker, businessman, and social activist who has devoted his many skills to helping homeless people. The Greyston bakery he established in Yonkers, New York provides jobs and job-training for people who need them. The adjoining Greyston Family Inn provides housing and life-skills training to many people in the community. Profitability is an important concept for Glassman; he believes that social service without it often results in romantic schemes that help no one. At the same time, he believes that investment in the people of a community makes good business sense and that effective outreach to people in need makes good customers.

Of course, Buddhism's practical orientation is long-standing. Its basic emphasis on escaping suffering and enabling others to escape suffering is evidence of that. But through exposure to American culture, the idea that Buddhism is spiritually therapeutic has developed in new directions that both borrow from and contribute to American ideas about spiritual growth, social action, and profitability. Purists sometimes object to the American tendency to make Buddhism a means of self-help and making life better, arguing that wanting to better appreciate life is the desire that most needs to be destroyed if we are to escape from suffering and attain enlightenment. But the influence of this American-style pragmatism on Buddhism is clear. While both Bornstein and Glassman believe that relinquishing attachment to things and to oneself is important, they also have a strong, and typically American, investment in the process of spiritual growth and in the happiness, satisfaction, and appreciation of life that such investment brings.

It is a long way from banishing Anne Hutchinson for failing to be a profitable member of her community in seventeenth-century Boston to Bernard Glassman's efforts to help make homeless people in Yonkers more profitable and less homeless, or to the efforts of American Catholic universities to link recruitment and retention to programs for undergraduate spiritual formation. And it is a long way from Hutchinson's insistence on the importance of personal religious experience to the religious self-confidence with which many American Catholics overlook the papal ban on birth control, or to Karma Lekshe Tsomo's argument that women bring freshness and vitality to American Buddhism. One would not want to minimize the distance between religion in New England in 1637 and religion in the United States today or the many significant changes that have occurred in the interim. But at the same time, we can also see threads of continuity in the emphasis on the primacy of religious experience and in the expectation of benefits that religious experience brings to individuals and their communities. These Puritan ideas have persisted and developed over time, shaping the habits and expectations that characterize American religion and culture.

BIBLIOGRAPHY

Bornstein, Sylvia (1995) *It's Easier Than You Think: The Buddhist Way to Happiness*, San Francisco: HarperCollins.

Clebsch, William A. (1964) *England's Earliest Protestants, 1520–1535*, New Haven, Conn.: Yale University Press.

Emerson, Ralph Waldo (1983) "Divinity School Address," in Joel Pore (ed.) *Essays and Lectures*, New York: Library of America.

Fields, Rick (1992) *How the Swans Came to the Lake: A Narrative History of Buddhism in America*, rev. edn, Boston, Mass.: Shambala Publications.

Glassman, Bernard and Fields, Rick (1996) *Instructions to the Cook: A Zen Master's Lessons in Living a Life That Matters*, Boston, Mass.: Shambala Publications audio imprint.

Gleason, Philip (1995) *Contending with Modernity: Catholic Higher Education in the Twentieth Century*, New York: Oxford University Press.

Hall, David D. (1968) *The Antinomian Controversy, 1636–1638*, Middletown, Conn.: Wesleyan University Press.

Ludwig, Robert A. (1995) *Reconstructing Catholicism for a New Generation*, New York: Crossroad Publishing Company.

Moseley, James G. (1992) *Winthrop's World*, Madison, Wis.: University of Wisconsin Press.

O'Brien, David J. (1994) *From the Heart of the American Church: Catholic Higher Education and American Culture*, Maryknoll, NY: Orbis Books.

Porterfield, Amanda (1992) *Female Piety in Puritan New England: The Emergence of Religious Humanism*, New York: Oxford University Press.

Tsomo, Karma Lekshe (ed.) (1995) *Buddhism Through American Women's Eyes*, Ithaca, NY: Snow Lion Publications.

Weber, Max (1958) *The Protestant Ethic and the Spirit of Capitalism* [1904–5], trans. Talcott Parsons, New York: Charles Scribner's Sons.

Chapter 7

Religion and the Culture of the Market in Early New England

Mark Valeri

The history of the relation between religion and the economy in early New England encompasses a remarkable change. Many of the original English settlers of Massachusetts Bay were Puritans, i.e. critics of the Church of England who adhered to the theological tenets of Calvinism and promoted a strict moral discipline over their communities. Puritans had long decried many of the most salient features of a growing market economy as the bane of England and the nemesis of a godly order in the New World. New England's economy nonetheless became integrated into a transatlantic system of commerce during the seventeenth and early eighteenth centuries. From 1630 through the 1710s, most Puritans had a pronounced habit of lamenting this development. They frequently excoriated market behaviors, from the most specific (such as demanding high wages during a labor shortage or borrowing money to speculate in land) to the most general (such as seeking profits for the sake of upward mobility). Yet by the end of the eighteenth century most leading religious thinkers, who claimed to be faithful heirs to the Puritans and true Calvinists, had ceased to issue their customary declamations. Many of them embraced a free-market system. American Calvinism was not born capitalist; but it certainly became capitalist.

There is a rich historiography that describes this development as the evolution of an original Puritan impulse toward modern economic rationality. Behind this line of argument stands Max Weber's *The Protestant Ethic and the Spirit of Capitalism*. Weber indicated how Calvinism might be construed as inherently modern in the sense that it legitimated moral self-regulation and entrepreneurial assertion. Calvinism, that is, taught individuals to regulate their behavior according to broad, internalized ethical principles rather than to the dictates of traditional social authorities that often prohibited economic innovations. Furthermore, a Calvinist stress on worldly activity as a means to personal sanctification shaped the capitalist personality by promoting the virtues of prudence (rational calculation of the future effects of one's business decisions), industrious-ness, and frugality.

Recent studies of early New England by Stephen Innes (1995) and Daniel Vickers (1994) have argued accordingly that Puritans viewed the settlement of New England as an entrepreneurial venture designed to glorify God through the accumulation of profits. Warnings against selfishness and materialism as well as exhortations to industry and frugality provided the moral guidelines for com-petition within the market. Puritans also embraced a market economy, Mark A. Peterson (1997) has maintained, because it funded the expansion of church settle-ments in New England.

Other historians have used Weber with more nuance. Perry Miller (1953) analyzed what he saw as contradictions within New England Puritanism: a medieval aspiration toward organic unity grounded on customary prescriptions for social behavior, and a modern drive for individuals to prosper in the world of commerce on its terms. He made much of that singularly New England literary genre, the jeremiad. Coming into vogue during the 1670s and 1680s, this form of sermon typically predicted God's judgment on New England for its supposed decline from the religious fervor and social concord of the first generation of settlement. Preachers especially lamented what they perceived as a loss of social cohesion and a rise of religious apathy – both of which attended, from their point of view, the commercial expansion of New England. Miller maintained that these jeremiads reflected a genuine sense of guilt. They also relieved that guilt and allowed New Englanders to rationalize their drive for profits and pursuit of social mobility. Modifying Miller, Stephen Foster (1991) has argued that the commer-cialization of New England was just one stage in a Puritan movement that always had been characterized by tensions between corporate solidarity and individual freedom, religious principle and practical expedience.

The following essay suggests a different line of interpretation. It does not neces-sarily contradict the above studies; but it does attempt to address some questions left by them. What accounts, for example, for the fact that religious leaders, lay and clerical alike, continued to issue protests against new economic behaviors through the early eighteenth century, despite legal and social accommodations to the market? Such protests may have served to relieve the consciences of merchants, but what underlying ideology sustained a sense of guilt in the first place? How can we explain furthermore why such rhetoric lost its currency over the course of the eighteenth century?

The answer to such questions may be found by allowing that seventeenth-century Puritans operated in a vastly different discursive world than that inhabited by later Calvinists. Rather than emphasizing the inherent modernity of Puritanism, then, this essay tracks the eclipse of a pre-modern ethos in New England's religious culture. From 1720 through 1750 leading religious thinkers in New England adopted theological and moral methods, associated with what we might for convenience sake call the Enlightenment, that aligned Calvinism with the cultural assumptions of the new economic order. This transformation helps to explain how Calvinists came to jettison the rhetorical and practical protest against the market and sanction the emergent economy. The examples of

John Cotton, Cotton Mather, Solomon Stoddard and Jonathan Edwards, with a brief postscript on John Witherspoon, provide the cases in point.

Religious commentary on commerce, to begin, depended on a distinction between economic production and the ethical apparatus of a modern market culture that developed through the seventeenth and eighteenth centuries. The story of Boston merchant John Hull and his reputation among the clergy of Boston is telling in this regard. Born in England in 1624 and immigrating to Massachusetts Bay with his parents in 1635, Hull became a prominent public official: Master of the Mint, Treasurer for the colony, a captain of the local militia company, an elected member to the colonial legislature, or General Court, and one of the founders of Boston's Old South Church. Hull invested profits from his silversmith shop in overseas trade. He eventually purchased six ships and developed a substantial mercantile business. He marketed American furs in England. He imported tobacco from Virginia and sugar from the West Indies. He bought manufactured goods from London and sold them to shopkeepers in Boston. He bought and transported fish from New England waters to Spain, and imported wine and iron in return. He sold textiles to New Yorkers, and shipped their whale oil to England.

Hull's biography illustrates the early growth of New England's economy. Puritans like Hull did not shy away from making profits from the production and exchange of goods. New England colonies were, after all, funded by Puritan and Anglican financiers in London who sought at least some return on their investments and established policies to that end. Subsistence farming and local trading initially characterized Massachusetts's economy. To the dismay of the colony's backers and settlers, it underwent a severe depression in 1640 and 1641, due chiefly to a drop in the number of new immigrants and the resulting scarcity of workers and consumers for local products. During the late 1640s and early 1650s, however, immigration rose again, and the economy recovered. New England farmers began to produce wool, hay, livestock, and cider for profit-making in colonial markets throughout British North America and the West Indies. Merchants such as Hull also began to work more actively to procure furs and timber for trade. Fishing ventures also began to produce profits. The governments of Massachusetts and Connecticut supported nascent manufacturing efforts as well, such as stone quarries, ironworks, mines, and shipbuilding.

By the time of Hull's death in 1683, signs of relative prosperity had appeared, along with the rudiments of a modern economic system. Farmers and merchants learned to anticipate the relation between excess production and market needs throughout New England, the Caribbean, and even Great Britain. Regional trading also grew, as merchants in Boston and shopkeepers in inland towns sold small amounts of consumer goods. By the beginning of the eighteenth century other indicators of a market economy appeared. Systems of credit expanded beyond local accounts to loans and investments that went through third parties and ranged across the Atlantic. Merchants invested in land on the frontier as a form of commercial speculation. A class of urban artisans and the unemployed poor gathered in Boston. By 1740, according to economic historians, New England had an integrated, if comparatively nascent, market economy. It bore only a distant likeness to the commercial worlds of London or Edinburgh, to be sure, but it was nonetheless a far cry from the rudimentary conditions of the first two decades.

When Samuel Willard, a minister at Boston's Old South Church, delivered Hull's funeral sermon, he analyzed the moral fortunes of New England in the midst of its newfound prosperity. Willard did not gainsay material wealth. He followed convention in eulogizing Hull as a merchant who had grown rich and remained godly. Hull gave his money to the church, served the government, and cared for the poor. Willard's funeral oration is striking, however, in its aloofness from the world of commerce in which Hull moved. The preacher spent more of the sermon attacking New England's infatuation with profits than extolling the merchant. Finding little to praise in Hull's way of making wealth, Willard did not attribute Hull's prosperity to the protocapitalistic personality traits of industry, energy, prudence, or patience. Providence, according to Willard, gave Hull his riches because Hull, unlike most merchants, had the communal virtues of loyalty to church, concern for neighbors, and self-sacrifice for the commonweal. Willard, like other religious leaders, approved of the fruits of productive labor and exchange. He nonetheless voiced a deep reservation about the emergence of a new social type: the entrepreneur driven by the law of profit-seeking in the market (Willard 1683).

Indirectly, and in a piecemeal fashion, Willard and other preachers limned (and disparaged) what historians today have labeled a "market culture." The term may stand for the nexus of economic behaviors, social theories, and ethical ideas that legitimated new modes of exchange in which goods, services, and credit were priced according to their supply and demand. Rather than defined by customary rules, canon law, or civil legislation, such prices fluctuated according to regional and international, as well as local, demand. A widespread use of paper money or other promissory notes (stocks, annuities, bills of credit) and an increasing reliance on credit integrated mercantile activities into a transatlantic network. Credit too changed, from a simple accounting of debts between individuals to a commodity, to be brokered or sold for profit. Apart from civil regulations, men and women in the market often determined the price of their goods, credit, or labor with the chief intent of maximizing their profits (Appleby 1978).

There were several sanctions for profit-seeking individualism. They ranged from the arguments of economic advisors to the court and lobbyists for overseas trading companies, who insisted that participation in the market enhanced national productivity and wealth, to contemporary ethical theories that defined self-interest as the inevitable and therefore potentially virtuous wellspring of all human activity. Proponents of a *laissez-faire* economy held that the exchange of goods and services could be construed as one expression of a universal and ordered system: regulated by natural laws (supply and demand) that were omnipresent but were invisible to, or at least distant from, the common shopkeeper or day laborer. Yet they were reasonable in that they produced prosperity and harmony. They linked individuals to an international network of sociability, transforming the market into a moral law.

More generally, one of the intellectual platforms for this market culture

– whether or not one took a market position on specific policies such as currency supply, price regulation, or poor relief – was the philosophical assumption that universal, rational laws ordered human affairs and bound individuals into an invisible social system. Stephen Toulmin has characterized this agenda in terms of the modern search for a cosmopolis: a civil society (polis) that duplicated the universal natural order (cosmos). Pre-modern modes of thinking in England and France, Toulmin suggests, rarely aspired to this universalizing goal. Oriented toward the solution of practical problems, they were premised on a localized context for moral method. Religious texts, customary values, and particular social conditions were the data of moral decision-making. The philosophical method that underpinned the market, in contrast, approached ethics as an analytical science. It described universal truths that, if followed, would lead to corporate peace and prosperity. Given various formulations by writers as diverse as Grotius, Hobbes, Locke, and Leibniz, this style of social analysis, in Toulmin's phrase, "decontextualized" human reason from historical particularities in search of "a unified science, and an exact language" (Toulmin 1990: 104). The willingness to envision and even create a universal language based on reason bespoke the urge to cultural self-fashioning. It was the linguistic analogue to, if not the fundamental expression of, the social ethos of the market.

The intellectual premises of Puritan moral thinking were incongruent with this full-fledged culture of the market. Anglo-American Calvinists attempted to contextualize moral thought in local communities and their disciplinary institutions. John Cotton, Puritan divine trained at Cambridge and a minister in Boston's First Church from 1633 to 1652, spent much of his career dealing with this issue. He took up the agenda set by an earlier generation of English Puritans such as the Cambridge divine William Perkins. Perkins waged an unsuccessful campaign to provide an alternative to the hierarchical system of discipline in the Church of England, which depended on the oversight of bishops. Like other Puritans, he criticized the episcopal courts as incapable of dealing with the day-to-day temptations of lay people. He envisioned local disciplinary bodies on the model of Geneva's Consistory: a body of lay leaders (elders) and pastors who kept a close watch over the lives of parishioners. In an effective system of discipline, according to Perkins, elders and ministers in the church examined individuals, counseling them or admonishing them to follow specific rules that touched on all aspects of social behavior, from sex to choosing one's vocation, entertaining friends to treating servants. He insisted that those who practiced market-driven activities such as usury – defined as making loans at a contracted rate that guaranteed a profit to creditors – hoarding goods, or raising their prices beyond customary limits, be excommunicated (Perkins 1608: 63–5, 734; 1611: 97–154).

Perkins modeled a theological ethics that would set later Puritanism at odds with the Enlightenment idea that moral analysis began with the deduction of absolute principles from the universal qualities of human nature. He made a direct application of the Bible to moral dilemmas in the context of particular social bodies: the family, the church, and the commonwealth. Nothing better typified this way of reasoning than the cases-of-conscience method, which consisted of a series of practical quandaries and their resolution according to biblical principles and contemporary social implications. Perkins addressed it to new modes of commerce. How much wealth should one seek? What clothing fashions were acceptable? How should one give alms? His answers were thoroughly alien to the standards of the market. One should not seek an income beyond what is necessary for a healthy life, should dress modestly and avoid especially French and Italian styles, and should give alms without reservation to all needy people. Perkins derived conclusions that pushed his readers to consider the meaning of the Bible for the circumstances of the local community (Perkins 1608: 728, 750–4; 1611: 305–62).

Cotton followed Perkins closely in this regard. Writing about a Christian's vocation, for example, Cotton began by locating the corporate context for economic decisions. Guided by the rules of the Bible, individuals should seek "the counsel of friends, and encouragement of neighbours" to determine which trade or vocation would be "ayming at the publique good," that is, the practical needs of "this or that Church, or Commonwealth." On the vexed question of usury, Cotton recommended the same method. He concluded that merchants should consult frequently with their Christian friends and business partners to determine the precise effects of their loan practices on their debtors (Cotton 1936: 319, 321).

Leaders in the Boston church initially attempted to turn this method into a system of corporate discipline. According to Puritan theory, the ideal church nurtured godliness by bringing before pastors and elders, or, in controversial cases, before the assembled congregation, those individuals suspected of vice. The church meted out discipline in the form of admonitions or excommunication. Cotton claimed that this disciplinary procedure was, indeed, the whole rationale for the Puritan settlement of New England. Ministers and lay elders in Boston's First Church gathered in council to examine and excommunicate members who presumed to set prices or wages by the impersonal law of supply and demand instead of by the organic needs of the community.

From 1630 to 1654, the church passed some forty sentences of excommunication, eight of them dealing with economic vices. The church censured Boston merchant Robert Keayne for making too great a profit from selling his wares. Keayne protested the facts of the accusation; but neither he nor his accusers doubted the church's prerogative to intervene in such matters. Ann Hibbon was admonished explicitly for acting as an autonomous economic agent. She insisted that some local carpenters had done shoddy work on her house, despite the fact that a church council had determined that the work was acceptable. She demanded compensation. Church elders demanded her submission to the guidance of the community, and excommunicated her when she refused (Pierce 1961: 31–3, 42–9).

During the 1650s and 1660s Boston's churches slowly abandoned these disciplinary efforts. The number of proceedings against commercial vices dropped to one or two a decade, and disappeared altogether during the early eighteenth century. This reflected the civil magistracy's consolidation of power over economic matters. The elected legislators of the colony determined to prevent a recurrence of the economic crises of the early 1640s by relaxing legal restrictions on prices and wages, supporting entrepreneurial ventures, and encouraging competition in the international market. These legal changes frustrated preachers such as Cotton. Elders who sat in church council, paid the clergy, and funded new churches, however, came to depend on a growing commercial economy. Attempts to maintain church discipline against behaviors that the government sanctioned, as a consequence, were deemed futile if not anachronistic.

Still operating in the discursive world of Perkins and Cotton through the first decades of the eighteenth century, many ministers issued complaints against Yankees who increasingly were prone to conduct their business according to the laws of the market. Increase Mather (1676), minister at Boston's Second Church and a widely known writer, spoke for many when he declaimed against the seemingly endless array of merchants who charged whatever price they could, speculated in land, bargained with the Indians, and profited from new mechanisms of credit. Mather, and other Puritans such as Samuel Willard and John Danforth, retained the moral method common to an earlier generation of Puritanism – contextual and historically-minded – and taught at Harvard through the 1720s.

Their jeremiads thus encoded an incompatibility between Puritan and market mentalities. They sounded an alarm against a culture that thrust individuals out of the organic community, with all of its particular circumstances and dilemmas, and out from under biblical precepts. Danforth (1704: 35) complained in this vein that New Englanders were all too willing to reject corporate restraints on their business dealings and project self-interest into a universal moral and economic law. "This *Sheba*, Self," Danforth wrote, had become so much an "*Idol*" that New Englanders regarded it as an "*Oracle*," even when its moral dictates contradicted the specific commands "spoken by the Lord Himself."

Cotton Mather, eldest son of Increase and also a minister at Boston's Second Church, as well as a prolific composer of sermons and tracts on nearly every conceivable subject of contemporary interest, attempted to remind New England of the ethical perspective of its founders time and time again. His *Lex mercatoria* of 1705 was a long reiteration of economic cases of conscience in the Puritan mode, including the usual warning against playing the market to get the best price. He made two original contributions. First, he updated the list of vices brought on by the market since the 1680s. Some New Englanders, for instance, had taken unjust advantage of the fact that Massachusetts's currency underwent sporadic but substantial periods of depreciation. They borrowed money at a low interest rate, delayed repayment, and thereby paid back their creditors with money that was worth less than the original loan.

Second, Mather argued that proper moral reasoning contradicted an ethics based on the laws of nature. A merchant who operated according to a "*State of Nature*," Mather claimed, "thinks, he may in the General *Scramble*" of the market "seize as much as he can for himself, tho' it should be never so much to the Damage and Ruine, of other men." God formed Massachusetts Bay, in contrast, as a community with peculiar obligations that went unrecognized by the rest of the world. Like most Puritans, Mather believed that New England existed under a special covenant according to which God promised corporate prosperity and peace on the condition that the people fulfill these obligations. In particular, they were to be guided by the commands of Scripture rather than by market mechanisms, and accordingly to consider the needs of their immediate neighbors and refuse to profit by their neighbor's loss. Mather thus recalled New Englanders to a rule-based, organic ethics. It was integral to Christianity itself, and the denial of such violated the baptismal vows that united Christians into a social body. "If you don't like my *Rules*," he concluded, "let me have them again; but then, Resolve to fill the world with as much *Rapine* and *Ruine* as ever you can; Resolve to be worse than *Pagans*" (Mather 1705: 11, 15).

One of the last Puritan utterances in the old method was Solomon Stoddard's *Cases of Conscience* in 1722. Like Mather, Stoddard, who was the pastor in the western Massachusetts town of Northampton, updated the specific issues under consideration. He lamented the current "oppression of the Country" by market-driven behaviors. Merchants from larger towns or cities sold their "Commodities" for "more than is meet," making egregious profits especially from people in "Country towns" such as Northampton. Debtors continued to make a profit to the harm of the creditors, often spending their loans on newly available consumer goods. Depreciation of the currency seduced people to raise their prices or demand more wages. The mobility offered by the market also tempted people to settle at a great distance from an established church, displacing them from the ministry of the local community. Stoddard reiterated the specific commands of Scripture that reprimanded such behaviors. He also liberalized requirements for admission to the sacraments in the church. He allowed those who had not undergone conversion (the customary requirement) to take communion. This was his attempt not only to encourage conversions through the sacrament but also to bring wayward citizens back into organic identification with a local moral community, the company of saints (Stoddard 1722: 1–2).

During the 1710s and 1720s, however, many New Englanders began to adopt a moral method that had the potential to provide a religious sanction for the new economy. Indications of this change were often subtle. Ministers abandoned the jeremiad. Divines stopped writing anti-market cases of conscience, or any cases of conscience for that matter. As taught at Harvard and Yale, academic ethics began to reflect rational systems of moral philosophy written in Britain. Many preachers began to discuss foundational moral principles that were much more congruent with the market than were the dictates of Puritan ethics.

One of the more significant figures in this turn was a grandson of Solomon Stoddard, Jonathan Edwards. Stoddard had opened the sacraments to the unconverted in a last-ditch effort to construct a community protected from the ethos of a market culture. Edwards tellingly attempted to close those same sacraments. He argued that the unregenerate had no business taking communion. He did not fear that such restrictions would release the ungenerate from their moral obligations because he thought that a sound moral theology could take its cue apart from the local communion of saints.

We should not overstate the point. Edwards was a transitional figure, and displayed a mixture of pre-modern and modern moral sensibilities. He promoted traditionally Calvinist doctrine: the utter depravity of human nature, the absolute need for divine grace, and the sovereignty of God over the process of conversion. When Edwards preached, especially early in his career, he derived from Scripture ethical prohibitions against specific market behaviors, and addressed them to the situation of his community. One of his longer ethical works, *Charity and its Fruits* (1989a), was a series of sermons that grounded moral reasoning on a New Testament text and drove home the organic obligations of Christian virtue. Furthermore, Edwards frequently criticized any version of natural theology or moral reasoning, such as deism, that challenged what he saw as the clear truths of the Bible.

And yet Edwards imbibed enough of a new, rational moral philosophy to think also in an abstract and analytical mode. He, like the Enlightened moderns of whom Toulmin writes, anticipated a universal ethical system that correlated natural law and divine revelation, transcended any one organic community, provided a means of communication between individuals only distantly connected, and resulted in a cosmopolitan society. He thought that moral decisions might be grounded on abstract reasoning on natural law, as long as such reasoning did not contradict orthodox doctrine. Edwards, in sum, experimented with a fashion of moral philosophy that other thinkers would use to sanction a free market.

He employed this new method only in part in his ethical treatises such as *The Nature of True Virtue* (1989a) but he also contemplated a systematic demonstration of how a rational moral philosophy could sustain Calvinism: a project that he mentioned but never completed, "A rational account." He proposed in it "to shew how all arts and sciences, the more they are perfected, the more they issue in divinity, and coincide with it" (Edwards 1980: 397). Edwards specifically was attracted to the rational ethics, if not the theology, of philosophical idealists such as Nicolas Malbranche and Samuel Clarke, who based moral reasoning on the premise that the human mind had an innate faculty for determining the qualities of virtue or vice in different social relations. So too Edwards drew on moral sense theorists such as the Third Earl of Shaftesbury and Francis Hutcheson, who maintained that all people had an instinct (sense) that benevolence was good, and that a disregard for the universal good of humanity was bad. Human existence was ordered, these rational moral philosophers contended, naturally to reward virtue with the sense of well-being and to punish vice with the sense of shame. Edwards learned from these theories a method to fuse natural moral principles and the idea of divine law. He was convinced, as Norman Fiering has put it, that "the rational laws of nature," which demonstrate the virtues of integration, order, and harmony, "must be accepted for what they are, the laws of God" for human society (Fiering 1981: 97).

In his private notebooks "The miscellanies" and "The mind" Edwards reflected on the value of abstract thought and language in themselves. God, Edwards observed, had ordered nature into a harmonious system of communication by natural laws. "Abstract ideas which we call universals" could be social expressions of these laws: modes of expression that allowed all human beings to communicate and unite with each other. The potential for an "agreement of languages" was evident not only in the common principle of reason but also in the very structure of language and the ways in which it operated to express the most complex ideas (Edwards 1980: 359–60).

Scattered ruminations on the nature of language hardly amounted to an explicit endorsement of free-wheeling capitalism. They nonetheless located Edwards within a discourse that legitimated a market culture. In this intellectual milieu it was possible for both merchant and minister to conceive of distant and universal modes of exchange that united individuals into a systematic, orderly, international society. Edwards, to illustrate, offered an ethics premised on the idea that true virtue was the union of an individual to the moral whole, which he called "being-in-itself," through the inner affection of benevolence. Common to the rational moral philosophy of the day, Edwards's conception of benevolence provided the intellectual framework for a description of moral virtue apart from the contingencies of local social relations. So in *On the Nature of True Virtue*, as in other works, Edwards expounded at great length on the virtues of such affection without reference to the practical moral quandaries of his community (1989a). In a similar line of reasoning, the new moral economists offered a social system premised on the idea that individuals who pursued private profits through industry and frugality were joined to an abstraction called the common good, or society. Honest labor in the market was virtuous in some universal sense, apart from its impact on immediate social groups.

Edwards speculated that the moral law, however distantly and even mysteriously, would unite well-motivated individuals into a harmonious and beautiful whole. His vision bore some analogy to Adam Smith's prospect of profit-driven individuals united by the hidden hand of the market into a rational and prosperous order. Calvinist that he was, Edwards never trusted the bulk of New Englanders to be well-motivated in fact. He urged the government to restrain commercial expansion. He continually returned, throughout his career, to a biblical and organic notion of moral obligation and sought to wound, rather than soothe, the consciences of businessmen who operated according to the laws of supply and demand. He did nonetheless entertain the idea that one day God's Spirit would be poured out to such an extent that regenerated individuals would command the market as well as being pious. It was no mere coincidence that on the rare occasions that Edwards commented on the future of economic exchange, he foresaw that the spread of "knowledge" and the arts of navigation would go hand-in-hand with increased trade, "communication," "prosperity," and social union on a universal scale, as temporal affairs moved toward "one orderly, regular, beautiful society" (Edwards 1989b: 483–5).

Edwards did not single-handedly change the shape of theological ethics in America. His adversaries in New England (critics of revivalism such as Jonathan Mayhew and Charles Chauncy), his partners in the Middle Colonies, and his students, the so-called New Divinity men, were engaged in a similar process of refashioning the fundamentals of moral theology. They went further than Edwards in providing a reconciliation between natural law and revealed religion. Focused on the sovereign and benevolent government of God over human affairs, they allowed for the claim that invisible moral laws bound self-motivated individuals into a social order. With all of his ambivalence, Edwards provided, however, an especially poignant example of how a Calvinist could retain Reformed doctrine, resist many of the individualist implications of the new economy, and yet consider alternatives to the moral methods by which earlier Calvinists had voiced a protest against the philosophical premises of the market.

The timing of this theological transformation marked a congruence between Calvinism and other cultural trends of the market. During the same decades that Edwards ruminated on his "Rational account" and speculated on universal social harmony, other New Englanders put into place equally compatible components of the new economic ethos. Bruce Mann has written of the growth of rational legal procedures in the 1720s, which replaced organic and localist models of debt and credit relations with an impersonal, and sometimes distant, means of economic negotiation based on contracts. Political historians have noted the maturation of colonial politics into a coherent and integrated system of government during the same period. The rationalization of accounting procedures, the growth of the popular press, the spread of newspapers, and even the increase of roads: all of these regularized and expanded New England's networks of communication to an unprecedented extent in the 1720s and 1730s. Together, they gave New Englanders more than the systemic means of commerce. They allowed people the conviction that they participated in a benevolent social order, even as they set prices and sold credit as individuals regulated only by impersonal laws of the market.

Other evangelical Calvinists were more sanguine about the implications of the market than was Edwards, who never displayed a fondness for the actual behavior of merchants and financiers. Harry Stout has suggested that itinerants such as George Whitefield adapted evangelical rhetoric for use in a mass-market culture. Frank Lambert has maintained that Whitefield and his American allies also employed commercial tactics, such as a widespread use of the popular press, that placed them squarely in the market-place. Christine Heyrman has contended that most New Lights in the coastal towns of Massachusetts thought that aggressive pursuit of profits in the market was perfectly consonant with religion and social cohesion.

Later Calvinists erased any trace of ambivalence remaining from their Puritan heritage. They exulted in the possibilities of an economic system bounded only by natural moral laws. The eventual successor to Edwards at the College of New Jersey, the Scottish-born Presbyterian John Witherspoon, exemplifies this completion of Calvinism's transformation into an ally of the market. Witherspoon began his lectures on moral philosophy in 1768 with the argument that Cotton Mather and his like were dead wrong in their moral method: their contextualized, biblical ethics. Witherspoon wanted to "meet" Enlightened unbelievers "upon their own ground, and to show them from reason itself, the fallacy of their principles." Witherspoon's intent was to draw on the method and premises of rationalists to defend Calvinism. He relied on Hutcheson, Pufendorf, and other philosophers who premised their systems on the virtues of human nature and the continuities between social and natural law (Witherspoon 1982: 64).

Indebted to Edwards's willingness to consider an alliance between a rational moral discourse and Calvinism, Witherspoon was unhampered by Edwards's scruples about the social implications of this method. Social exchange and harmony, Witherspoon contended, were negotiated not by customary rules, specific biblical texts, or local and corporate obligations, but by human contracts that assured the natural rights of individuals. Contracts were voluntary agreements. Witherspoon concluded that it was a natural law that individuals should set the terms of such contracts, whether they concerned loan rates, prices, land values, or even the worth of money, in ways that would most reward their labor and ingenuity, i.e. by a free market (Witherspoon 1982: 126-37).

Witherspoon was evidence enough that in the long term Anglo-American Calvinists became capitalists. There is more than one explanation for this transformation; but transformation it was. There was a world of difference between Cotton Mather and John Witherspoon. To the extent that the market became a social force in early New England, it bypassed a line of thought running from John Cotton through Solomon Stoddard. This consideration of the intellectual relation between religion and the market in early New England suggests that we rethink the importance of the Enlightenment for an understanding of the connections between Anglo-American Protestantism and capitalism. In its intellectual history, the eventual alliance between Calvinism and the market was less the outcome of an original social impulse or set of theological ideas than a concession to the philosophical agenda of the late seventeenth and eighteenth centuries.

Max Weber himself drew attention to this agenda when he portrayed Benjamin Franklin as the most salient illustration of how a Protestant ethos of self-discipline and rationality was integral to capitalism. Franklin, of course, was America's *philosophe* and a religious rationalist with little sympathy toward Calvinism. Weberians have explained the appropriateness of the illustration in terms of irony. Puritanism, we have been told, had unintended consequences, namely, the triumph of a market culture in America. Irony, however does not always serve well as historical explanation. Puritans, in fact, appeared too deliberate in their self-scrutinies, and too attentive to the meaning of their rhetoric, to admit of such an explanation. Puritanism, to put it simply, yielded not to ironic consequence but to other forms of thought. When Calvinists began to think like rationalists they left Puritanism behind. That transformation allows us to take rhetorical protests against the market seriously, and to explain the likes of John Witherspoon. Whether betrayal or progress, corruption or adaptation, this transformation signaled Calvinism's contribution to New England's market culture.

BIBLIOGRAPHY

Appleby, Joyce Oldham (1978) *Economic Thought and Ideology in Seventeenth-century England*, Princeton, NJ: Princeton University Press.

Cotton, John (1936) "The way of life" [London, 1641], in Perry Miller and Thomas H. Johnson (eds) *The Puritans: A Sourcebook of their Writings*, vol. I, New York: Harper & Row.

Danforth, John (1704) *The Profanations of Prosperity*, Boston.
Edwards, Jonathan (1980) "The mind," and "Outline of a rational account," in *The Works of Jonathan Edwards*, vol. 6: *Scientific and Philosophical Writings*, ed. Wallace E. Anderson, New Haven, Conn.: Yale University Press.
—— (1989a) *Charity and its fruits* [1852], *Concerning the End for which God Created the World* [1765], and *On the Nature of True Virtue* [1765], in *The Works of Jonathan Edwards*, vol. 8: *Ethical Writings*, ed. Paul Ramsey, New Haven, Conn.: Yale University Press.
—— (1989b) *A History of the Work of Redemption* [1774], ed. John F. Wilson as *The Works of Jonathan Edwards*, vol. 9: *A History of the Work of Redemption*, New Haven, Conn.: Yale University Press.
Fiering, Norman (1981) *Jonathan Edwards's Moral Thought and its British Context*, Chapel Hill, NC: University of North Carolina Press.
Foster, Stephen (1991) *The Long Argument: English Puritanism and the Shaping of New England Culture*, Chapel Hill, NC: University of North Carolina Press.
Innes, Stephen (1995) *Creating the Commonwealth: The Economic Culture of Puritan New England*, New York: W. W. Norton.
Mather, Cotton (1705) *Lex mercatoria: or the Just Rules of Commerce Declared*, Boston.
Mather, Increase (1676) *An Earnest Exhortation to the Inhabitants of New-England*, Boston, Mass.
Miller, Perry (1953) *The New England Mind: From Colony to Province*, Cambridge, Mass.: Harvard University Press.
Perkins, William (1608) *Workes*, vol. I, Cambridge.
—— (1611) *The Whole Treatise of the Cases of Conscience*, London.
Peterson, Mark A. (1997) *The Price of Redemption: The Spiritual Economy of Puritan New England*, Stanford, Calif.: Stanford University Press.
Pierce, Richard D. (ed.) (1961) "Records of the First Church in Boston,1630–1868," in *Publications of the Colonial Society of Massachusetts*, vol. XXXIX, Boston, Mass.: Colonial Society of Massachusetts.
Stoddard, Solomon (1722) *An Answer to Some Cases of Conscience*, Boston, Mass.
Toulmin, Stephen (1990) *Cosmopolis: The Hidden Agenda of Modernity*, New York: Free Press.
Vickers, Daniel (1994) *Farmers and Fishermen: Two Centuries of Work in Essex County, Massachusetts, 1630–1850*, Chapel Hill, NC: University of North Carolina Press.
Willard, Samuel (1683) *The High Esteem Which God hath of the Death of His Saints*, Boston, Mass.
Witherspoon, John (1982) *An Annotated Edition of Lectures on Moral Philosophy*, ed. Jack Scott, Newark, Del.: University of Delaware Press.

Part III

Religious Cultures in Transition

Introduction

The studies in the previous section addressed the issue of religious change from a long-term perspective, focusing on the persistence of social and intellectual themes rather than on institutional continuity. The institutional descendants of New England Puritanism and Virginia Anglicanism – the United Church of Christ and the Episcopal Church, respectively – still exist after many centuries, but in radically transmuted form. American religious history has not only witnessed the birth of a number of new movements – Mormonism and Pentecostalism are two dramatic examples – but is also characterized by the gradual metamorphosis of more established traditions over long periods of growth and change. Even these latter movements have now endured sufficiently long to be subject to these same inducements towards adjustment.

The great Weber himself addressed some of these issues of change in his notion of "the routinization of charisma," through which movements, like Mormonism, originally founded on the power of an individual's demonstration of apparent supernatural power, eventually become bureaucratized in the interest of orderly transmission. Almost any sectarian movement – the Quakers, Wesley's Methodism, revivalism – eventually succumbs to some degree of institutionalization or, like the Shakers and Father Divine's Peace Mission, dies out.

The pressures for change are manifold, and may come from within or without, from success or from adversity. Growth almost inevitably necessitates change. As a religious movement transcends its original, "effervescent" character, it has, as Weber argued, to develop structures for self-perpetuation. The emergence of these structures may in turn offend purists who believe that the "primitive" integrity of the movement has been forsaken and must be recaptured. Growth also introduces diversity, which inevitably leads to change and often to contention. Success over time also leads not only to institutionalization but also to respectability. Where new movements often attract the less affluent and sophisticated, their descendants, and new recruits, may reflect more comfortable situations and more cosmopolitan outlooks. This transformation may reflect some irony: the very virtues of discipline that the early movement in its rigor instilled may contribute to the material success and intellectual restlessness that later rigorists may interpret as signs of decadence and heresy.

Change may also be induced from without. Social issues, such as slavery, the sale of alcohol, or abortion, may come so centrally into public discourse that they cannot be avoided, and religious communities may divide over their response. Broader cultural themes may also have their impact. The persistence of participatory democracy as an irrepressible part of the "American character" has been so pervasive that few religious institutions – even the ultimately hierarchical Roman Catholic Church – have been able to avoid its impact. Economics may also play a role. Some religious movements may be fostered by economic privation, preaching a message of liberation and offering material relief. Others may be threatened by the same forces, and be forced to undertake serious internal reappraisal to rally support during hard times. Even the reclusive Amish have been unable to resist the incursions of technological change, and have had to devise a mechanism for continuous evaluation and selective appropriation of material novelty.

Russell Richey deals with American Methodism in the early Republic, as that movement's second generation of leaders struggled with issues such as democracy, centralization, race, ethnicity, and upward mobility in an attempt to fashion an organization and religious culture that would flourish in a rapidly changing and growing social order.

Beth Wenger examines the situation faced by the American Jewish community after the onset of the Depression of the 1930s. Jewish leaders adopted a variety of strategies to persuade their fallen-away constituents that institutional Judaism could offer them relief and meaning in the midst of economic hard times, but were unsuccessful in many of their attempts. Ultimately, the appeal of Zionism as an undergirding for American Jewish identity was to prove the most successful, if not the most overtly religious, means of revitalizing the community once prosperity returned.

Philip Barlow looks at the Latter-day Saints, or Mormons, over the broad perspective of their nearly two centuries of development. Barlow sees three periods of dramatic change through which a small movement gathered around a local prophet became transformed theologically, socially, and geographically into what is now a highly bureaucratized international organization.

Mary Jo Weaver discusses the impact of Vatican II, the ecumenical council held at Rome in the early 1960s, on the American Catholic community. Here the theological changes in a worldwide religious community combined with distinctively American social circumstances and subsequent reversals in emphasis at the highest levels of leadership to produce a church at odds with itself internally over the degree and manner to which change should be effected.

Chapter 8

Early American Methodism

Russell E. Richey

In the year 1816, Methodism thought anxiously about itself. It was a year that provided an unusually clear window into the soul of the movement. Or to switch from a visual to a temporal metaphor, in 1816 Methodism showed intense awareness of what it had been: of the passing of one day and of the beginning of another.

The passing of one day Methodism acknowledged in the deaths of leaders who had guided the movement from the beginning and who both effected and symbolized its unity. The *Minutes* in which the church meticulously monitored its every vital sign put the matter tersely. "Quest. 13. Who have died this year? 1. The venerable Francis Asbury – March 31, 1816." Eight others of the early leadership were also given obituaries (*Minutes* 1816). News of Bishop Thomas Coke's demise had only been minuted in 1815, Asbury's dominated 1816 and almost-bishop Jesse Lee's, also in 1816, would be noted in 1817. Governor Richard Bassett, one of Methodism's key lay leaders had died in 1815 (Wakeley 1875: 427–9, 460–5). Ezekiel Cooper, who preached a sermon on the death of Asbury, and subsequently published it "enlarged" to 230 pages, saw the whole history of American Methodism through the prism of this one life. Cooper affirmed:

> It is almost, if not altogether, impossible to give a narrative of his life and character, without incorporating with it, in some degree, the history of the Methodist Episcopal church. The one, is so intimately and essentially connected with the other, that they cannot well be separated, without injustice to the subject. The *Memoirs* of his life, must necessarily contain a considerable history of the Methodist church in America. And a faithful history of the church, must, as necessarily, give a history of his life. (1819: 59–60)

Methodism in 1816

Methodism's highest body, the General Conference of the Methodist Episcopal Church, held its quadrennial meeting in Baltimore, then the heart and soul of the church, its capital city, its place of greatest strength. It began its work with heightened consciousness of the changes through which the movement was going. In its first action of business, after the election of a secretary, the General Conference of 1816 received a petition "from the male members of the Methodist Episcopal Church in the city of Baltimore" to remove Asbury's remains there. The next morning an address by the departed Bishop Asbury was read. In the afternoon, an address by the surviving bishop, William McKendree, "was presented by himself, and read in order by T. L. Douglass." Several days later (Friday, May 10) the conference began its session late so that members could attend a "funeral" for Asbury (Wakeley 1875: 430–3). And after the addresses of Asbury and McKendree, conference established a committee to which it referred their remarks and "whose duty it shall be to report to the conference the different subjects in them proper to be committed to district committees." That body in turn reported out recommendations establishing six other committees: episcopacy, book concerns, ways and means, review and revision, safety and temporal economy (*Journals*, 124, 126, 128–9).

General Conference and the Business of Methodism

One day had surely passed. The dawn of a new day General Conference recognized by getting down to "business," to committee structure, to procedure, to order. It did so by referring espiscopal concerns – those of the dead Asbury as well as the presiding McKendree – to the several committees. The provision for and use of committee structure represented a looking ahead and would thereafter characterize Methodist governance, at all levels. Committees thereafter belonged to Methodist life, like so much else that had and would characterize the movement, adopted because they worked. "There was," noted Henry Boehm, "a vast amount of business done at the General Conference of 1816, and it was more methodical than formerly" (Wakeley 1875: 436).

The committee reports conveyed the sense of a new day, of much work to do, of tried and proven leadership slipping away, of crisis, of a clear perception that "new measures" were called for and now of new hands to put to the challenges ahead. The church clearly was in new hands, not just Bishop McKendree and the two new bishops elected at that conference, Enoch George and Robert Richford Roberts, but also those destined to be bishops like Joshua Soule and John Emory and near-bishops like Peter Cartwright. The church now boasted, for the first time, an American-born leadership.

It also featured governance on the American plan through a series of conferences – general, annual and quarterly – which some likened to a calendar and others to a machine with geared wheels. The general conference, which met every four years for a period of several weeks, possessed plenary authority; it was subject to a set of restrictive rules, which guarded central aspects of Methodist belief and structure and had elaborate procedures for emendation. General conferences had become a representative body; the representation was based on population, albeit of preachers rather than people, and was constituted also of preachers rather than people. Annual conferences, also composed of preachers, and quarterly conferences, which included the array of officers – presiding elders, traveling preachers, local preachers, exhorters, stewards, class leaders – we treat below.

In 1816, for the second time, General Conference assembled as a representative body; some of those attending, like Cartwright, had come great distances, from the southern or western edges.

> We had no steamboats, railroad cars, or comfortable stages in those days. We had to travel from the extreme West on horseback. It generally took us near a month to go; a month was spent at General Conference, and nearly a month in returning to our fields of labor. (Cartwright 1856: 110)

In the assemblage of General Conference, Methodism was aware of itself as a truly national church: popular, expansive, competitive, entrepreneurial, like the nation itself. But, like the nation, it was insecure, anxious, conscious of its vulnerabilities. The deaths represented such vulnerability. So also the present quality of its ministries. The Committee of Ways and Means worried over both "locations and the admission of improper persons into the itinerancy" (*Journals*, 148–52). The latter was something the church could, and thereafter strove to, do something about. General Conference empowered the bishops to a course of study, believing "an ardent desire for useful knowledge" if not "a collegiate education" to be essential to a gospel ministry (*Journals*, 149, 151). The next year, the Baltimore Conference received a quite impressive list of books and itemization of expectations for "candidates for the ministry" (Baker 1972: 132–3); Baltimore: 99–100).

The committee's other concern, the loss to the church through locations of its experienced, trained and pious "ornaments" was less readily addressed. These "locations" – the surrendering by itinerants or traveling preachers of their conference membership and ministerial status – had been a grave concern of Asbury's and continued to be an agony. What was to be done when the church's most experienced and gifted gave up traveling to marry, farm, and locate? What was to be done when these located or local preachers came to constitute two-thirds of the church's ministry, and to take a major responsibility for the church's pastoral service and evangelistic outreach? What was to be done about representing the insights, concerns, and interests of these bi-vocational ministers in the annual and general conferences that exercised over them authority, supervision, and governance over them? At this juncture, locations and local preachers raised questions about the elasticity in Methodist polity. In another decade, such inflexibility would bring crisis and schism.

Defining Methodism's Place in American Society

If the Ways and Means Committee looked around and back, the Book Committee looked ahead. It and the conference decided that the book agents "shall be chosen

from among the travelling preachers, and, by virtue of their appointment, shall
be members of the New-York Annual Conference, to whom, in the interval of
the General Conferences, they shall be responsible for their conduct in the book
business . . ." By this act, the church established a system of accountability and
oversight that tied agents, operations, and voluntary societies to its conference
governance structure.

The conference then urged the agents to "publish more small books and fewer
large ones" and also authorized a periodical, to be entitled "The Methodist
Missionary Magazine" (*Journals*, 171). Joshua Soule was put at the helm and did
move the Book Concern towards publications of Bibles, tracts and cheap items
that could be effectively marketed to Methodist readership (Pilkington 1968:
154–68). Nathan Bangs, who would succeed Soule at the Book Concern, symbolized Methodism's more serious engagement with American society. The year
1816 found him already engaged in the Calvinist controversy. He had taken up
the Arminian cause in public debate and in 1815 published *The Errors of
Hopkinsianism Detected and Refuted*. In 1816, he answered a responder in *The
Reformer Reformed: or, A Second Part of the Errors of Hopkinsianism Detected
and Refuted*. Another volume, *An Examination of the Doctrine of Predestination*
followed in 1817. Methodist doctrine suffered at Calvinist hands, so also did
Methodist ministry. To that affront responded Freeborn Garrettson, an experienced preacher and leader, earlier proposed by John Wesley for the
episcopacy, and tied by marriage to the Livingston political and social elites. In
A Letter to the Rev. Lyman Beecher (1816), he repudiated Beecher's inference
that competent ministry was confined to the Calvinist community and that the
country, in consequence, faced a crisis in meeting the needs of the West.

Nathan Bangs, looking back at these controversies, saw them as symptoms of
Methodism's increase "in number and respectability" and augmentation of its
"influence upon the public mind" and the consequent alarm of the Calvinist
"establishment" (Bangs 1860: III, 14–26). Methodists had their own solution to
ministry in the West. General Conference's Committee on Temporal Economy
took over the responsibility of configuring Methodism on the American landscape, dividing conferences, establishing their boundaries (*Journals*, 152–4).
Thus did Methodism catch up, formally and organizationally, with the rapid
expansion on to American frontiers, some of it initiated by appointment of itinerants into new areas, much of it undertaken by the lay men and women who
organized classes and by local preachers who moved west. The effective
Methodist response to Mr Beecher was in action rather than words.

Methodists, however, had their own version of Beecher's worry. The
Committee of Safety took into "consideration that part of the address relating to
the duty of preachers, to inquire whether our doctrines have been maintained,
discipline faithfully and impartially enforced, and the stations and circuits duly
attended" (*Journals*, 128). Composed of Joshua Soule, Enoch George, and
Samuel Parker, it concluded "that, in some parts of the connexion, doctrines
contrary to our established articles of faith, and of dangerous tendency, have
made their appearance among us, especially the ancient doctrines of *Arianism*,
Socinianism and *Pelagianism*." It found also the *Discipline* not fully enforced,

property not secured in Methodist manner, rules of dress ignored, discipline exercised without due process, preaching and visitation neglected. The committee itemized the problems in a set of eight resolutions. It expressed alarm at the worldliness that had crept within, notably in the building of finer churches and equipping them with pews: (3) "That the manner of building houses of religious worship with pews is contrary to the rules of our economy, and inconsistent with the interests of our societies" (*Journals*, 155–8). Another committee recommended changes in the ministry that would address some of these concerns. Worldliness proved both a problem and a cure. Among this committee's recommendations was one for more adequate ministerial housing, and one for better education through a course of study for candidates for the ministry. The latter, as we have already noted, became thereafter a Methodist institution.

General Conference also faced a number of issues that would continue to trouble the church in years ahead: petitions by local preachers for representations, efforts at "an amicable adjustment of certain differences between our Church and the British connection relative to Upper and Lower Canada," and whether to allow annual conferences some say in the selection of presiding elders. The latter was an issue that would not go away. Should not the preachers play some part in the selection of those who supervised and governed? After all, they enjoyed that seemingly "American" prerogative with respect to the bishops who appointed the presiding elders. So Samuel Merwin proposed the selection of presiding elders by episcopal nomination and conference vote. The matter was later dealt with by General Conference, McKendree relinquishing the chair. Bangs proposed a friendly amendment. After considerable debate, the motion failed by 42 votes to 60. Merwin and others made further efforts at refining the motion. The action continued for several days, over Sunday, but with the same outcome. Merwin moved towards the end of the conference "That the motion relative to the election and appointment of presiding elders is not contrary to the constitution of our Church." That, too, failed (*Journals*, 166–9, 151, 135, 140–64). General Conference did have a say in the matter of bishops and authorized and elected two new bishops, Enoch George on first ballot, Robert Richford Roberts on the second. A heightened political consciousness was another sign of Methodism's engagement with American society.

Another indicator of accommodation to American society was the church's stance on slavery. From an early abolitionism and mandate that its members and preachers free their slaves, the church had beaten a gradual retreat. In the face of Southern state legislation frustrating manumission, the Committee on Slavery conceded that "under the present existing circumstances in relation to slavery, little can be done to abolish a practice so contrary to the principles of moral justice. They are sorry to say that the evil appears to be past remedy." They therefore resolved to adjust the *Discipline* limiting prohibition against slave holders' holding office to states permitting emancipation (*Journals*, 169–70).

Conference's greater political sensitivity and interest in its business had been manifest in the selection of its delegates. In the 1815 meeting that selected its General Conference delegation, the New England Conference decided to proceed in democratic fashion:

Took up the business of choosing delegates to the next General Conference. Ascertained that this Conference have the right to send the number of twelve, it is moved that they be selected by choice rather than by seigniority, carried unanimously in the affirmative.

Then the Conference made its own judgment about the leadership of the Conference, in this instance confirming the bishop's selection of his presiding elders by electing them all to General Conference, a confirmation not always to be repeated in years ahead (New England Conference 1815: 212).

New England Conference

Presiding Elders, 1814	Delegation elected in 1815 to General Conference
Asa Kent	Asa Kent
Charles Virgin	Charles Virgin
Eleazer Wells	Eleazer Wells
Solomon Sias	Solomon Sias
Oliver Beale	Oliver Beal
Joshua Soule	Joshua Soule
	Elijah Hedding
	George Pickering
	Martin Ruter
	Philip Munger
	Joseph A. Merrill

Outside the MEC, others also struggled with what it meant to be Methodist in American society.

The German Americans

By 1816 the two German movements with affinities to the Methodists also witnessed the passing of their first generation leadership. Among the United Brethren, Martin Boehm and George Adam Geeting had died in 1812 and William Otterbein in 1813. In 1815 the Brethren held their first General Conference. They reworked a German translation of the *Methodist Discipline* to clarify the denomination's understanding of the various levels of conference and of ministry. For instance, they accepted a term episcopacy. Two years later, at the General Conference of 1817, two bishops were elected, Christian Newcomer (re-elected, in fact) and Andrew Zeller. A hymn book was also authorized and thereafter produced.

United Brethren struggles towards their place in American society involved sorting out relations with the English Methodists. For several years they had conducted negotiations with the Baltimore Conference (MEC) looking forward to unification. The two bodies had exchanged formal written overtures and sent delegates to one another's gatherings. By 1814, the Baltimore Conference concluded that the United Brethren were not willing to reach Methodist standards of discipline, licensing, itinerancy, record-keeping, and membership and declared it "unnecessary to continue the ceremony of annual letters" but left "the door of friendly intercourse open" (Baltimore 1809: 40–1; 1810: 46–7; 1811: 52–3; 1812: 59, 61; 1813: 68–70; 1814: 74, 78; Baker 1972: 110–12; Drury 1897).

Such friendly intercourse continued, as can be discerned from the travels of the UB episcopal leader, Christian Newcomer:

> Sunday, April 7, 1816 – I attended a Quarterly meeting in Hagerstown; and on the 13th and Sunday 14th – we had a Quarterly meeting at the widow Funkhouser's in Virginia. 15th – I reached at Mr. Hays'; 16th – at Christian Funk's, and rode to Abr. Niswander's and staid for the night. Visited others, and returned home on the 20th. Sunday, 21st – preached in the forenoon at Funks-town and at my home in the afternoon. 29th – I rode to Baltimore and lodged with Br. Hildt. 30th – This morning I visited Bishop McKendree; Asbury was no more, he had died a few days before near Fredricksburg, Virginia, on his way to the General Conference; in the afternoon I led a sister's class at Br. Hoffman's.
>
> May 1st, 1816 – The (Methodist) General Conference commenced its session this afternoon; at night I attended meeting in Oldtown and lodged with Hildt. (Hough 1941: 182)

From there Newcomer went on to the meeting of his own Eastern Conference, riding, preaching, lodging, and presiding over conference, sacramental meetings, quarterly conferences and camp meetings very much in the fashion of his English-speaking counterparts.

The other German-speaking, Methodist-like movement, the Evangelicals, had lost their founder, Jacob Albright, in 1808. The year 1816 also saw the death of George Miller, architect of episcopal government for that communion and the drafter of its first two Disciplines. Although ill, he began his autobiography July 1, 1815, and kept at it for four weeks: "in part I copied it from my papers, and partly wrote from memory." He died April 5, 1816. Biographer of Albright, author of *Practical Christianity*, teacher of holiness, and effective preacher, Miller had symbolized the transitions through which the Evangelicals were going in his crafting of order and orientation to American efficiency:

> This induced me to draw up business rules for the Conference, which were also adopted, and we could now do our business in accordance with these rules, so that the majority of votes decided all questions, and hence evils could be suppressed and good purposes promoted, without hurting each other's feelings, or offending the weaker brethren. Our Conferences hereafter became seasons of great grace, in which all were edified and encouraged. The Lord be praised who thus ordered it. (Yeakel 1883: 264, 249, 169–275).

By 1816 John Walter, the author and translator of hymns and compiler of the denomination's first hymnal had ceased traveling; he died two years later, in 1818 (Yeakel 1883: 129–68). In 1816, in its first General Conference, the Evangelical

Association selected the name by which it would thereafter be known, entertained a plan of union with the United Brethren, and appointed a head of its press (Behney and Eller 1979: 92–5). The Germans as well as the English were struggling with accommodation to American society.

African Methodist Independence

The year 1816 also saw the final stage of the long drama of African Methodist independence. In prior decades, Methodism had made a credible appeal to blacks, preached anti-slavery, and become a bi-racial movement. Baltimore, the heart of Methodism, had seen black membership double between 1805 and 1815, reaching virtual parity with white, as shown by the list of members for 1805 to 1816 (*Minutes*).

	White	*Black*
1805	1,205	702
1806	1,154	755
1810	1,170	750
1813	1,540	973
1814	1,673	1,101
1815	1,667	1,552
1816	1,954	1,430

However, as Methodism had gained in numbers, adherents among the propertied classes, and in respectability, it had also followed the "worldly" trend of accommodation to slavery and, in areas like Baltimore where free blacks abounded, of stripping blacks of rights and privileges. In the church that entailed continued segregation, resistance to acknowledging black aspirations for leadership and autonomy, and white control of black affairs.

For Baltimore Methodists, the years 1815 and 1816 registered the ambiguities and imperfections in the moral climate and in race relations. For those years the "Colored" class rolls attest that many African Americans, some one-seventh thereof, had their fill of white domination (Bilhartz 1986: 32–3). Beside name after name is an X, followed by the explanation "gone with Coker." These members had cast their lot with Daniel Coker, whose name, first on the list of local preachers, was also stricken through.

Coker led Baltimore African Americans into declaration of independence, the acquisition of separate property, and affiliation with Richard Allen, leader of the older, Philadelphia congregation. In 1816, "African" churches from Philadelphia, Baltimore, Salem (NJ), and Wilmington met in what would be reckoned the first General Conference of the African Methodist Episcopal Church (AME). The new church elected Coker bishop, turning to Allen only when Coker demurred. Under Bishop Allen the AME continued the Methodist witness against slavery and for freedom.

By this point also, the African Union Church, a smaller denomination, centered in Wilmington and led by Peter Spencer of that city, had also coalesced. The New York-based African Methodist Episcopal Zion movement would organize a few years later, but the Zion congregation was already in the struggles over conference membership and recognition of its own leadership that would eventuate in independence (George 1973; Gravely 1993: 106–24).

On a Conference Level

The 1816 *Minutes* specified nine annual conferences, staged so that the bishops could attend, beginning September 3, 1816 with Ohio and concluding with the Genesee on June 21, 1817. The Ohio Conference, meeting in only its fifth session, opened as appointed with Bishops McKendree, George, and Roberts presiding in its several sessions. The journal listed 54 members, 10 marked * as absent. Organization remained spare, not yet replicating the level of structure found at General Conference. D. Young was appointed Secretary. The three appointed stewards set about reckoning the yearly collections by the ministers and distributing as much towards equity as collections permitted, much as their constituent farmers would tally up after the crops were in. A book committee was appointed to look after the business the preachers ran in connection with the saving of souls (Sweet 1923: 140–50). The sale of Methodist tracts, hymnals, Bibles, and books was a significant source of income, for the individual preacher and for the conference. For instance, the list of sales by Benjamin Lakin in 1817 on Limestone Circuit attests something of Methodist reading habits as well as the importance of such colportage for the ministry (Sweet 1946: 698–709):

57	Catechisms	$3.56½
39	Hymn Books	34.12½
18	Kempis	5.62½
14	Hester A. Rogers life	10.50
14	Disciplines	5.25
14	Nelsons Journals	5.25
11	Portraitures	11.00
10	Allen and Baxter	5.00
7	Nester A Rogers lettrs	1.31¼
7	Testaments	7.00
	. . .	
2	Sets Wesley Notes	6.00
2	Sets of Fletchers Checks	10.00
TOTAL 236		148.58¾
	commission	17.83
NEAT PRODUCE		130.74¾

The Ohio minutes made no reference to a coincident camp meeting, but holding camp meeting and conference together was common practice. The work of the conference would be punctuated by services held in the camp. The most eloquent or powerful would be appointed to preach. Conversions and revivals resulted. Conference had its own spiritual intensity, occasioned by its serious task of reviewing candidates for ministry and examining the character of those in the several stages from trial to elder. This involved hearing of spiritual estate and religious pilgrimages, an inspiring and renewing process for the auditors as for the candidates. It also involved judging the fitness of persons for ministry, assessing their gifts, determining their orthodoxy. Such inquiry was not pro forma. In "An examination of the Characters & conduct of those remaining on trial, the Conference ordered that Othneel Talboot & Mathew Mahan should be laid aside" (Sweet 1923: 141). And conference extended similar scrutiny to those who, though not admitted to the traveling connection, would exercise pastoral oversight. In dealing with local deacons to be elected elder, it acted on one individual only after pointed queries on original sin and native depravity. Preachers expected and were expected to exercise spiritual leadership by being spiritual models. So the brothers

> [R]esolved by the Ohio Annual conference that it is inexpedient [sic] and imprudent for a travelling Preacher to dishonor himself by associating with the Free Masons in their Lodges.
>
> Resolved that this conference communicate by letter thro' the Presiding Elders their disapprobation to the Official men or Members of our Church associating themselves with the Free Masons either in their Lodges or Festivals. (Sweet 1923: 141–3)

Effective, revivalistic, expansive, missionary, entrepreneurial religious leadership measured itself by the souls committed to the Lord and the dollars committed to their own upkeep. So the conference journal featured two fairly elaborate charts. One page itemized by circuit the numbers in society, a total of 21,641 whites and 537 colored, on five districts. It accounted for an actual dip in membership from the prior year with a note: "The loss in membership due to the transfer of the Salt River District to the Tennessee Conference." The monetary accounting came in the stewards' report, fairly elaborate tables, one listing preachers, stations, amount of quarterage, defects, surplus and collections and appropriations, all endeavors to provide preachers their $80 salary; the other listing preachers with children over and under 7, the claims made, and very modest appropriations. For instance James Quinn had four children, claimed $80 and was granted $10 (Sweet 1923: 148, 145–7).

Conferences such as Ohio evidenced the fluidity of Methodism on its growing western edge. Circuits would grow into districts and then into conferences. Conferences periodically divided. Members, congregations, and ministers would then find new places within the expanding church. Ministers, in particular, changed conference affiliation easily in the west, as they had nationally in Methodism's earlier decades when the church had really a genuinely connectional ministerium, that is, a ministry in service to the entire church and understanding itself and committed to be appointable anywhere. The combined *Minutes* for 1816 evidenced this earlier national Methodist itinerancy in its obituaries. The once connectional character of appointments is clear in the career of one who died that year, Learner Blackman, native of New Jersey, converted about age 19, and admitted on trial in 1800 (*Minutes* 1815: 274):

1800	Kent Circuit
1801	Dover
1802	Russell (Va.)
1803	New-River (Va.)
1804	Lexington (Ky.)
1805	mission to Mississippi
1806	Presiding Elder, Mississippi
1807	" "
1808	Presiding Elder, Holston
1809	" "
1810	Cumberland
1811	"
1812	Presiding Elder, Nashville
1813	" "
1814	" "
1815	Cumberland

Already in the East and particularly in the South, ministry increasingly defined itself within, rather than across, conference lines; conferences stabilized themselves as geographical units; the ministry operated within regional and sub-regional lines; a sectionalized church was in the making.

Local Methodism

Methodism had no *Christian Advocates* to keep its parts aware of one another. The church connected itself by correspondence, minutes, and journals, and especially the movement of the itinerants, presiding elders, and bishops. The nerve centers of communication and of church life were the quarterly meetings. Particularly important was that held in late summer, frequently coincident with a camp meeting. The circuit then gathered to do its business, as prescribed by the *Discipline*. Business constituted only one part of the occasion. Religious ceremony and festival made the quarterly meeting the source of great power and appeal; there were love feasts, preaching in abundance, exhortation to suit, celebration of the sacraments, memorial services. Typically the entire circuit would be represented: the presiding elder, occasionally a bishop, the travelling preachers, local preachers, exhorters, stewards, the 'mothers in Israel' who nurtured life in the homes. Commonly, presiding elders and itinerants would attend one another's quarterly meetings, so the event would be well staffed top to bottom. Conversions and revival often resulted, partly because they were expected, partly because then Methodism gathered in the crowds that made revival possible, partly because the denomination focused its converting efforts on such occasions. At any rate, the quarterly/camp meetings loom large in the record and in retrospect.

On a weekly basis the class meeting and society or congregational gatherings constituted Methodist fare. The year 1816 saw the founding in Baltimore of what would eventually be a successor institution to the class meeting, namely male and female Sunday schools, the Asbury Sunday School Society and the McKendrean Sunday School Society respectively. The former was organized in a meeting chaired by Stephen Roszel; it operated initially in rented quarters, held classes Saturday evening and Sunday, outgrew its quarters and moved the next year into the Male Free School. The young "scholars" from this institution marched on Sundays to one of the Baltimore preaching houses. In the latter, organized at Eutaw Street Church, women took the instructional responsibilities and held the major offices: Sarah Hammond was president, Sarah McConnell, vice-president, Elizabeth Morsell, treasurer, Caroline Hammond, secretary (Baker 1972: 123–6). The explosion of the Sunday School lay in the future, so also the dramatic growth of the mission societies. Sex, age, and race stratification of the classes and race stratification of the societies proved common. Here Methodism showed its fractures. Baltimore Methodists constituted half the town's clergy and its social profile tracked that of the community as a whole (Bilhartz 1986: 23–38). Similar patterns pertained on Delmarva where Methodism no longer concentrated a third of its membership, as in 1784, but where some 20 percent of the total population adhered to the movement (Williams 1984: 72–87). Here, it seemed, Methodism needed a more "parish" style ministry.

Nevertheless, Methodism continued its circuit deployment of preachers, even for cities such as Baltimore, Philadelphia, and New York, where a number of churches had been acquired. In New York, for instance, preachers appointed there took responsibility for John Street, Second (Forsyth) Street, Fourth (Allen) Street, Two Miles Stone (Seventh Street), Greenwich (Bedford Street), and Duane Street plus Zion African and Asbury African. Caring for these were five stationed preachers, plus the MEC Book Agents, Joshua Soule and Thomas Mason, and J. Lyon, a located preacher. A plan of their appointments, actually a published plan, shows that itinerancy continued to be the norm. Only two of the churches are given in the plan shown here.

Frontiers: Respectability or the Poor?

The arrangement of rotating preachers through the appointments was to be a casualty of Methodism's prosperity, numerical growth, and aspirations for respectability. The eastern and larger towns increasingly desired station appointments that afforded an individual congregation with continuous, stable ministry. Leaders with New England experience, particularly Nathan Bangs, implored Methodism to take a leaf from the competition's book and recognize what effective congregational leadership could achieve. But that direction yielded the finer churches and the pew rentals that elicited General Conference concern. That

A six-week plan for the stationed preachers in the City of New York

Dates	John Street			Second Street		
	Morning	Afternoon	Evening	Morning	Afternoon	Evening
1. July 7	W. Thatcher	E. Washburn	L. Andrus	D. Ostrander	W. Thatcher	E. Washburn
2. July 14	E. Washburn	L. Andrus	T. Mason	W. Tahtcher	E. Washburn	L. Andrus
3. July 21	L. Andrus	J. Lyon	A. Scholefield	E. Washburn	L. Andrus	J. Soule
4. July 28	J. Soule	A. Scholefield	D. Ostrander	L. Andrus	T. Mason	A. Scholefield
5. August 4	A. Scholefield	D.Ostrander	W. Thatcher	J. Lyon	A. Scholefield	D. Ostrander
6. August 11	D. Ostrander	W. Thatcher	E. Washburn	A. Scholefield	D. Ostrander	W. Thatcher
7. August 18	W. Thatcher	E. Washburn	L. Andrus	D. Ostrander	W. Thatcher	E. Washburn

NB: (1) The stationed preachers will be held responsible for all the appointments assigned them on this plan, but they may provide substitutes when it is not convenient for them to attend themselves.

(2) Whenever a preacher is called on to attend in either of the African churches or state prison or almshouse he shall see that his place is supplied by local preachers, according to this plan.

(3) Preaching in the week as follows: Tuesday evening, Duane Street and Fourth Street; Wednesday evening, Zion African; Thursday evening, Second Street and Greenwich; Friday evening, John Street, Two Mile Stone, and Asbury African; to be attended as follows, namely, each preacher to preach in that church in which his appointment is the preceding Sabbath morning; the preacher who preaches in Duane Street on Tuesday evening, to preach also in Zion on Wednesday evening; and the preacher who preaches in Second Street on Thursday evening to preach also in Asbury on Friday evening.

(4) Sacraments. At John Street, Two Mile Stone, and Asbury African, the first Sabbath of each month; Zion African, second Sabbath; in Second Street and Duane Street, third Sabbath; and in Fourth Street and Greenwich the fourth Sabbath in each month.

(5) Leaders' meeting to be held in the lecture-room in Second Street the second Monday in each month, in the evening, and to be given out in all the churches the preceding Sabbath evening.

Source: Seaman 1892: 478–81

direction added economic stratification to the church's list of internal divisions. That direction also made it possible for Methodism to hold its own: to keep its own children, who, as they prospered, wanted the panoply of congregational services. The church was not of one mind on the matter and both accommodated and resisted genteel and congregational patterns.

Such tensions derived in part from the growing complexity of the movement. In more frontier areas, Methodism resembled the church that Asbury had known, sprawling circuits tying small societies into community and order and demanding itinerants as vigorous as before. A disordered frontier needed and got a unifying Methodism. In areas around Baltimore and the Chesapeake, where it came close to being an establishment, Methodism's frontier lay in its differentiation, in its capacity to relate to a society divided economically, socially, racially. Could Methodism minister to the poor as it increasingly claimed the middle classes? Could it hold the slaves and free blacks as it welcomed the slave-owners? Could it match in its leadership the educational and cultural attainments of its laity? And as Methodism accommodated itself to the cultures of East and West and North and South could it hold itself together?

BIBLIOGRAPHY

Baker, Gordon Pratt (ed.) (1972) *Those Incredible Methodists: A History of the Baltimore Conference of the United Methodist Church*, Baltimore, Md.: Commission on Archives and History, The Baltimore Conference.

Baltimore Conference (MEC), Typescript Minutes of the Baltimore Conference, Lovely Lane Museum. Used with permission from Edwin Schell (abbreviated Baltimore).

Bangs, Nathan (1860) *A History of the Methodist Episcopal Church* (4 vols), 8th edn, New York: Carlton & Porter (first printed New York: T. Mason and G. Lane for the Methodist Episcopal Church, 1838–41).

Behney, J. Bruce and Eller, Paul H. (1979) *The History of the Evangelical United Brethren Church*, ed. Kenneth W. Krueger, Nashville, Tenn.: Abingdon Press.

Bilhartz, Terry D. (1986) *Urban Religion and the Second Great Awakening: Church and Society in Early National Baltimore*, Rutherford, NJ: FDU Press.

Brugger, Robert J. (1988) *Maryland: A Middle Temperament*, Baltimore, Md.: Johns Hopkins University Press.

Cartwright, Peter (1856) *Autobiography of Peter Cartwright*, ed. Charles L. Wallis, New York: Carlton & Porter; reprinted 1956, 1984, Nashville, Tenn.: Abingdon Press.

Cooper, Ezekiel (1819) *The Substance of a Funeral Discourse . . . on the Death of the Rev. Francis Asbury*, Philadelphia, Pa.

Drury, A. W. (trans. and ed.) (1897) *Minutes of the Annual and General Conferences of the Church of the United Brethren in Christ, 1800–1818*, Dayton, Oh.: United Brethren Publishing House.

Fields, Barbara Jeanne (1895) *Slavery and Freedom on the Middle Ground: Maryland during the Nineteenth Century*, New Haven, Conn. and London: Yale University Press.

George, Carol V. R. (1973) *Segregated Sabbaths: Richard Allen and the Rise of Independent Black Churches, 1760–1840*, New York: Oxford University Press.

Gravely, Will B. (1993) "African Methodisms and the rise of black denominationalism," *Perspectives on American Methodism: Interpretive Essays*, ed. by Russell E. Richey,

Kenneth E. Rowe, and Jean Miller Schmidt, Nashville, Tenn.: Kingswood Books/ Abingdon Press.

Hough, Samuel S. (ed.) (1941) *Christian Newcomer: His Life, Journal and Achievements*, Dayton, Oh.: Board of Administration, Church of the United Brethren in Christ.

Journals of the General Conference of the Methodist Episcopal Church, I: 1796–1836 (1855), New York: Carlton & Phillips. (Text references are to the year 1816 unless otherwise indicated.)

Minutes of the Annual Conferences of the Methodist Episcopal Church for the Years 1773–1828, New York: T. Mason and G. Lane, 1840 (abbreviated *Minutes* and for 1816 unless otherwise indicated).

New England Conference (MEC), *Minutes of the New England Conference of the Methodist Episcopal Church . . . 1766 to . . . 1845* (2 vols) (typescript prepared by George Whitaker for New England Methodist Historical Society, 1912).

Pilkington, James P. (1968) *The Methodist Publishing House: A History*, vol. 1, Nashville, Tenn.: Abingdon Press.

Seaman, Samuel A., A.M. (1892) *Annals of New York Methodism Being A History of the United Methodist Church in the City of New York from A.D. 1766 to A.D. 1890*, New York: Hunt & Eaton.

Sweet, William Warren (ed.) (1923) *Circuit-Rider Days Along the Ohio. Being the Journals of the Ohio Conference from its Organization in 1812 to 1826*, New York and Cincinnati: The Methodist Book Concern.

—— (1964) *The Methodists: A Collection of Source Materials: Religion on the American Frontier, 1783–1840*, IV, New York: Cooper Square Publishers; first published in 1946.

Wakeley, J. B. (1875) *The Patriarch of One Hundred Years; Being Reminiscences, Historical and Biographical of Rev. Henry Boehm*, New York: Nelson & Phillips; reprinted by Abrahm W. Sangrey, 1982.

Williams, William H. (1984) *The Garden of American Methodism: The Delmarva Peninsula, 1769–1820*, Wilmington, Del.: Scholarly Resources Inc.

Yeakel, R. (1883) *Jacob Albright and His Co-Laborers*, trans. from the German, Cleveland, Oh.: Publishing House of the Evangelical Association.

Chapter 9

Synagogues and the "Spiritual Depression" in the 1930s

Beth Wenger

The story of American religion is often told in cycles of boom and bust. Periods of growth and contraction – measured in terms of church membership, belief patterns, and institutional expansion – have become part of the standard narrative of American religious history. By all accounts, the Great Depression was a low point for religion in America. During the thirties, both Jewish and Christian clergy complained of dwindling attendance at synagogue and church services and widespread religious apathy. This essay explores the ways that American synagogues responded to the challenges of the Great Depression and suggests that, despite membership losses and financial turmoil, the 1930s should not be interpreted merely as a period of religious decline but rather as a time of creative ferment in institutional Judaism.

In the history of the American synagogue the 1930s stand between two periods of enormous synagogue expansion. The 1920s synagogue building boom ended with the onset of the Great Depression and synagogue growth resumed only after World War II, when a new generation of Jews revived synagogue life on the suburban frontier. The Depression decade has generally been characterized as a period of stagnation and religious malaise in American synagogues. During the 1930s, synagogues struggled under heavy financial burdens and mortgage debts, watched their memberships shrink, and were often forced to curtail programs and dismiss personnel. And the fiscal crisis was only part of the problem facing Depression-era synagogues. Like their Christian counterparts, Jewish leaders identified a "spiritual depression" gripping the nation (Handy 1960: 3–16). The Depression threatened both the economic health and substantive role of synagogues. As Jewish leaders contended with the financial problems plaguing their synagogues, they also searched for some means to combat spiritual lethargy and transform the synagogue into a vital communal institution.

The Depression was an arduous and uncertain period for Jewish congregations, but it was also a time when Jewish leaders re-evaluated the synagogue's inner structure, communal role, and spiritual agenda against the backdrop of a changing American environment. The economic crisis did not radically transform American Judaism nor dramatically alter the character of the synagogue, but the Depression experience significantly contributed to the ongoing development of institutional Judaism. Confronted with fiscal crisis and religious apathy, Jewish congregations responded by broadening the synagogue's role, by linking synagogue policy and programs with American social and political developments, and by addressing the evolving needs and interests of American Jews whose ethnic identities extended beyond strictly religious concerns. Synagogues struggled through the Depression years and never succeeded in commanding widespread Jewish interest, but they emerged as institutions more determined than before to build an expansive and relevant religious agenda.

When the Great Depression struck American Jews had just completed a decade of unprecedented synagogue growth. During the 1920s scores of new congregations were built, memberships grew, and synagogue programming reached new heights. From 1916 to 1926 the number of American synagogues almost doubled. The late twenties saw New York Jews spend more than $12 million dollars on synagogue construction, with a significant portion of that money funding the building of synagogue centers. The synagogue center provided social, educational, and recreational facilities, all under the religious auspices of the synagogue. The typical synagogue center contained an auditorium and religious school in addition to a space for worship. More elaborate buildings might include a gymnasium, pool, and even a restaurant (Moore 1981: 122–47). The enormous growth in the number of synagogues and synagogue centers in the 1920s reflected the success and ethnic vision of second generation Jews, but it also involved a hefty capital investment. Confident of future growth and increasing membership, middle-class Jewish communities invested heavily in their synagogues and expected them to thrive.

The Depression brought this decade of synagogue growth to an abrupt halt and left congregations to contend with outstanding loans and formidable mortgage debts. After investing in elaborate buildings and expanding synagogue programs, many congregations suddenly had to struggle to remain fiscally solvent. At the height of the Depression, the president of the Brooklyn Jewish Center candidly explained to congregants, "Our annual interest of $22,000 on the $400,000 first mortgage is actually crushing us" (Brooklyn Jewish Center, Annual Report, 1933). Synagogues throughout the city experienced similar after-shocks from the 1920s building boom. During the Depression, virtually every congregation suffered from an inability to meet financial obligations. A 1936 sample of 456 New York synagogues reported a collective debt of over 14 million dollars.

The unfortunate combination of dwindling incomes and mounting deficits characterized synagogue experience in the 1930s. Rabbi Abba Hillel Silver, a leading figure in the Reform movement, pointedly assessed the state of synagogue affairs:

I was once asked whether I thought that Judaism would die in America. I answered no! the banks won't let it die! We built so many of our institutions on borrowed

money and mortgaged their future incomes. So that in this depression the leaders
of these institutions must wear themselves out in heart-breaking efforts to meet
budgets abnormally swollen by huge interest and amortization charges. (Silver
1932: 45)

In the 1920s, heavily mortgaged synagogues expected to meet their debts with
the dues from a steadily growing membership. Instead, many found themselves
with shrinking memberships, expensive facilities, and large deficits. Reform,
Orthodox, and Conservative congregations shared a common problem in the
Great Depression: their synagogues were in deep financial trouble.

The crisis of Depression prompted a reassessment of the previous decade's
synagogue expansion. Jewish leaders concluded that the progress of the 1920s
had been illusory, based on fleeting prosperity and grandiose plans rather than
true commitment to Judaism. "We are beginning to realize," explained one
Conservative movement publication, "that our duties and obligations to our
religion are not satisfied completely by erecting buildings and providing maintenance." Rabbi Mordecai Kaplan, a pioneer of the synagogue center movement,
acknowledged that "there is too much of a building craze," and attacked the
growing tendency "of relying upon the mere presence of the building to guarantee
a Jewish future." Less than two months after the Wall Street Crash, Kaplan
predicted that "the folly and the waste of putting up structures which are seldom
used and which involve a tremendous overhead will sooner or later become too
flagrant to be permitted to go on" (Mordecai M. Kaplan Diaries, October 10,
1930, December 5, 1929). Reflecting upon the hardships of the Depression,
Rabbi Silver echoed those sentiments, suggesting that, "perhaps in the future we
shall learn to invest more in the essential qualitative purposes and programs of
our institutions and less in brick and stone" (Silver 1932: 45).

As the Depression wore on, synagogues did re-evaluate the content of their
programming, but they had to contend first with urgent financial problems. Most
congregations instituted extensive, often painful, money-saving measures. They
began by scaling down their choirs and limiting synagogue hours and activities
(minutes of Congregation B'nai Jeshurun, Anshe Chesed, and Kane Street
Synagogue, 1931–33). In more drastic budget cuts, synagogues frequently
dismissed personnel, reduced salaries, and sometimes failed to pay their employees for months at a time. The Brooklyn Jewish Center "cut down expenses
in each and every department to rock bottom," operating on what Rabbi Israel
Levinthal called a "starvation diet." In addition to eliminating some of its maintenance and office staff, the Center reduced wages to all remaining synagogue
employees (Brooklyn Jewish Center Collection, 1933). By 1931, the Society for
the Advancement of Judaism (SAJ) had accumulated a $60,000 deficit and owed
its staff thousands of dollars in back salaries (Mordecai M. Kaplan Diaries, April
22, 1931, August 21, 1931). Officials at Kehilath Jeshurun went without pay for
as much as eight months at a time (Minutes of Congregation Kehilath Jeshurun,
June 1, 1932). In 1932 Brooklyn's Kane Street Synagogue told officers that they
"would have to wait indefinitely for their back salaries." One year later, Kane
Street abolished fixed wage scales entirely, determining its ability to pay

employees on a month by month basis (minutes of the Kane Street Synagogue, May 4, 1932, April 3, 1933). At Anshe Chesed, where finances were particularly strained, one board member recommended that, "All persons with whom we have heretofore had obligations to serve for salaries should be told in a spirit of fair play and honesty that if they remain it must be with the understanding that at this time, and until some practical financial plan can be evolved, we are not in a position to pay salaries (Minutes of Congregation Anshe Chesed, February 9, 1931). Salary cuts affected all those involved in the synagogue, including rabbis. Using tactful language, congregational minutes regularly reported that their rabbis had "declined" salary increases or "voluntarily contributed" their wages to the synagogue (minutes of Congregation Kehilath Jeshurun, November 9, 1931; minutes of Congregation B'nai Jeshurun, November 9, 1932). In some cases, congregations could not afford to pay even drastically reduced rabbinic salaries and dismissed their clergy altogether. At the nadir of the Depression, Kaplan noted in his personal diary, "Among those who are bound to suffer most keenly from the demoralizing effect of the present economic depression are the rabbis, the superfluousness of whose calling has become more conspicuous than ever. Most of my colleagues are going through torments of hell" (Mordecai M. Kaplan Diaries, July 2, 1931, April 23, 1931, October 4, 1932). Even at the most affluent synagogues, officers, teachers, and staff routinely remained unpaid for months while their congregations struggled to stay afloat.

Among the greatest obstacles facing synagogues was that they could no longer depend on steady income from membership dues. During the Depression, synagogue memberships plummeted in virtually every congregation. At New York's prestigious Temple Emanu-El, home to the city's most affluent German Jews, membership decreased by 44 percent during the 1930s (Meyer 1988: 307). The Brooklyn Jewish Center had hoped to attract 1,500 members by the mid-thirties, but instead struggled to retain just over half that number (minutes of Brooklyn Jewish Center, January 18, 1934). The precipitous decline in membership resulted not simply from lack of interest in synagogue life, but from the inability or unwillingness of many congregants to continue paying dues. During the Depression, many members formally resigned from synagogues or simply stopped paying dues. Congregational minutes from the 1930s contain frequent reports of members being suspended for failure to meet dues obligations, but most synagogues allowed congregants at least a year's grace period before removing them from the membership rolls. As a rule, synagogues developed policies that gave consideration to their congregants' individual circumstances, frequently waiving and postponing membership fees (Minutes of Congregation Kehilath Jeshurun, November 9, 1931; minutes of Kane Street Synagogue, February 27, 1933). Dues requirements were slashed in almost every congregation. Synagogues desperately needed to retain congregants and did whatever they could to keep members on their books.

In an era of economic contraction, synagogue membership often became an expendable luxury. The reasons for withdrawing from or declining to join synagogues varied, as did the individual experiences of Jews during the Depression. Many Jews affiliated with synagogues only to celebrate life-cycle events. Sydney

Evans, who grew up in Brooklyn, remembered that, "When the time came to be Bar-Mitzvahed [my family] joined . . . and when it was over, it kind of faded away." Evans explained that his parents, like so many other Jews in the thirties, were too preoccupied with the daily struggles of securing work and raising children to take much interest in the synagogue. Another Depression-era youth reported a different story, recalling that his father had attended synagogue regularly until his business failed. "With the Depression," he reflected, "things changed with my father even in religious practice. Before, he never failed to take us to the synagogue every single Saturday. After the crash he didn't seem to care anymore." For other Jews, lack of participation in the synagogue was more a financial than a psychological matter. Edwin Shapiro, who grew up in Flatbush, remembered celebrating his Bar-Mitzvah in 1934, but indicated that his parents did not belong to a synagogue because it "required some financial identity," which the family did not possess. Financial considerations drove the synagogue choices of many Jews. Irving Howe recalled that in his Bronx neighborhood, "The nearest synagogue, in a once baroque structure, was also struggling through the Depression, and as if to acknowledge reduced circumstances my own bar mitzvah took place not there, since that would have cost too much and probably made us feel uncomfortable" (Howe 1982: 3). Resigning from a synagogue was not necessarily the result of impoverishment; many congregants simply chose to eliminate synagogue dues from strained household budgets. As Mordecai Kaplan observed in the mid-thirties, "There is a growing tendency to treat synagogue affiliation as a luxury to be enjoyed when times are good and money plentiful. But as soon as the financial status of the members slumps, the affiliation is one of the first luxuries to be surrendered" (Kaplan 1981: 293).

Many Jews attended synagogue only on Rosh Hashanah and Yom Kippur and purchased tickets for those days alone. Stanley Katz recalled that his family bought High Holiday tickets every year. "You had a special ticket fee you would pay," Katz explained, "and you could attend holiday services without having to be an annual member." For Jews who had neither the income nor the desire to become regular synagogue members, High Holiday tickets provided a useful solution. Synagogues usually charged set fees for worship during Rosh Hashanah and Yom Kippur, the peak days for synagogue attendance. Many congregations offered free High Holiday admission to those who could not pay, but obtaining the free seats often required special application. The Institutional Synagogue, for example, explained that "upon application, unemployed people, home relief recipients and children will be given free seats." Yet many Jews would not submit to the humiliation of formally declaring impoverishment in order to gain admission to the synagogue. Despite the best intentions of congregations to serve the Jewish poor, most synagogues remained, in the words of Mordecai Kaplan, "the exclusive clubhouse of a homogeneous group," often alienating the poor and working class (Kaplan 1981: 292).

Many Jewish leaders hoped, perhaps mistakenly, that the Great Depression would spark a spiritual revival. Religious renewal efforts gained momentum with the implementation of the New Deal, as congregations mimicked and capitalized upon the spirit of Roosevelt's recovery programs. In 1933 Rabbi Herbert

Goldstein of the Institutional Synagogue urged Jewish leaders to seize the moment and initiate a meaningful revival program. "While the entire nation has enlisted in the very worthy cause of restoring economic prosperity to the United States, little has been done to repair the depleted state of our religious institutions," Goldstein insisted. "The best minds in the country have been drafted in the noble effort to bring back prosperity, but no religious or lay leaders have taken any steps to revive our weakened institutions." In the years after Roosevelt's election, religious leaders hoped to create a movement for spiritual renewal. Taking their cue from New Deal programs, Jewish, Catholic, and Protestant organizations united in a "Drive for Religious Recovery." The campaign urged complete attendance in churches and synagogues during one weekend in October of 1935. Known as "loyalty days," the two days of worship were advertised as a means "to show united leadership in spiritual recovery." Jewish organizations promoted the day as "loyalty Sabbath," using the slogan, "every Jew present and accounted for" (*Orthodox Union*, October 1933: 1; August 1935: 1). There is little evidence to suggest the realization of a religious revival, but Jewish leaders persisted nonetheless, hoping to capture for the synagogue what Roosevelt had promised for the nation.

Among all New Deal initiatives no Roosevelt program sparked as much rhetoric in religious circles as did the National Recovery Administration (NRA). Established in 1933, the NRA negotiated codes for industries, determining hours, wages, and rates of production. While Roosevelt proposed the NRA as a tool for economic recovery, synagogue leaders seized upon it as a polemic device. By using the political terminology of the New Deal, Jewish commentators articulated Jewish commitment to the national recovery effort while also attempting to emulate Roosevelt's far-reaching renewal tactics within Jewish life.

For religious leaders, the NRA not only epitomized the spirit of revitalization, but equally important, promoted the five-day work week. Jewish organizations hoped that Jews who were freed from Saturday employment would embrace the opportunity to observe the Sabbath. "The NRA will . . . revolutionize the Sabbath," declared the United Synagogue, which represented Conservative congregations, "the new standard of working hours for the individual means that the Sabbath will be a real day of rest" (Congregation B'nai Jeshurun Collection, October 3, 1933). Representatives from all branches of Jewish life embraced the promise of the NRA. Like many other rabbis, Herbert Goldstein made the NRA the subject of his 1933 Rosh Hashanah sermon, proclaiming to the congregation:

> I regard the NRA as singularly Providential for the restoration of the observance of the Sabbath. It will bring on I am sure (if only we seize its possibilities), a religious revival to both Jew and Christian. Work and physical enjoyment were rapidly supplanting rest and the religious exhilaration of the Sabbath. With the introduction of the five day work week throughout the nation, there will be one day for the recreation of the body and the other for the recreation of the soul.

Other Jewish leaders echoed Goldstein's sentiment, declaring that "the opportunity for which countless Sabbath-loving Jews have been hoping is at hand . . .

Now the 'I-would-if-I-could' Jew can, if he will, observe Shabboth [*sic*]"
(*Orthodox Union*, September 1933: 2). The NRA met with similar enthusiasm
from leaders throughout the Jewish community. The Synagogue Council of
America, representing the three major bodies of American Judaism, hailed the
NRA as a spiritual antidote, capable of "bringing the Sabbath back to the Jews"
(*New York Times*, December 16, 1933, p. 3). In fact, the NRA brought no
discernible change in Sabbath observance; American Jews rarely attended synagogue or set aside the Sabbath as a day of rest. The fervent enthusiasm about the
NRA and the five-day work week revealed much more about changes in synagogue strategy and rhetoric than it did about general patterns of religious
observance.

The possibility for greater Sabbath observance was not the only benefit that
religious leaders hoped to reap from the NRA. They also wanted to build a mass
movement for religious recovery modeled after Roosevelt's sweeping economic
programs. As Israel Levinthal proclaimed in his 1933 Rosh Hashanah sermon,
"We need an NRA in American Jewish life, a resolve on the part of every Jew
to bring about a recovery of those ideals that have given strength and vitality to
Jewish life in all the ages past." Levinthal outlined the symbolism of each letter
of the NRA acronym, explaining that the "N" represented the nationality of
Israel, both in Palestine and throughout the world; the "R" stood for the religion
of Israel, which he claimed required a "New Deal" in order to survive; finally,
the "A" emphasized the importance of action, of demonstrating Jewish commitment through deed (Brooklyn Jewish Center Collection, September 1933).

Jewish leaders capitalized upon the spirit of national recovery, using the NRA
as a springboard for promoting religious revival. In the fall of 1933, the United
Synagogue told its constituents that "the synagogue should meet the challenge
presented by the NRA. It should initiate the new era with the proclamation of
a Spiritual Recovery Act." Declaring its efforts an "historic event in the life
of American Jewry," the United Synagogue organized a National Recovery
Assembly with representatives from over 750 Conservative congregations and
associations. The major issues addressed by the Assembly – reviving the Sabbath,
channeling new leisure time produced by the NRA into Jewish educational,
cultural, and spiritual pursuits, and democratizing the synagogue in order to
attract a broader constituency – represented the central concerns of congregations from all branches of American Judaism. While Roosevelt's NRA was as a
useful and heavily exploited vehicle for calling attention to religious issues, its
primary contribution to American synagogues was to provide the rhetoric for
addressing key problems within organized Jewish religion (Congregation B'nai
Jeshurun Collection, November 12, 1933).

The pressing concern of most synagogues was attracting the interest of the
Jewish public. Critics of synagogue behavior emphasized that the Jew "does not
. . . reject the synagogue; he ignores it" (*Central Conference of American Rabbis
[CCAR] Yearbook* 1938: 205). During the Depression, religious leaders worked
to change synagogue atmosphere and address contemporary issues in an effort
to appeal to a broader segment of the Jewish population. They also attempted to
destroy the image of the synagogue as an elitist institution. With the spirit of

social democracy permeating New Deal politics, congregations emphasized the need to apply democratic principles to synagogue life. Bringing democracy to the synagogue meant accepting members regardless of financial status and including them fully in congregational affairs. At the National Recovery Assembly, the United Synagogue resolved to create membership categories "so as to enable the man and woman of the smallest means to share in the honors and responsibilities of the synagogue." The organization further declared that "financial and social snobbery should have no place in the synagogue. A true spirit of old-fashioned Jewish democracy should permeate every synagogal activity" (Congregation B'nai Jeshurun Collection, November 12, 1933). In fact, the democratic spirit had never been a vital element in American synagogues, which were generally supported and governed by an economic and social elite. The new emphasis on equality in the synagogue was a conscious attempt to broaden the base of congregational support, but equally important, it underlined the commonality of Jewish and American ideals and championed the cause of democracy. As Europe fell victim to right-wing political movements in the 1930s, American Jews became more concerned than before about preserving the principles of American democracy. The president of the Union of American Hebrew Congregations (UAHC) insisted that the synagogue, "cannot afford to overlook the trends and tendencies of present-day American life. In these days when democracy is everywhere on the defensive, we Jews must more than ever affirm it – and especially in the synagogue." By calling for democracy in Jewish congregations and mimicking New Deal programs, synagogues portrayed the essential harmony of Jewish ad American pursuits. The attempt to bring democracy to Jewish congregations was, then, both an effort to attract a larger synagogue constituency as well as part of the synagogue's response to the political and social climate.

The endeavor to heighten synagogue appeal and create relevant programming also included a new emphasis on the Jewish working class. "The bane of the synagogue in this country," insisted Mordecai Kaplan, "has been its confinement to the middle class" (Kaplan 1981: 427). At the National Recovery Assembly, United Synagogue representatives discussed ways to draw the masses of Jewish workers to the synagogue. They not only stressed the importance of attracting Jewish laborers, but also declared that "the synagogue must take an active interest in all problems affecting the worker, such as the relationships between employer and employee, exploitation of labor, [and] general problems of social justice" (Congregation B'nai Jeshurun Collection, November 12, 1933). The Reform movement acted most vigorously in the field of social justice, accelerating its efforts during the Depression years. As early as 1931, the Central Conference of American Rabbis (CCAR) formally endorsed federal public works projects, relief programs, unemployment insurance, and even encouraged industry profit-sharing. In order to implement its social justice program within the synagogue, the CCAR recommended that congregations employ only those firms that supported organized labor and collective bargaining (*Central Conference of American Rabbis* (CCAR) *Yearbook* 1931: 86–91). None of these programs succeeded in attracting large numbers of working-class Jews to the synagogue. Nevertheless, while institutional proclamations did not assure compliance or support for workers, the explicitly political role outlined for the synagogue was a significant innovation.

The themes of social justice and economic reform were not limited to the resolutions of national organizations, but also reiterated in individual synagogue programs and rabbinic sermons. Several congregations responded to the call for social justice with volunteer projects and fundraising efforts for the unemployed. With the implementation of relief programs, New York synagogues often served as unofficial liaisons between the jobless and the city's relief offices (minutes of Congregation B'nai Jeshurun, December 2, 1930). In addition, rabbis used their pulpits to draw lessons from the Depression experience. Rabbi Israel Levinthal, known for applying Jewish teachings to contemporary issues, told his audience that the "whole social structure needs revision. There is something radically wrong with an economic system that keeps men, who want and are able to work, out of employment." According to Levinthal, lobbying for social and economic reform could be equated with pursuing the religious goal of *Mishpat*, justice. A few years later, Levinthal put his theories into action by helping to mediate a labor dispute at Brooklyn's Beth Moses Hospital.

Not all rabbis agreed that the pulpit was the proper place to discuss contemporary social and economic concerns. As one Orthodox publication proclaimed, "We believe that the rabbi should not stoop to the discussion . . . of economic problems, for then he generally becomes sophomoric. He is not a teacher of economics, but of religion. What we need today is to make our people understand that our economic, social and political problems are basically personal religious ones" (*Orthodox Union*, February 1936: 3). But despite some detractors, the trend toward extending the realm of synagogue concerns to include the social and political arena persisted. During the Depression years, synagogues heightened consciousness and encouraged discussion about social and economic issues. Ultimately, religious leaders were more successful in formulating progressive social platforms than in attracting large numbers of Jewish workers to the synagogue. Nevertheless, the introduction of political themes and the focus upon social issues was one of the most meaningful changes instituted in Depression-era synagogues.

Some Jewish leaders anticipated that the economic crisis might revive religious enthusiasm. In both Jewish and Christian circles, hopes for a return to religion increased with the onset of the Depression. "Some religious leaders actually hailed the depression with rejoicing," explained a Chicago Theological Seminary professor, "since they had the idea that previous depressions had 'driven men to God' and felt that the time was overdue for men again to be reminded of the need to let the spiritual dominate the materialistic order" (Kincheloe 1937: 1, 94–5). Synagogue officials similarly hoped that the crisis might spark a spiritual renewal among American Jews. In 1932, the CCAR's president reminded his rabbinic colleagues that, "The rehabilitation of a disordered world presents to religious leaders an opportunity and a challenge." He urged synagogue leaders to "furnish the dynamic spiritual force to maintain the morale of people in these trying days," insisting that "if we religious leaders are equal to the task, the ultimate result of this depression will yet be a gain for things of the spirit" (CCAR *Yearbook* 1932: 155).

But the economic crisis did not precipitate a mass religious return. While some Jews undoubtedly found comfort in the synagogue, enthusiasm for Roosevelt and the New Deal and the daily challenges of Depression-era life far eclipsed religious concerns for most Jewish Americans. In examining the religious response to the Depression, the *Christian Century* reported that most Americans attributed the Depression to "the failure of human intelligence or the blind power of entrenched privilege, or both." Therefore, they opted to look for solutions in the human rather than in the divine realm. Moreover, Depression discontent did more to rally fundamentalist and reactionary movements than to reinvigorate mainstream religion. In the field of religion, the thirties are best remembered as the era of such leaders as Father Coughlin, William Pelley, Gerald L. K. Smith, and Father Divine (Marty 1991: 258–302). In 1937, New York's Social Science Research Council reported the meager accomplishments of organized religion during the Depression, concluding that the country's religious movements had not "reaped a large harvest during these lean years of economic life" (Kincheloe 1937: 95).

Jewish leaders joined the chorus lamenting the decline of religious devotion during the Depression years. As early as 1931 the Orthodox Rabbinical Association identified a "'spiritual depression' in American religious life" and vowed to prevent the economic crisis from bringing about a complete "moratorium on religion" (*New York Times*, August 11, 1931, p. 44). While pronouncements of doom about the imminent decay of Jewish life and impassioned pleas for greater religious commitment were hardly new to the American Jewish community, the Depression brought a sense of urgency to apprehensions about the Jewish future. Rabbis and synagogue leaders seized upon the metaphor of recovery, in part, because they perceived their institutions to be as morally and financially bankrupt as the nation as a whole. In the mid-thirties, one Jewish sociologist went so far as to claim that "the Jewish religion as a social institution is losing its influence for the perpetuation of the Jewish group" and predicted "the total eclipse of the Jewish church in America " (Engelman 1935–6: 44). As synagogue memberships plummeted, congregations struggled to remain fiscally solvent, and Jews looked elsewhere for personal and political solutions, the future of institutional Judaism looked particularly grim.

The Great Depression did not bring about a sudden lack of interest in Judaism, but rather exposed long-term trends in American synagogues. Even before the Depression, only a minority of American Jews were affiliated with synagogues and fewer attended regularly. In 1935, three-quarters of New York's Jewish youth reported that they had not attended any religious services during the past year. A 1929 study revealed that almost 80 percent of Jewish children in New York City received no religious training whatsoever and had never learned the Hebrew alphabet (Engelman 1935–6: 50–1). The lack of interest in the synagogue was nothing new to the American Jewish community; even during the enormous synagogue expansion of the 1920s, only a minority of Jews joined, supported, or attended congregations. But in the twenties, despite ongoing concerns about

religious apathy, synagogues were able to carry out and even expand congregational programming. The Depression revealed the narrow base of synagogue
support and brought to light the precariousness of relying upon a small group to
sustain Jewish institutions. For years, congregations had underlined the importance of reaching a broader constituency, but the economic crisis made that
need even more pressing. The Depression forced synagogue leaders to search for
some means to revitalize congregations and make them relevant and responsive
to the needs of Depression-era Jews.

Congregations had offered social and recreational activities long before the
Depression, but unemployment and limited working hours created more leisure
time, breathing new life into the synagogue's secular programming. During the
Depression, Jewish centers that housed pools and gymnasiums found their
facilities taxed to capacity. Between 1931 and 1935, while the Brooklyn Jewish
Center experienced dramatic losses in general membership, over four thousand
new members came to use its gym (Brooklyn Jewish Center Collection, January
16, 1934, January 17, 1935). Jews flocked to synagogue centers to use physical
education facilities and also to participate in social and cultural activities. "We
have more social, literary, and athletic clubs . . . today than ever before in our
history," declared Rabbi Goldstein, assessing the Institutional Synagogue's
programs in 1934. "This is due," he added, "to the present unemployment
situation. Our young people have more leisure now than ever before."
Depression-era synagogues underlined the importance of making the synagogue
a gathering place for youth, noting that "this leisure will shape the character of
the individual for good or bad." Since increased leisure time affected adults as
well as youth, several congregations initiated adult education programs that
attracted hundreds of men and women who wanted "to utilize the extra leisure
hours to some useful purpose" (Brooklyn Jewish Center Collection, January 18,
1934). The city's large Jewish centers sponsored the widest array of leisure-time
activities for both young and old, but even the smallest congregations organized
social programs, youth groups, sporting events, and cultural activities. The
United Synagogue insisted that Jewish congregations owed it to their members
to alter programming in response to Depression-era conditions and "to step in
and see that this leisure is used for spiritual and character building purposes"
(Congregation B'nai Jeshurun Collection, October 3, 1933). As the Depression
wore on, New York congregations became more convinced than ever that expansive synagogue programming answered the needs of Depression-era Jews and
provided a prescription to heal Jewish alienation from the synagogue.

Filling increased leisure time was only one way that Depression-era synagogues
hoped to widen their appeal. Many congregations also initiated practical
programs to improve Jewish economic status and employment options. Many
religious leaders believed that by actively working to better the Jewish economic
condition, synagogues could capture a central role in the lives of American Jews.
"In the direction of economic life, there is a great opportunity for the Synagog,"
one rabbi proclaimed. "When men and women, young and old, will see that the
Synagog is alive to their needs in the economic area of life," he optimistically and
mistakenly predicted, "their allegiance and devotion to Judaism will become

much stronger and more enduring" (CCAR *Yearbook* 1937: 244). Responding according to their own ideological positions, religious organizations proposed various solutions to ease the Jewish economic burden. At the 1937 meeting of the Reform movement's rabbinical conference, Rabbi Samuel Wohl proposed the creation of Jewish Economic Councils that would operate under the auspices of the synagogue (ibid.). Orthodox synagogues initiated some of the best-organized efforts to help Jews find jobs that would not require Saturday work. As early as 1930, Orthodox congregations in the Bronx joined forces to compile lists of employers willing to hire Sabbath-observant workers. New York's Young Israel, a modern Orthodox movement designed to appeal to American-born youth, provided more far-reaching employment services. The Young Israel Employment Bureau, first organized in 1925, expanded its activities during the Depression, offering both job placement and vocational training. The number of young Jews whose employment problems stemmed from a refusal to work on Saturdays was admittedly small. Nevertheless, Young Israel's efforts to secure jobs for Jews reflected the Orthodox movement's attempt to address Depression-era economic needs in accordance with its religious agenda. In the 1930s, synagogues across the Jewish spectrum not only brought secular programming into the house of worship, but also extended religious endeavors into the political and economic realm.

Behind religious employment efforts and various synagogue proposals to aid the Jewish economy lay real fears about Jewish status and security in America. Jewish employment bureaus and attempts to diversify the Jewish economic profile were, in part, a response to job discrimination and prejudice. Many non-observant Jews came to the Young Israel Employment Bureau because it offered protection from anti-Semitism and job discrimination. National and city-wide organizations played the most prominent role in combating anti-Semitism, but synagogues also responded to the growing threat. As anti-Semitism peaked in the 1930s, religious organizations worked even harder to maintain support from Jews, not only by devising schemes to preserve Jewish economic health, but also by arguing that participation in synagogue life helped to fortify Jewish self-respect in the face of anti-Semitism. In 1933 the UAHC provided a sample letter that congregations could send to members who had resigned from the synagogue. The letter emphasized that no matter what economic hardships members had endured, they could not afford "*not* to be a member of the Temple" because of the threat of anti-Semitism. The synagogue reminded withdrawing members that anti-Semites "are capitalizing the fact that a number of Jews are in the confidence of the Federal Administration and they are capitalizing the fact that men such as you and I have been reasonably successful in our respective fields." Retaining synagogue membership, according to the UAHC, was crucial in order for Jews to demonstrate loyalty and pride in the face of prejudice. Throughout the Depression synagogues became more concerned with raising Jewish self-respect. Synagogues joined the battle against anti-Semitism, hoping, often without success, that the struggle would produce "a more concentrated social energy and a finer spirituality" (Kaplan 1981: 76).

Many synagogues championed Jewish education as the best means to raise

Jewish esteem and struggled to keep their schools open. Officials at the Brooklyn Jewish Center admitted that "the apathy prevailing in the field of Jewish education" had resulted in a significant loss of students and a growing number of unpaid tuition fees, but the Center was proud of its ability to sustain educational programs "despite hard financial conditions" (Brooklyn Jewish Center Collection, January 17, 1935, January 16, 1936). The Institutional Synagogue's Talmud Torah experienced similar difficulties but also managed to stay afloat. Using the motto, "a religious education for every child, regardless of financial circumstances," the Institutional Synagogue school, like most in the city, struggled but did not collapse during the Depression years.

In virtually every Depression-era synagogue school, Zionism became a central concern. "Palestine . . . gives tone to everything that we do educationally," declared the president of the National Council for Jewish Education in 1934. "It is the leit motif in all our cultural efforts." The 1930s were a turning point in American Zionism, a decade that witnessed widespread support for the Zionist cause among both Jewish laity and professionals. By 1930, an estimated one in five Jewish families had at least one member who had joined a Zionist organization (Halperin 1961: 61–111). The American Zionist movement, which included a range of convictions from religious Zionism to socialist Zionism to cultural Zionism, grew substantially in the Depression decade, as American Jews responded to the crisis of European Jewry and came to believe that Palestine could provide both a refuge for Jews and a center for Jewish culture. Within American Jewish life, Zionism was not a movement that required Jews to relocate to Palestine, but rather an ideology that offered a foundation for Jewish identity and ethnic survival in America. Given the concern with maintaining Jewish identity and culture in Depression-era America, Jewish educators seized upon Zionism as a tool for Jewish renewal.

At a time when synagogues had little success in reviving religious devotion, Zionism offered a program capable of eliciting Jewish support and enthusiasm. "Jewish life . . . is precisely in the stage of trying to find itself – trying to find a new point of view to live today," declared one Jewish professional in 1933, claiming that "Zionism seems to offer the only possible substitute." In the midst of the Depression, historian Jacob Marcus observed that "Zionism has prevented the *morale* of many from completely collapsing . . . Zionism brings [Jews] comfort; it instills new hope in them by emphasizing the fact that they belong spiritually, at least, to a group with whom they share a tradition of a courageous past and the hope for a better future." (Halperin 1961: 25–6). For Jewish leaders searching for some means to invigorate American Judaism, Zionism offered a strong cultural message with far greater appeal than calls for renewed religious commitment.

The enormous expansion of Jewish youth groups in the 1930s testified to the power of the Zionist cause. Zionist-oriented youth groups grew rapidly in the Depression years, attracting thousands of new members. Nevertheless radical politics continued to command much greater allegiance from Jewish youth than did the Zionist movement, a fact that constantly frustrated Zionist leaders. Despite this, American Zionism did make significant inroads in the 1930s. Jewish youth who demonstrated little interest in religious worship often responded to the Zionist message, which was usually infused with a socialist spirit and a program for economic justice. Synagogue officials who lamented that Jewish youth were "indifferent to the spiritual intensity of their forebears," became convinced that cultural Zionism, with its emphasis on Jewish peoplehood and ethnic persistence, was uniquely capable of sustaining Jewish identity in the next generation.

Zionism certainly did not draw most Jews back to the synagogue, but it was quickly embraced as a key component of Depression-era synagogue life. By incorporating Zionism within the synagogue agenda, congregations broadened their message to reach a generation of Jews whose ethnic identities extended beyond religious concerns. As the Depression decade drew to a close, Zionism was poised to become a foundation for Jewish identity, preserving and enhancing ethnic consciousness both inside and outside the synagogue walls.

The Depression was a time of both crisis and consolidation in American synagogues, less a dramatic turning point than a period of hardship that accelerated ongoing trends in congregational life. The economic crisis neither heralded the demise of the synagogue as skeptics had predicted nor precipitated the religious revival for which leaders had hoped. In the 1930s, synagogues endured financial problems, membership loss, and spiritual malaise, but few congregations collapsed and most proved to be resilient. In 1933, Isidor Fine, president of the Brooklyn Jewish Center, jokingly remarked that despite the crisis, "the Brooklyn Jewish Center [had] kept its head above water . . . [and] in this respect we did better than Mr. Hoover" (Brooklyn Jewish Center Collection, January 19, 1933).

After World War II, American Jews initiated another synagogue-building boom which eclipsed the level of growth produced in the 1920s. In the post-World War II era, synagogue affiliation and religious school enrollment peaked as a new generation of Jews moved from urban centers to the suburbs (Wertheimer 1987: 123–32). The fiscal crisis that characterized synagogue experience in the Depression years disappeared in the postwar prosperity, but the lessons of the 1930s remained important to American congregations. Depression-era synagogues reaped few benefits from their efforts to heighten synagogue appeal by extending the religious umbrella to embrace social and secular concerns. Yet the much-heralded post-World War II religious revival owed much to the synagogue's expansive religious vision. American Jews of the 1940s and 1950s joined synagogues in unprecedented numbers, but attending worship services remained a minority phenomenon. The postwar revival was primarily a reflection of the Jewish desire to maintain ethnic identity, to associate with other Jews, and to educate Jewish children in the basic principles of Judaism. Although the blueprint for integrating the secular and the sacred emerged before the Depression, synagogues survived a decade of religious apathy and stagnation by refining the parameters of an inclusive religious agenda, laying the groundwork for an institutional Judaism in which religion and ethnicity were inextricably intertwined.

BIBLIOGRAPHY

Note: The following is an abbreviated list of sources used for this essay. A number of short quotations are from personal interviews, interview transcripts, and bulletins too numerous to cite here. A longer version of this essay, complete with full annotation, can be found in Chapter 7 of my book, *New York Jews and the Great Depression: Uncertain Promise* (1996), New Haven, Conn.: Yale University Press.

Archival sources and periodicals

Brooklyn Jewish Center, Annual reports, New York Public Library.
Brooklyn Jewish Center Collection, Joseph and Miriam Ratner Center for the Study of Conservative Judaism, Jewish Theological Seminary, New York.
Central Conference of American Rabbis (CCAR) *Yearbook*.
Congregation Anshe Chesed, New York, congregational minutes.
Congregation B'nai Jeshurun, New York, congregational minutes.
Congregation Kehilath Jeshurun, New York, congregational minutes.
Kane Street Synagogue, New York, congregational minutes.
Mordecai M. Kaplan Diaries, Jewish Theological Seminary of America, New York.
The New York Times
The Orthodox Union

Books and articles

Engelman, Uriah Zevi (1935–6) "The Jewish synagogue in the United States," *American Journal of Sociology* 41, pp. 44–51.
Halperin, Samuel (1961) *The Political World of American Zionism*, Detroit, Mich.: Wayne State University Press; reprinted Silver Spring, Md.: Information Dynamics, 1985.
Handy, Robert T. (1960) "The American religious Depression, 1925–1935," *Church History* 29/1 (March), pp. 3–16.
Howe, Irving (1982) *A Margin of Hope: An Intellectual Autobiography*, New York: Harcourt Brace Jovanovich.
Kaplan, Mordecai M. (1981) *Judaism as a Civilization: Toward a Reconstruction of American-Jewish Life*, Philadelphia, Pa.: Jewish Publication Society of America and Reconstructionist Press; first published New York: Macmillan, 1934.
Kincheloe, Samuel C. (1937) *Research Memorandum on Religion in the Depression*, Social Science Research Council Bulletin no. 33, New York: Social Science Research Council.
Marty, Martin E. (1991) *Modern American Religion*, vol. 2, *The Noise of Conflict*, 1919–1941, Chicago: University of Chicago Press.
Meyer, Michael A. (1988) *Response to Modernity: A History of the Reform Movement in Judaism*, New York: Oxford University Press.
Moore, Deborah Dash (1981) *At Home in America: Second Generation New York Jews*, New York: Columbia University Press.

Silver, Abba Hillel (1932) "The relation of the Depression to the cultural and spiritual values of American Jewry," *Jewish Social Service Quarterly* 9/1 (December), pp. 44–8.

Wertheimer, Jack (1987) "The conservative synagogue," in Jack Wertheimer (ed.) *The American Synagogue: A Sanctuary Transformed,* New York: Cambridge University Press, pp. 111–49.

Chapter 10

Shifting Ground and the Third Transformation of Mormonism

Philip L. Barlow

Twenty-three centuries ago Aristotle posed a problem: if a person were to replace the planks of a ship with fresh planks, one by one, at what point would the original vessel become a new one? Bearing in mind such difficulties of identity and continuity, it is nonetheless possible to suggest that the dominant form of Mormonism – the Church of Jesus Christ of Latter-day Saints whose head-quarters are in Salt Lake City – is in the midst of its third transformation. The original Mormon ark has become a new ship twice over, and is, as it approaches the twenty-first century, achieving its fourth incarnation. These transformations, moreover, are tied to the shifting physical terrain the movement has occupied and to believers' and outsiders' conceptions of this terrain. Mormonism's essence is religious, but geography has always conditioned the religion. A geographic lens can reveal otherwise obscure dimensions of the story.

The prospect of a meditation on geography is sure to prompt yawns somewhere. Those hoping to comprehend religion, however, ignore geography at their peril. The peril is severe, for example, if one aspires to know biblical religion yet fails to see that the Hebrew Bible is in part a vast tract probing the thesis, "This land is mine; God gave this land to me." Neither does one know Islam without exploring Muslims' Mecca-consciousness, nor Native American religion apart from the land and its products, nor Eastern Orthodoxy and Roman Catholicism without a feel for their respective locational groundings. Promised lands, sanctified cities, consecrated temples, sacred rivers, taboo forests, holy mountains, and hallowed directions all evoke the meshing of religion and interpreted space.

All this presses particularly on Mormonism. Millennialists by definition have doted on time, but Mormons have been yet more preoccupied with space. Sacred and secular space and their collisions have, indeed, helped to define the evolving Mormon ship, which rode in the nineteenth century on the turbulent waves of an expanding United States, and in the twentieth century on the tumultuous contraction of a once-large planet. Among the plausible ways to discern points at which the old ship became new, one may suggest four distinct stages of the movement: (1) the original Church of Christ founded in 1830 in New York state as the restoration of primitive Christianity, freshly complemented with a living prophet, the only legitimate priesthood, and the Book of Mormon; (2) the immensely more complex, geographically concentrated, and half-Hebraicized church-kingdom that, after rapid evolutions in Ohio and Missouri in the 1830s, achieved full expression first at Nauvoo, Illinois, in the early 1840s, and then in spatially magnified form during the next half-century in Utah Territory; (3) the still-western, post-1890 church, almost become an ethnic entity unto itself through its past geographic and social isolation, but shorn of its official theocratic character and striving for national respectability; and (4) the international "correlated" church that arose in the 1960s and began to come into its own as a new world religion in the latter decades of the twentieth century. It is this immense, expanding church, subject to a global program of reorganization, coordination, bureaucratization, and simplification of doctrine, curricula, and purpose that points to Mormonism's emerging shape for the twenty-first century.

In the Beginning

Place is not merely occupied ground, but space conceived as one thing rather than another. A sense of place was woven into the fabric of Mormon origins. So recurrent were the fires of religious fervor sweeping antebellum upstate New York that the region earned the label "burnt-over district." And it was just this region's tumult of revivals and religious opinions that perplexed the young Joseph Smith.

Working on his father's farm and engaged in a variety of pursuits, including the hunt for buried treasure by occult means (a quest not uncommon in his subculture and from which he later disengaged himself), young Joseph determined to ask God the way out of his spiritual confusion. In the spring of 1820, as he later recalled it, Smith beheld a vision of God and Christ, who instructed the boy, aged 14, to join none of the existing churches. Subsequent revelations confirmed that the original Christian church had fallen into apostasy at the end of the apostolic era. Smith learned too that he was the vessel through which God was about to accomplish a wonder: the restoration of "the fullness of the gospel," of the true church, of the exclusively authorized priesthood, and of a conduit – Smith himself – for ongoing revelation, the pre-eminent example of which was the Book of Mormon.

Beyond even the Bible, land consciousness saturates the Book of Mormon from its opening narratives. Produced by Smith's inspired translation of inscriptions on ancient gold plates, these narratives tell of the family and descendants of a Hebrew patriarch, Lehi. Prior to Judah's Babylonian captivity in the sixth century BCE, God led Lehi from Jerusalem and, like Moses and Abraham, into the wilderness and thence to a promised land: in this case America. The balance of the record centers on the long struggle of Lehi's descendants with God, with one another, and with and for the land. After a millennium of such struggle, one segment of these descendants annihilated the other in a relentless civil war, both sides having ignored the pleas and threats of their prophets. Among the last of these was Mormon, who recorded and edited the history of his people on metal plates. Buried, then revealed 1,400 years later to Joseph Smith, this record is, among other things, a treatise on sacred geography, a meditation on God's intent for America, a land "choice above all other lands."

Thus, in the early nineteenth century, the Book of Mormon proclaimed that God had long ago spoken to the "new" world and now spoke again. To a millennially-conscious antebellum people, intoxicated with the unencumbered possibilities open to them and the seemingly infinite room for expansion, yet at the same time cut off from traditional moorings, the Mormon record reconnected heaven and earth. In this it echoed the Bible, though with enhanced geographic and temporal proximity for its readers. To a young and still experimental American nation – exuberant, insecure, and chaotic in its new freedom from monarchy and church establishments – the Book of Mormon bequeathed the possibility of a religious authority, religious direction, religious security, and religious history. That history was a model of civilization gone wrong, a prophetic warning for the infant republic: heed God, or be destroyed even in the promised land.

Vitalized, then, by a new scripture, by a restored and exclusively authorized ancient priesthood, and by a prophet in ongoing communication with God, the new church organized formally at Fayette, New York, in April 1830 and rapidly attracted seekers.

The First Transformation

Little more than a dozen years later, Mormonism – now transplanted to the Midwest – had become something different. Rejected by its neighbors to the point of plunder and mob violence, Latter-day Saint theology had grown so distinct that believers ever since have felt obliged to defend their very real Christian allegiance. The small band of followers thriving in 1830 had expanded by 1844 to 30,000 souls. More remarkably, the church had, without surrendering its churchness, become also a kingdom – not merely a symbolic but an actualizing New Israel, at once religious, political, and economic; at once Christian, American, Hebrew, and esoteric. Its privately polygynous prophet served also as chief military officer over a considerable and largely independent branch of the Illinois state militia. The prophet and general was also mayor and king (or at least allegedly king, privately but apparently literally anointed). And the defensive army and church-municipality-kingdom over which he presided constituted the largest city in the state. Half of all Mormons resided in the environs of this city, and to it all were beckoned. The Prophet discarded Commerce, the worldly name of the incipient town, and rechristened it Nauvoo: Hebrew, he said, for "a beautiful place." With an astonishing vision, will, and faith, Joseph Smith consecrated this space, turning it into the sacred global vortex captured by Richard Bushman: "a funnel that collected people from the widest possible periphery and drew them like gravity into a central point" (1997: 5). And at the symbolic center of this center, at the city's high point, the Prophet directed construction of the temple, the ultimate Mormon sacred space, in which living Saints would ritually re-enact their cosmology; take or renew oaths of loyalty, virtue, and sacrifice; and vicariously perform ordinances for the dead as an aid in salvation. All this attests a breathtakingly rapid metamorphosis from the Mormonism of 1830. How had it happened?

Change had begun within months of the movement's birth back in New York. In Aristotelian terms, the planks of the original ship began early on to be replaced – or, more often, added to in ways that changed the ship's nature – though a new craft was not in full sail until the years immediately preceding Smith's murder at the hands of an Illinois mob in 1844. Revelations received by the Prophet spurred the transformation. Many of these were canonized in what became the *Doctrine and Covenants*, a volume Mormons came to accept as equal in authority to the Bible, but which they held to be less obscure, and more current and direct. Undergirding these revelations, shaping Mormonism's character and fortunes for the next century, was a command from God that all believers, in millennial preparation, should congregate in "one place upon the face of this land."

"The gathering," as this command came to be known, first became explicit in a revelation of September 1830. Shortly thereafter, Joseph Smith and many followers moved from New York to Ohio, joining Sidney Rigdon, an influential minister who brought his congregation of one hundred along with him in his recent conversion to Mormonism. For approximately seven years the town of Kirtland was a focus of Mormon activity, and by the summer of 1835, 1,500 to 2,000 Saints resided in the vicinity. The following year they dedicated a beautiful temple, one that still stands; it was a structure the Saints had been instructed by revelation to build even before understanding its full purposes. Earlier, in 1831, believers had established a second headquarters around Independence, Missouri, designated by revelaton as Zion: the future site of additional temples, the literal location of the primeval Garden of Eden, the spot where Christ would launch his millennial reign, and the true "center place" around which all other Mormon clusters were to become "stakes" in the tent of Israel.

Rather than dispersing in congregations throughout the land like other churches, Mormonism thus established two great enclaves, with plans for a series of carefully laid-out millennial cities. To gather was a divine invitation, an organizing principle prompting thousands of converts to arrive at great sacrifice, with high hopes. This spatial theology spawned profound consequences, though consequences and causes grew circular and complex as Smith proclaimed revelation upon revelation. Three tendencies, however, are crucial if one is to understand the movement's metamorphosis. First, Mormonism, newly gathered, turned toward the Hebrew Bible as well as to the New Testament, toward literal as well as symbolic enactments of these Testaments, and toward the esoteric while yet retaining traditionally Christian doctrines. Second, as these tendencies developed in the centers, many Saints – commonly those unable to gather – rejected new revelations that so changed the Mormonism they thought they had joined. Although accepting in principle the notion of continuing revelation, some were disturbed enough to leave the faith each time a new layer of revelation and practice was added to then-current understandings. Third, internal dissent, unfamiliar beliefs, and especially the geographic concentration of great numbers of adherents, with its potential to tilt local politics and economics, combined to terrify and anger non-Mormon citizens.

The theological implications of the first of these tendencies associated with the gathering, the Hebraicization of Mormonism, have been probed by historian Jan Shipps (1997). As Joseph Smith would put it in 1842, "We believe in the literal gathering of Israel and in the restoration of the Ten Tribes" and that "Zion will be built upon [the American] continent" – all in preparation for the personal reign of Christ on a paradisiacal earth. Not only were these prophecies soon to be; the Latter-day Saints were themselves called to build the new Zion and gather Israel. Thus arose Mormonism's impulse to become not merely the uniquely true church, but also a literal theocratic kingdom. Earlier, certainly, the Saints had shared with all Christianity the notion of "the new covenant," with its figurative conception of Gentiles' adoption into Israel. Indeed, Zion, temples, priests, and a covenant people had figured prominently in the Book of Mormon. But in the process of gathering physically together at their new centers in Ohio and Missouri in the 1830s and, in more developed form in Illinois in the early 1840s, Mormonism became something new.

Revelation after revelation pulled the Saints into a neo-Hebraic, yet still Christian, consciousness. Actual and planned constructions of temples set the Saints apart. In the temple at Kirtland Smith received visions: first of Jesus, then of Moses, Elias, and Elijah, who, in fulfillment of the prophecies of Malachi concerning the last days, committed to Smith the power and authority of, respectively, the ushering in of the gathering of Israel, the "dispensation of the gospel of Abraham," and the turning of "the hearts of the fathers to the children and the children to the fathers." Through such means, differentiations between New and Old Testament figures and concepts, already thinned in the Book of Mormon, were further eroded. This Hebraization of "restored Christianity" received its most controversial expression with the institution of polygamy; Joseph Smith felt called to practice it probably in the 1830s and demonstrably by 1841, though the doctrine was not made public until 1852, when the church felt comparatively safely ensconced in Utah Territory.

To this practice, in his last years in Nauvoo, the Mormon Prophet added a final constellation of esoteric doctrines: vicarious baptisms and temple ordinances for the deceased, pre-existent spirits, tiered heavens, the possibility for the righteous to progress eternally to godhood, the consequent notion of plurality of gods, and distinctive views on the nature of spirit, creation, intelligence, and the meaning of life. Taken together, and coupled with the gathered and explosively growing church-kingdom, it becomes clear that by the 1840s Mormonism had become something more and other than the simple restoration of priesthood, prophecy, and primitive Christianity it had proclaimed itself in 1830.

Made widely known, Mormon ideas may have been sufficient of themselves to prompt persecution from an intolerant culture. But wherever Mormons settled, even apart from irreducible religious prejudice, there was much to frighten and enrage their gentile neighbors: the sight of thousands of devout believers in antebellum America clustered in the scarcely tamed Midwest; bolstered by a sense of revelation, millennial expectation, and celestial destiny; wielding by their numbers and deference to their leaders a potential bloc political and economic power; and claiming for themselves and for God a physical Zion, with implied and explicit aspirations for the surrounding land. The Saints were run out of Kirtland in the wake of the collapse of their bank, internal disaffection, and external opposition to their alarming numbers. They were driven from Missouri under threat of the Governor's extermination order. And they were mercilessly expelled from Illinois in the bitter winter of 1846, launching one of the most dramatic recolonizations in American history. Those who stayed behind and organized separate Mormon churches were disproportionately those who had not gathered to Nauvoo, and those who construed metaphorically, or even denied, Joseph Smith's new kingdom developed there. Those who followed Brigham Young to the West constituted the New Israel.

Expansion in the West

After many deaths, untold suffering, and an exodus through the wilderness, a modern Moses led the largest remnant of Saints into the Salt Lake Valley to initiate what historian Charles Peterson calls "the most widely applied and formally practiced system of squatter's rights ever devised in America." To this valley, from across the continent and beyond, came believers, entering both sacred time and sacred space, intent to fulfill Isaiah's prophecy by making the desert blossom as the rose: "in the last days . . . the mountain of the Lord's house shall be established in the top of the mountains." Thus biblically conscious of their new terrain, the Latter-day Saints discovered that the setting of their new kingdom was more than an alluvial basin bounded by the peaks of the Wasatch Mountains. It was "Palestine turned around," a portentous climatic and terri-torial echo of mountainous Israel, with a river the settlers named Jordan flowing north from a fresh to a dead sea.

Mexico's Upper California, into which the Mormons entered in 1847, became Utah Territory in 1848, ceded to the United States in the aftermath of the Mexican War. The Saints immediately pressed Congress for recognition as a state, proposing a theoretical separation of religious and civil government, and also proposing ambitious physical boundaries: all of present-day Utah, most of Nevada, three-quarters of Arizona, a third of California and Colorado, and more than one-sixth of New Mexico, Wyoming, and Oregon. Half a century and seven proposed constitutions later, the US Congress would finally grant statehood to a severely reduced but still ample domain to be named Utah – but not until it forced fundamental change in Mormondom.

For Mormonism in Utah had not changed its fundamental character upon its transplantation to the West after 1847. What had happened, rather, was that this character, already established in Nauvoo, achieved the geographic – and therefore the psychic, social, economic, and political – separation from the dominant culture that it needed for expansive expression. Enabled by the immensity and isolation of the space available to them, Brigham Young and his followers enacted on a vast scale Joseph Smith's vision of a latter-day kingdom of Israel, complete with temples, an elaborate patriarchal order, openly plural marriage, a dedicated and covenanted people, and a theocracy patterned as much on the Hebrew Bible as on the US Constitution. Though they did attend services, pioneer Saints were less concerned about such matters as church attendance, in which their minds might focus on the kingdom to come in a heavenly realm, than in building the literal kingdom on earthly soil in the present. "Good crops of sugar beets" and "neatly built houses" were their most expressive signs of worship (Shipps 1985: 125, 188 n.35).

By 1850, 10,000 souls had already settled in remote Utah. Two decades later, when a railway spanned the continent and Ute natives no longer posed a serious challenge to white settlement, 86,000 resided there, more than 90 percent of them Mormons. By around the end of the century, when Mormon colonization came to a virtual halt, leaders had supervised the arrival of 100,000 immigrants (excluding their subsequent children) and had established more than 500 settlements, ranging from Alberta, Canada, to Sonora and Chihuahua, Mexico.

Despite this growth and territorial spread, Mormonism in the 1880s – fifty years after its inauguration – remained in jeopardy of extinction. The nation's Congress, zealous to annihilate polygamy and the Saints' political and commercial solidarity, had in the decades following the Civil War passed a series of laws that rendered polygamy a felony, disfranchised even those Mormons who were not polygamists (on the grounds that the church fostered the practice), and eventually laid grounds to seize Mormon assets by actually disincorporating the church. The underground became the new geography for practicing polygamists, including Mormon leaders, in retreat from US marshalls. Avoiding and subverting federal law became a badge of honor, as Mormon fathers for years moved secretly from house to house or even out of the country, and Mormon families painfully endured the siege. In 1890 the Supreme Court upheld the culminating anti-polygamy law (the 1887 Edmunds–Tucker Act) in a five-to-four decision. Within months, Church President Wilford Woodruff acted to rescue his institution from obliteration by issuing a manifesto discouraging the performance of "any marriage forbidden by the law of the land."

A great many Saints sighed in relief, both for polygamy's demise and for the prospects of less forceful expressions of America's disapproval. Others balked at the reversal of a practice for which they had sacrificed and in which their lives were enmeshed. Leaders continued privately to sanction and perform polygamous marriages, especially outside of the US where the act was not attacked, until well into the twentieth century. Even after 1904, when the church stiffened its ban on such marriages, two of the Twelve Apostles – officials who, along with the three-member First Presidency, form the highest echelon of Mormon governance – resigned their ordinarily life-long positions rather than submit to the new policy. A third apostle might well have acted similarly had he not died in 1906.

In little more than a generation, however, polygamy was dismantled among all but a few, who – excommunicated if discovered – continued their ways in secret or in separate, tribal sects. The official surrender of polygamy (on earth) and the informal surrender of Mormonism's self-contained social, economic, and political structures impelled the Saints to join the mainstream of the nation's cultural life.

The Second Transformation

The surrender also changed Mormonism, for the second time. The church-kingdom became a church again. The "kingdom" was spiritualized, made symbolic, equated with the church, or looked toward in heaven. Implications emerged only gradually.

Mormonism's physical geography did not change immediately and obviously after 1890, as it had with the first transformation in the 1830s and 1840s. Not until 1921 did church leaders discourage gathering to the Mormon cultural center in the West and begin to promote Zion as "the pure in heart" rather than as a physical boundary. And even then new converts long continued to view Utah as the homeland and to migrate there. What did change after 1890 was the Mormon psychic and political geography vis-à-vis the United States. Sacred space shrank from a broad and present kingdom to temple, church, home, and symbol. Near-millennial time reduced to sabbaths and the future. Leaders and other erstwhile polygamists emerged from the underground. The prospect of statehood loomed; national cultural fashions were less thoroughly taboo; and Saints bought goods from non-Mormon sources and aligned with Republicans or Democrats. A people two generations deep in alienation was about to become fully American again.

A measure of continuity with nineteenth-century Mormonism, of course, remained. Leaders and missionaries continued to teach long-standing doctrines about God, Christ, priesthood, and the restoration of pristine Christianity. And the Mormon character that had repeatedly enabled survival continued to express its genius for order, discipline, and obedience to authority – not least as the Saints reshaped the land. Wallace Stegner observed as much in "Mormon trees," the tall, straight Lombardy poplars that everywhere lined the ditch banks and fields in the valleys of Mormon Country prior to World War II:

Perhaps it is fanciful to judge a people by its trees. Probably the predominance of poplars is the result of nothing more interesting than climatic conditions or the lack of other kinds of seeds and seedlings. Probably it is pure nonsense to see a reflection of Mormon group life in the fact that the poplars were practically never planted singly, but always in groups, and that the groups took the form of straight lines and ranks. Perhaps it is even more nonsensical to speculate that the straight, tall verticality of the Mormon trees appealed obscurely to the rigid sense of order of the settlers, and that a marching row of plumed poplars was symbolic, somehow, of the planter's walking with God and his solidarity with his neighbors. (Stegner 1942: 23–4)

To Stegner in the 1940s, his rhetorical negations aside, the trees suggested long-standing Mormon traits: *were* Mormon traits externalized.

Still, the Saints had accomplished their transforming reconciliation with American society by 1950, which enabled a redoubled missionary outreach. Mormon emissaries bore a message increasingly free of what the public took to be the taint of its polygamous past. Through sermons of church leaders in the decades after 1890 the faithful heard less of Zion, kingdom building, eschatology, the apostasy of other churches, and the corruption of outside government; they heard more of the greatness of American institutions, good citizenship, and rapport with other faiths (Shepherd and Shepherd). Mormons borrowed more hymns from Protestant sources; put new stress on the Protestant (King James) Bible; made changes in their temple attire and ritual that rendered them less alien to the uninitiated, and codified their doctrines on deity in ways that, while still distinctly Mormon, shed some innovations of the Brigham Young era and showed influence of prevailing Victorian Protestant scholarship. A fresh aspiration for education appeared in efforts to enhance the intellectual respectability of Brigham Young University, to inaugurate a wider religious education system for young people of high school and college age, to use genuine scholars in the production of church lesson manuals, and even to sponsor a handful of promising students to seek graduate degrees in religion at such centers as the University of Chicago during the 1930s (Alexander 1986; Barlow 1991; Mauss 1994).

Never witholding criticism entirely, America nonetheless came to recognize the Saints as model citizens: thrifty, wholesome, cooperative, industrious, purposeful, patriotic, law-abiding, God-fearing, well-organized, and family-oriented. Rid (or bereft) of polygamy and persecution, the Saints aspired to the image, even while searching for less threatening distinctives to maintain a clear identity. For example, abstinence from alcohol, coffee, tea, and tobacco – a "word of wisdom" in Joseph Smith's time – now became a commandment, visibly differentiating Mormons from most others. Church attendance similarly achieved near-mandatory status, coupled with a heightened emphasis on the payment of full tithes and activity in Mormon temples. In general, the nineteenth-century corporate responsibility for maintenance of the literal kingdom's boundaries shifted, after 1890, to an individual responsibility in codes of conduct (Shipps 1985).

The church by 1950 grew to a membership of one million, and believers were more likely to have been born into the church than to have joined from outside. As late as 1959, 90 percent of all Mormons lived in the US. Eighty percent, indeed, lived in the western states, half of these in Utah, and the majority of this half within a fifty-mile radius of Salt Lake City. Most Mormons lived among other Saints in ways that encompassed virtually every aspect of their lives. The Mormon psyche still placed Zion (Utah) at the world's center; everywhere else was "the mission field." While gathering was officially a thing of the past, a narrow swathe of land running north–south in northern Utah formed the heart of a still-regional faith.

The Third Transformation

Something changed about 1960. Two things, actually, and these mutually dependent: the first was an explosive international growth that dramatically expanded Mormonism's horizontal geography. The second was the concurrent launch of a new administrative program to allow and direct that growth, initiated in Mormonism's vertical geography from the top down. Less obviously sensational than the appearance of angels in New York, bloodshed in Missouri, or open polygamy in Utah, these horizontal and vertical developments in combination were to transform Mormonism for the third time, spawning not merely a larger and relocated church, but a subtly altered entity.

In 1960, for the first time in the twentieth century, Mormons baptized more converts than Mormon children, the result of complex post-World War conditions, the more broadly acceptable entity that Mormonism had become, and a tremendously expanded and systematized missionary outreach. Within a single generation the church would grow many-fold, exceeding 10 million members by the late 1990s, when almost four times as many converts were baptized each year as were children of Mormon parents. Moreover, the dominant growth occurred not only outside the Mormon heartland, but outside of North America, though still in regions where things American were gaining influence. Suddenly, less than 15 percent of all adherents lived in Utah, and less than a third lived in the western US. After 1996, more Mormons resided outside than inside the United States as a whole, a trend with incalculable repercussions as the movement attempted to retain its soul while accommodating enough of the cultures in more than 150 nations to thrive in them.

Mormon authorities, not unrealistically, anticipate a membership of 35 million by 2020. One wonders what Mormonism is to look like when it boasts more Spanish- and Portuguese- than English-speaking believers, becoming a church whose administrative power remains in northern Utah, but whose demographic center lies in Mexico or even further south. How should the church respond to an image tied so closely to conservative elements in the United States that its chapels are bombed by offended political elements in Chile, its missionaries assassinated as American imperialists in Bolivia and Peru, its members pointed out by national officials as a plague to Mother Russia, its activities banned altogether in Ghana? Considered an affluent body in the late twentieth century, Mormon resources are challenged by a flood of new converts from impoverished regions of the globe.

Mormonism is more genuinely a "hemispheric church" (Mauss 1994) than a global one, with 85 percent of adherents living in the western hemisphere. Geographer Lowell C. Bennion has demonstrated how much of the regional cast of the faith remains, noting that the movement has grown rapidly only in restricted areas of the world, changing little in others, with virtually no presence in, for example, China and India. Nonetheless, the church is poised to enter such arenas when allowed, and its geographic consciousness, increasingly global, has been revolutionized in a single generation.

Emergent Mormonism is not, however, a church merely larger and more dispersed than heretofore, as with the nineteenth-century transplantation from Illinois to Utah. It is, rather, a different Mormonism: continuous with its origins but also as distinct from them as Aristotle's old ship become new, half its planks replaced. This is a movement whose swelling numbers, international spread, and uneven accommodations to those international contexts *in concert with* its streamlined program, simplified public theology, sacralized corporate sensibility, and bureaucratic mechanisms now in place to manage the global sprawl, have changed the institution the world encounters, and has changed the experience of being a Latter-day Saint. This is so despite the maintenance of what modern church officials have defined as the unchanging doctrinal essentials (noted earlier and variously expressed).

These "streamlined," "simplified," "corporate," and "bureaucratic" traits derive from a still-unfolding administrative program called Correlation. Correlation was and is a Mormon *perestroika* intended to consolidate the diverse workings of the church and to ensure that the Mormon priesthood is firmly in control of policy, doctrine, and programs. Nods in this direction occurred early in the twentieth century, but became full-scale policy only after 1960. Church leaders, in particular Apostle (later President) Harold B. Lee, saw Correlation as a divinely prompted response to an unwieldy organization whose auxiliaries (such as the Sunday School, the Primary (a Sunday School for children, though it sometimes met on weekdays), and the women's Relief Society) had grown too autonomous and redundant. Lee also was responding to what he saw as an encroaching worldliness that had insinuated itself with the Mormon embrace of American culture. Fundamentally, however, the change reflected the church's growth and the anticipated international growth to follow, a welcome problem that nevertheless put central control and perceived purity of doctrine at risk. Given this, and because the church was determined to identify in itself a core that could cut across all cultures so that (as diverse leaders and teachers began to put it) "the only culture we're bound by is the culture of the gospel," Correlation constituted in many ways a far-sighed, cost-saving, and perhaps inevitable development.

Space allows for only the barest suggestion of some of the changes, which have left no dimension of Mormonism untouched. A single church-wide Curriculum Department replaced the various committees that once functioned with relative freedom in each auxiliary. At all levels officials coordinated, censored, and simplified teaching manuals, which are now written and screened by committee. They consolidated into three magazines, respectively for children, youth, and adults, magazines and literature formerly produced by independent auxiliaries having independent budgets and agendas. Leaders imported highly efficient policies and styles from corporate America, and recruited to their ranks leaders experienced in such practices. They centralized and professionalized control over the church's welfare system, which is among history's most impressive. Church buildings, beginning even before the 1960s, became standardized and instantly recognizable across the nation – a formula with aesthetic limitations, but one saving untold money and reducing inequities between rich and poor congregations. Church finances came under more centralized control, easing and equalizing burdens for the burgeoning missionary force and assisting Saints in Third-World nations where Mormonism has grown so rapidly. Mandated church meetings were consolidated from their traditional format – two or three each Sunday, morning and afternoon, with additional sessions for the separate auxiliaries during the week – to a single three-hour block on Sunday only, leaving more time for families and lightening the burden for those forced to travel considerable distances to worship and to spend their entire sabbaths at church. Perhaps most importantly, the church collapsed its articulated mission into a three-pronged statement that has come to shape the consciousness of millions of participating members: "to proclaim the gospel of the Lord Jesus Christ" to every nation and people; "to perfect the Saints by preparing them to receive the ordinances of the gospel and by instruction and discipline to gain exaltation"; and "to redeem the dead by performing vicarious ordinances . . . for those who have lived on the earth."

For all its perceived necessity, however, Correlation has sired mixed offspring. These consequences too can scarcely be touched on here. The importation of corporate styles of management has grown incestuous, centralizing control at ever higher echelons of an already powerful hierarchy. General church authorities are drawn disproportionately from professionals trained in the law or in business or educational administration, with the unsurprising result that the concept of "management," under various sacralized rubrics, holds an increasingly elevated stature in the Mormon worldview. Educational materials that are not only simplified but simplistic have displaced a more substantive curriculum common in the generation prior to 1960, a move that has facilitated the catechizing of converts while often boring a generation of long-term Saints. Converts are comparatively easily swept into the church by a dedicated, huge, and highly organized missionary corps, but fewer than half of such recruits, superficially converted, remain active for even a single year, while untold energies are spent to reactivate them. The vast church education system has turned away from genuine inquiry and toward simple indoctrination, while Brigham Young University has retreated from traditional academic freedom and turned toward "institutional freedom." The perhaps unintended result of dissolving the relative autonomy of the women's Relief Society along with the other auxiliaries has been a decline in the power and visibility of women even in affairs that had theretofore been in their realm. The similarly incidental consequence of the consolidated schedule of Sabbath meetings into tight three-hour blocks has been an erosion in communication and connection among church members, especially among the great majority not living in Mormon centers in the western US, who thus have little contact with other Saints during weekdays and little time to visit and bond at church.

Conclusion

The rise of any broadly applied idea is apt to bear unforeseen results. It was so, for example, with the mechanical clock, invented in the late Middle Ages to facilitate monastic prayers. The clock brought more than convenience. It also spawned human beings who grew more time-conscious, who then became time-savers, and ended as time-slaves, living in frenetic desperation, quartz-powered gods strapped mercilessly to their wrists.

Just as devout men brought the world the clock, for good and ill, so the world of Mormonism now lives its correlated life. Anyone who underestimates the program's genius in focusing purpose and coherence while enabling vast international growth fails to understand this still-evolving religion. Correlation has fashioned a formula for success that the Mormon church has franchised into new congregations far and wide, no end in sight.

But achievement bears its dangers. The spectacular franchising of modern Mormonism parallels another, precisely contemporaneous, American success story. The fast food conjured by McDonald's is now offered in Paris, Tokyo, and Moscow as conspicuously as in Boston, Omaha, and Salt Lake City: "billions and billions served." In addition to the church's wrestling with its rapid recruitment but low retention of new members and its frequent strain with diverse cultures abroad, perhaps the underlying issue with which Mormon Christianity will have to struggle in the twenty-first century is the ultimate desirability of a final correlation. Can the corporate, consolidated, simplified, international church yield a spiritual diet more sustaining over time and across space than the physical nutrition of a Big Mac?

Whatever the answer to that question, the entanglements of Mormon space and Mormonism's past and future constitute a complex and intriguing case study, one that might prompt students of American religion to new explorations on a wide array of subjects. Mormonism's womb in New York's "burnt-over district"; the Book of Mormon's interpretations of and ambitions for the New World promised land; and the church's millennialist expectations for Israel and America generally and for Missouri and Utah in particular are examples of Mormonism's genetically geographical make-up. The doctrine of "gathering" and the movement's consequent transfers from New York to the mid- and far west; its isolation from and eventual reunion with the United States; and its international spread in the late twentieth-century have all given shape to what Mormonism, in its several transformations, has become. Probing analogous dimensions in other faiths, observers may notice that more is at stake in the intersection of geography, demography, and religion than simply "counting heads."

BIBLIOGRAPHY

Alexander, Thomas G. (1986) *Mormonism in Transition: A History of the Latter-day Saints 1890–1930*, Urbana, Ill.: University of Illinois Press.

Barlow, Philip L. (1991) *Mormons and the Bible: The Place of the Latter-day Saints in American Religion*, New York: Oxford University Press.

Bennion, Lowell C. (1995) "The geographic dynamics of Mormondom, 1965–95," *Sunstone*, 18/3: 21–36.

Brown, S. Kent, Cannon, Donald Q., and Jackson, Richard H. (eds) (1994) *Historical Atlas of Mormonism*, New York: Simon & Schuster.

Bushman, Richard L. (1997) "Making space for the Mormons," Leonard J. Arrington Mormon History Lecture Series No. 2, Logan, Utah: distributed by Utah State University Press.

Chidester, David and Linenthal, Edward T. (1995) *American Sacred Space*, Bloomington, Ind.: Indiana University Press.

Cornwall, Marie, Heaton, Tim B., and Young, Lawrence A. (eds) (1994) *Contemporary Mormonism: Social Science Perspectives*, Urbana, Ill.: University of Illinois Press.

Dialogue: A Journal of Mormon Thought (1996), 19/1 (Spring). (Guest-edited by Armand Mauss, the entire issue focuses on Mormon prospects in the twenty-first century.)

Hamilton, C. Mark (1995) *Nineteenth-Century Mormon Architecture and City Planning*, New York: Oxford University Press.

Mauss, Armand (1994) *The Angel and the Beehive: The Mormon Struggle with Assimilation*, Urbana, Ill.: University of Illinois Press.

Shepherd, Gordon and Shepherd, Gary (1984) *A Kingdom Transformed: Themes in the Development of Mormonism*, Salt Lake City, Ut.: University of Utah Press.

Shipps, Jan (1985) *Mormonism: The Story of a New Religious Tradition*, Urbana, Ill. and Chicago: University of Illinois Press.

—— (1997) "Joseph Smith and Mormonism," in James Duke and Mark Toulouse (eds) *Makers of Christian Theology in America*, Nashville, Tenn.: Abingdon Press.

Stegner, Wallace (1942) *Mormon Country*, New York: Hawthorn Books.

Chapter 11

American Catholics in the Twentieth Century

Mary Jo Weaver

American Catholicism in the twentieth century divides neatly down the middle in this way: Catholics born before mid-century were shaped by the vision and energy of the Council of Trent (1545–63) and Vatican I (1869–70), whereas those born after 1950 were introduced to a Catholicism challenged by the changes of the Second Vatican Council (1962–5). Tridentine Catholicism had a tendency to divide people into Catholics and non-Catholics, to defend itself against the treacheries of the world, and to hold fast to those eternal truths and transforming practices that promised everlasting life for the faithful. Sure of itself as the embodiment of God's will on earth, Catholicism was a closed system uneasy about democracy and hostile to pluralism. Catholics prayed fervently for the conversion of "obdurate Protestants" and "perfidious Jews." Tolerance was not a virtue. Defensiveness was. Post-Vatican II Catholicism struggles to be more at home in the world, less defensive, more focused on Christ's transforming presence in the daily situations of one's life. Still sure of itself as embodying an ancient tradition of values and spiritual insight, post-conciliar Catholicism accepts democracy and pluralism as rich soil for the growth of the church, and approaches Protestants, Jews, and non-Christian religions in a spirit of dialogue and in hope of mutual understanding. Toleration for opposing views is still not one of its virtues, but it could be.

When Pope John XXIII announced the Second Vatican Council in 1958, he called for an assembly of the world's Catholic bishops to address pastoral (not doctrinal) problems. Unlike the church in earlier centuries, Catholicism in the middle of the twentieth century was not divided over questions about the person and nature of Christ, or the best way to explain the real presence of Christ in the Eucharist. Its leaders were not scandalous rogues as in some earlier times, and its religious orders were not at war with one another. Since the modernist controversy at the turn of the century, there had been virtually no condemnations of heresy, no excommunications, no inquisitorial intrigues.[1] But times had changed and the pope saw that fidelity to the Gospel in the new age meant rejecting the Tridentine model with its suspicion of modernity, its defensiveness and isolationism. He was eager to address the modern world and to infuse Catholicism with a spirit of confidence as it approached the end of the millennium.

In Europe, Catholics were attempting to address a myriad of intellectual challenges to Catholicism (some left over from the Enlightenment, others rooted in the crisis of faith precipitated by two world wars). Theologians and scholars were involved in questions of liturgical renewal, engaged in dialogue with political philosophers, and hoped for greater participation of the laity in the life of the church. If American Catholics perceived no problems within their church, they may not have been paying attention. Garry Wills, in his provocative examination of 1950s Catholicism, exposed some of the cognitive dissonance that made renewal imperative.[2] Whether most American Catholics were aware of problems in their church or not, they joined with Catholics throughout the world to look at the "signs of the times" and to adjust their religious lives to accommodate to new challenges.

Catholicism, in fact, has always paid attention to the signs of the times, although not always with alacrity. Throughout its long history, it has exhibited a genius for holding on to a core set of values while accommodating to new languages, missionary strategies, disciplinary regulations, devotional needs, hostile philosophies, and modes of institutional organization. Its rhythms of change appear glacial in a fast-paced world, but they seem to work, especially in America. In a recent book, Charles Morris suggests that "America, and perhaps Australia and Canada, which derive from the same tradition, may be the *only* place where the Church really works."[3] American Catholicism, by reading the "signs of the times" in its own history, has come to the end of the twentieth century with a combination of wealth, activism, and dynamism that connects its believers with tradition and challenges them to find religious meaning in their relatively affluent, secular, pluralistic lives.

Signs of the Times in Different Contexts

In the first half of the twentieth century, the signs of the times for American Catholics were rooted in their nineteenth-century experience. They immigrated to this country in massive numbers to find a predominantly Protestant population fearful of and hostile to Catholicism. They were poor, often unable to speak the language, had very little control over their lives, and needed the shepherding they found in their parish churches. The insular subculture they developed – later called "ghetto Catholicism" – was initially a defensive reaction to a hostile environment and ultimately a way to glorify difference. In the nineteenth and early twentieth century an isolated existence was pretty much imposed on Catholics. When immigrants faced various kinds of discrimination, they found protection in the local parish that was both the center of their neighborhoods and the heart of their religious and social lives. By the early and mid-twentieth century, however, Catholics were more mainstream and middle class, more able to control their lives and less likely to encounter the flagrant discrimination that marked the lives of their parents and grandparents. The ghetto was no longer necessary, but it was comfortable and it served to preserve the faith, secure the loyalty of the working classes (a feat not accomplished in Europe), and provide an excellent means of education for subsequent generations. By mid-century, ghetto Catholicism was still alive in small towns and in some urban neighborhoods, but it was about to disappear.

The descendents of nineteenth-century immigrants live in a pluralistic and mobile society and do not choose their neighborhoods around an ethnic parish. Ghetto Catholicism as a defense against the world is no longer necessary. As the mainstay of social life and ethnic identity, it no longer works for most children of European immigrants. Increasingly in the twentieth century, and particularly since the Second Vatican Council, assimilated Catholics have inherited a set of problems that are distinctly American: they have to struggle with the opposing attractions of success and religion. If the American Revolution carried within it a general distrust of organized religion and a celebration of individualism, the great awakenings that marked the beginnings of American evangelicalism signaled a thirst for religion, and responded to desires for spirituality and community. This tension between individualism and community is played out in specific ways within American Catholicism. The religious ideals of Catholicism can conflict with the goals of the American dream, and the political ideals of America can conflict with the style of an authoritarian church.

The context of modern American Catholicism can be described in terms of the demise of the ghetto for a majority of assimilated Catholics, but not for a significantly large group of "new immigrants." The history of American Catholicism has usually been written in ways that exclude the major players: early histories were predominantly about bishops and priests, usually Irish and German ones. Although later historians have been more inclusive, we still do not have adequate historical accounts of the lives, devotional practices, dreams, and challenges of immigrant groups themselves. We know much more than we used to about women in the church, but are nowhere near arriving at the details of that story. And, until very recently, historians and assimilated American Catholics have virtually ignored Hispanic, black, and Native American Catholics. The trajectories of American Catholic triumph have not included them and they continue to face flagrant discrimination. The "ghetto Catholicism" that eventually protected European immigrants and enabled their success was originally forced on them by a context of Protestant hostility. The "ghetto Catholicism" experienced by Hispanic, black, and Native American Catholics has been imposed on them by the culture and reinforced by their fellow Catholics.

American Catholicism in the future will depend to some extent on the ways in which Catholics remember and negotiate the ghetto experience. For some Catholics today, "ghetto Catholicism" was (and is) the most effective means of preserving Catholic identity and therefore a refuge not to be relinquished easily. For others, it was (and is) a way station which protected the faithful as they learned to make their way in this new environment, a developmental stage which can well be left behind. However they perceive the virtues and vices of the ghetto,

Catholics can be challenged by this part of their past and their present to come to a more inclusive understanding of themselves and their religious identity in the future.

Styles of Leadership in Different Eras

The ghetto Catholicism of the pre-conciliar church accepted a style of leadership that was hierarchical, patriarchal, and in some ways patronizing. Authority moved from the top down: bishops and priests were the links between the faithful and God, standing in a chain of command that went from God to the pope to the bishops to the priests to the people. Obedience was a primary value. The priest was a "father" who was to be given the authority and reverence bestowed on a *pater familias*. One did not question father's judgment but gratefully accepted his counsel and admonitions, and sought divine forgiveness through his agency in the confessional. In the Middle Ages, this hierarchical model specified a set of obligations and privileges up and down the ladder that gave one a sure sense of place and a clear role in the mystical body of Christ. In a romantic rendering of benign patriarchy, twentieth-century Catholic movie priests like Bing Crosby's "Father O'Malley" and Spencer Tracy's "Father Flannigan of Boys Town" embodied the unselfish, familial leadership that characterized this model at its best. Those movie characters were created in and reflected a romantic view of American Catholicism in the 1940s and 1950s. Some people look back at them wistfully, and some conservative Catholics still welcome hierarchical and patriarchal models, but most American Catholics do not.

The Catholic Church in the latter days of the twentieth century is not as indifferent to hierarchy and patriarchy as it once was. Although Catholics still find the link between hierarchy and divine will comforting on a doctrinal level and acceptable in terms of administrative efficiency, they have replaced obedience with discernment in matters touching their personal lives. Many Catholics still address their pastors as "father", often coupled with his first name but without the same willingness to obey his teaching and follow his counsel as was true of their parents and grandparents. Many contemporary Catholics no longer go to confession; some see no need for it, others prefer to monitor the direction of their religious lives with spiritual directors or significant others. If mid-century novels and movies portrayed kindly, fatherly, priest-figures, today's movies show a more sinister side of priesthood. The shocking scandals around priestly sexual abuse and hierarchical cover-ups during the 1990s have seriously sullied the role of priesthood. As a Midwestern parish priest lamented several years ago in *Commonweal*, these scandals have made all priests, including innocent ones, objects of suspicion and weakened the priesthood just when it needs a new generation to carry on.[4]

Like other Catholics, priests reflect the times in which they were born and the ways they experienced formation. Those fully educated before the second Vatican council tend to have different understandings of church, liturgy, leadership, and preaching than those educated during and after the council. The most pressing problem for the future is the projected shortage of priests. The rates of decline in priestly vocations and the rates of increase in the Catholic population tell us that whereas there was one priest for every 1,300 Catholics in 1965, there will be only one priest for every 3,600 Catholics forty years later, in 2005. Statistics like these may account in part for the support most American Catholics give to women's ordination and optional celibacy, recommendations that would change the nature of priesthood altogether.

Matters of importance in the fifties, like the obligation to send one's children to a Catholic school, have not been observed for years. Many Catholics continue to send their children to Catholic schools, but their decisions are now based on the quality of education rather than on a sense of obligation to the teaching of bishops and priests. At a more fundamental and serious level, most American Catholics who then feel no need to leave the church over this disagreement have substantially rejected official Catholic teaching against artificial birth control. As divorce and remarriage have become part of American Catholic culture, many such couples continue to participate regularly in the sacramental life of the church even though such participation is expressly against the teachings of the Holy Father. On a level of lived experience, Catholics are willing to discern God's will for themselves and to disagree with some official teaching. As they see it – perhaps being shaped by American spirit – those seeking sources of moral values and spiritual fulfillment must decide the extent to which they will follow their chosen authorities. In matters of personal morality and sexuality, Catholics are out of step with church teaching and most of them to not see themselves as disobedient or as bad Catholics.[5]

The most direct challenge to hierarchical and patriarchal authority within the church has come from women. As I have shown, the intersection of the women's movement and the Second Vatican Council inspired a contemporary challenge to traditional religious authority.[6] Feminism in its late-twentieth century version has raised consciousness about the ways in which patriarchy identifies women with maternity and relegates women to complementary or stereotypical roles with church and family. Women have asked the church to take women's experience seriously as a datum of theological and spiritual reflection. Feminist theologians, women spiritual directors and liturgical co-ordinators, the Leadership Conference of Women Religious, the women who make up the overwhelming proportion of students in seminaries in the United States, and the women who keep the local church going with their time, energy, and devotion, have challenged the church to take its own teachings in justice seriously, to adopt leadership styles that are cooperative, inclusive, and enabling.

The Vatican reaction to the women's movement can be exemplified in part by its response to the issue of women's ordination. Opening the priesthood to women has the support of a majority of American biblical scholars and theologians. Most American Catholics favor it. There have been many books – historical, philosophical, practical – written about it, and whole organizations (American and worldwide) promoting it. Yet the Vatican has ruled not only that women may never be ordained, but that the issue may not even be *discussed*, a rather drastic and nervous response from an institution that invites discussion about nuclear war and capital punishment.

Leadership – locally, nationally, and globally – is one of the most vexing issues within the American church. At the institutional level, the church itself has struggled with models of centralized authority versus local initiatives for centuries. Conciliarism, collegiality, and local control are not simply modern issues: one can find desperate battles along these lines in the early church and in the Middle Ages. The locale for that argument in the century before Vatican II was Vatican I, a council that declared papal infallibility, marginalized the bishops, and favored the Curia. The struggle to find the right leadership model, therefore, is not a new one, but the terms of the problem today are significantly different and more challenging. However much one admires a priest, bishop, or the pope, the old deference is gone and obedience is no longer a primary value. Roman recalcitrance on women's issues coupled with the historical propensity of the American hierarchy to recruit and promote mostly Irish and German candidates for priesthood make the American church exclusive and alienating for many of its faithful. Today, both for practical reasons and as a matter of justice within the church, Catholicism is challenged not only to find a balance between papal and episcopal authority, but to reflect the racial, ethnic, economic, and gender diversity of its faithful in its ministries and leadership positions, especially priesthood.

Experiencing Catholicism before and after Vatican II

Devotional life

In the pre-conciliar church, Catholic life was experienced in a local parish that one might have been born into, married in, and been buried from. It was not unusual for families to spend several generations in the same parish, and their devotional lives there were not markedly different from those of their ancestors in earlier centuries. In most parishes, one could find two or three daily masses and a series of regular devotions (including the rosary, Stations of the Cross, novenas, forty hours devotions, and Benediction of the Blessed Sacrament). Mixed marriages (between Catholics and Protestants) were rare, sometimes done in the rectory rather than in the church. Funeral masses were celebrated in black vestments and were elaborate rituals of eternal drama featuring the exquisitely frightening language of the *Dies Irae* with its evocations of divine judgment and wrath and closing with the beautiful strains of the *In Paradisum*, asking the angels to conduct the departed into paradise.

American Catholics in the second half of the twentieth century also experience their religious lives in a local parish, but probably not the one into which they were born. Like other Americans, Catholics move around a great deal and may, even if in the same town, move from parish to parish in search of a congenial liturgy or a specific school situation. Their devotional lives are markedly different from those of their ancestors and even from their parents. In many parishes today there is not even one daily mass, and the variety of regular devotions no longer exists. Although one still finds Stations of the Cross during Lent, most of the old devotional forms have disappeared. Today there might be para-liturgical services, Scripture study groups, and small groups devoted to specific types of prayer (charismatic, for example, or Marian). Mixed marriages are more common and one sometimes finds both the priest and the minister of the Protestant partner at the altar. Funerals are celebrated in white vestments and are focused on the resurrection of the body. The music at funerals rarely evokes judgment: it tends to reinforce the idea that God is eager to protect the faithful and welcome them to eternal life.

Preaching

Before the Second Vatican Council, sermons were often based on the preaching outlines made from the catechism of the council of Trent. In order to counteract the religious confusion of the Reformation period, the bishops at the Council of Trent produced an extraordinarily rich compendium of Catholic teaching rooted in the Apostle's Creed, the Sacraments, the Ten Commandments, and the Lord's Prayer. In order to make the catechism more readily available for parochial preaching – the main purpose for which it was written – later translators prepared a course of doctrinal instruction that combined the teachings of the Council of Trent with the scriptural readings for all Sundays and holy days. The sermon program usually suggested a doctrinal and a moral subject for each week, using the week's readings and cross-referencing them to the appropriate parts of the catechism. Priests trained before Vatican II sought clarity of teaching in their sermons and aimed to present a confidence about Catholic truth. They presumed that people needed security and certainty about their beliefs and that doctrinal instruction was the primary purpose of preaching.

At Vatican II, the bishops put a primacy on Scripture. In order to draw the faithful into the richness of scriptural texts, they insisted that preaching focus on the readings of the day. Priests were trained to look for new insights into the life of Jesus and to make it more understandable and personally meaningful to people. In the years since the council, preaching tends to call the faithful to conversion, suggesting ways in which they can use the word of God to make the world into a better place. Preachers presume that people need to be challenged to open themselves to the transforming power of God's word as found in the Scripture. Sermon guides tend to be rooted in biblical studies and are aimed to help priests understand the context and meaning of particular passages. Preaching in the Catholic church before and after the council shares one feature: it is not very good. It was then and remains the weakest part of Catholic liturgical life.

Spirituality

In the pre-conciliar era, the church was seen as a unified reality, the same everywhere. The mass, an unbloody re-enactment of the sacrifice of the cross, was a transcendent event with a primary focus on the consecrated elements and on the power of the priest to change the bread and wine into the body and blood of Christ. The people joined their prayers with those of the priest and were encouraged to make themselves worthy to receive communion through regular confession. Most parishes sponsored regular "missions" in which visiting priests preached a dramatic style of repentance designed to draw people to the confessional and thence to a renewed life. In their spiritual lives, people focused on their sins and were helped to overcome them with prayer and penance.

Since Vatican II, the church understands itself as a more complex reality made up of distinct elements. The documents of Vatican II talk about the church as both a visible society and a spiritual community, united in doctrine, but with enormous diversity. Recovering the practice and understanding of Eucharist in the early church, the mass is a communal meal based on the Passover supper celebrated by Jesus before his crucifixion with the primary focus on the gathered congregation who, themselves, constitute the body of Christ. With its emphasis on participation, the church is understood as the people of God who offer and receive the gifts of bread and wine that become the presence of Christ in the Eucharist. Most parishes sponsor activities that involve people in small group activities designed to enhance prayer and responsiveness to the needs of the world around them. Most American Catholics no longer go to confession, but many of them seek spiritual direction and tend to focus on their own experience as a locus of divine activity in their lives. Catholics today can find many different types of spirituality available to them. Charismatic renewal groups focus on the gifts of the Holy Spirit manifest in their everyday lives. Jesuit retreats and spiritual directors, using *The Spiritual Exercises of St Ignatius*, encourage people to ask for a personal revelation from God that will help them direct their lives. Carmelite, Franciscan, Dominican, Benedictine, or Salesian spiritual directors bring the traditions and insights of their founders and saints to those in search of ways to understand God's love for human beings and the divine desire for union with humanity. Some Catholics seek combinations of Christian and non-Christian spiritualities (especially Buddhism) to enrich their lives.

Means of local involvement

Before the council, life in the parish offered people in a series of social support systems meant to keep their faith lively and involved. Holy Name Societies, Altar and Rosary Societies, Knights of Columbus, Daughters of Isabella, Sodalities, Catholic Youth Organizations, Catholic summer camps, Serra Clubs, all gave lay people ways to participate in the ongoing life of the church and to be connected with its traditions. Catholic teaching about the Mystical Body of Christ imagined the church divided into the "church triumphant" (those already in heaven), the "church suffering" (those in Purgatory on their way to heaven), and the "church militant" (those here on earth working toward their eternal destinies). The cosmic connections inspired a grand sense of community and had a logical spin-off in the notion of "Catholic action", various kinds of good works that joined the work of the laity to the ecclesiastical work of the bishops and the pope. Vocations to the priesthood and sisterhoods were seen as calls to participate in the highest forms of Catholic life. In the 1930s and 1940s, energetic social and liturgical activists got involved in new movements like the Catholic Worker, the Grail, or Friendship House, which were meant to address the needs of the poor, women, and blacks. All of these organizations responded to the signs of the times and the pressing needs of the pre-conciliar church.

Catholics were either poor or connected to the poor: the St Vincent de Paul Society in each parish looked after the needs of parishioners who were down on their luck. Social teaching from Leo XIII at the end of the nineteenth century through encyclicals of Pius XII in the middle of the twentieth century encouraged Catholics to help their fellow religionists with alms and work, and American Catholics responded with an astonishingly effective national network of hospitals, orphanages, homes for unwed mothers, and other philanthropic organizations. The emphasis was on helping the poor, not on changing the conditions of their lives in any structural way.

Today, those pre-conciliar societies are not as active as they once were. One still finds many of them, but with reduced membership and energy. At the same time, many people in parishes are involved in Bible study classes either at their own churches or in ecumenical groups. The desire to read and study a book that Catholics seldom read before the council is one of the hallmarks of contemporary Catholicism. Although Catholics might still talk about the "Mystical Body of Christ", they more generally talk about the body of Christ as the church itself and understand community in both local and global terms. Their activities on behalf of justice or social activism are no longer cast in the language of "Catholic Action" since they no longer think of the church so readily in institutional terms. The fact that vocations to the priesthood and sisterhoods are no longer abundant challenge Catholics in the parish to assume more responsibility for their own spiritual lives and to understand their lives as vocations within the body of Christ. The Catholic Worker and the Grail still exist – along with other ministries of social justice – but they are not apparently as attractive as they once were. Catholics involved in the local parish are often those with children in the school, or those who are interested in the parish council. Supporting the life of the parish is now often a matter of committee work, as various parishioners work on finances, liturgy, board of education, or spiritual life committees.

Assimilated European Catholics are generally no longer poor, but are still connected to the poor. Parishes have ways to address the needs of their members, but also encourage activism in the local community more broadly understood. Ecumenical activities often gather the energy of a variety of religious people to address problems of poverty, housing, hunger, and other socially dysfunctional issues. In addition to local initiatives, Catholics today are introduced to global understandings of poverty and injustice: today Catholic almsgiving and activism extends from the parish to the diocese, and out into the world. Catholics have always supported the foreign missions – sending a great deal of their money and many of their young sisters and priests to convert peoples in Africa, India, and China to Catholicism – but without much thought about underlying structures of injustice in those venues. Today mission strategy is characterized by adaptation and a desire to help marginalized people to address those aspects of their lives that perpetuate poverty and injustice. In some countries, especially in Latin America, missionaries are likely to be informed by "liberation theology," a reading of the Catholic tradition that teaches a divine "preferential option for the poor," and asks people to identify with the poor and help them to overcome the condition into which they have been born. American bishops have called on Catholics to examine themselves in relation to the poor of the country and of the world, to share what they have with them and to extend the kind of help that enables poor peoples to help themselves out of poverty.

Schools

One of the accomplishments of American Catholicism is its national network of Catholic schools. Before the council, schools were able to make room for parish children who could not afford even the minimal tuition cost because millions of sisters dedicated their lives to selfless service within the Catholic school system. Most children attended mass weekly, sometimes daily, and were instructed in the rudiments of their faith by way of the *Baltimore Catechism*, a compact and comprehensive presentation of the truths of the faith based on the genius of the catechism of the Council of Trent. Priests and sisters were trained with the manuals of Catholic theology (usually based on the work of Thomas Aquinas) and exuded confidence about what they taught. Children who knew their catechism knew the answers and could explain and defend their faith.

Catholic schools still exist, but without the presence of those sisters who insured inexpensive Catholic education. Today's Catholic schools are staffed by lay people who work long hours on pay scales substantially below that of their local school systems, but not so low that they can operate without significant tuition fees. Many of the sisters who still remain active in the church have turned their energies to inner-city schools, going where they perceive the need to be greatest. Many other nuns – usually not in traditional habits – now work in women's shelters and in situations of social distress that cause some conservative Catholics to long for a return of nuns to their former lives (full habits, obedience to the pope, and their work in schools). Religious instruction in post-conciliar Catholic schools is generally not taught from the *Baltimore Catechism*, but is still rooted in Catholic doctrine (the creed, sacraments, commandments, and prayer). There is often a greater emphasis on social justice than in the old system, and a desire to help children understand Catholicism in terms of community and the insights of Vatican II.

Membership

The church before the council was dominated by Irish and German peoples. They made up the majority of American Catholics for a long time and most of the bishops came from those ethnic traditions. Other European peoples – French, Italians, and Poles, for example – were part of the church, but the devotional style and general directions were set by the dominant groups. Black, Hispanic, and Native American Catholics suffered in the church the same discrimination they found in the culture and were seldom seen in predominantly white parishes. They were treated, in many ways, like peoples in the foreign missions: white priests and sisters were assigned to look after them as if they were in need of learning the European model of Catholicism. Their forms of devotion and worship were not welcome.

American Catholicism today has made some gestures toward black and Hispanic Catholics by appointing a few black and Hispanic bishops, but the challenges offered to the church by these "new immigrants" probably require more radical attention to the voices of those constituencies. The universality of the church – its multicultural reality – is astoundingly diverse even in this country. Those who speak Spanish as a first language are nearly a majority of American Catholics and along with black and Native American Catholics (not to mention Italians, East and South Europeans, and Asians) bring a set of experiences and needs that will very much shape the future of the church.

Concluding Theses

Vatican II was the most momentous event in the history of twentieth-century Catholicism and it is not unfair to say that one of the results of the council was a shift from a paradigm of obedience to a paradigm of discernment. The American church before the council responded to the signs of the times by adopting the defensive mentalities and doctrinal certainties of Vatican I and the Council of Trent. Those strategies served the American church well as they helped to assimilate millions of European immigrants and to protect them from the anti-Catholicism that marked American religious experience in the nineteenth century. The pre-conciliar church did a splendid job of educating its children and inculcating the faithful with the traditional values of a church that described itself as one, holy, catholic, and apostolic. By being obedient to the teaching of the church as handed down from the pope through the bishops and priests, American Catholics built an enormous and coherent system of interacting institutions in this country: churches, schools, philanthropic institutions, universities, professional associations, and civic organizations reflected a faith that was virtually monolithic. The universality of the church was celebrated in one language (Latin) and generally reflected a unified set of cultural assumptions (European).

In the second half of the twentieth century, and as the American church prepares to move into the next millennium, the times have changed and the self-understanding of the church has been shaped by Vatican II. In some ways today's challenges are similar to earlier ones: Catholics still want to educate their children in the values and practices of their faith, and church leaders still want a majority of Catholics to be faithful participants in the life of the church. In other ways, the challenges facing contemporary Catholics are different. There is an unfinished agenda attached to the Second Vatican Council that mandates more work in liturgical renewal, more attention to ecumenism and inter-religious dialogue, and greater inclusivity. Women, marginalized groups like Hispanics and blacks, and Third-World peoples increasingly understand themselves as the "people of God" with experiences and outlooks that can enrich the body of Christ. On the whole, Catholics are better educated and more theologically aware than in earlier times. Catholic theology, which used to be a clerical discipline, is now done by lay men and women who are often critical of the church and see the magisterium as an office within the church rather than as an authority over it.

American Catholicism at the end of the millennium exhibits a splendid variety of peoples, approaches to spirituality, devotional proclivities, and reactions to the directions taken by the church since the council. The very idea of valuing the experience of everyone as part of the discernment process makes some American Catholics uneasy and leads them to talk about the "Protestantization" of the Catholic Church. Without objective moral norms and a clear sense of obedience to the teaching authority of the church, they say, Catholics will splinter and lose their distinctiveness. Although it is true that Catholics attend church less frequently than in earlier times, there is no indication that Catholics have lost themselves in a morass of indifference. The Catholic experience is still distinctively sacramental, finding God's presence in everyday life and in the ritual actions of the church. The Catholic Church is comprised of simple believers who do not need to question their faith and of sophisticated believers who bring critical questions to their faith before they decide whether to believe it.

Reactions to the council include some who resist it, some who accept it selectively, and some who accept it wholeheartedly as a first step in a program of ongoing reform. All of these groups can find support in the council documents, which reflect a wide range of ideas and tend not to monolithic.[7] Although Catholicism tries to show a unified face to the world, there have always been different points of emphasis in understanding and appropriating Catholic teaching. One should not be surprised, therefore, to find interpreters of the council who focus on the mystery of the church as separate from the world along with those who see in the council a warrant for more involvement in the world. One can find interpreters who can find in the council documents the justification for a politically involved theology aimed at confronting social injustice along with those who stress traditional approaches to liturgy and religious life as keys to the future of the church.

In a 1995 interview David Tracy, one of the most productive and important theologians in the American Catholic Church, said that since the council Catholicism understands itself as *semper reformanda*, always reforming and in need of doing so. The three dimensions of a vibrant church, according to Tracy, are the mystical one (the piety, rituals and community life of the church), the intellectual dimension (theologies, philosophies, literature, and sciences related to the church), and the institutional factor (the explicit exercise of authority in the church). Each has its place and each has its particular temptations. Left to themselves without reference to the other parts, each can make wrong turns: the mystical element can become superstitious, the intellectual dimension can over-rationalize and divorce itself from mystery, and the institutional arm can find itself exercising power for its own sake.[8]

If allowed to do so, the American Catholic Church is capable of generating conversations that can lead to new understandings of its life and faith for the next millennium. It has managed to come this far without doctrinal splits, with a rich spiritual tradition, and a solid history of response to issues of social justice. Pressing pastoral problems today include: the future of the priesthood (including women's ordination and optional celibacy); the status of divorced and remarried Catholics; constructive conversations with homosexual Catholics; the implementation of new forms of ministry and spirituality; the inclusion of Hispanics, blacks, women and others previously left out of the mix; and the need to address pressing issues of ecumenical dialogue and Third-World Catholicism. Most American Catholics resist appeals to authoritarianism and are eager to discern the *sensus fidei* of the church as a whole. Unlike those who perceive the church as "finished," they are willing to cooperate in a maturation process that moves slowly but surely with confidence in the whole people of God.

NOTES

1 Let me gloss this sentence. The condemnation of modernism in the early years of the twentieth century was so severe that it stifled creativity and led to an atmosphere of intellectual fearfulness in the church. Pius XII (1939–58) made some moves that encouraged critical scholarship and renewal through his encyclicals *Divino Afflante Spiritu* (1943), permitting the use of modern historical methods by biblical exegetes; and *Mediator Dei* (1947), calling for the intelligent participation of the laity in the mass; but he also signaled a highly defensive posture with *Humani Generis* (1951) warning against the accommodation of Catholic theology to current intellectual trends.

2 Garry Wills, *Bare Ruined Choirs: Doubt, Prophecy, and Radical Religion* (New York: Doubleday, 1972). The first section, on memories of a Catholic boyhood, fifties Catholicism and the liturgical crisis, is still one of the best presentations of the rumbles beneath the surface of seemingly placid pre-conciliar Catholicism.

3 Charles R. Morris, *American Catholic: The Saints and Sinners Who Built America's Most Powerful Church* (New York: Times Books, 1997), p. 422.

4 John R. Dreese, "A priest looks at priest pedophilia," *Commonweal* 121 (April 22, 1994), pp. 11–14. Dreese says that because of these scandals, a "heavy pall hangs over the life of priesthood. Priests find their duties difficult and joyless. Some are ashamed to wear a Roman collar."

5 Thomas C. Fox, *Sexuality and Catholicism* (New York: George Braziller, 1995).

6 Mary Jo Weaver, *New Catholic Women: A Contemporary Challenge to Traditional*

Religious Authority (Bloomington, Ind.: Indiana University Press, 10th anniversary edition, 1994).

7 Daniele Menozzi, "Opposition to the council 1966–1984," in Giuseppe Alberigo, Jean-Pierre Jossua, and Joseph A. Komonchak, (eds) *The Reception of Vatican II*, (Washington DC: Catholic University Press, 1987), pp. 325–48.

8 "Reasons to hope for reform: an interview with David Tracy," in *America* 173 (October 14, 1995), pp. 12–18.

BIBLIOGRAPHY

Alberigo, Giuseppe, Jossua, Jean-Pierre, and Komonchak, Joseph A. (1987) *The Reception of Vatican II*, Washington, DC: Catholic University Press.

Burns, Gene (1992) *The Frontiers of Catholicism: The Politics of Ideology in a Liberal World*, Berkeley, Calif.: University of California Press.

Morris, Charles R. (1997) *American Catholic: The Saints and Sinners Who Built America's Most Powerful Church*, New York: Times Books.

Oates, Mary J. (1995) *The Catholic Philanthropic Tradition in America*, Bloomington, Ind.: Indiana University Press.

Weaver, Mary Jo, and Appleby, R. Scott, (eds) (1995) *Being Right: Conservative Catholicism in America*, Bloomington, Ind.: Indiana University Press.

— and — (eds) (1999) *What's Left: Progressive Catholicism in America*, Bloomington, Ind.: Indiana University Press.

Part IV

Popular and Material Culture

Introduction

The study of American religious history has undergone a number of paradigm shifts over the decades, as outlined in part in the general introduction. The earliest effort to interpret America's religious experience was that of the New England Puritans. In such works as Cotton Mather's *Magnalia Christi Americana* of 1702 these Calvinists employed the categories of Scripture – especially the Hebrew Bible – to come to an understanding of their own experience, interpreting the latter as providentially guided towards an ultimate realization of God's purposes through his new chosen people. This sense of providential guidance through historical development and of Protestant centrality persisted well into twentieth-century historiography, and was not directly challenged by more secular or pluralist readings until the late 1970s. Sydney Ahlstrom's recognition that the "Great Puritan Epoch" had ended with the election of a Roman Catholic president in 1960 was one of the first harbingers of a new interpretive paradigm, even though Ahlstrom himself had stressed the centrality of Puritanism in his own magisterial *A Religious History of the American People* of 1973.

The Puritan legacy has also been evident in American religious historiography in what has been called its *logocentrism*, that is, its focus on the centrality of the written and spoken *word* in religious life. Puritan – and, more broadly, Protestant – belief and practice have taken Scripture as the ultimate locus of divine presence and authority, and have correspondingly made the proclamation of God's Word, in preaching and theological writing, the most central religious activity. The normative study of American religion, then, involved describing the development of religious thought and institutions – primarily Protestant – from their (usually) European origins to their state in the present-day United States.

As "mainline" Protestantism began to lose its normative character in the broader society, and as scholars of non-Protestant background began to enter the academy, these assumptions about the proper practice of historical interpretation began to undergo some important modifications. Most obviously, it has become increasingly clear that American religious life no longer centers on the cluster of "mainline" Protestant denominations that for many decades had held sway both in theological and political communities of discourse and in the realm of religious historiography as well. Catholics, Jews, non-Christian religions, and previously marginalized strains of Protestantism such as Pentecostalism and fundamentalism now began to exert a significant role in the public arena and to demand an accounting by religious studies scholars.

In addition, many scholars began to realize that developmental accounts of religious leaders, institutions, and ideas were not sufficient to account for the religious experience of many Americans – even mainline Protestants themselves. Although the major denominations, their clerical leadership, and the theological traditions that informed their seminaries have certainly played an important role in the shaping of America's religious life, they have from the beginning existed in a counterpoint with other, more diffuse movements and practices that might collectively be called *popular* religion. Though highly diffuse, popular religion usually is characterized by a desire for direct contact with the supernatural, in such forms as emotional conversions, miraculous healings, and experience of the Holy Spirit in the form of glossolalia. Such phenomena may eventually become institutionalized, but generally begin in the context of grassroots dissatisfaction with more formal belief and worship.

Similarly, the realm of material culture, which had been minimized in traditional Protestant belief and practice, has now re-emerged as a central locus for study. Roman Catholics and other groups – Anglicans, Eastern Orthodox, as well as many Jews and Lutherans – had worshiped for centuries in a manner in which the proclamation of God's word was accompanied by a web of gestures and movements enabled by a variety of physical accompaniments: buildings, stained glass windows, paintings and sculpture, objects wrought in wood, metal, or even plastic, as well as the matter of everyday life in the form of bread, wine, oil, and water – or, more radically, poisonous snakes. This *sacramentalism* – the use of material objects as channels through which contact with the supernatural world is achieved, and which often involves the consecration of the realm of the everyday – constitutes an alternative theological and liturgical world to that of traditional American Protestantism.

The material dimensions of religion provide windows into a variety of other facets of the American experience as well. Anthropologists such as Mary Douglas have made it clear that the human body is the basis of much religious and political symbolism, and it does not take a great deal of imagination to realize the degree to which preoccupation with our own bodies pervades contemporary American culture. Physical well-being has thus been a theme in much official and popular religion, taking on a central role in movements and phenomena such as Christian Science, Seventh-Day Adventism, and the Catholic cult of the Virgin Mary at Lourdes: all, significantly, focused on female presences. Food preparation and consumption and sexuality are other body-centered areas of vital everyday activity in which women in particular have been involved and which have only recently begun to be investigated in their religious dimensions.

Jeanne Halgren Kilde concerns herself with a virtually indispensable aspect of religious worship: its physical setting. Throughout the history of Christianity, there has been a tension between religious buildings designed specifically to evoke a sense of the presence of the sacred – exemplified in pre-Vatican II Catholicism

– and those which are simply intended to provide an appropriate setting for preaching, such as the meetinghouses of Puritan New England. In the latter case, Protestants, like Jews, have often turned to secular models to find an appropriate functional setting for their worship. Kilde here discusses the adaptation of the secular arrangements of the theater to the needs of revival preaching, beginning with that of the eminent Charles G. Finney in the mid-nineteenth century. The consequences of this strategy proved to be considerable in reconfiguring the relationship of preacher and congregation.

Leonard Primiano explores the material dimensions of contemporary Roman Catholicism, beginning with a personal encounter in far-off Newfoundland that leads him back to his native Philadelphia. His pursuit of sources of Catholic material culture reveals dimensions of economics and marketing, popular and clerical taste, ethnic and class differences, the liturgical impact of Vatican II on American Catholic life, and the thin line separating "official" Catholicism from popular practices, including the syncretistic practices of Vodou and Santeria brought to this country by recent Caribbean immigrants.

Daniel Sack investigates the roles that food has played in American Protestant culture, in this case primarily through the careful longitudinal study of one representative congregation. Sack reminds us how central the preparation, serving, and consumption of food has proven in the life of many church communities, and how these processes exist in a dialectical relationship with other aspects of culture, for example, gender and age roles and norms. In addition, a shift in time of emphasis from the internal life of the congregation to reach out to those beyond its circle indicates a change both in social circumstances and a religiously informed response to those circumstances.

At the other end of the religious spectrum, *Marie Griffith* explores what seems to be a distinctively Protestant phenomenon of religiously-inspired diet books. Lacking the ascetic tradition of Catholicism, American Protestants have had to invent their own theological approach to matters of bodily health. However, the question of slimness as a cultural desideratum, even obsession, beyond issues of physical health leads into the issue of the dialectical relationship between Protestantism, especially in its contemporary Evangelical manifestations, and religious ideals and practices.

Bill Leonard reports on his experience as a participant-observer in one of the most notorious and least understood aspects of American Protestantism, the Appalachian cult of snake handling. Leonard argues that this often sensationalized practice is actually rooted firmly in more familiar traditions: Evangelicalism, fundamentalism, Pentecostalism, revivalism, and biblical primitivism. The handling of poisonous serpents in the course of Pentecostal services can best be understood as a kind of sacramentalism, in which the elements of the physical world can serve as channels for supernatural power.

Chapter 12

Architecture and Urban Revivalism in Nineteenth-century America

Jeanne Halgren Kilde

Religious revivals, characterized by large gatherings of people celebrating and participating in an emotional outpouring of Christian spirit, are closely associated with the spaces in which they occur. From Billy Sunday's revival tents to Billy Graham's athletic stadiums to Robert Schuller's glistening Crystal Cathedral, twentieth century revivalism brings to mind the image of a multitudinous audience seated in an amphitheater-like auditorium – a large space housing a semicircle of ascending seats radiating from a center stage – and focused intently on a magnetic speaker. However familiar the auditorium revival space is today, though, it was revolutionary in the nineteenth century and constituted an unprecedented and unique addition to the history of Christian church architecture. The origins of this spatial plan lay in the architectural iconoclasm of urban Protestant revivalists willing to favor utilitarianism over convention. Led by preacher Charles G. Finney, Presbyterian revivalists in New York City opted in 1832 to hold their revival meetings in a former theater, a space that proved remarkably facilitative of the revival agenda. As theater-like spaces were subsequently adapted by revivalists for later church buildings, however, they engendered an unexpected consequence. The new revival spaces reconfigured the relationship between the preacher and the audience, aligning the preacher with the actor on stage, and recontextualizing his or her performance and authority within a more audience-centered spatial dynamic. The space itself tended to favor charismatic preaching and enhance the authority of those individuals gifted in theatrical techniques while simultaneously ushering in new audience expectations for preacherly performance and the worship experience, and, as a result, giving audiences a new influence over worship. Although the theater-derived architecture that enhanced this audience-centered dynamic had limited influence among Protestant congregations in general during the middle decades of the nineteenth century, it resurfaced with great strength at two later points in US history: the late nineteenth century and the late twentieth century. Like the early development of the auditorium church space, each of these resurgences has been accompanied by a preoccupation with furnishing worship services that satisfy audience needs, desires, and expectations.

The religious revivals of the mid-eighteenth and early nineteenth centuries owed much of their success to the powerful, emotion-packed, mostly extemporaneous preaching of extraordinary speakers. A successful revival preacher could captivate a huge audience, using his words to fill them first with dread of their imminent and horrible doom and then with exuberant joy at their chance to be saved in the bosom of Christ. Like an actor, such preachers honed their oratorical skills and delivery with the goal of enhancing the emotional impact of their words on their audiences. Indeed, many successful revival preachers have owed a great debt to the theater itself. Noted eighteenth-century revivalist George Whitefield, labeled the "Divine Dramatist" by historian Harry S. Stout (1991), drew upon his early acting experiences to enhance the emotional impact of his preaching. Recognizing the power of performance, revivalists like Whitefield mimicked theatrical strategies, borrowing oratorical styles, and punctuating their sermons with exaggerated facial expressions and bodily gestures. Such strategies not only intensified the force and significance of the message, but also personalized an audience's experience of the sermon, encouraging witnesses to feel intimately engaged in the event. Savvy preachers soon learned the more emotive the performance, the more popular the preacher.

The buildings in which revivals were held, however, often frustrated revivalists' efforts to maximize the emotional impact of their preaching. In North America, Protestant worship space since the 1630s had consisted of variations on a fairly simple spatial theme: a single room, either square or rectangular, with a pulpit located on one wall and rows of seats facing it. This plan proved remarkably versatile, and Congregationalists, Anglicans, Presbyterians, Baptists, and Methodists adopted it through two centuries to serve their purposes. As revival spaces, however, these buildings left much to be desired. For one thing, the relatively small buildings could not accommodate large audiences. Whitefield's appearances, for instance, were noted for huge audiences that spilled out of the church buildings into churchyards and streets. Even when large audiences could squeeze into the buildings, their view of the pulpit was often obstructed by columns or galleries and those seated in the rear sections could often not hear the proceedings. Thus, these traditional spaces undermined revivalists' attempts to heighten the immediacy and emotional impact of their preaching.

The transformation of the traditional church plan commenced in 1832 when evangelical Presbyterians attempted to broaden the appeal of their denomination among the urban working classes. Within the rapidly growing city of New York (the population had more than doubled in the previous two decades to over 200,000 people) religious denominations were becoming markedly competitive. While the Methodists were proving quite successful in expanding their congregations by preaching to the working people of the city, the Presbyterians' erudite sermonizing and costly pew rentals (congregations supported themselves financially by renting their pews on a yearly basis) warned the working classes from their doors. A small group of wealthy businessmen, however, spurred by concern over the burgeoning urban population and what they perceived as its lack of moral grounding, decided to enhance the influence of Presbyterianism by eliminating pew rentals (hence their identification as "free church" Presbyterians) and providing preaching that was intellectually accessible to the urban population (Cole 1953). The leader of this group, Lewis Tappan, a merchant and abolitionist leader, hoped to establish a permanent free church congregation by attracting city dwellers with the revival preaching of Charles Grandison Finney, a man already well known for directing successful revivals in up-state New York.

Space was at a premium in the burgeoning city, however, and Tappan's search for a building in which to locate the new free church ended only when he discovered the foundering Chatham Garden Theater in the heart of the city. Ironically, immediate opposition to the plan to gather a religious congregation in a theater, a veritable den of wickedness, came from Finney himself. Could Christian authority hold sway in such a space? In a letter responding to questions Finney had raised about the enterprise, Tappan wrote an impassioned appeal:

> The *sensation* [emphasis in original] that will be produced by converting the place, with slight alterations, into a church will be very great; and curiosity will be excited . . . By taking this theatre & appropriating it for a church the whole city will talk of it, wonder and inquire [illegible]. We then have secured the attention of a vast multitude, and the measures subsequently taken will be made known to them. Strangers will be desirous of visiting this place, will talk about it when they go home; & they will be stimulated to similar efforts. It will have the effect of storming a redoubt, or taking cannon & turning them upon the enemy, as in an army. (Tappan to Finney, CGFP March 16, 1832)

Tappan's militaristic language highlights the extent to which meaning and authority were at stake in this move. Evangelicals condemned the theater with tracts, sermons, and newspaper articles denouncing the immorality that characterized both the actors' performances and the audiences' activities (Grimsted 1968). In moving into the Chatham, the free church Presbyterians were taking on this evil enemy precisely where he lived, for although the Chatham theater, built in 1824, had enjoyed a brief period of prosperity, a series of disappointing seasons had reduced its reputation. Like most theaters of the period, its third tier reputedly held prostitutes, and a saloon in the gallery kept the play goers liberally lubricated, but, more importantly, as an article in the May 2, 1831 issue of the *New York Mirror* explained, its fare of equestrian and circus shows at cheap prices marked the establishment as decidedly low on the social scale. Finney wondered whether "the location [was] too filthy, etc. for decent people to go there" and whether the "place [could be] made decent inside & out for the worship of God" (quoted in the letter from Tappan to Finney, CGFP March 16, 1832).

Upon obtaining Finney's rather reluctant approval, Tappan acquired a ten-year lease on the building and immediately commenced a strategic assault on the meanings previously associated with the space. He and his colleagues spread stories attesting to the power of their revival message within this former den of

Satan. Tappan, for instance, testified that during lease negotiations he and his colleague William Green, Jr. had convinced the owner of the building of the sinfulness of his involvement in theatrical enterprises. Similarly, theater lessee and circus manager William Blanchard was so overcome by the evangelicals' arguments that he wept and agreed to assist in converting the building to religious use. A reformed actor who had performed on the Chatham stage reportedly offered the first prayers in one saloon-cum-prayer room, and some thirty grogshops in the neighborhood closed shortly after the theater became a chapel (letter from Tappan to Finney, CGFP May 22, 1832,). Apocryphal though they may be, these stories show how the meanings associated with the space were negotiated and changed; what had once been a sinful place was fully "converted" into a spiritually powerful site. As Finney's close friend Herman Norton stated in a letter of April 10, 1832, "The Theatre we trust is taken out of the hands of the Devil & will hereafter become a Bethesda. Your voice will one day I hope be heard there proclaiming salvation where have stood the Gates of Hell" (CGFP). By announcing such a public victory over the meaning of this formerly sinful space, the free churchers bridged a critical gap between the immoral space of the theater and their Christian agenda, thereby creating the conditions under which the space could be legitimated for religious uses.

Finney and others who came to preach in the new Chatham Street Chapel immediately recognized the utilitarian benefits of theater space in presenting the revivalist's message. The 65 by 100 foot room could accommodate a large audience: some 2,500 people could be seated in the boxes that lined the walls of the house. In addition, the view of the stage from the boxes was excellent. The original "pit," or main floor, had been constructed at a fairly high elevation and also provided reasonably good views (Young 1973: 72–4). The free churchers, moreover, improved upon the pit seating by inclining the floor from the stage up to the first tier of boxes, a strategy for creating obstruction-free sightlines that was rare in American theaters of the period. Good acoustics also rendered the theater-cum-chapel superior to most large churches as a place for hearing sermons. As the *New York Evangelist* reported on May 12, 1832, despite some distracting noises from the perimeter during the initial service, "the speaker's voice was distinctly heard in all parts of the house." Thus, the building addressed the major limitations of traditional church spaces: inadequate size, sightlines, and acoustics.

The Chatham theater space also provided a number of additional benefits to revival preachers intent upon enhancing the emotional impact of their sermons. For one thing, it allowed the preacher much greater physical freedom. Traditional pulpits of the period were large, often ornamented, elevated boxes, which the preacher entered by mounting a narrow stairway of eight to ten steps. Once in the box with the door closed, the preacher was relatively fixed, as there was little room for movement. The audience, whether looking up from their seats below or across from the gallery, could see only the preacher's head and torso. Thus, the preacher could enhance his oratory with movement of his arms or upper body, but the pulpit restricted further motion. In contrast, the Chatham Street Chapel gave the preacher a whole stage with only a lectern, placed center-front, to impede the performance. The preacher could easily move about and use his full body in the delivery of the sermon.

The spatial dynamic, or relative power based on physical positioning, between the audience and the preacher was altered from the traditional models in this building. Power and authority in traditional churches was clearly designated by the imposing presence of the large raised pulpits that physically elevated the preacher over the heads of the congregants. This elevated presence, backed by the dignity and power of the preacher's ministerial office itself, left no doubt as to whose agenda and position was of greater consequence. While the Chatham stage sacrificed this architectural statement of clerical authority, it included an apparatus designed to establish power in a quite similar way, that is, by manipulating an audience's perception of the speaker and the performance by enhancing their visual impact. The proscenium arch, used on theater stages since the eighteenth century, accentuates a performance just as a frame accentuates the picture it surrounds, that is, by outlining the stage and directing the gaze of the audience into that space. Designed to underscore the difference between the framed (imaginary or extraordinary) space and the exterior (real or ordinary) hall, a proscenium privileges the authority of the performer by setting him or her apart from the world of ordinary experience. In the Chatham Chapel, the proscenium undoubtedly functioned similarly, emphasizing the performance and authority of the preacher. In fact, the proscenium stage proved superior to many elevated pulpits precisely because it catered to audience's needs, encouraging them to focus their attention on the stage.

Thus the theater space served to heighten the attention of the audience and underscored the authority of the preacher on the stage, properties that ultimately facilitated both the delivery and the reception of the revival message. From the revivalist's perspective, this was no small benefit. For a preacher such as Finney, whose power stemmed from his ability to transfix audiences with the immediacy of his message, this architectural setting magnified the impact of that message. His preaching style fitted comfortably into the theatrical space: he gesticulated, he raised his voice to great shrieks and lowered it to whispers, he scanned the crowd for sinners, dragging his piercing gaze from face to face, and he addressed individual sinners by name and publicly excoriated them (Weisberger 1958: 100–3). The Reverend Henry Ward of Boston, commenting on Finney's performance at Utica in 1826, condemned it as sham:

> He has talents, unquestionable talents, but no heart. He feels no more than a millstone . . . he is acting a cold, calculating part . . . His tones of voice, his violent, coarse, unfeeling utterance, his abject groanings, his writhing of his body as if in agony, all testify that he is a hypocrite, and yet I try not to be uncharitable. (Ware 1846: 179–81)

Whether sincere or fabricated, physical demonstrativeness was critical to Finney's success as well as to that of other revival preachers who stood before diverse and untested audiences with diminished access to traditional sources of clerical authority. The revival preacher delivered a message geared toward convincing those assembled of the centrality of their own responsibility for their eternal souls: a message that at its heart bred antinomianism (the idea that faith alone is needed for salvation and that the sanctified must follow divine law even when it conflicts with human law) and necessarily brought earthly, clerical authority into question. Revival preachers lost the cloak of traditional clerical authority as they postulated conversion based upon personal struggle with one's own conscience guided by God. They lost the cloak of intellectual authority as they condemned the educated ministry and exhorted extemporaneously in vernacular language (Hatch 1989). With such traditional avenues to power diminished, new sources for religious and social power had to be created if their revival message was to be heard. Personal power or charisma substituted for institutional, ecclesiastical authority, making preachers' success heavily reliant upon their ability to connect with audiences, on their ability to perform. The spaces of the theater were precisely what these preachers needed to enhance their performances because they allowed for greater dramatic expressiveness while maintaining preacherly spatial status (albeit on stage, not in a pulpit) and the incumbent authority it underscored. Although no record of Finney's thoughts on the performance-enhancing power of the Chatham space survives, his close associate, the Reverend Joel Parker, who preached in the Chapel many times, recognized the effectiveness of the space, declaring, "if I were to build a church it should be in this form" (letter from Tappan to Finney, CGFP March 22, 1832).

That Finney came to admire the theater as a preaching space is clearly suggested by his first attempt to design a revival space. Within three years of moving into the Chatham Street Chapel, Finney became involved in the designing of a new church to serve as the home for a segment of the growing Chapel congregation and as a site for the annual anniversary meetings of several religious and moral reform societies. The Broadway Tabernacle, completed in 1836, was conceived in the spatial terms of the theater. In contemplating a new building, Finney was particularly determined to bring as many people as possible within the sound of the voice in the pulpit, and, according to his memoir, his influence on the design was enormous:

> The plan of the interior of that house was my own. I had observed the defects of churches in regard to sound; and was sure that I could give the plan of a church in which I could easily speak to a much larger congregation than any house would hold that I had ever seen. (Finney 1989: 367)

When approached to design such a space, builder Joseph Ditto was singularly reluctant. As Finney remembered, "he [Ditto] objected to it that it would not appear well, and feared that it would injure his reputation to build a church with such an interior as that" (Finney 1989: 367). The design Finney envisioned and that was realized in the Broadway Tabernacle went far beyond the theatrical strategies of the Chatham Street Chapel, to draw directly upon the spatial arrangement of the classical amphitheater. As church architecture, the building was unprecedented in the United States, and it is perhaps not surprising that a builder would be suspicious of the project. Following the classical amphitheater plan, the Broadway Tabernacle's main floor was given over entirely to the audience; only the projecting stage and its background wall, reserved for the musical elements of the service, intruded upon the audience space. The room itself was square, with each side about 100 feet long. Within that space, a circular arrangement was inscribed, with the orientation of the room radiating from a somewhat off-center stage. A dome in the center of the ceiling emphasized this circular theme as did arcs of pews that curved around the pulpit-stage. While it is unclear whether the main floor sloped from pulpit up through the audience room (a bowl-like effect common in later buildings), the general thrust of the space was toward the pulpit, mimicking the inverted spatial cone of the classical amphitheater. The gallery encircling three quarters of the room (interrupted only by the organ case that surmounted the stage) held stepped ranks of seats, creating a profoundly vertical slope in the upper regions of the room and a distinct amphitheatre effect. Although the exact figures are not known, this audience room likely accommodated some two to three thousand people.

Dismissing traditional forms of ecclesiastical architecture, this building borrowed from two sources, the first and most familiar of which in the New York landscape was the circus amphitheater. In establishments like the popular Rickett's Circus, raked rows of seats encircled a center ring in which animal acts were performed. Intended to attract large crowds, these amphitheaters accommodated several hundred spectators, and cheap ticket prices ensured that the performances were well attended. The circus, however, remained a distinctly lower-class form of entertainment as urban elites considered its spectacle unrefined. In addition to this debt to the circus plan, Tabernacle shared much, architecturally and socially, with eighteenth-century German and French experiments in theater design. In an effort to eliminate the court theater with its dual focus on stage and royal box (opposite the stage) and create a theater space appropriate to the growing bourgeoisie, a few European designers had used amphitheater seating that focused attention exclusively on the stage. This plan leveled out hierarchy among audience members by giving each person a comfortable seat and good sightlines to the stage (Schwarzer 1994: 58). Legitimate theaters in the United States, however, would not draw upon this amphitheater design until the 1840s (McConachie 1992), making its use in the 1836 Broadway Tabernacle extraordinary.

The spatial dynamics in the amphitheater were also quite different from those in traditional churches. Allowing audience members to view one another, the curved rows of the amphitheater helped to create a strongly shared identity among audiences, merging them into a "corporate body" of undifferentiated social equals sharing a mutual agenda (Goodsell 1988: 38, 51, 198). When the new Tabernacle audiences gazed out at one another, they did, in fact, see a fairly homogeneous group. The Finney revivals had not attracted the urban poor as the free churchers had initially intended; instead, they appealed to more respectable religious and civic-minded individuals of the artisan and business classes. While it is unclear whether those who remained at Chatham differed significantly in socio-economic status from those who went to the new Tabernacle, the Tabernacle congregation quickly gained a reputation as a bastion of the reform-minded middle class. Their "corporate body" identity was reflected in and reinforced by the decision of the free church group to separate from the ecclesiastical power of the Presbyterian Church: upon their occupation of the new building, they renounced their denominational affiliation and declared the Tabernacle Congregationalist.

The new social ramifications of amphitheater seating complicated the question of authority within revival space. On the one hand, the Tabernacle's interior arrangement lent profound authority to a charismatic speaker, just as had that of the Chatham Street Chapel. Jutting out into the semicircle of seats, the stage was raised some five or six feet above the main floor of the house, and two fifteen-foot-high lamps flanked the lectern table centered at the front of the stage. The encircling (and perhaps raked) floor made the preacher's performance space readily viewable from three sides, and the speaker could see the congregants in all parts of the house. Although lacking a proscenium, the thrust stage of the Tabernacle had its own benefit, placing the speaker physically close to the audience. It also offered several visual elements to attract and rivet the audience's gaze. Choir members seated on risers behind the pulpit formed an intriguing, motion-filled background, and the pipes of the huge organ rose to the ceiling like a gigantic musical monolith behind the choir. Placing the preacher on a large, elevated stage quite near the audience, and making that stage visually interesting, the Tabernacle space, like the Chatham Street Chapel space, underscored the importance and authority of the preacher.

These new features also visually emphasized a new significance of music in the service. Under Thomas Hastings's direction, musical performance achieved an unprecedented prominence in the Tabernacle, which quickly attained a national reputation for the quality of its music. Services opened and closed with well-rehearsed pieces by choir or organist, thus adding a new form of performance to the service and raising audience expectations. These new visual and aural elements forced preachers on the Tabernacle stage into a competition of sorts for the attention of worshipers. As in the Chatham Street Chapel, clerical intellectual and spiritual authority existed in a new context, one that privileged dramatic performance, but the Tabernacle also encouraged new types of dramatic performance to flourish.

The arbiters of the stage performances, just as in the popular theater, were the people in the seats, and in the Tabernacle, their "corporate identity," enhanced by the space and their homogeneity, carried significant ramifications in this regard. Every aspect of the religious experience, both physical and spiritual, was designed to satisfy this homogeneous audience's needs. The building itself was constructed to facilitate the physical needs of each person to see and hear the stage performance. Similarly, the performances were gauged to address the needs of the soul, to elevate the people's spirits – through inspiring sermons and, increasingly, through heart-stirring music. Such overwhelming attention to congregational needs had the potential to eclipse clerical agendas, a situation more akin to that of the audience-driven theater than that of clergy-directed churches.

While one might expect that in this spatial setting preachers would heighten their theatricality in order to compete with the musical performances (and later in the century, many preachers did just this), Finney himself seems to have toned down the histrionics of his earlier years. Several commentators on his later preaching style have claimed that he depended upon reason and logic to move his audiences rather than the "soul-stirring appeals to the heart and conscience" although his "dramatic power" continued to be often cited. Why the change in style? As one friend suggested, the "peculiar circumstances in which [he had been] placed have led . . . to a discussion of abstract theological subjects" (Fletcher 1943: 31). The "peculiar circumstances" seem to have been those created by the unique spatial features and resulting corporate audience of the Tabernacle. Unlike the (supposedly) spiritually-bereft masses at which the Chapel revivals aimed, people needing to be persuaded that their eternal souls were in jeopardy, the Tabernacle audience was convinced of its spiritual needs and strongly Christian-identified. For Finney in the Broadway Tabernacle, the revival was over; he was preaching to the converted, and believers did not need to have their attentions seized and their souls wrested away from distractions. The more educated middle class audiences of the Tabernacle were less impressed by dramatic gestures than by well-reasoned arguments, and Finney, ironically, was forced back into a more traditional mode of asserting clerical power: appeals to intellectual authority and erudite language. His message and style changed to suit his new audience, much as theatre producers changed their shows and actors changed their performance styles to suit specific audiences. That Finney's style changed is indicative of the increasing power audience needs and expec- tations wielded over the form of religious services. His "performances" continued to be evaluated and hailed, and his oratorical power remained strong, but the Tabernacle audience held significant influence as well.

Although Finney went on to help design another amphitheater-like church in Oberlin, Ohio, in 1842, it was not only clear that the revival was over, but also that American Protestants were relatively uncomfortable with the theater-like spaces and the meanings attached to them. Those congregations that ex- perimented with the amphitheater features did so conservatively, usually by enhancing audience sightlines in their traditional sanctuaries, or audience rooms, by replacing the old box pews with the now common narrow slip pews and slanting each row toward the pulpit – making their audience rooms into auditori- ums but not amphitheaters. Plymouth Congregational Church in Brooklyn, for instance, constructed in 1850 to the specifications of charismatic preacher Henry Ward Beecher, consisted of a wide rectangular (almost square) room with a longi- tudinal axis terminating in a Tabernacle-like thrust stage surmounted by an organ pipe case. The floor, however, was level and seating was not semicircular. Even this period of limited experimentation with auditorium plans was soon curtailed, however, as the professionalizing of architectural practice and the growth of the Gothic Revival in the 1850s imposed new spatial and aesthetic criteria upon church building. The new trend cast aside auditorium seating experiments in favor of a neo-traditionalism (albeit Roman Catholic and Anglican) that imposed rigid social hierarchy and clerical authority on worship space. Baptists, Methodists and Presbyterians, building in the growing frontier towns of westwardly expanding America, overwhelmingly adopted Gothic facades and rectangular worship rooms ("naves" in the Gothic vocabulary) with longitudinal axes. The architectural iconoclasm of Finney and the revivalists was widely rejected, and as the traditional architectural forms regained hegemony so did traditional forms of clerical authority.

Amphitheater designs were, however, adopted fairly enthusiastically for impermanent rural revivals. Finney himself had a large tent constructed as an auditorium in which to conduct his revival meetings during his first years at Oberlin College, and large revival tents quickly became camp-meeting staples, sheltering hundreds of participants from inclement weather. Typically referred to as "tabernacles" these tents were gradually replaced by more durable wooden canopies. Such structures, occasionally closed off with canvas sides, remained prominent at camp-meetings through the century.

In the 1870s, however, over three decades after Finney's experiments in church architecture, the auditorium church design, complete with the inverted spatial cone of the amphitheater, resurfaced and achieved nationwide popularity on a scale undreamed of by Finney and its early developers. Between 1869 and 1910 not only did the construction of auditorium churches burgeon, but so did the inclusion of theater-derived features in these buildings. Across the country church designers adopted square and circular audience rooms and furnished their raked floors with rows of curved pews that radiated from a pulpit-stage. Horseshoe balconies swept dramatically around audience rooms throughout the country, as in Warren H. Hayes's Wesley Methodist Episcopal (1891) in Minneapolis and the "Mother Church" of Christian Science (1894) in Boston. Moreover, borrowings from theater became even more conspicuous. In the 1906 extension to the Boston Christian Science Church, architects Charles E. Brigham and Solon S. Beman installed three cantilevered galleries rising one above the next on the wall opposite the stage, an arrangement that was also used in the remodeled Tremont Temple in Boston. Upholstered flip-up theater seats replaced pews in many church auditoriums, including architect Stanford White's Lovely Lane Methodist Church in Baltimore (1884). The focus of these new church rooms was on the elaborate stage, usually placed either on the short wall terminating a longitudinal axis or in a corner, thus creating a diagonal orientation. Fully articulated and elaborately decorated proscenium arches defined these pulpit stages in Baptist, Methodist, Congregational, and Presbyterian churches. Theatrical lighting schemes drew upon new electrical technologies not only to draw attention to pulpit stages but also to ornament audience spaces. For instance, rows of marquis lights outlined the proscenium arch and gallery edges in Boston's Tremont Temple (1893) and similar lights lined the vaulting in architect Sidney Badgley's Pilgrim Congregational Church in Cleveland (1893). In addition, in at least one church, Richard Roeschlaub's Trinity Methodist Episcopal Church in Denver, opera boxes graced the elaborate proscenium.

Moving well beyond its roots in revival religion, auditorium church design was adopted by a wide variety of congregations in the closing decades of the nineteenth century, bridging gaps between revivalism, evangelicalism, and liberalism. On the one hand, the design resurfaced in revival buildings like the remodeled

Tremont Temple in Boston, the Ryman Auditorium (1889) in Nashville, and the Moody Memorial Church (1924) in Chicago. But amphitheater design was also adopted by evangelical congregations, such as the First Congregational Church (1887) in Minneapolis and the Trinity ME (1888) Church in Denver. Moreover, liberal congregations such as David Swing's iconoclastic Presbyterians adopted the plan. After holding services in McVicker's Theater in downtown Chicago, they enthusiastically supported the construction of Swing's Central Church (1880), designed specifically as a music hall with an oversized audience room, curvilinear seating with a very steep rise, and a half-octagon stage complete with wings and backstage space.

Just at the time Protestantism was undergoing enormous divisions and tensions from such external and internal challenges as scientific evolution, new biblical criticism and questions of social justice, this widely shared architecture linked disparate denominations, suggesting the coherence of, at least, a shared aesthetic. This shared aesthetic, however, derived less from religious sources than from the growing power of the urban middle class. In their attempts to gather respectable, middle-class members, late-nineteenth century congregations openly competed for celebrated preachers and professional musicians, and to accommodate them they turned to auditorium churches. Congregations banked on the hope that an up-to-date auditorium church offering an exemplary setting for music and oratory might attract, or keep, a celebrated preacher, and many congregations were willing to spend often in excess of $150,000 to provide such a space. Preacherly power seemed to be at a peak, and charismatic oratory assured certain preachers in these spaces extensive authority and influence over their audiences, a fact evidenced by the elevation to celebrity status of such individuals as Henry Ward Beecher, David Swing, and Dwight L. Moody. But the new auditorium churches also enhanced the audiences' experience, ensuring each member a good view and aural reception in a physically comfortable setting, which was maintained through the latest technologies in central heating and air-conditioning. In these buildings, middle class worshipers demanded and got services consisting of fine music and a good lecture. Such catering to the needs of audiences occurred on a level not dreamed of in the earlier Chatham Chapel or Broadway Tabernacle, and suggests that despite the authority of eminent speakers, a good deal of the power to influence and direct worship services in these Gilded Age churches lay ultimately in the gracefully curved and softly upholstered pews rather than on the stage.

This "golden era" of auditorium churches proved relatively brief, however. Despite their nationwide popularity, the design succumbed to changing aesthetic judgements after the turn of the century. With the late Gothic Revival of the second decade of the twentieth century, auditorium style was once again shunted aside by architectural orthodoxy. Liberal Protestant congregations turned to technologically updated medieval forms, imitating such world renowned buildings as England's Ely Cathedral or patterning their buildings on English parish churches. Other denominations favored Renaissance and neoclassical styles. Whatever historical style they adopted, church designers of the mid-twentieth century wanted to carry it through from the exterior vocabulary to the interior spaces. By the mid-1920s interest in amphitheater and auditorium plan churches had succumbed to the new fashions. Hundreds of auditorium churches across the country remain intact, however, including the Lovely Lane Methodist Church in Baltimore, the Luther Place Memorial Church in Washington, DC, and Pilgrim Congregational in Cleveland.

In more recent memory, this spatial strategy has enjoyed a new resurgence as Protestant congregations, again interested in attracting large numbers of worshipers, have opted to build large circular or polygonal auditorium buildings, located conveniently near suburban housing developments and major freeway nodes. Huge auditoriums, or "megachurches," like the Willow Creek Church outside of Chicago, draw thousands of visitors weekly. These congregations have grown out of the work of individual organizers who adapt the methods of business marketing to the religious situation. For instance, Willow Creek organizer Bill Hybels, conducted intensive market research into the desires and expectations of his potential religious audiences prior to constructing the church. In fact, he literally went door-to-door canvassing people about their attitudes toward church services. Hybels found that contemporary audiences considered traditional liturgies and sermons boring and irrelevant, and they desired services that kept their attention fixed (Lewis 1996: 14). Like nineteenth century audiences, contemporary religious audiences are quite comfortable with cutting-edge technological strategies designed to accommodate these desires. Consequently, Willow Creek's sanctuary includes not only an amphitheater design that accommodates an audience of over 4,550, but also sound amplification, video projection, and spot- and laser-lights, which physically help the audience see and hear the message as well as convey it in a way that captures and holds their interest. Again, just as in the nineteenth century, these performance-enhancing techniques have been borrowed from the secular theater and bring with them the same implications regarding audience power. Satisfying audience expectations, however, goes beyond the physical features of the auditorium. Willow Creek services include a variety of pop-music numbers as well as narrative skits, complete with stage scenery and props; these are designed to demonstrate the contemporary relevance of the Christian message and to maintain audience attention. Thus, audiences stated their demands and the megachurches met them. Not surprisingly, megachurches have been accused of presenting a watered down Christian theology to maintain audience comfort. Ultimately, this consumer-oriented approach demonstrates a signal shift in the balance of audience/clerical power toward the audience side.

Although most religious practices – including the investment of special status in a priestly or clerical class, liturgies and other rituals, and preaching – have always addressed the needs of the laity to some extent, the development and use of the amphitheater space in the nineteenth century represents a dramatic change, both in the religious needs being met and the means developed to meet them. Physical, not spiritual, needs attained great influence during the 1830s revival period and perhaps predominance by the late nineteenth century. Surely in the late twentieth century, physical and psychic comfort guide the megachurches' success. Meeting these physical needs, auditorium church spaces have encouraged an audience self-awareness, or corporate body identity, that has helped congregations achieve great influence in the formulation of religious services while, at the same time, rendering that influence markedly transparent. Yet the auditorium space remains beneficial to clergy as well, its continued attractions remaining those that first appealed to revivalists in the 1830s: large spaces, good sightlines and acoustics, elevated and thrust stages, proscenium arches, etc. All of these features do indeed assist the orator in presenting the message. In 1836 Charles Grandison Finney claimed that the Broadway Tabernacle was "altogether the most spacious, commodious, and comfortable place to speak . . . [he had] ever seen of its size" (Finney 1989: 367). This capacity remains a critical feature of the legacy of the amphitheater churches of nineteenth century urban revivalism, but to it we must add that amphitheater church space has also proved uniquely empowering to audiences as well.

BIBLIOGRAPHY

CGFP (Charles Grandison Finney Papers), Oberlin College Archives, Oberlin, Oh.

Cole, Charles C., Jr. (1953) "The Free Church Movement in New York City," *New York History* 34 (July): pp. 284–97.

Finney, Charles Grandison (1989) *The Memoirs of Charles G. Finney: The Complete Restored Text*, ed. Garth M. Rosell and Richard A. G. Dupuis, Grand Rapids, Mich.: Academie Books.

Fletcher, Robert Samuel (1943) *A History of Oberlin College: From its Foundation through the Civil War*, vol. 1, Oberlin, Oh.: Oberlin College.

Goodsell, Charles (1988) *The Social Meaning of Civic Space*, Lawrence, Kan.: University of Kansas Press.

Grimsted, David (1968) *Melodrama Unveiled: American Theater and Culture, 1800–1850*, Chicago: University of Chicago Press.

Hatch, Nathan O. (1989) *The Democratization of American Christianity*, New Haven, Conn.: Yale University Press.

Lewis, Michael (1996) "The capitalist: God is in the packaging," *New York Times*, July 21, sect. 6.

McConachie, Bruce A. (1992) *Melodramatic Formations: American Theatre and Society, 1820–1870*, Iowa City, Ia.: University of Iowa Press.

Schwarzer, Mitchell (1994) "The social genesis of the public theater in Germany," in John Zukowsky (ed.) *Karl Friedrich Schinkel: The Drama of Architecture*, Chicago: Art Institute of Chicago.

Stout, Harry S. (1991) *The Divine Dramatist: George Whitefield and the Rise of Modern Evangelicalism*, Grand Rapids, Mich.: William B. Eerdmans Publishing Company.

Ware, John Ware (1846) *Memoir of the Life of Henry Ware, Jr.*, Boston: J. Munroe.

Weisberger, Bernard A. (1958) *They Gathered at the River: The Story of the Great Revivalists and their Impact upon Religion in America*, Boston, Mass.: Little, Brown and Company.

Young, William C. (1973) *Documents of American Theater History*, vol. 1, Chicago: American Library Association.

Chapter 13

Postmodern Sites of Catholic Sacred Materiality

Leonard Norman Primiano

A few years ago, I received a telephone call from a former student living in the city of Corner Brook in western Newfoundland. He had taken my course on "Folk Religion," when I was a visiting professor at Memorial University of Newfoundland's Department of Folklore. Remembering my discussion of the contemporary veneration of Catholic saints, he had a request for me. Could I purchase and send him an inexpensive statue of St Joseph, patron saint of workers and the family?

Even though he was residing in the province's second largest city, and the island has a large Catholic community, he was having difficulty obtaining this Catholic religious object that his father believed was crucial for the selling of their home. My student told me that his father had heard that individuals were having success in selling commercial and residential real estate in the difficult economic times of the early 1990s by burying a statue of St Joseph in the back yard of the building or home in question. The method for burying and preserving the saint's statue (upside down or right side up, left in its box, in the back or front of the house, facing the house or facing the street, or next to the "For Sale" sign) had been transmitted and interpreted to this student's father in several variants, but it always included the ritual of digging up the image when the property was sold and installing it in a place of honor in the newly acquired home or business.

This home-owner became convinced of the efficacy of this particular practice and wanted to apply it to his own personal circumstances (see also Clark 1990; Pacelle 1990). He was, in fact, following an ancient Christian tradition of taking holy things such as the relics of the martyrs and saints and using them to transform or "sacramentalize" everyday life (Brown 1981). Christians continue to integrate into the mundane world material culture expressing Christian imagery and symbol. From hand-crafted items to printed media and mechanically produced objects, religious material culture has been and continues to be purchased and given for placement in the home, workplaces, modes of transportation, or on the person (Lepovitz 1991; Spamer 1930). This tradition can readily be observed when doing ethnographic work with religious individuals and regional or ethnic communities in North America (Cartwright 1981; Cooper and Sciorra 1994; Cosentino 1995; Dewhurst *et al.* 1983; Flores-Peña and Evanchuk 1994; Gizelis 1971; Halle 1993; Lange 1974; Lessard 1981; Milspaw 1986; Morgan 1998; Orsi 1985, 1996; Pocius 1986; Sciorra 1989, 1993; Shaner 1961,1972; Teske 1973, 1980, 1985; Turner 1982, 1983, 1990; Turner and Seriff 1987; Vlach 1989; Yoder 1988, 1990; Yoder and Graves 1989).

My student's request to purchase a statue of St Joseph prompted me to reflect on several interrelated folklife questions concerning religious material culture in the United States (Primiano 1997a). At the end of the twentieth century, what were the possible sites for the purchase of such religious objects in an urban American context, such as the city of Philadelphia where I was living? What did such an availability of religious materials for purchase by the contemporary audience say about the personal religiosity of Americans? In an ethnographic context, how do the individuals who purchased such articles make use of religious objects within their lives? This study is a response to the first two queries. It is concerned with how religious objects enter into the everyday lives of North Americans; which Christian traditions and ideas about the material world are expressed by these sites; and how retail stores stimulate the negotiation between Roman Catholic tradition and vernacular creativity of contemporary Catholics.

I choose to emphasize religious material culture as my contribution to this volume because it is still possible to study American religious history and never touch any artifact, see any image, or even visit a site that relates to the lived religion of the people who are the subjects of discussion. It is also quite possible to read texts on American religion and never see a religious object pictured (as happened to be the case with this volume) or even discussed within its narrative. American ecclesiastical art and architecture is, on the other hand, the one component of material culture study and American religious creativity frequently considered by scholars (Dillenberger 1984; Williams 1988, 1997). Such studies present an excellent foundation for understanding the material expression of religious institutions in America, but they present the material face of normative religion, not expressions of the people's belief. Only recently have some historical studies of American religious material culture and lithography been published that discuss the religious objects used or created by Americans (McDannell 1995; Morgan 1996, 1998). In *Material Christianity*, Colleen McDannell discusses Protestant catalogs and bookstores selling religious goods in America from the perspective of "Christian retailing," but she does not consider in much detail stores that sell Catholic religious articles.

My interest in Catholic imagery in general and St Joseph in particular took me to several retail establishments in the city of Philadelphia. I visited museum and church shops selling gothic style Christian artifacts, everything from medieval gargoyles, Renaissance angel figurines, and kitchen magnets to stained glass replicas of great cathedral art. I discovered folk art stores selling authentic

Mexican, New Mexican, Puerto Rican santos (antique and contemporary carved wooden statues of the saints or the crucified Christ); retablos (tin votive or devotional paintings of saintly subjects and personal miraculous events); and contemporary religious art produced for the tourist trade (plaster, clay, or papier mâché images of Our Lady of Guadalupe, patroness of the Americas, for example, resting in tin or wooden shrines) (Briggs 1989; Durand and Massey 1995; Giffords 1992; Kalb 1994). There were also retro-Catholic stores that specialized in selling mass-produced Catholic-inspired items (such as "Nun-Zilla," a wind-up toy image of a nun that "breathes fiery sparks as she walks" or "the Boxing Nun," a nun puppet wearing boxing gloves) and, more significantly, Catholic devotional objects from the first sixty years of the century (including plaster reproductions and statuary of Marian apparitions at Lourdes and Fátima).

I also found Afro-Caribbean botanicas selling candles marked with many images of saints, statuary of plastic and plaster, magical oils, and sometimes offering the opportunity for a session with a reader and adviser in a back room (Borrello and Mathias 1977; Murphy 1988:39-48). Often overlapping with botanicas in both materials and clientele are New Age/pagan/Wiccan shops or stores. These stores usually offer a wide selection of material representations (neolithic goddesses of old Europe, Druidic and Celtic symbols, the ancient Greek and Roman pantheon, Native American totems, Hindu and Buddhist statues, Roman Catholic iconography, and Afro-Caribbean votive images). They also stock candles, oils, stones and crystals, devotional books and periodicals, as well as drums and rattles, chalices and vessels, pentacles for ritual use both for wearing on the person and placing on an altar, and meditative and ritual music (See Adler 1986 for a representative discussion of Wiccan and pagan periodical literature found in these stores, as well as for a discussion of the communal diversity and overlap that these stores serve). The general public visits both botanicas and these metaphysical centers out of curiosity, general interest, as well as a syncretic desire to tap into the belief systems they represent.

The same could be said about traditional Roman Catholic religious goods stores, where it is possible to see the full spectrum of contemporary Americans who identify with the Roman Catholic tradition. Traditionalist, restorationist, and progressive Catholics may visit such stores, as well as Catholic-influenced or interested peoples, such as adherents of Vodou, Santería, etc.

My quest for an inexpensive statue of St Joseph finally led me to the St Jude Shop in Havertown, Pennsylvania, advertised in the archdiocesan newspaper, *The Catholic Standard and Times* as "the largest religious goods store." This store is located in a middle-class suburb of the ethnically diverse city of Philadelphia, known still for its conservative brand of Catholicism. This shop is the main branch of six sites under the corporate title, "St Jude Shop Inc.," which was described to me by one of its family owners, Mark G. DiCocco, as "a corporation whose principle operation is the whole [sale] and retail sale of religious articles, books, and church goods." This store had run out of inexpensive statues of St Joseph, and it was necessary for me to return to make my purchase. Further visits to this shop piqued my interest in such a thriving, contemporary source of religious goods, and the place of objects and stores in the total lifeways of contemporary Catholics.

Students of contemporary American religion frequently encounter examples of such "sacred materiality" (O'Connor 1994) in their fieldwork within not only Christian and Christian-influenced communities, but among non-Christian individuals and groups as well. The groups include but are not limited to Roman Catholics, Eastern Orthodox, Lutherans, Mormons, Pentecostals, Evangelicals, Afro-Caribbeans, Jews, Muslims, Buddhists, Native Americans, Neo-Pagans/Wiccans, and New Age believers. Researchers might recognize that the blessedness of material objects is a potent force within religious belief systems, but they do not know what to call it. Each culture and religious tradition articulates its own beliefs about sacred materiality and the form that it takes.

Within Roman Catholicism, the unique theological term used to express the relationship of the sacred and the material is "sacramentality" (Hufford 1987). Sacramentality has been described as the "notion that *all* reality is potentially and in fact the bearer of God's presence and the instrument of divine action on our behalf" (McBrien 1994: 1250). The principle of sacramentality . . . affirms that the invisible and spiritual God is present through the visible and the material, and that these are in turn made holy by that presence" (McBrien 1987: 441; see also Greeley 1988, 1989, 1990; Tracy 1981). For believing Catholics, a unique religious material culture exists reinforcing the Catholic attraction to sacramentality and the Catholic taste for sacramentals or material objects that assist worship or devotion.

The types of sacramentals that interest individual Catholics depend on their personal belief and practice, the type of family or ethnic Catholicism within which they have been raised, how they have been educated about Catholicism, and the locale or region of the country in which they live. The term "sacramental" is employed by Catholics to designate individual creations in a church: liturgical art objects (such as altars, chalices, vestments, monstrances, paschal candles) or church decorations (such as statuary, murals and frescoes, stained-glass windows). "Sacramentals" also refers to the objects used in daily liturgies (such as sacramental wine, candles, incense). "Sacramentals" can also describe material culture used as a part of the personal devotional life of Catholics (paintings or statues for the home and articles for use on the person such as relics, rosaries, medals, scapulars, crucifixes, holy cards, religious jewelry).

The history of the first religious goods stores to open in America dispensing objects imported from Europe or made in this country has yet to be written. It is, however, known that missionaries and European-trained clergy brought religious objects with them from the stores and monastic workrooms of Europe. An example is the holy cards that Bishop John Neumann, now canonized a saint and buried in Philadelphia, brought with him to North America from Bohemia. American religious historians, Ann Taves and Colleen McDannell, have noted that for an American Catholic prior to the Civil War the major sources of devotional books and religious objects, such as rosaries, scapulars, statues, and holy pictures were canvassers or peddlers, some of whom were Jewish; they "made the rounds of Catholic homes, schools, and churches" (Taves 1986: 10). As the

Catholic population grew, in the 1890s, established Catholic book publishers, who had been distributing religious goods to the peddlers and parish missions, expanded and newer businesses opened. Companies such as D. and J. Sadlier's and P. J. Kenedy and Sons in New York City, Benziger Brothers in Cincinnati, Krieg Brothers in Indianapolis, and the Herder Company in St Louis, offered a variety of Catholic materials for distribution to local stores. The manufacture of many forms of religious goods also expanded as a result of the increase of personal piety endorsed by institutional hierarchy, such as devotions to the Sacred Heart of Jesus and the Rosary (McDannell 1995: 167–73; Taves 1986: 21–45;). It was also stimulated by the growth of the American Catholic parochial school system with its need for books and objects to reinforce catechism lessons and the life of faith for Catholic immigrant children. The Victorian interest in filling the American home with material objects that nurtured Christian beliefs and values was another contribution to this process (McDannell 1986: 66; 1989; 1992; 1995). Such practices were also a natural transplantation and evolution of the devotionalism of European Catholic homes, which had their "holy corners" for centuries (Milspaw 1986).

One of the oldest religious goods stores in Philadelphia was Kilner's Church Goods which opened in 1888 on Market Street, and closed on Arch Street because of changes in urban buying patterns in June 1986. Its Arch Street location was by that time surrounded by shops selling pornography. Founded by Isaac Kilner as a business publishing mostly religious literature in Baltimore, this was the last of the religious-supply houses in an area that once contained five such stores. Kilner's even had its own relic of St Anthony of Padua, a signed and sealed document of the relic's authenticity from 1953, and a statue of the saint marking its entrance way. Here individuals would occasionally kneel and say a prayer or leave a written petition in the hand of the statue. Religious goods stores such as Kilner's are money-making enterprises that would not offer relics as, for example, does the shop connected to the Philadelphia Shrine of St John Neumann; here the saint's body is honored by the faithful who view his body in a glass altar (Kruesi 1995). In the case of Kilner's store, it was in response to a vow to the saint for a new Arch Street location that led to the placement of the relic at the entrance to the store. This relic (referred to in the tradition as a "first class relic" because it is a remnant of the body of the saint) gave the visitor a special feeling that the store itself was a sacramental. I myself recall entering this shop as a child in the late 1960s with its wooden floors and neatly displayed articles and books. The store reminded me of a church sacristy, with an atmosphere I recognized from service as an altar boy, and I was quite careful about what I touched in the store. Its musty smell and dim lighting added to the sensation of entering one of Philadelphia's many functioning turn-of-the-century churches, and the store was adorned with objects the way Philadelphia's churches were: a relic, statues, cards for the altar, candles. The only element missing was the flowers.

The back of Kilner's Church Goods contained the "Sisters Lounge," which included a small kitchen, a few sofas, a refrigerator, and a restroom, in an era when nuns did not enter public bathrooms. This lounge was one of the few areas in the archdiocese of Philadelphia where sisters could go and comfortably socialize with each other, as well as take their visiting nieces and nephews on Saturdays, the free day outside of their teaching duties in the classroom. The store owner would provide coffee, tea, and soft drinks for the women religious, and they would bring their own food. Though sisters from different orders did meet and converse as teachers in Philadelphia's parochial high schools, these women would seek refuge and the opportunity for conversation in an environment of sacred materiality here within a non-diocesan building, away from the public and the institutional church.

Kilner's Church Goods could be described as one of many establishments in the first half of the twentieth century selling objects called "Barclay Street art." The term refers to the Manhattan district housing French and other importers and producers of religious materials. This designation actually "became a derogatory term for books and objects that were cheap, vulgar, and pretentiously pious" (McDannell 1995: 170). Women religious whom I have interviewed, however, recall Barclay Street fondly as a Catholic cultural icon. Its presence was appreciated as not simply the name of a street or of Catholic consumer goods. This collection of businesses represented the existence of Catholicism in America as a thriving culture, the power of Catholic devotions and schools, and with so many sisters in habit, the significant presence of women religious in America.

As Kilner's and the stores on Barclay Street in New York City did in the past, the St. Jude Shop continues to serve both liturgical needs for the institutional church and its functionaries (priests, deacons, sisters, etc.), as well as the public. Considerable room in this retail establishment is devoted to the laity's desire for religious items. After opening this store in 1965, co-founders Louis and Norma DiCocco gradually established other stores, as well as wholesale and retail catalogue businesses. At the end of the 1990s, St Jude's was one of the top ten dealers of Christian religious materials in the continental United States. The circulation of their over 500 page wholesale catalogs exceeded 10,000, predominantly in churches and schools on the East coast. They distributed an equal number of retail catalogs. Since Louis DiCocco's death in 1993, the business has expanded even further to include Internet marketing and sales.

The Havertown St Jude Shop is located in a former supermarket that was renovated in 1981 into 12,000 square feet of retail space. This main store is attached to the more modest stone shop that housed the original business and now sells First Holy Communion dresses, veils, and suits as well as special occasion dresses. A cream-colored stucco facade and large windows reframed in gothic style were added to the exterior of the spacious showroom in 1996. From their positions along the sills, statues, such as a five foot St Jude, gaze through these clear windows on to the outside world. Instead of a shrine to St Anthony at its entrance, a marker to the right of the main exterior door bears a bronze plaque with an image of the entrepreneurial founder of the store. The inscription reads: "In Loving Memory of Louis R. DiCocco, Jr., Co-Founder of the St. Jude Shop, When Through One Man A Little More Love and Goodness, A Little More Light and Truth Comes Into the World, Then That Man's Life Has Had Meaning."

The large retail space with its plastered ceiling, exposed fluorescent lights, and worn tan carpet, occupies the front section of the store; storerooms and small offices are hidden from view in the rear. A central island on a raised platform allows cashiers to observe aisles lined with glass shelves where merchandise is displayed and glass cases where more expensive items are visible. Surmounting this central station and punctuating the otherwise smooth expanse of the plastered ceiling is an illuminated dome covered with gold wallpaper. Future plans call for this dome to be fitted with stained glass panels creating a skylight. These features seem to suggest a post-Vatican II sanctuary where the congregation sits around a centrally located liturgical space.

The St Jude Shop lacks the sacramental ambiance of the old-style religious goods stores I had visited as a child. Still, when I enter the building, I know immediately that I am in a Catholic site: the store is jammed with all manner of sacred things, religious objects, Catholic stuff. I encounter there a veritable explosion of Catholic sacramentals from the small image of St Jude screwed above the handle on the metal entry door to the First Holy Communion paper plates in a display to the right of the front windows. The St Jude Shop is a center for the observation of both past and present-day material expressions of Catholic personal piety, as well as of the Catholic communities that use them, all in one location. Myriad forms of sacred materiality can be found, objects deliberately made to complement the sacred mission of the Church, as well as normally secular objects which have been given a specifically religious reference.

Objects for personal use or for gift-giving are positioned in the front of the store, and church goods are placed in the rear. As you enter, you immediately find yourself before multiple images of the Virgin Mary in plaster, ceramic, and wood, as well as in framed prints. A variety of angel figures also inhabit the store's front section. Their diverse forms – dolls, ceramics, framed images, on glass, etc. – pay tribute to the American fascination with these spiritual beings at the end of the millennium. Family-themed collectibles such as German "Hummel" figurines join other secular gift items such as plates, stuffed animals, and picture frames.

As you move through the aisles, you observe displays organized around particular themes: angels, Confirmation, First Holy Communion, saints, rosaries, Marian apparitions. Here can be found objects made to commemorate both Catholic sacramental rites of passage and events in an individual's life such as First Communion and Confirmation certificates, "First Penance" rings; and guardian angel medals for the newborn's bed, crib, or carriage.

Wherever you turn in the St Jude Shop, hundreds of pairs of eyes peer back at you, a reminder that you are not alone. In a colorful display near the central cashiers are a multitude of statues of saints of every imaginable size and variety from St Patrick and St Frances Xavier Cabrini to St Peregrine and St Martin de Porres. Nearby is a generous assortment of inexpensive three- to five-inch statues of holy figures, what can be called Catholic plasticiana. Displayed on the right wall are images of the Infant Jesus, Jesus within the Trinity, the Suffering Jesus, the Sacred Heart of Jesus, and several variants on what could be called as the Second Vatican Council Jesus: the "laughing" Jesus, the bohemian Jesus, or my personal favorite, Jesus playing ice hockey. Adjacent to these prints stands a row of plaster statues in all sizes portraying Jesus as the child king, an image known in Catholic tradition as the "Infant of Prague." One or two regal outfits for devotional dressing of the royal image by the faithful normally accompany these statues, but most of them are dressed only in white ceramic gowns.

Throughout the showroom there is a multitude of crucifixes, crosses, scapulars, candles, vestments, and images of the heavenly pantheon represented on medals of gold and silver, as statuary of plaster, on small holy cards of paper or encased in plastic, and on iconographic plaques laminated with a passion. A multitude of rosaries makes for a colorful display: "egg" rosaries (i.e. a rosary enclosed in a tiny plastic egg); large and small wooden rosaries; crystal rosaries; one decade (i.e. ten-bead section) hand rosaries; pink, black, white, blue and glow-in-the-dark plastic rosaries. Holy water fonts, angelic hook racks to hang keys, and guardian angel light switch plates are all available for purchase, as are kitchen magnets with the Madonna glued on them (as well as light-bulb magnets proclaiming "Jesus Power and Light") and St Jude key chains. The traditional patron for safe travel is remembered here in the form of St Christopher magnetic plaques for the car, for the boat, and for the bicycle. I once found 1960s printed blessings of St Clare of Assisi, patron saint of television, to be placed on top of the set; Blessed Virgin Mary lamps and night lights; and even $1.50 "Marian Shrines" that are a cross between the Blessed Virgin Mary encased in a plastic torpedo and a Freudian analyst's dream. (For a Freudian analysis of the cults and devotions of Catholics, see Carroll 1986; 1989; 1992; 1996.) A few objects look carefully handmade, but most are obviously mass-produced.

Objects specifically related to the pro-life movement are gathered together in a display closer to the center of the store. A graphic reminder of how traditional images can be freshly negotiated by contemporary forces is the multitude of images of "Our Lady of Guadalupe," sold under the designation "the Virgin of the Unborn." This Marian icon, so significant to Hispanic Catholics in this hemisphere, has been appropriated by pro-life anti-abortion Catholics as a symbol of their cause on the basis of the traditional interpretation that Mary in this image appears pregnant (Elizondo 1995).

Eventually, the store even stocked a contemporary commerical response to property owners' interest in St Joseph's intercessory powers. Designated the "St. Joseph Home Sale Practice," this pre-packaged kit included printed instructions, petitionary prayers with printed image, and a small plastic statue of Joseph holding bread and a jug. On the reverse of the package was a drawing of a man either burying or digging up something at the back of his home.

The store sells objects to be used for prayer, and objects to make everyday living a constant devotion. Materials for the sanctuary, the parochial school room, the catechetical class, as well as the Catholic home are all available. Recordings of religious music, greeting cards, games as well as video documentaries of saints' lives, and classic films such as *The Song of Bernadette* are found in the second half of the store. The rear of the room is reserved for vestments, chalices, patens, cruets, flagons, and bells.

Books are also displayed beyond the central cashier station: Bibles, lectionaries, sacramentaries, aids for religious education classes, coloring books, missals, prayer books, devotional literature, a few scholarly texts by conservative Catholic authors. This is not, however, a book store which sells some religious articles. It is a religious goods store that stocks books and devotional pamphlets. You can find the documents of the Second Vatican Council, works of Thomas Merton and Pierre Teilhard de Chardin, papal encyclicals, but there are also many popular devotional books on apparitions of the Virgin Mary at Lourdes, Fátima, Garabandal, and Medjugorje, though excluding Our Lady of Bayside (Cuneo 1997: 175–94; Wojcik 1997: 60–96).

The store is representative of a general material culture of American Catholicism, which has incorporated older ethnic devotions and images. The St Jude Shop relates to Catholics as a generic American ethnic group rather than a particular group of ethnic Catholics. It reflects the homogenization and national-ization of Catholicism especially after the Second World War, when prosperity and the breakup of the ethnic neighborhoods caused a change in the Catholic evaluation of place and self (Fish 1982; Santino 1982). The acceptance by Catholics of material culture associated with Protestantism or non-denominational Christianity is also evident in the presence of certain images, such as *The Praying Hands, The Good Shepherd,* or Warner Sallmann's *Head of Christ* or *Christ at the Door,* as well as word-centered plaques and other objects (Lippy 1994: 185; Williams 1989: 141–2). Objects adorned with an appropriate inscription, prayer, or scriptural passage, are part of the Christian practice of transforming words into images.

The embodiment of scriptural words as images and the enhancement of word-centered documents has been cultivated by various denominations, for example, by the Pennsylvania Germans and their illuminated manuscript art called "fraktur." Still, one might ask which is primary: the words themselves or the images that they create? There is a sensibility over imagery for both Catholics and Protestants, whatever doctrinal investments since the Reformation may exist to the contrary. In his assessment of the popularly produced Protestant religious art of Warner Sallman, Morgan (1993, 1996, 1998) cites American Protestant memorates (first-person accounts of the supernatural) reporting miraculous experiences concerning the artist's famous *Head of Christ.* He also, however, stresses that it was Sallman's intention to "verify the literal character of the biblical text" (1993: 43). "The character of mechanical reproduction" of the New Testament stories in Sallman's work "serves to textualize the sacred image and therefore to make it acceptable to the Protestant community . . . Protestant believers feel safe *reading* the image of Christ" (1993: 43; 1998).

Catholics, however, feel safe *seeing* the image of Christ, and the Virgin Mary, and the saints. The fact remains that images are the foundation of the St Jude Shop. This store represents a pre-Vatican II Catholic understanding of sacra-mental culture which is centered on the visual, the sensual, and their innate association with the supernatural and the sacred. When individuals possess such a sensibility, they do not read an image, they *feel* it. This idea of "feeling" an image, of responding to it emotionally, is a way of articulating Catholic sensi-bility, i.e. the affective component of Catholic experience.

It is perfectly understandable that someone not familiar with Catholic culture would ask about such a setting as St Jude's: what exactly is going on here? What is this store all about? What does it all mean? The store as a site and the objects it displays carry complex, "multiple layers of meanings, uses, symbolisms, and connotations" (McAlister 1995: 306). Looking at all these objects of devotion and artifacts of belief, it is possible to see the Reformation controversies over mediated grace, purgatory and indulgences, and justification by faith and works come alive. The store also signifies the tension between the individual orientation of vernacular devotionalism, with its stress on personal salvation, and the communal sensibility of the institutional Church, an important principle of Catholic theology and practice. Within the study of vernacular religion (Primiano 1995; 1997b), particularly American vernacular Catholicism (by which I mean not the multitude of ethnic, regional, or cultural expressions of Catholic faithful, but the religious lives of the individual Catholic believers within such contexts), the St Jude Shop is a significant post-modern Catholic site. This space presents a notable opportunity to view an example of virtually every kind of devotional item used by and popular with Catholics both pre- and post-Second Vatican Council.

Researching the National Shrine of Saint Jude Thaddeus which opened in Chicago in 1929, Robert Orsi has noted that "devotionalism reached its peak in the 1950's, just prior to the Second Vatican Council" (1989: 78). The "popular devotions" of which he writes were stimulated especially by devotional periodicals, as well as "pastors and prelates of the airwaves, Catholic fiction, catechisms, sermons, religion classes, book clubs, moral handbooks, and so on" (1994: 582; see also 1996: 14–18). These devotions included expressions of both an immigrant piety and a "modern, indigenous post immigration piety" that "reflected the different experience of space and time among the immigrants' children; it did not simply replace the older devotional forms, but extended, supplemented, and (in some cases) reimagined them" (1991: 219).

A mark of the postmodern American Catholic community is its division over the necessity of employment of devotional objects to enhance personal piety. Starting with the Liturgical Movement of the twentieth century (Searle 1995: 783–785; White 1995: 71–114) and especially since the reforms of the Second Vatican Council (see the 1963 Constitution on the Sacred Liturgy), the institutional Church has made a concerted effort to stop paraliturgical activities during the celebration of the liturgy by the congregation (such as praying the rosary or other devotions). The goal is greater participation in the reformed Mass of Paul VI, which is said in the vernacular language of the region (White 1995: 115–40). The use of such personal sacramental objects as rosaries, prayer books, and holy cards during Mass or at other times has likewise been de-emphasized. Sacred materiality, of course, has not been dismissed in Roman Catholicism (see *Catechism of the Catholic Church* 1994: 1667–79), but its position within Catholic devotionalism has been questioned by the institutional Church. Council documents and later institutional writings direct clergy and laity to see the function of sacramental objects as expressions of the sacredness and holiness of a particular ritual action or occasion but not as sacred objects in and of themselves. So, for example, it is not the incense, candles, vestments, monstrance, or white communion wafer as objects which are important, but how they work holistically to enhance the significance, solemnity, and prayerfulness of the liturgy that matters. These items should be of fine quality because they are being used in important sacred ceremonies, but not because they are significant in and of themselves. The same thinking relates to personal piety: it is not the saint's statue or relic or holy card that is the center of attention in an act of prayer, but how these sacramental objects serve the goal of aiding in the quality of an occasion of prayer to God.

American Catholics at the end of the twentieth century are split in thought and action over the treatment of religious objects. Traditional and restorationist Catholics retain a more object-oriented subjective sacramentalism, while progressive Catholics support a more holistic and relational attitude toward religious objects. It is impossible to consider post-Vatican II American Catholicism and not recognize the differences in the traditions, quality, and style of both institutionally sponsored and lay practice in various regions of the United States. For example, parishes in dioceses of East Coast cities maintain a more traditional and conservative demeanor of Catholicism than do parishes in the Midwest. This phenomenon may be related to the general cultural formality of the East, or to the particular ethnic Catholic groups who settled there. For progressive Catholics, the St Jude Shop, filled as it is with religious articles, is an anachronism of the devotional past, the public face of the tradition that communicates nothing of its contemporary reality. For other communities, such as traditionalist Catholics or members of Afro-Catholic syncretic religions of the Caribbean including Vodou and Santería, the store and its contents represent what it means for them to be Catholic: participating in a magical mysterious religion where objects reflect and manifest the power of the sacred and the supernatural. Ironically, at any given time in the store, there can be a remarkably disparate assembly of shoppers, all constituting the late twentieth-century American Catholic Church: parish priests and campus ministers purchasing their church goods, housewives preparing for their own home liturgies, mambos buying some necessity for a Vodou ceremony not available at a local botanica, and grandmothers shopping for First Holy Communion gifts. The store services the contemporary American Catholic community in all of its surprising diversity.

The St Jude Shop embodies passive accommodations, intriguing survivals, active creations, dissenting impulses, and reflections on lived experience that mark the vernacular religion constantly emerging in everyday life (Primiano 1995). The items sold there have been flexibly employed both by a powerful directive church to create a compliant community of believers, and by equally resourceful individuals who have negotiated their own creative and personal experiences of God.

Many of the objects for sale in this store could be classified even by Catholics as nothing more than Catholic kitsch, religious theme junk with no spiritual value and little taste. Such a classification passes judgment on the beliefs of the individuals who buy from this shop. Given the sacramental nature of Catholic culture, all objects have the potential to become objects of belief. Such material culture forces scholars to reconsider the limiting designation, "kitsch," defined as "false art . . . often devised for mass consumption . . . meant to offer instant satisfaction of the most superficial aesthetic needs or whims of a wide public" (Calinescu 1987: 262; see also McDannell 1995: 163–7). The term "Catholic kitsch" designates rather the complicated amalgamation of affection and joy at the absurd or outrageous aspects of the ethnic, regional, and national expressions of the tradition within the American context. One has in some way to participate, for example, in the values and culture represented by such images as St Lucy holding plates with eyeballs, copiously bleeding stigmatics, or the mummified bodies of "incorruptible" saints kept in sitting positions at side altars for centuries, in order to appreciate why these objects are affective and meaningful. Such is the case whether they are categorized as folk art, popular representation, fine art, or even as kitsch. Such stores create an opportunity for a rich exposition of American Catholic religious folklife in the form of an ethnography of the senses of American Catholicism. They mark the change, and some could say rupture, in the visual, tactile, auditory, and olfactory experience of Catholics pre- and post-Vatican II.

When I look at this repository of Catholicism, I see not only institutional sanction for theological principles of intercession, mediation, and sacramentality, but also a deeper meaning as a vernacular religious sanction of the way ordinary people themselves continue to sacramentalize even the most humble or everyday parts of their lives. Passing the time in the St Jude Shop means not only encountering statues of St Joseph, the Virgin Mary, and other Catholic friends, but immersing oneself in a multitude of expressions of an ancient human impulse to objectify our gods and to seek a blessing for ourselves and the created world around us.

I did purchase an inexpensive statue of St Joseph and mailed it off to my student's father. He buried it as he had been instructed, and six months later his house was sold. And that plastic statue that I searched for all over Catholic Philadelphia is currently enshrined in the dining room of his latest Newfoundland home.

BIBLIOGRAPHY

Adler, Margot (1986) *Drawing Down the Moon*, Boston, Mass.: Beacon Press.
Borrello, Mary Ann and Mathias, Elizabeth (1977) "Botanicas: Puerto Rican folk pharmacies," *Natural History*, 86/7, pp. 64–73.
Briggs, Charles L. (1989) *The Woodcarvers of Córdova, New Mexico: Social Dimensions of an Artistic "Revival"*, Albuquerque, N. Mex.: University of New Mexico Press.
Brown, Peter (1981) *The Cult of the Saints: Its Rise and Function in Latin Christianity*, Chicago: University of Chicago Press.
Calinescu, Matei (1987) *Five Faces of Modernity*, Durham, NC: Duke University Press.
Carroll, Michael P. (1986) *The Cult of the Virgin Mary*, Princeton, NJ: Princeton University Press.
—— (1989) *Catholic Cults and Devotions: A Psychological Inquiry*, Kingston, Ont.: McGill-Queen's University Press.
—— (1992) *Madonnas that Maim: Popular Catholicism in Italy Since the Fifteenth Century*, Baltimore, Md.: Johns Hopkins University Press.

—— (1996) *Veiled Threats: The Logic of Popular Catholicism in Italy*, Baltimore, Md.: Johns Hopkins University Press.

Cartwright, Christine A. (1981) "Indian Sikh homes out of North American houses: mental culture in material translation," *New York Folklore* 7, pp. 97–111.

Catechism of the Catholic Church (1994) New York: Paulist Press.

Clark, Robin (1990) "Another sale! by St. Joseph," *Philadelphia Inquirer*, September 23, city edn, p. 1.

Cooper, Martha and Sciorra, Joseph (1994) *R.I.P. Memorial Wall Art*, New York: Henry Holt.

"Constitution on the Sacred Liturgy" (1966) Documents of Vatican II, New York: Guild Press.

Cosentino, Donald J. (ed.) (1995) *Sacred Arts of Haitian Vodou*, Los Angeles: UCLA Fowler Museum of Cultural History.

Cuneo, Michael W. (1997) "The vengeful Virgin: case studies in contemporary American Catholic apocalypticism," in Thomas Robbins and Susan J. Palmer (eds) *Millennium, Messiahs, and Mayhem: Contemporary Apocalyptic Movements*, New York: Routledge, pp. 175–94.

Dewhurst, C. Kurt, MacDowell, Betty, and MacDowell, Marsha (1983) *Religious Folk Art in America: Reflections of Faith*, New York: E. P. Dutton.

Dillenberger, John (1984) *The Visual Arts and Christianity in America: The Colonial Period through the Nineteenth Century*, Chico, Calif.: Scholars Press.

Durand, Jorge and Massey, Douglas S. (1995) *Miracles on the Border: Retablos of Mexican Migrants to the United States*, Tucson, Ariz.: University of Arizona Press.

Elizondo, Virgilio (1995) "Our Lady of Guadalupe," in Richard P. McBrien (ed.) *The HarperCollins Encyclopedia of Catholicism*, San Francisco: HarperSanFrancisco, pp. 594–6.

Fish, Lydia (1982) "Ethnicity and Catholicism," *New York Folklore* 8, pp. 83–92.

Flores-Peña, Ysamur and Evanchuk, Roberta J. (1994) *Santería Garments and Altars: Speaking Without a Voice*, Jackson, Miss.: University of Mississippi Press.

Giffords, Gloria Fraser (1992) *Mexican Folk Retablos*, rev. edn., Albuquerque, N. Mex.: University of New Mexico Press.

Gizelis, Gregory (1971) "The use of amulets among Greek Philadelphians," *Pennsylvania Folklife* 20/3, pp. 30–7.

Greeley, Andrew M. (1988) *God in Popular Culture*, Chicago: Thomas More Press.

—— (1989) "Protestant and Catholic: is the analogical imagination extinct?," *American Sociological Review* 54, pp. 485–502.

—— (1990) *The Catholic Myth: The Behavior and Beliefs of American Catholics*, New York: Charles Scribner's Sons.

Halle, David (1993) *Inside Culture: Art and Class in the American Home*, Chicago: University of Chicago Press.

Hufford, David J. (1987) "The love of God's mysterious will: suffering and the popular theology of healing," *Listening* 22, pp. 225–39.

Kalb, Laurie Beth (1994) *Crafting Devotions: Tradition in Contemporary New Mexico Santos*, Albuquerque, N. Mex.: University of New Mexico Press.

Kruesi, Margaret (1995) "Symptoms, signs and miracles: narratives of illness and healing at the St. John Neumann Shrine, Philadelphia, Pennsylvania," Ph.D. dissertation, Department of Folklore and Folklife, University of Pennsylvania, Philadelphia, Pa.

Lange, Yvonne (1974) "Lithography, an agent of technological change in religious folk art: a thesis," *Western Folklore* 33/1, pp. 51–64.

Lepovitz, Helena Waddy (1991) *Images of Faith: Expressionism, Catholic Folk Art, and the Industrial Revolution*, Athens, Ga.: University of Georgia Press.

Lessard, Pierre (1981) *Les Petites Images dévotes*, Quebec: Presses de l'Université Laval.

Lippy, Charles H. (1994) *Being Religious, American Style: A History of Popular Religiosity in the United States*, Westport, Conn.: Greenwood Press.

McAlister, Elizabeth (1995) "A sorcerer's bottle: the visual art of magic in Haiti," in Donald Consentino (ed.) *Sacred Arts of Haitian Vodou*, Los Angeles: UCLA Fowler Museum of Cultural History, pp. 304–21.

McBrien, Richard P. (1987) "Roman Catholicism," in Mircea Eliade (ed.) *The Encyclopedia of Religion*, vol. 12, New York: Macmillan, pp. 429–45.

—— (1994) *Catholicism*, San Francisco: HaperSanFrancisco.

McDannell, Colleen (1986) *The Christian Home in Victorian America, 1840–1900*, Bloomington, Ind.: Indiana University Press.

—— (1989) "Catholic domesticity, 1860–1960," in Karen Kennelly, CSJ (ed.) *American Catholic Women: A Historical Exploration*, New York: Macmillan, pp. 48–80.

—— (1992) "Parlor piety: the home as sacred space in Protestant America," in Jessica H. Foy and Thomas J. Schlereth (eds) *American Home Life, 1880–1930: A Social History of Spaces and Services*, Knoxville, Tenn.: University of Tennessee Press, pp. 162–89.

—— (1995) *Material Christianity: Religion and Popular Culture in America*, New Haven, Conn.: Yale University Press.

Milspaw, Yvonne J. (1986) "Protestant home shrines: icon and image," *New York Folklore* 12/3–4, pp. 119–36.

Morgan, David (1993) "Imaging Protestant piety: the icons of Warner Sallman," *Religion and American Culture* 3, pp. 29–47.

—— (ed.) (1996) *Icons of American Protestantism: The Art of Warner Sallman*, New Haven, Conn.: Yale University Press.

—— (1998) *Visual Piety: A History and Theory of Popular Religious Images*, Berkeley, Calif.: University of California Press.

Murphy, Joseph M. (1988) *Santería: An African Religion in America*, Boston, Mass.: Beacon Press.

O'Connor, Kathleen Malone (1994) "The alchemical creation of life (Takwin) and other concepts of genesis in medieval Islam," Ph.D. dissertation, Department of Religious Studies, University of Pennsylvania, Philadelphia, Pa.

Orsi, Robert Anthony (1985) *The Madonna of 115th Street, Faith and Community in Italian Harlem*, New Haven, Conn.: Yale University Press.

—— (1989) "What did women really think when they prayed to St. Jude?," *U.S. Catholic Historian* 8, pp. 67–79.

—— (1991) "The center out there, in here, and everywhere else: the nature of pilgrimage to the shrine of St. Jude, 1929–1965," *Journal of Social History* 25, pp. 213–32.

—— (1994) "'Mildred, is it fun to be a cripple?': the culture of suffering in mid-twentieth century American Catholicism," *South Atlantic Quarterly* 93, pp. 547–90.

—— (1996) *Thank You, Saint Jude: Women's Devotion to the Patron Saint of Hopeless Causes*, New Haven, Conn.: Yale University Press.

Pacelle, Mitchell (1990) "Some people will try anything except lowering the asking price," *Wall Street Journal*, September 17.

Pocius, Gerald L. (1986) "Holy pictures in Newfoundland houses: visual codes for secular and supernatural relationships," in Peter Narváez and Martin Laba (eds) *Media Sense: The Folklore–Popular Culture Continuum*, Bowling Green, Oh.: Bowling Green University Popular Press, pp. 124–48.

Primiano, Leonard Norman (1995) "Vernacular religion and the search for method in religious folklife," *Western Folklore* 54, pp. 37–56.

—— (1997a) "Folklife," in Thomas A. Green (ed.) *Folklore: An Encyclopedia of Beliefs, Customs, Tales, Music and Art*, Santa Barbara, Calif.: ABC-Clio pp. 322–31.

—— (1997b) "Folk religion," in Thomas A. Green (ed.) *Folklore: An Encyclopedia of Beliefs, Cutoms, Tales, Music and Art*, Santa Barbara, Calif.: ABC-Clio pp. 710–17.

Santino, Jack (1982) "Catholic folklore and folk Catholicism," *New York Folklore* 8, pp. 93–106.

Sciorra, Joseph (1989) "Yard shrines and sidewalk altars of New York's Italian-Americans," in Thomas Charter and Bernard L. Herman (eds) *Perspectives in Vernacular Architecture*, vol. III, Columbia, Mo.: University of Missouri Press, pp. 185–98.

—— (1993) "Multivocality and vernacular architecture: the Our Lady of Mount Carmel Grotto in Rosebank, Staten Island," in Luisa Del Giudice (ed.) *Studies in Italian American Folklore*, Logan, Ut.: Utah State University Press, pp. 203–43.

Searle, Mark (1995) "Liturgical Movement," in Richard P. McBrien (ed.) *The HarperCollins Encyclopedia of Catholicism*, San Francisco: HarperSanFrancisco, pp. 783–5.

Shaner, Richard H. (1961) "Living occult practices in Dutch Pennsylvania," *Pennsylvania Folklife* 12/3, pp. 62–3.

—— (1972) "Recollections of witchcraft in the Oley Hills," *Pennsylvania Folklife* 21, Folk Festival Supplement, pp. 39–43.

Spamer, Adolf (1930) *Das Kleine Andachtsbild vom XIV. bis zum XX. Jahrhundert*, Munich: Bruckmann.

Taves, Ann (1986) *The Household of Faith: Roman Catholic Devotions in Mid-Nineteenth-Century America*, Notre Dame, Ind.: Notre Dame University Press.

Teske, Robert Thomas (1973) "The Eikonostasi among Greek-Philadelphians," *Pennsylvania Folklife* 23/1, pp. 20–30.

—— (1980) *Votive Offerings among Greek Philadelphians: A Ritual Perspective*, New York: Arno Press.

—— (1985) "Votive offerings and the belief system of Greek-Philadelphians," *Western Folkore* 44, pp. 208–24.

Tracy, David (1981) *The Analogical Imagination*, New York: Crossroad.

Turner, Kay Frances (1982) "Mexican American home altars: towards their interpretation," *Aztlan: International Journal of Chicano Studies Research* 13/1–2, pp. 309–26.

—— (1983) "The cultural semiotics of religious icons: La Virgen de San Juan de los Lagos," *Semiotica* 47, pp. 317–61.

—— (1990) "Mexican-American women's home altars: the art of relationship," Ph.D. dissertation, Department of Anthropology, University of Texas, Austin.

Turner, Kay and Seriff, Suzanne (1987) "Giving an altar: the ideology of reproduction in a St. Joseph's Day feast," *Journal of American Folklore* 100, pp. 446–60.

Vlach, John Michael (1989) "Morality as folk aesthetic," in Robert E. Walls and George H. Schoemaker (eds) *The Old Traditional Way of Life: Essays in Honor of Warren E. Roberts*, Bloomington, Ind.: Trickster Press, pp. 28–39.

White, James F. (1995) *Roman Catholic Worship: Trent to Today*, New York: Paulist Press.

Williams, Peter W. (1988) "Religious architecture and landscape," in Charles H. Lippy and Peter W. Williams (eds) *Encyclopedia of the American Religious Experience*, vol. III, New York: Charles Scribner's Sons, pp. 1325–39.

—— (1989) *Popular Religion in America: Symbolic Change and the Modernization of Process in Historical Perspective*, Urbana, Ill.: University of Illinois Press.

—— (1997) *Houses of God: Region, Religion, and Architecture in the United States*, Urbana, Ill.: University of Illinois Press.

Wojcik, Daniel (1997) *The End of the World as We Know It: Faith, Fatalism, and Apocalypse in America*, New York: New York University Press.

Yoder, Don (1988) "Fraktur: an introduction," in *Pennsylvania German Fraktur and Printed Broadsides: A Guide to the Collections in the Library of Congress*, Washington DC: Library of Congress, pp. 9–19. Reprinted 1990 in Don Yoder (ed.) *Discovering Amerian Folklife: Studies in Ethnic, Religious, and Regional Culture*, Ann Arbor, Mich.: UMI Research Press, pp. 271–81.

—— (1990) *The Picture-Bible of Ludwig Denig: A Pennsylvania German Emblem Book*, New York: Hudson Hills Press.

Yoder, Don and Graves, Thomas E. (1989) *Hex Signs: Pennsylvania Dutch Barn Symbols and their Meaning*, New York: E. P. Dutton.

Chapter 14

Food and Eating in American Religious Cultures

Daniel Sack

Americans love to eat. They devote large spaces in their homes and significant parts of their incomes to preparing meals. They spend increasing amounts of money on commercially prepared food. They write – and buy – hundred of new cookbooks annually. And they are more likely to be overweight than any other society.

Americans are also deeply religious. They have one of the highest church attendance rates in the world. They have built large institutions for religious practice and nurture. And, in a supposedly secular age, large numbers of Americans continue to identify religious belief as important in their lives.

In such an environment food and religion are inevitably intertwined in American culture, from food rituals to food taboos. Everyone eats, from Native Americans to American Buddhists, and they frequently endow their eating with religious meaning. Nevertheless, both observers and participants are likely to take for granted the role food plays in religious life. They may see rituals and rules as either trivial or obvious.

Some scholars, however, remind us that food events are full of meaning. British anthropologist Mary Douglas says that "food is a field of action. It is a medium in which other levels of categorization become manifest ... Food choices support political alignments and social opportunities" (Douglas 1984: 30). Elsewhere (1975: 260) she states that "the meaning of a meal is found in a system of repeated analogies." In her view, the role of food in a society reflects that society's structure and self-understanding. Douglas and her followers have applied this insight in their studies of food events in settings as diverse as Native Americans in South Dakota and Italian-American Catholics in Philadelphia (Douglas 1984). In the work of Douglas and others, the study of food events opens an important window on religious behavior and belief.

But as the topics selected by Douglas's colleagues reflect, most studies of food and religion in America focus on cultures that appear "exotic." Anthropologists and folklorists are fascinated with the food practices of Jews and ethnic Catholics, which are rich with rituals and traditions. On the other hand, scholars tend to ignore food practices among white middle-class Protestants, which appear either boring – meals supposedly made up largely of Jell-O salads and coffee – or non-existent. Meanwhile much of the rest of the culture laughs at Protestant food events. The work of Garrison Keillor (1985) and such cookbooks as *Lutheran Church Basement Women: Lutefisk, Lefse, Lunch and Jell-O* are just two examples. Protestant cuisine appears as laughable or insignificant.

But we can learn more from Protestant church meals than just a good Jell-O salad recipe. Here I examine the role that food has played in the lives of mainline Protestant congregations. I argue that, for these Protestants, church meals both reflect and shape their relationships and value systems. In the words of anthropologist Clifford Geertz, they are both a model of and a model for the proper functioning of society (Geertz 1973: 93).

To trace the role food has played in the life of mainline Protestant congregations I will look at the experience of St Pauls United Church of Christ in Chicago. Over its more than one hundred and fifty years, the members of St Pauls have consumed tons of spaghetti, numerous salads, and countless cups of coffee. But, as Douglas would suggest, these dinners were more than just food. In their development they reflect changes within the congregation and in the larger society. And throughout, they have been analogies for the church's understanding of the world.

Historian of American religion E. Brooks Holifield argues that colonial-era churches were "comprehensive congregations," organizations designed to include all residents of a community and serve all their needs – spiritual, political, and social. After the American Revolution, however, changes in society forced churches to focus on specifically religious functions for voluntary and homogenous groups, making them "devotional congregations." The pattern changed again in the decades after the Civil War, giving rise to the "social congregation." Holifield writes that "in the late nineteenth century, thousands of congregations transformed themselves into centers that not only were open for worship but also were available for . . . nameless other activities." While New York pulpit prince Henry Ward Beecher encouraged seminarians to "multiply picnics," many congregations went one better than Beecher and built "gymnasiums, parish houses, camps, baseball teams, and military drill teams." These new measures were important in a rapidly growing country, as the churches hoped "that the new congregational activities could overcome the impersonality of large churches and synagogues, eliminate class distinctions, attract children and their parents, provide wholesome amusement for young people, and draw men more actively into congregational work" (1994: 39).

In a rapidly urbanizing and industrializing society, social congregations also sought to provide alternatives to the city's tempting entertainment. In rural America, churches were the only social centers available and thus could exercise some moral control over their members. The growing cities, however, provided too many temptations, particularly for young men and women. In such a setting, churches tried "to maintain influence over recreational choices by providing their own picnics and parties . . . If they could no longer comprehend a geographical region, they could still comprehend a wider spectrum of the activities of their members" (Holifield 1994: 43). In the urban environment, churches were just one competitor in the free market of entertainment; they knew that city dwellers had an almost infinite number of ways to spend their time and money – including on amusement parks, restaurants, pool halls, and the dreaded saloon. In this competition, the church had to use every tool at hand, including food.

For immigrant congregations such as St Pauls these social events were even more important. The church was founded as a congregation of the Evangelical Synod of the West, a German denomination centered in the Midwest; the Evangelical Synod joined in the Evangelical and Reformed Church in 1934, which helped to form the United Church of Christ in 1957. The congregation's charter members were all recent immigrants, and the church's primary language was German until early in the twentieth century. (That German heritage runs through the congregation today, even though only a few members are of German background.) The church served the immigrant community as a community center, where people could both feel at home and experiment with assimilation. It preserved ethnic solidarity and tradition against the homogenizing forces of the larger culture. It provided opportunities for young people to meet and court, encouraging endogamous marriage.

To meet these various social needs, congregations and denominations created a rich variety of social organizations in the late nineteenth century. Women's societies, founded to support missionary work, often became social groups as well. Men's groups, perhaps inspired by the rise of the Young Men's Christian Association, also served a mixture of missionary and social purposes. Perhaps most important were groups for young people, like the interdenominational Christian Endeavor Society, founded in 1881, and the Methodist Epworth League, founded in 1889. Alongside Bible study, social service, and evangelism, these organizations sponsored co-ed social events for their high-school-aged members.

By the end of the nineteenth century, St Pauls Church was a typical "social congregation." In 1869 a group of young men and women founded the *Jugendverein* or Young People's Union, which held social events and pushed the congregation towards greater integration in American society. Men in the church formed the Men's Club, the Ushers Association, the Edgewood Bowling Club, and the Athletic Association. In 1892 the congregation's women, under the leadership of the pastor's wife, formed the *Frauenverein* or Women's Union. In addition to their own social events, these "mothers of the church" took responsibility for taking care of the church building and cooking its meals.[1]

While these organizations had a variety of purposes – study, service, education – many of their meetings centered on food. The meals not only provided nourishment and fellowship, but also modeled the proper ordering of society. Many of the church's meals, particularly before mid-twentieth century, were not only strictly for adults, but also gender-segregated. In their program and their menu, these separate men's and women's meals reflected gender roles current in the larger society.

Starting in the early years of the twentieth century, the Men's Club held annual dinners at the church. To our more casual age, these dinners appear quite formal, mimicking the huge secular feasts of businessmen and fraternal organizations of their day. The menus were large, involving multiple courses (often with French names) and always including at least one kind of meat, usually beef. The club's annual dinner in 1913 was a four-course banquet, featuring trout and beef tenderloin and concluding with cigars. This menu was a common one for men's dinners in the early twentieth century; Laura Shapiro writes that "the dinners planned for men were mighty, sometimes blatant, symbols of maleness. Commonly recommended for a bachelor supper or a men's club dinner were saddle of mutton, woodcock, strong cheese, brown bread, and hard-crackers" (1986: 102). In this gendered understanding of food, a meal for men must be substantial – and include meat.

Like the menu, programs for the Men's Club dinners were weighty. The 1913 dinner, presided over by a toastmaster, was enlivened with a song from the men's quartet and the church's orchestra, a poem from the assistant pastor, and a special address by social gospel leader Graham Taylor, "A Church for the City and a City for the Church." The 1918 dinner attracted more than three hundred men to a room decorated with "many American flags . . . in harmony with the spirit of the evening." "Forty gracious young ladies waited on the tables, while twenty more women, some young and others not so young, worked like Trojans in the kitchen." As reported by to the church newsletter, the meal, again with a beef course, was "one of the finest meals ever served at a Men's Club dinner."

The club's meals changed as circumstances changed. The meals went into some decline during the 1930s, reflecting the pressures of the Depression and perhaps a decline in the availability of willing "ladies." After the Second World War, however, Men's Club dinners returned with enthusiasm. In 1948 the club's leadership announced in the newsletter that all future meetings would be preceded by a meal.

> We anticipate that the dinners will encourage more of our members to attend regularly, and will also spare the wives the trouble of preparing dinner on at least one night each month. We believe that most of you will agree that there is nothing quite like a good dinner to get any meeting on its way.

These meals were prepared by the women of the church and served by girls. By the late 1950s, however, men from the church's catering committee were sharing in the food preparation. In the church newsletter the group crowed about these men-cooked meals, "Do you know, that we have the best cooks in Chicago to prepare the delicious food served at our meetings?" A 1958 "Ladies Night" dinner featured a male member's famous fried chicken, as well as "fellowship, entertainment, and 'Gemutlichkeit'" in the form of games and group singing.

Women's organizations also revolved around food, with meals that were as feminine as the Men's Clubs dinners were masculine. One such group was the Dorcas Society, which was made up of younger women interested in studying the social issues of the day. The newsletter reported that members of the society felt that "joining in at coffee parties or being studiously present at all society functions, bringing good friends together from time to time for a pleasant pastime is well and good enough in its place, but the Dorcas society is organized for greater purposes." Nevertheless, the society did indeed eat at its meetings. A luncheon in 1938, the society reported, was quite enjoyable; "the hour that is spent around the festal board surely creates a friendly feeling and closer fellowship between one another."

Church meals for women, like these luncheons, had a culture – and a menu – all their own, reflecting gender expectations. For such meals a 1962 church "how-to" book, *How to Plan Church Meals* recommended "dainty, delicious sandwiches." The author argues that "sandwiches for the tea table are quite a different thing from the 'he-man' sandwiches you want for a picnic, or the meal-in-one you serve to teen-agers. They are delicate, made for nibbling – and looking pretty is far more important than providing nourishment" (Kirk 1962: 57). Or lunch may have been a salad, as recommended for women by a generation of domestic scientists. As Shapiro notes in her *Perfection Salad*,

> As a kind of non-food, the salad course had a non-nutritive function: it enhanced the femininity of the whole meal and made the scientific cook herself more socially palatable. Decorative, seemingly ephemeral, salads were perceived as ladies' food, reflecting the image of frailty attached to the women who made them. (Shapiro 1986: 100)

Whether fragile salads or dainty sandwiches, the menus for the women's luncheons were appropriately feminine.

Like the men, the women of the church also held more formal social events. A good example is the tea held to celebrate the dedication of the church's new parish house in 1952. The menu included "a plentiful supply of dainty tea sandwiches and cookies [which] added to the completeness of the occasion." The entertainment included a "delightful and well-known reader" performing her writings, including "humorous verses, stories about gardening, household experiences, and family living which everyone recognized as true to life. All were told in such a happy manner that everybody's spirits were refreshed." An annual event for the church's women, perhaps parallel to the Men's Club annual banquet, was the annual Easter Monday luncheon, the cooperative effort of the various women's organizations. In 1961 the menu included "potato salad, jello molds, pickles, olives, meat balls, ham, fried chicken, and all the rest of the goodies." Over a hundred and eighty women attended, "replete with all their Easter finery." A woman comedian doing Swedish ethnic humor provided the entertainment. Like the luncheons of the Dorcas Society, these formal meals modeled the femininity expected of the church's women.

Not all of the church's meals were exclusively for adults. The men's and women's organizations each invited their children to join them for the annual Mother-Daughter and Father-Son banquets, meals that reinforced these food-structured gender roles in the younger generation. For the Mother-Daughter banquet of 1934 the women produced a play called *Ruth, the Loyal*, extolling devotion to mother. In later years the mothers and daughters welcomed visiting entertainers, such as "the Gypsy Troubadours," a balloon artist, or a fashion show provided by the Cotton Council of America. Each of the banquets included singing (with songs such as "What a faithful friend is Mother," and "What a friend we have in Jesus") and concluded with a candlelighting ceremony, marking the passing of wisdom and tradition from mother to daughter. The Father-Son banquets were more obviously masculine, both in program and menu; in the place of poetry and songs of devotion, one such banquet began with a Boy Scout-led pledge of allegiance, with a dinner of roast beef followed by a tumbling act and Disney cartoons.

As the adult meals at St Pauls presented a model of society's gender roles, food-centered social events for the congregation's young people presented a wholesome model of youth, an alternative to dangerous adolescent activities. Wholesome church-sponsored programs for youth have a long tradition in American religious life. In the eighteenth century Jonathan Edwards gathered his Northampton youngsters into neighborhood groups for "lectures in social religion." Patricia Tracy writes that these "evening frolics became legitimized as 'social religion'" (Tracy 1979: 111). An Epworth League leader and creator of a pseudo-science called "phunology" argued in the early decades of the twentieth century that "young people will seek to satisfy the social instinct. It is God-implanted." But he warned that "if the church and the community do not provide their social life in other wholesome modes of expression for this God-implanted instinct, young people will seek outside the church for places, many of them un-desirable, or positively dangerous" (Harbin 1923: vii). It was up to the church to model a wholesome adolescence; it conveyed these models partially through food events. These activities were especially important to an immigrant church like St Pauls, as it sought to assimilate its children into the mainstream, while providing them a place to meet and court young people from the same ethnic group.

To serve these purposes, St Pauls put great emphasis on programs for its children and teenagers, reported – as always – by the church newsletter. Soon after the turn of the century the Young People's Union hosted a "necktie party" to encourage young men and women to socialize. "Each girl brought a necktie and an apron made of the same cloth. She would put on the apron and leave the tie at the door. As they arrived, each of the boys would choose a necktie, then enter the social hall to discover who was to be his partner for the evening." At a 1924 supper for the confirmation class, "the girls of the class furnished the enter-tainment while the boys furnished the best appetites and the noise, ably assisted, of course, by the girls. So it proved to be a real homelike party." In 1939 the congregation's youth welcomed the Young Peoples' Federation of the Chicago area to the church; the main course was an increasingly common treat, chop suey, which fortunately could be extended to satisfy the larger than expected crowd. The same year the Young People's League had a potluck Thanksgiving dinner. The church newsletter detailed the "simple" menu of "casserole dinners of noodles, vegetables and bean varieties, meat loaves, three kinds of potato salads, three varieties of cole slaw, salmon mold, five fruit and vegetable jello molds, potato chips, pickles, olives, bread and butter sandwiches, cakes, cookies, candy and coffee!" A member made the buffet table "look even more enticing, by directing two blue floodlights upon it." The "Chuck Wagon" at the Junior Congregation's western night features a menu that "was true Western style (at least the Council members who planned the meal seemed to think so) – beans, beans, and more beans, then dry bread, coffee, and doughnuts."

If the congregation worried about the temptations awaiting their young people after World War I, the anxiety reached a fever pitch in the 1950s. This was the era of *West Side Story* and *Rebel Without a Cause*. Anxious parents, worried that their children growing up in the city might join a gang or drive a Mercury over a cliff, turned to the church for help. In these years the congregation organized a variety of activities to keep the youth coming to church; the planners knew that if you feed young people, they will come. Confirmation class "graduates" were invited to join the junior high fellowship at a party, "and if you don't come, there is something wrong with you because they always have a very good time and I sincerely hope that you will become a very active member of that group for they do a great deal of good and have lots of fun as well." Another year's dinner provided "plenty of good fellowship" and an "Inspiring Film" on "teenage witness." In the late 1950s the church turned the basement of the new sanctuary into a "youth center and lounge," where the young adults "had a Smorgasbord supper followed by entertainment." In March 1961, the senior highs went swimming, and came then back to the church for pizza, which soon became a youth group standby. At the peak of the national folk music craze the youth group hosted a "Hootenanny," which attracted over one hundred teens from neighboring churches. "Pizza and coke were served by hard working mothers. When the evening was over, $33 was collected for the Mental Health Drive." The young people also presented three short plays as a "cafe-style theatre-in-the-round," that is, modeled after Chicago's increasingly famous Second City company. "Food? Of course . . . Pizza, beverages, and other refreshments (all soft!) will be sold at intermissions." Members of the congregation were urged to turn out and show their support for the young people's programs. These events kept the church's young people out of real nightclubs and in the church.

The years after World War II also saw the church take an increased interest in the nuclear family, seemingly threatened as it was by social and economic changes. To strengthen families, congregations like St Pauls organized "family nights." In 1962 the church sponsored "a Night of Knights" which "found our gym transformed into a kingly banquet hall as well over 200 'knights, ladies, and little jesters' enjoyed a scrumptious pot luck 'feast' and a delightful movie: 'The Mouse That Roared.'" A Mardi Gras in 1963 featured games, cartoons, and dancing for everyone (including "twisting for the teens"). In place of gumbo and jambalaya, the menu provided something most un-Cajun: hot dogs and taffy apples. The "Family Roundup" in 1966 had the same menu at the "chuck wagon," plus square dancing with the "Hi-Kickin' Chickens." An international night in 1967 brought out three hundred people for " lasagne, Swedish meat balls, chicken terriyaki [sic], and sauerkraut and bratwurst" prepared by families in the congregation. Guest performers from local Filipino, German, and Spanish American communities provided the entertainment. As the young adult group said about their own meetings, the family nights " brought all of us closer together, sort of like a big happy family." These social events aimed to strengthen the nuclear family and give it the church's blessing.

The church's food events through much of the twentieth century presented its members with models for society. Adult dinners reflected gender roles, youth events encouraged wholesome and churchly behavior, and family events strengthened togetherness. Changes in urban America in the 1960s, however, challenged these traditional models. Lincoln Park, the once stable neighborhood around St Pauls, changed as long-time German residents moved further away from the city-center. Large rowhouses were divided into small apartments, and housed a mixture of elderly residents and a growing community of single young people. By the early 1970s, as a result, the family night suppers and youth activities did not appeal to these new constituencies. One pastor observed after a picnic that many families and new members attended, but "missing in our family gathering, however, were older adults and single persons."

In response, the congregation created food-centered social events to welcome these missing groups. In 1977 the church planned a "Family of Faith Thanksgiving" dinner on the Sunday before Thanksgiving. "Invitations have been sent to our shut-ins and it is hoped that other members of St. Pauls who may have no family nearby will join us." The congregation's strategic plan of 1984 called for specific fellowship programs to reach the elderly. The outreach to young singles was even more important. In 1960 St Pauls had begun to sponsor a series of "after church 'coffee clatsches' [sic] for the young 'career' men and women who so often join us for morning worship but who yet remain strangers to St. Pauls and to each other." As the neighborhood revived in the 1970s, Lincoln Park became the haunt of Chicago's yuppies, and the church looked for ways to attract them. It opened the gym for a monthly volleyball game, mainly for the young adults. "We then retreat to a home where repast of various sorts are offered on a Bring Your Own basis (usually wine and cheese)." The church also started a monthly series of restaurant visits and hosted progressive dinners to attract more singles. Previous food events at St. Pauls modeled traditional gender roles and nuclear family structures. In response to a changing urban environment, the congregation adopted a more inclusive model, to accommodate single adults.

This shift also affected traditional family nights, in that they were broadened to include the whole congregation. The Family Life Committee wanted its meals to "be a time when groups of people having diversified interests (such as the volleyball group and the Frauenverein) could enjoy together some of the life at St. Pauls." In 1980 the Board of Elders organized a "prom night," but felt that it was "very important, given the theme, that this be 'billed' as an inter-generational event and that single people feel comfortable in attending." A Mardi Gras party several years later moved further from the "family night" model; the newsletter warned parents that there would be no events for children and so encouraged them to leave them at home. The food events reflected a change in the congregation and a shift away from traditional family models.

After the late 1960s, however, there were fewer large social events at St Pauls for a variety of reasons. Most practically, there were fewer volunteers available to make the food. In 1967 the pastor asked the Mothers Club "to cook and serve dinners for some of the church functions." While happy to help, they replied, "we could not give him a definite answer at this time because most of our members are working mothers, and this leaves it up to those few mothers who are at home (working)." This decline in volunteer time reflected a larger trend in the congregation, as members had less and less time for church activities. In 1985 the Congregational Life Committee abandoned its monthly "Fun 'n Games Nights" during daylight savings time, when people were distracted by other claims on their time. A year later the committee announced that it was reducing the number of church-sponsored social events "to prevent 'burn-out.'"

Alongside these more practical reasons, the 1960s saw a tide of theological and ethical critiques of church social events; these criticisms no doubt affected the leadership of St Pauls. Around the beginning of the decade, a group of social critics, most importantly Gibson Winter in his *Suburban Captivity of the Churches*, attacked Protestant "organization churches" for their "trivialization of the religious enterprise." Such churches were marked by "the bustle of activities which are only indirectly connected with the sacred aspects of religious life." Defined by their place in political and economic structures, organization churches become "a cult of consumption rather than mission and ministry" (Winter 1961: 102, 94, 79). Winter was not alone. Martin Marty warned readers that "laymen can become so organized and their activities so routinized that the machinery of church life, smoothly oiled, takes the place of the deity in many a hierarchy of values" (Marty 1958: 135). Critics such as Winter and Marty called the churches to turn their attention away from organizations and activities – like potlucks and family nights – and to focus on mission and ministry to the city.

In the face of this critique, liberal congregations like St Pauls shifted their food events from feeding their own members to feeding strangers. At St Pauls the "mothers of the church" had been doing this work for years. Often during the Christmas holidays, members of the *Frauenverein* and the Dorcas Society used to visit the indigent, taking food along. In 1940 the Dorcas Society distributed twenty-eight baskets of food at Thanksgiving and twenty-three at Christmas." The Christmas visit to the County Hospital brought gifts of 150 glasses of jelly, 337 boxes of cookies and candy, 30 shoulder capes, 200 oranges and 134 gifts for the 'forgotten men.'" This continued into the 1970s, as the women of the Dorcas Society and the Sunshine Club took Christmas fruit baskets to "the sick and shut-ins." Another group of women baked fifty dozen cookies for a Christmas party for the children of state prisoners.

In the 1960s, however, members of the church increasingly turned their attention – and their food – to urban problems. In 1968 the congregation helped to sponsor a summer education and work program for city youth, mainly minorities. "As with all teenage students they get extremely hungry while studying and working. To help solve the hunger problem, women in the congregations are preparing hundreds of sandwiches for daily lunches." As the neighborhood changed, more poor people appeared on the streets and in the houses of Lincoln Park. In response, a group of churches organized an open pantry to "provide food and other necessities for families which have been unable to make ends meet." Within nine years it had served over a half-million meals to needy families. The first Sunday of the month was "Pantry Sunday," when members brought contributions of canned goods to worship. Responding to a different needy group, the church also co-sponsored a weekly lunch for neighborhood seniors in need of a good meal. Another agency supported by the church hosted a Christmas dinner for street people. "Donations are needed: turkeys cooked, without stuffing, stuffing, salads, cranberry sauce, salads, desserts. Volunteers are needed for kitchen duty and to visit with the guests."

But while members of the church took food out to poor neighbors, it began to invite them inside as well, after a precedent was set in 1968. During the Democratic National Convention in Chicago, protesters against the Vietnam War gathered in a park near the church. When police used horses and tear gas to clear the park, the pastors of St Pauls opened the church as a shelter for young people fleeing the park and the streets. "They were invited into the gym and social hall to sleep. They were fed by some of the women of the church, many of whom could imagine their own children or grandchildren in this situation." The controversial decision divided the church, but it set a precedent for offering the church's hospitality to strangers.

With the gentrification of Lincoln Park and the deinstitutionalization of the mentally ill in the early 1980s, the neighborhood's homeless population grew. Working with three neighboring congregations in the fall of 1985, St Pauls opened its doors as a temporary overnight shelter during the winter months. By the end of that winter, the shelter had provided 3,594 "bed nights", as well as serving a hot meal. "The Shelter provides an opportunity to do something good 'for one of the least of these, my brothers, and sisters.' It also gives you a chance to meet and talk with our volunteers." Volunteers stayed the night to supervise the shelter, spent an evening preparing and serving a fresh dinner, or helped shelter guests in the laundry room constructed in one of the gym's locker rooms. The shelter served meals once a week during the summer months. Food service facilities, built in 1952 to serve St Pauls' "large, cordial family," with its "scientifically-ventilated and attractive dining hall-auditorium-gymnasium" in its "festive setting unsurpassed in church units," now welcomed shabby strangers as well as prosperous members.

The church's social concerns even appeared in its social events. In 1988, after the "relative failure" of "South of the Border Night," several board members and the pastors

> noted/surmised that people may not be regarding the church as a center of social life any more; that, in fact, they look upon the church as a center for volunteer activity in the community, and perhaps South of the Border would have drawn more people if it had been tied to fund-raising.

In a busy congregation like St Pauls, there seemed to be less time for socializing for its own sake, but people welcomed parties with a purpose. In 1985 "the Youth Group [hosted] an 'all you can eat' Pancake Breakfast on Sunday, November 24.

The proceeds will be used to support . . . [a] program for homeless and runaway teenagers." Another youth group pancake breakfast benefited Habitat for Humanity. Participants in a combination exercise and Bible study group, called "Exercise and Exegesis," began preparing and distributing sack lunches for the homeless. To support this work they sponsored "a St. Pauls Motherhood and Apple Pie Bake Sale on Sunday, October 18, during coffee hour." Members were invited to "come and get your just desserts!" "Whether baking or buying, be sure to take part in this worthwhile event that will feed both the fortunate and the less fortunate among us!" Church members also attended a shrimp boil on behalf of a denominational mission program on the Gulf coast. These food events were an analogy for the shift in the congregation's self-understanding and its mission, shift from being an inward-focused "organization church," a "social congregation," to a "socially conscious congregation."

Earlier decades had seen a flood of "fun books," resources for helping churches organize their social lives. Issued by denominational presses but aimed at an ecumenical audience, they had such titles as *Gay Parties for All Occasions* and *How to Plan Church Meals*, and described in detail a variety of seasonal parties for families, couples, and young people. The 1980s, however, saw the creation of what might be called a "serious fun book." *Simply Delicious: Quantity Cooking for Churches* provides some of the same helps found in earlier books – recipes, cooking hints – but they are helps for a very different church. The book seeks "to encourage local churches to be responsible about serving food."

> In a world where so many are hungry and malnourished, the church dare not be complacent about how much we eat, about how much we waste, and about the relationship between our greed and our neighbor's need. Also, in a nation where so many of us have serious health problems from eating too much and from eating unwisely, the church must call us to be good stewards of our bodies. (Winn 1983: 2)

In place of recipes for roasted meat and Jell-O salads, *Simply Delicious* features meatless meals and complementary proteins. In place of ideas for the Valentine's Dance, the book has hints on feeding street people and running a fast to learn about hunger. One chapter verges on heresy: "Kool-Aid and Cookies Have Had Their Day." *Simply Delicious* is a cookbook for a socially conscious congregation. St. Pauls even learned some lessons here. A newsletter urged prospective hosts and hostesses of its weekly coffee hour "to be creative with the refreshments you bring. Consider a fruit tray or vegetables and dip in place of cookies." This was the social hour of a socially conscious congregation

By looking at the food-centered social events at St Pauls Church, we have seen how these meals present models for society, and how those models changed. In the early years of this century, church meals for adults reflected gender roles in their menus and programs, while food events for young people tried to make adolescence wholesome and safe. But these models changed in response to the church's environment. In the baby boom decade after World War II, the church's social events centered on families, but shifted to include single adults as yuppies replaced families in the neighborhood. And in response to both neighborhood change and ethical challenges, the church turned its food events outward, to welcome strangers into its kitchen and dining rooms.

St Pauls' is not unique; American churches large and small include kitchens and fellowship halls. Investigating the use of food in other congregations would be equally illuminating, but similar methods would yield different results in a different religious community. A Hindu temple in Nashville, Tennessee, serves as a retail outlet for spices and grains needed for Indian cooking, while African-American churches in northern cities offer traditional southern cooking at congregational suppers. In both of these communities, the church's food events provide an element of "home" in what might feel like an alien environment. A Korean Presbyterian congregation wrestles over the menu and manners for church suppers, reflecting inner tensions over assimilation into the larger society. A "megachurch" builds a food court, to provide a place for evangelization and community creation. In each of these religious communities food plays a unique role; attention to that role tells us much about that community's understanding of itself and of the world.

The sources for investigating a congregation's use of food are rich and diverse. Much of the history is in print sources, such as bulletins, newsletters, and cookbooks, of course. Such an inquiry would also benefit from direct observation of social events, and from looking at the building's kitchen and social rooms. Good sources for investigating the role of food in congregational life are "fun books," guidebooks from denominational hints full of hints for organizing successful church social events. The recipes, games, and decoration ideas convey an entire way of life in a church setting.

Douglas and her fellow anthropologists argue that meals are a system of analogies to society and its structures. Applying this insight to something as prosaic as a Protestant church supper reveals richness in an unexpected place. Just as Douglas advocates "deciphering a meal," there is much to be learned from deciphering a church potluck.

NOTE

1 All unattributed quotations come from the newsletters of St Pauls Church.

BILIOGRAPHY

Douglas, Mary (1975) "On deciphering a meal," in *Implicit Meanings*, London: Routledge and Kegan Paul.
—— (1984) "Standard social uses of food," in *Food in the Social Order: Studies of Food and Festivities in Three American Communities*, New York: Russell Sage Foundation.
Geertz, Clifford (1973) "Religion as a cultural system," in *The Interpretation of Cultures: Selected Essays*, New York: Basic Books.

Harbin, E. O. (1923) *Phunology: A Collection of Tried and Proved Plans for Play, Fellowship, and Profit*, Nashville, Tenn.: Cokesbury Press.

Holifield, E. Brooks (1994) "Toward a history of American congregations," in J. P. Wind and J. W. Lewis (eds) *American Congregations* (2 vols), vol. 2, *New Perspectives in the Study of Congregations*, Chicago: University of Chicago Press.

Keillor, Garrison (1985) *Lake Wobegon Days*, New York: Viking.

Kirk, Jane (1962) *How to Plan Church Meals*, Westwood, NJ: Fleming H. Revell Company.

Marty, Martin E. (1958) *The New Shape of American Religion*, New York: Harper and Brothers.

Shapiro, Laura (1986) *Perfection Salad: Women and Cooking at the Turn of the Century*, New York: Farrar, Straus, and Giroux.

Tracy, Patricia (1979) *Jonathan Edwards, Pastor: Religion and Society in Eighteenth-century Northampton*, New York: Hill and Wang.

Winn, Grace (ed.) (1983) *Simply Delicious: Quantity Cooking for Churches*, Ellenwood, Ga.: Alternatives.

Winter, Gibson (1961) *The Suburban Captivity of the Churches: An Analysis of Protestant Responsibility in the Expanding Metropolis*, Garden City, NY: Doubleday.

Chapter 15

Fasting, Dieting, and the Body in American Christianity

R. Marie Griffith

Christian philosophers, theologians, and laypeople have long pondered the un-settling mystery of the human soul's relation to its fleshly body during earthly life: is the body simply an inert shell that houses the active spirit? Or a temptation-ridden obstacle to purity and holiness? A battlefield upon which God and Satan engage in war? Or a source of sanctified pleasure and goodness? Even if laypeople's treatments of these issues have rarely converged with those of theologians, these groups have shared a powerful need to scrutinize material–spiritual relations for their disclosures about human existence and ultimate purpose. It is to be expected, then, that ordinary bodily experiences relating to sexuality and birth, illness and healing, ingestion and digestion, to name only a few, have persistently received critical attention from believers struggling to understand and interpret their physicality within a Christian theological framework.

In turn, historians of Christianity have sought to understand the complexities of such struggles in various epochs, resulting in an impressive array of research on ideas and practices relating to the body in the Christian tradition. While no neat summary of this research is possible, it is quite clear that the changes in Christian bodily preoccupations over time, on the one hand, and the continuities between concerns and habits in different historical eras, on the other, are equally striking. For two thousand years, that is, a powerful, scripturally grounded ascetic tradition of disciplining and restraining the body has been interwoven with a strong inclination (also justified by Scripture) toward liberating and celebrating the body. The yoking of these distinct yet interrelated impulses has resulted in multiple historical permutations of belief and behavior, patterns that vary dramatically in different periods but that are nonetheless clustered around a set of common problems and practices.

Exhortations pertaining to food and eating have figured prominently in these historical patterns, especially practices of fasting and varied modes of feasting (such as the eucharist). Fasting, well established in the Mediterranean world long before Christianity emerged, became especially important in Christian communal practice during the early fourth century CE, used variously as a method of preparation for baptism, a means of purification, a sign of grief and mourning, a work of charity, or an expression of penitence and the desire for God's mercy. Augustine of Hippo warned Christians: "Above all be mindful of the poor so that you lay up in the heavenly treasury what you withhold from yourselves by a more frugal mode of life. The hungry Christ will receive that from which the fasting Christian abstains" (quoted in Bynum 1987: 35). Over the next several centuries, as historian Caroline Walker Bynum has richly documented, both the meaning and the practice of Christian abstinence changed significantly, so that by the thirteenth and fourteenth centuries preachers and theologians urged "spiritual more than physical abstinence" and frequently allegorized fasting to mean general restraint or moderation in all areas of life (pp. 42–3). Yet many Christians of the later Middle Ages, most of them women, decried this perspective as a dangerous compromise with the world, a relaxation of God's rules that would not find favor with the holy will. Instead of moderation, they chose the path of extreme asceticism, imitating and deeply identifying with the broken flesh of Christ on the cross through rigorous sacrifical fasting. For those like Catherine of Siena, who died of self-induced starvation at the age of 33, the only true nourishment came from Christ, and to rely merely on earthly food for sustenance was to commit the terrible sin of gluttony.

Theological prescriptions and lay practices pertaining to food abstinence and bodily discipline fluctuated in subsequent eras, and scattered examples of intense fasting among Christians, again mostly women, have continued to dot the historical record. Since the transformative religious revolutions of the sixteenth and seventeenth centuries, Catholics and Protestants alike have adapted and participated in the ascetic tradition, though always in very particular, localized ways. Martin Luther condemned as "folly" extravagant forms of fasting that destroyed the body; instead he recommended fasting in moderation, according to individual conscience and endurance, as a useful means of curbing fleshly desires that distract one from God and also as a way of taking care of the body so that it is strong enough to labor in service to others' needs. John Calvin held to a stricter interpretation of fasting as a necessary discipline for appeasing God's wrath, a view echoed in later groups like the English Puritans. The Church of England and the Roman Catholic Church fixed particular calendrical times for fasting – such as the Lenten period prior to Easter, Ember Days, Rogation Days, Fridays, and Vigils prior to certain holy festivals – but varied in the precise meaning given to "fasting" per se. The evolution of fasting in the Christian tradition, then is not one but many stories; and while this essay attempts to narrate one particular strand of events as they took place on American soil, there are, of course, many other narratives linked to and underlying this one.

From the colonial period onward, American Christians wrestled with questions about bodily asceticism and gluttony in ways that would, to all appearances, feel increasingly unfamiliar to their patristic and medieval forebears. While the religious critiques of greed and abundance – articulated alike by Puritans and Social Gospelers, radical Catholics and Holiness adherents – recall themes expressed by early and medieval Christian ascetics, an evolving fixation on bodily health and perfection in American Christianity represents a stark departure from the older emphasis on corporeal acts of penitence. Even more discordantly, the twentieth-century obsession with slender, tight bodies and the equation of extreme thinness with wellness and beauty bear only a distorted resemblance to the intense rituals of purification and self-denial that occupied Christians in earlier periods. Somehow, it seems, the kinship between body and soul has become dramatically reconceptualized, with significant help from men and women professing Christianity but focusing as much on the "promised land of weight-loss" as on the eternal Kingdom of God.

Understanding how this apparent mutation occurred requires solid historical contextualization. When did American Christians begin to worry about their weight, and why have many Christians couched that worry in theological terms? What precedents are there in American history for concern about food intake and body size? At what point did fasting cease to be a wholly spiritual practice and become a technique for weight reduction? What, finally, does Christianity have to do with the American diet obsession? It is possible to trace the modern American concern for keeping to the "right" weight back into eighteenth-century British sources and, from there, further back to a sixteenth-century work by an Italian nobleman, whose critique of "gluttony" – an old foe of Christianity, considered one of the seven deadly sins – would be cited for centuries thereafter. This essay documents that chain of influence, paying close attention to the growing anxiety about weight control and health among Christians of the eighteenth and nineteenth centuries and to the surge of diet literature and programs promoted by the faithful in the twentieth. While much work remains to be done in this area, it is quite evident that the transformation of fasting into dieting is largely a Protestant story; whether because they have retained a stronger hold on the older ascetic devotions and rejected the individualistic nature of dieting or because they have simply had concerns other than dietary reform to worry about, American Catholics (along with Jews and other religious groups) have not emerged in the record as zealous advocates of physical fitness. Yet it is equally evident that the history of American dietary practices is deeply linked to the history of American religion and that to examine the one is inevitably to gain insights into the latter.

Diet Reform in Eighteenth- and Nineteenth-century America

At the ripe old age of 83, Luigi Cornaro (1464–1566) began writing *La Vita Sobria*, translated into English as "A Sure and Certain Method of Attaining a Long and Healthy Life" or more simply "The Art of Living Long." Here Cornaro recounted the years of intemperate eating and drinking that had almost led to his death before the age of 40. Frightened by his Venetian doctors' remonstrances, Cornaro gave up gluttony for temperance and thereby managed to exchange his ill health for remarkable physical vigor and mental well-being. While most of Cornaro's prescriptions for health were typical of the Galenic medical tradition widely accepted in this period, he departed from this tradition in asserting that temperate living created a kind of safety barrier against sickness, making way for increased mental and spiritual alertness on earth and a strong chance of increased longevity. With a confident optimism that would deeply appeal to later Enlightenment thinkers, Cornaro assured his readers that God intended all humans of whatever condition or endurance to possess good health, happiness, and long life. The story of Cornaro, who lived to be over 100 years old, became a model for later health reformers; as historian James Whorton has noted, the "Cornaro tradition" of ideas (and of biographical narrative) "colored hygienic literature down to the 1830s" (1982: 19–20).

The great receptivity to Cornaro's ideas in the centuries after his death was conditioned by many factors, not least of which was the recovery by Renaissance humanism of classical ideas about the virtue of temperance and the promotion of moderation in daily living. Like the revival of symmetry, balance, and restrained simplicity in Renaissance art and neoclassical architecture, a renewed ethic of spareness and frugality appealed to Christians and Enlightenment critics of religion alike, an ethic easily recognizable in Benjamin Franklin's prescriptive advice (if not always exemplified in his life). What was singular about this "Cornaro tradition," however, was not merely its censure of excessive ingestion and its inducements to curb the appetite; critiques of gluttony, after all, were part of a venerable tradition in European Christianity. Rather, the distinguishing feature of Cornaro's thought and, even more, that of the Anglo-Americans who cited him voluminously in later centuries, was leanness of body and its linkage to health, vigor, contentment, moral uprightness, and, soon enough, beauty. Body size, rarely before viewed as a sign of moral uprightness or depravity, gradually became in the early modern period an index of physical, moral, and spiritual well-being; and fervent, conversionist accounts such as Cornaro's – "I once was fat but now am thin" – increased apace.

One of the most influential of these converts to bodily reduction was the Scottish-born London physician George Cheyne (1671–1743), who ballooned to 448 pounds while living a life of dissipation, until he realized his dangerous state of health. At this point he made a dramatic change in his habits, settling on a life-long regimen of milk and vegetables, regular exercise, proper sleep, and temperate drinking of wine. Reduced to a healthier weight and rid of the many illnesses that had accompanied his obesity, Cheyne wrote extensively about the physical and spiritual benefits of "diaetetick management" and its resulting corporal leanness in works such as *The English Malady*, *An Essay on Regimen*, and *Book of Health and Long Life*. Like Cornaro, whose work he had read in George Herbert's 1634 translation of *La Vita Sobria*, Cheyne conceived of health as a religious obligation and perceived "control of the body," as Bryan Turner has observed, to be "part of the religious calling" (1991: 161).

One of Cheyne's most important readers was John Wesley (1703–91), who similarly recommended a sober and temperate life in his *Primitive Physick* (1747), as well as in various sermons, letters, and journal entries. As a young man, Wesley praised Cheyne's writings to both his mother and the Bishop of London, noting that he himself had "been free (blessed be God) from all bodily disorders" since adopting Cheyne's regimen. Following Cheyne, as well as the disciplinary norms of his parental upbringing and the "Holy Club" at Oxford, Wesley vowed to eat a spare and simple diet comprised largely (and sometimes entirely) of "vegetable food" and water, with only moderate amounts of meat, beer, and wine included. Wesley's own writings make clear that his approach to diet, like his approach to all other aspects of daily living, grew out of both his sense of Christian duty (inspired by the scriptural emphasis on fasting) and his interest in maintaining overall health. His view is summarized in *Primitive Physick*: "The great Rule of Eating and Drinking is, To suit the Quality and Quantity of Food to the Strength of our Degestion [*sic*]; to take always such a Sort and such a Measure of Food, as fits light and easy on the Stomach" (pp. xiii–xiv). Wesley's book sold extremely well among the ordinary folk who were its intended audience, going through twenty-three editions during his lifetime and reissued for years after his death.

The combined influence of Cornaro, Cheyne, and Wesley pervaded the nineteenth-century popular and medical literature on diet. During the Jacksonian heyday of American reform movements, men such as Sylvester Graham, William Alcott, and John Harvey Kellogg crusaded for a revolution in American eating habits and portrayed dietary reform in redemptive terms. Temperance reformer and homeopathic physician Dio Lewis (1823–86) quoted copiously from Cornaro and Cheyne in *On Digestion*, his popular 1872 work recommending an abstemious diet and urging the eradication of supper. Lewis also cited Wesley, Benjamin Rush, and Franklin as exemplars of dietetic moderation (and, not coincidentally, of longevity). Recommending the abolishment of breakfast rather than supper, physician Edward Hooker Dewey taught that disease was often caused or abetted by gluttonous behavior and excess body weight and advocated both extreme and mild forms of fasting as a panacea for all ills. In his 1899 book *The True Science of Living: The New Gospel of Health*, Dewey especially singled out "these life-depressing, sin-enticing church suppers" as "untimely repasts that have to be most uncomfortably recovered from," and declared:

> No man can be a good Christian without *most extraordinary and persistent and ceaseless effort who is not physically well*. Your headaches and all your ailings, no matter how many or where they are located, are mainly the results of lifelong avoidable culture of sins against the body and against the soul, which often have to be confessed "with groanings that cannot be uttered" as to duly interpret the wrongdoing within. I would have you believe that headaches and bilious attacks are never anything less than direct humiliating evidences of excesses *at the table*. (1899: 244; italics in original)

Once again, health was advocated as a primary Christian duty, to be fulfilled by means of light eating and evidenced by a thin body.

The Cornaro tradition would continue, a few degress removed from its author, in Horace Fletcher (1849–1919), an American businessman stunned into self-examination at the age of 44 when a life insurance company refused to insure him because of his poor health and portly size. At the time, Fletcher was apparently prone to severe indigestion and other illnesses related to his extravagant food intake; but he shortly lost his excess pounds and regained his health by means of a two-pronged cure: "menticulture" (his version of positive thinking, inspired by New Thought) and thorough, prolonged mastication. Claiming to have improved upon the dietary methods of Cornaro and praised by readers from John D. Rockefeller to Kellogg and many respected physicians of the day, Fletcher wrote numerous books elaborating his ideas and encouraging a nation of gulpers and gluttons to eat only when hungry, to limit intake to whatever precisely appealed to the appetite, and to chew every bite until it had been thoroughly pulverized into liquid and was automatically swallowed. Any fibrous remnant that could not be liquidized should not be ingested but spat out as delicately as possible. One of the great benefits of Fletcher's system, and one that he publicized with high-pitched enthusiasm, was that it supposedly resulted in odorless and easily passable stools. Whether or not this was actually verified in the private chamber pots of his followers, Americans seized upon "Fletcherism" with a vengeance, discussing mastication, digestion, and evacuation with unrivaled ease and scrutinizing the size of their bodies with remarkable zeal.

A more extreme version of Fletcher's message emerged with Bernarr Macfadden (1868–1955), the American publisher and king of physical fitness in the early twentieth century. Though perhaps better known today for having founded such magazines as *True Romances* and *True Detective Mysteries* than for promoting exercise and regular fasting, Macfadden's teachings on health and beauty were widely distributed and followed during his early adulthood. The arrogant Macfadden himself was a laughingstock to many for obsessively developing and flamboyantly displaying his own musculature (as well as the bodies of the many skimpily clad women in his theatric exhibitions), but his magazine, *Physical Culture* (launched in 1899) as well as his many published books drew a wide audience of people concerned to improve their health. Among other things, Macfadden strongly emphasized the beneficial effects of fasting, thorough mastication, and a near vegetarian diet, as well as the evils of alcohol, tobacco, caffeine, and most of all gluttonous eating. Though his unconventional ideas about clothing (thought to be unhealthful, with nakedness his own preferred state of being), his unstable personal life, and his messianic bravado limited and eventually all but stifled Macfadden's popular appeal, his fervor about limiting food intake and fasting to cure disease received broad approval.

By the early decades of the twentieth century, Anglo-American diet reformers had achieved colossal success in their quest to demonize fat and preach thinness as necessary to personal salvation. The truism that converts are always the most fervid advocates within a faith well describes these reformers, as nearly all claimed to have been at an earlier time obese and tearfully recounted their corporeal reductions in histrionic, life-changing terms. Their diatribes against fat reveled in the most grotesque descriptions imaginable, some landing squarely in the realm of the absurd. In his preface to *Eat and Grow Thin: The Mahdah Menus*

(1914), Vance Thompson (who predictably claimed to have reduced from his former corpulence) exemplified the maudlin depths of this realm as he moaned:

> The tragedy of fat! One could write books, plays, poems on the subject. One thinks of the beautiful women one has known – loved perhaps – who have vanished forever, drowned in an ocean of turbulence and tallow; of actresses who filled one's soul with shining dreams – and now the dreams are wrecked on huge promontories; of statesmen and rulers who cumber the earth, now mere teeth and stomach, as though God had created them, like Mirabeau, only to show to what extent the human skin can be stretched without breaking. The tragedy of fat!
>
> An ancient man said: 'Plures crapula quam gladius'—gluttony kills more than the sword; but the saddest part is that it kills with a death more horrible. One may face with fair courage the lean and bony fellow with the scythe—meet him with grim fortitude; but the boldest man shudders at the thought of a fat death; as one who sinks in a sebaceous sea. (1914: 3–4).

Thompson and other diet writers of the 1910s and 1920s seemed to signal that the older devotional context for abstemious eating, in which fasting was undertaken as a godly discipline and not only a technique for improving health, had vanished, replaced by a shriller and more extreme gospel of thinness. In muted form, of course, the religious significance of diet would survive, as evidenced in the language of sin and morality that Americans have persistently used when discussing their own and others' food habits. But the assumption of earlier writers of a heathen world transformed into the Kingdom of God by means of dietary temperance sharply declined after the Progressive Era. Only at mid-century would Christian piety and diet reform enthusiastically reunite, creating a dramatically repackaged message that echoed the concerns about gluttony and corpulence evident as early as Luigi Cornaro while buttressing these concerns with the consumer-driven values of slenderness and beauty more characteristic of twentieth-century American culture.

Religious Diet Reform in the Twentieth Century

The earliest text to articulate this new message, and the first twentieth-century representation of the Christian diet book genre, was *Pray Your Weight Away* by Presbyterian minister Charlie Shedd (1957). Writing to an audience somewhat less jaded by diet books than later readers would be, Shedd managed to blend the comforting tone of a down-home preacher with the shrewd business sense of an enterprising fitness mogul. In his version of the gospel of slimness, portly bodies were condemned in the explicit language of sin and guilt, while salvation – that is, weight loss – was guaranteed by means of sustained prayer and true faith.

Those who purchased *Pray Your Weight Away* were treated to a tasty menu of helpful hints and reminders. "When God first dreamed you into creation," Shedd affirmed, "there weren't one hundred pounds of excess avoirdupois hanging around your belt." In line once again with the Cornaro tradition, the author proclaimed himself a fellow struggler who had once divested that much

from his own body and recommended various treatments for successful slim-
ming, including vocal mealtime affirmations such as: "Today my body belongs
to God. Today I live for him. Today I eat with Him." He also advised, as a useful
time-saver, combining daily devotions with fifteen minutes of calisthenics and
encouraged readers to follow his own regimen, which included executing karate
kicks while reciting the third chapter of Proverbs and timing sit ups to the spoken
rhythm of Psalm nineteen. With a heavy dose of positive thinking to balance his
rebuke of excess poundage, Shedd assured readers that beneath their bulk, "there
is a beautiful figure waiting to come forth. Peel off the layers, watch it emerge,
and know the thrill which comes when you meet the real you."

Shedd and his readers could have hardly foreseen the impending explosion of
Christian diet literature into a multimillion dollar industry, one that rode the back
of the American diet craze and capitalized on it by creating a message specially
geared to the evangelical multitudes. In the fifty years after *Pray Your Weight
Away* was published, American Christianity saw the rise (and sometimes fall) of
iconic groups and hopeful concepts like Overeaters Victorious, Believercise, the
Faithfully Fit Program, and the Love Hunger Action Plan. Episcopalian Deborah
Pierce composed *I Prayed Myself Slim* in 1960, describing how she was transformed from a 210-pound object of campus ridicule to a "high-fashion model"
in Washington. Seven years later *Devotions for Dieters* was published by pastor
Victor Kane, a book that was reprinted in 1973 and again in 1976. As Christian
diet literature underwent its first significant boom in the 1970s, Charlie Shedd
again led the way, as his 1972 book *The Fat Is In Your Head* remained on the
National Religious Bestsellers list for 23 months and sold more than 110,000
copies by 1976. Evangelist Frances Hunter produced *God's Answer to Fat* in
1975, a top religious bestseller that far exceeded even Shedd's numbers, with
1977 sales figures nearly matching Charles Colson's *Born Again* and the inspirational autobiography, *Joni*. Other striking successes in this period include
titles such as *Help Lord – The Devil Wants Me Fat!* (1977); *Slim for Him* (1978);
and *Free To Be Thin* (1979); the latter sold more than half a million copies and
spawned a virtual industry of diet products marketed by the author, including an
exercise video and a low-calorie, inspirational cookbook.

Along the way, women who had failed to lose weight on their own took a cue
from secular weight-loss groups like TOPS (for "Taking Off Pounds Sensibly"),
Overeaters Anonymous, and Weight Watchers, and began seeking help from
other struggling dieters, only adding a biblical dimension to these groups that
was unavailable elsewhere. For instance, Carol Showalter, the New York wife of
a Presbyterian pastor, gave up the strict regimen of Weight Watchers in 1972 to
form 3D (Diet, Discipline, and Discipleship), advertised as "a Christian counterpart to national weight-watcher programs"; it had expanded to more than 5,000
churches and 100,000 participants by 1981. About the same time, 248–pound
Neva Coyle, having failed at every commercial diet program she tried, turned to
the Bible, lost 100 pounds, and founded Overeaters Victorious in 1977, which
launched her successful career as a best-selling author and inspirational speaker.

This trend hardly faltered in the 1980s and into the 1990s. The later plethora
of publications included books on "spiritual discipline for weight control,"

"Biblical principles that will improve your health," and achieving "greater health God's way." Christian presses competed against each other as well as with non-christian presses as they published secular-sounding titles such as *The Diet Alternative* (1984), *The No Diet Fitness Book* (1985), *Gentle Eating* (1994), and *Power Living: Everybody's Health and Diet Book* (1996). While most of this literature was written by evangelicals, other Christians participated as well, including mainline Protestants; *The Serpent Beguiled Me And I Ate: A Heavenly Diet for Saints and Sinners* (1986) was written by Edward Dumke, an Episcopal priest. Mormons – LDS members – have published books such as *The Mormon Diet* (1991) and the fat-free, cholesterol-free *Mormon Diet Cookbook* (1992), which claim to provide the way for easy permanent weight loss. Even Christian Scientists, who deny the materiality of the body and believe that the true nature of human beings and the universe is nonmaterial spirit, have addressed the problem of excess weight and have advocated mental versions of diet control in a special issue of the *Christian Science Sentinel* (September 8, 1997).

More Christian diet groups also emerged locally and went national during the 1980s and 1990s. These included Houston-based First Place (founded in 1981 and later consolidated under the auspices of the Southern Baptist Convention), peaking with programs estimated at between 5 and 8 thousand churches across the country and in thirteen other nations, and also smaller programs such as Jesus is the Weigh and Step Forward to a New Healthy You (based on the 12-step recovery model). The largest of these has been the Tennessee–based Weigh Down Workshop (founded in 1986), a twelve–week Bible–study program offered in as many as 20 thousand churches and 60 different denominations (including Catholic and mainline Protestant) in the United States and beyond. That program gained new ground with founder Gwen Shamblin's 1997 book, *The Weigh Down Diet*, which sold 200,000 copies in the first two months after it was released by Doubleday and over a million within the year. More explicitly denominational programs have also emerged and been successful: The United Methodist Church has sponsored its own devotional diet program called "Body and Soul," with a thriving curriculum published by Abingdon Press. Robert Schuller's Crystal Cathedral has developed another (and not dissimilar) program called "Balanced for Life," which it markets to paying believers across the nation.

Christian exercise programs have also taken the country by storm. Catalogs from the Texas-based Christian Aerobic Resource have been successful at selling a vast array of Christian music tapes, workout clothes replete with religious slogans, and training manuals for "Faithfully Fit" aerobics instructors. In 1996, Sheri Chambers's "Praise Aerobics" video immediately went gold, fast selling over 50,000 copies to compete numerically with the latest offerings from pop music stars like Bon Jovi and Janet Jackson. The word "aerobics" itself, defining a particular form of vigorous cardiovascular exercise, was coined by a devout Southern Baptist heart surgeon, Kenneth Cooper, who built his gigantic fitness complex in Dallas as a monument to the harmony between physical and spiritual health. In Cooper's interpretation of the Bible, God commands human beings to glorify their bodies even as they strengthen their spirits. Leaders and participants involved in the many other Christian fitness enterprises in America would certainly agree, and they have worked vigorously to fulfill that command by the sweat of their brows.

All of these manifestations of the Bible-based diet culture, permeating a wide spectrum of American Protestantism, have expanded steadily and, especially since the 1980s, rapidly, with little ebb in sight. As in earlier historical periods, these latter-day diet reformers have promoted a variety of messages, some advocating fasting as a useful scriptural means for controlling one's weight and others urging against it, several advising a strict vegetable-based diet even as others proclaim the benefits of meat and dairy products (in moderation), some lauding the supposedly miraculous benefits of certain nutrients and vitamin supplements and decrying the toxins found elsewhere, while many more express a mainstream preference for dietary variety combined with frequent exercise. Like the wider secular diet culture of which Bible-based writers are in some sense part, there is no general consensus as to the best way of losing weight and maintaining thinness, but few if any authors question the belief that following God means watching one's figure. Only rarely are distinctions made between those whose obesity seriously affects their health and those who are merely a few pounds over the extremely lean ideal celebrated in the American advertising industry: none can afford to relax completely, for there is always room in the arena of Christian discipline for improvement.

Indeed, a 1997 study by a Purdue University sociologist, Kenneth Ferraro, added a new dimension to the analysis of Christian diet programs by arguing, on the basis of data collected in two national surveys, that religious people are statistically more likely to be fat than are nonreligious people and showing Southern Baptists to be the most overweight of all groups in the US. (Body weight was measured according to the standard Quetelet Index, better known as the body mass index or BMI.) Exactly why obesity should be statistically correlated with higher levels of religious practice and affiliation is unclear, and further contextualization along cultural, regional, and class lines is surely needed before drawing conclusions. Nonetheless, this research may begin to suggest one facet of the popularity of religious diet plans, since they are addressing what is at least perceived to be a serious health problem that seemingly affects church people as much as or even more than people outside church walls. What the research does not and cannot do, of course, is to critique the implicit norms and values that have come to govern both religious and secular language about weight and diet or to provide a historical framework for understanding the intertwining of Christianity and American culture in creating and sustaining these obsessions.

Bodily Obsessions and American Christian Culture

Plainly, Christian diet writers have not simply jumped on to the wider cultural bandwagon of obsessive weight-watching but have contributed to that culture in crucial and profoundly revealing ways. In fact, Christian concerns about the body and health in earlier historical eras gave powerful impetus to emerging therapies of bodily perfection, impetus whose reach and depth has only begun to be suggested within the parameters of this essay. At the same time, however, it must be noted that America's culture of thinness has deep and diverse roots well beyond the bounds of Christianity. These include the quest among occultist practitioners of magic for elixirs against illness and death in the perennial desire for longevity and eternal youth; the changing economics of food distribution in the early modern and modern worlds and the near tyrannical bodily fashions that have subsequently arisen among the privileged classes; and the counter-Christian worship of the self that has turned the body, again and again, into an idol of pleasure, allure, and power, gluttonous less for food than for prestige. Such historical events have meant that the relationship between Christianity and so-called "fitness" has frequently been one of antagonism and resistance as much as cooperation. Taking a broad perspective, this relationship looks less like an enthusiastic alliance *or* a thoroughgoing enmity than a confused (and confusing) ambivalence.

After all, Christian thinkers have always been wary of any religious pursuit that threatens to become an end in itself rather than a means of achieving greater spiritual maturity and Christian humility. The supposed distortion of ascetic pursuits like fasting clearly occupied the minds of medieval churchmen; they balked at the intensity of Catherine of Siena and also disturbed later thinkers like John Wesley, who may well have had this problem in mind when he wrote:

> The having our thought and affections centered on God, this is Christian simplicity; the having them in any degree uncentered from God, this is dissipation. . . . And whether our thoughts and affections are dissipated, scattered from God, by women, or food, or dress, or one or ten thousand petty trifles, that dissipation (innocent as it may seem) is equally subversive of all real virtue and all real happiness. (quoted in Wallace 1977: 200).

The amount of ink that has been spilled in addressing the issue of turning virtues into obsessions is evidence, if anyone needed it, that the balance called for by ascetic disciplines is extraordinarily difficult to achieve.

For the historian observing the food practices of American Christians, those who have sought a godly way of life but have been constrained to live amid the confines of the earthly world, such a balance is, indeed, hard to find. One is tempted to conclude that excessive dieting in the modern period, like extreme fasting in earlier periods, is but the flip side of gluttonous overeating, all being acts of near compulsion rather than moderation. But rather than resort to jaded explanations regarding supposed psychological neuroses, the question should be asked: *Why* has food retained such extraordinary symbolic power, not only among American Christians but among non-christians as well? Whatever conclusions emerge from future research, it seems clear that for the religious and secular alike the relationship between the soul and the body, a relationship whose complexities are traceable in attitudes toward pain and suffering, death and bodily remnants, filth and cleanliness, and any number of realms besides food and fasting, remains as elusive and as contested as ever.

BIBLIOGRAPHY

Brumberg, Joan Jacobs (1988) *Fasting Girls: The Emergence of Anorexia Nervosa as a Modern Disease*, Cambridge, Mass.: Harvard University Press.

Bynum, Caroline Walker (1987) *Holy Feast and Holy Fast: The Religious Significance of Food to Medieval Women*, Berkeley, Calif.: University of California Press.

Dewey, Edward Hooker (1899) *The True Science of Living: The New Gospel of Health*, Norwich, Conn.: Haskell.

Ferrarro, Kenneth (1998) "Firm believers? Religion, body weight, and well-being," *Review of Religious Research* 39/3 (March), pp. 224–44.

Griffith, R. Marie (1997) "The promised land of weight loss: law and Gospel in Christian dieting," *Christian Century* (May 7), pp. 448–54.

Nissenbaum, Stephen (1980) *Sex, Diet, and Debility in Jacksonian America: Sylvester Graham and Health Reform*, Westport, Conn.: Greenwood Press.

Schwartz, Hillel (1986) *Never Satisfied: A Cultural History of Diets, Fantasies and Fat*, New York: Free Press.

Shedd, Charlie W. (1957) *Pray Your Weight Away*, Philadelphia, Pa.: Lippincott.

Showalter, Carol (1977) *3D*, Orleans, Mass.: Rock Harbor Press.

Stearns, Peter N. (1977) *Fat History: Bodies and Beauty in the Modern West*, New York: New York University Press.

Thompson, Vance (1914) *Eat and Grow Thin: The Mahdah Menus*, New York: Dutton.

Turner, Bryan S. (1991) "The discourse of diet," in Mike Featherstone, Mike Hepworth, and Bryan S. Turner (eds) *The Body: Social Process and Cultural Theory*, London: Sage Publications, pp. 157–69.

Vandereycken, Walter and van Deth, Ron (1994) *From Fasting Saints to Anorexic Girls: The History of Self–Starvation*, New York: New York University Press; German edn published 1990.

Wallace, Charles (1977) "Simple and recollected: John Wesley's life-style," *Religion in Life* 46 (Summer), pp. 198–212.

Wesley, John (1764) *Primitive Physick: Or, an Easy and Natural Method of Curing Most Diseases*, 12th edn, Philadelphia, Pa.: Andrew Steuart; originally published 1747.

Whorton, James C. (1982) *Crusaders for Fitness: The History of American Health Reformers*, Princeton, NJ: Princeton University Press.

Chapter 16

The Bible and Serpent-handling

Bill J. Leonard

The scene is a small rural church somewhere in West Virginia, where a revival meeting is going on week nights and Sunday. The context is the Pentecostal-Holiness tradition, which embraces shouting, speaking in tongues and singing accompanied by guitar, drums and tambourines. Meetings are always lively affairs but sometimes very lively. Somewhere near the pulpit there is a box, about three feet long with a screen at one end and a padlocked lid. Eleanor Dickinson, in her study called *Revival!* (1974: 127), describes what happens: "At some time during the service, usually while music and dancing is also going on, a preacher will unlock the box, reach in and pick up one or more snakes. Anyone in the congregation may come forward and reach for a snake if he or she feels moved to do so. A person who has won the victory over the serpent may cry out 'hallelujah!' or 'Thank you, Jesus.'" (I know I certainly would.)

Dickinson quotes Elzie Preast, the pastor of the West Virginia church:

> But it does say, "They shall take up serpents." And Jesus is the one's doing the talking. Said, "They shall take them up." Well, I've got to do it, or somebody's got to do it, or else it makes Jesus out a liar, because if I tell you shall go out that door, it means that you've got to go out there, one way or the other. Now listen how it reads. "And these signs shall follow them that believe." Shall. Now if it said, "If you feel led to handle them, if you believe to handle them, it'd be kind of different. But it says, "These signs shall follow . . ." But the scriptures said that they shall pick up serpents, and somebody has to do that. If we don't do it, Jesus can raise up a people that will do it. (pp. 127–8)

I met my first serpent-handlers in the summer of 1990 while teaching in the Appalachian Ministries Education Resource Center based at Berea College, Berea, Kentucky. Mary Lee Daugherty, the director of that seminary consortium, is a well-known authority on serpent-handlers. She and David Kimbrough, then a graduate student at Indiana University, made arrangements for us to visit a homecoming service; it was held up a hollow from Berea on a blazing hot Sunday in June. Kimbrough was completing a dissertation on a segment of the serpent-handling subgroup that was largely related to the Saylor family (see Kimbrough 1995). It was through Kimbrough that I met Brother Arnold Saylor, patriarch of the family, Appalachian-born holiness preacher and serpent-handling pastor of the Highway Holiness Church of God in Fort Wayne, Indiana. Saylor presided but did not preach at the homecoming. He was friendly, open, and welcomed us gladly. He was also an amazingly articulate spokesperson for serpent-handling theology. At the homecoming about thirty people gathered for worship in a small grove of trees. With their permission I used my video camera to record the preaching, singing, shouting and yes, the serpent-handling – an event powerful and dramatic beyond my wildest expectations.

Yet it was Arnold Saylor who captivated my interest apart from the obvious fascination with the serpent-handling phenomenon itself. I attended his meetings during two summers and invited him to speak in my classes at the Southern Baptist Theological Seminary, Louisville, where I was then teaching. Saylor was one of the most amazing persons I have ever met and his death from heart failure in December, 1991 was a great tragedy for all who knew him. He was, in my view, an ecumenical serpent-handler, firm in his convictions, largely self-educated, and deeply concerned for human beings whether they handled the dreaded serpents or not. In July, 1991, Brother Saylor attended a foot-washing which marked the end of our summer term at Berea College and willingly participated in that "saycrament", as he called it. He washed feet in the company of a Byzantine Franciscan, several members of the Church of God, Cleveland, Tennessee, and assorted ordained women and men from across the theological and denominational spectrum, marvelling that such a diverse group could "take the saycraments" together.

"Do you believe in snake-handling?," one of my students asked a few days before Brother Saylor was to visit my class. "Believe in it?", I replied, "Why, I've actually seen it done!" It was after observing certain services and discussing it all with colleagues Daugherty, Kimborough and others, that I began to listen more carefully to the serpent-handlers and to ask what they are saying about the nature of religion, revelation, and mystery. Beyond all the caricatures what is it that the serpent-handlers are saying to the rest of us? In that effort, I found myself intrigued with the hermeneutic: the method of utilizing and interpreting biblical texts, oral and written, which the serpent-handlers demonstrate. My thesis, therefore, is that the people called serpent-handlers are in a real sense the ultimate biblical inerrantists. They carry the doctrine of biblical inerrancy – learned through oral tradition, not classrooms or books – to its logical or, some may say, its illogical conclusions. They make serpent-handling as described in Mark 16: 17–20 the ultimate test for validating what other American evangelicals call the "total truthfulness" of the Word of God. Likewise, their reading of this text provides a method for informing their rituals and their spirituality. The infamous passage, sometimes known to biblical scholars as the "false ending" of Mark, reads:

And these signs shall follow them that believe; In my name shall they cast out devils; they shall speak with new tongues; They shall take up serpents; and if they drink any deadly thing, it shall not hurt them; they shall lay hands on the sick, and they shall recover. So then after the Lord had spoken unto them, he was received up into heaven, and sat on the right hand of God. And they went forth, and preached every where, the Lord working with them, and confirming the word with signs following. (Mark 16: 17–20)

It is in their hermeneutical response to this text that the literalism, ritual and spirituality of Appalachian serpent-handlers take shape.

The study of hermeneutics, particularly as it relates to classic texts, is a popular and often controversial topic addressed by a wide variety of scholars. In this brief presentation, there is neither time nor space to survey the labyrinth of contemporary hermeneutical studies. For purposes of discussion, however, two introductory observations seem essential. First, conservative-evangelical-inerrantist scholars have given extensive attention to hermeneutical issues as a way of establishing a framework for their inerrantist approach to the biblical text. There are in fact many types of biblical inerrancy affirmed by a wide variety of faith traditions. In the words of the *Chicago Statement on Biblical Inerrancy*, inerrancy means "the quality of being free from all falsehood or mistake"; it is the concept that "Holy Scripture is entirely true and trustworthy in all its assertions" (Youngblood 1984: 237)

Conservative scholar Henry Virkler defines hermeneutics as "the science and art of biblical interpretation" (Virkler 1981: 45). As a conservative, he notes several issues affecting the way in which hermeneutical methods may be applied. He writes that people must first,

decide whether Scripture represents the religious theorizing of the ancient Hebrews, divinely-guided but not infallible writings of men, or divinely-guided and infallible writings written by men but initiated and superintended by God. We must also decide whether there is a single valid meaning of a text, or whether any individual application of a text represents a valid meaning. (p. 46)

Virkler also delineates other important hermeneutical issues, including: whether one believes that the divinely intended meaning "includes a fuller sense than the human author's"; determining "when a passage is to be interpreted literally, when figuratively, and when symbolically"; and the way in which one's "spiritual commitment" shapes the ability to comprehend "spiritual truth." Such issues are not lost on the serpent-handlers, although their application to a specific text (Mark 16) create considerable hermeneutical discomfort for most conservative inerrantists.

Second, this effort to examine the hermeneutics of serpent-handling is informed by certain observations made by David Tracy in *Plurality and Ambiguity: Hermeneutics, Religion and Hope* (1987). Tracy urges readers to give attention to the study of hermeneutics in its broad expressions. He writes:

We admittedly cannot offer a fully explicit account of the complex human skill of interpreting any more than we could offer such an account of any one of our other practical skills. Nevertheless, studying a variety of models for understanding this central but puzzling phenomenon can aid us in developing the practices necessary for good interpreters: those that enrich our experience, allow for understanding, aid deliberation and judgment, and increase the possibilities of meaningful action. (Tracy 1987: 9)

He concludes, "anyone can also learn interpretation theories (or hermeneutics). Then we may use these theories as they should be used: as further practical skills for the central task of becoming human." Tracy then cites Kenneth Burke's "fine dictum" as applied to "interpretation theory": "'Use all that can be used'"(Tracy 1987: 9). Doubtless Tracy did not have Appalachian serpent-handlers specifically in mind when he made those suggestions. Yet, if in the study of hermeneutics we are to use all that can be used, we might glance, at least, at this specific Appalachian subgroup and their methods of utilizing one smaller text to validate a larger one.

Serpent-handlers have been a popular topic of journalists, anthropologists, psychologists, and sociologists since the movement began around 1909. Newspaper and magazine articles abound, most written in response to the death of serpent-handling devotees as a result of snake bite or the ingestion of poison. Many focus on the group's legal battles against state attempts to impose certain sanctions on their services and their practices. Some of the more exploitative materials have created an image of serpent-handling as a widespread and normative form of Appalachian evangelicalism. Such is certainly not the case. Serpent-handlers are a tiny but provocative sect within the Protestant-Evangelical-Pentecostalism of the region. Recent scholarly works concentrate on such issues as their place within Appalachian culture and Pentecostal tradition, their unique theology, their psychological profile, and the psycho-sexual nature of their practices (Kane 1979 and La Barre 1962).

Yet Appalachian serpent-handlers should not be studied simply as religious mutants who demonstrate a bizarre cultic aberration within a vanishing cultural milieu. Rather, their approach to religion – in this case their hermeneutic – may help us understand something about the broader American religious context, particularly in certain of its popular expressions. Knowingly or unknowingly, Appalachian serpent-handlers have articulated popular arguments about the inspiration, authority, and inerrancy of Scripture in ways which might inform the methods by which others – conservative/liberal, evangelical/non-evangelical – approach those issues. In developing their interpretation of Mark 16 the serpent-handlers incorporate significant hermeneutical motifs evident throughout American Evangelicalism. They are heirs of such religio-social movements as revivalism, fundamentalism, and Pentecostalism. Likewise they give their own unique response to questions of New Testament primitivism, so important to those Appalachian religious groups which see themselves as Bible-believing Christians, and claim to trace their lineage back to the apostolic church.

Hermeneutics shape the unique rituals of the serpent-handlers and their accompanying spirituality. Again, David Tracy's comments inform an analysis of the serpent-handling hermeneutic. He writes:

> To encourage interaction between text and interpreter, it is helpful to find examples where the interpreter is forced to recognize otherness by confronting an unexpected claim to truth. So immune can we all become to otherness that we are tempted to reduce all reality to more of the same or to that curious substitute for the same we too often mean when we say similarity.(Tracy 1987: 15)

Tracy notes that when it comes to classic texts, i.e. the Bible, our "temptation to domesticate all reality is a temptation that any classic text will resist. The classics resist our ingrained laziness and self-satisfaction. Their claim to attention must be heeded." (ibid.). Serpent-handlers seem determined to resist domestication in both the text of Scripture and their own religious practices. Rather they are willing to risk their lives in every service of worship in quest of what seems the ultimate experience of otherness–a victory over poisonous snakes through complete reliance on an immediate apprehension of the power of God.

What then are the hermeneutical issues evident in this question and where do serpent-handlers fit in the debate over hermeneutics raging within segments of American religion? I would suggest that the hermeneutics of serpent-handlers draw on the influence of various religious traditions evident within that amorphous phenomenon sometimes referred to as American Evangelicalism. These traditions include revivalism, fundamentalism, Pentecostalism and an overall claim to biblical primitivism.

First, serpent-handlers reflect an "enthusiastical" religion born of American revivalism. Many of their worship services are specific gatherings for revival– protracted meetings to enliven the community of faith and call sinners to repentance. Every service is characterized by revivalistic, conversionistic fervor. My first experience of a serpent-handling was at an outdoor memorial service which had all the signs of a frontier revival meeting: multiple preachers, indigenous hymnody, shouting, glossolalia, shaking, jerking, tears, prayer, and praise. My second encounter with them came at a full-fledged revival meeting held outside Berea, Kentucky, in a building rented from another "holiness" congregation, as the sign outside indicated. It was a three day revival meeting led by Brother Arnold Saylor. That night a serpent was handled, but little time was given over to that practice. Rather, the occasion was dominated by music, prayers for the salvation of the unconverted, healing of the sick, and preaching: a lengthy discourse by Brother Saylor. Serpent-handling occurs within the context of a revival-like setting, what participants call "old timey religion." Above all, it seems, serpent-handlers are revivalistic conversionists. Their primary aim is to bring people to an experience of Christian salvation with sanctification by the Holy Ghost.

Second, their hermeneutic is constructed largely around arguments used by other evangelical fundamentalists to prove the absolute authority of Holy

Scripture and the total inerrancy of the biblical text. Clearly, serpent-handlers are among those who would be considered fundamentalists in their insistence that the Scripture is totally without error in everything it addresses. Although without formal theological training, they would agree with Henry Virkler that "if the Bible errs when it speaks on matters not essential to salvation, then it may be in error whenever it speaks about" essential matters of salvation, morality, doctrine, and community life. They would also agree with the so-called "slippery slide" argument promoted by many inerrantists. It suggests that "groups who begin by questioning the validity of small details of Scripture eventually question larger doctrines as well" (Virkler 1981: 31). Virkler and other inerrantists insist that hermeneutics is a major aspect of evangelical doctrine. Concerning a basic hermeneutical approach he concludes: "If we begin with the presupposition that Scripture does not contain errors, we are motivated to find an exegetically justi- fiable way of resolving any seeming discrepancy" (ibid.). Serpent-handlers would readily agree with this approach and claim that their beliefs, confirmed by their rituals, represent the ultimate verification of the proposition. As Arnold Saylor told my seminary class: "Whether you handle snakes or whether you heal anybody or speak in tongues or whether you drink any poison, you can't fight the Book" (Saylor, October 1991).

Quite simply, serpent-handlers believe that in their battle against the serpents they are confirming the Word of God. As they see it, if the Markan texts and accompanying rituals are not true, then the Bible itself is not true. If the serpent- handling rites cannot be practiced now as they were in the apostolic era, then the veracity of all Scripture may be called into question. Eleanor Dickinson inter- viewed one serpent-handler who noted: "Now I told you that we preach the gospel and God anoints for the serpents. Why that's confirming this word that I've just preached. Confirming it with the signs following" (McGuire 1981: 175). Implicitly or explicitly, therefore, the serpent-handlers perform a service for the entire Christian community. As they see it, they preserve the inerrancy of Holy Scripture even for those who do not practice the art of serpent-handling. By vali- dating the signs described in Mark 16, they protect the truth of Scripture for the church itself.

It is in the idea of "signs" that the Pentecostal element of serpent-handling becomes most evident. Serpent-handlers are fundamentalists but they are also Pentecostal-fundamentalists. As such, they not only affirm the inerrancy of events and details described in the biblical text, but also believe that those miraculous events may be repeated here and now. These are the "signs" of the true church carried on from the New Testament period to the present. In his work, *Vision of the Disinherited*, Robert Mapes Anderson suggests that, "All of the unusual events reported to have occurred on the first day of Pentecost were claimed by the early Pentecostals. . . . Indeed, all the signs, wonders, and miracles recorded in Acts and elsewhere in the New Testament were allegedly repeated in the early Pentecostal movement – and more" (Anderson 1979: 92). As these early Pentecostals saw it, apostolic signs and gifts did not die with the apostles but could be repeated by the Spirit anew in every age, particularly in the "latter days" as a prelude to the return of Christ.

Serpent-handlers continually insist that handling serpents was one of the signs of primitive, apostolic Christianity. They cite Mark's gospel and its comment that these signs "shall follow those that believe." The signs include speaking in tongues, casting out demons, drinking "deadly things," offering prayers for healing, and taking up serpents. Serpent-handlers observe that many Pentecostal groups speak in tongues, cast out demons, and anoint the sick. Why, they ask, do Pentecostals not fulfill all the "five signs" which "accompany the believers" including drinking poison and handling serpents? One preacher remarked: "They shall take up serpents. Didn't say they might, said they shall do it. And they shall lay hands on the sick and they shall recover. That 'shall' is a must and a will be" (McGuire 1981: 174). He continued:

> No, these signs is for all men. Because in a congregation of people you'll always find some unbelievers. It'd take something to convince them that this is God's word. Now when they live in the mountains and know that these serpents is deathly poison, kill, now when they live here and they see that and they know it, why, they see you do this thing after you have preached this word, why, they believe. They'll get off later to themselves and they'll say, 'There must be something to that. Nobody can do that unless God be with him.' And if they deny this word – if that is the word of God, taking up serpents – if they deny that . . . Why, they got it right here in the Bible to read. There ain't no interpretation to it. It's explained. And if they deny that, then they've denied the Word of God. (McGuire 1981: 174–5)

This statement reveals another aspect of serpent-handlers' literalist hermeneutic, the idea that there "ain't no interpretation to it." They are not giving an interpretation which may or may not be valid. Rather, they are simply carrying out the obvious directive of the biblical text.

As Bible-believing Pentecostals, serpent-handlers insist that all their rituals are governed by the power and "anointing" of the Holy Spirit. Preacher Robert Grooms comments:

> The Word is spiritually understood. And without the Spirit of the Lord, nobody can understand it. You can read the Bible, and without the Spirit you can make many meanings out of it, many things. But with the Spirit of God, you get the true meaning. That's what's wrong with a lot of churches today. They don't have enough of the Spirit to understand what the Bible really means. (Carden and Pelton 1976: 155)

This statement parallels comments by various evangelical-inerrantists, among them William J. Larkin, Jr. of Columbia Bible Seminary. He writes: "The illumination of the Spirit also aids in distinguishing between truth and error and in the ability to hold fast to the truth. . . . Not being subject to the judgment of others, the Christian does not need to adjust the truth to meet current cultural criteria" (Larkin 1988: 290). Where Pentecostals and non-Pentecostal evangelicals often part company is over the practice of certain "signs" or "gifts" of the Spirit- tongues, healing, and, in this case, serpent-handling. Did those experiences end with the apostolic age or are they to be recovered in these "latter days"? Those questions have divided evangelicals throughout this century.

It was the Pentecostal-Holiness movement which gave the serpent-handlers birth. Their founder, George Hensley, was an Appalachian Baptist who experienced the "new birth" among the Pentecostals near Cleveland, Tennessee shortly after the turn of the century, just as the Church of God, Cleveland, Tennessee was taking shape. In fact, Hensley and A. J. Tomlinson, a founder of the Church of God, were friends and co-workers early on in the movement. Like other Pentecostals, serpent-handlers are given to what Robert Anderson describes as, "literal-minded Biblicism, emotional fervor, puritanical mores, enmity toward ecclesiasticism, and above all, belief in a 'Second Blessing'" (Anderson 1979: 28). By 1909 George Hensley had simply applied fundamentalist-Pentecostal teaching and practice to the additional sign of serpent-handling as described in Mark 16. He would continue to carry out the practice until his own death, caused by a "serpent bite" in 1955.

Anderson notes that, "Fundamentalists had no real grounds for condemning the Pentecostals, since they merely carried Biblical literalism – the bedrock of Fundamentalism – to its logical conclusion" (Anderson 1979: 6). If this is true, then perhaps Pentecostals have less to condemn in the serpent-handlers since they appear simply to carry Pentecostal biblicism and spiritism to their logical conclusions.

At the heart of the serpent-handlers' fundamentalist Pentecostalism is a powerful belief in biblical primitivism. They believe that they are simply modeling the behavior of the early Christian church – that Jesus and the apostles handled serpents before them. Some base their assumption about Jesus's serpent-handling on John 20: 30: "And many other signs truly did Jesus in the presence of his disciples, which are not written in this book." They also cite 2 Timothy 2: 6: "The husbandman that laboureth must be first partaker of the fruits" (Kane 1970: 94). If serpent-handling is truly "Bible doctrine," then Jesus must have practiced it.

In his conversation with my seminary class, Arnold Saylor referred to Paul's experience with the viper as evidence of Paul's participation in the rite and a sign of God's power in preserving those bitten by serpents. In that account (Acts 28:3–5) Paul is bitten by a "viper" while gathering wood. Paul did not intentionally handle the serpent, Saylor admitted, but he commented, "Paul mighta not knowed that snake was in that bundle of sticks, but Jesus knowed. And He placed it there. It bit him but it was a sign to the people" (Saylor, October 1991). So serpent-handlers believe they are merely replicating the practices of the primitive church, giving evidence of the continuing power of God. In a sense, therefore, serpent-handling is a deadly form of apostolic succession whereby the gifts of the Spirit are passed along from generation to generation to those who manifest the "signs."

For them it is a simple matter of believing the Bible or not believing it. If the Scripture is wrong on serpent-handling, it may be wrong on the resurrection of Jesus or other crucial dogmas. Robert Grooms, a serpent-handling preacher, told one researcher: "We've got to take the Bible like it's written. If you're going to take part of it, and lay part of it down, you might as well let it all go. We need to abide in the Word and get the full meaning out of it" (Carden and Pelton 1976: 155). Serpent-handling is simply the contemporary observance of rituals begun in the primitive church.

Primitivism is also evident in the oral tradition which pervades the serpent-handling community. Indeed, the serpent-handling hermeneutic developed and is passed on largely through an oral tradition expressed primarily in sermonic exposition of a written or oral text. As I talk with them, listen to them, and read their interviews, I am struck by the way in which the serpent-handlers have acquired what for them seems a perfectly rational explanation for a powerfully spiritual experience, all without a single college or seminary course in biblical studies. Their hermeneutical principles, like their doctrines and much of their knowledge of Scripture itself, are passed on largely through sermons and other forms of oral tradition. Hensley, the founder, was illiterate. He was taught the Bible by his wife, Manda, whom some believe was the person who first developed the doctrine of serpent-handling. When he preached, she would stand by his side, reading passages of Scripture for him. His use of the text, therefore, came from memorizing passages as he had heard them read aloud (Kane 1979: 33) Others also reflect this kind of oral tradition.

Arnold Saylor told my class that when he was converted and "called to preach" sometime in the 1960s, his own father questioned the decision since Saylor could not read. Said Saylor, "I just told the Lord, I have the same Spirit in me that wrote the Bible, the Spirit will have to teach me." He acknowledged that if a student wrote him a letter, he would have to have his wife read it to him. But when it came to the Scripture, he could "read." Again, much of his knowledge of Scripture seemed to have come from oral tradition, hearing it read aloud, and committing large sections to memory.

Thus most of the doctrines of the church are passed on through the preaching. At first glance, the sermon appears to be an exercise in creative spontaneity as the preacher goes wherever the Spirit leads. Closer scrutiny, however, reveals a fascinating homiletical form in which holiness doctrines are articulated in colorful style and punctuated by the repetition of particular phrases and ideas which are passed on from preacher to preacher, generation to generation. Preachers learn to preach by hearing and repeating what they hear. Actually, many sermons demonstrate a kind of litany in which spontaneous phrases are tied together by the repetition of such phrases as "Praise God," "Thank you, Jesus," and "Hallelujah." These phrases allow the preacher to catch his breath and think about where he wants the sermon to go next.

Likewise, the community enters into the preaching experience. Young preachers are encouraged by the worshiping congregation. If they forget part of a Bible verse, someone will often prompt them. If they seem to have difficulty getting into the Spirit someone may call out, "Hep him, Lord, hep him." And, when the Spirit has run its course – particularly in younger, less seasoned preachers – women may pick up guitars and begin to sing, signaling that time is up. Doctrines, therefore, are seldom if ever written down. Rather they are passed on orally to and through the worshiping community.

The serpent-handlers are heirs of numerous traditions: revivalism, fundamen-

talism, Pentecostalism, and primitivism. These movements shape their hermeneutics and inform their response to critics. In fact, serpent-handlers turn the
fundamentalist-Pentecostal-inerrantist hermeneutic back on their conservative
critics in surprising ways.

Perhaps the most significant argument against the serpent-handling
hermeneutic and practice comes in the insistence of most biblical scholars that
the "long ending" of Mark 16 is not found in the earliest extant manuscripts
of the New Testament. The first accounts of this text come from a Latin version
found by Jerome in certain Greek manuscripts and a Greek version found in the
Washington Manuscript dating from the fourth or fifth century (Buttrick
1951–7: 916) If this is true, then one might conclude that the text is a spurious
one and has no place in the truly inspired, original manuscript of Holy Scripture.
Thus, critics say, serpent-handlers have built a hermeneutic on a text which
should never have been included in Scripture in the first place. Theirs is a false
dogma built on a counterfeit text.

The serpent-handlers are not fazed by this argument. First, they simply turn
the argument against their accusers. Why, they ask, if God is the author of all
Scripture and has given it as the authoritative guide of the church would God
permit spurious texts to remain in the Bible at all? How could God have gone to
all the trouble to inspire writers, preserve texts, and shape biblical materials have
tolerated any textual error however it got there? If God is not in control of the
Bible which we have, how could God be in control of the Bible at all?

Second, the discussion of original manuscripts and varied texts is simply lost
on serpent-handlers since their textus receptus is the King James Version of the
Bible, the infallible guide to old time religion. Third, their rhetoric provides their
best response. One declares: "The Bible is the Word of God! I have faith in the
Word of God. I believe this because the Spirit of God that's in me is the same
Holy Ghost that was in the disciples back there that helped write the Bible"
(Carden and Pelton 1976: 156). Another notes: "The Bible was written by holy
men of God. They were inspired by the Holy Ghost. None of the Bible can
possibly be wrong. I don't think God would have put 'they shall take up serpents'
in His holy book if it didn't belong in there. After all, I don't think anyone can
deny those are the words of Jesus" (ibid.: 156). And Pastor Alfred Ball, a well
known serpent-handler, explained:

> They stand up and say Mark 16: 17 and 18 ought to be torn out of the Bible, that
> it don't belong in there. Amen, I would like to know what they think about Exodus
> 4: 4, Job 26: 13; Luke 10: 19; and Acts 28 – they mention handling serpents. I
> wonder if they feel these verses belong in the Bible? We always urge people to find
> a church that teaches the scriptures. We never ask anybody to blindly believe
> anything we can't back up with Bible scripture. (Carden and Pelton 1976: 156–7)

Sister Mary Bailey continues:

> If the Word of God says to do something, I believe then that we had better do it.
> We better always obey the Word of God. Some say the sixteenth chapter of Mark

doesn't really belong in the Bible. Those were words spoken by Jesus. It does belong in the Bible. And they can't take it out. They can't ignore it. (Carden and Pelton 1976: 159)

Likewise, when charged with excessive literalism, the serpent-handlers return to the context of the text. Their snake-handling activity is simply one of the several signs evident in the apostolic church. They do not, for example, cut off their hands or pluck out their eyes as described in Matthew 5: 29–30 since that action is not one of the Pentecostal signs. If serpent-handling is wrong then so is praying for the sick, speaking in tongues, and anointing with oil. Arnold Saylor concluded: "I see it just like the Bible says. We don't try to change none of the book. The Bible says it's already been interpreted by the old prophets. . . . We just take it what it says" (Saylor, October 1991). Again, they insist that they are not interpreting the text but carrying out its obvious teaching.

As with any religious community, these believers articulate and "tangibilify" (as some Appalachians might say) their dogma in a variety of religious rituals, most distinctive of which are taking up serpents and drinking poison. While spontaneity dominates their worship services, it is a consistent spontaneity, characterized by common rituals and observances. Many of these parallel practices evident among other Pentecostal groups, evidence of a prevailing Pentecostal hermeneutic. They speak in tongues, anoint with oil, are often slain in the Spirit, falling to the ground under the Spirit's power. Many experience shakes, jerks, and other physical expressions of religious enthusiasm. Their music, accompanied by drums, tambourines, guitars and other instruments, is often based on "spirit songs" written by inspired members and passed on orally. Again, these rituals are evidence of a Pentecostal hermeneutic as observed in other Holiness-Pentecostal churches. Like other mountain churches they also practice immersion baptism and the washing of feet.

Their unique rituals, such as serpent-handling and poison drinking, take on sacramental qualities as they replicate the practices described in Mark 16. Thus Mary Lee Daugherty could write: "Knowing serpent-handlers to be biblical literalists, one might surmise that they, like other sects, have picked a certain passage of Scripture and built a whole ritual around a few cryptic verses. While this is true, I am persuaded, after years of observation, that serpent-handling holds for them the significance of sacrament" (Daugherty 1976: 233–4).

Serpent-handling, therefore, is truly an outward and visible sign of an inward and spiritual grace, perhaps the ultimate transubstantiation in which the living sacrament simultaneously offers both life and death. In this sense, the text itself comes alive and is put to the test every time the ritual is enacted. Belief in the inerrancy of Scripture is not merely a dogma to be believed, it is a participation with the Spirit of God in battle against the ultimate symbol of evil. For Daugherty, serpent-handling unites literalism, ritual, and culture. She concludes: "Each time they handle the serpents they struggle with life once more and survive again the forces that traditionally oppressed mountain people. . . . The handling of serpents is their way of confronting and coping with their very real fears about life and the harshness of reality as experienced in the mountains in years gone by and, for many, even today" (Daugherty 1976: 235).

The link between biblical text and faithful action is found in the "anointing," that inner assurance by which serpent-handlers claim the authority and the divine guidance to pick up poisonous reptiles. Indeed, the anointing seems the inward and spiritual grace which guides serpent-handlers toward specific outward and visible signs – rituals. It is at the heart of serpent-handling spirituality. The anointing is a spiritual sensation which comes over the believer often with physical effects. It may be described as a feeling, as "going cold" all over, a numbness, or a trance-like state (Kane 1979: 123–4). Whatever its expression, it is a sign of the protective power of God on the believer. Arnold Saylor identified it as a "shield" preserving the serpent-handler from danger. Kane quotes one devotee who claimed, "As long as that anointin' of God is on you, the serpent wouldn't hurt you. It could chew on you all day and it wouldn't hurt you" (Kane ibid.: 117).

Underneath the hermeneutic, therefore, lies a ritual that is what the serpent-handlers perceive and believe to be a profound spiritual, indeed, mystical experience – what David Tracy calls a sense of otherness. It is in this sense of otherness – spirituality – that an economically and politically powerless people justify their observances as significant not only for themselves, but for the entire church. They are literalistic dogmatists but they are also spiritualists who put their dogma to the test anew every time they worship, every time they take up a serpent.

Serpent-handlers, therefore, offer a valuable opportunity for interpreting the contemporary hermeneutical impasse between what David Tracy calls "fundamentalist readings" and "secularist readings." Tracy contends that these two perspectives are actually "reverse sides of the same effaced coin of certainty, mastery, and control." (1987: 101). Serpent-handlers claim certainty aplenty, but it is certainty which requires much more than intellectual verification. It is a certainty challenged every time they open the box of snakes.

Serpent-handlers challenge the rationalism evident among proponents of both modernity and fundamentalism. They claim to represent old timey religion – unapologetically primitive – in the modern era, yet they also press biblical inerrancy and Pentecostal spiritism to its limits. In that they may demonstrate what Tracy calls "a natural hermeneutical competence." He concludes:

That competence does not wait upon the results of debates over methods and hermeneutical theories. That natural competence belongs to all those who assume that, to understand any classic and its claim to attention, we must be prepared to risk our present understanding. That competence knows that we cannot simply distance ourselves from the classics as objects-out-there available for either passive contemplation or domination by means of the latest method. It is the competence of anyone willing to confront critically and be confronted by any classic. There can also be a natural religious competence that may illuminate the interpretation of the religious classics far more than even the most helpful modern techniques. (Tracy 1987: 103)

I submit that the serpent-handlers do just that. Behind their unnatural and dangerous practices may indeed lie a "natural religious competence" which sheds new light on old hermeneutical debates.

Whatever else one may say, however, students and critics of serpent-handling will surely agree on this: serpent-handlers are not boring. Tracy writes that, "patrons of certainty and control in the interpretation of religion are boring. And whatever else religion is, it is not boring. It is other, different, disturbing. It is not more of the same" (p. 101). At our first meeting, when I told Brother Arnold Saylor that I was a Baptist, he remarked: "I go to Baptist churches, they sing pretty. But you know, after a while, I just get a little bored." After being with Saylor and the serpent-handlers, I know exactly what he meant.

BIBLIOGRAPHY

Anderson, Robert Mapes (1979) *Vision of the Disinherited*, Oxford: Oxford University Press.

Buttrick, George Arthur (ed.) (1951–7) *The Interpreter's Bible*, vol. 7, New York: Abingdon Press.

Carden, Karen W. and Pelton, Robert W. (1976) *Persecuted Prophets*, South Brunswick, NJ: A. S. Barnes.

Daugherty, Mary Lee (1976) "Serpent-handling as sacrament," *Theology Today* (October).

Davis, Stephen T. (1977) *The Debate about the Bible*, Philadelphia, Pa.: Westminster Press.

Dickinson, Eleanor (1974) *Revival!*, San Francisco: Harper & Row.

Kane, Steven M. (1974) "Snake-handlers of Southern Appalachia," Ph.D. dissertation, Princeton University.

Kimbrough, David (1995) *Taking Up Serpents*, Chapel Hill, NC: University of North Carolina Press.

La Barre, Weston (1962) *They Shall Take Up Serpents*, New York: Schocken Books.

Larkin, William J. (1988) *Culture and Biblical Hermeneutics*, Grand Rapids, Mich.: Baker Book House.

McGuire, Marsha (1981) "Confirming the Word, snake-handling sects in Southern Appalachia," *Quarterly Journal of the Library of Congress* (Summer).

Saylor, Arnold, October 1991, class lecture, The Southern Baptist Theological Seminary, videotape.

Tracy, David (1987) *Plurality and Ambiguity: Hermeneutics, Religion and Hope*, San Francisco: Harper & Row.

Virkler, Henry (1981) *Hermeneutics, Principles and Processes of Biblical Inerrancy*, Grand Rapids, Mich.: Baker Book House.

Youngblood, Ronald (ed.) (1984) *Evangelicals and Inerrancy*, New York: Thomas Nelson.

Part V

Race and Ethnicity

Introduction

Race is one of the most charged terms in American discourse, and is also one of the most elusive. Anthropologists have long since abandoned the notion that physical characteristics such as skin color and facial features have very much intrinsically to do with cultural potential or behavior. Intermarriage in the American context has also weakened considerably the "purity" of racial identity, especially for those of non-European origin. On the other hand, it is obvious that one of the most salient features of American social history has been a tendency to ascribe to individuals fixed social roles and opportunities on the basis of such characteristics. The "color line" has been most decisively drawn in terms of "black" and "white": symmetrical, mutually exclusive, and ultimately metaphorical designations of African and European ancestral origin. "Brown," "yellow," and "red" have also been used to designate Latino, Asian, and Native American identity, but the lines here have been somewhat more porous, with intermarriage with Euro-Americans, for example, more of a socially acceptable option.

Not surprisingly, racial identity – or ascription – has played a major role in American religious life, with segregation within or among religious groups the norm, especially but by no means exclusively in the South. Early in the nineteenth century the color line had appeared within the Methodist movement, initiated by blacks dissatisfied with the discrimination they had experienced within predominantly white Northern congregations. In addition, the freeform patterns of worship that developed within the "invisible institution" of African-American folk Christianity in the slave-holding South resulted in a ritual style that ultimately influenced black churches across regional and denominational lines, with considerable impact upon white southern popular Christianity as well. By the late nineteenth century, some blacks also began to advocate separation of the races, an ideology that would later infuse the "black nationalism" of Marcus Garvey's African Orthodox Church and Louis Farrakhan's Nation of Islam. Although most "mainline" churches today welcome African-American members, patterns of separate worship have become so deeply ingrained that Sunday morning has been called the most segregated time in the American week.

Ethnicity is related to but conceptually different from race. In common usage, the term "ethnic" usually applies to subcultures – usually those of recent immigrants and their children – that exist in the American social context but maintain, out of choice or necessity, some significant distinction from the broader culture. Like race, ethnicity is a basis for maintaining difference from that broader culture, and may be perceived as quaint, intriguing, or threatening. Unlike race, ethnicity, at least by the time of the second generation, generally becomes elective: it can be performed or discarded at will as long as it is not reinforced by the distinctive external physical characteristics upon which race is constructed. Whether a group is "racial" or "ethnic" may vary with time: Jews were not too long ago regarded as a separate race – in Nazi Germany, to give a terrifying example – and the Irish only gradually came to be construed by native-born Americans as "white."

Unlike race, ethnicity carries with it the potential of assimilation, since it can presumably be discarded at will. Together with language and food customs, religion is an important component of ethnicity which, in the free American market of belief, can be abandoned together with garlic and accents. For many evangelical Protestants, Roman Catholics needed to shed their heretical ways in order to qualify as full Americans. For both Catholic and Protestant Christians, the conversion of non-believers such as Native Americans has at times been a high priority, and has usually involved the abandonment of traditional folkways in the process.

The decision as to whether to assimilate or not has for centuries been an important choice for newcomers (as well as for the aboriginal inhabitants of the continent). This has proven an issue not only for individuals but also for entire religious communities. American Jewry, for example, has evolved out of successive waves of immigrants – from the Iberian peninsula, the German states, and then from Slavic-speaking countries – with each wave speaking a different language as part of a broader cultural baggage. Assimilation became the watchword of the Bohemian rabbi-immigrant Isaac Mayer Wise and of the American version of Reform Judaism he led for decades from his temple in Cincinnati, while many Orthodox Jews argued for keeping a distance. The Roman Catholic Church in the United States coalesced from an even more complex ethnic amalgam – Irish, Germans, Poles, Italians, and Latinos, to name only the most numerous groups – and similarly divided internally over cultural strategies before a uniform "ghetto" culture emerged in the World War I era of nativist xenophobia and episcopal centralization.

Jewish and Catholic ethnicity are dealt with in various aspects in articles in other sections: see those by *Beth Wenger* and *Mary Jo Weaver* in III; *Leonard Norman Primiano* in IV; *Karla Goldman* and *Anne Rose* in VI; and *Paula Kane* in VII.

In this group of essays, *Joan Bryant* discusses debates about race and its relationship to religion in the public discourse of both blacks and whites during the nineteenth century. Despite attempts by reformers to persuade African-American churches that their segregated status was incompatible with Christian ideals, the pervasiveness of the color line resulted in the perpetuation of race-based denominations.

Albert Miller adds nuance to discussions of the nature of African-American religion by examining the development of evangelicalism within the black community. The emergence of the National Black Evangelical Association in 1963 is evidence that evangelicalism is not simply a white middle-class phenomenon, but also reflects a number of complex strains of religious identity within black Protestantism.

Michael McNally considers a number of Native American movements to examine the dichotomy often drawn between the historical character of European religion and the traditionalism of that of non-literate peoples. In looking at *Black Elk Speaks*, Hopi prophecies of the end of the world, the Muskogee revolt of 1813, and Ojibwa hymn singing, he finds much more complex interactions between tradition and change than is often suspected. In each case, selective adaptation has proven an effective strategy for negotiating life on the border of two cultural worlds.

Chapter 17

Race and Religion in Nineteenth-century America

Joan L. Bryant

Within weeks of launching his anti-slavery paper, *The North Star*, Frederick Douglass used its columns to publicly denounce "colored churches." Douglass possessed first-hand knowledge of religious institutions led by black Americans. After his escape from slavery in 1838 he had become a licensed preacher in New Bedford's African Methodist Episcopal Zion (AMEZ) Church. However, nearly a decade later, having long since abandoned the pulpit for the abolitionist circuit, he set out to convince his readers that the mere existence of churches like the one he once served was evil.

The juxtaposition of slavery and colored churches in abolitionist discourse was part of a distinct tradition within nineteenth-century reform movements. Churches served as a touchstone for reformers intent on establishing the immorality of race distinctions. Douglass was one of a diverse lot of religious and secular reformers who saw race at the root of the most glaring vices. This judgment led him and others to broaden the scope of culpability for social injustice and expand the parameters of moral responsibility for eradicating it. Individuals and institutions that made distinctions on the basis of race came to share blame with actual perpetrators of wrongs. Colored churches thus earned condemnation on the same terms as the "pro-slavery" churches that Douglass and other abolitionists so despised.

For the most part, opponents of colored churches stopped short of wholesale condemnation of race distinctions. Douglass, for one, maintained that, however unfortunate, it was necessary and even valid for colored people to establish political organizations along racial lines. Citing the social facts of racial difference, he argued that there was "neither good sense, nor common honesty, in trying to forget this distinction" (*North Star*, December 14, 1849). Similarly, Presbyterian minister Samuel Cornish, who himself ministered to segregated congregations, consistently argued that the peculiar social circumstances of antebellum free people of color demanded racially exclusive political organizations and special reform periodicals, like his own weekly, *The Colored American*. Yet Cornish also used his paper to condemn the existence of colored churches.

Several factors combined to make churches vulnerable to attacks that secular organizations sometimes escaped. The conviction that race constructions played a central role in perpetuating slavery and other forms of oppression led nineteenth-century reformers to question the concept of race itself. Because religion, in the form of biblical truths and Christian ideals, supplied the principle arguments against race, churches became an obvious target of scrutiny. Virtually all nineteenth-century churches were subject to criticism on these grounds, since racial segregation, whether between or within congregations, was the norm. However, the critical role churches played in shaping the collective existence of black Americans earned them special consideration. Throughout the century, churches provided the institutional foundations for communal networks within the black population. Their status as the most stable and visible black American organizations singled them out as valuable partners in social and political reform initiatives aimed at eliminating the racial foundations of American identity. However, their apparent unwillingness, as institutions, to repudiate race distinctions compromised their moral and religious authority among reformers.

The irony of this situation is readily apparent. One of the original purposes of independent black American churches was to overcome racial impediments to religious authority in institutions dominated by white Christians. Founders of these organizations hoped to transcend race by associating along racial lines. As Richard Allen explained to leaders of the Methodist Episcopal Church, what he and his fellow African Methodists wanted was "to regulate [their] affairs . . . as if [they] were white people" (Clark 1958: 367). Yet, in the process of assuming religious authority unfettered by race, colored churches implicated themselves in perpetuating the idea of race, along with the evils that reformers associated with it. They became a pivotal, if unwitting focus of efforts to eliminate the ideology of race that restricted participation in civil and political affairs.

The religious integrity of colored churches was among the first items that reformers challenged in their attack on race. Popular anti-slavery arguments provided them with a starting point. Abolitionists, as well as a host of other antebellum reformers, habitually rehearsed the Genesis account of creation and the apostle Paul's declaration that God made all nations "of one blood" as proof of the essential oneness of humanity. These texts established a principle of unity that reformers offered as evidence that there was no scriptural basis for dividing human beings into different races or species. Reformers invoked this principle to indict colored churches, along with all religious organizations founded on racial difference, for subverting the body of truths they professed to uphold.

Scientific theories of race that circulated in the mid-nineteenth century re-inforced the judgement that race distinctions were sinful. The "American School" of anthropology, led by Louis Agassiz, Samuel Morton, and Josiah Nott, all apologists for slavery, divided humans into races: Caucasian, Mongolian, Malay, Indian, and Negro, which purportedly developed from separate creations and comprised different, unequal species. In an effort to reconcile the notion of polygenesis with religious ideals, Agassiz argued that the true principle of human unity had nothing at all to do with physical reality. It signified, instead, a moral relationship rooted in individuals' feelings of connection and mutual obligation, even in the absence of common origins. Not surprisingly, opponents of race distinctions rejected this argument, which failed to sway even Christian defenders of slavery. Polygenesis simply confirmed the conclusion that race categories were, as Douglass explained, "artificial" constructs invented to support the notion that "nature" required the separation of white and colored people into different spheres (*North Star*, February 25, 1848). Douglass argued that because they organized on the basis of race, colored churches were guilty of perpetuating this deception. They were thus in direct violation of divine purposes.

More egregious than misrepresentations of biblical "fact" was church complicity in sustaining injustice. This charge hinged on the judgment that the social evils free people of color endured were not simply a function of individual prejudice, but that evil was intrinsic to the concept of race itself. Evidence of this connection emerged from everyday experiences of oppression. To illustrate the irredeemable character of race, William Whipper, the most consistent antebellum critic of the concept of races, rehearsed a litany of familiar wrongs, all of which were attributable to race. "Now what is it," he asked,

> that deprives us of the benefit of institutions of learning – churches – the social circles – schools – the mechanic arts – elective franchise – the privilege and protection of government – the favor of just and equitable laws – trial by jury – mercantile employment – riding in the stages and steamboats on equal footing with "white people," but the odious distinction in language, principle, and practice, that confers the boon of favor on those that are known by the distinctive appellation of "white people?" (*Colored American*, September 16, 1837)

Whipper's interpretation anticipated contemporary theories that characterize race as a discursive reality. In short, race was a discourse that did not simply justify social inequality and discrimination; it executed it. It constructed whiteness as a site of privilege and made distinct and inferior classes of people who were not deemed white. That was enough to call it sinful.

The implications of helping to sustain racial discourse were grave. As villainous as reformers made it seem for anyone to make race distinctions, it was worse for organizations and individuals who claimed public recognition as defenders of righteousness. Both William Whipper and Samuel Cornish maintained that no institution whose practices or name delimited participation according to racial classifications could represent "true" religion. Cornish accused all such entities of creating a *de facto* religious hierarchy that reinscribed political and social inequality. The result was a caste system that rendered some Christians unworthy of full fellowship and ecclesiastical authority. Although reformers interpreted this sin as corporate in nature, they singled out ministers for particular blame. It was wicked, they reasoned, for clergy to nurture arrangements that were, by definition, unrighteous. According to Whipper, pastors bore personal responsibility for violating Christian principles when they served in denominations that made racial distinctions.

Even as they targeted colored churches for specific criticism, most reformers avoided suggesting that these organizations were, in theory, any worse than those led by white people. To the contrary, the alleged crime of colored churches lay in their likeness to churches that invoked race to exclude, segregate, or deny authority to people who were not white. Critics saw them as partners in shaping a discourse and social arrangement that perpetrated the very wrongs they sought to overcome. The involvement of colored churches in upholding the concept of race prompted charges that they were equally guilty of transgressing God's moral order. Some reformers attributed this wickedness to the nature of American Protestantism. Like radical abolitionist William Lloyd Garrison, they came to view this tradition as bankrupt, because so many Protestant denominations either supported slavery or refused to actively oppose it. The discrimination that slaves, free people of color, and their sympathizers experienced in Protestant denominations suggested that belief in the natural inferiority of colored people was as central to the tradition as belief in God. Garrisonians such as William Whipper maintained that colored churches would have to disavow Protestantism altogether before they could establish moral and religious integrity. Otherwise, they would be doomed to reinscribe its racial doctrines.

Reformers who avoided wholesale condemnations of Protestantism were, nevertheless, critical of functional similarities between white and colored churches. For example, Douglass described their likeness in terms of the roles they both played in separating colored people from white people. He observed that colored churches functioned in the same way as the hated "negro pew." Both produced racial segregation. This commonality grounded his conclusion that the two arrangements were morally indistinguishable. The only difference he was willing to acknowledge was size. The divergent purposes of segregation were irrelevant.

Strategic considerations were as important as religious convictions in shaping reformers' assault on colored churches. These institutions robbed reformers of prized moral foundations on which to ground their opposition to discriminatory laws and policies, by appearing to maintain distinctions based on race, voluntarily. This was a particularly grievous offense, because moral arguments were such a valuable commodity for antebellum reformers. They afforded people who lacked official political authority with means for exercising power. Colored churches created problems of moral inconsistency for reformers. As corporate entities, they seemed to uphold some of the very practices that their individual leaders and members declared evil and tried to eradicate. The state by state disenfranchisement of almost the entire antebellum northern colored population was one such practice. Churchmen and other reformers protested these legislative enactments on the grounds that they constituted a "toleration of complexional difference" (*Colored American*, February 6, 1841). The existence of colored churches, as well as secular voluntary associations, for that matter, challenged the practicality of such claims. These organizations compromised the credibility of reformers who insisted that race distinctions were, in principle, unjust. Whipper was so vexed by this obstacle that he stopped just shy of arguing that defenders of racially exclusive organizations reaped what they had sown. He was tempted to say that they deserved disenfranchisement because of their failure to abandon institutional race distinctions. Douglass showed less restraint and charged that colored churches nullified protests against racial injustice altogether. He saw a sympathetic link between voluntarily segregated religious organizations and race discrimination in all other spheres, whereby the former was, in effect, an argument on behalf of the latter.

The threat of colonization confronted reformers with a different set of logistical issues. On the one hand, it reinforced convictions that the existence of colored churches was problematic. Free people of color were keenly aware of a connection between colonization efforts to remove them from the United States and the racial separation practiced by white churches. Samuel Cornish gave voice to widespread sentiment when he asserted that "the same spirit that would drive us from our country colonizes us in the churches" (*Colored American*, June 19, 1839). His charge did, in fact, capture the organizational arrangement of major colonization initiatives. Not only did clergy join with statesmen to found the American Colonization Society in 1816, but colonizationists boasted the support of prominent Protestant denominations. Governing bodies of Episcopalians, Presbyterians, Dutch Reformed, Methodists, Congregationalists, Baptists, Lutherans, Moravians, and the Society of Friends all gave official endorsement to the Colonization Society.

The numerous goals tied to colonization schemes – the elimination of slavery, political self-determination and social equality for people of color, and the Christianization of Africa – account for some of its broad appeal, especially among people with benevolent intentions. However, none of these objectives explain the ideological foundations of colonization, nor its perceived affinity to segregation in churches. Colonization, like religious separation, rested on the premise of racial difference. As Abraham Lincoln explained to a delegation of "freemen" on the eve of issuing the Emancipation Proclamation, "physical difference" made it necessary to remove the "colored race" from the country. His simple statement: "You and we are different races," conveyed the sense that colonizationists shared of the utter impossibility of free black and white people comprising a single nation (Lincoln 1996: 210). Given such arguments, it required little deliberation for reformers to draw direct parallels between colored churches and the colonization scheme. They cited the implicit, and sometimes explicit defense of the "propriety" of colored people worshiping with their "*own*" kind" as evidence that colored churches were, as Douglass argued, "a mere counterpart of colonization" (*North Star*, February 25, 1848).

Colonization proposals also focussed attention on the term, "African," which graced the titles of churches. This standard designation became increasingly unseemly in light of the Colonization Society's maxim, "Africa for Africans." Architects of the colonization scheme found biblical warrants for their agenda in the text that other reformers cited to oppose race distinctions. They pointed out that the same God who made all nations "of one blood" also designated where each should live. It was obvious to them that divine Providence intended Liberia for descendants of Africa, just as it had ordained North America for white Protestants. In response to such reasoning, free people of color laid unprecedented claim to American citizenship. More precisely, they defined for themselves the terms of United States citizenship, because the concept had no precise legal definition before the Fourteenth Amendment, apart from the 1857 *Dred Scott* decision that identified it as a precondition for rights that Negroes lacked. The broad consensus among free people of color was that birth constituted citizenship. This principle held sway at numerous mass meetings where they publicly condemned colonization as unchristian and anti-republican, denied that they were a distinct race or species, and identified themselves, collectively, as American citizens. Even leaders of the African Union Church, the first of the independent African denominations, declared on behalf of the free people of Delaware: "we disclaim all connexion with Africa" and insisted that colonizationists threatened their rights as Americans (Garrison 1832: 36).

As institutions, churches largely refrained from participating in this trend. They were ultimately unmoved by the rising tide of criticism it inspired, even from people who had no objections to the existence of segregated religious institutions. The African Baptist Church of Boston proved to be an aberration when, in the 1830s, it extended the disavowal of Africa to its name. To the undoubted delight of many reformers, the church renamed itself "The First Independent Church of the People of Color." The reason for this change, members explained, was that the term, "African," was "ill applied to a church composed of American citizens" (Horton 1993: 159). Yet even churches that retained the term agreed that it was something of a misnomer. "It is true," noted the Reverend George Hogarth of the African Methodist Episcopal (AME) Church in response to criticism; "we are not Africans" (Tanner 1884: 171). However, the apparent truth of the matter was less compelling than tradition and denominational boundaries. An historically continuous name, however unpopular, enabled AME Church leaders to successfully block apparently fraudulent claims to their property by "impostors" using similar designations. Practical considerations such as this one overshadowed other concerns.

Officials of the African Methodist Episcopal Zion Church, which until 1848 was known by varying titles, experienced similar tensions. Church leaders who opposed the designation, "African," tried to change the denomination's name on their own. In 1841, they issued a new church *Discipline* under two different names: the Wesleyan Zion Episcopal Church in America and the Colored Methodist Church in America. Opponents of this change successfully appealed to tradition to defend the existing designation, African Methodist Episcopal Church in America. They worried that a name change would undermine denominational coherence by confusing people who identified themselves as African Methodists.

The institutional concerns that burdened churches failed to diminish reformers' criticisms. The persistence of the "African" designation simply gave opponents of race distinctions further evidence of the inability of churches to provide consistent moral leadership. They interpreted this shortcoming in both strategic and ethical terms. The name "African" not only compromised claims to American citizenship, it functioned as a caste designation, particularly in the hands of colonizationists. Reformers thus concluded that churches that "defaced" their titles with the word violated divine laws to the same extent as those who engaged in practices that separated or excluded individuals on the basis of racial classification.

Agreement on the necessity of abolishing race distinctions in religious institutions produced no consensus among reformers as to what abolition entailed. To some it meant eradication of racially separate churches and denominations altogether. The principle aim, in this case, was to create institutional unity and equality among black and white Christians. Colored churches bore the brunt of this vision. Abolitionists such as Henry Bibb and Frederick Douglass maintained that the successful elimination of these institutions would constitute the first step toward destroying "complexionary" obstacles to justice and universal freedom. As they saw it, colored churches should be agents of their own destruction. The churches should disband, they argued, and demand participation as "equal Christians" in organizations controlled by white people.

Other reformers directed their energies toward eliminating religious appeals to race, rather than destroying institutions. Their primary aim was to demonstrate to the American public that the idea of races was morally indefensible. Principle was to replace race as the basis of religious association and authority, even if it failed to produce wholesale integration. Reformers such as Whipper reasoned that all churches could and should further this end by removing racial designations from their titles and refraining from practices that made race a basis of participation, membership, or access to authority. Yet none dared to suggest that the concept of race, the wrongs it justified, or caste would disappear if churches refused to make race distinctions. Instead, reformers predicted that racial discourse would simply never cease as long as churches, especially colored churches, persisted in using it. Everyday use gave it credence and kept it alive.

Criticism of colored churches elicited a somewhat restrained response during the antebellum period. Church leaders largely ignored or dismissed charges that their institutions perpetuated oppressive race distinctions. Discrimination in white churches, coupled with the conviction that colored churches had responsibilities that were peculiar to them, overshadowed concerns that critics raised. However, even the most staunch defenders of colored churches betrayed misgivings about the morality of race distinctions. For instance, the Reverend Lewis Woodson, mentor to black nationalist, Martin Delany, argued that colored churches served the special function of elevating colored people. The task of improving their moral condition was more important than any other religious endeavor. Woodson suggested that it was even more essential than anti-slavery efforts and attempts to eradicate racial bigotry. In his words, the "mere circumstance" of being free from slavery and discrimination would not make colored people worthy of participating in "polite and elevated society" (*Colored American*, December 2, 1837). Nevertheless, Woodson was careful to insist that he too opposed the discourse that rendered colored people a "distinct class." However, it was a social reality that he accepted.

Most religious leaders avoided attempts to devise moral imperatives for colored churches. They noted instead that practical necessity explained the existence of such institutions. Daniel Payne, who became one of the most prominent figures in the AME Church, agreed with reformers that there was no scriptural nor scientific validity in the idea of racial difference. An ally of opponents of race, he too cited the apostle Paul, as well as scientific arguments, as evidence of the unity of the human race. Despite this perspective, church leaders had to contend with the fact that colored churches were the only antebellum institutions where people could worship and exercise ecclesiastical authority without racial discrimination. Eliminating their churches was not an option. Yet Payne made concerted efforts to ensure that his denomination did not exclude anyone on the basis of race. He championed membership rights for the rare white person who wanted to join an AME Church. As a matter of Christian principle, he reasoned that the churches should be open to all.

In the aftermath of the Civil War, optimism replaced moral outrage as a primary motivation for questioning the soundness of colored churches. A new generation of free people reveled in the assurance that civil and political rights nullified the idea of races. It was as if by withdrawing federal support for slavery and other forms of oppression Congress had eradicated the racial discourse that upheld them. Popular notions held that freedom and rights meant that all Americans were, as an anonymous freedman put it, "one color now," (*New Era*, August 31, 1871). Reformers made similar declarations in public celebrations where they praised God for destroying the heresy of race. Ministers preached sermons declaring that the Fifteenth Amendment was God's voice opposing caste and reaffirming the oneness of humanity. Prospects for full, unfettered participation in civil society and political affairs prompted a sense of relief among many that their "race condition," as Douglass called it, was finished.

Optimism also muted the voices of antebellum opponents of colored churches. Most of those who lived to see emancipation abandoned their public objections as they became involved in Reconstruction reforms. Critics who had simultaneously defended exclusive secular initiatives now had little basis for condemnations. They themselves faced some of the same charges they had lodged against religious organizations. For instance, when Frederick Douglass and Presbyterian minister, Sella Martin, introduced their reform periodical, *New Era*, they were compelled to defend its commitment to the interests of colored people against accusations that colored newspapers fueled the very ideas that had sustained oppression. The editors took great pains to distinguish the benevolent purposes of their appeals to race from the "obsolete and unholy" notion that people of color constituted "a peculiar variety" of humanity (*New Era*, September 8, 1870). They argued that, despite the particularity of its focus, the paper gave no credence to biases founded on either color or sectarian allegiances; it identified with all people. This new context tempered Douglass's criticism of colored churches such that he abandoned his earlier injunction that they disband. However, he urged them to promote racial integration within their ranks, lest they be found guilty of consecrating color distinctions.

While external opposition waned, church leaders had to contend with challenges that emerged from hopefulness within their own ranks. Confidence that race would be expunged from the nation extended the focus of opposition beyond colored churches. Both black and white Protestants reconsidered the

validity and necessity of distinctions in religious endeavors. Methodist denominations were especially affected by this development. Of the major Protestant
traditions, their leaders launched the most aggressive assault on race after the
war. The former abolitionist, Gilbert Haven, led initiatives to eliminate appeals
to race in the Methodist Episcopal Church, North. With like-minded clergy
in New England and Louisiana he tried to eradicate racial segregation policies in
the denomination's churches, conferences, and schools and demanded an end to
the marginalization of its colored ministers in church government. These clergy
shared the judgment of antebellum reformers that it was blasphemous for
churches to maintain "anti-biblical" caste distinctions that effectively encouraged
racial hierarchies in other spheres. Yet their embarrassment at seeing their church
lag behind politicians in working to abolish immoral social arrangements com-
pounded the urgency of their cause. Among their chief concerns was that the
churches hindered the process of national unification by continuing to structure
their operations on the basis of race. Decrying his denomination's ongoing
espousal of race distinctions, Haven asked: "Shall the church wear these chains
after the State has dropped them from her limbs?" (*Zion's Herald*, April 10,
1867).

Haven's fellow clergy, both within and outside his denomination, worked to
ensure that the concept of races remained a guiding principle in the structure of
religious institutions. Race ideologies inspired and shaped proposals for organizational arrangements that, on the surface, appeared to transcend race
constructions. Even some of the most ardent proponents of abolishing racial
bases of association remained committed to racial doctrines that deemed black
people inferior to white people. One Reverend D. M. Wilson offered a scathing
rebuke of white Christians for fostering such inhospitable conditions in their
churches that the average colored person was driven to "that ecclesiastical
monstrosity, a *colored church*" (Wilson 1883: 270). He argued that segregated
churches surpassed slavery in alienating the races, and thus had the disastrous
effect of consigning colored people to spiritual "darkness." He was convinced
that colored people were incapable of practicing true religion by themselves. Only
with guidance from white people would their worship amount to anything more
than "senseless noise."

Similarly, leaders who worked against religious hierarchies based on race also
continued to observe social conventions derived from notions of racial difference.
For instance, although northern Methodists were compelled by Haven and others
to try to repair the breach that had given rise to African Methodism earlier in the
century, they remained committed to race distinctions. Architects of unification
plans, led by the Reverend Benjamin Crary, tried to ensure that race would play
no role in determining participation in church government or access to ecclesiastical authority. However, rather than attempt to eliminate all distinctions, as
Haven urged, they sought equality via racial segregation. To ensure that African
Methodists would retain access to positions of authority, unification proposals
stipulated that existing AME bishops would preside over "colored conferences,"
which would have equal representation in Church affairs. This arrangement was
no doubt intended to appease people who were opposed to interracial worship.

However, it went too far for African Methodist clergy who had looked to unification as a sign that the idea of race no longer held sway among Methodists. They rejected the plan, in spite its promise of ecclesiastical equality. Daniel Payne lamented that the proposal showed that the Methodist Episcopal Church, like American churches in general, remained infected with the *"virus"* of caste.

Ministers in predominately white denominations came to replace antebellum reformers as the primary disparagers of colored churches. These new critics indulged the fallacy that the inclusion of colored people on their church rolls somehow purged their organizations of race. The specter of race was readily apparent to them, however, in denominations led by black Christians. When faced with competition from African Methodists in proselytizing former slaves, northern Methodists forthrightly condemned the use of race categories as a basis of religious association. Ministers warned proselytes that it was wrong for any church to rely on racial foundations. Denominational periodicals publicly challenged the religious integrity of African Methodism with accusations that its institutional strength and identity rested on "the mere distinction of complexion" (Morrow 1956: 136–7). The critics suggested that African Methodists were morally unfit to evangelize freed people, because theirs was a "race church." They were accurate in noting that the church solicited converts with appeals to race. African Methodists themselves boasted that ties of "blood" and oppression made their denomination the most appropriate home for freed slaves. However, northern Methodists' focus on African Methodism obscured their own organizational innovations to maintain racially distinct congregations and conferences.

Allegations that colored people bore sole responsibility for race distinctions extended beyond the domain of Methodism. Colored churches, as a whole, faced similar accusations from white church leaders who found them unworthy of partnership in interdenominational reform initiatives. Congregational minister Washington Gladden, "father" of the Social Gospel, popularized this judgment in his imaginative account of ecumenical association, "The Christian League of Connecticut" (1882). Gladden pointedly asserted that the league had an obligation, not only to exclude colored churches from "Christian union," but to destroy them. Their crime, he explained, was in maintaining sectarianism on the basis of color, which was sectarianism of "the meanest kind." In his zeal to ensure that there was "no color-line in Christianity," Gladden somehow failed to notice the racial doctrines and distinctions that prevailed in the league's predominantly white denominations, including his own. He simply assumed that predominantly black denominations included and excluded people on the basis of race. He refrained from drawing any such conclusions about his denomination, which despite a policy rejecting race as a basis of association, maintained churches that organized along racial lines. Thus, in appearance, it was as much a "race church" as the colored churches Gladden hoped to eradicate and the white churches his league warmly embraced.

While defending themselves against charges from the new reformers, leaders of colored churches had to contend with internal opposition to race distinctions. The AME Church experienced particular difficulty, because some of its prominent clergy agreed with critics that it perpetuated the notion of race and was thus out of step with the pace of national progress. These ministers quit the denomination. The most public of the departures involved future Mississippi Secretary of State, James Lynch, who was editor of the church periodical, and Reconstruction Senator, Hiram Revels. Both men became ministers in the Methodist Episcopal Church, North. They were lured there by the promise of escaping association based on race, which Lynch identified as the "*vitalizing* force" of African Methodism. He was convinced that religious adherence to race distinctions was not only immoral, but had become unnecessary with rising acceptance of the idea of human unity. In his mind, racially separate churches were inseparable from the bigotry that led "democrats, conservatives and Southern Methodists only" to champion their existence (Gravely 1977: 265–6). Conscience compelled him to reject them by leaving what he saw as a "race church." Unfortunately, he and Revels soon found themselves allied with Haven, trying to forestall their new denomination's sanction of the race distinctions they had decried in African Methodism.

The magnitude of defections from colored churches that were motivated by racial considerations is unknown. However, it was significant enough to generate public concern among AME Church officials that opposition to race would deplete their ranks and weaken their cause. This apprehension inspired a stream of apologetic literature in defense of colored churches. Their own misgivings about the morality of race categories prevented most apologists from ascribing any intrinsic virtue to "race churches." Instead, they focussed on the achievements of African Methodism and the ongoing necessity for colored churches to serve as havens for people who might otherwise be excluded from full religious fellowship. Some countered the charge that colored churches were truly "race churches," explaining that they welcomed all people and counted white people in their ranks. However, most apologists conceded that, with or without exclusionary policies, colored churches were "race churches," just like all other American churches. Many shared Daniel Payne's conviction that only in a distant future would "the miserable, puerile and heathenish question of color" be annihilated. Ultimately, he argued, but solely through the power of divine intervention would "*Races perish*" (Payne 1884: 3, 6).

Gradual acceptance of the fact that the concept of race held unyielding sway in religious circles diminished tensions within colored churches. Calm was reinforced as post-Reconstruction exclusions dashed hopes that black Americans could have a full say in American life. External criticism of colored churches became virtually nonexistent. Reformers tacitly accepted W. E. B. DuBois's argument that long-standing appeals to a common humanity had proven to be an untenable basis from which to secure civil and political rights. Races were a fact of history.

Despite these developments, churches remained a critical center of race reform at the close of the nineteenth century. Church leaders who tried to resist popular trends became the primary critics of race. Foremost in this endeavor were African Methodist ministers Benjamin Tanner and Theophilus Steward. These reformers no longer focussed condemnations on religious institutions. Moreover, they largely refrained from citing religious evidence to denounce the idea of race. The resources of churches – the pulpit, press, schools, and lyceums – served as their forums for exhorting co-religionists of their duty, as citizens, to abandon racial discourse.

Steward and Tanner theorized that no popular government could extend its boundaries of participation beyond its notion of race. As long as black Americans were defined as a different race, they reasoned, they would be subject to different, unequal access to citizenship rights. Only a new configuration of race that was coextensive with existing parameters of citizenship could overcome this in-equality. Citing the Civil War as evidence, Tanner argued that if two governments could not rule the country, two races could not comprise the citizenry. "The one is the corollary of the other," he postulated, "one government, one race; and both purely American" (*Christian Recorder*, April 26, 1883).

Steward and Tanner failed to win even their fellow church leaders to their cause. In the end, they too yielded to the reality of race. Like Daniel Payne, they looked to a distant future for the eradication of races. Tanner expressed faith that God would abolish notions of racial difference and inferiority within the span of human history. However, Steward was less optimistic and envisioned the end of prevailing race constructions in an apocalypse that would begin the millennium.

Nineteenth-century reformers misjudged the pervasiveness of racial discourse in American society. They overestimated the capacity and willingness of churches to abolish the idea of race. Their failure to rid the nation of "race churches" reflects the historical fact that American churches heed social conventions as much as they shape them. As institutions, churches could not carry out what reformers viewed as an imperative of a commitment to transcendent truths.

BIBLIOGRAPHY

Christian Recorder (Philadelphia), April 26, 1883.

The Colored American (New York), September 16, 1837; December 2, 1837; June 19, 1839; February 6, 1841.

Clark, Elmer (ed.) (1958) *Journal and Letters of Francis Asbury*, vol. III, Nashville, Tenn.: Abingdon Press.

Garrison, William Lloyd (1832) *Thoughts on African Colonization*, Boston, Mass.: Garrison and Knapp.

Gladden, Washington (1882) "The Christian League of Connecticut," *Century Magazine* 25 (November), pp. 50–60.

Gravely, William B. (1977) "The decision of A.M.E. leader, James Lynch, to join the Methodist Episcopal Church," *Methodist History* 15 (July), pp. 263–9.

Horton, James Oliver (1993) *Free People of Color: Inside the African American Community*, Washington, DC: Smithsonian Institution Press.

Lincoln, Abraham (1996) Address on colonization to a deputation of colored men [1862], in Wilson Jeremiah Moses (ed.) *Classical Black Nationalism: From the American Revolution to Marcus Garvey*, New York: New York University Press, pp. 209–14.

Morrow, Ralph (1956) *Northern Methodism and Reconstruction*, East Lansing, Mich.: Michigan State University Press.

New Era (Washington, DC), September 8, 1870; August 31, 1871.

North Star (Rochester), February 25, 1848; December 14, 1849.

Payne, Daniel (1884) "Thoughts about the past, the present and the future of the African M. E. Church," *A.M.E. Church Review* 1 (July), pp. 1–8.

Steward, Theophilus G. (1888) *The End of the World, or, Clearing the Way for the Fullness of the Gentiles*, Philadelphia, Pa.: A.M.E. Church Book Rooms.

Tanner, Benjamin Tucker (1884) *An Outline of Our History and Government for African Methodist Churchmen, Ministerial and Lay*, published by B. T. Tanner, no place given.

Wilson, D. M. (1883) "It decides nothing," *American Missionary*, 37, p. 270.

Zion's Herald (Boston), April 10, 1867.

Chapter 18

The Rise of African-American Evangelicalism in American Culture

Albert G. Miller

Contrary to popular belief, not all black Christianity falls into the stereotypical categories of historic black denominational life. This paper traces the origin and development of the evangelical movement within the African-American Christian community in the United States. Scholars of modern Evangelicalism have difficulty adequately defining black Evangelicalism, identifying its origins, and making a clear differentiation between it and the historic black church tradition. The issues will be clarified and some historical connections will emerge between this movement and its larger white evangelical counterpart. It will also suggest ways in which it has differed from the traditional black church community, and ways it is similar. It focuses on a roughly seventy-year period, from just prior to the turn of the twentieth century to about 1963 and the founding of the National Negro Evangelical Association (NNEA). Use of the NNEA as a focal point will help identify a larger movement of African-American Christians which does not fit well into the typical classification of American and African-American religious movements in current historiography.

With the founding of the NNEA in 1963, we see the clearest presence of a segment of the modern Evangelicalism movement within the African-American community. The National Black Evangelical Association (NBEA), as it is now called, is an umbrella association of individuals, organizations, and churches. This movement is of the same theological genus as the larger, modern, white American evangelical movement. It is representative of the larger theologically conservative religious movement in the African-American community known as black Evangelicalism. While black Evangelicalism is certainly not limited to the membership of the NBEA, the NBEA is a paradigmatic of the religious movement that we refer to as contemporary black Evangelicalism. The NBEA's numerical strength is unknown, but in 1980 its leadership estimated its mailing list at 5,000, with an extended constituency of 30,000–40,000 (Maust 1980). James Davison Hunter indicates that:

the percentage of Evangelical blacks is lower than might be expected. Black religion has always been thought of as a "religion of the disinherited" – oriented toward salvation, revival, holiness, and biblical literalism – in a word, crudely Evangelical. Yet current data do not support this idea. Evangelical and mainstream Protestants each have roughly the same percentage of blacks. (1983: 49–51)

Yet the number of African Americans who self-identify as Evangelical or who support various versions of Evangelical theological tenets is unclear. In an interview, Kenneth Rollerson, Marketing Director of Urban Ministries Incorporated, the largest black and evangelically-oriented Sunday school material publisher, estimated that the number of African Americans who self-identify as evangelical or who support various versions of evangelical tenets exceeds 800,000. The black evangelical movement has spread to influence many denominationally-affiliated African-American churches as well as many independent churches. Taking as a model the white evangelical movement's focus on the media, many African-American evangelicals have flooded the mass-media markets of radio and television. Their conservative theological and evangelical tenets are challenging the historically black denominations as well.

Before the founding of the NBEA some scholars of Evangelicalism viewed black Evangelicalism's origin as a type of hatched egg without a mother hen. The difficulty of defining the black contingent of the movement is partly to do with grasping the diversity and intricacy of Evangelicalism as a whole. This modern movement had its beginning in the early twentieth century, when the fundamentalist–modernist controversy took shape after the defeat of the conservative Christian worldview hegemony in the Scopes trial of 1925. This trial pitted the Christian fundamentalist's creationist views against the secular humanist's evolutionary views. Modern American Evangelicalism was popularized with the rise of various televised revival preachers, the best known being Billy Graham. It was organized as a social movement under the umbrella of the National Association of Evangelicals in 1943. George M. Marsden, the evangelical historian, wrote:

> Evangelicalism includes striking diversities: holiness churches, pentecostals, black churches in all these traditions, fundamentalists, pietist groups, Reformed and Lutheran confessionalists, Anabaptists such as Mennonites, Churches of Christ, Christians, and some Episcopalians, to name only some of the most prominent types ... opinion surveys that test for evangelical beliefs typically find somewhere around fifty million Americans who fit the definitions. (1991: 5)

Marsden (ibid.) suggested that regardless of denominational affiliation, or lack thereof, evangelicals have in common certain theological traits. They share a belief in the historic "fundamentals" of the Christian tradition: the complete reliability and final authority of the Bible in matters of faith and practice; the real, historical character of God's saving work recorded in Scripture; personal eternal salvation only through belief in and trust in Jesus Christ; evidence of a spiritually transformed life; and the importance of sharing this belief and experience with others through evangelism and mission works. Yet even with this broad theological starting point, there is a debate over whether Evangelicalism is a coherent religious movement. Some argue that the term "Evangelicalism" has little descriptive value, owing to the diversity within the movement; others have argued that its members make up an extended family, a recognizable and definable whole (Dayton and Johnston 1991).

Most scholars who study the evangelical phenomenon have had a difficult time situating black Evangelicalism historiographically and tracing its development as a movement. The historiography has developed in two strands. One strand looks at the eighteenth- and nineteenth-century evangelical roots of the traditional black church and then jumps to the rise of contemporary black Evangelicalism with the founding of the NBEA, ignoring the important forces of the several decades before 1963. It suggests that black churches were either poor, "otherworldly" and emotively focused, or were middle class and theologically liberal. The works of Gayraud Wilmore (1998), Milton Sernett (1991), William Pannell (1975), and George Marsden (1991) exemplify this particular analysis, which omits the early twentieth-century influence.

The second revisionist strand, while paying attention to this interim period, does not sort out and identify the specific forces that led to the formation of the NBEA. William Bentley is representative of this view, which attempts to subsume black Christian life under an all-encompassing term, "Bible believers":

> Use of the term "Bible believer" may be deceptive. The tendency is to regard it as unsophisticated. Yet there is probably no better name to be used in describing a complex of belief-systems that spans the gamut from simple credulity to real profundity. (1975: 111)

This notion is supported by sociologist James Hunter (1983: 50). He and Bentley go on to say that most African-American Christians are theologically conservative and thus evangelical, but are unfamiliar with the nomenclature (Bentley 1975: 111).

The historic American black church, with all of its various denominational forms, has been a major component of classic American Evangelicalism. Around the end of the nineteenth century it had, like the movement as a whole, a strong moral and social agenda. It called for reform in the areas of personal piety, slavery, and discrimination. Exemplars of this historic movement included Philadelphia's African Methodist Episcopal Church, founded by Richard Allen in 1816, and Savannah's First African Baptist Church, founded by George Liele and Andrew Bryan in 1794. The classic evangelical movement continued after the Civil War in the explosion of the various black Methodists and independent Baptists churches throughout the country. Although the late nineteenth- and early twentieth-century modernist movement significantly influenced some of the black church's leadership there has always been a significant segment that sees itself as "Bible believing."

Neither of the historiographical views mentioned has given sufficient attention to formative influences of black fundamentalism in the early twentieth century. The first view correctly focuses on the beginnings before the twentieth century, but neglects the development of several small significant groups of African-American modern fundamentalists that were the genesis of the modern black evangelical movement. As for the second view, although it is true that most African-American Christians who affiliated with traditional and historic black churches were "Bible believers," there were also some who aligned themselves with the developing fundamentalist movement of the early twentieth century. The traditional African-American church subscribed to the theological tenets of Evangelicalism as congruent with its beliefs, which, as Bentley has suggested, spanned "the gamut from simple credulity to real profundity" (1975: 111). But some have argued that this church was an admixture of "the remnants of the (West) African 'sacred cosmos,' on the one hand, and Euro-American Protestant evangelical Christianity on the other" (Wimbush 1989: 141). The modern black evangelical movement, as it developed, placed more emphasis on the propositional aspects of faith than on experiential and ecstatic elements. This caused some strains between the black evangelical movement and the traditional black church, leading some black evangelicals to characterize the historic black church as "apostate and unbiblical." Conversely, some in mainline black churches labeled black evangelicals as doctrinaire and schismatic "fanatics" (Bentley 1988). These tensions go back from the NBEA to the very beginnings of black fundamentalism in the twentieth century.

In the remainder of this paper I will suggest a more accurate genesis of the modern black evangelical movement. Several areas should be looked at in developing a more comprehensive view of the early origins. They include certain leaders of the black Christian Brethren and Christian and Missionary Alliance Churches, and the involvement of various black Pentecostal church leaders in the broader black evangelical movement. I suggest that these are the most significant factors, among possible others that influenced the early years, and they deserve further research.

The black Plymouth Brethren churches, led by Berlin Martin Nottage, (1889–1966), were one of the earliest components of the evangelical movement. In 1904, while in their native home on the island of Eluthera in the Bahamas, Nottage – affectionately known as B.M. – and two of his older brothers, Whitfield, and Talbot, became Christians within one month of each other. By 1910, all three brothers had immigrated to New York to seek better employment, and had begun evangelistic work among the African Americans in New York, especially in Harlem. By 1914 they had established the first Brethren assembly (congregation) in that community in New York (Nottage: 121). The brothers, especially B.M., broke their strong ties to the West Indian Brethren community and began an aggressive evangelistic ministry in the black community of the United States, eventually establishing assemblies in St Louis, Muskegon, Terre Haute, Birmingham, Philadelphia, Richmond, Va., and Cleveland. T.B. and B.M. established the first African-American Plymouth Brethren assemblies in Chicago. By 1932, B.M. had founded the Bethany Tabernacle assembly in Detroit. He established five more over the next eleven years in Detroit (Nottage: 124). B.M.'s ministry stretched well beyond the bounds of the Brethren assemblies; he networked within the wider association of evangelical efforts. He was also a mentor to a group of younger men, some of who were to be influential in the NBEA: Marvin Printis, the first president of the NBEA; William Pannell, the professor of evangelism at Fuller Theological Seminary; and Howard Jones, a minister with the Christian and Missionary Alliance Church, and the first black associate of Billy Graham. B.M. became a well-known evangelist outside the Brethren circles. He was one of the earliest African-American speakers at the Moody Bible Institute's Founders Week celebrations and, in 1957, was one of the earliest blacks to have a weekly radio program on the Moody Bible Institute's radio station, WMBI. He seemed to have a large following, at least in the Chicago area, as evidenced by a successful WMBI radio rally held in a black church that drew 700 people and featured B. M. Nottage speaking on the life of George Washington Carver, the famous African-American scientist (Nottage: 124).

B. M. Nottage's sermons and speeches show the development of an early theological fundamentalism and criticism of the traditional black church. They reveal classic rationalistic or propositional Christian doctrine, as opposed to the more experiential and ecstatic tradition of some black churches. His intention in his sermons was to restore the faith of the "backsliders" (in this case those who were doctrinally impure, especially in the African-American church) and effect "the salvation of the lost and perishing all around us." Nottage followed typical propositional logic in developing his theology:

> Here are the *Facts of Faith* which I shall consider: Ruination, Redemption, Regeneration, Salvation, Justification, Sanctification, Unification, Glorification, Compensation, Subjugation, Damnation, Consummation [sic]. I wish to make it crystal clear, that our most Holy Faith rests upon solid and eternal facts. To know and heartily accept these facts is to produce and strengthen faith. "Faith cometh by hearing . . . the Word of God." (Nottage: 9)

His theology, as expressed in his sermon, "Divine dispensations," was representative of the pre-millennial dispensationalist theology of the early twentieth century, which emerged among the Plymouth Brethren and other fundamentalist groups. We gain a glimpse of the conservative theological beliefs held by this group. Contrary to Bentley's notion of "Bible believers" this body of black Christians clearly identified with the early fundamentalist groups. Nottage in the beginning of his sermon lamented that so few "of even God's own dear children know so little or nothing of our Heavenly Father's plans." He outlined the classic tenets of the pre-millennial dispensational tradition.

> [F]irst: The dispensation of Creation of the Heavens, the Earth and Angels. Second: The Creation of Man in Innocence. Third: Man After the Fall Under Conscience. Fourth: Mankind After the Flood, or Noah and Human Government. Fifth: . . . the Dispensation of Promise, God's Promises of Grace and Salvation to Abraham. Sixth: The Giving of the Law . . . The seventh, . . . the dispensation of Grace and Truth by Jesus Christ . . .
>   . . . [T]he eighth dispensation: The time of Great Tribulation . . . The Dispensation of the Kingdom will be the ninth, when Jesus . . . will sit on the Throne of David . . .

The tenth and last administration brings us to the end of Time or back to Eternity;
. . . the New Heaven and the New Earth . . . (Nottage: 27–8)

It is in Nottage's discussion of African Americans that we get a clear sense of
how this community of faith perceived the larger black church tradition. In the
chapter of his book entitled, "The American Negro" Nottage briefly traced the
history of African Americans through slavery and surveyed state population
statistics and the economic status of African Americans in 1963. He gave a favorable spin on the social condition of African-American life in both the North and
South, in spite of the overwhelming evidence of racial segregation in the United
States at the time. His perception of the increasing juvenile delinquency, crime,
divorce, illegitimacy rate, and crowded living conditions in the black community
as the effects of sin showed his conservative theological stance. "Sin, of course,
is the root of all this, and no effort should be made to excuse the Negro; but it is
true that the economic and social disadvantages placed upon him by American
society encourage and increase these problems" (Nottage: 27).

In "The Negro and religion" his focus shifted: decrying the general increase of
secularism and the decrease of Christian fundamentalist influences within society,
he focused on the effect they had on black religious denominations. Nottage
suggested that, "The Negro church is founded more largely on a sociological than
on a theological basis" (p. 75). According to him, either black churches led by
liberally trained ministers affiliated with ecumenical councils endorsed
modernism or black churches led by poorly trained clergy endorsed extreme
emotionalism.

> Many of its better trained leaders were instructed in institutions in which the
> doctrine of the plenary inspiration of the Scriptures is not held. A large number of
> pastors, on the other hand, who have not had the benefits of a higher education,
> condone and encourage extreme emotionalism. (Nottage: 83)

He said that there were, in various places, those churches in which "the fundamental doctrine of the Christian are taught and the Gospel of the Lord Jesus is
preached in clarity and power" (Nottage: 75). In essence, the forces that hinder
the "progress of evangelical Christianity" among blacks in the United States were
"Communism, Romanism, modernism, emotionalism and racial discrimination"
(pp. 75 and 83). The sermons did not at all elaborate upon Communism. One
assumes that its dangers were obvious enough not to need mentioning. Nottage
blamed the Catholic Church for siphoning off blacks from traditionally black
churches through their strong emphasis on parochial education and provision of
medical facilities in urban areas.

Besides criticizing the negative impact of modernism, ecumenism, and
emotionalism on the traditional black church, Nottage also raised the issue of
racial discrimination – a major barrier to attracting African Americans to
evangelical Christianity. His sermon is both a critique and a plea for support.

> Generally speaking, the "all welcome" sign on the doors of most evangelical
> churches does not include the Negro or some other minority group. Most Bible

conferences, Bible schools and colleges, Bible Camps, rescue missions and other Christian gatherings are not geared for the Negro. Usually he isn't welcome and is not allowed to enjoy such fellowship. He isn't exposed to that type of teaching which makes for godly character among white Christians. But if the Christian Church doesn't take the lead in treating the Negro as an equal and giving him spiritual help and Bible training, who will? This is a responsibility that cannot be ignored. (Nottage: 76–7)

That this passage was written at about the same time as the formation of the NBEA was not a coincidence. The African-American evangelical community had become frustrated with the lack of acknowledgment of its leadership and lack of support from white evangelicals. Originally, in 1963, the NBEA did not view itself as racially separatist, although since then it has been a predominantly black association. It did see itself as an association which focused its efforts on developing African-American leaders who would minister to black people in strongly fundamentalist way. From the beginning the social action commission raised social issues within the NBEA, yet major social concerns were not in the forefront. The NBEA concentrated instead on strategies for spreading its particular brand of Evangelicalism within the African-American community. During this early stage, many black evangelicals were frustrated with the white evangelical movement. This tension primarily sprang from what blacks perceived as white evangelicals' indifference and lack of sympathy for the evangelistic needs of African Americans. This eventually led some black evangelicals to charge their white counterparts with a spiritual "benign neglect." Eventually the charge of neglect evolved into a stronger allegation of racism.

The history of African Americans and their struggle for self-reliance in the Christian and Missionary Alliance (C&MA) movement suggests another significant source for the development of black Evangelicalism. The Reverend John Davis Bell (1888–1957) is one important example. He was the mentor for several individuals who were important to the development of the NBEA, including Howard O. Jones, its second president, and Ralph Greenidge who was active both in the NBEA and the C&MA.

The C&MA, founded in 1880s by A. B. Simpson, was a parachurch mission organization that eventually evolved into a denomination. It focused on evangelism, holiness, and missions with a strong interest in healing. African Americans associated with this movement almost from its beginning; churches were established in Cleveland in 1892 and Pittsburgh in 1893. Before the 1930s several black missionaries went to West Africa under the auspices of the C&MA, but by 1940 the C&MA had withdrawn support for black missionaries to Africa. The C&MA also had a developing mission, led by both blacks and whites, in the United States. Historian Dale Irwin has said, "We have seen here that the witness of the Afro-American churches within the C&MA against the sinfulness of racism and its hindrance of the Gospel has been a part of the movement since its infancy" (Irvin: 29). By the time Bell had become the black representative of all C&MA works in 1945, black C&MA workers had gone through several low points in the organization.

What was significant about Bell was his sense of independence from white control, his self-determination, and willingness to organize within the black C&MA. One gets a sense of this in a speech entitled "My Vision," given before a camp meeting of black C&MA members some time during World War II. While outlining a vision for the raising of funds, a black workers' rest home, an annual camp and prayer meeting that would organize the black C&MA work, he challenged the gathering not to be dependent upon whites, nor to be afraid of being labeled as segregationist:

> Some argue we are afraid of segregation. Well, we have always had the class, and this will go on until the end. I have given thought along this line also. If we would plan and do something for ourselves, we would find that the word "segregation" would not enter into our plans at all. The very fact that you do something to lift your people, that in itself demands the attention of the other fellow, and he desires to come among you. Can we stop here because someone disagrees with our plan or Vision [sic]? No, as I already stated, a "passion" is a thing that will not cease because it is opposed. It must continue because God is behind it and it must succeed. (Bell: 3)

Although Bell did not himself live to see the formation of the NBEA, many of his protégés did and were active in the organization of the black evangelical movement. Bell's sense of independence and self-determination was very evident. But he clearly was not a separatist; he was faithfully connected to the C&MA until his death, and encouraged the active participation of whites in the activities of African Americans. Yet he was a realist and he knew that blacks must organize themselves if they were going to be effective at evangelizing in the black community. Thus, through his example, independent action could already be seen to be a viable strategy for the NBEA.

Another significant influence on the development of the NBEA was a more traditional religious movement within the African-American community: the Trinitarian Pentecostal tradition as exemplified in the Church of God in Christ. The best representative of this movement is William H. Bentley.

Pentecostals did not emphasize propositional Christian doctrine as the Brethren did, although they had their own brand of dispensational theology. They also diverged, but to a lesser degree, from the C&MA and its devotion to missions. The black Pentecostal tradition was a sectarian movement that saw itself at odds with traditional black churches because of its own stress on sanctification, baptism in the Holy Spirit, and tongue speaking. Pentecostals clearly focused on the experiential and ecstatic side of the Christian tradition, although they also valued fundamentalist doctrines, because they were biblical literalists. And black Pentecostals, as all Pentecostals, regarded experience and not theology as of primary importance in the religious life. Black Pentecostalism remained isolated from the mainstream evangelical movement even longer than its white Pentecostal counterpart. The Assemblies of God, the largest predominantly white Pentecostal denomination, was a co-founder of the National Association of Evangelicals in 1948. Black Pentecostalism's perceived emotionalism further isolated them from the mainstream evangelical movement. Because most blacks and whites saw black Pentecostal churches as composed of poor and dis-advantaged there was also a class barrier. However, the image of black Pentecostals has changed dramatically in both camps (black evangelical and traditional black church), in part because of the increased social and class status of black Pentecostals since the 1960s. This is especially true for the Church of God in Christ, with its explosive growth and the attraction to it of many more middle-class parishioners.

Black Pentecostalism, like other traditionally black denominations, also differed significantly from the Brethren and C&MA traditions because it was independent of white control. It thus saw itself somewhere between the funda-mentalist variety of black evangelicals and the traditional black churches.

The early relationship between black fundamentals and black Pentecostals began, in part, around the same time that a few black Pentecostals, such as William Bentley, ventured beyond their home church denominations in pursuit of education and theological training, to attend liberal colleges and seminaries, where they were introduced to evangelicalism. Bentley obtained a BA degree from Roosevelt University in 1956 and was the first African American to receive a BD degree from Fuller Theological Seminary in 1959; he was one of the founding members of the NBEA and its president from 1970 to 1976. Another seeker of education was Bishop George D. McKinney, Jr. of the Church of God in Christ and a past president of the NBEA. Bishop McKinney graduated from Arkansas AM&N (Agricultural and Normal College at Pine Bluff) and later, in 1956, received a MA in theology from Oberlin School of Theology.

Bentley was critical of the theological limitations of his Pentecostal colleagues because of their little formal training, but he also appreciated the sound Christian foundation that they had.

> Those of us who came from the Pentecostal-holiness tradition were well aware that many of our ministers had but little formal training, but we also knew that they knew the Lord God, were led by the Holy Spirit, and preached and taught us and their congregations the truth according to that Word. (Bentley 1988: 31)

Bentley used the words "Bible believers" to define the larger black traditional Christian community partly because he represented a small but significant part of the movement that had come out of a black Pentecostal church tradition. (Bentley became a Christian in the Church of God in Christ and later affiliated with the United Pentecostal Council of the Assemblies of God, Incorporated. He served as its National President from 1981 to 1989). Pentecostals differed in some areas of theology and liturgy with their early black fundamentalist counterparts but clearly saw themselves as upholding the fundamentals of the Christian tra-dition. At the same time, they clearly identified themselves as part of the traditional black religious community.

> There were those of us, in the decided minority during our founding years, who were proud products of the mainline Black denominations. Agreeing with our

teachers . . . regarding the presence of much emotional excess [in the traditional black church], we nevertheless knew the difference between the baby and the bath water. We felt that a church which has enabled, indeed, took the leading place as the Afro-American institution of our racial and ethnic survival, and had simultaneously become the generating place of more than the lion's share of Black creativity could not be as far from redemption as its detractors, Black or white, thought it to be. (Bentley 1988: 30–1)

It is noteworthy that it was the Pentecostals, such as Bentley, who challenged the NBEA in areas of black theology, black culture, social action, and rethinking black evangelical's relationship with the African-American church. This came about partly as a result of the Pentecostals' encounter with broader and more liberal theological thinking and their rootedness in a black church tradition. This desire to save the evangelical black church baby from being thrown out with the emotional and modernist bathwater was the impetus behind black Pentecostals' exploration of wider trends within the African-American community, including black nationalism, black theology, and social action.

There were, of course, other influences that helped to make up this movement, which need further research. These include: Bible schools established to serve this early black movement; the many women who were local and foreign missionaries and founders of mission and Bible schools to serve the neophyte fundamentalist African-American community; various white evangelical para-church organizations that emerged during and after World War II and were involved with African-American leadership and mission efforts; and the various African-American, independent, evangelical organizations that emerged before and after 1963.

Each of these three movements contributed different characteristics to the formation of the NBEA. The Brethren brought a strong propositional theology, the C&MA a mission tradition and desire for self-reliance, and the Pentecostals an independent black church ethos and a strong experiential theological tradition. What the three movements have in common is a desire to evangelize the African-American community, to find a strategy for carrying out this mission, and to embrace a fundamentalist theology that differed from traditional African-American churches.

Evangelicalism has heretofore been seen primarily as a white and middle-class phenomenon. The picture is more complex: I hope, by showing the diversity within the evangelical movement, to have deepened our understanding of its development. Seeing the intricate history of African-American institutions during the twentieth century, should enable greater appreciation of black religion in general.

BIBLIOGRAPHY

Bell, John Davis "My vision," The Christian and Missionary Alliance Archives, Colorado Springs, Colo. (MS received September 11, 1981).

Bentley, W. H. (1975) "Bible believers in the black community," in D. F. Wells and J. D. Woodbridge (eds) *The Evangelicals: What They Believe, Who They Are, Where They Are Changing*, Nashville, Tenn.: Abingdon Press, pp. 108–21.

— (1979a) *National Black Evangelical Association: Evolution of a Concept of Ministry*, rev. ed, Chicago: The Author, P O Box 4311).

— (1979b) *The Meaning of History for Black Americans*, Chicago: National Black Evangelical Association and the National Black Christian Students Conference.

— (1988) *National Black Evangelical Association: Bellwether of a Movement, 1963–1988*, Chicago: National Black Evangelical Association.

Dayton, D. W. and Johnston, R. K. (eds) (1991) *The Variety of American Evangelicalism*, Downers Grove, Ill.: Inter Varsity Press.

Hunter, J. D. (1983) *American Evangelicalism: Conservative Religion and the Quandary of Modernity*, New Brunswick, NJ: Rutgers University Press.

Irvin, D. "Much land to be possessed: black churches of the early Christian and Missionary Alliance," The Christian and Missionary Alliance Archives, Colorado Springs, Colo. (MS received 1984).

Marsden, G. (1991) *Understanding Fundamentalism and Evangelicalism*, Grand Rapids, Mich.: Eerdmans.

Maust, J. (1980) "The NBEA: striving to be both black and biblical," *Christianity Today* (June 27), pp. 58–9.

Nottage, B. M. (n.d.) *Facts of the Faith*, ed. H. A. Rylander, Detroit: privately printed.

Pannell, W. (1975) "The religious heritage of blacks," in D. F. Wells and J. D. Woodbridge (eds) *The Evangelicals: What They Believe, Who They Are, Where They Are Changing*, Nashville, Tenn.: Abingdon Press, pp. 96–107.

Sernett, M. G. (1991) "Black religion and the question of evangelical identity," in D. W. Dayton and R. K. Johnston (eds) *The Variety of American Evangelicalism*, Downers Grove, Ill.: Inter Varsity Press, pp. 135–47.

Wilmore, G. S. (1998) *Black Religion and Black Radicalism: An Interpretation of the Religious History of Afro-American People*, Maryknoll, NY: Orbis Books.

Wimbush, V. L. (1989) "Biblical historical study as liberation: toward an Afro-Christian hermeneutic," in G. S. Wilmore (ed.) *African American Religious Studies: An Interdisciplinary Anthology*, Durham, NC: Duke University Press, pp. 140–54.

Chapter 19

Religion and Culture Change in Native North America

Michael D. McNally

As students of North American religious history, how many of us feel confident that the mental maps we carry of our subject adequately appreciate the hundreds of Native American traditions that enrich the religious landscape? In the introductory courses we teach or take, in the surveys we write or read, in the constructs we devise to make sense of the whole, are we satisfied with our sense of how Native traditions matter in North American religious history? I suspect not, and for a variety of reasons. Among those reasons is a widely held perception that Native American traditions are not quite at home in history. Native traditions are often perceived to be so exotic as to be incomparable to the so-called historical religions of the West. They are often seen to be organized to prevent change over time, not to move naturally with it. These religions have often been viewed as reservoirs of timelessness, holdouts of a receding pre-Columbian past that deny what Mircea Eliade famously called "the tragedy of history"(1949). Through a cyclical "eternal return" to sacred times, the myths and rituals of traditional Native religions have often been seen to work against the grain of linear time, of change, of history.

What then does one do with the dramatic changes so clearly undergone by Native American communities in the centuries since historical contact with Europeans? What do timeless traditions have to do with change? Adequate answers to such questions have long evaded scholars because of a habit of thinking about Native religions in terms of an opposition between the *traditional* and the *historical*. On the one hand, traditional religions are said to exist in purest form prior to European contact, in the days when the buffalo roamed free on the Plains, in the days well before the "last of the Mohicans." If such traditional religions belong in the historical era at all, they are seen to persist in fragmented ways after contact; and only to the extent that a Native community has remained unassimilated.

In stark contrast to such traditional religions, conventional wisdom has placed a category that fuses together the phenomena that register change over time: conversions to various Christian denominations and hybrid movements prompted by rapid change in the post-contact historical era. In effect, such an opposition places "authentically Native" traditions solidly outside history – before contact, before historical change – and consigns the career of those traditions after contact to a rather second-class status. At best, they become "survivals," aggregates lacking a logic of their own, brief flashes of exuberance on their way off the stage of history. At worst, they become derivatives of the colonized experience, examples of the collapse of tradition under the weight of history. Either way, tradition and history seem to be mutually exclusive, and Native religions consistently have been interpreted in terms of the commotion between them. If traditional religions are without history and the historical religious phenomena are beyond the reach of the traditional, neither is understood on its own terms. This essay will introduce the reader to the larger subject of Native American religions by means of four examples representing a variety of ways that Native *traditions* have been and remain in *historical* motion. Before turning to those illustrations, however, I wish to frame the discussion by identifying the root causes of misunderstanding, and drawing on an emerging body of scholarship to chart a course of inquiry that places Native American religions more meaningfully in larger narratives of American religious history.

While scholars have recently done much to correct the sense of the timelessness of Native religions, consider the extent to which it remains entrenched, if subtly, in scholarly practice. Native American religions are frequently confined to the first chapter of our American religion textbooks, and they are usually covered in the first lecture in our introductory courses. In the structure of such endeavors, Native religions help set the stage for the historical drama of religion in the US, but they often recede from the stage once the drama begins. If they return at all, it is typically for cameo appearances that serve to illustrate how the traditional has eroded. Even such a well-documented movement as the Ghost Dance is seldom viewed as a genuine tradition. The Ghost Dances were ceremonial complexes of renewal that swept many Native peoples of the Great Basin and Plains into the idiom of prophecy, dance, and ritual as the appropriate response to the injustices of the reservation era. But the Ghost Dances are often seen as desperate, even pathetic, attempts to erase the tragedy of history by appealing to traditions shown to be already deteriorating.

Informed by such treatment in courses and books, most of us would find it difficult to recognize Native American religion if we were to encounter it today. Thinking that European contact sealed the fate of traditional religions, many of us would be somewhat incredulous were we told that a Native community at the end of the twentieth century still holds that the world's fate relies on the proper performance of annual world renewal ceremonies. By the same token, many of us would find it jarring to imagine a "real" sweat lodge in the trampled mud of a prison courtyard, a pipe ceremony at a protest roadblock, or a funeral ceremony held under the bright lights of a high school gym.

I want to suggest here that the first step toward redressing the problem is to think afresh of Native American religious traditions as at home in history. Just what might it mean to be at home in history? Given the power of tradition and the violent dispossession of tradition that has characterized so much of that history, I do not mean to suggest, as some historians recently have, that significant Native American traditions can be explained away by identifying their historical roots in colonial encounters with Euro-Americans. Native religions may work to transform ordinary experiences of time and space by tapping into the power of the sacred in ways that suggest its *timelessness*. But that said, the fuller consequence of these religions lies in their *timeliness* as resources in the survival of that violent history. Indeed, many Native people today understand their spiritual traditions to be the most cherished resources at hand in the ongoing struggle to survive as communities. Language, ceremony, songs, stories, and spiritual knowledge are precious to Native communities, and perhaps now more so than ever, as they negotiate a way to live as distinctive communities at the brink of the twenty-first century. Here, religion is less concerned with the denial of history, as Eliade would have it, than with the facing of it.

With our vision trained on either the traditional or the historical to the exclusion of the other, we would find our historical understanding obscured as well. Indeed, we must ask ourselves whether the "religion" that we think we see is really there. In my brief travels with Anishinaabe, or Ojibwa, communities in Minnesota, my inquiries as a religionist have often met with some consternation. I have been told – on too many occasions to overlook – some version of the following: "We don't have a religion; we have a way of life." There is a great deal of material packed into such a statement. At the least, it carries the conviction that religion is not solely a matter of the spiritual, or the supernatural, or the immaterial. Behind the point is also a spiritual posture that does not easily identify religion as a discrete segment of culture, but rather sees it as ideally integrated into economics, politics, environment, art, and society. Perhaps the fervor with which many people say "we have no *religion*" in this sense is a sign of times when the very possibility of that integration is threatened by the political, economic, and social structures of contemporary American life. Taking the remark seriously here at the outset can help enrich our understandings of the place of the religious in Native ways of life, and in turn, the place of Native American religious traditions in American religion generally.

The problem here is one of boundaries: the boundaries within "culture" and the boundaries between "cultures." On the one hand, the problem concerns the boundaries thought to distinguish religion from the rest of culture. On the other, the problem concerns the nature of the boundaries thought to obtain between and among the various Native American religions: those between traditional and historical, and those among culture-specific tribal religions, various denominational forms of Native Christianity, and new inter-tribal religious movements. The boundaries by which we organize Native American religions in our heads are often far afield from the boundaries that actually obtain in the lives of Native American communities. It might be pedagogically useful to distinguish traditional religions, those religions falling within the boundaries of tribe, culture, or particular geographical landscape, from other innovations of the post-contact culture change. But if we assume that the boundaries we employ to help make sense of

Native religions actually arise in the lives of Native communities, we risk over-looking perhaps the greatest lesson to be learned: the centrality of religion in the process of culture change.

Once underscored by disciplinary boundaries between anthropologists and historians, this framework recently has been called into question by scholars in both fields. Native communities have consistently understood their religious traditions to be rich and timely resources in struggles to negotiate the demands and possibilities of a history of colonization and dispossession. But it has been only recently that ethnohistorians, anthropologists, and religious historians who write about them have begun to show how religion often plays the lead role in mediating culture change. Indeed, it is often religious beliefs and especially prac-tices that establish the continuity of community identity and meaning while negotiating the changes necessary to community survival.

At the heart of the newer way of viewing Native traditions is a redrawing of the boundaries on the basis of a revised understanding of what we mean when we speak of *culture*. Much of earlier twentieth century cultural anthropology has given us a sense that a "culture" is a well-bounded whole, a coherent system of symbols that is, at rest, static, and in principle, designed to fend off change and to promote equilibrium. If culture is naturally stable, then cultural change is an anomaly. When traditional cultures "collide" with Euro-American cultures in the wake of contact, they are said to undergo a process of what mid-twentieth-century anthropologists called "acculturation." For example, "Ojibwa culture" is understood to remain largely intact until "it" collided with the culture of French fur traders and Jesuits in the seventeenth century, or with the culture of Protestant Anglo-American missionaries in the nineteenth. The story thereafter is a more or less predictable one of cultural erosion, occasional revitalization, but almost always acculturation. Acculturation was something so "given" that one distinguished anthropologist (Hallowell) undertook extensive research using Rorschach ink-blot tests to compare and contrast its extent among various Ojibwa communities in Manitoba. (1955: 345–57).

If we approach Native religious traditions as at home with change and at home in history, we can also envision how understandings of those traditions might be more at home in our larger understandings of the narrative of religion in North American history. These thoughts follow Joel Martin's recent call for a post-colonial narrative of Native American religious history (Martin 1997). By "post-colonial," Martin means a posture toward writing and reading history that identifies more thoroughly how uneven power relations have given shape to Native American religious histories while appreciating more fully the agency of Native communities as co-producers of that history. To retell Native American religious history, then, would be simultaneously to leave behind the view that Old World meets New World in favor of a view that a number of new religious worlds were being improvised in the contact among Native Americans, Africans, and Europeans in North America, while "de-centering" that story to appreciate how Native traditions have shaped history, not merely having been on the receiving end of it.

Crucially, Native American communities have co-produced that history without necessarily sharing the same linear view of history that historians take for granted. Calvin Martin and others have alerted us to how historians must account for the fact that Native people have often imagined their place in time in ways that are neither anthropomorphic or contingent (1987). In this regard, Eliade's metaphor of the "eternal return" through myth and ritual to sacred time is apt. But the eternal return itself can be seen as a strategy for acting in time and history. Perhaps it is the very timelessness effected by certain ceremonies that becomes the principle of their timeliness. In this respect, the Ghost Dance could be a useful example to illustrate how ceremony addresses the tragedy of history, rather than denying it. The manner in which such traditions are at home in history is perhaps debatable, but the fact that they help make history is not.

What would a fresh appreciation of Native American religious history along such lines look like? In what follows, I will appeal to four specific examples to show what we gain by training our eyes not on either tradition or history at the expense of the other but on something that can entail both. In these examples, we can perhaps appreciate the *historicity of the traditional,* and the renewed *"traditionality" of the historical.* Taking seriously the warnings of literary critic Gerald Vizenor against the academic habit of reducing the complexities of Native experience to the static realities of a photograph, I wish to undertake a kind of snapshot that blurs its images to suggest motion, that points beyond its own borders, and that points beyond its capacity to freeze what resolves to keep moving (Feld 1990; Vizenor 1989). To do so, I have chosen four images that frustrate the conventional boundaries between the traditional and historical and show the timeliness and relevance of Native American religious traditions.

(How) Does Black Elk Speak?

A 1931 collaboration between a Lakota holy man named Black Elk and an ambitious poet named John Neihardt resulted in a book that has become a classic text of Native American religion. *Black Elk Speaks,* published the following year, gained an exceptionally broad and enthusiastic following in the counter-cultural movements of the 1960s and 1970s, among them the American Indian Movement. In his forward to a recent edition of *Black Elk Speaks*, Vine Deloria, Jr. notes that for the "contemporary generation of young Indians who have been aggressively searching for roots of their own in the structure of universal reality," *Black Elk Speaks* "has become a North American bible of all tribes" (Neihardt 1979: xiii). Perhaps what captured Native and non-Native imaginations alike was the promise of unity and relatedness in Black Elk's great vision, the crux of the entire book. Concerning the great vision received as a youth, the author recalled:

> Then I was standing on the highest mountain of them all, and round about beneath me was the whole hoop of the world. And while I stood there I saw more than I can tell and I understood more than I saw; for I was seeing in a sacred manner the shapes of all things in the spirit, and the shape of all shapes as they must live together like

one being. And I saw that the sacred hoop of my people was one of many hoops that made one circle, wide as daylight and as starlight, and in the center grew one mighty flowering tree to shelter all the children of one mother and one father. And I saw that it was holy. (Neihardt 1979: 43)

The book traces Black Elk's life as it threads through the milestones of his people's recent history: the battle of Little Bighorn/Greasy Grass where George Armstrong Custer met his fate, the near-annihilation of the buffalo, Buffalo Bill's Wild West show, the famine and disease of the early reservation era, and the Ghost Dance movement of the late nineteenth century. *Black Elk Speaks* reaches its climax with the bloody massacre of the Ghost Dancers at Wounded Knee, South Dakota in 1890. Looking upon the massacred bodies of innocent Lakota women, children, and men in the bloody snow, the author laments the loss of the dream of the sacred hoop wherein all things might have been restored to their proper relation:

And so it was all over. I did not know then how much was ended. When I look back now from this high hill of my old age, I can still see the butchered women and children lying heaped and scattered all along the crooked gulch as plain as when I saw them with eyes still young. And I can see that something else died there in the bloody mud, and was buried in the blizzard. A people's dream died there. It was a beautiful dream. (Neihardt 1979: 270)

For the reader who has just traveled along with Black Elk through the narrative of his life, this is perhaps the book's most powerful and lasting passage: "A people's dream died there. It was a beautiful dream." But a spate of recent scholarship has challenged whether it was indeed Black Elk who did the speaking. Transcripts of Neihardt's interviews with Black Elk indicate no such speech on Black Elk's part, and lend compelling support to the conclusion that Neihardt had taken poetic license and had cropped and retouched Black Elk's story for the sake of poignancy. Here was the final scene of an American tragedy: the vanishing Indian and the vanishing possibility of an Indian view of all things being related (Demallie 1984). Recent biographers of Black Elk have shown how Neihardt's editorial program further obscured how complex a religious figure Black Elk really was. He was indeed recognized as a traditional Lakota healer and holy man, but he was also a rather committed Roman Catholic catechist, a respected lay preacher. Baptized Nicholas Black Elk in 1905, he conducted thenceforward a dialogue between his Roman Catholicism and his Lakota tradition, filtered through a life of continuous service to his community as a spiritual leader. Half a century later, much has been made of the invention of Black Elk on the part of a burgeoning readership hungry for tragic images of beautiful, dying Native American visions that once were but no longer are. However, Demallie argues persuasively that although the "end of the dream" speech in question was Neihardt's and not Black Elk's, Neihardt was indeed seeking to capture the old man's melancholy concerning his dream and the sense of responsibility he felt for his people's plight (1984: 55).

Revisiting *Black Elk Speaks* in light of this idea has perhaps allowed Black Elk to speak anew by placing him in history as a complicated figure acting strategically for the betterment of his people and in obedience to his vision. But the effort has, in turn, arguably done Black Elk another kind of disservice. To view him merely as Neihardt's invention is to deny Black Elk's agency in the collaboration. Black Elk, after all, was no bumpkin. For example, while on tour with Buffalo Bill's Wild West Show in England, he evaded his chaperones and struck off to see Europe on his own. He later resurfaced in Paris, where he had lived for a time and had fallen in love. One should think no less of Black Elk's savvy when it came to his collaboration with Neihardt. After an immediate rapport had formed between them, he shared his story with Neihardt, apparently out of a sense of sacred obligation to extend his vision of renewal at a time of duress for his people. Black Elk took Neihardt ceremonially as a son, and their interviews proceeded in a ceremonialized fashion under Black Elk's direction. As Demallie puts it, "Neihardt perceived Black Elk's religion in terms of art, Black Elk perceived Neihardt's art in terms of religion" (1984: 37).

Curiously, *Black Elk Speaks* contains few overt references to Black Elk's Christian leanings, and the publication of the book in 1932 concerned Jesuit missionaries at the Pine Ridge Reservation because it depicted the aging catechist and pillar of the Lakota Catholic community as a resolute holy man still engaged with traditional Lakota religion. The conspicuous absence of references to his Christian influence has fueled a number of competing interpretations of the Black Elk of *Black Elk Speaks* (see Holler 1995). Was the Black Elk of the 1930s disaffected with his Christianity, eager to return to the traditions and vision of his youth by the time of Neihardt's visit? Or had his Christianity always been something of a ruse – an outward vehicle for an inwardly Lakota worldview?

Underlying the debate about the voice of the "real" Black Elk is the premise that "Lakota tradition" and "Christianity" are two clearly-bounded "isms" competing for Native souls. Perhaps missionaries viewed the matter this way, but interpretations that begin with this premise risk overlooking the possibility that Black Elk's own spiritual resolve did not find itself in a kind of religious either/or-ism. Indeed for many Native people – Black Elk perhaps among them – sacred matters are fundamentally matters of mystery that defy the attempts of the ordinary intellect to make complete sense of them. Besides, as the series of visions chronicled in *Black Elk Speaks* makes clear, the Lakota tradition made room for new visions, new songs, and new ceremonies.

For most of those who have seen fit to quote the "end of the dream" speech from *Black Elk Speaks*, its rhetorical power rests on the image of a traditional religion on its way out, tragically obsolete in an era when neither the buffalo nor the Lakota people move freely on the Plains. An aged, melancholy Black Elk telling of the end of his dream signified the end of the *traditional*, making his dream common property: a beautiful, safe, literary museum piece for all to see and share. But to suggest that the book is fundamentally Neihardt's invention is also to eclipse the powerful presence of Nicholas Black Elk in the book.

Black Elk can be viewed as a figure that brings the traditional and the historical into sharp focus: not as two inherently antagonistic entities in the midst of which he could be neither fully Lakota nor fully Christian. Black Elk was no mere relic of a bygone Lakota traditionalism, no mere mouthpiece of a traditional way that was now rendered obsolete with the collapse of the traditional way of life. Rather, as some recent studies have shown us, he was a resourceful spiritual leader who opted to collaborate with Neihardt because he wanted to extend his vision. He was one who may very well have sought to chart a new course through the sincere interplay of both Lakota and Christian religions (Holler 1995).

Hopi Prophecy: Time out of Time?

Another example of how traditional beliefs and practices breathe the atmosphere of new historical circumstances can be seen through Armin Geertz's recent interpretation of the dynamics of prophecy among today's Hopi community in northern Arizona. Among the Hopi, prophecies are afoot concerning the imminent end of this current world. Geertz shows how enmeshed the prophecies are with issues of Hopi history, identity, and politics. The prophecies speak of the inevitable consequences that face a world out of balance. Because they also incorporate the encounter with Europeans at the heart of the Hopi myth, published accounts of the prophecies have gained a wide readership among non-Native people. Books such as Frank Waters's *Book of the Hopi,* for example, have for years filled Native American shelves in bookstores from Santa Fe to Harvard Square. But the broad audience has a rather shallow appreciation for how the prophecies represent creative Hopi attempts to make sovereign sense of the historical circumstances in which they find themselves. Opposite the title page to Geertz's book is a telling photograph of Hopi elder Thomas Banyacya standing with Elizabeth Taylor and Jon Voight at a Hollywood event. Of the three, it is clearly Taylor and Voight who look star-struck.

The prophecies are far more than exotic stories that grant white people a central place in Hopi mythology. For Hopis, the prophecies remain firmly rooted in familiar Hopi narratives about the emergence of people into this current world. While narratives of end times vary among Hopis, each narrative centers on the return of Maasaw, the spirit who taught the Hopis how to live faithfully on the earth, over which Maasaw presides. Hopi narratives of origin teach that people emerged from a chaotic underworld through a place of emergence onto the surface of the current world. It was Maasaw who initially granted the people permission to emerge to the present world, after they agreed to follow his way of humility. When the people failed to live up to their promise, Maasaw granted them only "temporary residence," declaring that they must make their own way, and that he will "return to cleanse or punish them" (Geertz 1994: 331). The prophecies also converge on the notion that two brothers, one white and one Hopi, parted ways with respective portions of a stone tablet message. At some point, the white brother will return from the East and either "help" or "punish" the other brother for the misdeeds of the Hopi (depending on the version) and Maasaw's final purification will usher in a new world order.

As such, the prophecies and their interpretations bear directly on the historical encounter with European Americans and address issues of cultural contact. While Geertz reports that it is unclear when the Hopi prophecies emerged on the historical landscape, he observes that, on Hopi grounds, the prophecies precede the coming of Europeans and thus recast the tragedies of the past and the challenges of the Hopi future in a larger, indigenous framework. Through a kind of intellectual sovereignty, this framework helps the Hopi come to grips with the violence of contemporary experience and renders that experience as not simply the outcome of historical contingency, but as a meaningful consequence of the Hopi story. At this juncture in Hopi cultural history when the community faces a crossroads, the prophecies support a sense of profound agency in the Hopis' "symbolic control" of their destiny.

Hopi prophecies provide a traditional framework with which to make sense of historical experience, but Geertz explores how remarkably supple and responsive the prophecies are as resources of tradition. Less matters of "prediction" than "thread[s] in the total fabric of meaning," the prophecies are given to a wide range of variations and, in turn, lend themselves to changing interpretations that speak anew to differing circumstances (Geertz 1994: 324). In recent years, the prophecies have been transposed into the English language, have appeared in the printed word, and have reached audiences far beyond the customary controls guaranteed by oral transmission.

It is the prophecies that enable Hopis to assimilate their existence in history, associated as it is with the coming of Europeans and their rule, into a larger "cosmic vision" bearing the authority of Hopi tradition. Through the arts of prophecy, experiences of marginality in American society can become recentered. Displaced experience in a world out of balance can become resituated in terms of a Hopi center. "The idea of the end of the world," Geertz concludes, "is a strategy for living in the world" (p. 339).

The Muskogee Sacred Revolt

Just as we can view Black Elk and Hopi prophecy as illustrations of the historicity of the traditional, so can we fruitfully revisit religious movements that appear as historical novelties to appreciate how they remained rooted in traditions. There has been a refreshing awareness in recent scholarship of the central role of the sacred in many Native American movements that emerged in direct response to the colonization and dispossession of the eighteenth and nineteenth centuries. Such movements as the Handsome Lake Religion of the Senecas, the Ghost Dance, and the Peyote traditions are fascinating for the ways they marked dramatic changes in the social and moral order brought on by new historical circumstances (Mooney 1896; Slotkin 1956; Wallace 1972) The changes were often sweeping and varied. Among other things, they reconfigured gender roles, they placed a new emphasis on the afterlife, they helped forge an inter-tribal Native identity, and they generated spirited anti-colonial critiques of Euro-American society.

Perhaps these movements have attracted so much attention because they furnish evidence of religious change in direct response to post-contact history. Unlike the case of so-called *traditional* Native religions, such "new religious movements" offer freer access to the historian working from text-based sources. Usually, a movement's origins can be traced directly to a prophetic figure whose biography can be researched in archives and confidently written up. The result is a refreshing appreciation for the responsiveness of Native religions to the shifting demands of historical circumstance. Nevertheless, a danger lies in so emphasizing the novelty of such movements that crucial connections to indigenous traditions are eclipsed, for these movements were firmly grounded in what had come before.

We need not understand new movements like the one led by the Seneca prophet Handsome Lake as anomalous new visions simply filling the cultural vacuum left in the wake of colonization, or simply compensating for the loss of cultural coherence (*contra* Wallace 1972). Instead, we can appreciate how they serve as positive indigenous reappraisals of tradition, new visions that arise meaningfully from within the framework of tradition. Because the movements improvised to such an extent on those traditions, and because they were willing to borrow traditions across the conventional boundaries of tribe and culture, they may seem radically disjunctive. One might think, for example, that the Lakota version of the second Ghost Dance was not "authentically Lakota" because of its "pan-Indian" nature and because its source lay with a Paiute prophet in distant Nevada. The Ghost Dance might be construed as a desperate search for meaning from afar to fill a void of cultural incoherence at home.

Joel Martin offers an alternative model for understanding pan-tribal new religious movements in his treatment of the sacred dimensions of an early nineteenth-century movement among the Muskogee, or Creek, people of Alabama and Georgia (Martin 1991). With the collapse of the deerskin trade and, in turn, the collapse of the inter-cultural "middle ground" that had developed between the region's Native peoples, Euro-Americans, and African Americans, a large segment of the Muskogee community was drawn into an anticolonial movement, one that bucked all odds stacked against it. Poorly armed but spiritually convinced that their actions obeyed divine commands to purge their lands of colonizing presences, Muskogee people took a stand. They did so despite the military might of the U.S. and despite the fragility of Native communities destabilized after decades of divide and conquer strategies. The Redstick revolt, so named for the red clubs they carried, erupted among seven to nine thousand Muskogee and like-minded Native neighbors in July, 1813. The Redsticks tried unsuccessfully to link their movement with related movements in the North famously associated with Tecumseh and Tenskwatawa, the Shawnee prophet. By March of the following year, when United States forces had extinguished the revolt, two thousand rebels had died. Twenty years later, the vast majority of Muskogees were forcibly removed to lands west of the Mississippi.

The Redstick revolt had been fueled by a surprisingly wide range of different cultural and religious sources, an array that came together not as the patchwork solution of a culturally deprived, desperate people, but as a coherent response to spiritual direction (Martin 1991). The spiritual direction that visited Muskogee prophets fused together the ritual practices associated with the Muskogee's annual world renewal ceremony, the dance traditions of neighboring tribes, apocalyptic traditions filtered to the Muskogee through the Christianity of African Americans, and elaborate rituals that symbolically purified the land and community of colonizing influences. "Restoring the symbolic boundaries between Indians and whites," Martin observes, "became a religious duty, political revolt a sacred cause" (Martin 1997: 163). Although much of the anticolonialism was directed at external threats, the Redstick revolt was also driven by a rigorous anticolonial critique directed internally at those Muskogees who had departed from age-old land and community ethics for fuller integration into the American economy and society, as part of their own strategies for negotiating history.

The Redstick rebellion, representative indeed of numerous other prophetic movements that swept through Native North America in the late eighteenth and nineteenth centuries, was anti-colonial without being derivative of colonial experience. It was innovative, even eclectic, in posture, but in ways that were rooted in visionary experience and that made sense in the idiom of Muskogee tradition. Most importantly, the Redstick revolt demonstrated how profoundly religion mattered in the Muskogee's response to their historical circumstances. "Colonialism may have pushed," Martin concludes, "but even more important, the sacred pulled Native American peoples into a new religious world"(1991: 182).

Native and Christian? Ojibwa Hymn Singing

It is a fact that many Native people today identify themselves as Christians. Can it be that they are both "Native" and "Christian" at the same time? Of course it can, but the fact that conventional wisdom assumes they cannot bespeaks the entrenched nature of the false opposition between the *traditional* and *historical* (Treat 1996). The emergence of various Native Christian communities is seldom the straightforward outcome of conversion or acculturation in the wake of the collision of cultures. To be sure, the message of Christianity and the cultural assumptions with which missionaries associated it were new to Native people. Further, the history of missionary exchange involved a deeply disturbing dimension of cultural coercion and violence (Tinker 1993). But Native Christians have not simply been on the receiving end of missionary history. They have improvised in creative and complex ways on both Christianity and their respective traditions. To illustrate this, we can fruitfully turn to a rich tradition of hymn-singing among Minnesota's Ojibwa, or Anishinaabe, people. This is but one of many stories of Native Christianity, and it may not be representative of those Native Christian communities that view their religion in sharp relief from their indigenous traditions. But the story of Ojibwa hymn-singing does evoke a sense of how Christian forms can become, at least for a significant number of Minnesota Ojibwa, consistent with and even emblematic of indigenous traditions.

Beginning in the 1830s, Protestant missionaries in the western Great Lakes promoted translations of their favorite hymns into the Native language.

Missionaries touted the hymn as a particularly effective means for rooting out Indianness and for inculcating an Anglo-American, evangelical, agrarian way of life. For their part, Ojibwa people listened intently to the new songs – even more intently, missionaries feared, than they listened to the spoken Word. Accustomed for generations to the practice of sharing new songs across cultural boundaries, Ojibwa people began to incorporate the hymns into their repertory. By the 1870s, when Ojibwa communities were confined to reservations, and more subject to the discipline of the mission and the Indian agent, the practice of hymn-singing appears to have taken on more urgency. Although missionary documents seldom refer to the sermons, theology, and structure of Native-led gatherings, references abound to the hymn-singing frequently heard in those gatherings. The missionaries who documented the practice typically encountered the singing in church, but it is clear that the music they occasionally heard had its own momentum and was most at home in distinctively Anishinaabe spaces: the tarpaper shacks that dotted the reservation and the temporary dwellings at maple sugaring or wild rice camps. The performances in these non-church settings were elaborately ritualized, the province of particular groups of men and women respectively known as "singing and praying bands." Led by respected elders, these groups met almost nightly in prayer meetings where hymn singing, prayer, counsel, and food were exchanged. Resources were pooled to keep food on the table, pay for community burials, and purchase capital equipment like ploughs and oxen. Singing groups traveled widely in the community, sometimes bearing witness to other Anishinaabe people and sometimes singing through the night at the sickbeds and deathbeds of the community. The music impressed missionaries as particularly soulful. It was always sung *a cappella* to a slow and solemn tempo, and was interspersed with long ceremonial speeches.

It was not simply for the beauty of the voices that missionaries relished the chance to hear familiar tunes sung in the Native idiom. Missionaries were hopeful that what they were hearing was nothing less than the "sound of civilization." As they listened, they were watching closely for evidence that the outward form was truly registering inner realities of cultural transformation. For example, in 1881, Episcopalian Bishop Henry B. Whipple wrote:

> I am always deeply touched with their singing. The *wild* Indian voice is harsh. Nothing could be more discordant than their wild yell and hideous war song. The religion of Christ softened this; their voices became plaintive, and as they sing from the heart their hymns are full of emotion. (Whipple 1881)

Because missionaries expected so much of it, Native hymn-singing was decidedly on display when performed in their presence. The conspicuous absence of the drum and dance made hymn-singing a different matter altogether from other Anishinaabe sacred music. Moreover, the sung texts of the hymns told Christian stories. Though they often used words highly charged with the idiom of indigenous religious thought, the hymn texts were not deemed comparable to the incantational words through which other sacred Anishinaabe songs brought spiritual power to bear. In these respects, missionaries were not entirely wrong when they construed hymn-singing to be a kind of performed devaluation of Ojibwa tradition, an accommodation to the missionary enterprise and a marked departure from the spirituality of the drum, dance, and dream.

But a closer look reveals that accommodation was not the whole story, for the sometimes subtle ways that Ojibwa singers ritualized singing made room for the continued performance of Ojibwa tradition. The hymns, after all, were no casual matter. They were sung by discrete groups of singers that were not unlike Ojibwa drum societies in their commitment to music-making as part of a larger way of life and tied to a higher standard of conduct. Sung by night, in prayer meetings and increasingly at funeral wakes, hymns became indigenized as associated with moments of particular challenge in the life of the struggling, often starving, reservation communities. In these highly ritualized performance contexts, the songs no longer meant merely what they meant at the level of text. They drew on indigenous understandings of the power of song to transform, to restore right relations within a community torn by factionalism and disease, and to restore right relations between the people and the spiritual sources of life.

If those Anishinaabe people who sang hymns were performing their accommodation to the Christian tradition, they were also performing their resolve to invest that religion with distinctively Anishinaabe ways of valuing land, community, and spirituality. This would explain the frequency of references to hymn-singing and the apparent centrality of the practice at wakes and other charged moments in the life of a community trying to negotiate difficult reservation circumstances. Like Black Elk, the singing and praying bands were trying to integrate the old and the new as a spiritual foundation for the continuation of a viable Anishinaabe way of life.

The tradition of hymn-singing remains vital one hundred years later on the reservations of northern Minnesota, where it takes an important place on the contemporary religious landscape. As was true in the 1870s, hymns are still sung by discrete groups of singers who consider music-making to be part of a larger calling that involves a high standard of ethical conduct and spiritual mettle. The music is still associated largely with the funeral wakes held at night in parish halls, homes, and gymnasiums, where the singers come, often unsolicited, to offer the gift of spirited singing in the Native language. The Ojibwa hymns are still sung *a cappella*, and are also still sung so slowly as to resemble the chanting of syllables rather than the conveying of the meaningful content of words and sentences. Given the tragically low rates of fluency in the Native language, few people today understand the lexical meaning of the songs. Yet, at many wakes, a visit by "the singers" can play a critical role in the grieving process.

There is an intriguing irony to this story. For many Ojibwa people today, the singing of those same hymns that were promoted by missionaries in order to eradicate what was distinctive about Ojibwa culture has become a profound expression of a distinctively Ojibwa value system. And, at least on the White Earth reservation, the elders who sing those songs in the Native language are widely regarded as among the more traditional people of the community.

But is the story really that ironic after all? If our view of religious culture is already in motion, we are prepared to see how this particular form of sacred song could become, over time, a part of a traditional Anishinaabe way of life. There are indeed some Anishinaabe people who do not share this spiritual connection to Native-language hymns. For them, the hymns may be emblems of the violence and dispossession that the historical encounter with European Christianity represents to them. But even such critics accord an uncommon level of respect for the elders who sing the hymns at wakes. As one hymn singer reflected, the Anishinaabe tradition had such respect for the fundamental mystery of the sacred that it had always made room for new songs, new visions, and new stories. In this instance of Native Christianity, tradition and history are far from incompatible; instead they are mutually reinforcing.

Conclusions

These four snapshots of native religion indicate the historical motion of Native American religious traditions. Though a more thorough exploration of each is warranted, these brief glimpses at Black Elk, Hopi prophecy, the Redstick rebellion, and Ojibwa hymn-singing show how myth, ritual, and the resources of religion have been at the center of Native people's efforts to survive. In each case, religion has mediated the tensions between continuity and change by conjoining tradition *and* history in important ways.

It is Pueblo novelist Leslie Marmon Silko who perhaps most artfully illustrates the complex relationship between tradition and history, as well as the centrality of the sacred in mediating the two. In her novel, *Ceremony*, the protagonist is a Pueblo veteran who has returned home from the Second World War to a life of alienation and illness. His wanderings are continually beset by unidentified hostile forces, which Silko's characters refer to as "the witchery." His struggle reaches a turning point in a conversation with a spiritual leader named Old Betonie, a recluse who lives on a foothill overlooking Gallup, New Mexico. Surrounded by stacks of telephone books, newspapers, and calendars – the ritual paraphernalia with which the holy man performs his unconventional prayers for the world – Old Betonie tells him:

> At one time, the ceremonies as they had been performed were enough for the way the world was then. But after the white people came, elements in this world began to shift; and it became necessary to create new ceremonies . . . [T]hings which don't shift and grow are dead things. They are things the witchery people want. Witchery works to scare people, to make them fear growth. But it has always been necessary, and more than ever now, it is. Otherwise we won't make it. We won't survive. That's what the witchery is counting on: that we will cling to the ceremonies the way they were, and then their power will triumph and the people will be no more. (Silko 1977: 126)

From this moment on, Silko's protagonist begins to see what it is that ails him and what he must do to set things aright. The witchery, as it happens, includes the lie that real things do not change.

Because change happens, tradition and history have always met in Native American religions. Native cultures have been in motion since long before Columbus set sail. What has changed since Columbus is the way that colonization has constrained the capacity of Native communities to respond to change on their own terms. Indeed, for all the thoroughgoing diversity among hundreds of distinctive Native religious traditions, their most striking common denominator may be the shared historical experience of colonization and dispossession. Far from rendering traditional religions obsolete, these historical circumstances have curiously underscored tradition, heightening the urgency with which Native communities muster the resources of tradition in response to rapid change. Whether a native community symbolizes and experiences the sacred in corn, cattail pollen, cactus buttons, or thunderbirds, whether their stories teach that human beings first emerged from an underworld, migrated from the East, or transformed after a flood, each Native community has turned to its spiritual resources to help navigate history. If our books and lectures can show Native religious traditions in this kind of historical motion, we will not only find more specific and satisfying ways to integrate Native American traditions into our larger narratives. We will also dramatically enrich our appreciation for how religion matters in the history of North America.

NOTE

I am grateful for the assistance of Devon Anderson and Jenna Merritt in this endeavor.

BIBLIOGRAPHY

Demaillie, Raymond (ed.) (1984) *The Sixth Grandfather: Black Elk's Treachings Given to John G. Neilhardt*, Lincoln, Neb.: University of Nebraska Press.

Eliade, Mircea (1974) *Cosmos and History: The Myth of the Eternal Return*, trans. Willard Trask, Princeton, NJ: Princeton University Press; first published 1949.

Feld, Stephen (1990) *Sound and Sentiment: Birds, Weeping, Poetics, and Song in Kaluli Expression*, Philadelphia, Pa.: University of Pennsylvania Press.

Geertz, Armin (1994) *The Invention of Prophecy*, Berkeley, Calif.: University of California Press.

Hallowell, A. Irving (1955) *Culture and Experience*, Philadelphia, Pa.: University of Pennsylavania Press.

Holler, Clyde (1995) *Black Elk's Religion: The Sun Dance and Lakota Catholicism*, Syracuse, NY: Syracuse University Press.

Martin, Calvin (ed.) (1987) *The American Indian and the Problem of History*, New York: Oxford University Press.

Martin, Joel (1991) *Sacred Revolt: The Muskogees' Struggle for a New World*, Boston, Mass.: Beacon Press.

Martin, Joel (1997) "Indians, contact, and colonialism in the Deep South: themes for a post-colonial history of Amerian religion," in Thomas Tweed (ed.) *Retelling U.S. Religious History*, Berkeley, Calif.: University of California Press, pp. 149–80.

McNally, Michael D. (1997) "The uses of Ojibwa hymn-singing at White Earth: toward a history of practice," in David D. Hall (ed.) *Lived Religion in America*, Princeton, NJ: Princeton University Press, pp. 133–59.

—— (forthcoming) *Ojibwe Singers*, New York: Oxford University Press.

Mooney, James (1896) *The Ghost Dance Religion*, Washington, DC: Bureau of American Ethnology.

Neihardt, John (ed.) (1979) *Black Elk Speaks*, Lincoln, Neb.: University of Nebraska Press; first published 1932.

Rosaldo, Renato (1989) *Culture and Truth*, Boston, Mass.: Beacon Press.

Silko, Leslie Marmon (1977) *Ceremony*, New York: Penguin Books.

Slotkin, J. S. (1956) *The Peyote Religion*, Glencoe, Ill.: The Free Press.

Tinker, George (1993) *Missionary Conquest: The Gospel and Native American Cultural Genocide*, Minneapolis, Minn.: Fortress Press.

Treat, James (1996) *Native and Christian: Indigenous Voices on Religious Identity in the U.S. and Canada*, New York: Routledge.

Vizenor, Gerald (1989) "Socio-acupuncture: mythic reversals and the striptease," in Calvin Martin (ed.) *The American Indian and the Problem of History*, New York: Oxford University Press, pp. 180–91.

Wallace, Anthony F. C. (1972) *The Death and Rebirth of the Seneca*, New York: Random House.

Whipple, Henry B. (1881) in *Minnesota Missionary* IV, no. 10 (July).

Part VI

Gender and Family

Introduction

As in much of American history, women enjoyed very limited visibility in studies of American religion until the advent of modern feminism during the late 1960s radically shifted academic angles of vision. Such women as were visible – Anne Hutchinson, Harriet Beecher Stowe, Ellen G. White, Mary Baker Eddy, Aimee Semple McPherson – were generally those who attracted attention, often of a negative or ambiguous sort, through their controversial teachings and behavior and flamboyant personalities. These women, to be sure, are entitled to a prominent place in religious history, but the matrix in which their careers are to be assessed has shifted considerably with the entry of large numbers of women into the historical profession (among them nearly half of the contributors to this volume).

One reason for the scarcity of women in the annals of American religion lies in the institutional fact that, with minor exceptions, women were barred from the ordained ministry in almost all major denominations until well into the twentieth century (and are still excluded from that role by Roman Catholics, Eastern Orthodox, Orthodox Jews, most Southern Baptist churches, and a number of other conservative groups). Even in Roman Catholic women's religious orders, where women were able to exercise substantial executive authority in administering schools and hospitals as well as convent life itself, an ethic of self-effacement generally kept their leaders, not to mention the rank and file, out of the historical spotlight. Since religious, like other, historiography tended until recently to focus on institutions and those who attained public prominence within their leadership, it is not surprising that this inattention should have been the case.

As social historians have shifted the perspective on the study of women's roles in American religious history, the nineteenth century has emerged as especially crucial. It was a time when many women were forced to sort out the implications of the disruptive changes that beset American society during these decades. In an agriculturally based colonial society, when their energies were needed as part of a collective family enterprise, there was little leisure for most women to devote to public or cultural matters, except perhaps for churchgoing. As an emergent market economy gave rise to a substantial middle class, however, the role of women became more problematic as their economic functions shifted. A doctrine of "separate spheres" emerged, in which men operated in an often amoral public world of commerce while women were designated the moral guardians of home and family. While some women accepted this division as suited to the nature of things, others directly or indirectly challenged its limitations. Many enterprising and committed women began to appropriate the realms of religion, reform, and education as extensions of this domestic sphere in which they could exercise their "proper" role. Middle-class Catholic, Protestant, and Jewish laywomen organized and staffed the innumerable voluntary societies that began to arise early in the nineteenth century and concerned themselves with every manner of good work from foreign missions to anti-slavery to immigrant relief. It is in this institutional context that many of the ideas were forged and skills developed that would eventually be channeled into more secular challenges to the notion of a constricted "women's sphere."

In the realm of religion proper, as Carolyn Haynes points out in her contribution, women have been historically far more visible in pews than in the pulpit (although, as Karla Goldman notes, women were invisible to men in traditional Jewish services since they were sequestered in a balcony). American women have thus always played a substantial but not highly visible role in congregational life from colonial times until well into the twentieth century. Even from this vantage, however, women have not been without influence. Ann Douglas, in her *The Feminization of American Culture* (1977), argued that during the nineteenth century Protestant women in particular formed a tacit alliance with male clergy in creating a distinctive religious ethos; in it traditional Calvinist rigor was displaced by a "feminized" piety and theology stressing the nurturing and maternal rather than the judgmental character of the Christian deity. Popular fiction, much of it written by what Nathaniel Hawthorne dismissed as "that damned mob of scribbling women," also contributed materially to this transformation of sensibility through the sentimental work of Harriet Beecher Stowe, Elizabeth Stuart Phelps, and a host of others. A parallel phenomenon was the feminization of Roman Catholic piety through pious practices such as devotional exercises focused on the Sacred Hearts of Jesus and Mary, during roughly this same period.

This section might be prefaced by *Amanda Porterfield*'s essay in section II, in which she reflects on the implications of the career and personality of the Puritan "heresiarch" Anne Hutchinson.

Karla Goldman addresses the transformation of Jewish women's roles in the nineteenth century in the broader context of changes in the role and even the architecture of the synagogue. Although Reform Judaism especially brought women from their traditional place in the balcony into ground-floor seating with their families, the constriction of religious and social activities by the synagogue itself left them little room to exercise religious influence. It was only the later challenge of Eastern European immigration that provided them with new roles in an expanding sphere of synagogue activity.

Carolyn Haynes deals with the Protestant realm, in which the "separate spheres" doctrine was especially powerful. She argues that Christian feminists adopted a variety of strategies, some confrontational, others more subtle, in attempting to expand their impact on the religious sphere. These included extensive activity in the realm of education, reform, and missions, as well as theological attacks on traditional Calvinism.

Anne Rose studies the nineteenth-century family as the mediator of religious experience. At a time when the forces of modernity were eroding the ascription of religious identity on the basis of family membership, growing numbers of Americans were exercising newly won rights of free choice arrived at through romantic attraction. Not only this, they were also crossing religious boundaries in choosing mates. How spouses of differing backgrounds accommodated one another, especially in the raising of children, often proved to be a matter of complex negotiation.

Chapter 20

Reform, Gender, and the Boundaries of American Judaism

Karla Goldman

A central marker of the reform and Americanization of the synagogue in the nineteenth century was the changing shape of public religious life, an evolution that was expressed both in synagogue design and in the changing configuration of activities and interests associated with Jewish institutions and community. The shifting boundaries of nineteenth-century public Jewish religious life reflected a variety of concerns and pressures emerging from interaction with the American environment, yet all such changes must be seen in light of the defining character of women's presence in the nineteenth-century synagogue. A focus upon the discrete reconfigurations of the American synagogue's physical and communal structure reveals the extent to which the shape of public American Judaism has been determined by the space given to women's physical presence in the synagogue and to their presence in synagogue activity and life.

Like many European synagogues, America's earliest synagogues, built during the colonial era, adopted the sanctuary design introduced by Amsterdam's Spanish-Portuguese Jewish community during the seventeenth century. These synagogues integrated lateral balconies, used as women's galleries, into a symmetrical building design. American synagogues replicated this layout, yet the second synagogue building in what was to become the United States, Newport, Rhode Island's 1763 Touro Synagogue, adjusted the design by including a balustrade with a low rail, thus dispensing with the additional grids, curtains, and lattice-works that marked European versions of this space. This innovation was repeated in subsequent American synagogue buildings, including Charleston's Beth Elohim built in 1794, New York's Shearith Israel building from 1818, and Philadelphia's 1824 Mikveh Israel.

This adjustment in the physical structure of American synagogues reflected a consciousness on the part of Jewish synagogue leaders of a need to reframe women's presence and status in public worship. These leaders were sensitive to observations like that of one 1744 non-Jewish visitor who described the gallery assigned to women at New York's Shearith Israel, built in 1730, as being much like a "hen coop" (see Goldman, *Beyond the Gallery*, for citation references). In addition, evidence of attempts to regulate where women should sit within the gallery and of actual fights in the gallery between fathers hoping to secure specific seats for their daughters suggests that unlike what we know about European synagogues at this time, unmarried women actually attended on a regular basis.

An 1825 letter from Rebecca Gratz in Philadelphia which noted that "we all go [to the synagogue] Friday evening as well as on Saturday morning - the gallery is as well filled as the other portion of the house" implies that in this community women had begun to understand synagogue attendance as one expected and regular aspect of their religious duties. Similarly, an 1853 petition from fifteen women at Cincinnati's Bene Israel congregation, in which they identified themselves as "the ladies who regularly attend divine worship," indicates that some American Jewish women had begun to understand their own identity as Jews in relation to the synagogue. This was an unprecedented situation within a tradition in which the synagogue had always been principally a male sphere and women's religiosity had centered on the home.

Eventually, continued adjustments to the gallery could no longer contain the weight of women's presence and the pressure of societal expectations that a woman's religious nature should be evident through her presence in the church as well as through her piety in the home. Ultimately, the synagogue had to be reconfigured to respond to the changing ways in which American Jewish women were expressing their religious and Jewish identities.

In 1851, a breakaway Albany congregation led by reformer Isaac Mayer Wise adopted the mixed-gender use of family pews when the group moved into a former church building and adopted the existing design rather than build additional balconies to create the customary women's gallery. Similarly, three years later, Temple Emanu-El in New York took over and utilized the existing family pews of the church building that they had bought for synagogue use. Within the new Emanu-El building, family pews were one component of a wide range of revisions of traditional synagogue practice; they included an abridged liturgy, elaborately orchestrated organ and choir music, emphasis on a service leader who intoned the worship service in distinguished and modulated tones, and a regular vernacular sermon. These innovations displayed prominently in the 1854 synagogue of Temple Emanu-El, which was patronized by some of the nation's most prominent and distinguished Jews, offered an influential model which other communities could adopt as the pattern for an Americanized Judaism. It is worth noting that all of these reforms found parallels in German Reform efforts, except for mixed seating which remained an exclusively American innovation until well into the twentieth century.

Women never could have been integrated into the main congregation at Emanu-El, if the congregation itself had not been transformed. In traditional Jewish worship settings the male congregants played a vital part in the proceedings, participating in the Torah service and other aspects of the service. Although a traditional service would have a leader, it was understood that he mainly marked time for the congregation as each individual made his own way through the liturgy. By contrast, services at Temple Emanu-El were all led and orchestrated by a reader – who having been taken from the reader's traditional position in the midst of the congregation, and moved to an elevated position at the front of the sanctuary – became the center of attention and of the service. One observer of the new Temple Emanu-El described a service in which "The minister and reader do all the praying, the organ and choir perform the music." The congregants themselves had been transformed into spectators: "the visitors appear as mere dummies . . . the visitor acts no part, but that of *auditor* . . . . except for an occasional rising from the seat, the congregation does not participate in the worship." Women became emancipated just in time to become part of an assembly that was rapidly losing its identity as a traditional *kahal* (community); the congregation was now often referred to as an "audience." Women did gain a sort of equality with men as worshipers in the sanctuary, but it was a role that had already been greatly devalued. Women had gained the right to join men in the shrinking role of congregant.

An emerging Reform Judaism at mid-century, building upon Emanu-El's model, found expression in the many opulent synagogues that appeared in America's urban centers from New York to San Francisco in the years after the Civil War, all proclaiming the achievement and refinement of America's Jews. These temples were home to a self-conscious and focused effort, driven by German-trained rabbis, to create a public Judaism that would satisfy the needs of an Americanized Jewish population. Acculturated congregations hoped to associate themselves with the decorum and respectability of religious sanctuaries occupied by established members of America's social and religious elites.

Apart from a few determinedly orthodox settings, all of these new homes for an Americanized Judaism emphasized the repositioning and integration of women within Jewish religious space. Male Jewish leaders saw the introduction of this innovation as completely consistent with their drive for respectability. The 1863 annual address of the president of the Indianapolis Hebrew Congregation proudly reported that in the congregation's new building, "Ladies & Gentlemen are seated together, which" as he pointed out "is nothing more than civilization demands." And women occupied the family pews of these magnificent temples in force, coming to dominate regular synagogue attendance as men increasingly attended to business concerns on the Jewish day of rest.

The success of the mid-nineteenth century American Jewish reformers in shaping a decorous and refined synagogue ceremonial into the dominant expression of Judaism had perhaps unforeseen consequences for American Judaism's ability to elaborate new public identities for women beyond that of synagogue-goer. This reorientation of worship space and gender roles within the synagogue, which Reformers would later describe as an act of emancipation for women, had decidedly mixed effects. In Christian churches, woman's numerical dominance of the pews was reinforced by her central role in general church-related activity. Historians have described the years after the Civil War as an era when the expansion of Christian women's work for benevolence and social reform was incorporated locally and nationally into organizations that gave life and vitality to churches and to church work. Since Jewish women modeled their synagogue attendance on patterns identified with American churches, we might have expected the integration of women into the synagogue to be accompanied by a galvanizing of women's energies, in order to serve the needs of the synagogue in a manner akin to that demonstrated by activist Christian women. Yet the integration of women into the main sanctuary of the synagogue was part of a larger movement that reoriented the synagogue *away* from just the kind of engagement and activity that female presence and energy was bringing to so many American churches and Christian denominations.

The effort to present an impressive ceremony in a magnificent edifice became so much the focus of congregational concerns for acculturating Jews, that the many activities that had been associated with earlier synagogue-communities tended to fade away. In 1859 one traditionalist congregational leader in Cincinnati reported that, despite the efforts of an ambitious reforming rabbi, "with the exception of having the choir with female singers we have no change in the service." Yet despite this claim, and even though the process of ritual reform may indeed have been stalling, the Jewish community of Cincinnati had already been transformed. Issues that had formed the core of congregational concerns for years had quietly disappeared. Since the arrival of the city's two activist reform rabbis Isaac M. Wise and Max Lilienthal, the city's most conservative congregation had dispensed with its ritual bath (*mikveh*), its committee on religious rules, its "killing committee," which had supervised the community's provision of Kosher meat, and its ritual slaughterer. By divesting their synagogues of the many day-to-day concerns of Jewish life, Cincinnati's acculturating Jews and their rabbis narrowed the synagogal sphere to the specific realm of public worship, its conduct and its setting. In the process, and with other congregations across the country, they helped to redefine the parameters of Jewish life.

In most communities a Reform emphasis on refining and rationalizing synagogue ritual rendered many of the various communal activities that had been associated with the synagogue suddenly irrelevant. Many extra-synagogal services and organizations which had been connected with the congregations, such as Ladies' Benevolent Societies, tended to fade into the background or dissolve entirely. Women's groups associated with synagogues had often been important fund-raisers and loan-sources when ante-bellum synagogue building costs were in the range of around $10,000. Although women's fund-raising efforts continued in many localities, their contributions became proportionately less significant in the years after the Civil War, when suddenly Jews were erecting edifices that cost hundreds of thousands of dollars. Women continued, both individually and collectively, to present congregations with gifts that had long fallen in the province of women to give: specifically Torah mantles, covers for the reading desk, and especially curtains for the ark. But there was nothing regularized about their efforts, which arose in response to particular requests. Women's contributions to their congregations did not represent the work of sustained organized groups pursuing a systematic plan of work or a continuing purpose.

As before the advent of mixed seating, the emancipated ladies of the Reform temple had little authority over any aspect of synagogue activity, even over those activities which late twentieth-century observers would simply assume had been given over to women. Records indicate that many responsibilities that might have been assigned to women were assumed by men. The board of trustees of Cleveland's Tifereth Israel in the 1870s and 1880s, for example, regularly formed male committees to decorate the synagogue for special events and to organize picnics for the school children. One explanation or perhaps result of this situation was that in this period the congregation actually took responsibility for very few matters besides those relating to the synagogue building, worship, and school.

Although women continued to play important roles most particularly in congregational religious schools, their benevolent and educational work was often subsumed under male supervision. The school director of San Francisco's congregation Sherith Israel captured this situation when he responded to a recommendation that the congregation employ a lady principal. "We do not approve it," the director declared in his 1871 report to the congregation, "Without venturing upon an argument on the question we unhesitatingly affirm that only under the leadership of qualified men can the School prosper. Ladies however can assist in the work."

A trend towards centralization in philanthropy also undermined women's activism. The charitable role which so many women's groups had assumed in Jewish communities was often subsumed into community-wide charity groups that were not directly affiliated with congregations and did not generally have women as leaders. Cincinnati's female benevolent societies continued to exist but, with the establishment of a general Relief Society, their work became proportionately less important. In many cities, the existing ladies' societies simply became contributors to other male-led distributing groups.

Even in Philadelphia, where Rebecca Gratz and numerous other committed women had established societies and institutions such as the Hebrew Sunday School Society whose good work was powerfully identified with female leadership, the work of benevolent women clearly had lost its salience. The Jewish Foster Home established in 1855 was, with the exception of organized relief for sick and wounded soldiers of the Civil War, the last major independent effort of Philadelphia's German Jewish women. And even this organization was ceded to male leadership in 1874 when the female board of directors was replaced by a male board of managers, assisted by "Ladies of the Associate Board."

The American Jewish attempt to prove that the American synagogue could be seen as a parallel to the churches of respectable Christian denominations had created a truncated religious community limited to the purposes of preaching, governance, and formalized worship. Jewish men found fuller communal expression through the elaboration of a network of secular Jewish clubs and societies, like the Bnai Brith. Women's access to such organizations was much more limited. Paradoxically, a series of reforms, including mixed choirs and mixed seating, intended to emancipate women in the synagogue left them with a defined public religious space but little to do.

Reform's initial solution to the problem of woman's synagogal denigration in a society which honored women as religious exemplars did not prove sufficient.

Like the traditionalists before them they still had to struggle with the dichotomy between American expectations of female religiosity and the religious roles available to Jewish women in America. A resolution of this tension occurred in the 1890s, when a combination of circumstances opened up the possibility of more active roles for women among America's acculturated Jewish population which in turn helped to reframe the parameters of public American Judaism.

First of all, the opening of a flood of immigration by Eastern European Jews beginning in the 1880s gave Americanized Jewish women who had little connection with the grassroots objects of Christian women's activism like temperance and missionary work, something to do. The creation of new women's organizations or the reframing of old ones to serve the needs of new immigrants was quickly reflected in the founding of the National Council of Jewish Women in 1893, a national organization that gave impetus to an expansion of women's organizational life at the local level.

In many locales, women remained a vital part of congregational and community efforts to welcome and support the hundreds of thousands of immigrant Jews, who continued to stream into the United States, halted only by World War I and the immigrant restriction acts of 1921 and 1924. Yet, as social service agencies arose to serve this population and much of the immigrant aid work became professionalized, the benevolent work performed by Lady Visitors was increasingly marginalized. Rather than retiring back to their homes, women who had entered organizational life to help immigrants learned to shift the focus of their efforts.

Instead of gathering as *ad hoc* groups of women to advance particular and limited congregational projects, women started to undertake their responsibilities on a permanent organized basis as congregations turned to them to look to the physical, charitable, and social needs of the community. The activation of female energy for the benefit of the congregation was a critical component in an effort by the graduates of the recently established Hebrew Union College to re-expand the synagogal sphere beyond the narrow scope of worship. Another wave of synagogue building in the 1890s and early twentieth century brought massive temple complexes. They were intended not only to frame respectable Jewish worship but to house the expanding and variegated institutional life that could no longer be contained in older buildings that consisted of little more than sanctuaries.

In their efforts to adapt traditional culture to a modern way of life, acculturating Jews aspired to a particular American religious aesthetic. By attempting to enact a decorous and orderly synagogue worship style, they followed the example set by middle- and upper-class American Protestants. In so doing, they distinguished themselves from both the raucous scenes of traditional synagogues and the often disreputable fervor of American camp meetings and revivals. Within this carefully delineated aesthetic space, they recognized that gender arrangements worked as sensitive barometers of gentility.

Accordingly, the Reform temple, built as an ornate and monumental home for Jewish religious identity, ceremonially and symbolically granted women worshipers equal status with male congregants. But this synagogue full of women nonetheless remained a male-defined sphere, guided spiritually by male rabbis and financially by male boards of trustees. Although this did not substantively distinguish male-led American synagogues from male-led American churches, Jewish Reformers were unable to find a way to construct substantive responsibilities for women within an institution that continued to be governed by the assumption of exclusive male membership and leadership. The expansion of activity and space that characterized the synagogue of the 1890s reflected the realization that a vibrant synagogue needed to be in touch with life beyond the sanctuary. With the expansion of public Jewish religiosity, acculturated Jewish women finally found appropriate ways to emulate the activism of Christian women and yet remain identified with Judaism.

Every major transformation of the American synagogue was, thus, integrally associated with major redefinitions of the place that women were to take within and outside their walls. The earliest American synagogues distinguished themselves from their European antecedents and contemporaries by opening up the women's gallery, breaking down the barrier that had concretized the ritual marginalization of women in public Jewish worship. The introduction of family pews in the synagogues of most of America's acculturating Jews shortly after mid-century signaled a reform effort that put institutional constructions of Judaism squarely in the synagogue. When Reform and other American rabbinical and lay leaders, towards the end of the nineteenth century, faced the reality, created by this extreme emphasis upon creating decorous ritual, of enervated and lifeless synagogues, women again played a central role in transforming synagogue structure and emphasis. The contributions and energies of women, organized into congregationally-oriented groups, allowed their synagogues to expand beyond the sanctuary into a broadened expression of Jewish religious and institutional life.

Women's steady presence within the nineteenth-century American synagogue constituted an evolving claim upon communal identity and status, which ultimately helped to redefine the communities of which they were a part. This pattern would be replicated in the twentieth century, when shifts in the American cultural climate raised the question of women's right to serve as figures of religious authority. For many years women in synagogue sisterhoods had sustained much of the communal, social, and, practical aspects of congregational life. These decades of service established the legitimacy of the call for recognition of the value and worth of women's participation within their religious communities. The record of women's invaluable contributions to liberal American synagogues made it difficult to argue that women's rights in that sphere should be any less than that of men. Like earlier innovations which shifted women's religious identity, the ordination of the first American woman rabbi in 1972 signaled a profound restructuring of the encounter of modern Jews with the traditions of Judaism, just as it signaled a major redefinition of synagogue leadership and life. Attention to the gendered history of the American synagogue offers the important information that even within a tradition that has often been portrayed as immune to the impact of women's participation and contributions, the impact of gender tensions in shaping communal religious life and experience has not been limited to the feminist and "post-feminist" eras. Women's presence at public worship redefined the physical structure of the synagogue in eighteenth- and mid-nineteenth-century synagogues. The ability of late-nineteenth-century acculturated Jewish women to create and participate in institutions of their own transformed the face of Jewish institutional life. In their quest to create a properly American Judaism, late-nineteenth-century American Jews, just like their late-twentieth-century counterparts, had to reconcile the demands of traditional culture with the ever-shifting societal ideals for women's roles and religious identities.

BIBLIOGRAPHY

Bodeck, Evelyn (1983) "'Making do,' Jewish women in philanthropy," in Murray Friedman (ed.) *Jewish Life in Philadelphia, 1830–1940*, Philadelphia, Pa.: Institute for the Study of Human Issues.

Goldman, Karla (1995) "In search of an American Judaism: rivalry and reform in the growth of two Cincinnati synagogues," in Jeffrey S. Gurock and Marc Raphael Lee (eds) *An Inventory of Promises: Essays on American Jewish History in Honor of Moses Rischin*, Brooklyn: Carlson Publishing.

—— (forthcoming) *Beyond the Gallery: Finding a Place for Women in American Judaism*, Cambridge, Mass.: Harvard University Press.

Jick, Leon A. (1976) *The Americanization of the Synagogue, 1820–1870*, Hanover, NH: University Press of New England.

Kaufman, David (1998) *Shul with a Pool: The "Synagogue-Center" in American Jewish History*, Hanover, NH: University Press of New England.

Stern, Meyer (1895) *The Rise and Progress of Reform Judaism, Embracing a History made from the official Records of Temple Emanu-El of New York, with a Description of Salem Field Cemetery*, New York.

Wischnitzer, Rachel (1964) *Synagogue Architecture in the United States*, Philadelphia, Pa.: Jewish Publication Society.

Chapter 21

Women and Protestantism in Nineteenth-century America

Carolyn Haynes

Writing on etiquette and American society in the 1830s, Frances Trollope explained the vital presence of women in Protestant churches by quipping that "it is from the clergy only that the women of America receive that sort of attention which is so dearly valued by every female heart throughout the world" (quoted in Marty 1986: 98). While Trollope's interpretation of why women were drawn to religion may be controversial, her assumption that women dominated the country's Protestant congregations in the nineteenth century was not. Numerous foreign writers, from Alexis de Tocqueville to Harriet Martineau, who visited and systematically observed nineteenth-century American society, noted the ready and vital presence of women in almost every religious gathering. By the second half of the nineteenth century, close to 75 percent of churchgoers were women; by century's end, women comprised the overwhelming majority of the domestic and foreign missionary force. Throughout the century, they were pivotal in founding and organizing numerous benevolence organizations and served as the principal educators in Sunday schools. As early as 1870, 165 women listed themselves a ministers, and many more served as prayer leaders, deaconesses, and evangelists.

Beyond constituting the majority of Protestant congregations, observers and historians have also underscored that women's presence strongly impacted Protestant theology and worshiping practices. Termed by contemporary scholars as the "feminization" of religion, this influence amounted to a greater emphasis on a merciful and loving God, a more feminine and suffering image of Christ, a stress on feelings over reason, and a decline in harsh Calvinistic doctrines such as predestination and infant damnation. Historians have varied in their interpretation of the significance of woman's influence on nineteenth-century US Protestantism. In her influential book, *Dimity Convictions*, Barbara Welter argued that women accepted religion more out of weakness than out of choice:

Whether in the divine or human order, woman was constantly urged to be swept away by a torrent of energy, not to rely on her own strength which was useless, to sink into the arms of Jesus, to become absorbed and assimilated by the Divine Will – in other words, to relax and enjoy it. The fantasies of rape were nourished by this language and by the kind of physical sensations which a woman expected to receive and did receive in the course of conversion. (1976: 92–3)

Other scholars, such as Nancy Cott, have disagreed with Welter and argued that not only was women's affinity to Protestantism understandable, it also afforded them a means of self-affirmation and political empowerment:

[R]eligious identity . . . allowed women to assert themselves, both in private and in public ways. It enabled them to rely on an authority beyond the world of men and provided a crucial support to those who stepped beyond accepted bounds – reformers, for example. . . . Religious faith also allowed women a sort of holy self-ishness, or self-absorption . . . In contrast to the self-abnegation required of women in their domestic vocation, religious commitment required attention to one's own thoughts, actions and prospects. (1977: 139–40)

Unlike Welter, who deemed Protestantism disadvantageous to women, Cott said that it helped women to gain a protected measure of liberation, a newfound public voice, and an escape from conventional social restraints. Some scholars have gone so far as to term this Christian-based empowerment a form of "soft," "maternal," or "domestic" feminism and to argue that it gave women an accept-able way to affect limited gains in women's rights. Cott, however, as well as several other historians, has asserted that while Evangelicalism may have granted women some personal authority, it ended up reinforcing conservatism because it perpetuated a rhetoric of traditional female values. According to her, in order to enter into the political campaign for women's rights and become more radical feminists, women ultimately had to disengage themselves from "the convincing power of evangelical Protestantism":

What precipitated some women and not others to cross the boundaries from "woman's sphere" to "woman's rights" is not certain but it seems that variation or escape from the containment of conventional evangelical Protestantism – whether through Quakerism, Unitarianism, or "de-conversion" – often led the way. (Cott 1977: 204)

For Cott and others, Protestantism may have served as a means of temporary feminine empowerment, but it ultimately was not congruent with feminism.

In this essay, I will argue that the interplay between feminism and Protestantism was more fluid and variegated than Cott and others have pre-viously recognized. Indeed, some women used, appropriated, modified, and altered evangelical Protestantism to forge a more public and liberating role for themselves and to fashion a moderate form of Christian feminism. Yet, others, such as Elizabeth Cady Stanton, whom many scholars have deemed the forerunner of the modern-day, secular-based feminist, also utilized Protestant rhetorical forms and methodologies to advance their women's rights agenda. The difference, however, between Stanton's form of feminism and that of the Christian feminists is that instead of relying on evangelical ways of thinking, she drew from the older Common Sense thinking endemic to the Reformed tradition.

Despite the fact that a diversity of religions emerged and flourished during the century and that shortly after the Civil War, the Roman Catholic Church constituted the largest Christian communion in America, the nation nevertheless was considered a Protestant country dominated by white denominations of British origin. Because Protestantism was embedded thoroughly into the fabric of American men's and women's lives, it comprised part of what Pierre Bourdieu terms one's individual "habitus." For Bourdieu, the habitus is "a system of internalized, embodied schemes which, having been constituted in the course of collective history, function in their *practical* state, for *practice* (and not for the sake of pure knowledge)" (1984: 467). As an internalized scheme, nineteenth-century Protestantism formed both a generative and structuring principle: it enabled individuals to recognize possibilities for action, while it also prevented recognition of other potentialities.

As a corollary to the Protestant habitus of this period was a rigid notion of gender roles. Women were relegated to any form of activity that occurred inside the newly privatized middle-class home; men, by contrast, were assigned to the competitive and chaotic public world of politics and capitalist enterprise. As Morgan Dix, rector of Trinity Church in New York City, described it, "Man's is the outer life, woman's the inner. . . . He is eminently the doer, the creator, the discoverer, the defender. His intellect is for speculation and invention; his energy for adventure, for war and for conquest" (1883: 19). According to another prominent clergyman, Daniel C. Eddy, "Home is woman's throne, where she maintains her royal court, and sways her queenly authority. It is there that man learns to appreciate her worth, and to realize the sweet and tender influences which she casts around her . . . and there she fills the sphere to which divine providence has called her" (1859: 23).

Scholars have termed this call for dualistic gender norms "separate spheres"; and although ministers such as Eddy perceived these norms as universal and providential, interestingly they were not propounded by clergy prior to the rise of nineteenth-century capitalism and industrialism. Betty DeBerg notes that before the nineteenth century Christianity typically portrayed woman as the deceptive Eve figure and man as the moral exemplar. According to her, the separate spheres ideal arose as a way to explain and stabilize the changing economy, rising middle class, and growing urbanization (1990: 14–19). By constructing the home as a safe, moral refuge from the ruthless world of business and assigning women to it, men were able to assuage their own guilt (for participating in capitalist exploitation) and to justify their own exclusive claim to public power. Men were "sacrificing" their own morals in order "to secure [the home's] maintenance, progress, and defence . . . [and by extension] to assist in the maintenance, in the advance, in the defence [sic] of the State" (Dix 1883: 20). In response, women were to sacrifice their public aspirations and to "endure any amount of suffering, of toil, and even of injury . . . [and not to] listen to those unthinking women who tell you [that] you will be trampled upon unless you assert your rights, and speak for yourself" (Wise1987: 122).

However, despite Protestantism's call for women's subjugation and confinement, many women found Protestantism to be a means for self-empowerment and leadership. The Christian feminists reiterated the conservative ideals of separate spheres but not as an expression of subordination. By assuming a public voice and leadership roles under the auspices of a church that forbade them entrance into the public sphere, these women reinterpreted the evangelical gender norms and simultaneously exposed them as privileged, constructed interpretations rather than innate, divinely decreed laws. By unseating the church's conservative authority within the confines of the church itself, they functioned as secret rebels.

Gaining public leadership roles and power under the aegis of the church was no easy feat, particularly given the church's stand against women in the public sphere. Indeed, Protestant clergy regularly castigated women who transgressed their role or – even worse – who openly called for women's rights with every imaginable invective from "Amazonian disputants" (Wise 1987: 85) to "leprous dregs of corruption" (Burnap 1848: 204). Reverend Hubbard Winslow's statement is typical:

> Oh how fallen . . . is she when, impatient of her proper sphere, she steps forth to assume the duties of the man, and, impelled by false zeal, with conscience misguided, does as even man ought not to do – when forsaking the domestic hearth, her delicate voice is heard from house to house to house, or in social assemblies, rising in harsh unnatural tones of denunciation against civil laws and rulers . . . What a sad wreck of female loveliness is she then! (Winslow and Sanford 1854: 24–5)

Faced with the threat of these denunciations, the Christian feminists softened their demand for a public role by couching it in the rhetoric of Christian separate spheres. For example, Frances Willard, president of the Woman's Christian Temperance Union, underlined woman's maternal instinct in her call for woman's right to preach and to vote: "Mother-love works magic for humanity . . . Mother-hearted women are called to be saviors of the race" (quoted in Hardesty1981–2: 97).

In addition to underscoring essentialized views of woman as maternal, domestic, pious, virtuous, the Christian feminists typically dressed in ways traditional clergy would approve. Lay minister and best-selling advice-writer Hannah Whitall Smith, for example, earned the honorific, "angel of the churches," because of her blond hair, tall stature, and traditional attire. Evangelist and lay preacher Amanda Berry Smith was a "smooth-skinned woman with a well-proportioned body that she chose to clothe in a simple, Quaker-like dress and scooped bonnet" (Dodson 1988: xxxiii). Sojourner Truth, civil rights and woman's rights activist, reportedly dressed herself regularly in Quaker garb. Frances Willard's attire was considered ladylike and fashionable; she usually wore velvet or silk dresses in brown or black with a blue ribbon or white or ivory lace around the throat and a tasteful bonnet that she removed when she spoke. These women's traditionally feminine demeanor and rhetoric enabled them more readily to gain public forums and favorable receptions. Willard, president from 1879 to 1898 of the largest organization of women in the nation's history, was so celebrated that one historian deemed her "Woman of the Century" (Hardesty 1981-2: 25). As lay preachers and lecturers, Amanda Berry Smith, Lillie Devereux Blake, Sojourner Truth, and Hannah Whitall Smith often spoke to enthusiastic crowds numbering in the thousands. Because they presented a palatable exterior appearance and rhetoric, these women were able to influence other women to follow their lead. As one historian asserts, because "Willard's rhetoric and strategy used an appeal to 'home protection,' which was an extension and adaptation of the ideology of separate spheres," she provided the opportunity for many women to venture into the world of moral, social, and political reform (DeBerg 1990: 29). Under the aegis of a militant temperance organization designed as a vital protection for the home and children, Willard granted women permission to do whatever they wanted in the public sphere and compelled men to praise them for it.

Beyond dressing in traditional ways and utilizing separate spheres rhetoric, these women advanced a number of arguments to increase their opportunities for religious and secular leadership. One of the most common ways they asserted their right for public participation was to emphasize the importance of certain tenets of evangelicalism. Unlike Reformed Protestants, who conceived of God as a merciless ruler who admits to Heaven only a predestined few, and who valued educated clergy and abstract systems of theology, evangelicals believed that anyone can will to be, and thus can be, saved. Hence, evangelicalism emphasized pragmatics over speculative doctrine, the importance of personal calling over clerical authority, and a loving over a judgmental god.

This accent on experience, calling, emotion, and compassion directly facilitated the entry of women into leadership roles within the church and society. Although in the late nineteenth century such higher educational institutions as Oberlin College, Boston University, and Garrett Biblical Institute were increasingly admitting women into their theological seminaries, a woman enrolled in a higher theological institution was still a rare occurrence. Without access to equal formal educational opportunities, Christian feminists not only underscored evangelicalism's accent on personal experience, they specially aligned women with it. Wrote Frances Willard, "Men preach a creed; women declare a life. Men deal in formulas, women in facts. Men have always tithed mint and rue and cummin [sic] in their exegesis and their ecclesiasticism, while the world's heart has cried out for compassion, forgiveness and sympathy" (1978: 47). By cloaking themselves with the banner of feminine experience rather than of masculine theology, they were able to theologize and take active roles in church and society without seeming to encroach on clerical authority or disrupting women's feminine status.

Accentuating the call of emotions over the dictates of abstract theology, women could justify their impetus to speak, sing, or act by attributing it to the

Holy Spirit. Lay preacher Eliza B. Rutherford, for example, suddenly was struck by the spirit at a Texas camp meeting:

> God called me to preach the gospel. He plainly revealed to me that I was to do the work of an Evangelist. When I recognized His voice calling me to this work, I answered: "Here I am Lord! I am wholly consecrated to Thee. I belong to Thee to go where and when you want to send me and by your power will do your whole will." (quoted in Dayton 1984: 65)

At the time of her revelation, Rutherford was married to a poor farmer and had rarely ventured beyond her small hometown. The Holy Spirit provided her an emphatic and irrefutable justification for renegotiating her life. When Virginia Broughton's husband objected to her decision to become a missionary, she responded, "I belong to God first, and you next; so you two must settle it" (quoted in Brooks Higginbotham 1993: 132). Only in the name of something as legitimate and long-standing as orthodox religion could women bring themselves to challenge the supremacy of their husbands and fathers. Thus the Christian feminists may not have perceived total submission to God as oppressive or confining because it allowed them to oppose male authority in the present world and to follow new, non-traditional paths.

The Christian feminists' strong allegiance to a deity over man was further fueled by the fact that their conception of God contrasted sharply with the stereotypical male. Hannah Whitall Smith, for instance, repeatedly drew the analogy of God as the loving mother or parent and the consecrated believer as a child in the Father's house. Sojourner Truth saw Christ "as a friend, standing between me and God, through whom, love flowed as from a fountain" (1991: 69). Similarly, Amanda Berry Smith frequently sang a song in which she proudly proclaimed, "I am married to Jesus." The image of God or Jesus as a loving partner offered Christian feminists an alternative not only to the stern Calvinist god, but also to the their dominating fathers and husbands.

Beyond valorizing experience, personal calling, and a loving god, the Christian feminists found scriptural support for their newfound public roles. Locating biblical justification for women's public leadership was especially important since conservative ministers routinely used scriptural evidence to verify separate spheres and women's subordinate status. As the conservative Reverend Winslow pronounced, "How any person of sober mind can read such scriptures and not perceive that they recognise an important distinction between the appropriate virtue and duties of the sexes, I am unable to perceive" (Winslow and Sanford 1854: 16). To reinforce their version of separate spheres, Winslow and other clergy frequently upheld the creation story and a few Pauline injunctions (I Corinthians 11: 8–9 and 14: 34–5; Ephesians 5: 22–4; I Timothy 2: 13–15) which, they claimed, directly legislated woman's subordination to man and her relegation to the domestic sphere. Moreover, they routinely adverted to such biblical women as the gentle Ruth, the reverent Hannah, the munificent Dorcas, and the meek Mary as virtuous examples for nineteenth-century women to emulate. Exemplary scriptural women, according to these writers, are particularly "remarkable [for] their strictly feminine deportment. From the wife of Abraham to the wife of Aquilla, there was none who forgot her subordinate station" (1854: 75–6). To drive their point home, ministers also paraded before their feminine congregants tales of biblical villainesses, such as Rebecca, Jezebel, and Herodias, who exemplify the pain, wretchedness, and condemnation brought on by disobeying the separate spheres doctrine.

When confronted with counterexamples of strong, virtuous, and public biblical women such as Deborah, Huldah, or Anna, these ministers tended to denigrate them or downplay their significance:

> Deborah, though she was a very wise woman and judged Israel, did not go at the head of the army. Huldah was endowed with the prophetic gift; but she does not stand forth prominent in the civil and religious history of the Jews. Anna, though she devoted herself to the service of God in the temple, did not at all go beyond the bounds of female modesty and propriety. Miriam led the songs of her countrymen after the triumph at the Red Sea. The daughters of Philip by no means stand forth in any public capacity. (Duren 1868: 26–7)

To reinforce their circumscribed view of women, these ministers employed selective literal and ahistorical readings of the Bible. As the celebrated minister J. L. Neve writes, "the Holy Scripture is source and rule of all faith and practice . . . If we can not believe that . . . Paul, under the guidance of the Holy Ghost, said something that is true and binding to-day just as well as at the time of the founding of the church, then we are on dangerous ground" (quoted in Zikmund 1982: 96). Neve's argument typifies the ministers' unwavering dedication to biblical inerrancy, literalism, objectivity, and universality, to uphold the fiction of separate spheres and their own authority.

Because the conservative argument was so biblically-focused, the Christian feminists were compelled to question their method of biblical interpretation and to promote an alternative, woman-oriented hermeneutics. As Willard eloquently expressed it, "The mother-heart of God will never be known to the world until translated into terms of speech by mother-hearted women" (1978: 46–7). For feminists, women provide a much needed check and perspective on masculine biblical scholarship: "We need the stereoscopic view of truth in general, which can only be had when woman's eye and man's together shall discern the perspective of the Bible's full-orbed revelation" (Willard 1978: 21).

What they had in mind by women's biblical exegesis was drawn primarily from historical criticism, a German-derived, liberal form of biblical scholarship. Rather than accept the Bible as the arbiter of universal, immutable truth, historical critics viewed the scriptures as a product of historical evolution, offering insights into the divine while also bearing the thought patterns and presuppositions of the time of its composition. Thus these critics took on the task of segregating the human-made parts from the divine treasure and questioned the authorship, translations, and content of some of the most sacred books of the Bible. As Lucretia Mott pointed out, "[A]ll the advice given by the apostles to the women of their day is [not] applicable to our own intelligent age; nor is there any passage of Scripture making those texts binding upon us" (quoted in Behnke 1982: 129).

Relying on historical criticism, one of the Christian feminists' most common interpretive strategies was to place what they perceived as objectionable verses in their historical context. For example, in reference to Paul's call for feminine silence in the church, Willard pointed out that

> places of worship, in the age of the Apostles, were not built as they are with us, but that the women had a corner of their own, railed off by a close fence reaching above their heads. It was thus made difficult for them to hear, and in their eager, untutored state, wholly unaccustomed to public audiences, they "chattered" and asked questions. (1978: 30)

Paul's command for women "to remain in silence" represented a sort of compromise; he was avoiding new grounds for opposition while allowing women to enter church life more actively than before.

A second strategy Christian feminists used was to invite readers to focus on the overarching spirit of the Bible rather than on isolated passages. As Whitall Smith remarked, "[T]he Bible is a book of principles, and not a book of disjointed aphorisms. Isolated texts may often be made to sanction things to which the principles of Scripture are totally opposed. I believe all fanaticism comes in this way" (1985: 58). Similarly, Willard bemoaned ministers who demand woman's silence in the church as commanded by Paul but overlook the apostle's specific exhortations against braided hair, gold, pearls, and expensive attire (1978: 20). Toward this end, they called for readers to compare Scripture with Scripture to uncover the Bible's general truths and to use their own faith and conscience to determine which verses were still binding and which were mere local historical injunctions.

Inspired by some of the radically new translations and interpretations of the Bible that emerged in the late nineteenth century, the Christian feminists considered the possibility of forged or mistranslated scriptural passages. For example, Ellen Battelle Dietrick questioned the validity of the anti-feminine portions of Paul's writings because they did not correspond to other parts of his writing where he lauds active, commandeering women: "In view of the whole of what is given us as Paul's life and letters, we must pronounce the woman-despising passages palpable forgeries and very bungling forgeries at that" (1897: 106–7). Other women quibbled with male scholars' proclivity to translate and interpret passages according to their own biases: "The word translated 'servant' occurs twenty times in Paul's writings. Sixteen times it is translated 'ministers.' Three times it is translated 'deacon.' Only once it is translated 'servant' and it is rather singular that the single exception is where the word it used in reference to Phebe" (Hunter, quoted in Dayton 1984: 27). For these women, the Bible was to be read in manifold ways: with historical knowledge, the guidance of one's individual conscience, a healthy and informed skepticism, and accurate translations. By opening up more possibilities for biblical interpretation, these women felt they were carving out new opportunities for themselves and for Protestantism itself. Mary Cook avouched, "God is shaking up the church – He is going to bring it up to something better, and that too, greatly through the work of women" (quoted in Brooks 1983: 37). The arguments Christian feminists used for women's public role were, on some level, heard because women did find new avenues for leadership, particularly under the aegis of the Protestant Church. In fact, their greatest strides came in three areas: reform organizations; missionary and deaconess work; and the ministry. Women's entry into all three areas was, for the most part, a feminist victory given its novelty and the initial conservative opposition to it. But these gains were not easily achieved.

Protestant women's earliest reform efforts came in the arena of education. Using the argument that education would bring about a more virtuous society, pioneers such as Emma Willard, Mary Lyon, and Catharine Beecher began demanding increased opportunities for women to attend school and for curriculum changes that would reflect their belief that women had the same intellectual capacity as men. Catharine Beecher, for instance, proclaimed that while she may not have been trained in the best colleges as were her brothers, she felt fully equal to them in terms of intellect. Beecher perceived that socialization rather than innate qualities accounted for the apparent differences in man's and woman's intellect. As an outgrowth of this belief, she, Willard, and Lyon all opened higher educational institutions for women in the early part of the century. Although all three of these founders believed that most girls would and should become devoted wives and mothers, they nevertheless introduced subjects – such as Latin, geography and history – formerly taught only to boys. According to them, an educated woman would better be able to assist her husband and children in taking on virtuous public leadership roles. Not until the latter half of the century would educators openly take on the task of preparing women for public career opportunities.

As the century progressed, women – particularly those in the middle and upper classes with leisure time – became involved in a range of social reform efforts: abolition of slavery, better treatment for Native Americans, prison reform, mental health, prostitution, orphanages, and temperance. Women's widening interest and participation in social reform can be attributed in part to their participation in evangelical revivals, especially those led by Charles Grandison Finney. Beginning in the late 1820s, Finney instituted new evangelistic measures which quickly became widespread practice. In addition to praying for people by name, colloquial preaching, and the institution of "anxious benches," this grand evangelist encouraged women to pray and testify in public. Moreover, he advocated postmillennialism, or the view that Christ will return only after humans have perfected society. Consequently, social reform became intimately bound with revivalistic evangelicalism. Among his converts and followers were some of the most successful female reformers of the century: Lucy Stone, Antoinette Brown, Elizabeth Cady Stanton, Frances Willard, and Phoebe Palmer. Inspired by Finney but with little concrete help from him or other male church officials, women, from 1835 on, began organizing Protestant-based reform groups themselves. Most of these groups – including the Colored Female Religious and Moral Society of Salem, the Maternal Association, the Female Mite Society, the Female

Charitable and Benevolent Society – were ecumenical in emphasis, thus drawing Protestant women from all denominations.

Although it espoused an evangelical philosophy, the Woman's Christian Temperance Union attracted thousands of women from a range of Protestant backgrounds. Because it was the largest and most influential of women's reform organizations, its history is emblematic of the development of women's social reform work. As the century progressed, the temperance movement had moved from a single-issue and evangelical orientation to the establishment of a national society, espousing a primarily secular political agenda. In the early years (1830s–1840s), women's temperance societies had been organized through churches, and men were given the public leadership roles. Female temperance reformers relied on moral suasion (visiting afflicted homes, appealing to individual sinners) rather than on political action to effect their goals. By the 1870s, women's temperance had become more politicized. During the period known as the Woman's Crusade (1873–5), women boldly halted the sale of alcohol in selected saloons by picketing and holding lengthy meetings in them. Although this militant period was short-lived, it did provide inspiration for the formation of the WCTU (1874), whose national political character represented a very different model from the local, church-based, antebellum organizations. The WCTU was highly organized at the national, state, and local levels, giving unprecedented numbers of women opportunities for public leadership (two million by 1897). Believing that alcoholism could not be separated from other social problems such as women's economic dependency, domestic burdens, and political disempowerment, Frances Willard as president of the WCTU from 1879 to 1897 took on a broad social agenda which included a free kindergarten movement, better municipal sanitation, federal aid for education, separate correctional facilities for women, Protestant ecumenicism, and women's rights.

Despite Willard's far-reaching social agenda, her influence was limited. Most of the WCTU members were far more conservative than she; and during and especially after her presidency, its conservative members helped to push through such repressive legislation as the Comstock law, Sunday blue laws, censorship regulations, the increased punishment of prostitutes, and prohibition. Yet, even though the WCTU reformers still believed that there was a proper place and duty for women, they nevertheless attracted several hundred thousand American women and prompted them to work at many reforms which those same women, a generation earlier, would have thought improper for their sex. Thus, by the end of the nineteenth century, Christian feminists may have still utilized a Protestant separate spheres rhetoric; but in practice, they no longer adhered to its prescription. Yet, despite their increased political power, the WCTU and other Protestant women reformers did little to reform the church power structure itself.

A similar trend toward greater autonomy and liberation occurred in the women's foreign missionary movement. As in the reform movement, women first became involved in missionary work through men, as missionary wives. Fueled by a zeal for Protestant manifest destiny and a conviction in their own capacity for submission and self-denying love, women accompanied their husbands to rescue "heathens" in ancient dark lands. For the educated woman convert eager for adventure and leadership, the role of missionary wife was appealing. Once in the field, her power and influence often expanded as the male missionaries found they had little access to the domestic realm. Thus women quickly became key to the hope for world evangelization. By mid-century, "female assistant missionaries" (or single women) were called to the field and quickly began to outnumber ordained males.

After the Civil War, women's missionary work burgeoned. Beginning with Betsy Stockton – the first single woman missionary – who traveled in 1823 to Hawaii, women not only ventured into the both the foreign and domestic fields, they also began founding and controlling their own organizations. These post-bellum missionary societies afforded thousands of women the opportunity to plan and administer wide-reaching programs for the first time. With the Women's Union Missionary Society (developed by women from six denominations in 1861), women founded female missionary societies in all denominations except the Congregational Church, which was organized by male leaders in 1869. While many of these societies were subsidiary to and dependent upon denominational boards (in the Episcopal Church), some served as supplemental offshoots of denominational churches (e.g. the African Methodist Episcopal and Congregational women's boards); and a few were fully independent (e.g. the Methodist Episcopal society). Moreover, although women in these societies typically began locally, they often banded with other women to form regional and national programs. By 1900 the women's societies supported 389 wives, 856 single women missionaries, and 96 doctors. They were responsible for creating numerous orphanages, hospitals, schools, and dispensaries all over the world. Thus they forged powerful feminine networks with women in remote areas of the nation and globe.

Women's missionary work provided an outlet for creativity and energy that made it possible for individual women to expand their own spheres and to improve the conditions under which other women and people lived. Believing that Christianity offered women greater liberation and better conditions than did other religions, women missionaries were convinced that by spreading the gospel they were ameliorating the situations of women around the globe. And indeed female missionaries did more than evangelize; they also often taught women to read and write, provided medical care, and dismantled sexist marriage customs, and as Elizabeth Clark points out, "[m]issionaries were heroines, often household names, to the women they left behind" (1986: 382). Yet, despite the benefits to the missionaries and those they served, the movement had some drawbacks. Not only did these women fail to recruit many new converts, they at times adopted ethnocentric and imperialist attitudes toward their "heathen" sisters. Moreover, as Barbara Welter has pointed out, the women's missionary movement rose into prominence only because the profession was no longer as prestigious for men. Additionally, since it did not arise within the established church hierarchy (but rather as an auxiliary to it), the movement failed to challenge the church's masculine power structure directly. Finally, it may have diverted the women missionaries and the Protestant Church from confronting directly the issues raised by the women's rights movement: "The *Woman's*

Evangel wrote of women's work in missions as a 'happy solution of the difficulty' when a woman found it hard to reconcile her religion and her rights, agitating her own and 'the public mind, creating warm discussion and angry debate'" (Welter 1980: 123). These shortcomings, as well as the missionaries' reliance on separate spheres rhetoric, may have served to dissuade these women from taking on political women's rights issues.

Although the female missionary movement had definite drawbacks and may not have propelled the women's rights agenda, it seemed to offer one benefit: it might have opened some people's minds to the possibility of women's ordination into the ministry. After all, women missionaries effectively assumed most of the typical responsibilities of a minister. Such, however, was not the case in most denominations. Despite women's gains in the missionary field, the struggle for women's right to preach was arduous. While liberal denominations such as the Unitarians and Quakers offered women early opportunities for lay preaching, they did not officially ordain them until much later. Several scholars have noted that in actuality it was evangelicals, and particularly those denominations with congregational polity, that served as the pioneers. Once he began teaching at Oberlin in 1835, Charles Grandison Finney ended up attracting several prominent women students, such as Lucy Stone and Antoinette Brown. In 1853, Brown became the first woman to be ordained in the country. Churches following presbyterial or episcopal polity moved much more slowly. Not until 1955 did northern Presbyterians approve the ordination of women, and Episcopalians failed to do so until 1977. And even when women did attain ordination, they were often not given access to the leadership positions and opportunities available to men. Today, women ministers still face longer periods of unemployment, lower salaries, and fewer leadership roles in national ecclesiastical organizations.

In all three areas of action – reform organizations, missionary work, and ministering – women gained greater opportunities for leadership, mobility, and creativity. Yet they often did so by propagating and then covertly expanding a doctrine of separate spheres and by arguing for women's rights implicitly rather than explicitly. As a result of their Christian-based and covert feminist strategies, these women were often estranged from their more radical feminist sisters, such as Elizabeth Cady Stanton, who overtly advocated women's rights and often combined that advocacy with a condemnation of Christianity. For example, in an 1888 article for the *North American Review*, Stanton fumed,

> A consideration of woman's position before Christianity, under Christianity, and at the present time shows that she is not indebted to any form of religion for one step of progress, nor one new liberty; on the contrary, it has been through the perversion of her religious sentiments that she has been so long held in a condition of slavery. (1885)

Sparked by her frustration over women's immersion into Protestantism, she assembled a group of white, middle-class, educated women to produce *The Woman's Bible*, a set of commentaries on scriptural passages that they deemed of special interest to women. Yet, rather than rely on liberal historical critical principles or Evangelicalism to carve out new power and space for women as did the Christian feminists, Stanton took a surprising approach. Despite her anti-clerical and anti-Christian rhetoric, Stanton utilized a way of thinking and hermeneutics popularized by the fundamentalist Reformed clergy: Scottish Common Sense Philosophy. But she did so, not to advance the spread of white, masculine Protestantism as did the fundamentalists, but instead to expand the political rights of women. Such a reliance is surprising given that fundamentalist clergy vehemently denounced her project. James H. Brookes, for example, decried the *Woman's Bible* as "that miserable abortion . . . that is only the impudent utterance of infidelity" (quoted in DeBerg 1990: 1). Yet on the other hand her use of fundamentalism may have been ingenious in that she ended up turning the anti-feminist impulse of fundamentalism on its head.

First propagated in the eighteenth century by the Scotsman Thomas Reid and his students, Scottish Common Sense thinking gained popularity in the US in the early nineteenth century. From 1790 to 1870, it served as a shaping force for all Protestants and for mainstream American culture. Put simply, Common Sense accepted the premise that truth is approximately the same for everybody everywhere and propagated the notion that everyone can understand the world directly, through sensory perceptions. After the Civil War, however, this system of thought vanished from mass culture and from liberal Protestant circles as a result of new patterns of economic organization, the restructuring of higher education, and the upsurge of Darwinism and Kantian idealism. No longer were most Protestants able to enjoy complete faith in the power of the individual to understand truth so easily. With the onslaught of modernism, Common Sense thinking waned. Indeed, the only Protestant group to continue to cling to this philosophy was the fundamentalists. And curiously, in *The Woman's Bible* project, Stanton also utilizes it heavily. Repeatedly, she calls on her readers to interpret the Bible "with their own unassisted common sense" (1974: II, 159) and to read the "unvarnished texts in plain English" (I, 8) and "in harmony with science, common sense, and the experience of mankind in natural laws" (I, 20).

Like Stanton, the fundamentalists believed that truths about the world or religion must be gained from strict induction from irreducible facts of experience. Charles Hodge, one of the most celebrated of the Princeton Reformed scholars, affirmed that God "gives us in the Bible truths, which, properly understood and arranged, constitute the science of theology. As the facts of nature are all related and determined by physical laws, so the facts of the Bible are all related and determined by the nature of God and of his creatures" (1974: I, 3). Similarly, Stanton contends that this inductive approach yields infallible and patent truth: "What seemed to me to be right I thought must be equally plain to all other beings" (quoted in Welter 1975: xxii). For her, no matter who the reader is, the Bible leads to one ultimate conclusion: It "does not exalt and dignify woman . . . The spirit is the same in all languages, hostile to her as an equal" (Stanton 1974: I, 12).

The Bible for both Stanton and the fundamentalists should be read straight-forwardly; neither culture nor context need be taken into account. In fact, at the celebration of his fiftieth year as professor at Princeton, Hodge proudly proclaimed that "a new idea never originated in this seminary. . . . The Bible is the word of God. That is to be assumed or proved. If granted, then it follows, that what the Bible says, God says. That ends the matter" (quoted in Hodge 1800: 521). Stanton correspondingly employs an absolutist methodology:

> In my exegesis, thus far, not being versed in scriptural metaphors and symbols, I have . . . merely comment[ed] on the supposed facts as stated. As the Bible is placed in the hands of children and uneducated men and women to point them the way of salvation, the letter should have no doubtful meaning. What should we think of guide posts on our highways, if we needed a symbolic interpreter at every point to tell us which way to go? (1975: I, 64)

Stanton and the fundamentalists both contend that the more liberal historical readings of the Bible are speculations, rather than plain facts. For them, Common Sense reason offers surer grounds of knowledge than hypothetical flights of fancy or personal emotion. Princeton theologian B. B. Warfield warns future theologians that an overreliance on "intrinsic evidence," that is, "the testimony [or emotional feeling] which each reading [of the Bible] delivers," can open "the floodgates to the most abounding error" (1887: 85). Stanton also implores her women readers to reject their "sentimental" and "blind" feelings of reverence for God and the Bible and to face the literal truth (1974: I, 10, 11).

In keeping with Stanton's and the fundamentalists' endorsement of literalism is their bifurcation of the natural and supernatural orders. According to Stanton, "church doctrine based not upon reason or the facts of life, issued out of crude imaginings; phantasms obstructed from truth, held in check the wheel of progress" (1974: II, 22). Thus, "natural" happenings signify truth, and supernatural events are produced through either ignorance or an overactive imagination. Stanton explains the raising of Elijah in a chariot of fire as follows: "Much of the ascending and the descending of seers, of angels and of prophets which astonished the ignorant was accomplished in balloons – a lost art for many centuries" (II, 72). Like Stanton, the fundamentalists insist on a definite break between the natural and supernatural realms and tend to abandon the idea that supernatural forces are intervening dramatically and miraculously at every moment. Charles Hodge tended to view miracles as more or less aligned with the laws of nature and science: "The truth on the subject [of miracles] was beautifully expressed by Sir Isaac Newton, when he said . . . 'God is the author of nature: He has ordained its laws: . . . He governs all things by cooperating and using the laws which He has ordained'" (1871: I, 622). For both Stanton and the fundamentalists, the emphasis is placed on the external not the internal, the objective rather than the subjective, the natural over the supernatural, and uniformity over diversity. Both groups strip their exegeses of the text's historical vicissitudes and multiple meanings in order to lay open, naturalize, and eternalize their own absolute but antithetical positions. Stanton and her radical feminist partners sought to remedy the gender inequities in this world, while the fundamentalists were concerned with spreading the gospel, in part by maintaining a gendered hierarchical dualism.

Despite contemporary scholars' claim that Stanton's feminism was secular – even anti-Christian – her stance does not represent a complete emancipation from Protestant ways of thinking. Indeed, in actuality, Stanton often found Protestant clergy receptive to her feminist message:

> In 1874, during her speaking tour of Michigan on behalf of a woman suffrage referendum, she enthusiastically noted that ministers of all denominations invited her to speak on suffrage in place of their Sunday sermons. "Sitting Sunday after Sunday in the different pulpits with revered gentlemen . . . I could not help thinking of the distance we had come since that period in civilization when Paul's word was law . . ." In 1883, after preaching in a London pulpit on the topic, "Has the Christian Religion Done Aught to Elevate Woman?" she admitted privately that, although her sermon had focused on the negative, a strong case could be made for a positive interpretation. (Banner 1988: 156–7)

Stanton's real complaint, then, was not so much with Protestantism *per se*, but with the slow progress of the feminist cause. In 1886, she wrote Antoinette Brown Blackwell about this frustration: "I feel like making an attack on some new quarter of the enemies [*sic*] domain. Our politicians are calm and complacent under our fire, but the clergy jump round the minute you aim a pop gun at them like parched peas on a hot shovel" (quoted in Kern 1990: 373). For political reasons, she chose to feature clerical resistance over accommodation and to totalize all of Protestantism as evil; but in actuality, her arguments drew from and, in a sense, overturned – for her own feminist ends – late-nineteenth-century fundamentalism.

Despite the fact that they took varying approaches, both the Christian feminists and the radical feminists drew from Protestantism in multiple ways. The basic difference between the two groups is that the Christian feminists, unlike Stanton, did battle against specific anti-feminine outrages without rejecting Protestant clergy, doctrines, and sacred texts altogether. As a result, not only did their calls seem less threatening to the general – and still largely Protestant – public, but they were also able, because of their outward Protestant behavior, to thwart the standard conservative charges of mannishness or heathenism – charges that some scholars claim effectively helped to undermine many of the radical feminist causes. In addition, these women avoided launching *ad hominem* attacks on conservative clergy and instead tended to accentuate their similarities with them. For instance, despite her public disagreement with the anti-suffrage views of Reverend Morgan Dix, Lillie Devereux Blake opened her book by praising him as "a man of great learning, of wide culture, and of much excellence of character, a man whose broad benevolence has made him a benefactor to many" (1883: 6).

The Christian feminists may have been able to achieve a certain limited effectiveness through their conciliatory rhetoric and conservative demeanor. A woman's rights agenda that recognized and at least partially reconciled itself with Christianity was no doubt more appealing to *fin-de-siècle* women and men still thoroughly ensconced in church life than was radical feminism. As Ruth Bordin notes,

Elizabeth Cady Stanton . . . most often chose "confrontation and a high moral stance" over political maneuver and compromise. Unlike Willard, Stanton was an enthusiast, not a politician. She was always forthright in speaking her mind. Willard was an inveterate dissembler and a clever and effective insinuator. She played the role of sweet conciliator whereas Cady Stanton assumed the stance of militant radical. Stanton herself recognized Willard's talent for conciliation. When in March 1888 Willard appeared before a United States committee investigating suffrage as a representative of the International Council of Women, Cady Stanton, who was making the arrangements, scheduled Willard as the final speaker, believing she would leave the committee in a friendly mood. (1986: 104–5)

The Christian feminists' ability to "mime" conservative Christianity enabled them to forge alliances with prominent clergy. Frances Willard made several references to ministers as among the most amenable of male professionals to women's enfranchisement, and contemporary historians also cite the liberal clergy as particularly loyal to the women's rights cause. Moreover, according to several scholars, legislators tended to be significantly more receptive to Christian feminists than to radical feminists. Mary P. Ryan, for example, explains that

[b]ecause [these] women did not convert the nineteenth-century political sphere into a feminist forum about sexuality does not mean that they were merely pawns in a male-dominated sexual politics. While clearly second-class citizens, women did batter away at the urban political system, winning concessions here and there, imprinting their ideas on public debates, and adding their perspectives to the array of conflicting interests that influenced policy decisions. (1990: 129)

It was the religious feminists rather than the radicals who could initiate legislation against wife abuse and other anti-feminine crimes precisely because they did not openly support divorce. In the late nineteenth century, feminists could either do battle against specific outrages against women without attacking the institution of Protestantism, or they could assail Protestantism while remaining vague about the circumstances that required it (as did Stanton); they could not do both. Stanton could oppugn Protestant clergy and the Bible, but as a result, she was not able to push forward much successful legislation and church reform or accrue a large following of supporters. Conversely, the Christian feminists may have been able to effect some changes within the institutions of religion and politics but at the expense of offering an expansive, revolutionary feminist vision.

The fact that the Christian feminists were more favorably received by larger audiences in their own time than the radical feminists does not necessarily mean that they constituted a "better" model for feminists either then or now. Moreover, although the radical and Christian feminists frequently disagreed with each other, they were also in many ways mutually dependent. One of the main reasons why the Christian feminists could position themselves in the strategically beneficial position of conciliator is that Stanton and her band so publicly voiced their views and cleared a space in which mainstream feminists could more freely and safely play. And one of the reasons Stanton could receive notoriety among the public in her own time and admiration among feminists today is partially because her views contrast so colorfully with those of her religious sisters.

While each group served as an important point of comparison for the other, neither group had the ultimate answer for women's problems. In fact, in at least one significant way, both groups fell regrettably short of forging a fully egalitarian and progressive social vision. Carolyn DeSwarte Gifford reports that in the 1880s the WCTU ran a suffrage advertisement with an insidious racist undertone. This image portrayed a prim, well-dressed and lily white Frances Willard encircled by ethnically and class-coded representatives of three other non-voting groups: idiots, Native Americans, and insane males. Many of these advertisements carried the ironic title, "American Woman and Her Peers," with the following caption:

> The incongruity of the company Miss Willard is represented as keeping is such as to attract and excite wonder, until it is explained that such is the relative political status of American women under the laws of many of our states.
>   No one can fail to be impressed with the absurdity of such a statutory regulation that places women in the same legal category with the idiot, the Indian and the insane person. (quoted in Gifford 1986: 107)

Similarly, shortly after African-American males were awarded the vote, Stanton spoke out:

> If American women find it hard to bear the oppressions of their own Saxon fathers, the best orders of manhood, what may they not be called to endure when all the lower orders of foreigners now crowding our shores legislate for them and their daughters. Think of Patrick and Sambo and Hans and Yung Tung, who do not know the difference between a monarchy and a republic, who can not read the Declaration of Independence or Webster's spelling-book, making laws for Lucretia Mott, Ernestine L. Rose and Anna E. Dickinson. (Stanton et al. 1881–1922: II, 353)

Because both the Christian feminists and the radical feminists necessarily drew from the larger Protestant culture (albeit in different ways), they both – for better and for worse – inevitably were imbued with its assets and weaknesses.

Despite these regrettable shortcomings, both groups exemplify the manifold ways women – enmeshed in a shifting, dynamic historical period – utilized Protestantism to find a public voice. Not only did they help to forge a new, softer form of Protestant theology, they effected (in the name of the Church) major educational and social reforms, carved out a place for themselves in the ministry, and launched powerful and varied arguments for women's right to public power. Without their efforts, neither the Protestant Church nor the feminist movement would enjoy the rich diversity of ideas, voices, and talent that they do today.

BIBLIOGRAPHY

Banner, Lois W. (1988) *Elizabeth Cady Stanton: A Radical for Woman's Rights*, Boston, Mass. and Toronto: Little, Brown.

Behnke, Donna A. (1982) *Religious Issues in Nineteenth-century Feminism*, Troy, Mich.: Whitson.

Blake, Lillie Devereux (1883) *Woman's Place Today*, New York: J. W. Lowell.

Bordin, Ruth (1986) *Frances Willard*, Chapel Hill, NC: University of North Carolina Press.

Bourdieu, Pierre (1984) *Distinction: A Social Critique of the Judgement of Taste*, trans. Richard Nice, Cambridge, Mass.: Harvard University Press.

Brooks, Evelyn (1983) "Feminist theology of the black Baptist Church, 1880–1900," in Amy Swerdlow and Hanna Lesinger (eds) *Class, Race and Sex: The Dynamics of Control*, Boston, Mass.: G. K. Hall, pp. 31–59.

Brooks Higginbotham, Evelyn (1993) *Righteous Discontent: The Women's Movement in the Black Baptist Church, 1880–1920*, Cambridge, Mass. and London: Harvard University Press.

Burnap, George W. (1848) *The Sphere and Duties of Woman: A Course of Lectures*, Baltimore, Md.: John Murphy.

Clark, Elizabeth B. (1986) "Women and religion in America, 1870–1920," in John F. Wilson (ed.) *Church and State in America, a Bibliographical Guide: The Civil War to the Present Day*, vol. 2, New York: Greenwood Press, pp. 373–401.

Cott, Nancy F. (1977) *The Bonds of Womanhood: 'Woman's Sphere' in New England, 1780–1835*, New Haven, Conn. and London: Yale University Press.

Dayton, Donald (ed.) (1985) *Holiness Tracts Defending the Ministry of Women*, New York: Garland.

DeBerg, Betty A. (1990) *Ungodly Women: Gender and the First Wave of American Fundamentalism*, Minneapolis, Minn.: Fortress Press.

Dietrick, Ellen Battelle (1897) *Women in the Early Christian Ministry*, Philadelphia, Pa.: Alfred J. Ferris.

Dix, Morgan (1883) *Lectures on the Calling of a Christian Woman, and Her Training to Fulfill It*, New York: D. Appleton.

Dodson, Jualynne E. (1988) Introduction, in Amanda Berry Smith, *An Autobiography: The Story of the Lord's Dealings with Mrs. Amanda Smith, the Colored Evangelist* [1893], ed. Henry Louis Gates, Jr., New York and Oxford: Oxford University Press, pp. xxvii–xlii.

Duren, Charles (1868) "Place of women in the church, in religious meetings," *The Congregational Review* 8/39 (January), pp. 22–9.

Eddy, Daniel Clark (1859) *The Young Woman's Friend: Or, The Duties, Trials, Loves, and Hopes of Woman*, Boston, Mass.: Wentworth, Hewes.

Gifford, Carolyn DeSwarte (1986) "Home protection: the WCTU's Conversion to woman suffrage," in Janet Sharistanian (ed.) *Gender, Ideology and Action: Historical Perspectives on Women's Public Lives*, New York: Greenwood Press, pp. 95–120.

Hardesty, Nancy A. (1981–2) "Minister as prophet? Or as mother?" in Hilah F. Thomas and Rosemary Skinner Keller (eds) *Women in New Worlds: Historical Perspectives on the Weslayan Tradition* (2 vols), Nashville, Tenn.: Abingdon Press, pp. 88–101.

—— (1984) *Women Called to Witness: Evangelical Feminism in the Nineteenth Century*, Nashville, Tenn.: Abingdon Press.

Hodge, A. A. (1980) *The Life of Charles Hodge*, New York: Charles Scribner's Sons.

Hodge, Charles (1871) *Systematic Theology* (2 vols), New York: Charles Scribner's Sons.

Kern, Kathi L. (1990) "Rereading Eve: Elizabeth Cady Stanton and the 'Woman's Bible,'" *Women's Studies* 19/3–4, pp. 371–83.

Marty, Martin E. (1986) "The Protestant majority: the struggles of women," in *Protestantism in the United States*, 2nd edn, New York: Charles Scribner's Sons, pp. 97–107.

Ryan, Mary (1990) *Women in Public: Between Banners and Ballots, 1825–1880*, Baltimore, Md. and London: Johns Hopkins University Press.

Stanton, Elizabeth Cady (1885) "Has Christianity benefitted woman?," *North American Review* 14 (May).

—— (1974) *The Original Feminist Attack on the Bible (The Woman's Bible)*, 2 Parts, introd. Barbara Welter, New York: Arno Press.

Stanton, Elizabeth Cady, Anthony, Susan B., and Gage, Matilda Joslyn (eds) (1881–1922) *History of Woman Suffrage* (6 vols), New York: Fowler & Wells.

Truth, Sojourner (1991) *Narrative of Sojourner Truth; A Bondswoman of Olden Time, With a History of Her Labors and Correspondence Drawn from Her "Book of Life,"* ed. Henry Louis Gates, Jr., introd. Jeffrey C. Stewart, New York and Oxford: Oxford University Press.

Warfield, Benjamin B. (1887) *An Introduction to the Textual Criticism of the New Testament*, New York: Thomas Whittaker.

Welter, Barbara (1974) "Introduction," in Elizabeth Cady Stanton, *The Original Feminist Attack on the Bible (The Woman's Bible)*, New York: Arno Press, pp. v–xxxiv.

—— (1976) *Dimity Convictions: The American Woman in the Nineteenth Century*, Athens, Oh.: Ohio University Press.

—— (1980) "She hath done what she could: Protestant women's missionary careers in nineteenth-century America," in Janet Wilson James (ed.) *Women in American Religion*, Philadelphia, Pa.: University of Pennsylvania Press, pp. 111–25.

Whitall Smith, Hannah (1985) *A Christian's Secret of a Happy Life* [1870], Westwood, Conn.: Barbour.

Willard, Frances (1978) *Woman in the Pulpit* [1889], Washington, DC: Zenger.

Winslow, Hubbard and Sanford, Mrs John (1854) *The Benison: The Lady's Manual of Moral and Intellectual Culture*, New York: Leavitt & Allen.

Wise, Daniel (1987) "Bridal greetings: a marriage gift in which the mutual duties of husband and wife are familiarly illustrated and enforced" [1851], in Carolyn De Swarte Gifford (ed.) *The American Ideal of the "True Woman": Women in American Protestant Religion*, New York: Garland.

Zikmund, Barbara B. (1982) "Biblical arguments and women's place in the church," in E. Sandeen (ed.) *The Bible and Social Reform*, Philadelphia, Pa.: Fortress Press, pp. 85–104.

Chapter 22

Religious Individualism in Nineteenth-century American Families

Anne C. Rose

The family, at first glance, does not seem a place of religious experience or a source of personal beliefs. Religion might more properly be found in public observance – perhaps the reading of sacred texts or performance of ritual – or in the dilemmas of conscience and ecstatic visions of the individual psyche. Families, by contrast, satisfy mundane needs of breadwinning, housekeeping, and child-rearing. Surely parents reinforce Sunday school lessons, but few of us identify homes with spirituality.

Yet earlier generations believed firm piety and right practice were rooted in kinship. In the Bible, Abraham pledged obedience to God on behalf of his household and offspring. Circumcision was the sign of a family covenant (Gen. 17: 1–27). Christianity left room for differing emphases. Although Jesus taught that "he who loves father or mother" or "son or daughter more than me is not worthy of me" (Matt. 10: 37), Paul worked to preserve families divided by the conversion to Christianity of one spouse. If "a brother has a wife who is an unbeliever, and she consents to live with him, he should not divorce her"; a Christian wife should likewise be faithful to an unbelieving man (1 Cor. 7: 12–13). These texts positioned Christianity between messages to sacrifice or honor family bonds. Cloistered celibacy was an ideal of the Middle Ages, along with the sacrament of matrimony. Protestants reinterpreted Jesus's words to counsel spiritual transcendence within marriage. When Martin Luther left the monastery, wed a former nun in 1525, and fathered six children, he understood the symbolism of his actions: salvation, though not achieved in family life, would be nurtured by domesticity.

This appreciation of the religious role of families grew out of a sense that piety was an expression of commitment rooted in daily life. Judeo-Christian thinking fully grasped the social dimensions of faith. Morality protected order, ritual bound communities, and tradition linked generations. Families, as agents of socialization and inheritance, were inseparable from the purposes of religion.

Today new perspectives permit us to miss these connections between religion and family. Secularism encourages us to associate worship solely with the Sabbath, and families seem no more than adjuncts to congregations. Flourishing individualism, supported by the key role of freedom in American political thought, downplays family ties. We expect to find religious interest, if at all, in spiritual self-expression and participation in voluntary associations.

This essay seeks to return our attention to the family as a mediator of religious experience. It focuses on a historical transition that took off in the nineteenth century: families once hierarchical in structure and uniform in belief gave way to households that coped with doctrinal diversity fostered by equality at home. The Puritans had envisioned fathers supervising wives, children, and servants in the practice of right religion. The family was at once a microcosm and foundation of the commonwealth. But by the nineteenth century, patriarchs faced the limits of their rule. Lyman Beecher (1775–1863), one of the century's leading Protestant evangelists, witnessed all of his eleven children desert his Calvinist theology for innovative understandings of faith. Jacob Mordecai (1762–1838) used his mastery of Jewish learning to respond to Christian polemicists. Only three of his thirteen children married Jews, however; some, swayed by the Christian gospel, were baptized. No less, only one daughter in the large family of the Irish-born publisher Mathew Carey (1760–1839) married a Catholic. He did not live to read the hostile accounts of the Inquisition written by his Protestant grandson, the historian Henry Charles Lea. These fathers responded to the children's independence with disappointment and sometimes with anger. The rise of diverse beliefs among kin did not portend the end of religious commitment, however, or the breakdown of family. Families, bending to accommodate individuality, gradually let go of religious conformity and learned to live with dissent.

Nineteenth-century Americans were willing, often anxious, to try new things. They were people eager for journeys: from place to place, toward greater social status, to unexpected religious convictions. It was this self-assertive temper that introduced religious differences into families. Sometimes the clash of opinions was a by-product of secular events, perhaps an upwardly mobile marriage. Crises of faith, with equal force, upended domestic religious arrangements. In all cases, willfulness combined with thoughtfulness about religion to produce family dramas.

Individual Aspirations and Family Faiths

In the early republic, young Americans claimed the right to free choice in marriage, even if the pursuit of happiness challenged scriptural rules to take a partner of the same faith. The assumption that marriage might serve personal gratification exposed mating to secular pressures. Desires for assimilation, success, and romance – commonly working together – united religious outsiders and insiders. The persuasiveness of worldly motives, however, did not produce neglect of religion or homogenization of doctrines. These were households that tolerated differing views.

Jewish men who wed Christian wives enacted a story of upward mobility shaped by the inequality of American religions. The romance of loving someone unlike oneself framed the pragmatic tale of ambition: genteel women were swept up in the outsider's determination, aspiring men swayed by the confidence of the well-born. Moses and Solomon Mordecai, Jacob's sons, left the family's successive homes in North Carolina and Virginia to become a lawyer and doctor respectively. In 1817, Moses married a Christian in Raleigh; Solomon did the same in Mobile in 1824. Judah Benjamin and David Yulee – both born in St Thomas, both attorneys, and eventually United States senators – also took Christian wives. Benjamin married into the New Orleans Catholic gentry in 1833. David Yulee's father-in-law, following Yulee's wedding in 1846, was a former governor of Kentucky. Advantageous matches for the husbands, the marriages nonetheless admitted affection. "Sweet tempered, amiable," and "well informed" were the words Solomon Mordecai chose to describe his fiancée to his brother Samuel in 1824 (Mordecai, Mar. 29, Duke). When Moses, now widowed, married his wife's sister the same year, his bride resisted her family. The "Miss Lanes & their aunt are so much opposed to it," Moses's sister Ellen told their sister Caroline (Jan. 10, Duke). Nancy Lane wed Moses because she followed her heart.

These families lived a double religious life that weighed heavily on the Jewish spouse. Although the men kept a measure of religious independence, Christianity became the family faith. Husbands, though unbaptized, were often treated ritually as Christians. Moses Mordecai was buried in a Christian cemetery over the objections of his Jewish kin. Judah Benjamin was married by a priest. Being folded into Christian society was one of the points of intermarriage; yet few men expected to become Christians. Solomon Mordecai's baptism in 1859, thirty-five years after his marriage, attests equally to his gradual absorption of Christianity and his tenacious sense of himself as a Jew. These were men who kept one eye ahead and the other behind. David Yulee assured his wife in 1848 that he was reading the sermons she advised (Yulee, May 14). Soon writing, in turn, to his father, Moses Elias Levy, he pledged his "affectionate interest in you," but vowed to be "responsible only to God" for his "religious views" (May 21, 1849). Yulee belonged to a Presbyterian church when he died in 1886. Even so, in the 1860s he had compiled two handwritten volumes of his father's writings on Jewish philosophy. More Christian than Jewish, Yulee remained suspended between religions and stood at a distance from his Christian kin.

Social power and romantic love combined in another way to bring diversity of faiths to households: successful Protestant men felt free to make religiously risky matches. Status was not the goal of these marriages, but the condition. Stephen A. Douglas and Zebulon Vance, members of the United States Senate, wed Catholics in 1856 and 1880 respectively. The element of scandal was not lost on observers. The wife of a former senator, herself a Catholic, gossiped to her daughter that Douglas's "Lady" is "a Catholic, was married by the Priest, etc. etc." (Maria Ewing to Ellen Sherman, in Ewing, Jan. 15, 1857). A minister in Vance's home state of North Carolina warned him that the wedding "would produce a shock" (Vance to Florence Martin, in Vance, Mar. 3 [1880]). Neither man was deterred by public opinion. Protected by their prestige, they acted on their desires. Both were widowers of Protestant wives, in love with young women. Adele Cutts, beautiful by all reports, was twenty-two years younger than Douglas. "I am *heart hungry* to see you," Vance implored Florence Martin, and "almost went crazy over your allusions to your wedding garments!" (in Vance, Mar. 15, 1880 [Mar. 1880]; all italics appear in the original texts). These middle-aged men had adhered to acceptable paths and now chose to disregard religious taboos.

They did not anticipate that private conflicts would be stirred by their own prejudices. Vance nearly lost his bride when he resisted the promises required for a marriage dispensation by the Catholic church. After he met with Archbishop Gibbons, he consented to religious freedom for his wife and to the baptism of future children. But "I had heard from childhood about the diabolical craft of the priests," how they "came between man & wife, dethroning him," he confessed to Florence. Catholicism threatened to "wound my conscience and degrade my manhood, as well as rob me of the love and respect of my people" (in Vance, Mar. 4 [1880]). The crisis past, the Vances sought a religious middle ground. Still unmarried, Vance felt guilty about dining out one Sunday and walking in the park, "contrary to our Presbyterian way of spending the Sabbath." "Your church I am aware does not agree with mine as to the sanctity of the Sabbath day," he continued, thinking ahead, "but still I *know* we will agree in welcoming its quiet hours" (Apr. 18, 1880). When Florence visited Asheville in the Carolina mountains after the wedding, she was distressed that there "was no church here." "I *must*," she told her husband, "have church" (Sept. 19, 1880). The couple lived mainly in Washington. The religious issue, never quite resolved, pushed the Vances toward self-understanding and forbearance.

These instances of marrying up or down cast light on religious individualism in families. They show the power of secular motives in democratic society. Seeking happiness, whether conceived as assimilation, gratified love, or simply exercising one's will, couples initially slighted their differences of belief. The stories show, too, that the religious outcomes were unpredictable. Egalitarianism had entered the family, and women had a voice in determining the household's observance. The families also reveal that individualism had two faces: integrity and isolation. Although family members were not required to concede their convictions, each one might have to practice his or her religion alone.

The depth of the cultural forces uniting dissimilar partners can be measured by mixed marriages among Jewish women. For decades, they watched their brothers wed gentiles, but rarely did so themselves. Conservatism about family religion, eroded elsewhere, still bound these daughters. In 1878, however, a Cincinnati newspaper carried the headline, "Daughter of a Rabbi Weds a Christian" (*Enquirer*, May 20). This was an elopement, shameful to the father – and Reform leader – Isaac Mayer Wise. But similar matches followed. Rachel Berenson became the wife of Ralph Barton Perry, the Harvard philosopher, in an Anglican ceremony in 1905. Rose Pastor married a son of the financier Anson Phelps Stokes in an Episcopal service the same year.

These turn-of-the-century families combined old and new traits: though religious inequality continued to deter Jewish practice, common intellectual interests were the foundation of marriages. Protestant culture still tended to absorb Jewish spouses. Helen Wise Molony, with a loyalty to Judaism of a rabbi's child, did take her own daughter regularly to services at Isaac Wise's Plum Street Temple. Rachel Berenson Perry, however, left no record of religious activity in Cambridge, and Rose Pastor Stokes, despite her outspoken socialism, wore a cross at her wedding. This inattention to Judaism was less a sign of their eagerness for legitimacy than the subordinate role of religion in their marriages. These women was intellectually accomplished, and they accepted men of similar talents. Helen Wise published fiction, Rachel Berenson had a master's degree from Radcliffe, and Rose Pastor wrote a newspaper column. Not surprisingly, they married, respectively, a lawyer, professor, and left-leaning philanthropist. It must have been easy to accede to the customs of the Protestant majority – perhaps a Christian wedding – because the couples connected most deeply in their secular passions.

Even so, free society did not displace religion, despite the complexities it brought to family faith. Iphigene Molony, the little girl who accompanied her mother on Saturdays to her Grandfather Wise's temple, told an interviewer in 1964 that she never "cared much for the forms of religion," yet, along with her Jewish husband, " we always regarded ourselves as Jews" (Bettman questionnaire). Ambition, love, and companionship produced mixed marriages and injected uncertainty into household religion. Individualism in worship was a source of religious change, however, more than decline. Indeed, democratic culture unleashed intense spirituality side by side with temporal aspirations. Conviction equally challenged the religious harmony of families.

Private Spiritual Journeys and their Consequences for Kin

Nineteenth-century Americans felt free to act on their religious impulses. Whether more or less pious than men and women of other eras, they behaved independently in spiritual matters. Democracy favored making choices. The separation of religion from the state invited the proliferation of denominations. Widespread literacy and education encouraged people to form and express their own opinions. In a society of free agents, the result might have been feverish individualism. Yet most Americans were members of families. Personal religious odysseys took place in households and tended to draw relatives along.

The period's great diaries were a sign of Americans' enthusiasm for constructing a sense of self. Journals kept by Ralph Waldo Emerson (1820–80), George Templeton Strong (1835–75), James A. Garfield (1848–81), and Mary Boykin Chesnut (1861–65), for example, were chronicles of observation and reflection. They were also a medium of spiritual exploration available to laypeople as part of daily life. Diarists inevitably revealed the relation of their religious questioning to their families' practice.

Indeed, the journals' thoughts remained self-contained to a surprising extent. This was a culture enamoured of both privacy and domesticity, and family members were permitted a guarded space to develop their views. James A.

Garfield, raised in the Disciples of Christ, used his diary in a traditional Puritan spirit as an instrument of self-discipline. As a student in Ohio in 1852, he vowed to spend time "communing with my old friend, my journal": "I must enter my own soul and survey it more than I do" (1967: 1: 126, 139). Distressed at his own "chilling indifference," "spirit of scepticism [sic]," and complacency in "living an objective life," he nonetheless continued to record his excitement about books and frustrations with romance (1: 186, 214, 308). The Puritans would have recognized his struggles with temptation, but frowned on his concessions. Garfield's marriage in 1858, Civil War service, and early political career left little time for self-communion. Yet the diary remained open to religious thoughts. "Why not better to let sin alone," he wrote in 1867 after hearing a fire-and-brimstone sermon, "and preach mercy and righteousness?" (1: 367). Garfield loved his family. "At home," he sighed in 1868, "Sweet Home" (1: 444). But the journal was his refuge, and it was here that he dealt most freely with doubt and belief.

George Templeton Strong experienced a deep religious change with seemingly as little effect on his family. His diary – quizzical, witty, and opinionated – recorded his development. Rejecting the Calvinist drama of sin and salvation for the sacramentalism of the historical church, he left Presbyterianism for Episcopalianism. Jonathan Edwards was distasteful, and Strong wondered "how any man can believe what his own heart and the spirit of truth and reason which God has implanted in every mind must every moment testify to be a lie" (1952: 1: 117). John Henry Newman, the British Tractarian, was "glorious," by contrast, in 1841, "the only modern sermons I ever could read with satisfaction" (1: 162). Clearly serious about religion, Strong exercised his independent judgment by taking swipes at foe and friend. The Transcendentalists fell to his pen for their "Deistical New England Socinianism"; the Episcopal clergy had "sensual pig-faces," much like a "fourth-rate snob" (1: 169, 2: 220). Sarcasm was as much a part of his religious commentary as reports on New York churches or discussions of doctrine. Almost absent, however, was information on his family's religion. The hasty baptism of his month-old son, critically ill, appeared in the journal in 1851, as did his mother's funeral in 1853. Yet on the whole his household's churchgoing must be inferred from Strong's own. The diary was so much an adjunct of private religion that it admitted little about family habits.

The religiosity of these men, situated in the midst of domesticity but self-enclosed, helps explain how many nineteenth-century American families lived with diverse beliefs. Families expected individual reflection, allowed privacy, and tolerated differences. Spirituality is rarely unchanging, however, or kept in predictable channels. Personal convictions found their way into family discussions, at times with subversive effects.

Women who lived through spiritual transformations often initiated communication with female kin. Whereas men such as Garfield and Strong relished their independence, women seemed to experience autonomy as loneliness. Wishing to share their thoughts, they created intimate circles within families. Sophia Ripley and Charlotte Dana, who were cousins, corresponded regularly after their conversions to Catholicism in the mid-1840s. It is "a strange sort of lonely life,"

Sophia wrote from Brooklyn in 1855. "I don't hear a Catholic word spoken from morn[in]g till night" (in Ripley [1855?]). The childless wife of a radical Protestant, Sophia was as solitary as her cousin, an unmarried daughter in an Episcopal home. "Charlotte carried on the R. Cath. [sic] service for the servants," her brother Richard noted in his journal, "in the little room" (Dana 1968: 2: 500). Small wonder Sophia believed, as she told Charlotte, that "sympathy between beings of the same kindred" forms "a mystic tie of union that binds them" (Ripley, Sept. 12, 1846). The women's correspondence centered on hopes for their families' conversions. Speaking of her husband, Sophia confided in 1857, "I am daily moved to tears by some instance of the drawing nearer of his heart to the church" (Sept. 18). Here, in a combination of evangelism and longing for unity of family beliefs, was the potential for domestic religious upheaval.

The secret correspondence of Ellen Mordecai, Jacob's daughter, was linked to successive family conversions from Judaism to Christianity in precisely this way. Although contact among Mordecai women was clandestine, changes of heart were less easily hid. Exactly when Ellen became a Christian by conviction is unclear, but it was surely not family news. In 1859, at age 68, she instructed her niece, also named Ellen Mordecai, to make sure "my christian letters," marked with a cross, "by no *possible* mischance . . . be left in the *folds* of 'the family letters.'" "Oh," she reflected, "how *frightful* to think of!" (Mordecai, Feb. 6, UNC). Ellen had long worried about unsympathizing readers. "I am very careful of all your letters," her sister Caroline assured her in 1835, "& have burned nearly all" (Mordecai, July 5, Duke). Fearful as Ellen was of the opinions of her Jewish kin, her correspondents were less able to suppress their beliefs. Caroline was baptized in 1834 and cut off by their father. Rachel, another sister, became a Christian on her deathbed in 1838, after Ellen summoned a minister to administer the sacraments. She was a guest in Solomon Mordecai's home in Mobile in 1859, the year of his baptism. Ellen assured Solomon, she told her niece, that "if he were baptised [sic] it need never be known in Rich[mon]d" in their Jewish family. Is "not this change of heart in your dear Uncle a blessing prayed, more than hoped for by us[,] poor *faithless* creatures as we are?" (Mordecai, Feb. 6, UNC). For decades, Ellen's hidden fervor met and stirred her relations' spiritual longings. Living with anxieties of disclosure and hard feelings of betrayal, the Mordecais witnessed recurring personal crises that produced deep family divisions.

In classic Puritanism, conversion bonded the family. The reception of grace secured the individual's submission to overlapping obligations: covenants with God, church, state, and family. Nineteenth-century America, by contrast, contained numerous denominations, and conversion, at times, meant the choice of a new faith. In families less reserved than the Mordecais, one conversion might precipitate all into crisis.

Widespread Protestant anti-Catholicism made becoming a Catholic especially taxing. Converts were not stopped, however, by fears of family distress. Wilhelmine Easby-Smith of Tuscaloosa, who entered the church in 1862, grasped the precariousness of her position. Her husband, William Russell Smith, had been a Know-Nothing politician in the 1850s and now served in the Confederate army.

As his third wife, she was raising stepchildren as well as her own. His nativism, the wartime setting, and her responsibility for other mothers' children induced Wilhelmine to hide her intentions. The night before she took first communion, William paled and "went out" when she revealed her plan, "shutting the door with enough force to make me understand how deeply he was offended" (Easby-Smith 1931: 139). She had an inheritance and would separate from William, if necessary, to live with her children and mother in Washington, DC.

Yet the result was more complex than alienation of husband and wife. The Smiths entered a lifelong – and friendly – religious truce. Love combined with good humor to persuade William to acquiesce in his wife's conversion. On their fourteenth wedding anniversary in 1868, his gift to her, as usual, was a funny poem. "The Honey-Moon" wonders if the moon's "golden ray" will "pass away," but ends reassured that "she" is "as bright as she was wont to be on that espousal night" (Smith Papers). With each of its fifteen lines marked by a calender year of their marriage, the lyric conveys the lighthearted affection that moderated their differing views. William consented to the Catholic upbringing of their children and the stepchildren still living at home. On their side, the Catholics in the household agreed, one daughter recalled, to avoid religious discussions. Even so, their piety worked a slow but decisive effect: William became a Catholic on his deathbed in 1896. The starting point for what became a family religious journey was Wilhelmine's private conviction. Her decision set in motion forces that divided, changed, and finally reunited her kin over a period of many years.

In the end, however, fervent religious individualism might produce its opposite: a single household faith imposed by the convert's will. Beliefs arrived at by reflection could awaken thoughtfulness in kin, but intolerance also inhered in faith. There was no question about the conversion of the family of Orestes Brownson when he became a Catholic in 1844. "He thinks for a dozen men," wrote his friend Isaac Hecker: Brownson had been a Presbyterian, Universalist, religious skeptic, Unitarian, and Transcendentalist in succession before he accepted Catholicism (Hecker 1988: 322) . His wife Sarah, led by Hecker to see the truth of Catholic doctrine, was not forced into the church. Even so, new Catholic commitments subsumed the family. Channing Brownson, 10 years old and named for the famous Unitarian preacher, became "William Ignatius." The older boys, some recently at school in the Transcendentalist community at Brook Farm, entered Catholic academies. John and Henry later studied for the priesthood, and Sarah, the only daughter, married a convert nearly as old as her father.

Behind this family transformation was the father's religious passion. "He impressed me with an idea of fear, that I can never overcome," Orestes, Jr., told his brother Henry in 1890. As a Protestant minister "in a great loose silk dress," their father "used to preach with all the seriousness of life & death": "His whole soul was in his metaphysical, philosophical & theological studies and he saw not that what interested him could not interest his son Orestes" (Henry Brownson Papers, Apr. 6). Utterly independent-minded, Brownson narrowed his family's choices by his fervency. Newfound belief extended its own authority.

The ambiguous effects on families of personal faith underscore the persistence of piety in a democratic age. Secular dreams of freedom were matched by a searching religious spirit. Both challenged families with disagreements and un-certainty. No less, religious institutions had to rethink traditional ways of approaching households.

The Public Religious Connections of Unconventional Families

In Judeo-Christian culture, families were the building blocks of religious commu-nities. Fathers, as heads of households, mediated between church or synagogue and his kin. A single member of a congregation – perhaps a widow – was anomolous; so was mobility from faith to faith. Nineteenth-century American families, increasingly dynamic and divided, threatened to pull the accustomed social rug out from beneath institutions. A willful laity compelled leaders to seek new measures to cope with families of unexpected kinds.

Few domestic situations were as vexing as the events that followed the con-versions to Catholicism in the mid-1830s of Pierce and Cornelia Connelly. For the Catholic church, the couple's spirituality upset delicate balances in its values, setting the stage for the transformation of Pierce's fervor into anti-Catholic aggression. His desire to enter the priesthood was predictable. He had been an Episcopal minister in Natchez, Mississippi, led to Catholicism by his study of patristics. Cornelia, too, accepted the Catholic faith; even more, in 1841, though a mother of three children, she acceded to the dissolution of her marriage and a vow of chastity. The Catholic clergy, however, was divided. Although the Pope favored the Connellys' religious vocations, other prelates sacrificed the family reluctantly. Indeed, it was Pierce's recovery of conjugal feeling that subverted his faith. In 1848, Cornelia took final vows in England and became the first Superior of the Society of the Holy Child Jesus. Pierce, though ordained, was as outraged as a cuckolded husband. Vowing to *"rescue my blessed wife from the hands of devils,"* he launched invectives against "coarse" priests who practice "impure casuistry" on "gifted women" (Con-nelly, in *Positio*, 1: 307; *Reasons*: 19). In 1849, he filed suit in the English courts to reclaim his wife. By the time he lost the case in 1858, Pierce had returned to the Episcopal Church. Cornelia's purported abduction, in the meantime, became a staple of no-popery literature.

The Catholic Church was buffeted by Pierce Connelly's ardor, naivety, and prejudice. In his headlong rush to sanctity, he did not quite grasp the distinction between celibacy and marriage: a priest had no conjugal rights. This was also a textbook case of Protestants' love–hate relation with Catholicism. Pierce's longing to enter holy space became, on the rebound, imaginings of conspiracy. With no deep understanding of Catholicism or himself, Pierce brought internal discord and external controversy to the church. His admiration of apostolic succession was a sign of his discontent with the era's individualism; yet his behavior was willfulness run wild. Religious institutions, used to exercising control of families, now struggled to keep up. The prospect of encountering exemplary piety, such as Cornelia's, was matched by the headaches of un-disciplined conviction.

Interfaith families inspired more coherent institutional responses than conversions. Perhaps this was because secular interests counterbalanced piety in mixed marriages, averting tumultuous fervor. Intermarriages were far more common, however, than cases of conscience. Bureaucratic solutions addressed the strain of ministering to congregations composed increasingly of parts of families, but could not restore the household securely to the center of worship.

Catholics and Jews, with more to lose by intermarriage perhaps than the dominant Protestants, debated, legislated, and communicated with families in nearly identical ways. The unacceptability of mixed marriage was beyond dispute; conflict arose over solutions. Rabbi Isaac Leeser denounced the unconventional conversion of a gentile wife, without *beit din* or *mikveh*, in 1860. She "is as much out of the pale of Israel as she was before that *mockery* of Judaism was exhibited" ([Lesser] 1860: 262). Similarly exasperated, a canon lawyer in the 1920s titled an essay, "Should dispensations for mixed marriages be absolutely abolished?" "Yes, they should," the author answered decisively: the "frequency and ease" of obtaining them "has practically wiped out the consciousness among Catholics of the very serious prohibition of the Church against mixed marriages" (Woywood, 1928: 703). Long-standing controversies produced official resolutions. In 1909, the Central Conference of American Rabbis ruled that interfaith marriage was "contrary to the tradition of the Jewish religion and should therefore be discouraged by the American Rabbinate" (quoted in Jacobs 1981: 98). In the Catholic church, the 1917 Code of Canon Law clarified the grounds for a dispensation. Policy aside, some rabbis and priests issued pledges to mixed couples concerning the religious training of children. Priests used printed forms as early as the mid-nineteenth century; rabbis, less receptive to compromise, still typed their own after 1900. The fact is, however, that as clergy pushed interfaith families away with one hand, they extended the other.

Indeed, families of divided beliefs might live comfortably on the margins of religious communities. Making peace required a relaxed outlook from laity and clergy. The Atlanta household of Esther La Rose Harris, married in 1873 to Joel Chandler Harris, was, with the exception of her husband, vigorously Catholic. The children received Catholic training, priests visited as guests, and Esther and a daughter corresponded with bishops on friendly terms. Joel, raised a Baptist, all but admitted his early prejudice. One author, he confided to a daughter-in-law Julia in 1907, spent his "time slamming Catholics because he is ignorant of their beliefs and practices[;] but I used to be even more ignorant than he is, so that I can put myself in his place and enjoy his books." "It requires a lifetime for most of us to put ourselves in the places of others," he concluded, "in order to deal charitably with them" (Harris, July 4). The tolerance of priests and kin sustained the Harrises religiously. Even more, the persuasive force of his family's Catholicism convinced Joel to become a Catholic before his death in 1908.

The Harris' success as an interfaith family rested on the underlying commitment of household and church to religious practice. Esther and Joel did not see their differences of opinion as an invitation to secularism. Nor did the clergy equate Joel's persistent dissent with the family's loss to the church. Both sides could imagine that the public religious connection of some kin might serve as a basis for worship.

The Family as a Site of Religious Experience

The domestic outcome of religious individualism was, ironically, the accented importance of households as places of spiritual change. Freedom, whether expressed in nineteenth-century America as worldly desire or strenuous piety, eroded the religious uniformity of patriarchy. Family religion became uncertain; in a democratic mood, everyone seemed to affect the final balance. Families in the past, working in tandem with churches and synagogues, cemented orthodoxy. Now more autonomous and internally diverse, they did not supply answers as often as they posed questions. It is not surprising that family religion became more open-ended in democratic society. But it is crucial to see that the presence of doctrinal variety and spiritual transformation did not eclipse the household's religious role. Indeed, the intricacies of domestic religion made family relations all the more decisive in shaping the spiritual choices of individual kin.

BIBLIOGRAPHY

Bettman, Iphigene Molony, Genealogical Questionnaire, May 9, 1964: American Jewish Archives, Hebrew Union College-Jewish Institute of Religion, Cincinnati, Oh.

Brownson, Orestes, Family Papers: Orestes Augustus Brownson Papers, Archives of the University of Notre Dame, Notre Dame, Ind.

Brownson, Orestes, Jr., Letters: Henry F. Brownson Papers, Archives of the University of Notre Dame, Notre Dame, Ind.

Connelly, Cornelia and Pierce, Family Letters: in *Positio: Documentary Study for the Canonization Process of the Servant of God Cornelia Connelly (née Peacock) 1809–1879* (4 vols), Rome: Sacred Congregation for the Causes of the Saints, vols 1–3, 1983, vol. 4, 1987.

Connelly, Pierce (1852) *Reasons for Abjuring Allegiance to the See of Rome: A Letter to the Earl of Shrewsbury*, Philadelphia, Pa.: Herman Hooker.

Dana, Richard Henry, Jr. (1968) *The Journal of Richard Henry Dana, Jr.* (3 vols), ed. Robert F. Lucid, Cambridge, Mass.: Harvard University Press.

Easby-Smith, Anne (1931) *William Russell Smith of Alabama: His Life and Works*, Philadelphia, Pa.: Dolphin Press.

Evans, Eli N. (1988) *Judah P. Benjamin: The Jewish Confederate*, New York: Free Press.

Ewing, Maria Boyle, Letters: Ellen Ewing Sherman Papers, Henry E. Huntington Library, San Marino, Calif.

Franchot, Jenny (1994) *Roads to Rome: The Antebellum Protestant Encounter with Catholicism*, Berkeley, Calif.: University of California Press.

Garfield, James A. (1967) *The Diary of James A. Garfield* (4 vols), ed. Harry James Brown and Frederick D. Williams, East Lansing, Mich.: Michigan State University Press.

Harris, Joel Chandler, Family Papers: Joel Chandler Harris Papers, Special Collections, Robert W. Woodruff Library, Emory University, Atlanta, Ga.

Hatch, Nathan O. (1989) *The Democratization of American Christianity*, New Haven, Conn.: Yale University Press.

Hecker, Isaac T. (1988) *Isaac T. Hecker, The Diary: Romantic Religion in Ante-Bellum America*, ed. John Farina, New York: Paulist Press.

Jacobs, Walter (1981) "Reform Judaism and mixed marriage," in Elliot L. Stevens (ed.) *Central Conference of American Rabbis Yearbook 1980*, 90, pp. 86–102.

[Leeser, Isaac] (1860) "Interesting Jewish ceremony: reception of a Christian female proselyte," *The Occident, and American Jewish Advocate* 17, pp. 261–2.

Mordecai, Jacob, Family Papers: Jacob Mordecai Papers, Special Collections Library, Duke University, Durham, NC.

Mordecai, Jacob, Family Papers: Jacob Mordecai Papers, Collection 847, Special Collections, University of North Carolina, Chapel Hill, NC.

Morgan, Edmund S. (1966) *The Puritan Family: Religion and Domestic Relations in Seventeenth-Century New England*, rev. edn, New York: Harper and Row; first published 1944.

Perry, Rachel Berenson, Diaries and Letters: Ralph Barton Perry Papers, Harvard University Archives, Nathan Marsh Pusey Library, Harvard University, Cambridge, Mass.

Ripley, Sophia Dana, Letters: Dana Family Papers, Massachusetts Historical Society, Boston, Mass.

Rose, Anne C. (1998) "Interfaith families in Victorian America," in Karen Halttunen and Lewis Perry (eds) *Moral Problems in American Life: New Perspectives on Cultural History*, Ithaca, NY: Cornell University Press.

—— (forthcoming) "Some private roads to Rome: the role of families in nineteenth-century conversions to Catholicism," *The Catholic Historical Review*.

Smith, William Russell, Family Papers: William Russell Smith Papers, Collection 1873, University of North Carolina, Chapel Hill, NC.

Strong, George Templeton (1952) *The Diary of George Templeton Strong* (4 vols), ed. Allan Nevins and Milton Halsey Thomas, New York: Macmillan.

Vance, Zebulon Baird, Family Papers: Zebulon Baird Vance Papers, Division of Archives and History, Department of Cultural Resources, State of North Carolina, Raleigh, NC.

Woywood, Stanislaus (1928) "Should dispensations for mixed marriages be absolutely abolished?", *The Homiletic and Pastoral Review* 28, pp. 703–11.

Yulee, David Levy, Family Papers: David Levy Yulee Papers, Small Collections 13329, American Jewish Archives, Hebrew Union College-Jewish Institute of Religion, Cincinnati, Oh.

Zipser, Arthur and Pearl (1989) *Fire and Grace: The Life of Rose Pastor Stokes*, Athens, Ga.: University of Georgia Press.

Part VII

Intellectual and Literary Culture

Introduction

The "logocentrism" – that is, the focus on verbal discourse – that the American Puritans brought with them as part of their Calvinist heritage insured from the beginning that words and ideas would not be lacking as distinctively American strains of religion began to develop. New England, not surprisingly, was for long in the forefront of theological disputation while the "genetic history of the New England theology" wound through several centuries of metamorphoses in which Calvinism became increasingly attenuated. The "New England way" – the distinctive pattern of church-state collaboration couched in the rhetoric of a restored Israel – was expounded during the seventeenth century in the context of a "federal theology," in which God's covenantal relationship with his new chosen people was explained in a Calvinist matrix at enormous length in an endless flow of sermons and treatises.

As the internal cohesion of the New England commonwealths began to erode during the eighteenth century, latter-day Puritan thinkers such as Jonathan Edwards began to appropriate the new philosophical vocabulary of the Enlightenment to interpret the Calvinist heritage to contemporaries tempted by a growing variety of religious options. Edwards, who is today hailed by many scholars (and conservative religious practitioners) as the greatest of America's religious thinkers, focused particularly on one issue that had nagged Protestants from the early days of the Reformation: lacking the sacramental apparatus of the Catholic Church, how can I be assured of my salvation? Edwards attempted to hold the line against an emergent liberal party that downplayed Calvinist doctrines of divine sovereignty and predestination on the one hand, while simultaneously attempting to restrain what he perceived as the excesses of a new evangelical party for whom the emotional experience of conversion was sufficient proof of divine forgiveness and favor.

During the nineteenth century, Edwardsean and other versions of strict Calvinism began to yield in popular favor to both of these newer strains of thought. Revivalism, in which Edwards himself had been an early and effective participant, grew increasingly detached from its Calvinist moorings, and became an effective strategy in the growing religious marketplace of competing denominations. Liberal Protestantism, on the other hand, tended to find adherents especially in such affluent and cosmopolitan locales as Boston. Liberalism, which reached its fullest flowering within urban "mainline" churches in the Victorian era, bespoke a confident faith in which God's judgment was eclipsed by his goodness and the possibilities of human moral and cultural achievement seemed endless. Such optimism was tempered during the crises of the twentieth century in the neo-Orthodox writings of Paul Tillich and the Niebuhr brothers, which in turn yielded to the social concern of feminist and African-American theologizing.

Religious thought, however, was not confined to the churches and nascent theological seminaries. As the hold of organized religion began to erode during the nineteenth century, especially among the intelligentsia, new takes on the impact of Calvinism on the American experience began to emerge in the fiction of Nathaniel Hawthorne, Herman Melville, Mark Twain, Ralph Waldo Emerson, Harriet Beecher Stowe, and others now regarded as "canonical" authors. Some, like Emerson and Henry David Thoreau, presented alternative philosophical systems around which theologically liberated Americans could order their lives. Others, like Stowe, contributed to a not-so-gradual erosion of Calvinism's grip on the Protestant imagination by introducing alternative images of God through their fictional characterizations. Still others, like Hawthorne, Melville, Twain, and Harold Frederick, went even further in speculating subversively on religious questions far beyond the bounds of institutional propriety.

Nor was religious thought confined to Protestants. As Jewish and Roman Catholic communities began to grow in number and sophistication, indigenous strains of speculation began to develop within their midsts. The relationship between their respective traditions and American culture – Protestant in origins, secular in tendency – became a major theme for Catholic thinkers from Orestes Brownson in the antebellum era to Jesuit John Courtney Murray at the time of Vatican II, as well as for Jewish writers such as Reform leader Isaac Mayer Wise. By the mid-twentieth century, issues such as the meaning of the Holocaust and the existential encounter between the divine and the human began to displace the implications of Americanization, as these communities grew more comfortably assimilated. Religious themes also emerged prominently in fiction, as in the satires of Catholic J. F. Powers and Jewish Philip Roth.

A beginning for this section, as for the previous one, might be found in *Amanda Porterfield*'s essay in Section II, which deals with the major strains of Puritan thought that have had impact in surprising ways in modern American religious experience.

Ava Chamberlain contributes a detailed study of Jonathan Edwards's thought on the perennial Protestant issue of the certainty of salvation and the varieties of hypocrisy, conscious or otherwise, which its quest might engender.

Mary Kupiec Cayton examines the culture of revivalism in the Connecticut Valley during the late eighteenth century, reflecting on the its relationship with the particular circumstances of Connecticut society during that era.

Leigh Eric Schmidt picks up on Chamberlain's theme of hypocrisy, but now sites it in the literary and religious ferment of the early nineteenth century and relates it both to the social disorder of the time as well as to present-day lamentations about the erosion of trust in society.

Lawrence Snyder discusses the "religion of humanity" that emerged among Victorian liberals as an attempt to construct an alternative spirituality that would meet the religious needs of Americans living in an age of growing relativism and skepticism.

Paula Kane takes up the issue of Catholic culture in the twentieth century, by which time American Catholics had become thoroughly immersed, if not entirely absorbed, into the broader world of cultural production: fiction, graphic arts, film, painting and sculpture, and the other genres of expression that constitute "culture" in the artistic sense. As she concludes, American Catholic culture is not now, and probably never has been, as homogenous and "orthodox" as traditionalists might wish, but instead reflects many broader currents at work in the United States and beyond.

Chapter 23

Jonathan Edwards on the Relation between Hypocrisy and the Religious Life

Ava Chamberlain

Nineteenth-century America produced two compelling fictional portraits of its colonial Puritan past. In *The Minister's Wooing* Harriet Beecher Stowe refused to judge "the truth or the falsehood of those systems of philosophic theology" that were "the principal outlet for the proclivities of the New England mind." Although eventually rejecting her own Calvinist heritage, Stowe maintained that "as psychological developments" these theological systems had "an intense interest," and she displayed by her depiction of Samuel Hopkins's piety the "grand side to these strivings of the soul," which she described as "one of the noblest capabilities of humanity" (1978: 24). Few today share Stowe's admiration for the Puritans. Much more common is the view constructed by Nathaniel Hawthorne in *The Scarlet Letter*. His depiction of Arthur Dimmesdale indelibly fixed in the American imagination the image of Puritans as hypocrites who "go about among their fellow-creatures, looking pure as new-fallen snow; while their hearts are all speckled and spotted with iniquity of which they cannot rid themselves" (1961: 98). And modern culture, which ranks authenticity among its highest values, continues to associate the rigorous piety of the Puritans with conscious pretense. However, this presumption of insincerity obscures Stowe's sense that the Puritans are not morally offensive but psychologically interesting. To defend this claim I turn to the writings of perhaps the greatest American Puritan theologian, Jonathan Edwards.

Jonathan Edwards was born in 1703 in East Windsor, Connecticut. His father was pastor of the church in East Windsor, and his mother was the daughter of one of the most prominent ministers in the Connecticut River Valley, Solomon Stoddard. The only son in a family of eleven children, Edwards was raised to enter the ministry. He received his education at Yale College, which had been established in 1701 as a more traditional alternative to the increasingly liberal Harvard. He was ordained in 1727 as the assistant to the aging Solomon Stoddard, and after his grandfather's death in 1729, he was installed as full pastor of the church in Northampton, Massachusetts. He remained there for more than twenty years, moving in 1750 to the Indian mission at Stockbridge, Massachusetts when a controversy in his congregation over the qualifications for communion resulted in his dismissal. In 1757 he was offered the presidency of New Jersey College (Princeton), but five weeks after his installation, in March 1758, he died of complications of a smallpox inoculation.

The defining event of Edwards's tenure in Northampton was the Great Awakening of the early 1740s. Revivalism, however, characterized his pastoral work from the outset. A series of sermons that Edwards preached in 1734 on justification by faith sparked a revival in Northampton, which lasted for more than a year and spread to several neighboring towns along the Connecticut River Valley. *A Faithful Narrative* (1737), Edwards's popular account of this revival, which was published in both England and America, established his international reputation as an evangelist. In the wake of George Whitefield's 1740 tour of Massachusetts and Connecticut, the revival that historians in retrospect have called the Great Awakening spread throughout New England. During this period Edwards distinguished himself as a "powerful preacher," first delivering the sermon "Sinners in the Hands of an Angry God" in July 1741. More importantly, he displayed for the first time during the Awakening his powerful intellect. To address the increasingly vociferous Old Light criticisms of the revival, Edwards wrote a series of treatises designed to vindicate what he suspected was nothing less than the anticipatory tremors of the millennium. *The Distinguishing Marks of a Work of the Spirit of God* (1741) gave the New Lights an effective technique for defense of the revival and established Edwards as its leading apologist. He continued this defense in *Some Thoughts Concerning the Present Revival of Religion* (1743), and brought the series on the revival to a close with *Religious Affections* (1746), his most mature and philosophically sophisticated work to date.

In the late 1740s Edwards decided to substitute for the broad policy on church admissions that had prevailed in Northampton since the days of Stoddard a more rigorous one that required applicants to give a narrative account of their conversion experiences. This innovation precipitated the controversy that resulted in his dismissal from Northampton and his acceptance of a missionary post in the western Massachusetts wilderness. In Stockbridge Edwards devoted little of his time to sermon composition, generally repreaching old texts that he delivered to the native Housatonics awkwardly through a translator. Instead, he wrote a series of treatises intended to counter the increasing popularity of theological liberalism in the trans-Atlantic evangelical community. In *Freedom of the Will* (1754) and *Original Sin* (1758) Edwards primarily engaged representatives of the English Enlightenment to defend the determinism and depravity integral to the traditional Calvinist view of human nature. Edwards also wrote *On the Nature of True Virtue* and its companion piece *Concerning the End for which God Created the World* while in Stockbridge, although they were posthumously published in 1765. In these two dissertations Edwards extended his polemic against theological liberalism by constructing a view of moral agency wholly dependent upon a subordination of the human will to the sovereign will of God. By his death in 1758 Edwards had laid the foundation for a new American school of divinity that would dominate theological debates well into the nineteenth century.

Many contemporary assessments of Edwards's greatness have rested exclusively on his penchant for philosophical speculation, attempting to "enhance Edwards's reputation as a philosopher by finding him to be essentially a modern mind trapped in an antiquated vocabulary" (Tracy 1980: 6). Edwards does distinguish himself by his use of liberal Enlightenment thought to pursue his conservative theological agenda. The influence of John Locke's epistemological views pervades both his private notebooks and his published writings. For example, in *Religious Affections* he uses the concept of a "new simple idea" to depict the activity of grace in the regenerative process. And in *Original Sin* he uses a Lockean interpretation of personal identity to defend the doctrine of innate depravity. Similarly, in *True Virtue* Edwards both appropriates and undermines the ethical sentimentalism of such British moral sense theorists as Francis Hutcheson, Lord Shaftesbury, and David Hume. According to this interpretation Edwards is interesting not because he was a Puritan theologian but because he was a modern philosopher. For example, Perry Miller considered Edwards's doctrinal positions "barbaric" but maintained that he "repays study because . . . he speaks from an insight into science and psychology so much ahead of his time that our own can hardly be said to have caught up with him" (1981: 328, xxxii). Like Hawthorne, Miller was offended by the apparent cruelty and probable hypocrisy of colonial Calvinism. To appreciate Stowe's insight requires a shift in perspectives.

This perspective will begin to emerge if we distinguish between the form of hypocrisy modern American culture associates with the Puritans and that which complicates Edwards's view of the religious life. Modern-day hypocrites willfully deceive by constructing a false facade of virtue or piety. They know that appearance contradicts reality and consciously intend to maintain this counterfeit posture. So construed, religious hypocrites are simply ordinary hypocrites acting in a religious context. They advocate monogamy but commit adultery. They profess to love God as a means to make money or acquire power. But the nature of such deception is structurally no different from that of the politician whose apparent patriotism masks his greed or the woman who disguises her infidelity by fabricating conjugal contentment. Although assuming different poses, each of these hypocrites commit the same transgression. They represent themselves to others in a way they know to be false. That the dissimulation occurs in a religious context does not fundamentally alter its character.

By contrast, in Edwards's thought hypocrisy primarily signifies not the self-conscious and willful intention to deceive others. The deception of others is included in the meaning of the term, but it is a secondary by-product of the hypocrite's own self-deception. Genuine religious hypocrisy entails a false profession of faith created by a claim to grace made in the absence of its corresponding inner condition. However, this incongruity between appearance and reality results not from a conscious intent to deceive. Edwards's hypocrites represent themselves to the world in a way they sincerely believe to be true, but because they deceive themselves their self-presentation is false. It is this element of self-deception that distinguishes religious hypocrisy from its ordinary counterpart and New England Puritanism from its modern stereotype. As ordinary hypocrites Puritans offend modern sensibilities by their lack of authenticity, but as a people whose very hope for salvation rested upon a tragically uncertain foundation, the Puritans are interesting.

Religious hypocrisy is but one example of the fundamentally deceptive character of Edwards's worldview. Following Plato and Augustine, he portrays reality to be – like a hall of mirrors – a confusion of appearances and reflected images. The vigilant Christian always suspects that things are not as they seem. Rigid morality and shrill piety likely mask the hypocrite. Absolute judgment may obscure inner error. Reality contains one certainty, the truth of the revelation of Jesus Christ, but appropriation of this truth risks confusion with its counterfeit. No facet of Edwards's thought is free of the complexity created by the problem of indiscernible counterparts. Indiscernible counterparts are apparently identical pairs of objects having radically distinct ontological identities. They may be numerically distinct objects, such as two members of the same church or two acts of charity for the poor; or the confusion may be created by viewing one object from two different perspectives. Nevertheless, their resemblance is deceptive; being apparently identical, it is difficult to differentiate the genuine from the counterfeit or to isolate the features that distinguish between them.

In Edwards's theology the gap between appearance and reality becomes a chasm. It separates grace from nature, the antitype from the type, the invisible from the visible church, genuine from counterfeit affections, and true virtue from ordinary morality, to name only a few of the indiscernible counterparts that confuse his concept of reality. Nevertheless, how to distinguish the saint from the hypocrite is the central form the problem of indiscernible counterparts takes within Edwards's theology. Following Thomas Shepard, Edwards distinguishes between "two sorts of hypocrites." Evangelical hypocrites "are those that are deceived with false discoveries and elevations; which often cry down works, and men's own righteousness . . . but at the same time make a righteousness of their discoveries, and of their humiliation, and exalt themselves to heaven with them." Legal hypocrites, on the other hand, "are deceived with their outward morality and external religion; many of which are professed Arminians, in the doctrine of justification" (1959: 173). Both sorts of hypocrite mislead others with their false piety, but their condition is defined primarily by self-deception. They misinterpret the evidence and reason from false premises, incorrectly concluding either that their religious experience or their moral behavior is a certain sign of grace. Edwards developed his views concerning evangelical hypocrisy during the Awakening of the early 1740s, and he articulated a comprehensive critique of legal hypocrisy in his Stockbridge writings. I will consider each in chronological order.

The Structure of Counterfeit Piety

It was the period of religious revival extending in New England from 1734 to the mid-1740s that first complicated Edwards's understanding of the religious life. Edwards advocated an evangelical understanding of Calvinist Christianity that emphasized the role of the emotions in both the act of conversion and the practice of the Christian life. As a consequence, he thought that the rhetorical use of terror in preaching was an effective means of convicting sinners, and that religious affections were a necessary expression of true Christian faith. During the Awakening itinerant evangelists, such as George Whitefield from England and Gilbert Tennent from the New Jersey, spread this style of preaching and this understanding of Calvinism throughout New England. As a result, the churches divided into the pro- and anti-revival factions that were called the New Lights and the Old Lights. Although Edwards was a loyal New Light, from the behavior of the radical revivalists he gained new insight into the nature of religious hypocrisy. "I once did not imagine that the heart of man had been so unsearchable as I find it is," wrote Edwards in 1741. "I find more things in wicked men that may counterfeit, and make a fair shew of piety . . . than once I knew of" (1972: 285). The Awakening demonstrated to Edwards that experimental religion's very dependence upon the affections made it vulnerable to self-deception. It tended to produce hypocrites because it falsely identified sudden, unusual, and overpowering emotional and physical experiences as evidence of divine grace.

The problem of evangelical hypocrisy dominates all of Edwards's revival writings, but in *Religious Affections* he most fully articulates a mechanism for unmasking counterfeit piety. He begins by examining the complex of characteristics generally associated with revival religion; for example, that religious affections are raised very high and have great effects upon the body; that they come with Scripture texts remarkably brought to mind, and are pleasing to the truly godly; that they occur in various kinds all in the expected order, and incline their subjects to spend much time in religion, praising, and glorifying God. Emphasizing the role of reason in the religious life, Old Light critics of the revival tended to maintain that affections such as these were certain signs of hypocrisy. In contrast, the radicals viewed them as certain signs of conversion. Arguing that they "are no signs one way or the other, either that affections are such as true religion consists in, or that they are otherwise," Edwards agreed with neither side of the debate (1959: 127). The subjects of such experiences could be either saints or hypocrites; that New Lights used them as evidence of salvation, therefore, generated the first pair of indiscernible counterparts addressed by Edwards.

These experiences do not discriminate between saints and hypocrites because they do not indicate the operation of a gracious cause. For example, when Edwards first preached "Sinners in the Hands of an Angry God" in Enfield, Connecticut, his auditors reportedly cried so loudly that he had to interrupt his delivery of the sermon. Any evangelical minister would take this as an encouraging response, but if we apply Edwards's own logic to this event, no member of the Enfield congregation would be warranted in concluding, on the basis of this experience alone, that he or she had been saved. Through the intervention of divine grace, some may have been saved, and because "the mind can have no lively or vigorous exercise, without some effect upon the body" this transforming experience would have caused a physical response (1959: 132). But it is equally likely that they experienced these intense emotions because of some natural cause, such as a weakened constitution or an overactive imagination. Because experiences such as these may have either a gracious or a natural cause, they are not a sufficient foundation for a genuine assurance of salvation. Edwards insists that "if there be a great deal of true religion, there will be great religious affections" (p. 127). Consequently, saints desire such experiences as perquisites of grace, but if they use them as grounds for assurance they run the risk of hypocrisy. Taking great affections as a standard of measurement, therefore, sinners are indistinguishable from saints. Hypocrites are deceived by this semblance of true piety, which confuses more than clarifies the religious life.

One technique that Edwards uses to identify those religious experiences that are inadequate grounds for assurance may be called the devil-comparison method. Edwards articulates this method in what is perhaps the most striking example of indiscernible counterparts in his writings, the sermon "True Grace Distinguished from the Experience of Devils," which was first preached in 1752. Edwards takes as his text for this sermon James 2: 19: "Thou believest that there is one God; thou doest well; the devils also believe and tremble." He draws from this text a description of the religious beliefs and experiences of the devil that mirrors in almost every particular genuine evangelical Christianity. "The devil," according to Edwards, "is orthodox in his faith; he believes the true scheme of doctrine; he is no Deist, Socinian, Arian, Pelagian, or Antinomian" (1858: 457). Because he was "educated in the best divinity school in the universe, viz. the heaven of heavens," the devil's knowledge of God's nature and the works of his providence, including the redemptive activity of Jesus Christ and the content of the Holy Scriptures, far exceeds anything of which human beings are capable (p. 455). Furthermore, the devil responds to this speculative knowledge with the affections of fear and longing for salvation, making his religion even more closely resemble true spiritual conviction.

Edwards uses the religious experience of the devil to formulate a test to differentiate between saints and hypocrites: "Nothing in the mind of man, that is of the same nature with what the devils experience, or are subjects of, is any sure sign of saving grace" (1858: 451). By means of this devil-comparison method Edwards eliminates as an adequate foundation for assurance not only a wide variety of religious affections but also orthodox belief and accurate doctrinal knowledge. Using all of these features of the religious life as a standard of measurement, the saint is indiscernible not only from the hypocrite but also from the devil. But because the devil is by definition excluded from God's salvation, his religious beliefs and experiences cannot be the effect of saving grace. They therefore function as a negative criterion against which human beliefs and experiences of similar appearance may be judged inadequate.

The devil-comparison method is related to another technique Edwards uses to distinguish between gracious and counterfeit affections, which may be called the devil-causation method. According to Edwards, the devil is one of the most pervasive causes of counterfeit affections. He can "counterfeit all the saving operations and graces of the Spirit of God" and all "those operations that are preparatory to grace" (1959: 158). By means of these counterfeits, he "deceives great multitudes about the state of their souls" and "establishes many, in a strong confidence of their eminent holiness, who are in God's sight, some of the vilest hypocrites" (p. 88). Evangelical hypocrites, therefore, serve on the front line in the devil's campaign against the advancement of the kingdom of heaven. By mixing counterfeit religion with true Edwards believes the devil precipitated the decline of every revival in Christian history and insidiously works to discredit the cause of evangelical religion. He therefore states as a test, "That only is to be trusted to, as a certain evidence of grace, which Satan cannot do, and which it is impossible should be brought to pass by any power short of divine" (p. 159). An assurance of salvation built upon experiences within the scope of the devil's agency is at best false confidence and at worst devil-induced delusion. But Edwards eliminates these experiences not only because they may promote the devil's campaign of deception; they are also inadequate because of their status as natural phenomena.

Originally created by God, the devil is a natural being in the broad sense of the term. In his intercourse with human beings he is constrained to use natural means. According to Edwards, his primary vehicle of operation is the imagination. Unlike nineteenth-century romantics who exalted the creative powers of the imagination, Edwards consistently maintains a pre-modern view of the imagination as "the devil's grand lurking place, the very nest of foul and delusive spirits" (1959: 288). This faculty affords the devil his only direct access to the human soul. By stimulating impressions on the imagination he exercises his powers to deceive. Therefore, evangelical religion's approbation of the imagination promotes counterfeit affections and hypocritical faith. During the Awakening people "had impressed upon them ideas of a great outward light" and called it a "spiritual discovery of . . . Christ's glory"; they "had ideas of Christ's hanging on the cross, and his blood running from his wounds" and called it "a spiritual sight of Christ crucified"; they "had a lively idea of a person of a beautiful countenance smiling upon them" and called it "a spiritual discovery of the love of Christ to their souls" (1959: 211–12). Despite their extraordinary character, experiences such as these are not reliable evidence of salvation. It is likely they are caused by the devil to beguile the sinner by a false sense of assurance. But more fundamentally, imaginary ideas are an inadequate foundation for assurance because they are natural ideas, composed of external ideas similar in kind to those perceived by ordinary sensation. Even if God acts upon the imagination by his common grace – as Edwards frequently notes he did in the case of Balaam – the experience is not saving.

By the operations of common grace, God "assists natural principles to do the same work to a greater degree, which they do of themselves by nature" (1959: 207). In this assisting capacity, God at times impresses ideas upon the imagination to produce visions. Unlike the devil, God does not aim to deceive the sinner, but the visionary experiences caused by God are functionally equivalent to those caused by the devil. When "the Spirit of God impresses on a man's imagination, either in a dream, or when he is awake, any outward ideas of any of the senses, either voices, or shapes and colors," he does so in the same way as the devil, by "impressing, in an extraordinary manner, the ideas that will hereafter be received by sight and hearing" (p. 207). Common grace may also cause high affections that have great effects upon the body. It may assist reason in its speculations about religious matters and enhance natural conscience's apprehensions of right and wrong, as it does in the legal humiliations preparatory to conversion. But in all these instances "'tis no more than nature moved, acted and improved; here is nothing supernatural and divine" (p. 207). Intense emotions that strongly affect the body, voices, visions, and all manner of imaginary ideas play a role in the religious life, but only as epiphenomenal attributes. Taken together they present a composite portrait of religious hypocrisy. "Nothing hinders but that all these things may meet together in men," writes Edwards, "and yet there be nothing more than the common influences of the Spirit of God, joined with the delusions of Satan, and the wicked and deceitful heart" (pp. 182–3).

The only distinguishing characteristic of truly gracious affections is a cause qualitatively distinct from all forms of natural agency. "Affections that are truly spiritual and gracious," writes Edwards, "do arise from those influences and operations on the heart, which are spiritual, supernatural, and divine" (1959: 197). This characteristic is not a sign in the proper sense of the term, for it is not an externally observable feature of the affections. It is an *a priori* criterion that analytically distinguishes the saint from the hypocrite and truly gracious affections from their many counterfeits. It establishes that the cause of the affections is "entirely above nature," and something "which no improvement of those qualifications, or principles that are natural, no advancing or exalting of them to higher degrees, and no kind of composition of them, will ever bring men to" (p. 205). According to Edwards, at the moment of conversion God infuses in the sinner a "new spiritual sense." This sense allows the saint to experience not simply a compound of natural external ideas but a "new sensation or perception of the mind, which . . . could be produced by no exalting, varying or compounding of that kind of perceptions or sensations which the mind had before" (p. 205). Perceiving "the transcendently excellent and amiable nature of divine things," this new sense alone is capable of sorting out the confusion of indiscernible counterparts that complicate Edwards's vision of the religious life (p. 240).

This new sense is that characteristic picked out as unique to the saint by the devil-comparison method. According to Edwards, the perception of God's holiness "is the only thing that can be mentioned, pertaining to the devil's apprehension and sense of the divine Being, that he did lose" when he fell from heaven (1858: 468). Therefore, it also picks out those "things, wherein those affections which are spiritual and gracious, differ from those which are not so, and may be distinguished and known" (1959: 127). For example, that the affections are attended with a spirit of humility, that they produce a change of nature by softening the heart, that they manifest a beautiful symmetry and proportion, and increase the desire for greater spiritual attainments, are features that distinguish truly gracious affections from their counterfeits. Unlike intense emotional and physical reactions, which may be caused by either nature or grace, these distinguishing signs are the necessary effect of only one possible cause. Consider evangelical humility, which is one of the principal signs of truly gracious affections. It is the "sense that a Christian has of his own utter insufficiency, despicableness, and odiousness, with an answerable frame of heart" (p. 311). Edwards contrasts it with the sense of sinfulness, guilt, and exposure to God's wrath that he calls legal humiliation. Legal humility is not counterfeit humility; it is a condition experienced prior to conversion that is caused by the natural effects of common grace. Its evangelical counterpart, however, is by definition a post-conversion experience caused by the supernatural effects of saving grace. No increase in the degree of self-abasement can transform legal humiliation into its evangelical counterpart. Although the humility that characterizes the genuine saint will be weak and inconstant, it is qualitatively distinct from legal humility because it necessarily results from a perception of God's holiness. If there is evangelical humility, or any of the other certain signs, it is therefore valid to infer that the subject of this affection is a genuine saint.

The validity of this inference does not, however, guarantee its practical application. The certain signs of grace are not simply a list of symptoms that mechanically distinguish between saints and hypocrites. Although they identify *a priori* the genuine saint, *a posteriori* identification is complicated by the fact that each of the certain signs itself has a counterfeit counterpart. For example, hypocrites may mistake legal for evangelical humility, confusing the natural with the gracious affection. And they may exhibit a facsimile of evangelical humility that is incorrectly identified as the real thing. Hypocrites "are deceived about themselves as to this matter," writes Edwards, "imagining themselves most humble, when they are most proud, and their behavior is really most haughty." Through a combination of self-deception and spiritual pride, they manufacture "a swelling, self-conceited, confident, showy, noisy, assuming humility," which is the counterfeit counterpart to genuine self-abasement (1959: 319). In *Religious Affections* Edwards exposes the structure of counterfeit piety to construct a foundation for experimental religion with built-in protections against self-deception. He catalogues the indeterminate and distinguishing signs of grace "to convince hypocrites" and to help true saints "detect false affections, which they may have mingled with true" (pp. 196–7). However, a duplicitous tendency within sinful human nature, encouraged by the subtle workings of Satan, generates counterfeit counterparts for every apparently distinguishing sign. Contrary to modern preconceptions, therefore, Edwards's understanding of Christian faith is not defined by dogmatic certainty, nor did he depict Puritan piety simply as a mask for insincerity. A multiplicity of deceptive appearances, which distort human perception of reality and frustrate the need for assurance, make anxiety and not certainty the hallmark of the religious life.

True Virtue and its Counterfeits

After his involvement in the Great Awakening debate a new polemical context gradually led Edwards to address a new pair of indiscernible counterparts. In the late 1740s Old Light critics of the revival, influenced by the philosophy of the British Enlightenment, began to formulate a liberal alternative to Puritan orthodoxy. Called "Arminians" because their thought resembled that of the Dutch theologian Jacobus Arminius (1559–1609), these liberal divines re-conceptualized the traditional Calvinist view of God, human nature and the means of salvation. Identifying perfect goodness and not absolute sovereignty as God's primary attribute, Arminians rejected such doctrines as innate depravity and double predestination, which appeared inconsistent with divine benevolence. As a consequence, they advocated an elevated view of human nature. Having a natural capacity for true moral goodness, people needed God's assistance to strive for salvation but did not require radical transformation of their faculties by saving grace to eradicate the effects of congenital sinfulness. And although the liberals thought it just for God to punish proportionately volitional and conscious sin, they considered eternal damnation the work of an infinitely cruel, not merciful, deity.

Aware of the increasing popularity of theological liberalism in New England, Edwards began in the latter 1740's to plan to write "something particularly and largely on the Arminian controversy, in distinct discourses on the various points in dispute" (Dwight 1830: 250). Although temporarily distracted from the proposed project by the communion controversy in Northampton, he vigorously pursued it once settled in Stockbridge. The four major treatises that Edwards wrote while in Stockbridge together comprise a sustained polemic against Arminianism. In *Freedom of the Will* and *Original Sin* he defends the moral deter-minism of traditional Calvinism and its foundation, innate depravity. And in *Concerning the End for which God Created the World* he challenges the liberal assertion that God designed the world primarily as a vehicle to promote human happiness. However, it is in *On the Nature of True Virtue* that Edwards explicitly defends what he calls elsewhere the "one grand principle, on which depends the whole difference between Calvinists and Arminians." Contrary to the liberal view, he contends in this treatise "that the grace or virtue of truly good men not only differs from the virtue of others in degree, but even in nature and kind" (1985: 523).

Calvinist divines maintained that God, as an expression of his sovereignty, ulti-mately established the standards of praise and blame applicable within the human community. Because of the inherent sinfulness of human nature, all human acts were blameworthy because they were necessarily the effect of a depraved will. Only through the passive and unmerited reception of divine grace did human agency acquire true moral worth. This divine standard of judgment at times conflicted with the norms of morality that commonly operated within the human community. Common morality could judge an action to be a virtuous contri-bution to the well-being of society, which from God's perspective appeared sinful.

Arminian theologians rejected this distinction between divine virtue and common morality, maintaining instead that human nature had an innate capacity for true moral goodness. Freed from the constraints of original sin, human agency was guided by the operation of a natural moral sense that established universal standards of praise and blame. Even God, as an expression of his goodness, subjected himself to moral norms equally applicable to all rational creatures. Therefore, all acts that were praiseworthy from the human perspective likewise merited God's approbation, and people by nature could meaningfully contribute to their own salvation.

Edwards viewed Arminianism as a form of hypocrisy, and his method of exposing its flaws was conceptually similar to that which he used against the radical New Lights during the Awakening. Unlike evangelical hypocrites who mistook the effects of an overheated imagination for the influences of saving grace, legal hypocrites failed to recognize the counterfeit status of ordinary morality. By maintaining that human beings had an innate capacity for truly virtuous action, they identified as pleasing to God behavior which was pleasing only to themselves. Nevertheless, both evangelical and legal hypocrites were deceived by appearances and based their assurance of salvation upon inadequate evidence. Therefore Edwards engaged not only in *Religious Affections* but also in *True Virtue* the problem of indiscernible counterparts to discredit the claims of his theological opponents. The former treatise asked "What is the nature of truly gracious affections?" and the latter, "What is the nature of true virtue?" Edwards's response to both these questions was consistent. Truly virtuous acts, like truly gracious affections, had as their cause an internal principle of grace, while their counterfeit counterparts could be sufficiently explained by natural agency. However, because of the shift in polemical contexts, the method Edwards used in *True Virtue* to articulate this response differed from that of *Religious Affections*.

In *True Virtue* Edwards does not use the language of evangelical Christianity. Absent from this treatise are such terms as hypocrite and saint, sin and grace, deception and assurance, which were the common vocabulary of both Edwards and the radical New Lights during the Awakening. To explode the arguments of his opponents from the inside, he appropriates in this treatise the vocabulary of British moral sense theorists, such as Francis Hutcheson and Lord Shaftesbury, which was employed by New England Arminians in their reconceptualization of Calvinism. Similarly, in *True Virtue* Edwards adopts a new theoretical apparatus to distinguish the genuine from its counterfeit counterparts. The causal analysis, which dominates *Religious Affections*, can be found in *True Virtue*. In this treatise Edwards does emphasize the natural foundations of those principles that masquerade as truly virtuous morality. Because he is addressing a new opponent, however, this causal analysis does not substantively contribute to his argument. Arminian divines maintained that human beings have an innate capacity for genuine moral action. To identify the natural foundations for this capacity will support, not undermine, their claims. To expose ordinary morality as counterfeit virtue, therefore, Edwards uses a different approach to the problem of indiscernible counterparts, an approach first articulated by Plato in his analogy of the cave found in Book VII of *The Republic*.

To illustrate the self-deception of ordinary existence, Plato depicts a race of beings who falsely believe that the shadows they perceive on the wall of the cave in which they live are substantial beings. They abandon this false belief only when they transcend their limited perception of reality by leaving the cave and adopting a more comprehensive view. Similarly, Edwards maintains that the moral principles liberal theologians identify with true virtue assume that appearance only when viewed from a limited, internal perspective. A more comprehensive perspective reveals them to be counterfeit. Some "actions and dispositions," Edwards writes, "only seem to be virtuous, through a partial and imperfect view of things." They may "appear beautiful, if considered partially and superficially," but "would appear otherwise in a more extensive and comprehensive view, wherein they are seen clearly in their whole nature and the extent of their connections in the universality of things" (1989: 540). This more extensive view discloses that natural morality is a compound of several useful, but fundamentally non-moral, principles.

Edwards rests his argument against the Arminian concept of morality on two shared presuppositions. First, he concurs with the Arminian definition of virtue. "It is abundantly plain by the Holy Scriptures," he notes, "and generally allowed not only by Christian divines but by the more considerable Deists, that virtue most essentially consists in . . . general love of benevolence, or kind affection" (1989: 541). This initial agreement on the definition of virtue entails a second common presupposition, that actions motivated by self-love cannot be virtuous. Benevolence is a public affection that promotes the general welfare; by contrast, self-love is a private affection that promotes the interest of a single individual. "Such a private affection," Edwards asserts, "will be against general benevolence, or of a contrary tendency; and will set a person against general existence, and make him an enemy to it" (p. 555). Beginning from these two presupposition, he proceeds to demonstrate that natural morality has only the appearance of virtue. If viewed from a more comprehensive standpoint each of the principles of natural morality are structurally identical to self-love.

According to Edwards, self-love frequently assumes the appearance of virtue when it extends its reach beyond the self to include other individuals within its circle of interest. If viewed from a limited perspective such affections as love of family, love of neighbor, or love of country appear virtuous because their object is a collective group larger than the self. From an external standpoint, however, the semblance of virtue disappears. The self, as a discrete entity, is so obviously a partial object that no great distance is required to perceive its limitations. Private affections that are broader in scope require a more comprehensive standpoint to reveal their counterfeit character. "The larger the number is that private affection extends to," observes Edwards, "the more apt men are, through the narrowness of their sight, to mistake them for virtue." The larger the scope the more "the private system appears to have the image of the universal system" (1989: 611). Despite this appearance, affections such as these express a private interest that conflicts with the true public good; their moral worth is, therefore, equivalent to that of self-love.

Private affections are not only structurally identical to self-love, they may also be caused by this amoral affection. Self-love functions as a motive to love others when the interests of the larger group promote those of the self. Affection extends beyond the self because "a man's love to himself will make him love love to himself, and hate hatred to himself" (1989: 578). Love of others – be it family, party or country – whose interest corresponds with self-interest, therefore is essentially an expression of self-love. However, Edwards's opponents assert that human beings have a natural capacity for truly virtuous action because they have an innate moral sense that operates independently of self-interest. Edwards concedes that the "moral sense so much insisted on in the writings of many of late" is the "sense of moral good and evil, and that disposition to approve virtue and disapprove vice, which men have by natural conscience" (p. 596). Like the other principles of ordinary morality, however, natural conscience is not an innate capacity for disinterested benevolence but a counterfeit counterpart of genuine virtue. It primarily operates by means of the principle of reciprocity, or "the inclination of the mind to be uneasy in the consciousness of doing that to others which he should be angry with them for doing to him, if they were in his case, and he in theirs" (p. 589). But the principle of reciprocity itself is an expression of two fundamentally non-moral factors.

Edwards claims, first, that the principle of reciprocity is a manifestation of self-love. Reciprocity depends upon a natural human capacity for substitution, whereby individuals form a conception of the feelings and desires of other people by sympathetically imagining themselves in the other's place. The uneasiness that results from a consciousness of inconsistent behavior is, therefore, the effect of self-love. When natural conscience operates according to the principle of reciprocity it is self-love, and not disinterested benevolence, that determines its standards of praise and blame. Second, if natural conscience ever acts independently of self-interest its operation is regulated by another non-moral capacity, the disposition to delight in symmetry and proportion. Edwards admits that the principles of natural morality have a kind of beauty or excellency, which is the foundation for their approbation. This beauty "consists in a mutual consent and agreement of different things in form, manner, quantity, and visible end or design," and it is called by such names as "uniformity, symmetry, proportion, harmony, etc." (1989: 561–2). It is because of their symmetry and proportion that such objects as an equilateral triangle, a human face or a work of art are considered beautiful. But Edwards also maintains that symmetry and proportion explain why certain moral relations are considered beautiful.

Acts of justice, for example, merit approbation because of the harmonious agreement manifest in returning good for good and evil for evil. To fulfill one's obligations to family or country also is judged beautiful because these actions are a proportional response to benefits received. Being structurally identical to the beauty of physical objects, however, the beauty of these moral relations cannot be genuine. The "disposition to approve of the harmony of good music, or the beauty of a square, or equilateral triangle" cannot be "the same with true holiness, or a truly virtuous disposition of mind" (1989: 573). It is a counterfeit beauty that manifests itself only within a private sphere and that conflicts, like self-love, with the beauty of general benevolence. Similarly, the principle of reciprocity has a beauty that consists in the "natural agreement, proportion and harmony between malevolence or injury and resentment and punishment; or between loving and being loved, between showing kindness and being rewarded" (p. 593). Like other manifestations of proportion and symmetry, therefore, reciprocity has only a private beauty, which when viewed from a more comprehensive standpoint loses its appearance of virtue.

Deceived by their limited view of reality, Arminians mistake natural morality for true virtue. Although correctly defining virtue as public benevolence, they identify as the constituents of morality principles that are fundamentally private in scope. According to Edwards, truly virtuous benevolence is an affection so broad in scope that external to it there is no standpoint from which to assume a more comprehensive perspective. He, therefore, identifies the object of this maximally comprehensive affection as "Being in general." "True virtue," he asserts, "most essentially consists in benevolence to Being in general." It is "that consent, propensity and union of heart to Being in general, that is immediately exercised in a general good will" (1989: 540) In contrast to all limited private affections, love to Being in general encompasses the totality of existence, including both God and creation. Its appearance of virtue, therefore, cannot be transcended to reveal a private, non-moral reality. It is a genuinely public affection, because the distinctions between public and private, external and internal, fail to apply.

Virtuous benevolence does not exclude love to individual people or private systems of being, such as family or country. Private affections will not promote an interest in conflict with the public good if they are subordinate to the more comprehensive interest of Being in general. Drawing upon the medieval concept of a hierarchy of being, Edwards asserts that "that being who has the most of being, or the greatest share of universal existence, has proportionably the greatest share of virtuous benevolence" (1989: 550). Love to Being in general manifests itself as a hierarchy of loves, the highest of which is love to God. A truly virtuous person has, therefore, a supreme love of God, and private affections, if subordinate to this love, do not express an interest opposed to the public good, but consent to the general system in a harmonious unity of hierarchically ordered ends.

Love to God is the quality that distinguishes true virtue from all its counterfeit counterparts. Private benevolence may expand its scope to embrace "the whole world of mankind, or even all created sensible natures throughout the universe," but if this love is neither "exclusive of union of heart to general existence and of love to God, nor derived from that temper of mind which disposes to a supreme regard to him," it is not truly virtuous (1989: 603). The principles of natural morality may even produce a kind of love to God, although one based upon a self-interested perception of benefits received or desired from God. Natural morality, therefore, has an appearance of virtue that mimics in almost every particular a genuine love of benevolence. This imitation virtue, being useful to society, merits approbation according to ordinary standards of praise and blame. Unlike his liberal contemporaries, Edwards saw no conflict between self-interest and *natural* morality. Natural standards of praise and blame are meaningful from a perspective internal to their private system of operation. A more comprehensive standpoint does not negate their usefulness but their religious significance.

In his argument with the Arminians, Edwards used the new language of the Enlightenment to defend the traditional Calvinist claim that from God's perspective none of the capacities of unredeemed human nature merited approbation. Because each of the principles of natural morality was incompatible with genuine public benevolence, only the supernatural principle of God's redeeming grace remained as a possible foundation for true virtue. The pair of indiscernible counterparts Edwards considered in *True Virtue* therefore coincided, in degree of difference and means of discrimination, with the pair he considered in *Religious Affections*. Flanked on either side by hypocrites, he constructed in these treatises a means of distinguishing evangelical Christianity both from a shrill piety and from a self-righteous moralism. That Puritanism today is associated with each of these qualities is testimony to the ultimate historical ascendancy of its counterfeit counterparts.

The End of the Counterfeit Counterparts

Edwards believed self-deception to be the cost of inhabiting a fallen world. In the absence of redemption, people were not only sinners but hypocrites. They confused nature with grace, mistaking either their religious experience or their moral action as reliable evidence of salvation. The fall was a beguilement, for the devil convinced Eve to disobey God's command by deception, and the history of the work of redemption was itself the process by means of which humanity's congenital hypocrisy was overcome. In *Concerning the End for which God Created the World* Edwards describes salvation history as a gradual elimination of the distinction between true religion and its counterfeit counterparts. He compares the gap between the external and internal perspectives to "two lines which seem at the beginning to be separate, but aim finally to meet in one, being both directed to the same center" (1989: 459). From the internal standpoint, the convergence of these two asymptotic lines is a process occurring in time. As they approach one another the distance between private and public diminishes, gradually eliminating the more comprehensive perspective that reveals the private to be counterfeit. From the external standpoint, which is functionally equivalent to the divine point of view, this image of convergence becomes one of union. Having "a comprehensive prospect of the increasing union and conformity through eternity," God views the relation as "an infinitely strict and perfect nearness, conformity, and oneness" (p. 443). The final salvation of the elect is, therefore, a realization in time of this eternal union. Even the damned will adopt on Judgment Day a quasi-public posture, although God will undeceive them not as an act of redemption, but to display to them the justice of their imminent condemnation.

From the divine perspective, which is undistorted by counterfeit counterparts, the elect appear one with God. They are "brought home to him, united with him, centering most perfectly in him, and as it were swallowed up in him"

(1989: 443). A certain knowledge of this union was, however, denied the saints prior to death. Although they were capable, through the operation of saving grace, of genuine public benevolence, they were not fully delivered from the limitations of the private perspective prior to the final consummation of the work of redemption. Saints were able to obtain an assurance of salvation that was sufficient to prevent despair, but the continuing presence of sin after conversion perpetuated the possibility of self-deception and prevented absolute certainty. To inhabit a universe of indiscernible counterparts was, therefore, a strenuous form of existence. To wait a lifetime to obtain but an imperfect assurance of salvation required fortitude and high tolerance of insecurity. Edwards's vision of Christian piety combined doctrinal certainty with frequent worry about hypocrisy. Confident in the truth, vigilant Christians had to be relentlessly suspicious of themselves.

These apparently contradictory impulses made Puritanism a fragile faith that was ultimately unsustainable in the modern world. During Edwards's lifetime the metaphysical system that supported a robust concept of religious hypocrisy was already beginning to break down. Radical New Lights advocated a form of piety less perplexed by deceptive appearances and more responsive to the need for assurance. Arminian divines maintained that human reason was so expansive a faculty that no more comprehensive perspective was available to render its judgments suspect. During the nineteenth century this breakdown was accelerated by forces on both the right and the left. Frontier revivalists embraced immediate experience, and moral reform societies emphasized the natural capacity for disinterested benevolence. Liberalism continued the association between religion and hypocrisy but did not identify hypocrisy as self-deception. It began to equate external piety with inner wickedness and to portray evangelical ministers as high-level confidence men who preyed upon the needs and weaknesses of their flock. Projecting this worldview back upon his Puritan forebears, Nathaniel Hawthorne perceived a way of life not complicated by self-deception but corrupted by conscious pretense. Considering the problem of indiscernible counterparts in the theology of Jonathan Edwards can help us recover Harriet Beecher Stowe's sense that the Puritans were an intensely interesting people.

BIBLIOGRAPHY

Danto, Arthur C. (1981) *The Transfiguration of the Commonplace: A Philosophy of Art*, Cambridge, Mass.: Harvard University Press (on indiscernible counterparts).

Dwight, Sereno (1830) *The Life of President Edwards*, New York.

Edwards, Jonathan (1858) "True grace distinguished from the experience of devils," in *The Works of President Edwards*, vol. 4, *Forty Sermons on Various Subjects*; reprint of the Worcester edn, New York.

—— (1959) *The Works of Jonathan Edwards*, vol. 2, *Religious Affections*, ed. John E. Smith, New Haven, Conn.: Yale University Press.

—— (1972) *The Distinguishing Marks of a Work of the Spirit of God*, in *The Works of Jonathan Edwards*, vol. 4, *The Great Awakening*, ed. C. C. Goen, New Haven, Conn.: Yale University Press.

—— (1985) *The Works of Jonathan Edwards*, vol. 7, *The Life of David Brainerd*, ed. Norman Pettit, New Haven, Conn.: Yale University Press.

—— (1989) *Two Dissertations: I: Concerning the End for which God Created the World, II: On the Nature of True Virtue*, in *The Works of Jonathan Edwards*, vol. 8, *Ethical Writings*, ed. Paul Ramsey, New Haven, Conn.: Yale University Press.

Hawthorne, Nathaniel (1961) *The Scarlet Letter*, ed. Scully Bradley, Richmond Croom Beatty, E. Hudson Long, and Seymour Gross, New York: W. W. Norton; first published 1850.

Miller, Perry (1981) *Jonathan Edwards*, Amherst, Mass.: University of Massachusetts Press; reprint of 1949 edn.

Nagel, Thomas (1986) *The View from Nowhere*, New York: Oxford University Press (on the relation between internal and external viewpoints).

Shklar, Judith N. (1984) *Ordinary Vices*, Cambridge, Mass.: Harvard University Press (contains an interesting discussion of hypocrisy).

Stowe, Harriet Beecher (1978) *The Minister's Wooing*, Hartford, Conn.: The Stowe-Day Foundation; first published New York, 1859.

Tracy, Patricia J. (1980) *Jonathan Edwards, Pastor: Religion and Society in Eighteenth-century Northampton*, New York: Hill and Wang.

Chapter 24

The Connecticut Culture of Revivalism

Mary Kupiec Cayton

Fall in the hills of western Connecticut can take your breath away. Yellow-golds, reds, dark and bright greens, brown-oranges, and flecks of not-quite-purple shimmer in luminous glory above rough outcroppings of granite and greenstone. There and then you may be tempted to think the attentive human soul able to find its ways beyond its own boundaries and briefly taste the possibility of something magnificently more than itself.

The price exacted for the privilege of living in such a land, however, can be substantial. Winters are long and cold, springs and summers, if splendid, are short. More mundane settings may be less dramatic, but they are often also more fertile. Extracting a living from that land has never been easy for peoples whose way of life hinged on settled agriculture, as did that of the sons and daughters of the Puritans who displaced the hunters of the Mohegan and other tribes in the early eighteenth century. New Englanders always had the mixed fortune of rooting themselves in a land that often demanded gallons of sweat for every morsel it yielded. Connecticut in particular gave up grudgingly its modest bounty of corn, wheat, rye, peas, hemp, flax, and tobacco, except in the fertile plains of the Connecticut Valley above what would become the city of Middletown and in the province's coastal plain along Long Island Sound. The hills and rocks that jut out or lie hidden just below the rolling contours of the land are unfortunately no farmer's friends. No wonder that by the mid-nineteenth century, Connecticut eventually became a land of peddlers, tinkers, mechanics, clockmakers, and gunsmiths. Banking on human ingenuity turned out to be a much better bet than gambling one's life on the fickle land.

In another place perhaps, where spring lingers for weeks on end before drifting into a languorous summer, time might take on different rhythms. But for the agricultural people who dwelled here, strenuous stretches of rough living were punctuated by seasons of heady abundance – seasons of grace flowing from nature itself. Even if you knew about when you could expect them (if they were going to come at all), or what you could do to help bring them about, you could never be sure that they would arrive on time or yield enough to tide you through the leaner months. You could prepare for them by working and hoping and doing what you knew to do, but when all was said and done, what happened finally depended on something other than your own efforts.

None of this is to suggest that the people who lived in this land of occasional richness were predestined to give their symbolic descriptions of their inner and outer lives any particular form or substance. The ways people construct their social and moral universes depend on many things: the traditions and languages they inherit for speaking about the world; those that they encounter from elsewhere in the course of their lifetimes and that get incorporated into or replace older traditions; leaders who dramatize and give new shapes to the common-sense understandings underlying their lives like bedrock. Nevertheless, if most of the inhabitants of this region for a century or more chose to represent their fundamental sense of how life was as something vast and inscrutable, beautiful yet relentless and exacting, demanding of enormous effort that might finally go unrewarded, it should not surprise us. How they lived, both physically and emotionally, had its seasons of richness and plenty, interludes toward which they looked expectantly as they went about the backbreaking work of building lives on rocky soil. Some, not surprisingly in a land of scarce resources, became flinty themselves and querulous, bent on getting the best of a bargain or of their neighbor. Connecticut became a land of such Yankees. Others turned toward the meetinghouse, a place where they could wait expectantly for the remarkable seasons of grace that an almighty and inscrutable God sent from time to time to some of those who were prepared and ready. They, along with their neighbors in the western reaches of Massachusetts to the north, gave rise to a culture of revivalism that came to be a fundamental feature of their outlook on life.

Today historians nearly always begin their discussion of revivals in New England with the theological and evangelical work of Jonathan Edwards and George Whitefield in the 1730s and 1740s, which in retrospect has come to be called the First Great Awakening. Revivals were communal times of attention paid to matters of the spirit. Often initiated by the self-conscious preaching of a minister or ministers who petitioned God for a seasonable outpouring of his grace, these cyclic occurrences produced conversions and church admissions among notable numbers of people in a community or region. The prospective subject of God's grace went through a predictable sequence: first self-doubt; then despair and abhorrence of her inescapable tendency to sin, often accompanied by tears and acute depression; then an elevation of mood, as the individual conceived that she might be a subject of God's grace; and finally (if the experience bore good fruit) a perception of peace and surety derived from an experiential sense of God's grace making over the sinner's recalcitrant human disposition. Revivals and awakenings were not anything new in the mid-eighteenth century. We know that as early as the 1670s, Solomon Stoddard, minister at Northampton, Massachusetts, in the Connecticut Valley, and grandfather of Edwards, led revivals at his frontier outpost of those grown cold in heart. Stoddard, in an era of apparent decline of the fervor associated with the faith once delivered to the Saints, had come to advocate a theology with vaguely Arminian overtones: works and an appropriate disposition might help to bring on the freshets of saving grace that God alone could send. Church activity and participation, particularly in the Lord's Supper, was for Stoddard a means by which the grace of God could effect conversion. Though God, of course, saved, men might take what measures they would to set the stage for God's work. From this point on in New England's history, we encounter scattered references to revivals and awakenings, most localized and limited in duration. In New England, writes Jon Butler, efforts at renewal and revival "appeared as early as the 1670s, and reappeared in major forms in the 1680s, the 1730s, and the 1760s, with a major peak between 1740 and 1745" (1990: 177). Revivals of experiential religion occurred periodically throughout New England, but most especially in the back country, from at least the fourth generation of settlement onward. They appealed especially in frontier regions, areas of high mobility or of social and economic disruption. There, according to Harry Stout, they "represented para-families of uprooted young people who found in the churches a stability that was lacking when they moved away from the well-established communities of closely knit families their parents inhabited" (1986: 188–9).

Nevertheless, the revivals of the 1730s and 1740s were different enough from earlier efforts that historians in retrospect have given them a name: the Great Awakening. Whether or not the series of revivals represents a coherent enough intercolonial phenomenon for us to view them as a discrete event – and Butler for one has argued that to do so may be anachronistic – certainly in New England it is clear that such an event, or series of events, occurred, and with important repercussions. Beginning with Jonathan Edwards's conversion of over 300 in Northampton in 1734, a series of revivals spread up and down the neighboring Connecticut Valley, following patterns of communication and trade that had been developing in earnest over the prior three decades. The visit of the prominent English itinerant prodigy George Whitefield – powerful of voice and mien, and already advertised to colonials through news reports in papers throughout the colonies – set off another round of revivalism and itinerancy in Connecticut and Massachusetts in the 1740s. Most heated in frontier areas, in towns in their second generation beginning to undergo outmigration, and in volatile urban settings, the revival fires touched many.

The Awakening also marked some significant changes in the colonial New England religious order. What it accomplished was twofold. First, it wrested from the Congregational religious establishment in Connecticut, and to a lesser degree in Massachusetts, some of the exclusivity of religious control that it had formerly held. Separatist Baptist congregations now had the right, along with Episcopalians, to "sign off" from support of the standing order and to direct their tax monies to the support of their own clergy. Second, the Awakening articulated a discourse of experimental religion that would provide a means rhetorically to institutionalize the revival experience. In other words, there now existed a common language for talking about, invoking, and recreating the revival experience in the lives of pastors, congregations, and ministerial associations so inclined. In New England as a region, that language was largely embodied in Edwardsian theology, an anti-Arminian expression of what it meant to experience the grace of God in the life of man. This body of divinity, articulated first and most forcefully by the brilliant if controversial pastor at Northampton, Jonathan Edwards, provided a powerful theoretical statement of the necessity for conversion and for the purification of both heart and church that typically happened in local, and now regional, revivals. Using Edwardsianism and its numerous derivatives, proponents now had a language which coupled an insistence on the necessity of experimental religion with explanations of the ways in which that conversion occurred. That man could not bring about his own conversion by force of will was a cardinal tenet of the theology. But that the conversion was tangible and necessary was not less a part of it.

Untangling the complex theological webs spun out of Edwardsianism and the legacy of the Awakening in eighteenth-century New England is no easy task. William Breitenbach (following Sidney Mead) identifies three theological tendencies resulting from the Awakening, only the third inspired by Edwards. Liberalism, a rationalist theology, developed in part in opposition to the kind of revival emotionalism that Edwardsianism captured. Old Calvinism was a theology with rationalist components: it was based in traditional covenant theology, and preparationist (that is, reliant on external measures to prepare the way for conversion) but not revivalistic or evangelistic in nature. New Divinity, the theological heir of Edwardsian Calvinism, emphasized pure churches, tangible conversions, and the ultimate sovereignty of God. Joseph Conforti's work suggests a further division between "New Divinity" and "New Light" theology, "New Light" being the broader term for those experiencing and advocating experiential conversions in the Awakening. The New Divinity, he argues, refers more narrowly to certain species of New Lightism developed out of Edwards's work by such ministers as Samuel Hopkins and Joseph Bellamy. Appealing mainly at first to congregations in backwoods areas and pastors who settled there, Hopkinsians (as they came to be known, at first pejoratively) emphasized the sovereignty of God and minimized the role that human beings might play in their own conversions (although they were still expected to take advantage of the means which God might utilize as channels of grace). Moreover, they interpreted Edwards's abstract dictum that true love of God consisted of disinterested love of Being in general to mean more concretely the necessity for disinterested benevolence towards one's neighbor. This love was the cement that held society together. Moderate Calvinists, in contrast, though revivalistic in orientation or at least not opposed to it in theory, were less attuned to the ideal of disinterested benevolence, which in its most extreme formulation, became articulated as "the willingness to be damned for the glory of God."

Edwards's unified legacy, despite differences in its interpretation, was an emphasis on revivalism and church purity. That fact is important to the story of later evangelical activity in Connecticut and Massachusetts in the early nineteenth century in two respects. First, both the theology of the Awakening and the revival tradition strongly influenced the group that would provide the leadership for conservative Congregationalism against liberal Unitarianism early in the nineteenth century and which would favor the organization of an expansionist, benevolent form of evangelical Congregationalism. Second, the grassroots membership of their churches would consist in large part of people who grew up in one way or another associated with that revival-oriented tradition. In other words, the roots of New England's Second Great Awakening, the vast movement of church organization and social reform that functioned as an important cultural force in the first third of the nineteenth century, lay firmly in traditions exemplified and codified by the First.

Visible evidence of Edwards's continuing inspiration as icon of a revival tradition in New England can be seen in the publication history of his works in that region prior to 1840. Between 1731 and 1839, at least 118 works authored by Edwards were published or reprinted in the United States, 85 of them after his death in 1758. The bulk of the works published during Edwards's lifetime issued from presses in Boston – as did the vast majority of imprints of any sort in colonial Massachusetts. After the Revolution, however, editions of various of Edwards's works – particularly those centering on conversion, anti-Arminian religious psychologies, and the hoped-for millennium to grow out of the awakenings and revivals – were reprinted in a number of places, from Edinburgh, Scotland, to Lexington, Kentucky. Increasingly, as the number of printing presses increased in the early Republic and they become widely dispersed across the countryside, volumes of Edwards issued forth to make him a steady seller. After 1786, Boston no longer held a near monopoly on publishing Edwards's works, and in fact lagged behind other locations. Now, the wisdom of Edwards was reproduced on presses in such places as Stockbridge in Massachusetts, Suffield in Connecticut, Exeter in New Hampshire, and Portland in Maine. Presses in twenty-two different locations in the years between 1786 and 1815 printed Edwards – either through altruism or expectation of pecuniary rewards. The works of liberal figures from the period show no such widespread dispersion.

The legacy of Edwardsian revivalism lived on longest and received its most developed articulation in the Connecticut and Massachusetts backcountry. From the 1760s on, much of the ministerial training in and for Connecticut went on in "schools of the prophets" conducted by Edwards's followers and interpreters – Joseph Bellamy in Bethlehem and Litchfield, Connecticut, Samuel Hopkins in Great Barrington, Massachusetts, and Stephen West in Stockbridge. So pervasive was this so-called New Divinity influence on the Connecticut Congregational ministry in the last half of the eighteenth century that one-third of the men filling Connecticut pulpits by 1792 had been trained in the New Divinity.

The New Divinity movement had its deepest roots in Connecticut in the western counties of Hartford and Litchfield. The last settled in the colony, these areas also maintained great homogeneity much longer than other areas of the state, with Episcopalianism in particular showing its weakest representation in the state there. The clergy of the region were tightly connected into a network, keeping each other informed of their activities, and the revival impulse alive consistently throughout the latter half of the century. Nearly all of them had been educated at Yale, and nearly all were from modest social and economic backgrounds. Usually they were sons of farmers or artisans rather than of merchants, ministers, or other professionals. For them, the move into the ministry was one of upward mobility, even if the parishes where they eventually settled typically provided no lavish living.

New Divinity ministers kept revivals a common fact of life in an area covering much of western Connecticut and Massachusetts, New York, Vermont, and New Hampshire. With the spread of transportation networks and commercial farming through Litchfield County came the network of revivals and revival activity. Just as word of Edwards's work of salvation at Northampton had sparked similar occurrences up and down the Connecticut Valley in the 1730s, the New Divinity revivalism of such agents of awakening as Edward Dorr Griffin of Litchfield spread throughout western Connecticut and Massachusetts from the 1790s through the 1810s. This later period of revival was marked by this difference, however: a newly prolific religious press printed accounts of revival activity, spreading word of them in a systematic way and regularizing expectation of their periodic appearance. In 1747 Edwards's *Humble Attempt to Promote Explicit Agreement and Visible Union of God's People* called for "concerts of prayer" among the churches to petition God to send the gift of spiritual awakening. Half a century later, religious periodicals such as the *Connecticut Evangelical Magazine*, the *Massachusetts Missionary Magazine*, and the *Panoplist* promoted the notion that it was these hoped and prayed-for times that most deeply tied churches together. The magazines published accounts of revivals as they occurred; they celebrated the mighty work of God, thereby igniting a hope for such seasons of grace in the faithful of congregations grown "stupid" or "senseless." And often the wish begat the thing itself. The more aware of revival activity elsewhere a church was, the more likely its own shower of spiritual refreshment would follow.

Why the "Land of Steady Habits" should have given rise to an especially strong culture of revivalism at the end of the eighteenth and the beginning of the nineteenth centuries is an interesting question. Economic and demographic factors surely played some role, as did institutions developed in an effort to restrain and contain burgeoning diversity of sentiment. Over time, a powerful church establishment developed, and that establishment came to adopt revivalism as its hallmark.

Economically Connecticut's inability to sustain large-scale agriculture produced patterns of settlement and migration that lent themselves to revivalism. Over time younger sons of agricultural families migrated outward, first to new parts of the colony and later to new parts of the nation, seeking fertile land to support their families. Religious unsettlement followed the settlers to new regions, and ministers instigated attempts to restore religious community and to make its presence tangibly felt: hence, revivals. Nevertheless, it is also true that in some areas of long and continuous settlement, it was often the sons and daughters of the most well-established families in town who found themselves the subjects of revivals.

Perhaps a more complicated explanation lies in certain factors and conditions in particular regions of Connecticut, which led to the nurturance of a culture of revivalism there. Parts of Connecticut were remarkably homogeneous in character, in terms of the ethnic derivation of the population, its occupations, and its political and religious attitudes. No substantial in-migration to the state took place directly from Europe until the mid-nineteenth century. Most of the residents of Connecticut had parents, grandparents, or great-grandparents who had come from Massachusetts. Moreover, much of the predominantly farm population of the colony, then state, were isolated in small villages and hamlets where trade, such as it was, was conducted mainly with nearby villages. By 1820, only three places – Hartford, New Haven, and Middletown – had a population of more than five thousand. More than half the population lived in towns of two to three thousand, with only the prime agricultural areas approaching anything like a dense population. No central economic nexus developed there comparable to Boston in the Bay State. Some meat and grain from the state was sold in New York, some exported to the West Indies. Most Connecticut farmers, however, remained mainly subsistence farmers well into the nineteenth century. A spirit of localism reigned in many parts of the state, and with it, tribalistic beliefs in church harmony, purity, and homogeneity of belief. Inbreeding and relative isolation led to a strain of conservatism, as did the out-migration of many of the young. Leaving for land or opportunities for economic advancement elsewhere, they robbed the towns and villages of a potentially dynamic part of its population. It was in these sorts of places that conservative revivalist culture developed and flourished through much of the eighteenth century.

It was a culture that its proponents began actively to try to export by the last decade of the eighteenth century and the first of the nineteenth. Connecticut's progeny often saw the state as the source of a distinctive, and superior, culture: the mother of the highest, best, and most virtuous style of life that the new republic had to offer. Timothy Dwight, soon to be the first evangelical president of Yale College and mentor of nearly all Congregationalism's evangelists of the early nineteenth century, in 1794 published *Greenfield Hill*, an encomium to the simple and virtuous yeoman farmers of his state. In it, he held up their style of life as the one best designed to preserve the virtue and fortunes of the republic:

> The happiness of the inhabitants of Connecticut appears, like their manners, morals, and government, to exceed any thing, of which the Eastern continent could ever boast. A thorough and impartial developement [sic] of the state of society, in Connecticut, and a complete investigation of the sources of its happiness, would probably throw more light on the true methods of promoting the interests of mankind, than all the volumes of philosophy, which have been written. (1794: 169)

Jedidiah Morse, Connecticut-born and later the major polemicist for orthodoxy in Massachusetts against its liberal opponents, praised Connecticut in his *American Geography* (originally published in 1789) as "a well-cultivated garden, which, with that degree of industry that is necessary to happiness, produces the necessaries and conveniences of life in great plenty" (1794: 354). Ironically, the homogeneity of population and sentiment that resulted in some measure from rural isolation became a positive virtue to be wished for and extended to those peoples and areas not nearly so fortunate. If one could not homogenize the backgrounds and circumstances of the heterogeneous lot that would become the basis for American cities and new western settlements in the nineteenth century, one could hope for purity and homogeneity of belief and ideology as the next best thing.

By no means did a tendency to value revivals and awakenings, at least of the Congregational sort, characterize all the denizens of the Nutmeg State. Taken as a whole jurisdiction, Connecticut was home to a thriving religious pluralism as early as the 1750s and 1760s. Or rather, some portions of the state saw the rise of dissenting sects and non-Congregational denominations. The established religion of Connecticut was Congregationalism, and it remained so until 1818, the next-to-last state to divest itself of a religious establishment. (The last was Massachusetts, in 1833.) Nevertheless, despite the homogeneity of Connecticut's people in so many respects, many contested the legitimacy of the religious establishment, beginning in the middle third of the eighteenth century. Revivalism came to be the common coin of the realm in part in response to plural-izing impulses within the state – some of which, ironically, began themselves in revivalism.

How to weave the story of orthodox Congregational revivalism into the tale of religious protest against the standing order is a complicated one, and it entails following out two threads. The first concerns the threat to the establishment posed by Connecticut Episcopalianism, and the ways in which the relatively strong presence of that denomination affected the shape of the Congregational establishment. The second involves the even more formidable challenge of the Separates, a group that emerged in the Great Awakening, and the adaptations standing order that Congregationalism made to circumvent their influence.

Anglicans first made their presence felt in a serious way in Connecticut in 1722, when Timothy Cutler, then rector of Yale College, along with a tutor and five neighboring ministers, abandoned Congregationalism for Anglicanism. As a result of this religious mutiny among some of Connecticut's more visible minister-intellectuals, the College thereafter required of its officers assent to a creedal statement. Significant departure from it was grounds for dismission. No coinci-dence, then, that Yale remained, both officially and in fact as far as the faculty was concerned, a bastion of orthodoxy, perhaps the principal legacy of Episcopalianism to Congregational orthodoxy. (Harvard, in contrast, did not.) Moreover, Episcopalians grew in number in reaction to what they perceived as the excesses of the Awakening. Second only to Congregationalists in wealth and prestige by the time of the Revolution, the Connecticut Anglican Church followed only Virginia (61) and Maryland (34) in number of Episcopal clergy, with 22 in the state in 1792. From mid-century, Episcopalianism served as a rationalist, lati-tudinarian alternative to Calvinism, obviating the necessity for a Congregational liberal alternative. Much of the well-to-do and Arminian element was diverted into a distinct denominational space. ("Upper-class deists in Connecticut tended to enter the Episcopal church," writes William McLoughlin; "in Massachusetts they became Unitarians" (1971, 2: 1026.) Connecticut Congregationalism thus remained more theologically conservative, and more uniformly so, than in its Massachusetts neighbor to the north.

Calvinist orthodoxy, of course, was not necessarily the same thing as support for revivals and awakenings, at least in the first half of the eighteenth century, as the great upheaval of the 1730s and 1740s makes clear. Old Light Calvinists, who were in the majority at Yale as elsewhere in the colony at the time, bore the brunt of New Light protests against the corruption of the existing religious order. These latter broadcast the dangers of an "unconverted" ministry untouched by the fires of experimental religion. Itinerants breeched parish boundaries that had heretofore marked the dominions of settled pastors. Even at Yale, New Light students such as David Brainerd were dismissed for their bad habit of judging others' states of grace. (Brainerd took Tutor Chauncey Whittelsey to task for having "no more grace than a chair.") Revivals became, in short, an acute and serious danger to the authority of the standing Congregational order. It was precisely the "uncontrolled" revivals of the Great Awakening and its aftermath that presented Connecticut's Congregational establishment with the gravest threat to the legitimacy of its authority.

As a direct result of the rise of marked dissent, however, the Congregational elite found ways to close ranks, and to insure tighter clerical control over church institutions. From the adoption of the Saybrook Platform in 1708, ministerial associations in Connecticut had had legal power to make certain kinds of decisions regarding the licensing, ordaining, and dismissing of ministers, and had the final say in ecclesiastical disputes. Connecticut gradually developed a form of Congregationalism that was more centralized than that of Massachusetts, and in which ministers were willing and able to put up a much stronger battle against attacks on their cultural authority. A General Association met regularly and provided an avenue of communication among the local associations and a means of coordinating their efforts. Ministerial consociations licensed ordinations and ruled on matters of church discipline. Their rulings no longer had the force of law after 1784, but by that time consociational government was firmly established, as was the expectation of clerical leadership on a regional level. Moreover, ties with the more self-consciously hierarchical Presbyterian Church, beginning in 1766 in an effort to keep an Anglican episcopate out of the colonies, encouraged a number of the Congregational ministry and laity of the state to see themselves as Presbyterians in spirit if not in fact. Others aspired to the organizational clarity of the Presbyterian-like polity as a way of insuring stronger church discipline and clerical influence.

The result institutionally was a tendency to greater ministerial control of belief and practice than under the looser Cambridge Platform in Massachusetts. A hostile observer, one John Wood, wrote of the state that

ancient superstition and prejudice of custom have established an hierarchy, which is directed by a sovereign pontiff, twelve cardinals, a civil council of nine, and about four hundred parochial bishops. The present priest, who may be honored with the appellation of Pope, is Timothy Dwight, President of Yale College. (1802: 373)

Though clearly something of an overstatement, Wood's judgment of the power of Connecticut's Congregational clergy finds clear echoes in Lyman Beecher's nostalgic recollection of Election Day in a state where the standing clergy held enormous religious and political power:

> All the clergy used to go, walk in the procession, smoke pipes, and drink. And, fact is, when they got together, they would talk over who should be governor, and who lieutenant governor, and who in the Upper House, and their counsels would prevail. . . [T]he ministers had always managed things themselves, for in those days the ministers were all politicians, they had always been used to it from the beginning. (Beecher in Storrs 1957: 22–3)

By the last decades of the eighteenth century, this clergy had come increasingly to bank its identity on regional organizations and professional networking that provided safeguards against challenges to authority on the local level.

Many of them also turned to revivalism as the spiritual tradition in which they had been trained, and as a means by which properly awakened hopefuls would shore up both church membership and, not incidentally, the leadership of the pastor whose preaching had become the instrument of God's grace to them. Though ministers preached revivals as visitations of God's grace, they came increasingly over time to emphasize preparing for them and encouraging their expectation among their parishioners. In fact, from the time Solomon Stoddard preached emotional revivalism in his Northampton parish from 1713 to 1729, awakenings (when they took the right form) often functioned as a vehicle for augmenting the power of a pastor. The minister, particularly the newly installed one, prayed and preached in hopes of a season of grace. Depending on the tradition of the particular church in question – or on his own ability to persuade church members to defer to him – he might judge the authenticity and spiritual reliability of particular experiences as the hopeful related them. As conversion added to the numbers in his church, he gained more leverage in potential struggles with the laity. His preaching became central to the collective life of the parish, and religious excitement impelled parishioners to attend more closely. As the position of the clergy as a provincial elite came under increasing attack in the latter half of the eighteenth century, no wonder ministers welcomed times of spiritual refreshment with gratitude. If God made awakenings, there was no doubt but that ministers benefited from them.

By the 1790s and 1800s the Connecticut Congregational leadership had adopted revivals and awakenings as the surest path to spirituality and moral order. Edwardsianism of one form or another had become the dominant theological strain in the rural "schools of the prophets" that trained Connecticut's Congregational ministry. By the latter third of the eighteenth century, even Yale presidents such as Ezra Stiles and Timothy Dwight openly advocated prayer for awakenings. For them and others of the clergy, the major threat to faith and the good moral order of society had come to lie less in the over-exuberance of dissenting religious enthusiasts than in the religious indifference, secularism, or infidelity of the rising generation. The Connecticut General Association resolved in 1795 to encourage "extraordinary prayer for the revival of religion and the advancement of Christ's Kingdom upon the earth" (cited in Shiels 1976: 21). Beginning in 1800, the *Connecticut Missionary Magazine* published news of local revivals in the hopes of stimulating a disposition to them elsewhere. Once large numbers of the Congregational establishment came to adopt revivalism as an expectation of communal spiritual life, the relatively cohesive institutional structures that Connecticut Congregationalism had developed over time to counteract erosion of church authority helped to spread that revivalism. Common practices over time became institutionalized, codified, formulaic. By the beginning of the nineteenth century, Connecticut Congregationalism was poised to export both its revivalistic practices and its awakening-oriented preachers as the embodiment of "the faith once delivered to the saints."

Students of the religious history of this period are apt to describe the evangelical impulse of the early nineteenth century in New England as largely a matter of theology. Orthodox Calvinism kept at its center a belief in human depravity and in the truth of the doctrine of the Trinity long after other strains of Congregationalism attenuated or abandoned them. It clung to and revised emphases on experimental religion and tangible conversion. In fact, this kind of orientation is neither surprising nor unreasonable. These things, after all, were what the publications of this group emphasized, what they themselves said they were about. Their theology flowered into an abundance of organizations for the reform of society on the basis of their theological premises: societies for the reformation of morals, for the suppression of intemperance, for the distribution of Bibles and tracts, for the conversions of Indians and infidels, for the training of an evangelical ministry. Their fledgling bureaucracies used new modes of technology and new forms of organization to spread what they believed was "the faith once delivered to the Saints." Though their impulse was certainly theology-driven, we ought also to be aware that for them – as for many today – theological truths functioned as expressions of cultural ones as well. A revival was not just a religious process that sprang from a particular theological orientation; it was also an emblem of a particular way of understanding human life and human experience, and one that came from a particular kind of cultural setting.

Cultures, of course, are not simple things. They must be sturdy enough to survive a variety of conditions, and sensitive enough to register changes in life conditions of the people who comprise them. So it was with the broad-based culture of revivalism, born in Connecticut and its western Massachusetts hinterlands, which took shape and flourished over the course of nearly a century. Though certainly part of a cosmopolitan and transatlantic phenomenon, it was at the same time exquisitely attuned to the physical, social, economic, political, and emotional conditions of life in the localities from which it sprang. Revivalism provided a common cultural language that was malleable enough to adjust to a variety of circumstances and to metamorphose as conditions required. Under the right circumstances, it shored up the power of a largely rural ministerial gentry whose power was in danger of waning, though it could also be used to undermine that power. It gave rise to expansive forms of organization in a time when political and commercial networks also were inexorably broadening beyond face-to-face transactions of localities; regional and national connections were beginning to have an influence on the lives even of those living in out-of-the-way villages and hamlets. It gave the sons and daughters who were leaving Connecticut at an extraordinary rate a way of holding on to the cultural traditions that had shaped their experience and ways of thinking about the world. As the eighteenth century gave way to the nineteenth, Connecticut Congregationalism's ways of thinking and talking about human experience were poised to transcend the hills, valleys, villages, and hamlets that gave birth to them. Something that contemporaries would identify as a Second Great Awakening was in the offing. Its repercussions would be beyond anything that Solomon Stoddard could have imagined.

BIBLIOGRAPHY

Breitenbach, William (1984) "The consistent Calvinism of the New Divinity Movement," *William and Mary Quarterly*, 3rd ser. 41, pp. 241–64.

Butler, Jon (1982–3) "Enthusiasm described and decried: the Great Awakening as interpretive fiction," *Journal of American History* 69, pp. 305–25.

— (1990) *Awash in a Sea of Faith: Christianizing the American People*, Cambridge, Mass.: Harvard University Press.

Conforti, Joseph A. (1981) *Samuel Hopkins and the New Divinity Movement: Calvinism, the Congregational Ministry, and Reform in New England between the Great Awakenings*, Grand Rapids, Mich.: Christian University Press.

— (1995) *Jonathan Edwards, Religious Tradition, and American Culture*, Chapel Hill, NC.: University of North Carolina Press.

Dwight, Timothy (1794) *Greenfield Hill: A Poem*, New York.

Keller, Charles Roy (1942) *The Second Great Awakening in Connecticut*, New Haven, Conn.: Yale University Press.

Kling, David W. (1993) *A Field of Divine Wonders: The New Divinity and Village Revivals in Northwestern Connecticut, 1792–1822*, University Park, Pa.: Pennsylvania State University Press.

Lee, W. Storrs (1957) *The Yankees of Connecticut*, New York: Henry Holt.

McLoughlin, William G. (1971) *New England Dissent, 1630–1883: The Baptists and the Separation of Church and State* (2 vols), Cambridge, Mass.: Harvard University Press.

Morse, Jedidiah (1794) *The American Geography, or, A View of the Present Situation of the United States of America*, London.

Purcell, Richard J. (1963) *Connecticut in Transition: 1775–1818*, Middletown, Conn.: Wesleyan University Press; originally published 1918.

Rohrer, James R. (1995) *Keepers of the Covenant: Frontier Missions and the Decline of Congregationalism*, New York: Oxford University Press.

Shiels, Richard Douglas (1976) "The Connecticut clergy in the Second Great Awakening," Ph.D. dissertation, Boston University.

Stout, Harry S. (1986) *The New England Soul: Preaching and Religious Culture in Colonial New England*, New York: Oxford University Press.

Valeri, Mark R. (1994) *Law and Providence in Joseph Bellamy's New England: The Origins of the New Divinity in Revolutionary America*, New York: Oxford University Press.

Wood, John (1802) *The History of the Administration of John Adams, Esquire, Late President of the United States*, New York.

Chapter 25

Trust and Confidence in American Religious History

Leigh Eric Schmidt

In a series of articles published early in 1996 entitled "The Politics of Mistrust," the *Washington Post* concluded ominously: "America is becoming a nation of suspicious strangers, and this mistrust of each other is a major reason Americans have lost confidence in the federal government and virtually every other major national institution." The newspaper, with the help of researchers at Harvard University and the Kaiser Family Foundation, had the survey data to give numbers to this cultural observation. In 1964, 54 percent of respondents thought that most people could be trusted; by 1995 that figure was down to 35 percent, and the numbers for those who expressed trust in the federal government had collapsed, down from 76 percent to 25 percent. Even President Clinton added a corroborating voice to the sobering statistics, noting "a pervasive loss of trust in the country, not just in political institutions but in the way Americans feel about each other." As one 26-year-old woman lamented, "I can't trust anyone" (*Washington Post*, January 28, 1996, A: 1, 6–7; February 4, 1996, A: 1, 20–1).

Sociologists and political theorists have been working overtime in the late 1990s to document as well as explain the plight of trust and confidence in American life. Robert D. Putnam's analyses have been particularly influential as he has sought to specify the forms of social capital that make a democracy work and to fathom the strong correlation between social trust and civic engagement. Put epigrammatically, those who trust, join; those who join, trust; those who distrust, drop out of civic and community life – from the churches to political gatherings. Putnam sees a grave decline in both civic participation and social trust in the culture, starkly evident in steady membership declines over the last thirty years for an array of voluntary associations from the PTA to the Red Cross to Masons to bowling leagues. For Putnam, the erosion of civic connectedness and social trust is explainable by multiple economic and cultural forces (from changing patterns of women's work to the fraying of marriage to the rise of big government to race relations). But, for all this multiplicity, he concentrates on one factor pre-eminently: television viewing and its deleterious, privatizing effects on civic involvement, associational membership, and public trust (on average, television watching absorbs at least 40 percent of each American's free time).

With church-related groups being the most prominent type of voluntary association in the culture, Putnam necessarily includes analysis of them. Though declines in church involvement have been less dramatic than the breakdown of engagement in other sectors, they remain noteworthy: a downturn in attendance at church-related groups since the 1960s of about one-sixth, with the growing dominance of small support groups potentially further undermining the civic significance of religious associations. Also, to be added to these associational questions are those of trust in religious leaders and institutions, and the Gallup polls on this suggest that churches and clergy have shared in the wider decline of confidence. There has been an "erosion of confidence" in "organized religion" from a high of 68 percent expressing trust in 1975 to a low of 52 percent in 1989; the figure edged back up to 57 percent in a subsequent Gallup poll, but in the mid-1990s the churches have now dropped from first to third in institutional confidence behind the military and the police (Gallup 1996: 57–60). The reasons given for these drops in participation and confidence in religious institutions would have to be as manifold as the forces sorted out to explain the wider cultural "crisis" in trust and associational life, but the suspect most often fingered bears a strong resemblance to Putnam's chief culprit; not television *per se*, but the sensationalist media attention given to religious scandals. With a series of exposed ministers, evangelists, and priests, organized religion took a prime-time beating in the late 1980s, because of which it forfeited the people's trust. The majority of Americans came to see TV evangelists as "dishonest," "insincere," and "untrustworthy," and this spectacle of lost credibility was broadly corrosive: Confidence in the honesty, integrity, and probity of ministers in general dropped from 67 percent in 1985 to 55 percent in 1990 (Gallup 1990: 54–7; Gallup and Jones 1989: 144–5).

The recent sociological analyses of social trust and civic engagement have not had a strong historical component, documenting instead a largely generational decline in social capital and concentrating explanatory energies on recent socio-economic changes and technological shifts. These are important projects addressing huge practical concerns: how to restore faith in government, nurture civic associations, rebuild community networks, facilitate economic development, and revive neighborliness. But, however thoroughly they are buttressed by statistics and graphs, one wonders whether these sociological and political diagnoses go to the religious heart of the dilemmas over trust and suspicion, credibility and mistrust, confidence and skepticism, joining and detachment. It seems fair to ask, especially for a historian: What might a longer view tell us about some of the enduring problems over trust in American religion and culture that are so devilishly recurrent (and hence far more haunting) than the passivity of couch potatoes and the seaminess of the latest scandals? How might a denser historical perspective complicate the current model of decline, which moves from a long Tocquevillean period of "spontaneous sociability" and "generalized social trust" to a new society of suspicious strangers (Fukuyama 1995: 281, 308–11)? The contemporary sociological literature has called attention to a crucial set of problems for voluntaristic, democratic, market societies – ones that are especially important for American culture as the civic intensity of the World War II generation comes to a close. But, what happens when these "new" concerns over the crisis of trust are turned into something "old," when the perspective is shifted from primarily politico-economic questions about what makes democratic capitalism work to religious quandaries about trust, authority, knowledge, and skepticism, when long-term sources of distrust are highlighted rather than recent losses in confidence in specific leaders, organizations, and institutions?

Where this rich contemporary literature has addressed materials before World War II, the most common reference point has been Alexis de Tocqueville's *Democracy in America* and the United States of the 1830s and 1840s. And certainly Tocqueville's focal concerns with civic associations and with religion in the workings of democracy make him and his era good starting points for historical comparison. Tocqueville saw the United States as a nation infatuated with "the principle of association"; there were organizations to promote any and every cause: "public safety, commerce, industry, morality, and religion." Of all those "habits of the heart" and favorable connections that helped maintain this new republic, Tocqueville singled out the Christian religion as the most important (Tocqueville 1945, 1: 198–9, 310). It provided the fixed moral parameters and social restraints within which liberty could flourish.

Tocqueville's confidence in the joined sovereignty of religion and the people in the United States seemed unbounded, but *Democracy in America* contained the specter of mistrust in the very midst of its most devout affirmations: "Religion in America takes no direct part in the government of society, but it must be regarded as the first of their political institutions; for if it does not impart a taste for freedom, it facilitates the use of it. . . . I do not know whether all Americans have a sincere faith in their religion – for who can search the human heart? – but I am certain that they hold it to be indispensable to the maintenance of republican institutions." Elsewhere Tocqueville performed the same sleight of hand, offering with the left the notion that "in the United States the sovereign authority is religious," then with the right "consequently hypocrisy must be common." The whole religious stabilization of the republic seemed to be based on a deceptive civic performance, something of a confidence trick of showing and hiding. "As those who do not believe conceal their incredulity, and as those who believe display their faith," Tocqueville concluded, "public opinion pronounces itself in favor of religion." Tocqueville did not unpack this point that the surface appearance of faith often masked incredulity but others – from Voltaire to Paine to Melville – were all too ready to search the human heart. In the wake of the Enlightenment and democratic revolution, Tocqueville warned, people were caught in strong currents, always in danger of being borne away "from a faith they love to a skepticism that plunges them into despair" (Tocqueville, 1: 314–16, 324–5; 2: 23–5).

Those anxious doubts about hypocrisy and hidden-but-deepening skepticism should have been enough to suggest that Tocqueville's associational principle and his confidence in religion were more fragile than firm. But his observations contained still other cracks of distrust. The social and intellectual realities of a relatively fluid democracy – one of high mobility and individualistic propensities – made for another epistemological problem. Americans seemed to be

> constantly brought back to their own reason as the most obvious and proximate source of truth. It is not only confidence in this or that man which is destroyed, but the disposition to trust the authority of any man whatsoever. Everyone shuts himself up tightly within himself and insists upon judging the world from there. (Tocqueville 1945, 2: 4)

The ascent of private judgment put people on their guard, made them skeptical and mistrustful of religious claims as well as other authorities. The American churches had to counteract both this individualism and what Tocqueville saw as its consequence, an "instinctive incredulity of the supernatural." (This last observation runs very much counter to common notions of the vibrant flourishing of Christianity and the supernatural under democratization, but it is actually very suggestive; any faith Americans grasped was necessarily a small raft in a sea of skepticism about other competing religious authorities. Incredulity about the supposed humbug, imposture, and fraud of innumerable other religious claimants was necessarily a dominant "instinct" in a pluralistic and competitive religious marketplace.) Tocqueville's concerns were pressing: Would religion really be able to perform its regulating functions, or would sovereign individuals find themselves endlessly swinging between skepticism and credulity, always eager to "laugh at modern prophets" and at the same time prone to "a fanatical and almost wild spiritualism" (Tocqueville 1945, 2: 4, 10, 25–7, 142–3)?

Tocqueville pointed to an important set of predicaments hidden within the apparent successes of Christianity in the 1830s and 1840s. Confidence in religious institutions was always partial and problematic, and the splinters of mistrust, skepticism, individualism, hypocrisy, and derision regularly put Tocqueville's faith in religion "to purify, to regulate, and to restrain" this democratic experiment to the test (Tocqueville 1945 2: 27). Social trust was frail, and the sociability contained within civic and religious associations was all too easily depleted and fragmented. These weaknesses were woven into the cultural fabric of Protestantism, the Enlightenment, and the marketplace, each of which will be examined in turn.

Wolves in Sheep's Clothing: or, Protestant Forms of Distrust

In the antebellum world, as in other periods, Christians were often presented as the embodiment of trust and the bearers of goodwill, and Tocqueville wanted religious associations to flourish for that very reason. In that prototypical world of suspicious strangers, Melville's steamboat *Fidele* in *The Confidence-Man* (1857), religious souls were common emblems of charity; with Christian compassion and humanitarian sympathy, they trusted mission fundraisers, philanthropic organizers, and New-Jerusalem dreamers to be what they seemed.

At the outset of his novel, Melville makes a Methodist minister the defender of a crippled black beggar against those who deem him "a sham," a "painted decoy." "If, next to mistrusting Providence, there be aught that man should pray against," the Methodist preaches, "it is against mistrusting his fellow-man. I have been in mad-houses full of tragic mopers, and seen there the end of suspicion: the cynic, in the moody madness muttering in the corner; for years a barren fixture there; head lopped over, gnawing his own lip, vulture of himself." Melville soon turns the minister into a hypocritical performer only superficially committed to charity, but it is the devout – an Episcopalian clergyman or a "sister in good standing" – that are most ready to express confidence in strangers and their varied schemes, such as the Asylum for Seminole Widows and Orphans. These Protestant folks dwell in the shadow of Melville's recurrent pericope: "Charity believeth all things" (Melville 1989: 12–19, 43–4, 56–9).

But, as Melville suggested, the problem of whom to trust and why was not easily resolved, and in actuality antebellum Protestants often drew the circle of confidence very tightly. They cultivated a multivalent piety of suspicion, three examples of which will suffice: hypocrisy, Satan, and Roman Catholicism. Duplicity and deception were classic Christian preoccupations, and the on-going cultural absorption with hypocrisy – with fallen ministers and wayward evangelists, with Ephraim Avery and Elmer Gantry – has its roots in the religious world itself (Silk 1995: 80–90). The impossible longing of Puritans to make the invisible state of the soul visible always carried the attendant fear over the presence of hypocrites within their small, gathered congregations. How could one trust the religious professions of others? How could one know that these experiences of grace were genuine and not counterfeit? How easy was it to impersonate godliness? In a recurrent nightmare of the biblical imagination, wolves in sheep's clothing stalked Puritan saints and their evangelical heirs.

Take one example of this fearful and deadly masquerade, out of near endless possibilities: a popular Protestant devotional book, *Religious Emblems* of 1848. First the reader is given the dread image of hypocrisy, the ravening wolf decked out as a sheep, then the double gloss of a poem and a short prose exhortation:

> See in the distance, there, those harmless sheep;
> Nor watch or ward at any time they keep; . . .
> The shepherd slumbers in the noontide's shade,
> His flock forsaken, and his trust betray'd.
> The wolf draws near, in sheepskin shrewdly dress'd,
> He bleats aloud, and mixes with the rest;
> They prick their ears, and look with some surprise,
> But can't detect him in his deep disguise.
> He marks his time; when they are all asleep,
> He slays the lambs, and tears the silly sheep.

In an unstable social and religious world, where ministerial oversight has attenuated – "the sheep wander on, without any to control their movements" – false teachers move in, preying on Christian gullibility. "True Christians are honest themselves in their professions of piety, and unsuspecting of others; they do not mistrust. This exposes them to the schemes of hypocrites." The wolf in sheep's clothing is the archetypal confidence man: "He begins by cant; he talks gospel truth sometimes; he insinuates, wheedles, and flatters, until he has gained confidence" (Holmes and Barber 1859: 106–8). Such disguised wolves, so the authors warned, were everywhere in the 1840s; it was enough to teach Christians that their first instinct should not be trust, but suspicion. These pious admonitions favoring skepticism over confidence came with considerable authority – the Bible itself. As Melville wryly pointed out, it is the "True Book" that "teaches distrust," which leads to a disquieting circularity in which Christians are asked to trust a text espousing mistrust (Melville 1989: 314–15, 322–3).

Satan was the impresario of this masquerade. In the lived religion of colonial and antebellum America, the Devil was an extremely active presence, and certainly news of his recent demise has been greatly exaggerated; 70 percent of Protestants still say they believe in the Devil, and 65 percent of Americans as a whole affirm Satan's reality, and in the mid-1990s the numbers were going up, not down, unsurprising perhaps given the wider growth of mistrust in the culture (Gallup 1996: 20). The Devil was the father of lies, and belief in him added to the Christian sense that the world was filled with ill-intended deceivers, malevolent drifters out to do the Devil's work. As the impostures of the mysterious ventriloquist, Francis Carwin, come to light in Charles Brockden Brown's *Wieland* of 1798, he is readily understood in demonic terms by the Wielands, a family with a marked heritage of Protestant enthusiasm. After Carwin's "divine" voices have managed to derange the family's republican home and even inspire murder, Clara cries out to her God-mad brother, "There is thy betrayer. He counterfeited the voice and face of an angel, for the purpose of destroying thee and me. . . . He is able to speak where he is not. He is leagued with hell" (Brown 1994: 200). Satan was not just a terror for Gothic romances, but a wily agent of popular dread, always threatening to disguise himself even as an angel of light. The evangelical Protestant world was filled with illusory appearances, with diabolic stratagems and counterfeit voices. Satan's various frauds made distrust a necessary habit of the Christian heart, and shifty strangers, like Carwin, particularly warranted suspicion.

Apart from Satan, the Wielands should have known that Carwin could not be trusted, for in his wanderings he had studied with a Jesuit in Spain, and for Protestants there were few surer signs of a dangerous capacity for protean dissimulation than Roman Catholicism, the Society of Jesus especially. To Protestant moralists, Jesuit casuists were long viewed as the ingenious advocates of deception through such subtle practices as mental reservation and equivocation, and their "undercover" missionary strategies for survival under Protestant persecution included concealment, misrepresentation, and fake identities. Hence Protestants regularly saw Catholic priests and missionaries as con men, experts at disguise and dissimulation. To offer an example from the most notorious anti-Catholic piece of the period, Maria Monk's *Awful Disclosures of the Hotel Dieu Nunnery* of 1836:

One point, on which we received frequent and particular instructions was, the nature of falsehoods. On this subject I have heard many a speech, I had almost said many a sermon; and I was led to believe that it was one of great importance, one on which it was a duty to be well informed, as well as to act. "What!" exclaimed a priest one day – "what, a nun of your age, and not know the difference between a wicked and religious lie!" . . . [A] lie told for the good of the church or Convent, was meritorious, and of course the telling of it a duty. (1977: 71–2)

Roman Catholicism was a religion of lies, a casuistic system of deception, the other to Protestant sincerity and plain speech, and the convent itself was an elaborate web of pious illusions: misused confessionals, secret rites, subterranean chambers, and sneaking priests. What Protestants saw in Catholics were those accomplished at "the arts of deception," and while the former made themselves out to be devout innocents imperiled by popish imposition and trickery, they simultaneously steeled themselves to Catholic wiles with a far-reaching discipline of mistrust. Also, as the sensational promotion of the exposed Maria Monk suggests, some Protestants learned to value (covertly) what they saw as the Jesuit *modus operandi* and what Augustine had long ago excoriated: the use of lying and subterfuge in the service of truth (Monk 1977: 71–2, 146–7).

In the 1830s and 1840s, Tocqueville's golden era of civic and religious association, Protestants were awash in a sea of suspicion. Hypocrisy, Satan, and Roman Catholics all made the religious world seem populated by subtle impostors. Protestant mistrust hardly ended there; there was considerable theological, liturgical, and class-based wariness of one another (Congregationalists of Methodists, Disciples of Presbyterians) and endless leeriness toward Swedenborgians, spiritualists, Universalists, Jews, Adventists, Freemasons, mesmerists, phrenologists, Mormons, and kindrid sectarian impostures. The piety of Protestants, despite constant professions of guileless trust and sincerity, entailed intense distrust of others; every sheepish look had to be probed. Incredulity and debunking were the necessary concomitants of the rise in Christianization and the consolidation (however tenuous) of Christian authority. In the uncontainable eclecticism and multiplicity of democratized religion, mistrust became all the more a Protestant reflex. Any newfound faith was inevitably hard-won, built on a series of disavowals, negations, and exposures, and social trust was hence a sharply bounded religious construction.

Pious Frauds: or, Enlightenment Forms of Suspicion

Enlightened skeptics, like Tom Paine and Elihu Palmer, were adamant that all revealed religion was a social construction. "Every new religion, like a new play," Paine wrote in a stinging essay on religious dreams, "requires a new apparatus of dresses and machinery, to fit the new characters it creates" (1945, 2: 845). Paine, Palmer, and other radical deists would not be party to Tocqueville's old game of enlightened dissimulation or "mental lying"; they would parade their incredulity for all to see (I: 464). Where utilitarian considerations had appeal to

more moderate inquirers such as Franklin or Adams, Paine would have no truck
with those who, on pragmatic or wishful grounds, embraced illusion:

> It is possible to believe, and I always feel pleasure in encouraging myself to believe
> it, that there have been men in the world who persuade themselves that what is
> called a *pious fraud* might, at least under particular circumstances, be productive
> of some good. . . . The persons who first preached the Christian system of faith, and
> in some measure combined with it the morality preached by Jesus Christ, might
> persuade themselves that it was better than the heathen mythology that then
> prevailed. From the first preachers the fraud went on to the second and to the third,
> till the idea of its being a pious fraud became lost in the belief of its being true; and
> that belief became again encouraged by the interests of those who made a livelihood
> by preaching it. (I: 504–5)

The exposure of Christianity for what it really was – a socially produced system
of deception for the purpose of garnering power and money for clerics – freed
the mind of the enlightened individual to explore the only true source of revelation, the universal laws of nature, which "no human invention can counterfeit"
(Paine 1945, I: 482).

The Enlightenment's hermeneutic of suspicion made Protestant versions of
mistrust seem tame. For radical deists, all scriptural authority, the very notion
of God's Word, was disavowed, and the supernatural buttresses of such claims
– miracles and prophecies – were "always to be suspected," if not rejected
outright as clever "legerdemain." Under this deistic view, prophets were the ultimate impostors, guilty of the pretense of claiming to speak God's words. As Paine
related,

> Those to whom a prophecy should be told, could not tell whether the man proph-
> esied or lied, or whether it had been revealed to him, or whether he conceited it;
> and if the thing that he prophesied, or intended to prophesy, should happen, or
> something like it, among the multitude of things that are daily happening, nobody
> could again know whether he foreknew it, or guessed at it, or whether it was acci-
> dental. A prophet, therefore, is a character useless and unnecessary; and the safe
> side of the case is to guard against being imposed upon by not giving credit to such
> relations. (1945 I: 505, 510–11)

The epithet of impostor, founded on ancient images of prophetic guile, was a
rhetorical construct endlessly replicated and extended by the enlightened, indis-
criminately applied to one prophet after another on the American scene, from
Joseph Smith to Robert Matthews to Joseph Dylks to Andrew Jackson Davis to
Mary Baker Eddy (Silk 1994: 91–105). With the prophetic impostor, as with the
hypocrite, the conviction was that in naming the fake, in exposing the humbug,
the truth would be manifest. But, as the unmasking of prophets as self-deceived
fanatics or outright frauds became an all-encompassing pursuit, any claim to
revealed truth, to prophecy and miracle, was threatened with enclosure within
the withering category of imposture.

Suspicion of the supernatural was not only a rhetorical strategy but also a set of practices. "There are performances by sleight-of-hand," Paine observed, "and by persons acting in concert that have a miraculous appearance, which when known are thought nothing of. And besides these, there are mechanical and optical deceptions. There is now an exhibition in Paris of ghosts or spectres, which, though it is not imposed upon the spectators as a fact, has an astonishing appearance." To go on believing in divine miracles, in the face of these celebrated exhibitions, was, Paine suggested, to degrade "the Almighty into the character of a showman." Paine's linkage of skepticism to showmanship was significant: entrepreneurs of the Enlightenment turned the supernatural into entertainments about the real and the illusory; the tricks of conjurers into mechanistic demonstrations; occultist wonders into the commodities, curiosities, and gimmicks of popular museums. Magic and wizardry did not so much decline in late eighteenth-century America but instead were transformed, absorbed into the commercial culture and made ambiguous agents of the Enlightenment (Paine 1945, 1: 508).

In *Wieland*, Carwin's ventriloquist act is the apt emblem of Paine's call for the modern, skeptical turn. Part of the family's problem is their active religious imaginations; Clara and her brother, for all their republican virtue and Lockean empiricism, are all too ready to attribute supernatural agency to Carwin's mysterious voices. "My opinions were the sport of eternal change," Clara despaired. "Sometimes I conceived the apparition to be more than human. I had no grounds upon which to build a disbelief." Torn between faith and skepticism, the Wielands fail at suspicion, and Carwin's deceptive art dupes them, providing a potent "lesson to mankind on the evils of credulity" (Brown 1994: 165, 181–2, 194). The novel's moral was soon acted out as various ventriloquists toured the country in the early republic, and their shows, however marvelous, suggested that such strange voices were not supernatural or diabolic, but a practiced art of misdirection, mimicry, and entertainment. The enlightened turned magical knowledge into a playful tool of naturalistic explanation.

Confidence Men: or, Market Forms of Deception

The market economy has had the most impact on the way historians think about notions of confidence, credit, trust, and duplicity in American culture. In *Worlds Apart* Jean-Christophe Agnew helped make market relations a matter of cultural history by focusing on the uneasy exchange between theatrical practices and commercial experiences, on how the Puritan moralists of London's market society reframed notions of the self, authenticity, and credibility in part through demonizing the masquerading artifice of the stage. Beyond London in the new United States, the most dramatic consequences of the market revolution were delayed into the first decades of the nineteenth century. Karen Halttunen's picture of the middle-class obsession with sincerity and transparency in the 1830s and 1840s in *Confidence Men and Painted Women* suggests a set of concerns parallel to those highlighted by Agnew. In an abstracted market economy and in stranger-filled cityscapes, social identities were hard to anchor and harder to read. With the apprenticeship system breaking apart and colonial forms of patriarchal authority in disrepair, young men entered an unpredictable marketplace needing to turn their "character" into vendible forms of trustworthiness. At the same time, they had to avoid the seductions of various confidence men or, even more gravely, the temptation to become one themselves – that is, a protean performer who severed "the link between surface appearances and inner moral nature" (Halttunen 1982: 42). The right forms of etiquette, manners, and fashion became indispensable for creating relatively dependable signs of middle-class honesty, reliability, and candor. But theatricality and masking had always been built into the courtesies of the courtier, and middle-class folks could not escape the fox. Despite the dissonance with lingering Puritan and republican convictions, as Halttunen suggests, the middle class gradually learned to accept, even embrace, the stage, the *theatrum mundi*.

In the last decade historians and sociologists of American religion have become increasingly attentive to how the culture of the market has affected the nation's religious life, and one of the most salient aspects of this discussion has been the convergence of itinerant evangelism, the theater, and the commercial revolution. As several recent works have argued (for example, those of Harry Stout and R. Laurence Moore), the evangelical movement (George Whitefield pre-eminently) transformed the minister from the holder of a sacred office within a hierarchic social order to a well-publicized performer of a theatrical itinerancy within a relatively fluid marketplace. This model of ministry helped keep Christianity competitive in a voluntaristic society and helped make its goods – Bibles, devotional works, sermons, journals, as well as less tangible items like the new birth – saleable along with other merchandise of the expanding commercial culture. Exploiting all the latest advertising and promotional techniques of the emergent consumer society, these roving preachers made Protestantism entertaining, popular, dramatic, enterprising, and marketable.

That shift to a theatrical, market-driven model of a minister's authority was a double-edged sword; it tendered both the potential adulation of popular celebrity and a pervasive wariness toward bamboozlement. In practice, the evangelist often ended up reinforcing a shape-shifting view of the self – one of dramatic impressions, artful poses, manipulated surfaces, and mastered strategies – exactly what Protestant moralists worried would happen to social identity in a market society. The evangelist's "show" spawned a nearly inescapable suspicion of popular preachers as hucksters and charlatans, as actors and hypocrites. The attack in 1835 on Jedidiah Burchard, one of Charles Grandison Finney's more flamboyant imitators, for "his theatrical, deceptive, and money-making exhibitions" captured this cultural refrain. The writer warned people to

> be upon their guard against the *wily arts* of this prince of impostors – this 'Simon the sorcerer' – who is filching *thousands* of *dollars* from his deluded followers, of various sects, and then laughing in his sleeve at their credulity. . . . His very look – his movements – his affected sighs, were enough to convince every unbiassed mind, that he was as heartless and artificial as a play-actor. I can say in truth that I read

him through, in a moment. . . . All his movements were *slow* and *studied* to *theatrical exactness.* . . . The house at once became a *theatre.* (Streeter 1835, iv, vi, 14–17)

This view of evangelists as swindlers and frauds became a venerable one in American culture, from attacks on Whitefield and Finney to the fictional assaults of Harold Frederic and Sinclair Lewis to film versions in *Marjoe* and *Leap of Faith.* The revival preacher, often at the heart of Protestant hopes for America's redemption, also became one of the culture's most familiar con men, a drifting stranger, a theatrical hypocrite corrosive of the very social trust needed to make the market and the republic work.

The expansion of the market depended on trust: among producers, wholesalers, and retailers in far-flung networks and between merchants and consumers in proliferating shops and stores. The commitments of the devout to honesty, diligence, and plain-dealing were supposed to help maintain confidence within a commercial culture devoted to competition and profit. Trust was so important, in part, because it was such a precious commodity in a market society fraught with unbelievable promotions, countless humbugs, rampant counterfeiting, and manifold adulterations. *Caveat emptor,* or as the barber's admonitory sign reads in the *Confidence-Man,* "NO TRUST" (Melville 1989: 4). Religion was made part of the turbulent culture of the market, and from that encounter it garnered not only entrepreneurial energy and popular relevance but also a reputation for deception, profiteering, counterfeiting, and fraudulence. Distrust and suspicion were endemic to this economy, and the questions asked of the confidence man were of necessity asked of religious leaders as well: Was the performance real or was it all an act? Where was the money going? Were the proffered wares of enduring quality? Why choose this brand (of faith) over that?

Religion did not simply take on the market's instabilities, but contributed its own forms of mistrust and deception to the deep crisis of confidence that plagued American society in the 1830s, 1840s, and beyond. Religion, Tocqueville averred, was a regulating, stabilizing, associational, trustworthy force in this rambunctious democratic society, but his own caveats about hypocrisy, skepticism, individualism, and unrestrained acquisitiveness suggested that he shared many of Melville's doubts. The current crisis of trust needs to be read against the older plight of confidence: "Did you never observe how little, very little, confidence, there is? I mean between man and man – more particularly between stranger and stranger. In a sad world it is the saddest fact," says one of Melville's shady strangers to another who "seemed a collegian" (Melville 1989: 34). These deeper religious, epistemological, and market predicaments have very much stayed with us (as the recent sociological work of Putnam, Fukuyama, and others so amply demonstrates), and at least for that small, skeptical, academic tribe of poststructuralists the quandaries have only intensified in a "postmodern" world of indeterminacy, simulation, virtual reality, and truth as a mask of power. Attending to these deeper historical problems may not help to resolve the contemporary crises over trust and confidence – their very depth suggests their tenacity – but it should lend perspective and perhaps not a little perseverance.

BIBLIOGRAPHY

Agnew, Jean-Christophe (1986) *Worlds Apart: The Market and the Theater in Anglo-American Thought, 1550–1750*, Cambridge: Cambridge University Press.

Brown, Charles Brockden (1994) *Wieland; or The Transformation*, Oxford: Oxford University Press.

Fukuyama, Francis (1995) *Trust: The Social Virtues and the Creation of Prosperity*, New York: Free Press.

Gallup, George, Jr. (1990) *Religion in America 1990*, Princeton, NJ: Princeton Religion Research Center.

—— (1996) *Religion in America 1996*, Princeton, NJ: Princeton Religion Research Center.

Gallup, George, Jr. and Jones, Sarah (1989) *100 Questions and Answers: Religion in America*, Princeton, NJ: Princeton Religion Research Center.

Halttunen, Karen (1982) *Confidence Men and Painted Women: A Study of Middle-class Culture in America, 1830–1870*, New Haven, Conn.: Yale University Press.

Hatch, Nathan O. (1989) *The Democratization of American Christianity*, New Haven, Conn.: Yale University Press.

Holmes, William and Barber, John W. (1859) *Religious Emblems: Being a Series of Emblematic Engravings, with Written Explanations, Miscellaneous Observations, and Religious Reflections, Designed to Illustrate Divine Truth*, Cincinnati, Oh.: Henry Howe.

Melville, Herman (1989) *The Confidence-Man, His Masquerade*, Oxford: Oxford University Press.

Monk, Maria (1977) *Awful Disclosures of the Hotel Dieu Nunnery of Montreal*, Salem, NH: Ayer.

Moore, R. Laurence (1994) *Selling God: American Religion in the Marketplace of Culture*, New York: Oxford University Press.

Paine, Thomas (1945) *The Complete Writings of Thomas Paine* (2 vols), ed. Philip S. Foner, New York: Citadel Press.

Putnam, Robert D. (1995) "Bowling alone: America's declining social capital," *Journal of Democracy* 6 (January), pp. 65–78.

—— (1996) "The strange disappearance of civic America," *American Prospect* 24 (Winter), pp. 34–48.

Silk, Mark (1995) *Unsecular Media: Making News of Religion in America*, Urbana, Ill.: University of Illinois Press.

Stout, Harry S. (1991) *The Divine Dramatist: George Whitefield and the Rise of Modern Evangelicalism*, Grand Rapids, Mich.: Eerdmans.

Streeter, Russell (1835) *Mirror of Calvinist Fanaticism, Or Jedidiah Burchard and Co. during a Protracted Meeting of Twenty-Six Days in Woodstock Vermont*, Woodstock, Vt.: Nahum Haskell.

Tocqueville, Alexis de (1945) *Democracy in America* (2 vols), New York: Vintage Books.

Washington Post, January 28, 1996, A: pp. 1, 6–7; February 4, 1996, A: pp. 1, 20–1.

Chapter 26

The Religion of Humanity
in Victorian America

Lawrence W. Snyder, Jr.

As the end of the nineteenth century approached, former rabbi Felix Adler asked aloud what many Americans were whispering, namely "Have we still a religion?" No longer satisfied with the liberal faith of his childhood, the Columbia University professor defected from Reform Judaism and, in 1876, founded the Society for Ethical Culture in New York to promote the cause of "ethical religion." For Adler and those who followed, traditional theism with its fearsome God of miracles and judgment had become an outgrown faith rooted in superstition and fear, a faith both inane and immoral. Popular religion, he complained, violated the moral and intellectual sensibilities of enlightened society. However, the soulless negations of agnosticism did not provide any comfort for the human spirit. In their speculations about a "First Cause," contemporary philosophers, it seemed, had merely replaced the abstract God of revelation with an equally aloof "pale, bloodless shadow of the mind." Thus, when asked about the future of religion, too many intelligent men and women could only shrug their shoulders in doubt and confusion. Yet Adler remained optimistic. The passing of supernaturalism did not mean the death of religion, but its liberation. Once released from the chains of ignorance and fear, a new "ethical religion" would be free to satisfy the spiritual demands of the modern age. "The essence of religion," he announced, "is the going out of the soul of man toward the infinite." And that "search after the infinite" was nothing more nor less than "an aspiration after the just, the pure, and the good" (Adler: 9). In short, Adler made humanity both the subject of religious experience as well as the object of its devotion.

Adler was not alone in voicing his dissatisfaction with the religious options of his day. Almost a decade earlier, in 1867, similarly disaffected Unitarians led by Octavius Brooks Frothingham had bolted from their Christian denomination and formed the Free Religious Association in order "to promote the interests of pure religion, to encourage the scientific study of theology, and to increase fellowship in the spirit." During the postbellum period the FRA was the most visible and inclusive liberal association in the United States, bringing together Unitarians, Ethical Culturalists, Hicksite Quakers, Universalists, spiritualists, Comteans, and even Reform Jews. American free religionists also established outposts in Europe, such as Moncure Conway's South Place Ethical Society in London, and in India through their support of the indigenous Brahmo Samaj. Supporters of free religion promoted the new association as a "spiritual anti-slavery society" that would champion the cause of progressive religion worldwide. They sought a universal religion that would transcend the parochialism and supposed primitivism of the historic faiths with a gospel of human betterment and global fraternity.

In the years following the Civil War several prominent religious liberals like Adler and Frothingham abandoned the familiar territory of theism and revelation, and set out for new spiritual lands. They articulated a form of religious humanism as an "alternative altar" for those Victorians who had rejected the supposed anachronistic dogmatism of orthodoxy yet were unwilling to forsake the cause of religion altogether. For them, a new "Religion of Humanity" was preferable either to the awkward compromises of Protestant liberalism or the pale negations of philosophical agnosticism. This religious humanism reflected the aspirations of a unique religious culture – a distinct, multilayered social expression of a shared worldview – reflecting and transforming the religious and cultural values of postbellum America.

Historians have long recognized the final decades of the nineteenth century as a "critical period" in the history of religion in the United States. Social change and intellectual upheaval challenged the custodians of traditional orthodoxies to come to terms with the new realities of modernity. The conservative response to these threats has been well documented by histories of American evangelicalism, most notably George Marsden's *Fundamentalism and American Culture* (1980). Also well known is the story of those liberal Protestants who sought to save Christianity by embracing modernity and revising traditional theological categories. What has been missed in the telling, however, is the appearance of a third religious option: an alternative piety that attempted to go beyond the trappings of theism to redefine religion along anthropocentric lines. By looking at the emergence of religious humanism, we begin to see that the spiritual world of late Victorian America was exceedingly complex. For those who could no longer believe in the God of revelation, the Religion of Humanity offered a way to maintain faith and religious piety in an age of skepticism and scientific irreverence.

By any measure, the seven decades stretching from 1830 to 1900 (roughly corresponding to the reign of Victoria in Britain) was a remarkable period in the history of the United States. Rapid urbanization, mass immigration, war, expansion of the frontier, and the advance of the sciences all coincided by the early twentieth century to transform the young nation into an industrial and imperial power. For America's faithful, the nineteenth century was indeed a puzzle. On the one hand, American Protestants at mid-century could legitimately claim success in their efforts to Christianize the nation. Awakenings, moral crusades, and a spirited missionary effort had expanded a Protestant empire across the continent, and even the world. Moreover, a network of voluntary societies and denominational structures led by clergy with power and access to the public sphere had created a *de facto* religious establishment with huge cultural influence. And yet all was not well. The dramatic transformation of American civilization in the postwar years created enormous social pressures that challenged the stability of that same establishment. More serious was the rise of organized unbelief that appeared in the wake of post-Darwinian science, and the popularization of the conclusions of the Higher Criticism. These, together with the emergence of the comparative "science of religion," and the general acceptance of the evolutionary method in the modern university all seemingly conspired to undercut the authority and uniqueness of biblical revelation. Ironically, even as revivalist Dwight L. Moody appeared to capture the hearts of America's faithful, the iconoclastic Robert Ingersoll seemed to make infidelity almost fashionable. Evangelicals and liberals alike recognized that the acids of modernity were eroding the foundations of historic faith. For many Victorians, then, there was a genuine crisis of faith as the continued existence of Christianity, even religion itself, seemed very much in doubt.

The crisis was most acute for America's intellectuals, those of the educated class who took seriously their roles as guardians of higher culture and morality in the broader society. For many, assumptions about the intelligibility and beneficence of Nature and Nature's God had been called into question by the 1859 publication of Charles Darwin's *The Origin of Species*. More important, celebrated philosophers such as Herbert Spencer and Thomas Huxley had expanded the original hypothesis about living things to include a new model for interpreting the whole of human experience and reason, including the origins of religion. The orderly and purposeful universe revealed in the pages of sacred scripture was now replaced by a chaotic world of historical circumstance and random chance. What could be confidently "known" was thus restricted to those natural phenomena which could be empirically observed and explained. As historian D. H. Meyer has noted, the general acceptance of this new, post-Darwinian "scientific method" by most nineteenth-century intellectuals was not simply a change in biological theory; it constituted a fundamental "*change of mind* among western thinkers" (1976: 62). The emergence of unbelief as a plausible intellectual option in the Victorian era was predicated upon the acceptance of science as an alternative to the Christian metaphysic. It was no longer necessary to posit the existence of God to explain the universe or the workings of the natural world. That transition left many sensitive souls stranded somewhere between doubt and faith. It was in this spiritual vacuum that the Religion of Humanity offered an alternative religious world.

The current of Victorian humanism flowed through the broad channel cut by the tradition of American freethought. Of course, radical religious dissent had a long and venerable history in the United States prior to the Gilded Age. The specter of infidelity, whether real or imagined, had been a staple of evangelical preaching since the Puritans, and even helped to define the limits of orthodoxy in the raucous religious market of the young republic. The list of notable, homegrown "infidels" of the antebellum era included the revolutionary deists Thomas Paine and Thomas Jefferson, the utopian Robert Dale Owen, and social reformer Francis Wright. Freethought was a diffuse movement that drew upon immigrant sources as well, as in the case of Czech and German anti-clericalism. By the late nineteenth century secular assemblies could be found in towns from New York to Oregon, and freethought journals such as *The Truth Seeker* enjoyed a national readership. Freethinkers were by nature a fiercely independent lot, united only by their mutual distrust of organized religion and its creedal boundaries. Their infidelity ranged from the pantheistic musings of Ralph Waldo Emerson to the scientific skepticism of John Fiske. Never a cohesive movement, freethought was rather a cacophony of dissenting voices, an assortment of gadflies and prophets, rationalists and romantics who preached skepticism and doubt as the religious virtues of the modern age.

Although much of Victorian freethought was decidedly secular in orientation, the self-styled "free religion" movement pursued a distinctly religious agenda. Late in 1872, O. B. Frothingham, president of the FRA for its first eleven years, published the first of four editions of *The Religion of Humanity*, the most comprehensive statement of the aspirations of free religion. He suggested that "Religion of Humanity" more accurately portrayed the "young Liberalism" than did the older but rather amorphous label "radicalism." While the latter term correctly indicated the relation of the old faith to the new, it failed to provide a blueprint for the construction of a modern religious system. Frothingham railed against the "older Liberal Church" that had not gone far enough in repudiating the supernaturalism and dogmatism of the past. The Christian Liberalism typi- fied by Unitarianism had indeed liberated humankind from the oppressive doctrines of total depravity and predestination, but had left it shackled to an abstract deity and a cosmic Christ. The mythic resurrection of Jesus, he argued, did not represent the exaltation and empowerment of a first-century prophet. Instead, it symbolized the potential of the human race to construct its own provi- dence, build its own heavens, and work out its own salvation. Emancipation from the past would allow human nature to vindicate its own divinity. According to Frothingham, "religion is the emblem – human nature is the creating power" (1975: 25). And although wary of system building and creedalism, the Religion of Humanity offered a plan for building the new spiritual edifice.

Frothingham's influential manifesto was widely read, and quickly became the theoretical center holding together the various and sometimes contradictory impulses that characterized free religion. As these radicals struggled to define the new shape and role of religion in the modern world they often disagreed. Such noteworthy free religionists as Samuel Johnson and T. W. Higginson continued to identify themselves as Transcendentalists, celebrating the universal theism of Emerson. This "intuitional school" of free religion was often opposed by others in the movement, most notably the philosopher Francis E. Abbot, who championed the cause of "scientific theism" by rejecting the idealism of Transcendentalism in favor of a more thoroughgoing empiricism. By contrast, Frothingham shifted discussion away from concerns over epistemology and cosmology. Instead, the three basic tenets of the Religion of Humanity were its opposition to supernaturalism, the quest for universality, and its commitment to humanitarianism. The "primary principle" affirmed that religious truth was not divinely revealed, but was instead an unfolding of those natural impulses common to mankind rationally interpreted and applied. From this it could be further asserted that the various historic religions were but the unfortunate divisions of the one reality. The Religion of Humanity, therefore, sought to discover the universal spiritual truths hidden beneath the facade of the historic religions, thereby bringing unity to a divided race. The goal of this "new faith," then, was the enlightenment and elevation of the human condition in the present world.

The roots of this humanism were found most directly in the theological and institutional developments within American Unitarianism, the standard bearer of Christian Liberalism in the nineteenth century. In 1841 the celebrated Transcendentalist preacher Theodore Parker sparked a controversy among the Unitarians when he announced that the Bible, and even Jesus himself, were but "transient" authorities whose power rested only in their faithful witness to that which was genuine and permanent in religion. Indeed, the "simple Christianity" taught by Jesus was true only if it measured up to the higher standards of an "Absolute Religion" – a faith of pure morality grounded in the perfect love of God and neighbor. Despite attempts to excommunicate him from the Unitarian fold, Parker could not be pressured into surrendering either his pulpit or the right to be called a Christian. However, the continuing struggle to come to terms with the meaning and essence of Absolute Religion took many of Parker's disciples well beyond the confines of the Christian faith.

The effect of the Transcendentalist critique had been to transfer spiritual jurisdiction from external authorities such as the Bible and church to the interior authorities of the individual conscience and the human soul. The intuitional philosophy of Emerson and fellow Transcendentalist Orestes Brownson essentially moved religion away from the worship of transcendent divinity and toward a cultivation of the universal "religious sentiment" common to humanity. And, although Parker was convinced that a simplified Christianity at least approximated the Absolute Religion, those following in his wake were not so sure. Indeed, an entire generation of liberals looked to Transcendentalism as the herald of a modern reformation of liberal religion. In his reading of Emerson, for example, a young Felix Adler found inspiration for his own anthropocentric and ethical spirituality. Likewise, the rejection of the finality of Christianity in favor of the sovereignty of the individual conscience led Frothingham and other young "Parkerites" to seek a less restrictive confederation in the name of "free religion."

The FRA and Ethical Culture societies were not the only purveyors of religious humanism in Victorian America, however. During the late 1860s, disciples of the French philosopher August Comte established several societies in New York promoting the "Church of Humanity." These "worshiping positivists" attempted to implement Comte's complex "second system" of social and religious reform on the basis of the findings of "Positive science." Though never large nor attractive to the masses, the various Positivist societies and clubs did attract some influential New Yorkers, and the Comtean influence on American philosophy and theology was significant.

Free religionists were often pressed to distinguish themselves from the Comteans. Positivism, too, replaced the Christian God with an "idealized human collectivity," instituting an elaborate program of secularized sacraments, saints, and priests in the hopes of appealing to both head and heart. Although there were some resonances between Positivism and the naturalistic piety of Frothingham and Adler, their humanism owed more to Emerson than to Comte. Indeed, Frothingham thought it unfortunate that the phrase "Religion of Humanity" had become associated with Comte, who despite his coining of the phrase, had "corrupted and perverted" the ideas of the solidarity of humankind and the immortality of the race by manufacturing a system more mechanical than spiritual. It seemed artificial and contrived. Frothingham described it as an "ambitious mausoleum" established in a "spasm of sentimentalism" that merely secularized "the monarchical and Romanist tendencies" with its own scientific priesthood and humanist liturgies. The greater difference lay in the systemic critique of the emergent industrial culture by the Positivists. Whereas most free religionists followed Frothingham in supporting the individualism and capitalist economy of American democracy, the Comteans sought a more radical restructuring of the social order based upon the laws of science and reason. Although Positivist leader Thaddeus B. Wakeman was a member of the FRA and even addressed the association at its 1878 annual meeting in Boston, the Religion of Humanity was understood in distinctly non-Comtean terms by most American free religionists.

The religious humanism of Frothingham and Adler also competed with Christian modernism, with which they still shared a great deal. Prominent liberal clergymen such as Henry Ward Beecher blended evangelical piety and scientific naturalism into a "New Theology," which often paralleled the interests of free religion and ethical culture. In fact, the same "modernist impulse" that transformed American Protestantism in the late nineteenth century also inspired the Religion of Humanity. They shared three fundamental assumptions: the need for theology to adapt to modern realities, the belief that God was revealed within nature and human culture, and an expectation of continued moral and spiritual progress of human civilization. Free religionists and Protestant liberals alike were committed to intellectual freedom and the use of the scientific method to transform religion in the modern era.

The Religion of Humanity differed from Christian modernism, however, in its rejection of theism as an adequate foundation for contemporary religious faith and practice. While many Protestants expressed a desire to be liberated from the constraints of tradition in order to accommodate the faith to modern realities, they continued to affirm that any recognition of the "Brotherhood of Man" was essentially linked to the "Fatherhood of God." Strip away the historic accretions of ecclesiastical authority and dogmatism, and Christianity remained fundamentally theistic. The radicals disagreed. Theological speculation about and worship of such a "hidden God," the One unknown and unknowable, provided no basis for a religion relevant to human needs. All claims to revelation from outside were rejected as preposterous and even blasphemous. Indeed, this was "a God who sends no private messages and receives no private audiences!" Declared

Frothingham, "The *human element in mankind* is the Christ of Humanity" (1975: 46, 25). The Religion of Humanity went beyond the theological innovations of the modernists by interpreting divine immanence to mean that whatever was "godlike" was to be found solely within the realm of human experience. While humanity was perhaps not the ultimate source of divine light, it was the limited incarnation of a limitless and otherwise hidden God. This was not the sentimental deification of the entire race, however. That which was uncivilized, brutish, demoralized, or insane could not be considered expressions of the Absolute. Rather, divinity was embodied in the potential for moral progress of collective humankind, and actually manifest in its best literature, art, philosophy, religion, and civilization. Such anthropocentric piety thus went far beyond the cultural immanentism of the Christian modernists. God was not merely revealed in the progress of civilization; human history was his autobiography.

The rejection of traditional theism in favor of a naturalistic and anthropocentric worldview was certainly fraught with peril. To be sure there was a real danger that in pulling up the anchor of Christian tradition, the free religionists might get caught in the riptide and be marooned on the shoals of atheism. In 1859 Henry Bellows, President of the National Conference of Unitarian Churches, had said as much. Bellows warned that the "suspense of faith" occasioned by the Protestant contempt for institutions coupled with the rise of scientific naturalism was a threat to national piety and the greatest contributor to secularism. Frothingham, however, was content to live with the ambiguity and religious uncertainty that resulted from the abandonment of theism. Creeds were mere memorials or high water marks of long-dead ideas, whereas doubt indicated the presence of spiritual vitality and power. According to Frothingham, "In honest doubt is all the live faith that exists" (1975: 317).

If it was their Victorian confidence in progress that allowed the radicals to make doubt virtuous, it was considerations of practical virtue, and not metaphysical speculations, that inspired the Religion of Humanity. A doctrine of the hidden God was deemed essential to the development of the race. Specifically, it promoted the intellectual, spiritual, and moral improvement of humanity by forcing the race to look inward and rely on its own resources. Frothingham argued that belief in an intrusive God led inevitably to moral sloth as humanity abdicated its own ethical responsibilities through the elevation of a transcendent lawgiver. Moral obligation required spiritual autonomy.

It was primarily for such practical reasons that the agnosticism of Spencer and Huxley was not an appealing option. Frothingham, for example, found the Spencerian concepts of law, order, and force to be too "overbearing" and materialistic. Moncure Conway complained that agnosticism was overly concerned with the existence of a First Cause, which was not really a religious problem at all. More important, according to Adler, was the fact that agnosticism failed either to provide a suitable basis for the construction of an ethical theory, or to satisfy the spiritual needs of ordinary men and women. Adler referred to the stunning work of David F. Strauss as an example of the the new philosophical critique of religion. And, while Adler found Strauss's criticisms of othodox dogma correct, he remained disappointed that the German scholar failed to replace the old with something new and vital. "Strauss sought to construct a religon from the head," he declared (p. 15), "He forgot that religion is of the heart." For those Victorians who still longed for spiritual nurture, the Religion of Humanity offered something more.

It still remained for partisans of the New Faith to explain how this anthropocentric piety in any way still constituted a religion. It had, of course, obvious appeal to freethinkers and religious dissenters who had drunk deeply at the well of Victorian individualism. What was more difficult was how to reconcile the principles of free inquiry and spiritual autonomy with the need for community and the desire for expansion. It was unclear, then, what institutional form, if any, the Religion of Humanity could or should take. How could apostles of religious humanism spread their gospel without routinizing and systematically defining it at the same time? If the Religion of Humanity was to survive as an alternative religious world for Victorian liberals, it was clear that iconoclasm alone would not suffice. Advocates would have to move from merely tearing down the older religious world to actually constructing a new one. In that light, the New Faith required a comprehensive metaphysic that explained the world around them in terms consistent with the natural sciences and the new learning. But it would also have to provide devotees with the ethical and ritual means to sustain a community of the enlightened faithful in the modern world.

Despite the fact that Frothingham and Adler never seemed quite sure how to harness the Religion of Humanity without domesticating it, they nevertheless devoted their careers to the effort. For twenty years, Frothingham proclaimed this radical gospel to the faithful of the Independent Liberal Church in New York City. The society was home to Transcendentalists such as George Ripley, founder of the ill-fated Brook Farm, and poet Christopher P. Cranch, as well as an assortment of "materialists, atheists, secularists, [and] positivists." Frothingham's sermons, almost all of which were extemporaneous, were regularly printed in the New York papers. His reputation as a fine orator was no doubt responsible for an audience that averaged between six and seven hundred. Yet for all its progressivism, the Sunday services did not differ greatly from those in Unitarian churches, with the notable exception that scripture readings often came from secular literature or sacred texts other than the Bible. And rather than abandoning the traditional Sunday school, Frothingham substituted an expanded afternoon children's service that included a "simple and anecdotal" homily, collective recitations, singing, and responsive readings from his own successful *Child's Book of Religion*, first published in 1866. Frothingham's exercises sought to combine the spiritual and the natural, and thus contribute to the "domestication of faith." He saw his congregation as a model of the broadly liberal and rational faith described in his *Religion of Humanity*.

Similar attempts to institutionalize the humanist impulse could be found in "free churches" across the country from the 1870s through the 1890s. In the Northeast, William J. Potter's First Congregational (Unitarian) Society of New Bedford, Massachusetts and Minot Savage's Church of the Unity in Boston offered examples of successful humanist congregations that retained their Unitarian affiliation. Both Savage and John White Chadwick of the Second

Unitarian Church in Brooklyn considered themselves "Cosmists," and preached a message that owed as much to Spencer as it did to Emerson. The spirit of religious humanism was not restricted to the eastern seaboard, however. Congregations belonging to the Western Unitarian Conference centered in Chicago were as often as not aligned with the denomination's radical wing, and thus gave voice to the humanist gospel throughout the Midwest. This was particularly true of female Unitarian clergy on the frontier. Women such as Mary A. Safford and Eleanor E. Gordon who pastored congregations in Iowa, for example, preached a liberal gospel that sounded very much like that of the free religionists. On the other side of the Atlantic, South Place Ethical Society became known as "the congregation of the world," and the flagship of the Religion of Humanity in Britain. When Conway was appointed as full-time minister in 1864, South Place, with a seventy-year history of liberalism, was near collapse because of declining membership and a lack of stable leadership. Almost immediately, the fortunes of the society improved as freethinking Londoners flocked to hear the energetic young American. Over the next two decades, Conway effectively reshaped the society in his own image, making it the most popular liberal congregation in London.

Committed as they were to the continuation of congregational life, the radicals were necessarily concerned with liturgical matters. Were they to pray or not? And if so, to whom or what? Which hymns, if any, were appropriate? From which texts were they to read? While each society answered these questions differently, free religionists in general were keenly aware of a void left by the loss of the Christian Bible from its authoritative position. Their acceptance of the conclusions of higher criticism and its anti-supernaturalism, together with their espousal of the universality of the religious sentiment, left the Religion of Humanity without a functioning canon. To address this need, free religionists regularly called for the creation of a universal bible that would be broad enough to reflect the spiritual insights of all the great traditions, yet practical enough to be used both in private devotions and in public worship. The need for such a collection had been voiced by early Transcendentalists such as Amos Bronson Alcott, who often referred to Asian scriptures to support their idealist critique of orthodoxy. In fact, Margaret Fuller's *Dial* – the unofficial literary organ of Transcendentalism – regularly featured the "Ethnical Scriptures" which reprinted classic spiritual texts in serialized form. The most successful of these collections was certainly Moncure Conway's *Sacred Anthology,* first published in 1874. It became the text of choice in many free churches across the country, including Frothingham's. As indication both of the reputation of the volume and the international character of the movement, Conway even found the *Anthology* being used by a freethought association in Sydney, Australia a decade after its publication. Between 1872 and 1900, no less than six anthologies of world scriptures were published in an effort to provide independent liberal congregations with a body of literature suitable to express the universality of the new faith. These volumes also sought to legitimate this liberal quest to a Victorian culture steeped in biblical imagery and traditional authority. Even if the Bible had become a mere icon for many Americans during the Gilded Age, an appeal to scripture, even someone else's scripture, lent the movement an air of authenticity.

Just as some sought to address the canonical issue through the creation of a "World Bible," others struggled to confront the more vexing liturgical problem. However loudly Victorian humanists might rail against the empty pomp and circumstance of orthodox ceremonialism, there were still babies to be named, young people to marry, and loved ones to bury. And, if rituals are the "condensed symbols" of a religion, those who seek to establish or perpetuate a new faith ignore it at their peril. Aware of the need for such ritual structure, these new evangelists set out to find one. Many Unitarian congregations, for example, continued to use the standard hymnals, but revised the texts to reflect liberal sensibilities. "Joy to the world, the Lord is come" was reborn as "Joy to the world, let reason reign." In addition, there were also new anthologies of original verse composed and published alongside selected (and often rewritten) older hymns and prayers. In 1877, freethinker D. M. Bennett of the Liberal and Scientific Publishing House in New York published the first edition of *The Truth Seeker Collection of Forms, Hymns, and Recitations* specifically "for the use of liberals." Over the next two decades a spate of similar collections appeared, including *The Liberal Hymn Book* (1880), the *Cosmian Hymn Book* for "Liberals and Ethical Societies" (1888), and the FRA's own official *Souvenir Festival Hymns* (1899). There were also attempts to provide a humanist perspective on the celebration of those significant rites of passage. One of the most successful of these was *Orders of Service for Public Worship* (1896) compiled by Anna Garlin Spencer for use at her Religious Society, of Bell Street Chapel in Providence, Rhode Island. Together these new hymns and liturgies were designed to provide a ritual structure for the new faith.

As good Victorians, the humanists connected religion with the promotion of an ethical public life. For these liberals, the public institution of religion remained an important social fact, by supporting the morality of self-restraint through the elevation of an idealized humanity. "Worship" was seen as a celebration of the human spirit rather than devotion to an absent and unknown deity, and thereby keeping faith with the fundamental premise of the Religion of Humanity. Observers pointed out that science, politics, and recreation were already replacing God in the hearts of many. Secularism was a fact of modern life. Unfortunately, those lesser pursuits could not move the human spirit to the higher plane of ultimate concerns and universal truth. In short, religion was still necessary to promote morality and protect the social good. Only such an anthropocentric piety, it was believed, would promote the humanitarian sentiments necessary to ameliorate the social ills of the modern industrial society.

In an 1889 address before the alumni of the Harvard Divinity School, free religionist Moncure Conway told his audience that they were witnessing the dawn of a new religious age. Indeed, a new light was shining on the world as science and natural philosophy shifted the spiritual orientation of the race from heaven to earth. The apparent end of the Christian era, which seemed to be the source of so much doubt and confusion, did not mean the end of western civilization, and should not be feared. Moreover, the death of the transcendent God of revelation had prepared the way for a resurrection of humanity. The "humanization of religion" was, he argued, the natural course of spiritual and intellectual development. Exclaimed Conway, "Religious evolution begins with man adoring the universe, and ends with the universe adoring man" (1889: 142).

The Religion of Humanity never became the religion of the future as Conway and others believed that it would. Looking back a century later, Frothingham, Adler, and their colleagues remain minor players on the stage of American religious history. Although the Free Religious Association survived into the twentieth century, it never attracted a popular following, or inspired the radical reformation of religion of which its partisans dreamed. Most of the "free churches" were unable to remain viable past the tenure of their founders. Frothingham's own Independent Liberal Church in New York closed within months of his retirement in 1879. Generally, only those congregations that had maintained a connection to Unitarianism were able to survive. By contrast, the Ethical Culture movement had more staying power. Adler and his disciples successfully established societies throughout the United States and Great Britain, until his death in 1933. Still, sixty years after his death the institution he founded could only claim some thirty congregations and around two thousand members nationwide. Clearly, the expected "humanization" of religion did not come, at least not in the way they had expected.

One apparent reason for this failure was that supporters of the Religion of Humanity within the FRA and Society of Ethical Culture were never able to organize or work together effectively. Free religionists were by nature a contentious lot, and the association remained divided by philosophical differences throughout the 1870s and 1880s. Leaders of the FRA, the larger of the two organizations, found it exceedingly difficult to unite a movement founded upon the principle of the absolute freedom of the individual conscience. More troubling were practical questions about how the far the movement could, or should, institutionalize its efforts to promote liberal religion and related causes. Controversy over that issue eventually led to the resignation of Adler as president of the FRA in 1882. As Frothingham's successor in that position, Adler was repeatedly frustrated in his efforts to organize the association more effectively for growth, or to involve it in specific social reform efforts. His departure permanently split the free religion and ethical culture camps, thereby weakening each. In retrospect, the religious humanism of ethical culture was more activist and less speculative than that of most free religionists.

The clearest legacy of the Religion of Humanity was its effect on American Unitarianism. Nearly thirty years after the radicals first left in protest to form the FRA, the 1894 National Conference of Unitarian Churches met in Saratoga, New York and adopted a resolution that virtually canonized the principles of free religion. Although the new constitution remained nominally theistic and Christian, those were no longer prerequisites to fellowship and ministry within the denomination. The Saratoga formula thus made official what Frothingham and the radicals had been agitating for all along, namely a religion committed to intellectual freedom, natural piety, and human betterment. Thus, as the twentieth century dawned, American Unitarians awakened to the fact that they no longer needed or sought the patronage of the Christian modernists; their liberalism had taken them in another direction. The emergence of a new movement for "Religious Humanism" in the 1920s directly reflected the anthropocentric piety of its Victorian predecessor and clearly indicated the movement of Unitarianism out of the shadow of the Christian tradition.

Despite its failures, the Religion of Humanity offered men and women of the Gilded Age a way to deal with the spiritual crisis of their era. The moralist tone, the stress on individual responsibility, and the confidence in science of this humanist spirituality all reflected those values of Victorian culture that made this faith an attractive option for those who felt abandoned by orthodoxy. Through its naturalist metaphysic and liturgical revisions, the Religion of Humanity presented a comprehensive religious world that addressed the intellectual and spiritual crisis of Victorian America.

BIBLIOGRAPHY

Adler, Felix (n.d.) "Have we still a religion?," in O. B. Frothingham and Felix Adler (eds) *The Radical Pulpit*, New York: D. M. Bennett, pp. 1–18.

Conway, M. D. (1889) "The humanization of religion," *The Unitarian Review* (August), pp. 138–50.

Frothingham, O. B. (1975) *The Religion of Humanity*, Hicksville, NY: Regina Press, first published New York, 1873.

Harp, G. J. (1991) "'The Church of Humanity': New York's worshipping positivists," *Church History* 60, pp. 508–23.

Hutchison, W. R. (1976) *The Modernist Impulse in American Protestantism*, Cambridge, Mass.: Harvard University Press.

Marty, M. E. (1961) *The Infidel: Freethought and American Religion*, New York: World Publishing Company.

Meyer, D. H. (1976) "American intellectuals and the Victorian crisis of faith," in D. W. Howe (ed.) *Victorian America*, Philadelphia, Pa.: University of Pennsylvania Press, pp. 59–77.

Persons, S. (1947) *Free Religion: An American Faith*, New Haven, Conn.: Yale University Press.

Turner, T. (1985) *Without God, Without Creed: The Origins of Unbelief in America*, Baltimore, Md.: Johns Hopkins University Press.

Versluis, A. (1993) *American Transcendentalism and Asian Religions*, New York: Oxford University Press.

Warren, S. (1943) *American Freethought, 1860–1914*, New York: Columbia University Press.

Chapter 27

American Catholic Culture in the Twentieth Century

Paula M. Kane

From Immigrant to Ethnic to American

In 1900 Catholics in America numbered about 12 million, or about 16 percent of the national population. The vast majority were descendants of the waves of immigrants who had arrived since the mid-1800s from Germany and Ireland, and between 1880 and 1924 from Germany, Italy, and Poland, plus some Eastern-rite Catholics of Slavic origin. Between 1920 and 1960, once freed from the demands of survival, Catholics experienced growing assimilation. Wherever there were favorable socioeconomic conditions, such as stable employment and income, a flourishing subculture, often called "ghetto Catholicism," emerged. The first transformation of this era's neighborhood and parish-centered life occurred after World War II, when Catholic main-streaming was accelerated dramatically by several factors: the ideological unity provided by anti-communism; the GI Bill of Rights, providing college and graduate education to more Catholics than ever before; and the movement of educated Catholics with young families from cities into suburban homes, jobs, parishes, and schools. The era of Vatican II (1962–5) and its aftermath provide another cultural turning point, as divisions between Catholic conservatives, who opposed the Council's results, and progressives, who favored them, emerged. Since 1965, intra-Catholic tensions have continued, while the presence of new immigrant groups, and an undeniable diversity of moral and political opinions among Catholics has led to efforts by the hierarchy to re-define American Catholicism without succumbing to acrimonious debate. In 1995, Catholics in the US numbered over 60 million, about 23 percent of the total population. It is projected that by 2020 Spanish will be the native tongue of more than 50 percent of American Catholics, a marked shift from the domi-nation of Catholic polity by Irish and Euro-Americans. In 1996, nearly one-third of the population growth in the US resulted from net immigration.

Recent Catholic arrivals reflect the vitality of African, Asian, Caribbean, and Hispanic voices from which new formulations are emerging. Material culture is represented here in such working-class art forms as murals, home altars, and indigenous textiles and crafts. Popular religiosity is also visible in the popularity of botanicas, healers, and pilgrimage shrines, and syncretic forms of Afro-Caribbean religions.

In its broad contours, twentieth-century American Catholic culture has been shaped by internal and external forces: the rise and fall of its separatist sub-culture; the assimilation of post-immigrant generations into the middle class; consumption habits and political allegiances related to class identity; the waning of natural law theology as an overarching theological, moral and aesthetic ground; the legacies of idealism, organicism and universalism; demographic, intellectual, and scientific developments. Catholic culture may be interpreted as the product of a broadly diffused ethos derived from parish-centered spirituality and sociability, expressed through devotional practices, and mediated by priests, nuns, and sisters, which is assumed in what follows.

This article confines itself to three components of Catholic culture in the twentieth century: literature, the visual arts, and mass media. These topics have received scant attention, even despite the fact that Catholics are shockingly underrepresented in the arts. Here, Catholic culture is not defined as American devotional and theological writing, nor as intellectual history, nor as journalism and publishing, which have been well served elsewhere.

American Catholics and Literature

To begin assessing a Catholic cultural role, one might ask: Is a Catholic different from other Americans? What elements make a cultural artifact representatively Catholic? Must an artist or the artistic subject, or both, be Catholic? Does religious identity explain more than class, gender, generational, linguistic, national, and racial, factors? How should Catholic cultural production be evaluated in the twentieth century?

Catholic commentary itself has not been coherent on these points. The most marked difference appears between and pre- and post-Vatican II outlooks. One preconciliar stream of thought has espoused a tradition of intellectual parochialism, as in the definition of a Catholic writer by Bishop Norbert Gaughan, as one still going to church (Gandolfo 1992: 19–20). By contrast, Giles (1992) has argued that the critical distinction among Catholic writers is that between cradle Catholics and converts, which might illuminate the diverse work of converts Joyce Kilmer, Robert Lowell, George Santayana, Allen Tate, and Tennessee Williams, whose vision of America was often unsympathetic to the culture of immigrant Catholics. Yet a third, hybrid approach is offered by novelist Valerie Sayers, who finds herself inspired not only by "the land of capitalism and individualism, with all its particularly American idiosyncrasies," but also by atypical Catholics like Flannery O'Connor, who generally wrote about non-Catholic subjects.

Catholics themselves have often accepted the Church's tactic of ranking authors by their institutional loyalty. With refreshing candor, Flannery O'Connor remarked that the Catholic writer is obliged to pay attention to reality "as we see it manifested in this world of things and human relationships" (As quoted in Tynan 1989: xiv). Some non-Catholic observers, notably Richard Hofstadter, contended that Catholics recognized Catholic writers only belatedly, if at all. In general, Catholics have not agreed upon whether their literary endeavors should represent "religion" or "reality," and even about who is a Catholic author. Until quite recently, religion was supposed to take precedence over art, which was judged by narrow standards of orthodoxy and morality. Many classics of modern American fiction, for example, were condemned by the Catholic Church, a legacy of the Inquisition's Index of Prohibited Books.

Further difficulties in defining a Catholic role in American culture are demonstrated by the absence of this topic in historical surveys of American literature. Among standard reference guides to the literary history of the United States (published by the university presses in Cambridge, Columbia, Oxford), none includes an entry headed "Catholic literature." The updated *Cambridge History of American Literature* (ed. Sacvan Bercovitch, 2 vols, 1994), for example, indexes "Catholicism, Catholics" with subheadings: "and colonization; and Great Schism; and idolatry; in Mexico; and Puritans; see also missions, missionaries." The absence of "Catholic literature" suggests that Catholics are nearly invisible as subjects who write. Although literary critics often cite the opposition between Catholic and Protestant as America's central imaginative dialectic, they have slighted the contributions of Catholics. Moreover, wherever Protestants from the British Isles predominated, Catholics were condemned for being too worldly (symbolized by a sexually threatening or power-hungry clergy), and for being too otherworldly (symbolized by Catholic "superstitions" and "foreign" rituals). The Protestant version of the Roman Catholic in America, from Puritan ministers to Mark Twain to Paul Blanshard portrayed Catholics through a lens of four contrasting forces: the alien, the erotic, the conspiratorial, and the anti-democratic. Few, if any, Protestant novelists approached the subtle and often admiring portraits of Catholicism found in Nathaniel Hawthorne and Henry Adams.

The function of Catholics as the Other in the Protestant imagination typifies the former's second-class status. But by the 1800s anti-Catholicism also functioned as an indirect conduit for the tensions within mainstream Protestant culture (Franchot 1993). Hence, the negligible Catholic literary presence in colonial and antebellum America may reflect not only the success of Protestant efforts to suppress it, but also that society's festering gender, racial, and class disputes. This dynamic may be less apt now, when there is limited value in grouping writers by their religion, and when Catholics are no longer marginalized. Certainly Theodore Dreiser, F. Scott Fitzgerald, Katherine Anne Porter, Louise Erdich, Mary McCarthy, Jack Kerouac, William Kennedy, Paul Theroux, and Donald Barthelme are hardly intelligible only as Catholic authors. In fact, while critics have spoken of a "Jewish fiction" and a "Protestant temperament," Paul Giles claims that there is no homogeneous American Catholic literature.

Yet there survives a tradition of middlebrow fiction and humor by and about Catholics such as the work of John R. Powers (*Do Patent Leather Shoes Really Reflect Up?* 1975), which has little appeal outside a Catholic audience. Jon Hassler's dozen novels and the work of Mary Gordon may be the exceptions. A genre of priest-centered and priest-authored novels and nonfiction has endured in the writing of Greeley and Hassler, James Carroll, Joseph G. Dever, Ralph McInerney, J. F. Powers, Henry Morton Robinson, Walter Murphy, Edwin O'Connor, and Paul Wilkes. Two women, Caryl Rivers and Kit Reed, have been able to transcend a parochial formula to engage broader concerns about religion in the modern world (Gandolfo 1992: 116). They represent a marked difference in tone and content from the preceding generation of women writers such as Phyllis McGinley, known for her humorous light verse, and Sister Madeleva Wolff, college president and activist for women's higher education, who did not question their own Catholicity however they might chafe at the limits the Church placed upon women.

As a consequence of their oppression at the hands of Protestants, Catholics generated a myth of their own uniqueness. Although this defensive posture is typical of a subordinate group in any cultural struggle, some critics have suggested, to the contrary, that the doctrinal rigidity of Roman Catholicism was remarkably similar to New England Puritanism. Rather than providing evidence of uniqueness, therefore, it is more likely that American Catholic writing absorbed the social and economic transformations that affected the United States generally since its establishment in 1776: the transition from oral to print culture; from ethnic homogeneity to diversity; from communal to individualist values; from small-scale production to industrial wage labor, to corporate capitalism and multinational capitalism. The operation of these forces however, has not prevented Catholic writers from asserting the existence of some "Catholic spirit" informing their work, a tactic to establish Catholic identity as distinct from, and possibly superior to others. Catholic fiction thus continues to reflect an ongoing conflict between being Catholic and being American. At the end of the twentieth century it has become common to speak of the twilight of religion and of ethnicity among Americans of European ancestry, a process with obvious implications for post-immigrant Catholics.

Catholicism and the Novel

In addition to the difficulties of defining an American Catholic culture and of understanding Catholic literature within a Protestantized society there are tensions within Catholicism stemming from the historical antipathy between the Church and the quintessential modern literary genre, the novel. As Mary Gordon remarks, "The artistic ego, a product of the Renaissance, coincided with the loosening of the grip of the Church over the hearts and minds of women and men" (Gordon 1988: 47). The decline of the Church's authority conflicted with its premodern, organic, worldview emphasizing a text's fidelity to Catholic dogma and to the "community of faith" (Giles 1992: 205). Even though convert Orestes

Brownson had contended in the nineteenth century that the novel or the poem would do more to foster Catholicism in America than theological tracts and polemics, the novel was an unlikely potential site for Catholic innovation even if it had potential as an alternative to Protestant individualism. Thus the institutional church tended to disparage novels and oppose progressive artistic movements. Further, the church's theological antipathy to modernism and condemnation of the "heresy" of "Americanism" probably had negative consequences on cultural output after 1900. Catholic fiction emerged within and against the Church's insistence upon art's communal and catechetical functions. Little has been written by or about Catholic art and social class, in part owing to the church's resistance to materialist interpretation, and in part because before 1950, the predominant location of Catholics in America was the industrial working class. Overall, nineteenth-century Catholic literature "is almost wholly bereft of serious artistic value" (Messbarger 1971).

The pre-Vatican II American Catholic novel was measured by its fidelity to religious orthodoxy (Gandolfo 1992: p. xi). Unfortunately, whatever critical potential Catholic had to offer was lost between 1884 and 1900 – a moment of "failed promise" (Messbarger 1971). As Catholics became Americanized, their hostility toward American society waned. Consequently, after 1900 Catholic fiction increasingly internalized and reflected secular values. This process need not be irreversible, but any opposition will necessarily be working against modernizing forces. After 1935 a Catholic subculture resurfaced briefly, only to fade in the 1950s as Catholics left their cultural ghetto in search of the American dream.

Regionalism and Localism

Catholic authors have expressed the regional variations of American writers in general. Regionalism has been well developed among Southerners, including Catholic converts Allen Tate, Caroline Gordon, and Walker Percy, members of the "Southern mandarins" who joined the Church in the 1940s and 1950s. Catholicism provided a refuge congenial to the antimodernist, anti-industrial sentiments already expressed by Tate and his colleagues in *I'll Take My Stand* (1930), the manifesto of the Southern agrarians. Conversion to Catholicism apparently did not improve Caroline Gordon's writing, which has been called propagandistic. Because of the lukewarm response to her post-conversion fiction, Gordon turned increasingly to literary criticism. She did, however, model a bohemian in *The Malefactors* (1956) on Dorothy Day, herself a radical journalist prior to her 1927 conversion. In the 1990s the comedic-melodramatic novels of Valerie Sayers, such as *Due East*, set in a fictionalized version of her hometown of Beaufort, South Carolina, represent the New South, minus Gordon's didacticism.

Regionalism has also flourished among the Catholic urban enclaves of the Northeast and Midwest. Andrew Greeley's novels explore Irish Catholics of Chicago; J. F. Powers and Jon Hassler feature Minnesota; William Kennedy writes of Albany; Edwin O'Connor of Boston. Louise Erdich's work explores themes of cultural absorption and resentment among Native American Catholics. Southwestern Catholicism has been reverentially treated in the novels and non-fiction of Paul Horgan (1903–95), although his well-known study of Archbishop Lamy, *Lamy of Santa Fe* (1975) has recently been criticized as ethnocentric by Chicano priest-poet Angelico Chavez. Horgan's many awards included two Pulitzer Prizes for historical writing.

Catholic fiction continues to provide a barometer of demographic change and regional diversity. Although Portuguese, Spanish, and French Catholics preceded the Famine Irish in the Americas, the latter dominated the North American Catholic Church between 1850 and 1950: nearly all of the bishops, priests, and nuns, and most published writers were Irish or Irish American. More recently, Italian novelists Mario Puzo and Richard Gambino have produced best-sellers. A profound recent demographic shift from white ethnicity to a Spanish-speaking community inhabiting regions of the Atlantic rim, West, and Southwest is imperfectly characterized by the term "Hispanic." Among this community at least three major geocultural regions are represented: Mexicans and Chicanos in the Southwest; Cubans, Puerto Ricans, Dominicans, and Afro-Caribbeans; and Central Americans, primarily Salvadorans. Chicano writing, the product of ethnic movements for self-determination, has gained national audiences with authors such as Rudolfo Anaya, Richard Rodriguez, and Sandra Cisneros, and poet Bernice Zamora. Chicanos and Puerto Ricans have made brave experiments in interlingual texts.

Hispanic fiction is characteristically hostile to the Catholic Church, finds Padilla, which has "a shaky place in nearly all Chicano literature written during the last thirty years" (Padilla 1989: 1). Thus Chicano authors "work within a discursive formation that has hardened against traditional Church teaching." Chicano writing expresses alienation from the Church and hostility toward priests who supported the elites against the people in the Mexican Revolution of 1910. Exemplary novels include Jose Villarreal's *Pocho* (1959) and Anaya's *Bless Me, Ultima* (1972). While the oppositional strategy of Chicanos may be most effective when it seriously explores the ideological impact of church teachings rather than merely caricaturing its easy targets, for contemporary Chicano writers the community always comes first. In Hispanic fiction, therefore, emphasis on communal values as the core of Catholicism supersedes any institutional focus and offers sharp challenges to the American ethos of individualism. Moreover, Latino religious skepticism and anticlericalism may resonate with modernist themes of other Catholic ethnicities. The Hispanic literary presence is consonant with broader cultural interest in "multi-culturalism," the exploration of "difference," and the rise of educational movements devoted to instilling values of tolerance and mutualism through the teaching of international texts. Overall, it mirrors a change in global Catholicism from a Eurocentric and East–West faith, to a de-centered Church polarized along North–South lines.

Periodizing Catholic Literature

Although numerous contemporary literary critics have abandoned the tradition of periodizing literature, nevertheless three broad phases of Catholic fiction have been remarked in the United States: the classical, innocence, and modern paradigms. In the nineteenth century, Catholic novelists conformed to the classical formula that art must serve a didactic function. Catholic Gilded Age fiction was sentimental serial stuff that demonized Protestants and disguised sermons as novels. The productivity of women writers at this time relates closely to the emergence of the cult of domesticity, Catholic publishing houses and book clubs, and the expansion of a parochial school system. Popular women authors who spanned the nineteenth and twentieth centuries include Mrs. James Sadlier of New York; in Massachusetts, Katherine Conway and Louise Guiney; in Pennsylvania, Eleanor Donnelly and the iconoclastic Agnes Repplier; in Missouri, Lucille Papin Borden, member of an aristocratic St Louis family. In San Francisco, Kathleen Norris, orphan of a middle-class family, married the brother of naturalist author Frank Norris, yet continued the genteel standards of the eastern establishment, combined with Catholic advocacy of large families and opposition to birth control. Norris was asked by her publisher to mute her Catholicity in response to market demands.

Victorian women authors gradually spoke less of church dogma and more of true Catholic womanhood, a subtle shift indicating their intersection with Protestant bourgeois culture. By the 1950s Catholics had not produced feminist novels perhaps because, once again, the moment of Catholic entry into the middle class coincided with a postwar return to domesticity. However, at least one of Margaret Culkin Banning's forty books advocated family planning, although her heroines were otherwise demure and subservient. Mary McCarthy (*Memories of a Catholic Girlhood*, 1957) represents a strand of Catholic existentialism centered on the themes of rebellion against childhood conditioning. Christopher Durang's play, *Sister Mary Ignatius Explains It All For You* (1981) likewise expresses adult disillusionment with the Church's formulaic indoctrinations. Terrence McNally has treated gay and Catholic themes in his dramas, which include *Corpus Christi* (1997). In Manhattan, the conservative Catholic League for Religions and Civil Rights sponsored a letter-writing campaign against the play, which represents a modern re-telling of the Passion through the character of "Joshua." One feminist heir to McCarthy is Mary Gordon, whose *Final Payments* (1978) is an indictment of the Catholic cult of female self-denial and suffering. A gentler recollection of the Irish Catholic milieu appears in the novels of Alice McDermott (*At Weddings and Wakes*; *Charming Billy*). As Gandolfo notes, Andrew Greeley's female characters have been criticized for the presumption that suffering abuse is part of being a woman (Gandolfo 1992: p. 64). Greeley's persecuted women are models of salutary suffering, while his priests are paternal, all-knowing figures. Theologically conservative and weakly plotted, Greeley's potboilers are at odds with many of his own sociological findings about contemporary Catholicism. A heritage of Catholic women poets includes Louise

Bogan, Sister Madeleva Wolff, Sister Therese (Florence) Lentfoehr, and Jessica Powers.

In its second phase, the "innocence" paradigm, American Catholic culture must be read in dialogue with European Catholic anti-modernism, rooted in the church's reaction against the French Revolution. With the defeat of monarchy, the European Catholic Church became the remaining bastion of political and aesthetic conservatism, mobilizing radical rightists and romantics to defend Catholicism as the source of national identity. From 1789 until Vatican II Catholics emphasized the superiority of spiritual values, in contrast to secularists who spoke of material progress through science, economics, or politics. Catholic fiction of this era usually involved a formulaic plot in which the protagonist must choose between the path of Christian virtue, family loyalty, and objective morality, and the road to ruin symbolized by hedonism, sexual immorality, or divorce. Although "the chaos of modern thought and the breakdown of objective moral order" was the implicit guiding assumption of most Catholic writers, their fiction was narrowly focused upon questions of personal morality (Sparr 1990).

The Catholic revival which produced novelists such as Belloc, Chesterton, Greene, and Waugh in England, and Bernanos, Bloy, and Mauriac in France, affected American Catholic culture as well. But it is not surprising that Americans, once liberated from purely didactic writing, also expressed something of their nationalism through the motif of innocence. Consequently, Catholic novels written between 1935 and 1950, the heyday of ghetto Catholicism, defended the Church's moral certainty and idealism and rejected America's relativism. This confessional subculture began to diversify in the mid-1930s, owing to social factors (the Great Depression), and intellectual and theological change (exposure of college students to the neo-scholasticism of Dawson, Maritain, and Gilson, new papal social teachings, European integralism, and new Christological emphasis on the Mystical Body). Introduction to European fiction, poetry, and theological titles was fostered by the London firm of Sheed and Ward, which had opened a New York City branch in 1928, soon becoming the largest Catholic publishing house in the English-speaking world, a title now held by the Paulist Press. Editors George Shuster and Michael Williams also played significant roles in promoting Catholic literature, while Walter Romig published the series, *The Book of Catholic Authors*, and related reference guides.

Between 1935 and 1960, when the social realist novel emerged, Catholic literature generally portrayed a homogenous ethnic and religious community trying to preserve its own unity "by suppressing any threat of difference" (Giles 1992: 134). Nonetheless unorthodox Catholic voices did emerge in the 1940s and 1950s, notably Jack Kerouac, who discovered the rhythms of jazz and blues music and the mystique of eastern religions. Fueled also by nostalgia for his French-Catholic roots in Lowell, Massachusetts, Kerouac's eclectic Franciscan spirituality has been compared by Giles to the spirit of Zen: "nondogmatic, nonjudgmental, and concerned with the grace of nature rather than the strictures of morality" (p. 413). Likewise, convert Thomas Merton was an anomaly in 1940s Catholicism, for protesting American imperialism, militarism, and materialism. Merton, who became a Cistercian monk in 1949, published some sixty books, including his best-seller autobiography, *The Seven Storey Mountain* *(1947)*. Catholics have at least one contribution to postwar science fiction in *A Canticle for Leibowitz* (1959), by Walter Miller, Jr., who converted in 1947. Even in its mid-century expressions of "innocence," Catholic literature moved to embrace a universalist Americanism and skepticism simultaneously (Giles 1992).

The most significant change in tone and subject matter for Catholic writing occurs after Vatican II. If Americanism in the twentieth century has meant allegiance to the principles of individualism, capitalism, democratic republicanism, and expansionism, then Catholics who were once hostile to these ideals generally embraced them, even if remaining mostly unconverted to modernism's belief in the autonomy of art from truth and morality. Since Vatican II, American Catholic novelists, responding to the church's theological *aggiornamento* and engagement with social realities, produced fiction derived from personal experience. Within this third, modern paradigm, Catholicism has been both a benevolent, nurturing influence as well as a source of rebellion in art. *Bare Ruined Choirs* (Garry Wills, 1972) and Rodriguez's *Hunger of Memory: the Education of Richard Rodriguez* (1981) are but two evocations of the Council's impact on culture. Elsewhere, postconciliar fiction encountered Vatican II through the recurrent image of the loss of a parent. Still other Catholics rejected the church's engagement with modernity and demanded a return to earlier didactic formulas.

The new interiorized focus of modern Catholic fiction represents an acculturation to the American gospel of pragmatism and heroic individualism, related to the upward social mobility of Catholics. In the 1840s, it was possible for convert Orestes Brownson to state, "Our theology determines our ethics, and our ethics determines our aesthetics." While contemporary society no longer privileges ethics over art, as recently as the 1950s Paul Horgan claimed that art and prayer were inseparable activities. Since then, writers who consider themselves stylistically and thematically influenced by Catholic roots may be more likely to agree with Mary Gordon that "Great art need have nothing in it of the ethical, although the greatness of some great literature is enhanced by ethical components. But some is not . . . This is why I say that the esthetic and the religious are not necessarily one" (Gordon 1988: 50). The severing of the artistic from the ethical has been a vexed question for modern writers still willing to call themselves Catholic. Still, modern and postmodern variations on agnosticism and atheism represent themes of doubt, fragmentation, and de-centering of the self that are not exclusively Catholic. The novels of David Plante and Andre Dubus, for example, affirm highly individual values and a compartmentalized kind of faith that are not tied to the historical heritage of Catholicism. This is a far cry from the caveat imposed by a nineteenth-century priest against six categories of bad books: "1. Books which are plainly about very bad things; 2. many novels; 3. idle books; 4. bad newspapers and journals; 5. superstitious books; 6. Protestant books and tracts."

Visual Arts

Arguably, film, video, and popular music have replaced literature as the premiere cultural icons of the late twentieth century. American Catholics were never a force in the modernist movement that, with the advent of Abstract Expressionism, made New York City the center of the art world. But they did contribute the king of pop artists, Andy Warhol, whose ethno-religious roots in Slavic Pittsburgh reveal the Church's undeniable iconographic influence. Another influential pop artist was Corita Kent, IHM, whose colorful upbeat serigraphs, posters, banners became politicized by the mid-1960s, drawn to civil rights and anti-war themes via her acquaintance with Cesar Chavez and the Berrigans. Sister Kent left religious life in 1968, gaining recognition for her commission for the US Postal Service's best-selling "LOVE" stamp. Something of a mass-marketed Catholic aesthetic can be said to be present now as kitsch: ancient traditions of visual piety are being revived in body tattooing, among street gangs, and on T-shirts utilizing such devotional images as the Virgin of Guadalupe and the Sacred Heart of Jesus.

Although no contemporary artists categorize themselves as "Catholic," there are painters, sculptors, and musicians who explore their religious backgrounds subtly via a preoccupation with subcultural strategies in general, including three urban Catholics born in the 1950s: Mike Kelley, Robert Gober, and Andres Serrano. Kelley, drawing from his Detroit working-class roots and parochial schooling, is regarded as a conceptual and performance artist now associated with Los Angeles. He confronts viewers with disturbing images and ideas, notably a fascination with trash, rubbish, and debasement, reflections on masculinity, and what Elisabeth Sussman terms "an aesthetics of failure" (1993: 27). Sculptor Robert Gober chooses familiar and even banal objects and renders them unfamiliar. A museum installation of his figure of the Madonna with a storm culvert piercing her body caused controversy in Los Angeles in 1997. In photography, the theatrical, erotic, painterly, and disturbing images of Brooklyn-born Andres Serrano rely heavily upon Catholic influences; they include a Latino-Catholic aesthetic and the visual rhetoric of Baroque art. Some are offended by Serrano's use of shocking images, which act as stand-ins for spiritual values. Yet, by playing with the heritage of Christian dualism and an artistic lineage from Caravaggio, Mantegna, Goya, El Greco, and Zurbarán, Serrano addresses traditional themes: the relation between the seen and unseen, between meaning and instability of meaning. His photos of corpses in morgues, religious statues submerged in various fluids, and Ku Klux Klansmen in hooded regalia overwhelm the viewer with an avalanche of associations, "ranging from utter disgust to an atavistic return of the fear of God" (Arenas 1995, unpaginated).

If Serrano's art merges the eschatological and the scatological, nonetheless his images must be understood as scenes from the political dramas of the 1980s, when the so-called "culture wars" erupted. Certain artists and funding institutions (even the National Endowment for the Arts) were scapegoated as symptoms, if not even causes, of social ills. The attacks on Serrano, as well as on Robert Mapplethorpe and other, more avant-garde artists or makers of issue-oriented or identity-based art, need likewise to be placed in the context of the Reagan administration's backlash against individual rights, homosexuals, unions, and federal funding for arts organizations.

While it was a single photograph, *Piss Christ*, (1987) that brought Serrano notoriety when it was torn up by a US Senator in May, 1989, the image – a standard mass-produced plastic crucifix floating in yellow fluid – was but one of a series which included classical statuettes submerged in various fluids. Using milk, blood, and urine, the artist found new ways to look at and through familiar symbols. Serrano's work is valuable because it transcends a Catholic subculture to universalize his subjects. Within a Catholic milieu, however, his photographs represent the diversity of the Catholic population and the persistent desire of art to shock the bourgeoisie. When many liberal Catholics joined the protest against Serrano, decrying obscenity in art and the desecration of sacred images, it appeared that Catholics had not entirely thrown off the priggish aesthetic standards of the Code for Movie Production. The Code, authored by two Catholics in the 1930s to save Hollywood from itself, was enforced for decades by the film rating system of the Catholic Legion of Decency.

In liturgical art, the tradition of reform inaugurated by Virgil Michel (1890–1938), a Benedictine monk of St John's Abbey, Minnesota, still flourishes. Associated at the outset with Maurice Lavanoux (architecture and decorative arts), Adé Bethune (woodcuts and engravings), Frank Kacmarcik (architecture), and Justine Ward (Gregorian chant), the spirit lives on in William Schickel of Ohio (a collaborator of Marcel Breuer and Pietro Belluschi), and others who work within the modernist aesthetic to produce liturgical environments inspired by Michel and publicized by the journal he founded in 1926, *Orate Fratres* (now *Worship*). While Michel's great hope was to join liturgy to a quest for social justice, his impact on the arts and education was significant as well, advocating churches and interiors that facilitated public and participatory liturgy. In sacred architecture, tension persists between Catholic liturgical requirements, modernism's cerebral severity, and architectural forms associated with ethnic varieties of Catholicism.

Motion Pictures, Television, and Popular Culture

Catholics were not present in Hollywood merely as its film censors, but also became prominent directors and actors. In the formative years of the western, John Ford became its quintessential shaper, perhaps marrying the idealism of Catholicism to the vastness of the American frontier. Frank Capra, Francis Ford Coppola, John Huston, and Martin Scorsese have identified a Catholic visual and moral sensibility in their movies. The term "Capra-esque" has come to mean an optimistic vision of human nature and good neighborliness, embodied in the figure of the populist hero battling an evil system. For Warhol, maker of short soap operas and soft-core pornography in the sixties, and for directors Scorsese and Robert Altman, cinema became an unapologetic mass-culture substitute for high culture.

As a result of the hegemony of television and motion pictures, images may have supplanted texts as the place where Catholics, and American in general, formulate and enact their identities. While many have condemned the godlessness of the movie industry, Scorsese, for example, defended his controversial 1989 adaptation of Kazantzakis' novel, *The Last Temptation of Christ* (1955), as "my attempt to use the screen as a pulpit in a way, to get the message out about practicing the basic concepts of Christianity" (Gandolfo 1992: 44). Elsewhere Scorsese has commented, "I believe there is a spirituality in films, even if it's one which cannot supplant faith." Independent filmmaker Ed Burns scored a surprise success with *The Brothers McMullen* (1995), which explored the place of moral traditions in an Irish Catholic family. *Dead Man Walking* (Tim Robbins, 1995) dramatized Sister Helen Prejean's campaign against capital punishment. With cheeky vulgarity, Kevin Smith's *Clerks* limned the sexual morality of (Catholic) adolescents toiling for minimum wages in a Jersey convenience store. *Priest* attempted to handle serious issues dividing pre- and post-Vatican II Catholics; *Household Saints* deals with cycles of ethnicity from the novel by Francine Prose of the same title; *Sister Act* and numerous imitators only parodied religious life. Occult Catholic themes of demonic possession, exorcism, miraculous cures, and stigmata appear with regularity in television shows such as *The X-Files*, while detectives, cops, and lawyers from urban Catholic backgrounds became the moral conscience of such series as *NYPD Blue* and *Law & Order*. As comedians, Catholics did not have a venue equivalent to the Jewish "Borscht belt." Nonetheless Gracie Allen, Art Carney, Jackie Gleason, and Bob Newhart have delighted generations of Americans with their wit and physical comedy. In the sixties and seventies, iconoclastic George Carlin, a self-proclaimed lapsed believer, performed a stand-up monologue entitled "I used to be an Irish Catholic," derived from his boyhood and parochial schooling on the fringes of Harlem.

Music

Self-taught pianist, composer, and arranger Mary Lou Williams (1910–981) dominated the jazz scene for five decades. After her conversion to Catholicism in 1956 at the affluent St Ignatius Loyola Church in Manhattan she produced numerous jazz settings of sacred texts and three complete masses, all of which have been performed internationally. A major shift in the role of music in liturgy was ushered in by Vatican II, when it became the heart of participatory worship. At the high end, C. Alexander Peloquin has been a leading composer, while at the parish level, Catholics embraced many "folk" hymns by the the priests and seminarians of the 1970s and 1980s known as the "St Louis Jesuits."

Singers and actors Harry "Bing" Crosby (1903–77) and Frank "The Voice" Sinatra (1915–98) expressed the tribal longings and identifications of Irish and

Italian Catholics, among others. Crosby, while starring in many lightweight Hollywood comedies with Bob Hope and Dorothy Lamour, was best known for his sentimental song recordings such as "White Christmas" and "Silent Night." Arguably the best vocalist and stylist of the twentieth century, Sinatra's reputation as "Ol' Blue Eyes" was marred by rumors of his connections to organized crime. In contemporary pop music, Frank Zappa's often blasphemous lyrics are a generation's assault on religious pomposity and moralism. The Catholic and Italian-American roots to Madonna Ciccone's songs have been remarked, as have the motifs of redemption and social justice in the lyrics of New Jersey native son Bruce Springsteen.

Conclusion: Disintegration Or Renewal?

What is the future for American Catholic culture? Thomas Kuhn has observed that new paradigms emerge imaginatively rather than rationally, consequently any medium may become a potent source for re-imagining Catholic culture in the next millennium. Because no Catholic avant-garde emerged with modernism, and because a Catholic modernism appeared only tardily, much Catholic writing and criticism is still mired in the dogmatism of older paradigms. The emergence of postmodernism, however, which celebrates and bemoans the pluralism of American society and the indeterminacy of identity, has resonated in fiction by Dubus and Plante, whose individualized faiths bear little relation to the Church of history and tradition. Among young Catholic artists and thinkers can be found the same rebellious marks of alienation and anti-confessionalism. A cultural preference for autobiography and a "return to narrative" suggests that the personal is all that can be known. Mary Gordon's hybrid identity, uncovered through discovery of her Jewish father's hidden past in *The Shadow Man* (1996), may become one exemplary text. Multifaceted Catholic autobiographies are also charted in Paul Theroux's *My Secret History* (1989) and in *Days of Obligation: An Argument with my Mexican Father* (1992), Richard Rodriguez' meditation on being a Chicano homosexual Catholic. Conservative Andrew Sullivan struck an autobiographical chord in *Virtually Normal* (1994), tackling religious and social arguments about homosexuality. Women have anthologized memoirs, short stories, and poems about childhood and sexual identities in *Catholic Girls* (Sumrall and Vecchione 1992), *Catholic Girlhood Narratives* (Evasdaughter 1996), and *Chasing Grace: Reflections of a Catholic Girl Grown Up* (Manning 1996). Contemporary painting and sculpture express similarly gendered and psychologized concerns.

Opposing these personalized narratives are Catholic conservatives embodying the standard resentments of white ethnics. Paradoxically, in rejecting ethnic pluralism and the welfare state, they attack the very "liberal" politics and legislation of the 1960s that had propelled them into the mainstream. The political shift during the 1980s that saw Catholic Democratic party stalwarts joining the conservative faction of the Republican Party or supporting third-party populists suggests that the fading of ghetto Catholicism participates in a general cultural crisis about the limits of liberalism. Catholic liberalism, as embodied by an ideal-istic Americanized Catholic whose life followed the contours of the Depression, World War II, and the Cold War, has died without a well-defined paradigm to replace it. Catholics born after Vatican II face declining economic expectations, disconnection from a Catholic artistic and intellectual heritage, and suspicion of moral regimentation and patriotism – realities that coexist bewilderingly with a worldwide resurgence of religious fanaticism, fundamentalism, and theocratic nationalisms.

As artists continue to unmake the old stereotype of Catholic art as forever trapped in themes of guilt and sin, some new paradigm is unfolding whose outlines can be tentatively enumerated in four areas: first, lay dissatisfaction with certain official Church teachings; second, the loss of natural law theology as a unitive force; third, the rise of gender, racial, and sexual politics to challenge static, ahistorical dogmas; finally, contact with new ethnicities. Nostalgic resis-tance to these trends endures among conservatives who continue to try to revive an imaginary Catholic golden age. At the opposite extreme, the so-called youth of "Generation X," described as apathetic, apolitical and anti-dogmatic, nonetheless have incorporated their faded religious roots into media-dominated postmodern culture. Old and new ethnicities still serve as a point of departure in the arts, even when they parody religious traditions.

The current vogue for "identity politics" and renewed attention to the mean-ings of ethnicity highlight the impossibility of a simple and singular notion of identity, and render the notion of "American Catholic culture" a complex phenomenon. As the twentieth century closes, the Catholic Church still inspires artists and writers, but in a different fashion than for the three earlier paradigms. Surprisingly, while signposts of Catholic culture have largely disap-peared in the postindustrial West, American Catholics still attend mass in healthy numbers. While a priest shortage and the aging population of clergy and women religious signal an impending institutional crisis, their impact on the arts and media is less clear. In some regions, Catholics are moving into emotive, spirit-filled churches, often Pentecostal, or embracing the postmodern demand for "designer religions," tailored to suit personal taste. In this context, the tra-ditional polarization in American history between Protestant and Catholic seems less relevant.

BIBLIOGRAPHY

"American fiction and Catholic culture," special issue, *U.S. Catholic Historian* (1987) 6/2–3.

Arenas, Amelia (1995) "The revelations of Andres Serrano," in Brian Wallis (ed.) *Andres Serrano: Body and Soul*, New York: Takarajima Books.

Brinkmeyer, Robert H. (1985) *Three Catholic Writers of the Modern South: Allen Tate, Caroline Gordon, Walker Percy*, Jackson, Miss.: University of Mississippi Press.

Evasdaughter, Elizabeth N. (1996) *Catholic Girlhood Narratives: The Church and Self-denial*, Boston, Mass.: Northeastern University Press.

Franchot, Jenny (1993) *Roads to Rome: The Antebellum Protestant Encounter with Catholicism*, Berkeley, Calif.: University of California Press.

Gandolfo, Anita (1992) *Testing the Faith: The New Catholic Fiction in America*, New York: Greenwood Press.

Giles, Paul (1992) *American Catholic Arts and Fictions: Culture, Ideology, Aesthetics*, Cambridge and New York: Cambridge University Press.

Gordon, Mary (1988) "Getting here from there: a writer's reflections on a religious past," in William Zinsser (ed.) *Spiritual Quests: The Art and Craft of Religious Writing*, Boston, Mass.: Houghton Mifflin.

—— (1991) *Good Boys and Dead Girls and Other Essays*, New York: Viking.

Halsey, William M. (1980) *The Survival of American Innocence*, Notre Dame, Ind.: University of Notre Dame Press.

Messbarger, Paul R. (1971) *Fiction with a Parochial Purpose: Social Uses of American Catholic Literature, 1884–1900*, Boston, Mass.: Boston University Press.

Padilla, Genaro M. (1989) "The Catholic Church in Chicano literature," in Daniel Tynan (ed.) *Biographical Dictionary of Contemporary Catholic American Writing*, New York: Greenwood Press.

Sparr, Arnold (1990) *To Promote, Defend, and Redeem: The Catholic Literary Revival and the Cultural Transformation of American Catholicism, 1920–1960*, New York: Greenwood Press.

Sumrall, Amber Coverdale and Vecchione, Patrice (eds) (1992) *Catholic Girls*, New York: Penguin/Plume.

Sussman, Elisabeth (ed.) (1993) *Mike Kelly: Catholic Tastes*, New York: Whitney Museum of American Art.

Tynan, Daniel (ed.) (1989) *Biographical Dictionary of Contemporary Catholic American Writing*, New York: Greenwood Press.

Index

102–3; moral dilemmas of the market, 96–102
Capra, Frank, 400
Carely, Matthew, 320
Carter, Jimmy, 52
Carter, Robert, 69
Cartwright, Peter, 110, 111
Cases of Conscience (Stoddard), 99
Catherine of Siena, 217
Catholics: African Americans, 264; and Anglicans, 66–7; banned books, 392; change in mass ritual, 54; consumption of religious goods, 189–95; converts to, 324–8; devotional life, 159–60, 190, 196; education, 163; election of Kennedy, 171; ethnicity, 49, 155–7, 195, 244, 390; fast days, 217; feminism, 158–9, 165; film, TV and popular culture, 157, 400–1; future in American culture, 402–3; growth of population, 41; holistic attitude, 196–7; immersion in culture, 335; influence on American literature, 391–8; interfaith marriage, 321–2; internal diversity, 7; issues for the future, 166; joins with Protestantism against Asians, 19; St Joseph's statue to sell property, 187; leadership and priesthood, 157–9, 160; material culture, 173, 188–98; mission work, 163; modern approach, 151–2; music, 401–2; nativism reacts against, 37–8; nuns, 191–2; papal authority, 67; personal spirituality, 58; pluralism, 3; population growth, 37; postmodern community, 196–8; Protestant suspicions, 371–2, 392; regional literature, 394–5; renewal of spirituality, 88–9; sacramentalism, 190, 196–8; saints' relics, 191; Second Vatican Council, 51, 53–4, 108, 159–66, 195, 398; social support, 161–2; spirituality, 161; trend towards internal authority, 83–4; varied membership, 164; visual arts, 398–400; *see also* Irish Americans; Italian Americans
Cayton, Mary Kupiec, 334
celibacy: Peace Mission, 28; Pierce Connelly's confusion, 327; priests, 53; Shakers, 27
Central Conference of American Rabbis (CCAR), 131, 132–3
Ceremony (Silko), 283
Chadwick, John White, 385–6
Chamberlain, Ava, 334

Chambers, Sheri, 224
charismatic worship, 55
Charity and its Fruits (Edwards), 100
Chatham Street Theater/Chapel, 176–9, 181
Chauncy, Charles, 101
Cheney, Richard, 68
Chesnut, Mary Boykin, 323
Cheyne, George: *Book of Health and Long Life*, 219–21; *The English Malady, An Essay on Regimen*, 219
Child's Book of Religion (Frothingham), 385
Chinese Americans: anti-Chinese campaign in California, 12–19; immigrants retain non-Christian beliefs, 13–16; kinship, 15; restriction of immigration, 19; syncretic blend of religious practices, 15
The Chinese in America (Gibson), 12–19
Christian Aerobic Resource, 224
Christian and Missionary Alliance movement, 265–8
Christian Coalition, 52
Christian Endeavor Society, 205
Christian modernism, 383–4
Christian Scientists, 25–6, 32; diet, 224; religious innovation, 25–6; theater-style churches, 183
Christianity: appeal of different practices, 67; challenged by Victorian humanist religion, 380–9; effect of Depression on organized religion, 133; erosion of trust in churches, 367; failure of established churches, 68; honoring family ties, 319; influence of women on Jewish women, 294–5, 298; and Ojibwa hymn singing, 280–2; science and philosophy, 379–80
Church of England: desertion by patriotic Americans, 72; fast days, 217; formality and decorum, 67–8; *see also* Episcopalians
Cincinnati: synagogues, 295, 296
civil rights movement: identities, 44–5; marginalized social groups, 8; questions church authority, 51; reaffirmation of African culture, 55–6
Clark, Elizabeth, 310
Clarke, Samuel, 100
class: influence on church design, 184; Jewish working class and poor, 128, 131; Pentecostalism, 267; revivalism, 180–1; upper and middle of Virginian Anglicans, 76–8
Clinton, Bill, 366
Coke, Bishop Thomas, 109
Coker, Daniel, 116